A Beautiful Way

DISCIPLESHIP
ESSENTIALS

A Beautiful Way
An Invitation to a Jesus-Centered Life
by Dan Baumann

The Leadership Paradox
A Challenge to Servant Leadership
in a Power-Hungry World
by Denny Gunderson

Learning to Love People You Don't Like
by Floyd McClung

The Chicken Farm and Other Sacred Places
The Joy of Serving God in the Ordinary
by Ken Barnes

A Fresh Look at Fear
Encountering Jesus in Our Weakness
by Dan Baumann

DISCIPLESHIP
ESSENTIALS

A Beautiful Way

An Invitation to a Jesus-Centered Life

Dan Baumann
with Mark Klassen

YWAM
PUBLISHING
P.O. Box 55787 / Seattle, WA 98155

YWAM Publishing is the publishing ministry of Youth With A Mission (YWAM), an international missionary organization of Christians from many denominations dedicated to presenting Jesus Christ to this generation. To this end, YWAM has focused its efforts in three main areas: (1) training and equipping believers for their part in fulfilling the Great Commission (Matthew 28:19), (2) personal evangelism, and (3) mercy ministry (medical and relief work).

For a free catalog of books and materials, call (425) 771-1153 or (800) 922-2143. Visit us online at www.ywampublishing.com

A Beautiful Way: An Invitation to a Jesus-Centered Life
Copyright © 2005 by Dan Baumann

Published by YWAM Publishing
a ministry of Youth With A Mission
P.O. Box 55787, Seattle, WA 98155

Third printing 2015

ISBN 978-1-57658-481-1

Library of Congress Cataloging-in-Publication Data

Baumann, Dan, 1963–
    A beautiful way : an invitation to a Jesus-centered life /
by Dan Baumann with Mark Klassen.—1st ed.
        p. cm.
    ISBN 978-1-57658-481-1
    1. Spiritual life—Christianity. 2. Christian life. 3. God.
I. Klassen, Mark, 1967– II. Title.
    BV4501.3.B39 2004
    248.4—dc22   2004021550

Printed in the United States of America

To my dear friends Randy and Edie Thomas. Thank you so much for all your love and for your encouragement over the years to teach and encourage young people to find "A Beautiful Way." I am so grateful that you have believed in me and released me to do what God has asked me to do.

—*Dan*

To Alexis Ayn and Dania Kay, my beautiful daughters, in hopes that you will learn to love Jesus and that you will lead others in your generation to discover the beauty of following him.

—*Mark*

Contents

◼ Acknowledgments

From Dan

I want to thank my friends at YWAM Trinidad, Colorado, who helped me with this project. Pete, Josanna, Becky, Edie, Jessica, Tasha, Cat, thanks for all your help and input. I also want to thank Misha and Lionel Thompson and Geoff and Janet Benge for your input into the book.

I want to thank my parents, Hans and Gunila Baumann. I love you! Thanks so much for believing in me and encouraging me to see this project happen.

I want to deeply thank Mark Klassen for helping me write this book. Your friendship, godliness, and commitment to excellence have inspired me greatly. Thank so much for all the long hours you have invested into this book. Thanks too for modeling the message of *A Beautiful Way.*

I want to thank Amy Klassen and Alexis and Dania Klassen for releasing Mark to work many hours on this project.

I want to thank Tom, Warren, Marit, and all of the staff of YWAM Publishing. Thanks for believing in Mark and me and encouraging us to write this book.

I want to thank Loren Cunningham, the founder of YWAM. Two years ago, you challenged me to write a second book. Your words have been a deep source of encouragement to me.

Mostly, I want to thank my Lord and Savior Jesus Christ. You are "A Beautiful Way." It's all about you!

From Mark

It's one thing to be blessed with good friends; it's another thing to be blessed with the opportunity to work closely with those friends. I thank God for the opportunity I've had to work with Dan Baumann on this book. Thanks, Dan, for giving me a chance and letting me help. You are an inspiration to me in many ways, but nothing impresses me more than your simple love for Jesus.

Our friends at YWAM Publishing, especially Warren and Marit, have been so positive and helpful throughout the process. Thanks also to Janet Benge for reviewing an early draft for us and gently suggesting needed improvements.

I'd like to express appreciation to my friend and present employer, Frank Ens, who gave me much freedom and encouragement during the writing. I'd also like to thank my friend Jonathan Quapp, who has faithfully stood by me in prayer throughout these past couple of years, including the year of writing. Thanks also to my family, both sets of parents and siblings, who have consistently shown interest in this book and offered valuable support and encouragement along the way. And to Dave Manuel, Ryan Harder, Greg Watt, Darrel Spenst, and Larry Wiebe, thanks for your friendship over the years and for encouraging me, each in your own way, to write.

Spouses often receive the final acknowledgement in book writing, and now I know why. No one in my life has sacrificed more during this project than my wife, Amy. At times it has been challenging for us, but she has amazed me once again with her patience and grace. Amy, I love you.

Introduction

Dear friends,

Jesus said, "I am the way" (John 14:6), and those who follow him discover that it is a *beautiful* way.

As Christians we are all on this journey of discovery. We are being convinced that we have found in Jesus something that is far more beautiful than anything we have ever experienced or imagined. As I sit down to write, I am excited about the opportunity I have to share my heart with you as it relates to the incredible journey we are on.

In 2001 my first book, *Imprisoned in Iran,* was published. It tells the story of my trip into Iran to explore possible service opportunities, my nine weeks in prison on a false charge, and my miraculous release. Since then I have had the privilege of sharing my story in many different settings around the world. As I have done this, many people have asked me, "How did you ever get from living in California to being in prison in the Middle East? Tell us about your walk with God and how Jesus has led you." Those questions have challenged me to think more about the experiences and principles that have shaped my own walk with God and also about how I could more effectively share my faith journey with others. This second book, then, is the result of that thinking.

This book has three parts: Believing, Trusting, and Serving. They represent key aspects of the spiritual life: learning to believe the truth about God's character, interacting with

God in ways that nurture trust, and then giving ourselves in service to others. Although there often seems to be a logical progression from one to the other, these areas are interrelated in terms of how God transforms our lives, and God's dealings with us cannot necessarily be traced specifically in this order. It is my hope that as you read each part, God will use it to continue the work of transformation that he is doing in your life.

Most of all, *A Beautiful Way* is an invitation to a relationship. It's about following Jesus. It is not an invitation to a career in global missions. Though this is the calling God has chosen for me and for many others, the principles that I write about apply equally to those who are working a nine-to-five job, those who are going to school, or those who are working at home. Whatever your career or life situation, you are invited to embrace a life that is completely centered on the person of Jesus.

My heart longs for each one of us to discover more and more of the life that Jesus offers to us and to let go of everything that distracts us and prevents us from finding it. It is with this longing that I want to share my own journey with you and invite you to walk alongside me as we explore *a beautiful way* together.

Your brother,
Dan

Part One

Believing

The journey begins with *believing*. More than simply belief in God's existence, I want to address belief
in terms of how we understand God's character and
how this affects our relationship with him. No one
can expect to find *a beautiful way* unless they encounter the God who freely offers it to them and longs
for them to find it. Chapters 1 and 2 focus on two
key aspects of God's character: his personal love and
his goodness. There is, of course, more to God than
these two characteristics, but these are crucial for us
to understand, and it seems to me that many Christians today are in the midst of a great struggle within
themselves to believe these things about God.

Chapter One

God's Personal Love

For great is your love toward me.
—*Psalm 86:13*

This is love: not that we loved God,
but that he loved us and sent his Son
as an atoning sacrifice for our sins.
—*1 John 4:10*

God always takes the first step. Before we ever loved God, he loved us. Before we ever invited him into our lives, he extended an invitation to us. Without that invitation we would be without hope. If God were not interested in being in relationship with us, we would have absolutely no way of reaching him and no chance at all of discovering meaning for our lives. We would be lost.

As Christians we believe in God as the Great Initiator. There is nothing more foundational to our faith than the belief that God is reaching out to us in love. Nothing else brings more meaning to human existence than the fact that our Creator is committed to initiating relationship with us.

It is this *downward* motion—God toward us—that distinguishes Christianity from all other religions. Instead of us reaching up to heaven to find God, we believe that God is reaching down to earth to find us. Our Creator has not left us alone to figure out why we are here. There is meaning to our lives: we are loved by God.

A Christian high-school student was once told, "Everything you do for God will be the overflow of intimacy with God." The statement made an impact on the young man. After hearing it, he pondered long and hard over what intimacy with God could mean. Deep in thought, he walked down to a nearby river and began to throw rocks. As another rock splashed into the river, the young man heard an inner voice ask the question, *Can I throw rocks with you?*

He didn't think much of it at first, but when he heard it again, he questioned himself about whether or not it could be the voice of God. He quickly concluded that it could not be, convincing himself easily that God was not interested in such a mundane activity. But he kept hearing the voice over and over again, until finally he stopped, turned to heaven, and said, "God, I think you're asking to throw rocks with me. But why? Why would you want to throw rocks with me? I mean, you're concerned about the world and all its problems. You can't possibly care about throwing rocks with me."

Then he heard the voice again, with even greater clarity, *I want to throw rocks with you because you want to throw rocks. I just want to hang out with you and do whatever you are doing. I just want us to be together so that our friendship can grow.*

In amazement, the young man replied, "That's it?" believing now that he was actually talking to Jesus.

That's it, Jesus replied.

It was on that day that I—Dan Baumann, a normal fifteen-year-old—began to realize that Jesus was madly in love with me. He loved me when I was having my personal devotions or sharing my faith, but he was just as much in love with me when I was relaxing, watching a movie, or throwing rocks. Jesus loved me without conditions and without restraints! From that day forward, as an ordinary kid growing up in Southern California, I became more and more aware of Jesus' personal love for me. More than anything else, Jesus wanted to be my friend and to hang out with me at every possible opportunity. I was totally amazed! How could the God of the universe love me like that!? Wow! What do you do when you are loved like that? For me, in that moment, I was changed, and all I wanted to do was to love God back.

> *"Everything you do for God will be the overflow of intimacy with God."*

Maybe you have had your own experience like this, when God revealed to you how much he loves you. It may have been similar to mine, or it may have been very different. It may have been a series of experiences. Maybe these experiences are etched forever in your heart, or maybe you have allowed their details to become clouded with negative experiences. We need to recall these moments in our lives when God's personal love became real for us. And if we don't feel we've ever experienced this kind of affirmation from God, we need to ask God for our own evidence of his personal love. He is more than eager to answer this kind of request.

The love of God is at work all around us. Of course, from our human perspective, we don't always see all of what God is doing on our behalf. When he is actively drawing us to himself, we can be quite unaware of it. When he was choosing us, we didn't know about it. When he was softening our hearts toward him, we didn't understand what was happening within us. This is why, in many cases, we talk about how we found God rather than how God found us. But when we come to faith and accept the perspective of the Scriptures, we learn to believe that God's action comes prior to our action. We still grapple with the mystery of it all, but we agree with the words of Jesus, "No one can come to me unless the Father who sent me draws him" (John 6:44). When we are personally awakened by God's loving action toward us, we realize that our role in the relationship is one of *response*. God's great love sets us free to respond. It invites a reply. God speaks; we answer. He acts; we react.

> God's great love sets us free to respond.

This understanding of God as the Initiator helps us to maintain a God-centered perspective on our lives of faith. It saves us from thinking that it's all up to us. We must be careful not to be led astray to believe that our salvation is the result of anything other than God's initiation. When the apostle Paul writes about our salvation, he says, "It's God's gift from start to finish! We don't play the major role" (Eph. 2:8–9 MSG). The apostle John also goes to great lengths to protect us from a self-centered spirituality when he emphasizes in the fourth chapter of his first letter that "love comes from God" (v. 7), that "God is love" (vv. 8, 16), and that "we love because he first loved us" (v. 19). The only way to understand our Christian lives is to begin with God's love toward us, not our love toward him.

Nothing exhibits God's love and his commitment to relationship more than the sending of his Son, Jesus Christ: "This is how God showed his love among us: He sent his one and only Son into the world that we might live through him" (1 John 4:9). God could not have made it more clear to us. In the sacrificial death of Jesus, God spoke to us, saying, "I love you, and I have made a way for us to be in relationship with each other."

The death was necessary because of sin. According to God's law, "without the shedding of blood there is no forgiveness" (Heb. 9:22). But instead of the temporary substitution of animal sacrifices, which were offered regularly according to the Old Testament law, Jesus Christ came to earth to die as the perfect sacrifice, offered once for all. Instead of us facing our own death sentence because of our sin, Christ faced it for us. And in providing a way for us to be forgiven, God dealt with the one thing that kept us distant from him. He made it possible for us to be together with him, to be at peace with him. That's what atonement is all about. Our sin separated us from him. We were estranged, alienated from our Creator. In fact, we were dead in our sin, unable to help ourselves, unable on our own to remedy our hopeless situation. We needed God to make a move toward us. In Jesus, he did. The apostle Paul says that "God was reconciling the world to himself in Christ" (2 Cor. 5:19).

This commitment to relationship becomes even more amazing to us once we understand that, in our sinful state, we were not only helpless before God but hostile toward him. In our sin we were enemies of God (Rom. 5:10). Thankfully, God loves his enemies. As we pushed him away, he was still reaching out to us. Through the death of Christ, he effected a transformation on our behalf, changing us from his enemies into his friends. He disarmed us, not through coercion but through an amazing act of unconditional love. Paul says that "God demonstrates his own love for us in this: While we were still sinners, Christ died for us" (Rom. 5:8). God did not wait for us to clean up our lives before he saved us. Contrary to the common *un*biblical saying, God helps those who *cannot* help themselves.

> **Although God is not ignorant of your failures, he does not focus on them.**

Where does this leave us? What does it do for you to know that God loves you like this? How will you respond to God's loving invitation to relationship? Even though God has made the first move, there comes a time when he waits for us to move.

Sometimes, however, we hesitate. We doubt. We resist God's love. Even though we may easily and eagerly admit to the facts about God's love for humanity, somehow we still find it hard to believe that God is deeply in love with each one of us as individuals. As we look within ourselves, we sometimes struggle with the idea that God's love is personal and he wants to prove this love to each one of us in specific ways. Instead of living under the power and freedom of God's affirmation, we allow ourselves to focus on our own inadequacies and limitations. One of the ways it becomes evident is when, at the end of the day, our minds dwell on two things: what we have done and what we haven't done. Hopelessly we evaluate the day based on the tasks that we did or did not accomplish, and more often than not, we feel guilty about both or either of these things. This leaves us going to bed at night feeling insecure, anxious, and unloved.

If you are like me, you have often struggled with this kind of heaviness. It was during my years at university that these pressures began to take their toll on me. After I graduated from high school in Southern California, I attended a Christian school in Illinois called Wheaton College. It was there that I began to learn how important it was for me to get beyond my own cramped perspective and take into account *God's* perspective on my life.

Basically, I learned to go to bed at night with one thought on my mind, and that was "God loves me." There is nothing else more important than that. Learning to rest in God's love changed me. It brought me peace and security that nothing else could bring.

No matter what has happened in your day, Jesus wants you to go to bed at night remembering that one simple truth: God loves you. Although God is not ignorant of your failures, he does not focus on them. Because of what Jesus accomplished on the cross, you are justified in God's eyes. He is consumed with a love for you and wants you to be assured of that love at the end of every day.

I can already hear many of you saying, "But . . . ." Yes, we can all think of many reasons why God shouldn't love us, but the simple truth is, he does. No matter what has happened today, he loves you. He loves you as you close your eyes to sleep, and he is excited in the morning as you begin another day with him.

We need to make it a practice to remind ourselves of God's love for us each night before we go to bed. Maybe we need to read a psalm, sing a worship song, or even just say, simply, "Thank you, God, for loving me."

When we do this, it helps us to rest in God's love. It also prepares us for our tomorrow. Knowing that God's mercies are new every morning (Lam. 3:23), we can move on from our yesterday, even when it is tainted by failure. So often, we cause ourselves to come under a heaviness that leads to depression and disillusionment because we are so inwardly focused and lose sight of his unconditional love for us. God invites us to experience a love without limits, a love that is not based on what we do.

Despite this open invitation from God, it is often difficult to maintain this understanding. If you are like me, it is a constant struggle.

After I graduated from college in 1988, I joined an international missions organization called Youth With A Mission (YWAM). Over the years I traveled extensively with the mission and actively pursued a variety of service opportunities.

> God invites us to experience a love without limits, a love that is not based on what we do.

Once while I was with YWAM in the States, I had an experience that tested my grasp of God's love for me. I was relaxing and playing billiards one day when a thought ran through my head: *Am I really doing what's best right now? I could be serving God overseas or preaching somewhere. What am I doing here playing this game? Am I missing God's best?*

As I thought about it, I was reminded of the simple truth that God's love for us is not based on what we *do*. God does not love us more because we are doing something we may consider more spiritual or useful. My feelings of guilt were based not on the truth of God's unconditional love but rather on the idea that I could somehow earn that love. As I continued to play billiards, I worked through some of this in my mind and began to affirm some simple truths: *Nothing can separate me from the love of God. He loves me right now! Nothing I do can make God love me more. Nothing I do can make God love me less.* As I pondered these things, the peace of God filled my heart and mind.

Of course, God's love for us should not inspire laziness. We will look at this later in the book, but the issue here is our motivation—why we do the things we do. What happened to me while I was playing billiards was that I had a greater revelation of his love for me. The more we understand God's love, the more we will want to love him back. Our actions, then, are to be inspired by love and gratitude and not by some sense of guilt or obligation.

Two stories early in the Gospel of John beautifully demonstrate the personal love that Jesus has for each one of us. The fourth chapter (vv. 1–42) describes Jesus' encounter with a woman at a well. As the woman of Samaria approaches the well, Jesus initiates the conversation with a simple question: "Will you give me a drink?" We are told in the text (v. 9) that Jews did not associate with Samaritans, and the woman's response to Jesus reveals her genuine surprise: "You are a Jew and I am a Samaritan woman. How can you ask me for a drink?"

Jesus then turns the conversation away from the water in the well to a "living water" that he is eager to share with the woman. The woman is intrigued by the offer and is drawn deeper into conversation with this man Jesus. When he begins mysteriously to expose some relationship problems in her personal life and history, the woman perceives that she is indeed speaking with someone very special. But still there are significant things that separate them, most importantly their religion. When Jesus judiciously breaks down this barrier as well and convinces her that his offer of life is equally open to Samaritans, she can do nothing but receive his love.

Despite a variety of reasons why Jesus shouldn't interact with this woman, he communicates a deep and personal love for her, a love that transforms her. Jesus boldly breaks down barriers of race, religion, sex, and reputation and calls this woman to a life of meaning and wholeness. Even though Jesus knows her personal flaws and frailty, he accepts her and wins her heart. And it is this love that inspires her and finally commissions her to invite others to meet this man and to experience his love.

Even though there are many things that legitimately separate you from Jesus, not least of which are your personal failings, Jesus loves you and is eager to convince you of his personal love.

> *What would you say if God said to you, "What do you want?"*

The next chapter of John (5:1–15 MSG) tells a similar story of transformation. This time Jesus approaches a man at the Pool of Bethesda. The man has been ill and sitting beside the pool for thirty-eight years when Jesus asks him, "Do you want to get well?"

The man answers, "Sir, when the water is stirred, I don't have anybody to put me in the pool. By the time I get there, somebody else is already in." This man only sees one way to get well, and he can't achieve it. He has tried many times, but it eludes his grasp. You can hear the hopelessness in his voice.

Then Jesus tells the man, "Get up, take your bedroll, start walking" (v. 8), and the man is healed. He is instantly able to pick up his mat and walk.

Jesus comes to this man to bless him, to meet his need. When all hope is gone and there seems to be no other way, Jesus appears on the scene. He walks into our lives in the same way. He comes to heal and to make whole. This is who

Jesus is. He is very committed to our personal lives, whatever needs and desires we have. He knows what we long for, and he longs to grant us our requests even before we ask. The man beside the pool thought he was forgotten, but he wasn't. Even though you may at times feel the same way, forgotten and without hope, Jesus is there for you.

For the lame man by the pool, I'm sure Jesus' question, "Do you want to get well?" came as a surprise. *Who was this man, asking such bold questions?* We need to understand that God desires to interact with each one of us in this kind of intensely personal way. What would you say if God said to you, "What do you want?" Are you ready and willing to be specific with God?

A young woman named Debbie had recently been challenged by another believer to ask God to reveal himself to her in a very specific way. Debbie responded to the challenge and prayed silently to God, asking him to give her a dozen long-stem, peach-colored roses and a ring for her finger that would be a reminder of his personal love for her.

After a few days a van pulled up to the place where Debbie worked. The driver told the secretary at the front desk that he was working for a florist and there had been a mistake in their order that day. They had some extra long-stem, peach-colored roses, and he wondered if anyone there could possibly make use of them.

Not knowing anything about Debbie's prayer, the secretary decided to surprise her friend and fellow believer with the roses. She accepted the roses from the driver; then, with a borrowed key, she slipped into Debbie's apartment and put an arrangement of a dozen long-stem, peach-colored roses into a vase.

When Debbie walked into her apartment later that day, she was overwhelmed by the specific answer to her prayer.

Shortly afterward a Christian couple who had been friends with Debbie for some time invited her out for dinner. At dinner they shared with her that recently they had had an impression that they should give her something, a special gift that had been in their family for many years. They handed her a box, and inside was a beautiful diamond ring. Overwhelmed again, Debbie put on the ring. She wore it as a reminder of God's personal love for her.

God wants to prove himself to each one of us. It may not be the same for you as it was for Debbie, but he wants to show you that he loves you.

One recent example from my own life came in the fall of 2002. I was asking God for a new Bible, and I felt like he was challenging me to be specific about what I wanted. So I asked specifically for a navy blue NIV Study Bible. I even specified that it didn't need to be brand new. After praying, I was content to see how God would provide. A week later, however, I was near a Christian bookstore and thought that maybe I should just buy my new Bible. As I walked through the doors, I felt God encourage me to wait for his provision in another way. The following week I had a similar experience at another bookstore in another city. Again I felt God say, *Wait.* But this time I also felt that he said the Bible would be provided for me next week during my visit to Texas. Sure enough, on the last day of my visit to a church in Waco, my hosts, unaware of my prayer request, took me to a lost and found box in the church and asked simply if I needed a Bible. When I said that I did, they answered, "Take whichever one you want." I looked down into the box, and right before my eyes was a used navy blue NIV Study Bible. Go, God!

Does God want to surprise you with his personal love in very specific ways? I want to challenge you to ask God to surprise you today with how much he loves you.

On another occasion God allowed me to be involved with one of his personal surprises for someone else, a man named Mark.

I met Mark in 1998 in New York, one year after I had returned to the United States after a harrowing experience in prison in Iran. In 1997 I had traveled into Iran with a friend of mine named Glenn to explore the possibility of future service opportunities within the country. On my way out of the country, I was detained by Iranian authorities and put into prison unjustly, charged with espionage. I was imprisoned for nine weeks before I was miraculously released.

> *Ask God to surprise you today with how much he loves you.*

I will tell more of my experiences in prison in the pages that follow, but upon my return to the States, I had many opportunities to share my story. On one occasion I was asked to speak in a church in New York. As I prayed about the invitation, I felt quite sure that I should go. However, as I walked into that church on a Sunday evening, dressed in my typical casual attire, I immediately felt out of place. The feeling was probably so strong because everything else in the church building seemed to me to be perfectly in place, including every man and boy in a suit and tie. When the pastor approached me, he looked me up and down and, with disdain in his voice, asked, "Are you the guest speaker?"

"Yes," I said hesitantly.

"Just give us your testimony about getting out of prison," he replied abruptly, leaving little doubt that he was expecting someone more impressive than me.

Struggling with uneasiness and insecurity, all I wanted was for that service to end and to quickly get on a plane heading home. But after I finished sharing my story, I was approached by a man who greeted me with tears in his eyes. He began, "Sir, my name is Mark, and I'm not from here. I was driving through this town tonight when I felt the Lord challenge me to walk into this church and listen to the preacher. A few weeks ago, God spoke to me about making restitution for several crimes that I had committed before I was saved. I did what God told me to do, but tomorrow I go into prison to serve a three-year sentence. After hearing you speak tonight, I know that the Lord will help me and that he will give me strength to endure."

Mark and I embraced, and we prayed together. As I left the church that evening, I had no doubt about why God had brought me there. I was greatly encouraged as I thought about God's personal love for Mark. What a privilege to be a part of God's surprise in his life.

The personal love that God has for each one of us is shown in many and various ways. Sometimes God brings us special encouragement. Sometimes he provides exactly what we need. Sometimes God shows his love for us in how he protects us from harm. Even though God holds the entire universe together, he also watches over each and every individual. Many times I have been amazed to see God's hand of protection upon my life.

Between 1988 and 1993, while serving with YWAM, I helped administer an eye hospital in Kabul, Afghanistan. On one occasion I went with a team from the hospital to run an eye clinic in the northeastern part of the country. The village where we were based was high up in the mountains (11,000 feet above sea level), and we had to walk for two days just to get there. The mountain trail was narrow and dangerous. On the way I tripped on a rock and stumbled off the trail. I fell onto a smooth boulder and quickly began to slide down the side of it. There was nothing to stop me, and as I glanced down, all I could see below me was a drop of at least one hundred feet. In a panic I cried out to God. As I continued to slide, I could see a little six-inch shrub sticking out of the rock. In desperation I grabbed for it, and to my amazement it held me and stopped me from falling. I held on to it long enough to gather my senses and to find a crack in the rock where I could brace myself. From there I slowly climbed back onto the trail. Once on the trail again, I looked down at the tiny shrub, knowing that it was nothing short of a miracle that it had kept me from plunging over the cliff. Somehow God had intervened and saved my life!

> *Even though God holds the entire universe together, he also watches over each and every individual.*

However, that is only part of the story of God's intervention at that moment in my life. Three years later, Maria, a friend from Brazil, approached me and inquired bluntly about my safety three years earlier, "Dan, were you ever in danger of losing your life back then?"

I immediately recalled the accident on the trail in the mountains of Afghanistan. "Yes," I said, "I almost fell off a cliff."

Maria then proceeded to tell me about the night three years earlier when she was awakened from her sleep and prompted by God to pray for my safety and for the sparing of my life. This kind of thing happened very rarely in her life, so she was careful to journal the details of the awakening. As we talked further and compared notes, we concurred that Maria had been called to pray at the precise time I was in danger on the trail!

God cares deeply for each one of us. He loves us in a profoundly personal way. I believe that he is prepared to convince us of that in ways that are quite obvious. We only need to open the door to the possibilities.

In Revelation the apostle John records an invitation from Jesus: "Behold, I stand at the door and knock; if anyone hears my voice and opens the door, I will come in to him and eat with him, and he with me" (Rev. 3:20 RSV). Jesus desires this kind of intimacy with each and every believer. He invites each one of us to open the door and to experience his personal love for us. As we do, we will be changed forever.

Chapter Two

God's Goodness

How great is your goodness, which you
have stored up for those who fear you.
                                    —*Psalm 31:19*

Taste and see that the LORD is good.
Oh, the joys of those who trust in him!
                                    —*Psalm 34:8 (NLT)*

G od is for you. He has your best interests in mind. He
wants you to find enjoyment in life. God is good,
and he wants each of us to experience his goodness. This is
exactly what the Bible affirms again and again, both in the
New and the Old Testaments. Throughout biblical history
God's people celebrate God's goodness.

Despite these affirmations, we sometimes still think of
God as a tyrant, someone who is withholding good from us and
trying to make things difficult for us. We may not say it, but
sometimes we think it. Is it possible that God is mean rather
than good? Does he have cruel intentions? Do you sometimes
think that he is trying to make life miserable for you?

During my imprisonment in Iran, I questioned God's goodness. I was innocent of the crimes of which I was accused, but would God come to my defense? In the midst of my loneliness and despair, it was an incredible struggle for me to acknowledge that it was God's good intention to bless me there in prison. I had believed in the goodness of God, but now I was confronted with something that threatened to disprove it. Alone in my prison cell, I was miserable. I thought I might never again see my friends and family. I thought I might never again walk freely in the sunshine. I was beaten regularly, and I could often hear others being beaten and even executed. I was stricken by fear, knowing that, at any moment, I might be the next to be executed. Often I lay curled up in the corner of my cell, shaking, crying, and cringing at any sound. Even though God had rescued me from many other difficult situations in the past, there in prison my hope was gone. I believed that this time God would *not* deliver me. And there was nothing within me that could muster up the faith to believe otherwise. Despair had set in at its deepest level.

For those who have read my prison story, you know about the day when this despair drove me to attempt suicide in my cell. It was only by God's grace that my attempt failed. Afterward, as I lay on the ground sobbing, Jesus met me in a miraculous way. I knew in that moment that Jesus was with me and that he would carry me through the rest of my time in prison.

Through that experience I began to realize that no matter how much pain and loss I was suffering, I still had what was most important to me—my relationship with God. Even though I had lost most of the other things that brought meaning and enjoyment to my life, no one could take away my faith. No one could separate me from God.

As I turned to the Scriptures there in my cell, particularly the Psalms and the Gospels, my faith was renewed. I saw in the lives of David and Jesus the understanding that even while we are experiencing pain and loss in other areas of our lives, we can still experience joy in our relationship with God. In fact, it is the pain that pushes us to God. It depends entirely on what we see as most important. There in prison God was challenging my values and clarifying for me what was ultimately most essential for my well-being.

Though it was a painful process, I was truly thankful for what I was learning. I was growing closer to God, and as my vision of Jesus became more and more clear, my circumstances became less and less significant. Though my situation didn't change, my perspective did. In the gloom of my cell, once again I was able to say with confidence that God is good.

Think about the trials you have encountered in life. What have you learned from them? How have you been strengthened through them? If you value the development of Christian character in your life, then you will be able to endure trials with this godly purpose in mind. It doesn't necessarily decrease the pain you may experience in the midst of the trial, but it will give you perspective. It will allow you to see beyond the immediate pain and to find joy and solace in God.

This is what James writes about in his letter to the churches: "Consider it pure joy, my brothers, whenever you face trials of many kinds" (James 1:2). Why? That sounds almost crazy unless we, like James, place a high value on spiritual growth and maturity. According to James, the reason why you should get excited about difficulty in your life is simply "because you know that the testing of your faith develops perseverance . . . so that you may be mature and complete" (vv. 3–4).

Whatever the source of difficulty in our lives, God is committed to doing something good in each of us. He is committed to cultivating growth in our lives. If we understand this, we will be able to endure the times of testing, but if we lose sight of God's good intent, the difficulties in life will drag us down and we will resist God's purpose.

A friend of mine, Misha, was only twenty-one years old when doctors told her she might never walk again. They also told her it would be impossible for her to have children. She had already suffered for years with a debilitating condition, and now she was losing hope. Twenty-three different medications and supplements had been prescribed to help her deal with the pain, but she was exhausted both physically and emotionally. She was afraid of becoming bitter and didn't want to allow anger to delude her. Maybe worst of all, she felt very alone. Misha's faith pushed her toward God, but she wasn't sure what to expect from him. Bedridden, she was isolated from her friends. She hoped to be married, but who would ever want to marry her like this? At times she was afraid of what she would do to herself if she got really hopeless, and for that reason she would not keep her medications next to her bed.

> God is committed to doing something good in each of us. He is committed to cultivating growth in our lives.

It was in the midst of this despair that God spoke to Misha, asking her, *Do you believe that I am good?* At first she didn't know how to take the question. Misha knew God existed. She had experienced his love. She was committed to following him. But the question about his goodness was difficult for her. She thought about war, about cancer, about poverty. She thought about her own challenging situation and the pain she was experiencing. It was easy to question the goodness of God, but she also knew that there was plenty of evidence that he is good. For Misha it came down to a simple choice. She chose to believe in God's goodness. She chose to embrace what he had allowed in her life. She reasoned within herself that if it was by faith that she believed in God's existence, and by accepting what the Bible said, and by testing it with her own experience, then she would have to wrestle in the same way with God's character, whether or not he was good. This process would be hard at times, but she would allow God to prove himself. And God was faithful. Though the struggle was intense, in the midst of it all, God proved himself time and again. Then, five years later, at the age of twenty-six, Misha was healed. God intervened in her life in a miraculous way, removing the sickness and the pain.

Now thirty-one, she is happily married to a wonderful man, and they have been blessed with two children. The challenges, however, continue. During the birth of their second child, Misha and the baby almost didn't survive the delivery. At one point in the crisis, doctors thought that even if their lives were spared, one or both would be brain damaged. Instead, both were healthy.

Through it all Misha testifies to a renewed sense of God's presence in her life. She boldly agrees with David that "the LORD is gracious and compassionate, slow to anger and rich in love. The LORD is good to all; he has compassion on all he has made" (Ps. 145:8–9). It doesn't mean that she has answers to all her questions. She also doesn't expect to live without pain and suffering. But Misha is eager to affirm that God is good.

As we seek to understand the goodness of God, it is helpful to return to the Garden of Eden, where the relationship between God and man began. Here we see God's original intent. *Eden* means pleasure in the original Hebrew, and the second chapter of Genesis describes the home of humankind as a place of incredible beauty and abundance. It was filled with good things created by God for Adam and Eve to enjoy. From the very beginning, we see that it is God's desire and plan for humankind to experience pleasure, to enjoy life.

Moreover, it is important to understand that one aspect of being created in the image of God is that we experience maximum pleasure in the context of our relationship with him. We were created for relationship with him. So, ultimately, Eden was pleasurable for Adam and Eve because God was there with them and they were able to experience an open, unhindered relationship with him.

For us this simply means that we will only experience the fullness of God's goodness if we are in relationship with him. Of course, people can experience a generous measure of God's goodness even without acknowledging him. Atheists are still able to enjoy sunsets and to experience love in relationships, but if God is not acknowledged, then what is ultimately most pleasurable in this life—relationship with God—is unattainable.

The test for all of us comes when we are challenged to question the value of our relationship with God. Do we really believe that there is nothing more valuable or pleasurable in this life than knowing God?

Maybe the most basic form of testing that we encounter is the result of the freedom of choice that God has given us. We are constantly confronted with the choice either to obey or disobey God, to believe or disbelieve. This freedom to choose was presented to us first in the Garden of Eden. In Genesis 2:16–17, God says to man, "You are free to eat from any tree in the garden; but you must not eat from the tree of the knowledge of good and evil." Because we know the end of the story, it may seem that God is merely giving man the opportunity to sin, but it's more than that—God also gives man the opportunity *not* to sin, or rather, the freedom to choose obedience.

As we face this freedom, it is our understanding of the character of God, and especially his goodness, that instructs our choices. If we believe God to be good, we will more easily trust him and more willingly do what he says. As long as Adam and Eve chose to obey God and trust his ways by not eating from the forbidden tree, they walked in the path of blessing and were thus able to enjoy all that God had given them. In the same way, when we walk in obedience, trusting in God, choosing his will, we are most able to enjoy his goodness.

> Do we really believe that there is nothing more valuable or pleasurable in this life than knowing God?

Of course, as we have noted, this path of blessing is not devoid of difficulties. But we need to see each challenge along the path as an opportunity to choose obedience and, in so doing, to express our love for God and embrace his goodness.

It's critical for us to catch a glimpse of what God was doing when he gave us this freedom. God was taking an incredible risk. He made himself vulnerable to us. He took the risk that we might learn to live without him. We might learn self-sufficiency, to live our lives and even to enjoy the good gifts he has given us in his creation while ignoring or even turning our backs on our relationship with him. In this way, the freedom that God has given us is a simple test. Will we take seriously our responsibility to value and maintain our relationship with God? Or will we neglect the relationship and choose to forget

God? How are you responding to this test right now in your life?

In the Garden of Eden, we see Adam and Eve choose disobedience. God's goodness is spurned, and their world falls apart. The relationship of trust between God and mankind is violated, and the community between Adam and Eve is broken.

The short passage of Scripture (Gen. 3:1–24) that we refer to as "the Fall" centers on a dialogue between Eve and a serpent (vv. 1–5). The issue in question in this conversation is the goodness of God. The serpent, here being used as an instrument of God's enemy, plants a seed of doubt in Eve's heart. Eve is tempted by the attractive fruit, but at a deeper level she finds herself believing the claim of the serpent, that God is perhaps not as good as she at first believed.

We all struggle with doubt. In fact, honest doubts and questions reveal faith's presence in our hearts, not its absence. But what we do with our doubts is critical. In the example of Eve, we have what *not* to do with doubts. In fact, as soon as she continues in conversation with this deceiver, she falters. She finds herself altering what *God* has said, expanding his command by adding "and you must not touch it" (v. 3). Then, instead of going to God or to her husband with her doubt, she isolates herself with the serpent and ends up believing his lie. Eve is at odds with her Creator. She thinks she knows what's best. In the end, she sets herself up as her own god, her own ruler. She rejects God's way and chooses her way.

This is, forever, the nature of sin. When we sin, we challenge God's authority and put ourselves on the throne. We disbelieve in God's goodness. We assert that we know what is best for ourselves. Sin is an act of defiance against God. When we sin, we are choosing a pleasure or a course of action of our own design instead of that which God intends for us; we're placing ourselves and our wants above him. Of course, part of the pain of disobedience comes when we realize that we have chosen a *lesser* pleasure or a less fruitful—perhaps even destructive—course of action. We have forfeited what is best.

Why do we sin? Why would we ever choose something less than what is most valuable and, in the end, most pleasurable? Because we do not see things clearly. Our faculties are impaired. Our souls and minds and hearts are completely darkened by a sinful nature. We are diseased, terminally. We are wounded, fatally. We are lost, eternally.

> *Ultimately, it is in Christ that we are able to experience all the good that God has intended for us.*

We have only one hope: that God will come looking for us and help us, just as he did with Adam and Eve in the Garden of Eden. After they had sinned, they were hiding from God. In Genesis 3:9 we have one of the most beautiful and amazing verses in the whole Bible: "But the LORD God called to the man, 'Where are you?'" In the same way, wherever our sin has left us, God comes to us and calls out, "Where are you?"

We run away from God, and God runs after us. This is unconditional love. This was the mission of Jesus Christ: "For the Son of Man came to seek and to save what was lost" (Luke 19:10). God wants to draw us to himself and convince us of his great love and goodness. It is his mission to find us and heal us and help us to choose again what is truly good.

Ultimately, it is *in Christ* that we are able to experience all the good that God has intended for us. This is what the apostle Paul has said so emphatically in his letters to the churches.

And perhaps in no other letter has he said it better than in his letter to the Ephesians. In the first chapter of that letter he writes, "Long, long ago he decided to adopt us into his family through Jesus Christ" (1:5 MSG). Through this adoption we have the inheritance and all the rights that come from being children of God. We can't even begin to fathom that. Why would God adopt us? He has. It was decided long ago. During Paul's time, in the Roman Empire, an adopted child was chosen by the family and thus had a greater value than a naturally born child. So when Paul says this, he is showing that we have greater value because God specifically chose us.

> As Christians we are not primarily in a religion, or in a teaching, or in a state of mind — we are in a Person.

Just when I think I'm able to grasp his goodness, there is more. In verse 7, Paul says, "Because of the sacrifice of the Messiah . . . we're a free people—free of penalties and punishments chalked up by all our misdeeds" (MSG). Wow, we are free! How many times have I based my walk with God on what I have done or what I haven't done? So often I've felt like I needed to do penance for my sin because it was just too ugly for the grace of God to cover. But Paul testifies that we are free from punishment for *all* of our misdeeds. And that means *all* of them, all of our sins from years ago, six months ago, yesterday, today, and for the rest of our lives. We are free. That is good news.

Throughout the book of Ephesians, as well as in his other letters, Paul uses the term *in Christ* over and over again. What does it mean to be "in Christ"? It is a description of intimate association. As Christians we are not primarily *in* a religion, or *in* a teaching, or *in* a state of mind—we are *in* a Person. We are invited to lose ourselves in this relationship. Jesus said, "If anyone would come after me, he must deny himself and take up his cross and follow me" (Mark 8:34). Being found "in Christ" requires radical self-denial and surrender. However, the very next verse affirms that it is actually in denying ourselves for Christ that we discover ourselves in Christ: "For whoever wants to save his life will lose it, but whoever loses his life for me and for the gospel will save it" (Mark 8:35). When we submit ourselves to Christ's authority, we are also entrusting ourselves to his goodness. Jesus commands our obedience but also promises our ultimate well-being. He calls us to die to ourselves, that we might live *in him.*

I would encourage you to pick up a newer translation of the Bible, such as *The Message,* and read through Ephesians, especially the first two chapters, with one prayer in mind: "God, show me your goodness." And it is my prayer that God would overwhelm you with his goodness just as he did with Paul.

When it comes right down to it, what we need most is a greater revelation of who God is. There is so much that we don't understand about him and so much that we misunderstand. In fact, most of the problems we face in our lives of faith stem from misconceptions about who God is.

After spending many years serving God in Central Asia, I was for a time back at home in the United States. During that period, I was struggling within myself over where I should be living and serving God. On the one hand, I was sensing that God was leading me to be in the U.S. for a while. On the other hand, I had this nagging notion that God would be more pleased with me if I were serving him overseas.

My inner turmoil was based on a misunderstanding: I believed that God showed preference toward missionaries and that somehow I could earn his favor simply by moving to another part of the world. I was very wrong, and I had no peace in my heart until God brought clarity to my confusion and affirmed that my worth was not based on where I was serving him.

As we struggle with limitations like this, we must learn to come before God regularly with a simple prayer: "God, give me a revelation of who you are today." We should pray this not only for ourselves but for others as well because nothing else will change our lives more than a deeper knowledge of God. The more we pray this prayer, the more we will desire to experience it. It will become our passion to know God, and the more we know him, the more we will yearn for more of him.

> "God, give me a revelation of who you are today."

What an amazing journey we are invited to embark on—a relationship with our Creator. What an amazing treasure we have—the opportunity to know God personally. Truly, there is nothing more beautiful, nothing more wonderful, nothing more extravagant that our hearts could desire. This is precisely what the apostle Paul was captivated by when he wrote, "I consider everything a loss compared to the surpassing greatness of knowing Christ Jesus my Lord" (Phil. 3:8).

Is it the cry of your heart to know God? Are you willing right now to lose everything else, as Paul was, in order to gain Christ, in order to go deeper in your relationship with God? If you are unsure about the answers to questions like these, then you have probably allowed other things to cloud your understanding of who God is. But right now God longs to prove himself to you and to bring you to that place of knowing that nothing else is more important than your relationship with him. God longs to captivate your heart. If you are ready and willing to go deeper with God, then brace yourself for the adventure of your life!

It was the author of Hebrews, when writing about faith, who wrote, "For whoever would draw near to God must believe that he exists and *that he rewards those who seek him*" (11:6 RSV, emphasis added). If we are to enjoy and cherish a relationship with God, we must believe in not only God's existence but also his character, that he is good and that he desires to grant us an experience of that goodness.

When we believe this about God, it presents us with the inspiring possibility of trusting him, of giving ourselves wholeheartedly to a relationship with him. It is to this topic, trust, that we will now turn our attention.

Part Two

Trusting

God has shown us that he is not only capable of relationship with us but that he is committed to it above all else. He has given himself to us, and in turn he invites us to give ourselves to him. This response on our part can generally be described as *trust*. Just as in any relationship, it requires something of us, an opening of our hearts. In the following three chapters I will discuss three aspects of this giving of ourselves to God: responding to the call to intimacy, dealing with fear, and hearing from God.

Chapter Three

Intimacy with Jesus

"Come, follow me," Jesus said.
                    —*Mark 1:17*

Remain in me, and I will remain
in you.
                    —*Jesus, John 15:4*

O ne day as Jesus was walking beside the Sea of
Galilee, he encountered some fishermen. First, he
approached two brothers, Simon and Andrew, in the midst of
their work. He called out to them, "Come, follow me, and I
will make you fishers of men." Immediately the two men left
their nets and followed him. Next, the same thing happened
with another set of brothers, James and John, also working
along the shores of the sea.

What would it be like today if Jesus walked into your
workplace and did what he did on that day beside the Sea
of Galilee? We don't know much about the situation on that
day when Jesus met these fishermen, but what we do know

is amazing, and it merits some further reflection as we think about God's desire for intimacy with us.

Here are these men at work, fishing, doing what they have always done and probably what their fathers had done before them. They seem to be absorbed in their regular routine when a man walks up to them and invites them to follow him. We don't know if they had ever seen this man before, but apparently, without a question, without any delay, they followed. We may ask about whether or not this was a wise decision, whether or not it was the responsible thing to do. What about their jobs? What about their families? This man told them nothing about the future aside from an obscure promise of transformation, that he would give them a new mission in life and change them into "fishers of men." It seems that, at that point, he offered them nothing more, except himself. And yet they followed.

> **This call to discipleship was first and foremost an invitation to intimate friendship.**

It was the person of Jesus that attracted these fishermen. This call to discipleship was first and foremost an invitation to intimate friendship. Jesus called them to himself—"Come, follow me"—and they obeyed. He was more than just another religious teacher—he was speaking with authority about life and death, and he was offering life itself. The prospect of following this man, of being near to him and receiving from him, was suddenly worth more to them than anything else. These fishermen were captivated by the person of Jesus. His authority compelled them. His love awakened them. His grace energized them.

Is it any different for us today? Jesus hasn't physically walked into our workplace or our school, but he has walked into our lives and called us to be his disciples. He has spoken those same words into our hearts: "Come, follow me." We have been amazed at his unconditional acceptance of us and inspired by his confidence in us. We have been invited into intimate relationship with Jesus, and we have responded to his call.

The lives of the disciples took a radical turn when they encountered Jesus. Some years later, after his death and resurrection, Jesus appeared to a man named Saul, whose life was similarly transformed. Saul was formerly a zealous member of a group of Jewish teachers called the Pharisees, and he was actively involved in opposing those who followed Jesus. However, one day, on his way to further harassments, Saul was dramatically confronted by Jesus, who asked him a simple question: "Saul, why are you persecuting me?" Immediately Saul realized the error of his way. The encounter also left him physically blind. But Jesus arranged for a meeting between Saul and a local believer named Ananias. This Ananias prayed for Saul, and Saul experienced both a physical healing and a spiritual rebirth. After further fellowship with local believers, Saul began to take a lead role in proclaiming the gospel of Jesus, and it was not long before he became the prominent leader in the early church, known as the apostle Paul.

Paul's testimony has an important place in the New Testament. It is recounted three times in the book of Acts (in chapters 9, 22, and 26), and it is also reflected upon frequently in Paul's letters to the churches. It was during my imprisonment in Iran that Paul's testimony had a profound impact upon me. I was privileged to have my Bible with me in prison, and I was especially drawn to Paul's letter to the Philippians, a letter he wrote while he was imprisoned for the cause of Christ. One of the resounding themes of that letter is joy and contentment. Paul sums it up near the end of his letter, when he exhorts his readers, "Rejoice in the Lord always. I will say it again: Rejoice!" (4:4).

> I am the vine; you are the branches. If a man remains in me and I in him, he will bear much fruit; apart from me you can do nothing.
> —Jesus in John 15:5

As I sat in my prison cell, I thought to myself, *How could Paul write so much about rejoicing while sitting in prison?* But the more I read that letter, the more clear it became to me. Paul teaches that a heart that is captivated by Jesus is able to endure any hardship. The joy in Paul's life had nothing to do with his circumstances but everything to do with his relationship with Jesus. At the end of the letter, Paul states that he has learned the secret of contentment (4:12), and we would be sadly amiss if we concluded that it was anything other than the intimacy of his relationship with Jesus. Knowing Jesus was everything to Paul. Everything else was not simply secondary but so secondary that he considered it rubbish (3:8). He was enthralled by the person of Jesus. All of Paul's accomplishments (of which he had many) were rubbish in comparison. All of his hardships and struggles were equally unworthy of distracting him from Jesus. Aside from imprisonment, Paul had suffered a wide variety of tortures, misfortunes, and deprivations (which he lists in 2 Corinthians 11:23–28). All of this faded into insignificance for Paul compared to the value of knowing Jesus. Intimacy with Jesus was his life.

There are many passages of Scripture that have challenged me in the area of intimacy with Jesus but none more than the words of Jesus himself in John 15. After three years with his disciples, Jesus begins to focus more and more on his departure and to prepare them for life without his physical presence. It would have been very difficult for these dedicated disciples to imagine life without Jesus. How would they survive without him?

Jesus answers this question in John 15. He uses a familiar image, that of a vine, and he invites the disciples to relate this image to their relationship with him. His message is clear: "Remain in me, and I will remain in you. No branch can bear fruit by itself; it must remain in the vine. Neither can you bear fruit unless you remain in me. I am the vine; you are the branches. If a man remains in me and I in him, he will bear much fruit; apart from me you can do nothing" (vv. 4–5).

It's a simple lesson but very profound. Jesus is calling his disciples to intimacy. It involves both an invitation ("remain in me") and a promise ("I will remain in you"). Even after his physical departure, Jesus will be with his followers by the Holy Spirit, and his followers will be with him as they acknowledge his presence. The metaphor helps to define for the disciples how they will continue to follow Jesus after his departure. Their sole responsibility will be to stay connected to the vine, to nurture their relationship with Jesus. Intimacy with him will still be a reality through the Holy Spirit, and as they maintain that intimacy, their lives will reveal the evidence of it—they will bear fruit.

As we consider these truths for our own lives, we need to appreciate the simple fact that fruit grows on branches that are connected to the vine. So often we assume that bearing fruit is, somehow, our own responsibility. We strive to produce the evidence of our faith. We worry about proving to others that we are worthy. We compete and we perform. But all the while we are distracted from the very thing that allows for fruit in our lives—intimacy with Jesus.

Maybe it seems too simple. Maybe it seems too easy. But the truth is, if we remain connected to Jesus, the fruit will happen. In some ways it is a mystery that large luscious fruit appear on skinny dry branches. In the same way it may be surprising to us and to others that beautiful things emerge from our lives. But the source of life is not in the branch itself. It only passes through the branch from the vine. Just as the branch receives its life from the vine, so we receive life from Jesus.

It is humbling to remember that we are branches and not vines. We need Jesus. We can accomplish nothing of lasting value without him, and yet with him we have such incredible potential. I learned this in a new way as I sat in prison for nine weeks in Iran. During that time I came to the end of myself. How could I bear fruit while sitting alone in a prison cell? The answer was simply by abiding in the vine. In my despair and loneliness, I clung to Christ, and now as I look back on that time, I can see how, in many ways, it was the most fruitful time of my life. Not only was God developing my Christian character and deepening my faith and trust in him, he was also using me to draw others to himself, even without my knowing of it. To my amazement, God used me to reveal his love to those around me. Before I left prison, I saw some profound changes in the hearts of the prison guards, the interrogator, and the judge.

The key is that Jesus will cause us to be fruitful. We may have strategies on fruitfulness and formulas and books that tell us how to achieve it. But in the end Jesus is all you need. You need only to remain in him and then watch what he will do with your life.

This posture of trust, of letting the life of Jesus flow through us, brings us deep and lasting joy. In John 15:11 Jesus says, "I have told you this so that my joy may be in you and that your joy may be complete." Jesus invites us to find ultimate joy and satisfaction in him. He is all we need. If we are looking elsewhere for this fulfillment, we are looking in vain. No amount of money can deliver the same kind of joy. No other relationship, no job, no drug—nothing—can give us joy like Jesus himself can.

> Jesus is all you need. You need only to remain in him and then watch what he will do with your life.

There is a small book that has had a great influence upon me and many others in helping to understand the life of abiding in Christ in practical terms. It is called *The Practice of the Presence of God,* written by Brother Lawrence, a seventeenth-century monk. Brother Lawrence tells of his simple life in the monastery, where among other things he carried out daily duties in the kitchen. It was his goal to continually acknowledge God's presence with him. In the midst of whatever he was doing, he would maintain a silent and secret conversation with God. It was not an easy task, but Brother Lawrence persevered. And just as Jesus promised in John 15:11, this devout monk also experienced the joy of abiding in Christ. He wrote, "There is not in the world a kind of life more sweet and delightful than that of a continual conversation with God. Those only can comprehend it who practice and experience it."*

One of the practical things we must do in order to abide in Christ is to seek to keep our whole lives centered on him. This

* Brother Lawrence, *The Practice of the Presence of God* (New Kensington, Penn.: Whitaker House, 1982), p. 29.

involves a daily challenge to prioritize our activities. From a young age, I learned to meet this challenge with what I call a "list approach" to priorities. I would simply make a list of the things that were most important in my life, something like this:

1. God
2. Family
3. Ministry
4. Friends
5. Recreation

Whether or not I wrote them down, I made these lists all the time and tried to order my day according to them. Sometimes I succeeded at this, and sometimes I did not.

As I have walked with the Lord now for many years, I have found some serious problems with this way of prioritizing. For example, it seems to me that when we involve ourselves with any of the priorities other than the first, which is God, we tend to leave God behind. We begin to view certain daily activities as secular, and so we don't invite God to be a part of them. Conversely, we think of other things as sacred, such as Bible reading and prayer, and we can find ourselves doing those things out of a performance orientation, thinking we can actually secure God's love for us by doing them. I also have found that when I prioritize this way, I am not allowing God to be in control. Instead I'm trying to run my own life and only fitting in God where I can, or where I really feel I need to. I don't allow for God's timing in things, and so I miss out on experiencing the freedom in following his leading. We may give God some time first thing in the morning as we rush through a few Bible verses and say a few quick prayers, but often we then find it easy to leave God out of our lives for the rest of the day. This is certainly not the kind of approach that was modeled by Jesus or by his disciples.

> We need to think of God as the sun in our lives. He is at the center and his light shines into every part of our lives.

I now prefer another priority system, one that I simply call a centering approach. This is where Jesus is at the center and everything flows out from my relationship with him. Think about our solar system, with the sun as its center. Everything revolves around the sun and is affected in some way by the light of the sun. We need to think of God as the sun in our lives. He is at the center, and his light shines into every part of our lives. This approach acknowledges that everything in our lives needs to be affected by God's presence. Nothing is outside of his eager interest. And as we submit our whole selves to him, nothing we do is outside of his influence. This is what I believe Jesus modeled for us, which he affirmed in statements like, "I do nothing on my own" (John 8:28; see also 5:30). He was always listening for the voice of the Father and paying attention to what God was doing in each and every situation. In the same way, everything we do needs to be influenced by our center, our relationship with God. We always need to be conscious of our Lord and his priorities, his desires. This way Jesus is involved in everything we do.

How do we decide what is right to do during the day? If God says that we need to spend time with this friend for the next couple of hours, then we should do it wholeheartedly, not feeling that we are neglecting our families or our other friends. Or what if we have peace about going to a movie with a friend? Is that somehow less spiritual than spending time in personal devotions? Of course not! If we have a sense that God is leading us, then we need not worry about the other priority. Now, is it better to pray for two hours or to do something else? Neither is better! The question is rather one of obedience. This is true freedom. It's best to do what we feel Jesus is leading us to do. That is best! Nothing else! The more Jesus rules and reigns in our lives, the more freedom we experience.

> *Everything we do needs to be influenced by our center, our relationship with God.*

Not all Christians are familiar with this kind of intimate interaction with Jesus. Until they discover that this can be a reality for them, the list approach functions as a viable option. But if intimacy with Jesus is possible, then the centering approach becomes the more exciting way to live out that relationship.

However, other Christians *prefer* to live by the list approach because, in fact, they are happy to leave God out of most of their lives, even if they regularly give him some of their time. In other words, they want to run their own lives. They want to be in charge of their jobs, their money, and their free time. How sad this is! It only shows a lack of understanding of who Jesus is. Really, the more we know him, the more we will want to have him ruling our lives. Who better to run our lives than the one who made us and loves us? Jesus wants the best for us. But many people have closed God out of their lives because they fear that he will tell them to do something they don't want to do, or that he will ask them to give up something they don't want to give up.

I remember when I first arrived at Wheaton College in 1985. I had looked for a Christian college where I could pursue my studies and also grow in my faith through chapels and Christian fellowship. During my first weeks there, however, things did not go as I had planned. It was much more challenging academically than I had expected. Friendships were very hard for me to make, and the chapels, in my opinion, were boring. In short, I hated it at Wheaton.

Then, in the third week, things got even worse. During a football game, I broke my arm in four places and was hospitalized for five days. As I returned to campus with a clumsy cast on my arm, I vented my frustrations to God: "What in the world is going on? I came here for all the right reasons, but it's all been going wrong!"

> **Who better to run our lives than the one who made us and loves us?**

It was there in my deep frustration that God met me. It was there that I heard him ask me a simple question: *Dan, what is the most important thing in your life?*

To that I answered, "You are, and my relationship with you."

Then he challenged me again: *Dan, is your relationship with me really more important than anything else?*

This time I paused, and after some thought I could only say, "It's supposed to be." At that point I realized that my relationship with God wasn't everything to me. If it had been, then the trials I was experiencing at school would not have affected me in the same way. The next day I repented and asked Jesus to captivate my heart once again.

During the next two weeks, he answered that prayer and more. I experienced a complete transformation. Not only did I begin to love being at Wheaton and to make friends more easily, but I had learned more about what Jesus described in the Beatitudes: "You're blessed when you feel you've lost what is most dear to you. Only then can you be embraced by the One most dear to you" (Matt. 5:4 MSG).

As I have taught on the topic of centering our lives on Jesus, one issue that frequently comes up is how this approach relates to our times of quiet devotion and prayer. This question has challenged me to think quite differently about personal devotional time. Setting aside time for personal devotions has been a very significant part of my Christian life, but sometimes I have made the mistake of using that time as an excuse to neglect prayer throughout the rest of my day. We don't just enter God's presence during our personal devotions; he is always with us. We need to appreciate times of solitude, but we also need to learn, like Brother Lawrence, to practice his presence throughout the day, no matter what tasks we are involved in. Our personal devotions are only part of each entire day spent with Jesus.

I am also often asked about how the centering approach relates to raising children. During my childhood I often heard it implied that ministry needs to come before everything else, including family. More recently the emphasis seems to have switched, placing family ahead of ministry.

In my mind, we need to have a God-centered focus on *both* ministry and family, but since I don't have children, I have asked my friends and family members who are parents how they have dealt with this issue. I have received a variety of answers. Both my sisters and their husbands have been serving God in India for many years, and they have raised their children in that context. They have remained faithful to both ministry and family, not only by entrusting their children into the loving care of their heavenly Father, but also by allowing those children to be involved in the ministry themselves. Instead of ranking these priorities, they have worked at maintaining a healthy interaction between ministry and family.

> *The centering approach develops a wholehearted reliance on Jesus. It forces us to always go back to him.*

I once asked Loren Cunningham, the founder of Youth With A Mission, for his perspective on this. Somewhat puzzled, he answered simply, "It's not about ministry or even about family, it's just about God. It's about doing the next thing God has told you to do." When his two kids graduated from high school, they honored their parents publicly for centering their lives on God. I hope I can live this model out when I have a family of my own.

When we begin to live more and more by a centering approach, it brings up the obvious question, how do I know what the Lord wants? Later (in chapter 5) we will discuss the issue of hearing God's voice, but here it may be enough to say that it is not always easy to know what the Lord wants. He doesn't necessarily tell us in each and every situation. Sometimes discerning the will of God in a particular situation is a process.

Whatever the challenge, we need to remember that God is most concerned about the condition of our hearts, that they are fully submitted to him and centered on him. When we keep asking the question, "Lord, what do you want?" it helps us to stay focused. We only need to be sure that we are ready and willing to obey when he does make known his will to us.

In this way the centering approach develops a whole-hearted reliance on Jesus. It forces us to always go back to him, and that is precisely what he wants. Frequently running to him to find out the next thing to do can often be a struggle, but I have learned to see the struggle as a gift because the struggle pushes us to prayer and into further dependence on him. It deepens the relationship between us and God. Again, this is exactly what Jesus wants. Intimacy is his desire.

> The more you center your mind and heart on Jesus, the more you will have his mind and his heart for the situations you encounter throughout your day.

In some ways a centering approach is very difficult. It requires more from us than prioritizing and the giving of parts of our lives to God—it demands *everything*. But its demands are far outweighed by the joy it brings by helping us stay connected to Jesus and reliant on him in the whole of our lives. It helps me to understand what happened at the Sea of Galilee when Jesus called the first disciples. Those disciples realized what Jesus was requiring of them. They didn't just rearrange their priorities, they gave up everything to follow him.

It seems to me that this is similar to what the apostle Paul had in mind when he challenged the Colossian believers, writing, "Since, then, you have been raised with Christ, set your hearts on things above, where Christ is seated at the right hand of God. Set your minds on things above, not on earthly things" (3:1–2). The more you center your mind and heart on Jesus, the more you will have his mind and his heart for the situations you encounter throughout your day.

I love how Loren Cunningham talks about the life that is centered on Jesus. "I want to lean so hard on Jesus that if he moved, I would fall down." That's a beautiful way! I want to be so dependent on Jesus that if he moved, I'd have to move as well. I'd fall over without him at my side. It's similar to Peter's response when Jesus asked if the disciples would abandon him as others had done. Peter said, "Lord, to whom shall we go? You have the words of eternal life" (John 6:68). Indeed, we are completely lost without Jesus at our side.

It has often been said that the last words Jesus spoke to his disciples before he ascended into heaven are of supreme importance. The command of Jesus to "go and make disciples of all nations" (Matt. 28:19) has deeply inspired me to invest my life in serving others. It has challenged me to be willing to do anything and go anywhere for Jesus. But something that has impacted me almost as much is what Jesus *didn't* say upon his departure. He didn't tell his followers a lot about *how* to fulfill their mission. He didn't present them with a long list of tasks and responsibilities. It's amazing to think about how little he actually left with those disciples. How would they have felt? I would think that they probably felt quite overwhelmed with the idea of continuing what Jesus had begun. It probably seemed almost laughable, as they looked around at one another, that they were the chosen ones to see the kingdom of God come to earth.

For these simple men, the sweetest of Jesus' parting words must have been the very last, as recorded in the Gospel of Matthew, "And surely I am with you always, to the very end of the age" (Matt. 28:20). In the midst of all their questions and potential confusion, these words must have sounded beautifully reassuring. The disciples didn't need a formula or a detailed how-to manual. They needed Jesus, and that is what they got. Jesus promised them himself, his continued presence with them. He invited them to a relationship with him that they would continue to nurture by faith. He said, "I am with you."

> We don't have a formula, a guaranteed strategy, or a how-to manual. We have what the disciples had — Jesus himself. What could be better than that?

Jesus would have us hear the same words today. Just as the disciples were left with a daunting task and a simple promise, so we have the same task and the same wonderful promise. Jesus will be with us as we each go into "all the world," whether that means going into the classroom, the workplace, the house next door, or around the globe. We don't have a formula, a guaranteed strategy, or a how-to manual. We have what the disciples had—Jesus himself. What could be better than that?

Jesus called the disciples, and he calls us, to run to him all day long with everything. He is with us. We have relationship with him. Words cannot express how amazing this reality is. If you receive anything from this book, receive this: Jesus is with you and longs for relationship with you. This is what life is all about.

Chapter Four

Dealing with Fear

There is no fear in love. But perfect
love drives out fear.

—*1 John 4:18*

For God has not given us a spirit of
fear and timidity, but of power, love,
and self-discipline.

—*2 Timothy 1:7 (NLT)*

The fact that Jesus is always with us wherever we go
doesn't mean that we don't encounter fear as we follow
him. On the contrary, the life of faith is filled with risk and
uncertainty. There is often much to fear, and it is quite natural
and normal for us to be afraid. However, in the very midst of
this, Jesus calls out to us and says, "Do not be afraid." It is not
as much a command as it is an invitation to face those fears
and to trust in him. It is in the loving embrace of Jesus that
we experience perfect love and find the courage and strength
to overcome that which makes us afraid.

The apostle Peter was a man of great zeal and emotion.
One stormy night he and some of the other disciples were

out on a boat in the Sea of Galilee (see Matt. 14:22–33). In the midst of the storm, Jesus appeared and approached them, walking on the water. The disciples didn't recognize him, so they were terrified until Jesus spoke to them, "Take courage! It is I. Don't be afraid." At that moment, Peter spoke up boldly and said, "Lord, if it's you, tell me to come to you on the water." Peter was willing to step out. He was willing to face his fears and to take the risk of faith.

> I want to simply obey. I want to step out in faith and walk on water.

Jesus responded to his challenge and said, "Come." I love how Jesus dealt with Peter. He saw his faith and rewarded him, though I'm sure the other disciples couldn't help but roll their eyes as they listened to Peter's latest outburst.

So what did Peter do? He got out of the boat and walked on the water toward Jesus. Peter experienced a miracle! So often when we hear this story, we focus on what happened next, when Peter took his eyes off of Jesus and began to sink. But we need to appreciate what happened before that—Peter walked on water!

What would that have been like for Peter? Was he at all hesitant as he stepped out of the boat? Did he touch the water with one foot first to test it out? What would *you* have done? I probably would have said, "Sure, Lord, I'd love to come to you on the water. Just provide a way, maybe another boat, or maybe you could part the lake like you parted the Red Sea for Moses. You make a way and I will come."

All that seems to have mattered for Peter was the invitation that Jesus gave him: "Come." Everything else at that point became unimportant. Whatever else was going on around him and within him, he was able simply to focus on God and walk toward the open arms of Jesus. In many ways it doesn't matter that Peter's faith wavered moments later. He was already closer to the arms of Jesus than any of the other disciples. And when he did begin to sink, Jesus was there to catch him. Peter was the only one who experienced the miracle; the others only witnessed it.

I don't know about you, but I want to be like Peter. No matter what Jesus asks me to do, I want to step out in faith. No matter what others may think. No matter how crazy or impossible it may look. I want to simply obey. I want to step out in faith and walk on water.

Sadly, our fears often keep us from stepping out in faith and obeying God. As I travel and teach, I hear many Christians, young and old, talk about their fears. Ten common fears that I have come across are:

1. The fear of loneliness
2. The fear of man
3. The fear of death
4. The fear of rejection
5. The fear of being misunderstood
6. The fear of pain
7. The fear of not having financial security
8. The fear of failure
9. The fear of missing God's will
10. The fear of the unknown or of change

These are all fears that I have personally experienced and continue to face. Many who know about my international adventures have come to me and said, "Dan, you are so courageous to have done all that you have done." But those who know me better know about my many struggles with fear. I'm sure that as you read a list like the one above you are able to identify the fears that plague you as well.

In some ways I wish I could offer a simple way to do away with fears, but I cannot. I can only testify to the fact that God has helped me to overcome many and various fears, and I am increasingly experiencing God's victory over fear. I assure you that God can help you in the same way.

> The remedy for every fear is the same: a deeper trust in God and a growing confidence that he will care for us and help us through any challenge that we face.

Though I will not deal here with each of the listed fears individually, I want to deal with fear in general by offering examples from my own experience.

First, it is evident that these fears tend to overlap, and often it is difficult to understand the nature of the fear that we are experiencing. However, the remedy for every fear is the same: a deeper trust in God and a growing confidence that he will care for us and help us through any challenge that we face. We need to realize that there is no fear that can keep us from obeying God. Fear can never become an excuse to run away from God. If anything, fear should drive us into the arms of God.

One of the most difficult personal struggles I have encountered has been the fear of being alone, and specifically the fear of never getting married. I remember sitting in the church at my younger sister's wedding and thinking about the fact that Christina was four years younger than I and yet married before me. God had provided for her but why not for me? I struggled with discouragement. I've also watched most of my friends get married and have children, and I've asked the Lord whether or not I would ever get married myself. I don't feel that God has spoken much to me on the issue.

As this fear surfaces and even as depression sometimes sets in, I have learned to run to God and to surrender it to him. Who is able to meet my deepest social and emotional needs? Jesus alone. Whether we are single or married, if we don't believe that he is enough, then we grasp for satisfaction in other things. There is so much more to know about Jesus, so much more to experience. I have told myself again and again that ultimately Jesus is all I need. To be honest, sometimes even though I know that is true, and maybe it is the right thing to say, I struggle to really believe it. Every time we feel that he isn't enough, we need to ask God to reveal more of who he is. He will be faithful to answer that prayer and to increase our understanding of who he is and of his ability to meet all of our needs.

> *There is no fear that can keep us from obeying God.*

I know that many have battled with this fear and that it has caused many of us to be hesitant about fulfilling what God has called us to do. This can be especially true when that calling will take us overseas. When I first went to Afghanistan, I knew that my prospects of getting married out there were slim, and sometimes that reality frustrated me. I needed to be reminded again and again that Jesus knows our needs. He knows our deepest desires. He wants to meet each of us where we are and take care of all our needs. He is completely trustworthy.

In Romans 8:15 Paul writes, "For you did not receive a spirit that makes you a slave again to fear, but you received the Spirit of sonship. And by him we cry '*Abba,* Father.'" This wonderful truth affirms again that our fears, including the fear of being alone, are dealt with in the context of relationship. As children of God we are invited to trust in our heavenly Father and watch our fears be dethroned by his intimate love.

I am amazed as I watch my nephews and nieces grow up, and I have been especially struck by the trust they have in their parents. I have a vivid memory of one of my nephews jumping off a table into the arms of my brother-in-law. He trusted his father and had complete confidence that he would catch him. God desires that each one of us would test him in the same way. He is completely trustworthy as we step out in faith.

Another fear I have often encountered is the fear of man. One of the most intense and trying times during my imprisonment in Iran was when I was put on trial. Facing two death sentences, I was brought into a courthouse to make them official. I was led before the judge and told to take my place on the witness stand. The judge looked at me intently and said, "Mr. Baumann, tell us why you came to Iran."

I took a long pause as I considered what to say. The judge waited for my answer. The video cameras also waited. I was scared and intimidated as the fear of man gripped me. But as I thought and prayed, I knew I had to be honest. There was no substitute for my integrity. I knew that they might kill me if I answered honestly, but I had to tell the truth about why I came to Iran.

As I opened my mouth to speak, something stronger than fear rose up within me. The Spirit of God was giving me courage and confidence. I looked directly at the judge and said, "I came to Iran to tell people like you about Jesus Christ."

I would like to say that those words came easy, but the truth is I struggled to speak and I was much afraid. But God gave me the grace to proclaim my faith despite my fears. He gave me strength to share my heart and to testify about Jesus. The more I shared, the stronger and bolder I became and the less my fears beset me.

> *Our fears are dealt with in the context of relationship. We are invited to trust in our heavenly Father and watch our fears be dethroned by his intimate love.*

The growing freedom that I experienced as I stood before that judge was indescribable. He had the power to order my execution right then and there, and yet I knew that even death could not separate me from God. If this was to be my time to leave this earth, then I was ready. On that day in the Iranian courtroom, I realized I was free. My fear had been overcome.

More recently, early in 2001, I was given the opportunity to visit Baghdad, Iraq. The Ministry of Religion in Iraq had extended an invitation to Christian leaders from around the world to come visit the country, view the effects of foreign sanctions, and assess the humanitarian needs. A friend of mine invited me to accompany him on this tour. I saw it as a unique opportunity to visit this needy country. As I prayed about the trip, I felt a peace about going and sensed that it would be a significant time for me.

Despite this initial confidence in prayer, as the date of departure came closer, the fear of man again surfaced in my heart. I was reminded of some of the details of my imprison-ment in Iran. I feared that the Iraqi authorities could do to me what the Iranian authorities had done in the past. During the weeks leading up to the trip, on more than one occasion, I seriously considered backing out. But I knew that the Lord wanted to bring me to a deeper level of trust in him. I knew that I needed to walk through this situation and allow my faith to be tested.

In May 2001 my friend and I headed to Jordan, where we picked up our visas and boarded a bus headed for Baghdad. Despite my fears, Jesus met me at every step of the way. As I walked by faith, the fears had less and less of a hold on me. It was a fabulous journey. We had a wonderful time interacting with the Iraqi people and visiting the ancient cities of Baby-lon, Ur, and Nineveh. My love for Iraq and its people grew strong, and as I left, I was so thankful not only that Jesus had given me that opportunity to go but also that he had given me the courage to face my fear.

Sometimes fear arises in our hearts when our obedience has the potential to affect others negatively, when it brings others into a place where *they* are vulnerable to pain or injury. I faced this kind of difficulty when I returned home after my time in prison in Iran. I was approached by a group of Iranian Christians who seriously questioned my decision ever to enter Iran. They reprimanded me for putting the national believ-ers at risk. Indeed, some of the believers that we contacted in Iran had subsequently been questioned and imprisoned them-selves. This was incredibly difficult for me. I struggled within myself, trying to reconcile the confidence we felt about going into Iran with the trouble it had caused. The very people in Iran that we had sought out to love had been hurt in the wake of our visit. Had God really called us into Iran? As I wrestled with this, I recalled how confident we were that God had led us to make the trip for the purpose of exploring future service opportunities. I knew in my heart that, as far as we were concerned, we had done what Jesus had asked us to do. We had trusted and obeyed.

> It is important to be aware of risk, but as Christians we shouldn't base our decisions on it.

A few months later, after this initial turmoil, I received some very encouraging words from Loren Cunningham. He affirmed that there is honor in doing what God has asked us to do, whatever the consequences for ourselves and others. We must leave the results of our obedience in God's hands. Of course we need to give serious consideration to how our actions will affect others, but we also must trust God that what he asks us to do will, in the end, be the best for all those involved. Again, our responsibility is to trust and obey. Yes, we need to be sure of our guidance, but in the same way that we entrust ourselves into God's hands, we also need to entrust the lives of others into his hands.

The more we step out to trust in God, the more we will be confronted with decisions that involve some element of risk. In Western society today, we avoid risk at all costs. We have made a god out of security and safety. When we must take a risk, we are encouraged to carefully calculate it and to methodically minimize it. There is some wisdom in this, but we have taken it to an extreme. It is important to be aware of risk, but as Christians we shouldn't base our decisions on it.

Risk comes not only to the person heading out into potentially dangerous situations but also to those who care about them. Parents, for instance, take a risk in releasing their children to follow their own callings. Even though I don't have children, I know that it can be a considerable challenge—and a high calling—for parents to trust God with their children's lives. I admire my own parents for how they have released all three of us to the purposes of God. Each of us has lived in Asia for many years and faced a variety of hardships. Elisabeth, my older sister, has lived in India and Nepal for the past twenty-two years and was once imprisoned in Nepal. I was imprisoned in Iran and before that spent many years in the war-torn country of Afghanistan. My younger sister, Christina, lived for years in India's northernmost state, Kashmir, considered by the U.S. State Department to be one of the most unsafe places in the world. Were my parents crazy to let us live in such risky and unsafe environments? They would say no. In fact, my parents have considered it an honor to release their kids to Jesus in this way. The more they trust in him, the more they realize that he is trustworthy.

> *The safest place in the world is in the center of God's will.*

I remember hearing about the first public prayer meeting that my mother attended after she received the news of my imprisonment in Iran. She prayed, with great boldness and courage, "Lord, I ask that Dan would not be released from prison until all of your purposes are fulfilled." Mom is intense. What kind of a mother would pray that kind of a prayer? One who is totally trusting her son into the care of her heavenly Father. One who has had a glimpse of eternity and longs for God's eternal purposes to be fulfilled in her own life and in the lives of her children. I'm glad, though, that there were others praying for my quick release!

Ultimately we have nothing to fear. Jesus loves us, and he invites us to be confident in that love. As we seek to obey him, we are not called to assess the risk involved and determine whether or not obedience will be beneficial or safe for us. We are simply called to trust and obey.

So often, even as Christians, we try to assess situations according to our own limited notions of safety. We are consumed by this. It's such a priority for us. We will not do certain things just because of the risk involved. In the face of this kind of thinking, we need to affirm that the safest place in the world is in the center of God's will. If God really does care for me, then this is what I must believe. According to some, I have made many *unsafe* decisions in my lifetime, but never have I regretted trusting in God. I have made my home in different war zones. I have been held at gunpoint. I have endured imprisonment. But in the midst of it all, despite many fears, I have known the goodness of the Lord, and my confidence in him has only been strengthened.

Some may wonder how I came to the place where I was so confident with these big decisions. The only answer I can give is that this kind of trust is a natural outcome of everyday relationship with God, living out the centered approach (as discussed in chapter 3). As you get to know God more intimately, you know that you can trust him with everything.

One of the things that I have learned over the years is that there are no big and small decisions in trusting God. Whether we are trusting him with which movie to watch, which house to buy, what to do on our days off, or what to do as we travel overseas, it's all the same. Everything is about trusting God.

God calls each one of us to take risks, to make ourselves vulnerable in a variety of ways. When God asks you to do something that seems risky or unsafe, go to him in prayer. Bring your fears and anxieties before Jesus. He will take care of you. Don't allow those fears or the feelings of being unsafe to determine your decisions. Simply trust and obey.

Risks to our physical safety are not the only challenges we may face. Sometimes God asks us to take financial risks. Just as we may make decisions based on what we think is financially prudent or possible, we may hesitate to obey God until we know we have sufficient funds to cover our costs. But the words of Jesus are always challenging in this regard: "Seek first his kingdom and his righteousness, and all these things will be given to you as well" (Matt. 6:33). Jesus is committed to taking care of us. He will provide for us.

> *Seek first his kingdom and his righteousness, and all these things will be given to you as well.* — Matthew 6:33

Those serving with YWAM have many stories to share about God's financial provision. I had the privilege of being very close to one of those stories. I was attending a discipleship program in Holland. One of the girls in our school, Alisha, felt that God wanted her to join the program's outreach team going to Hong Kong. She needed about US$1,200 to cover her costs. After many weeks of praying and asking God to provide, Alisha had only $250, so she gave up on the idea of going on the outreach. The day came for her team to leave, and with many tears and frustrations, she went to the airport to see them off and say her goodbyes. While she was at the airport, a woman she didn't know walked up to her and asked, "Are you with YWAM?"

When Alisha said she was, the woman continued, "Well, last night I was awakened by the Lord, and he told me to come here today to the airport and to give you this." The woman gave Alisha one thousand dollars. She couldn't believe it! She had a wonderful outreach in Hong Kong. Oh, that we would have the grace not to let money stand in the way of doing what God has called us to do.

Sometimes we give in to fears and miss the opportunity that God is giving us at the moment. I have done this many times. On one occasion, six months after my release from prison in Iran, I was given the opportunity to return to Afghanistan. For many reasons I had a deep sense of peace that God was leading me back to Kabul, in part to help me face my fears about returning to that area of the world. I had invited a friend of mine, Chad, to come with me on the trip. At that time the only way into the country was overland from Peshawar, Pakistan. After arriving in Pakistan, we realized that it would take a couple of days to complete the paperwork necessary to enter Afghanistan. As the day approached, fear gripped my heart. It became overwhelming for me, and on the day before we were to leave, I decided that I would not go. It wasn't a decision I made in prayer. It wasn't that I sensed God had changed my plan. I simply gave in to my fears.

My friend Chad decided to go alone, and as I hugged him goodbye early that next morning, my heart was filled with shame. Not only had I disobeyed God, but I had let down my friend, whom I had planned to host in a country I loved. God, however, was gracious. Even while I was still in Peshawar waiting for Chad to return, the Lord began to encourage me and to show me the many other wonderful things he had in store for me, but all I wanted to do was grovel in my failures for a while. But Jesus, wonderful Jesus, had other plans. He wanted to lift up my head and lead me on. He was eager to give me another chance. Somehow my failure didn't exhaust his grace. The failure just opened up another opportunity. Six months later God opened the door again, and I had the privilege of returning to Kabul, where I spent two wonderful months.

Despite such testimonies to God's grace, we often still struggle with a fear of failure. I've learned a lot about God's perspective on our failures as I've thought about how children learn to walk. I watched carefully as my nephew Caleb took his first step and fell to the floor. How did his father respond? Did he say, "Oh well, son, you tried, but you failed. Sorry, I guess you can't walk. You had your chance, but you blew it"? Of course not! That would be ludicrous. But often this is how we think God responds to our failures. Caleb's father didn't focus on the fall; he focused on the step: "Look, my son is walking!" God is the same with us. He doesn't focus on our failures. Like a loving father, he is eager to pick us up when we fall and is excited for us to try again.

Learning to trust in God is a process, and along the journey we begin to understand more and more about his character, enabling us to trust him more. As we walk out this adventure with God, our lives are filled with opportunities to take steps of faith, often requiring us to face the uncertain and the unknown.

In 1989, while I was working in Afghanistan, the Soviet forces withdrew from the country. Due to the civil unrest that followed, all the foreign workers were encouraged to evacuate. I went to Thailand for a few weeks to decide what I would do next. While there I asked the Lord to speak to me about what he wanted me to do for the next couple of months. I felt that he spoke to me about going to the northwestern part of China to spend a few weeks praying for the Uyghur people. (The Uyghurs are a Turkic Muslim people numbering about ten million and considered to be unreached with the gospel.)

After wrestling with God about this for a while, I finally decided that I would have to obey him. So I secured a visa for China, then went to a YWAM training center nearby to ask if anyone there knew someone in the Uyghur area of northwest China. One man that I talked with said, "Yes, I think there's a man named Mike Brown from Australia who is a friend of YWAM and is studying the language up there, somewhere in the province."

I thought to myself, *I need more than this to go on.* The next day I brought my concerns to the Lord, praying, "Lord, I need more specifics. I need a contact up there. This Mike might be up there somewhere, but that province has a population of over twenty-five million people. I need someone with a specific address." Again heaven was silent.

> Learning to trust in God is a process, and along the journey we begin to understand more and more about his character.

After a few days, still with very little to go on, I left for China. I arrived in Beijing, uncertain and afraid, thinking to myself, *Why did I ever allow myself to come here?* I walked out of the airport and saw two young Japanese men standing at a tourist center. I hadn't yet found anyone who spoke English, so I approached them and asked, "Do you speak English?"

"A little," they replied.

Without hesitation I blurted out, "I want to stay with you tonight." They looked at each other briefly and agreed. At least I had someone I could talk to.

My plan was to go to the train station in the morning and book a ticket on the next train leaving for the city of Urumchi in the northwest. When I came to the counter and told the woman there what I wanted, she replied, "The next train for Urumchi leaves in four days."

"What?!" I blurted out. "But I need to go tomorrow."

I did not have the money to stay longer in Beijing, and besides, I hadn't come to China to visit Beijing. And surely my new Japanese friends didn't expect me to stay with them that long. But apparently I had no choice. As I began to walk away from the counter, the woman called out to me, "Sir, by the way, the train ride to Urumchi lasts ninety-two hours."

I stopped, turned around, and said, "Ninety-two hours?"

The woman smiled and said, "Yes, sir."

Four days later I said goodbye to my Japanese friends and boarded the train for Urumchi. After ninety-two hours I arrived in the city at 6:00 AM and was greeted with subzero temperatures. I had met one Chinese person on the train who spoke some English. He told me about the many universities and other institutions in the city of two million people and offered to take me to the largest university and drop me at the front gate.

> Are you trusting in God, or do fears rule your life?

Soon I stood at that gate, freezing. It was still dark outside, and the city seemed very barren. As I stood there, hopelessness began to set in. What in the world was I thinking back there in Thailand? There is no way that I will find this Mike Brown. Why did I allow myself to come here? God would have forgiven me if I had disobeyed, but at least I wouldn't have been in this mess. In my desperation, I turned my head toward the sky and cried out to Jesus, "Lord, I need you. I have no idea what to do."

Immediately, as clearly as I have ever heard the Lord, he spoke to my heart. *Dan, walk to the center of the campus.* I did. *Now make a right turn and walk down this pathway until you reach that big building.* Once I got to the building, I heard him say, *Now go inside and stand in the corridor for twenty minutes.*

By now I was beginning to question this whole escapade more and more. I thought to myself that I must be losing it. It was crazy. As I stood there, many students walked by me and stared at me, and I stared at them. After twenty minutes, God spoke again, *Now walk to the end of this hallway and knock at the last door on the left.*

As I was walking, I saw a man come in from a hallway ahead of me and begin walking in the same direction. He went into the last room on the left. I arrived at the room and knocked. As he opened the door, I couldn't believe my eyes. He was another foreigner, a German studying at the university. He invited me in, and we began to speak in English. Then I asked him if he had ever heard of a man from Australia named Mike Brown who was studying the local language somewhere in this province.

He replied, "Yes, Mike is a good friend of mine. He lives right here in the city and is studying at another university. I can take you right to his room." I sat there stunned. Then tears began to well up in my eyes. All the anxiety and fear that I had up until that moment was quickly fading away. Jesus, wonderful Jesus, had come through again. This was one of the greatest miracles I had ever experienced. If I had disobeyed back in Bangkok, I would have totally missed out on this moment. As my eyes turned to heaven, I could see Jesus with a big grin on his face looking down on me and saying, *My son, I love you. Thanks for coming here.*

Minutes later I was sitting with Mike Brown. We talked for hours. I told him the story of how I found him, and we marveled together at the goodness and faithfulness of God. Mike invited me to spend the next few days with him and then arranged for me to be hosted by some friends of his in another part of the province about five hundred miles away. I cherished my time among the Uyghur people, spending much of those three weeks praying for them. Afterward I returned to Beijing and then back to Thailand. What an adventure with Jesus! Oh, the beauty of learning to trust in him.

Are you trusting in God, or do fears rule your life? Whatever it is that you are afraid of, Jesus is inviting you now to face that fear and to trust in him. Remember, it is the presence of his perfect love in our hearts that will give us the courage and strength to overcome our fears.

Chapter Five

Hearing from God

The LORD came and stood there, calling as
at the other times, "Samuel! Samuel!"
  Then Samuel said, "Speak, for your
servant is listening."
                              —*1 Samuel 3:10*

My sheep listen to my voice;
I know them, and they follow me.
                              —*Jesus, John 10:27*

Communication is vital in any relationship. Our capacity to hear God's voice is an essential part of our relationship with him. As we open the Scriptures, we encounter a God who speaks. In the very first chapter of Genesis, it is recorded that God *spoke* the world into existence: "And God said, 'Let there be light,' and there was light" (1:3). And as soon as Adam and Eve were created, God interacted with them in a conversational manner—both God and man were able to speak and be spoken to. We see the same kind of thing throughout the Scriptures—God's people hear God's voice. God is intensely interested in individuals, and he desires to communicate in intimate ways with each and every person.

In all of my travels, including a wide variety of speaking engagements, I have found there to be more interest in the topic of hearing God's voice than in any other topic. It is a critical issue among Christians today, especially young people. The church is crying out for understanding and clarity on this topic.

In some ways, however, this subject is daunting. It seems that when it is addressed, it often raises more questions than it offers answers. If the topic of hearing God's voice has been a point of frustration and confusion for you, I would encourage you to focus your attention on God and allow him to give you fresh insight and inspiration on this matter. Rather than seek answers to questions, we need to be refreshed in our faith.

First, we should not be looking for some formula on the topic of hearing God. There aren't three easy steps to figure this out, even though sometimes it seems that's exactly what we want. Hearing from God is relational, not mechanical. It is very much related to trusting and following, as John 10:27 affirms: "My sheep listen to my voice; I know them, and *they follow me*" (emphasis added). In that passage Jesus uses the metaphor of sheep and their shepherd to stress that the capacity to listen comes quite naturally as we spend more and more time with Jesus. Sheep know the voice of their shepherd so well because they hear it all the time. They know the voice because they know the shepherd. Jesus invites each one of us to spend time with him and to become familiar with his voice.

God speaks to us for different reasons, sometimes to affirm us, sometimes to convict us or correct us, and sometimes for some other purpose. Although these purposes are often intertwined as God communicates with us, in this chapter I want to focus specifically on the area of *guidance*—how God gives us direction in our lives.

God also speaks to us in many different ways. However, for the purpose of gaining insight into some of those ways, I will highlight four of them in this chapter: (1) through an inner voice, sometimes called the still small voice; (2) through Scripture; (3) through other people; and (4) through his peace in our hearts.

It was the prophet Elijah who heard the voice of God as "a gentle whisper" (1 Kings 19:12), or "a still small voice" (KJV). Many Christians have come to use this term for the way in which God guides us through an inner prompting in our hearts. No matter what term we use to describe this subtle voice, it is an experience to which many Christians throughout the ages have given testimony.

> *Hearing from God is relational, not mechanical. Jesus invites each one of us to become familiar with his voice.*

One of the times in my own life when God spoke to me in a very clear way through an inner voice was when he first called me to go overseas. In September 1983, while I was in my first semester of college, I was praying in the quietness of my room on what was a very ordinary day. As I was praying, I heard a voice within me say, *Dan, I want you to go to Ashkhabad as a missionary for me one day.*

To my knowledge, I had never even heard the name "Ashkhabad" before that day, so I questioned what I had heard. Maybe I had put too much salsa on my burritos that night. But as I sat in my room, the name "Ashkhabad" kept ringing in my heart. I decided to get up and look at the world map on my wall. Sure enough, there in the south-central part of the Soviet Union was a state called Turkmenia, and its capital city was Ashkhabad. I stood there stunned.

Again I questioned what I had heard. *Could this be for real? Could God be calling me there?* I reasoned further in my own mind, *But the Soviet Union is a closed country. People don't go there as missionaries.*

Despite my initial doubts and questions, I cherished these words as if they were from God. In the days to follow, I eagerly listened for confirmation from God. I wanted to see the writing on the wall. I expected to hear his voice again, to bring clarity to this call. But it never came. I soon realized that I was left with two choices: I could hide the words in my heart and walk in the direction they led, or I could discount the experience altogether and move on. Even though I still had my doubts about the experience, I could not disbelieve that it was actually God who had spoken to me. I chose to hold on to this call from God and to wait patiently for further guidance. I was confident that God had led me to go to college, so I continued my studies, trusting that God would work out the details of this call in his time.

Over the next few years, I went through much testing in regard to this call to serve God in Ashkhabad. As I mentioned the idea to friends, most of them thought that I was crazy and that I should drop it. Many were surprised that I persisted for years to keep the dream alive in my heart. Sometimes being at college in the American Midwest seemed to me to be walking in the opposite direction from this call to Central Asia.

In October of 1991, eight years after the initial experience of hearing God speak to me about Ashkhabad, the world watched as the Soviet Union crumbled and various states became independent countries, Turkmenistan being one of them. In those events I could not help seeing a door opening for me.

Less than a year later, in September 1992, my opportunity came. I will never forget the occasion when I first flew into Ashkhabad. I landed at the airport about 3:00 AM. As I got out of the plane, I knelt down on the tarmac and wept. With tears streaming down my face, I looked up to heaven and prayed, "Lord, nine years ago you told me that I would come here. Though I doubted it many times and others laughed, today I am here. Thank you, Jesus, for letting me hear your voice and for fulfilling your words to me." (Although I was only there for two days on that first trip, I've returned there on several occasions to spend prolonged times of service.)

When God speaks to us through an inner voice, it may often be easy to disregard it as merely the product of our imaginations. At any given time, our minds are flooded with a variety of ideas and impressions. But as we practice listening and responding to these special promptings, we learn to distinguish the sound of God's voice in the midst of all the other sounds.

For many Christians, one of the most common ways that God speaks is directly through a passage of Scripture. It happens in various ways, but often, when the Scriptures are being read, a certain portion will come alive for us and speak directly to our hearts. Somehow God uses that scripture to uniquely address our own situations. Sometimes, as well, while we are praying or thinking, God will cause us to recall a specific passage of Scripture that will speak to us in a particular way, or God may bring to mind a certain portion of Scripture that we are then to share with someone else, for their encouragement.

Of course, we can never *force* God to speak to us, though sometimes we may try. When I was in high school, I attended a prayer meeting where we were encouraged to wait on the Lord in silence. As we did, I was determined to receive a scripture from God. Sure enough, the words *Obadiah, verse 9* popped into my head. *Wow!* I thought to myself, *this actually works. It must be from God because it's such an obscure verse.* As I looked it up, it became obvious to me in my spirit that it wasn't from God at all. Although I laughed at myself, I also realized how inappropriate and ridiculous it was to try to *make* God speak to me.

> We can never force God to speak to us, though sometimes we may try.

On another occasion, while I was in prison, God spoke to me through the Scriptures in a very profound and comforting way. On the twenty-first day of my imprisonment, I had this sense that God wanted me to open my Bible and that he would speak to me. So I grabbed my Bible, and it opened to the tenth chapter of Daniel. Immediately my eyes focused on verses 12 and 13, and I was amazed at what I read: "Do not be afraid, Daniel. Since the first day that you set your mind to gain understanding and to humble yourself before your God, your words were heard, and I have come in response to them. But the prince of the Persian kingdom [which was centered in modern-day Iran] resisted me twenty-one days. Then Michael, one of the chief princes, came to help me, because I was detained there with the king of Persia." God was speaking directly into my situation at that moment and giving me hope. It is amazing how comforting that was for me while I sat alone in prison.

We cannot expect God to speak to us in the same way each time we open the Scriptures. Sometimes, as we read, we may simply grow in our understanding of God's truth. This also is the work of God's Spirit and is certainly no less an impartation of God's grace. Any time that God's truth shines into our hearts, we could say that we are *hearing* God's voice. But there are times when the Holy Spirit addresses a specific scripture to a specific situation in our lives, and we find ourselves being spoken to in a more decisive way.

A third way that God speaks to us is through other people. God uses friends, parents, pastors, and others in our lives to make known his will to us. Their wisdom and advice is God's way of leading and guiding us.

Four years ago I was leading a group on an outreach into Tibet. We arrived in Kathmandu, Nepal, and prepared to go overland from there to Lhasa, the capital of Tibet. Before we left for Tibet, one of my friends on the team, Jerome, came to me and asked if we could smuggle Tibetan Bibles into Lhasa. Without hesitation I told Jerome that it wouldn't be wise because it could cause us problems at the border. But later that night, as I was seeking the Lord, I came under strong conviction that I had made that decision out of fear rather than faith. The truth was that I didn't really want to pray about it because I didn't want to deal with the danger we could be in through defying the authorities this way. As I confessed my reluctance to God and began to pray for this situation, it became clear to me that I should listen to what God was speaking through Jerome and plan to smuggle the Bibles into Tibet.

As we left Kathmandu, each of us on the team had about five Tibetan Bibles packed into the bottom of our backpacks. At the border we passed by all the guards and officials without any problem, and once we arrived in Lhasa, we were able to distribute the Bibles.

The Scriptures, of course, are filled with examples of people speaking on God's behalf, sometimes even without their awareness of it. However, as in the above example, we must also discern within ourselves whether or not the words of the other person are meant to be taken as divinely appointed for us.

A fourth way that God speaks to us is simply through the presence of his peace in our hearts. Of course, God's peace should be present in our hearts however God is speaking to us, but often, as we seek God for guidance and commit our ways to him, we get a sense of peace about pursuing a certain direction and that is enough for our decision. This is by far the most common way that God makes his will known to us. I'm sure that most of us could think of many examples from our own lives of how God has guided us in this way. Of course, it also needs to be said that it is often the absence of God's peace that helps us to know that some options are not to be pursued.

> As we seek God for guidance and commit our ways to him, we get a sense of peace.

I had a profound experience of this latter scenario a few years ago. Several months before I visited Iran and was subsequently imprisoned, I was visiting my sister Christina in New Delhi, India. After much prayer together, Christina and I decided that we would take a short trip into Iran. We proceeded to acquire our visas and purchase our airline tickets. However, three days before we were to leave, I no longer had any peace in my heart about making the trip. After some questioning and testing, I was still faced with this lack of peace. After another day of waiting, I knew I had to back out. I couldn't make a trip like this without a sense of God's peace. Although my decision made things difficult for my sister and for our relationship, we canceled the trip. One week later Christina found out that she was a couple of weeks pregnant. It is very likely that if we had gone together into Iran at that point, we would have both ended up in prison, as I did months later. I am so thankful to God that he withheld his peace and prevented us from going at that earlier date. As it turned out, it was during my imprisonment some eight and a half months later that Christina had a baby boy, who was given *Daniel* as his middle name to honor the uncle he might never meet.

It should be noted here that a lack of peace is very different from fear. Both can prevent us from pursuing a certain option, and from someone else's perspective, the difference may be hard to detect. In our own hearts, however, the difference should be quite clear. Whereas fear grips our hearts and paralyzes us, a lack of peace sets our hearts free and enables us to look at other options. When we give in to fear, we are left with guilt; when we respond to a lack of peace, we quickly discover a new sense of peace as we explore a different path.

As we seek to hear God's voice, we need to remember that God leads us in different ways at different times in our lives. There is no one "right" way for him to guide us, better than any other. It is entirely up to him to choose just how he will make known his will to us in a particular situation. We simply need to remain sensitive to the many ways there are of hearing from God.

I have also found that often, after God guides us in a specific direction, we experience a time of testing. At that point we need to persevere. We need to hold on to what God has spoken to us and walk in the direction in which he has led us. This also seems to be the occasion when the enemy comes in to tempt us and to misdirect us. Just as the serpent tempted Eve, so the enemy would come to us with the question, "Did God really say . . . ?" We must be aware of the schemes of the enemy and resist him. If we persevere in faith, we will see the promises of God fulfilled.

On rare occasions, as we are walking in obedience to what God has already spoken to us, God will speak again and alter our direction. This experience really puts our trust in God to the test, but hopefully we come through it with a stronger faith in him.

> *We need to hold on to what God has spoken to us and walk in the direction in which he has led us.*

This is seen clearly in the story of Abraham and Isaac, in Genesis 22. God had fulfilled his promise to Abraham and Sarah and miraculously provided them with a son. Isaac was the promised child through whom God's plan of salvation would be carried on. But then God tested Abraham and asked him to sacrifice Isaac as a burnt offering. In an amazing act of trust, Abraham took his young son up a mountain, built an altar, arranged wood upon it, and then bound Isaac to the top. As Abraham took hold of the knife to slay his son, the angel of the Lord stopped him. Abraham clearly having passed the test, God told him not to touch the boy and instead provided a ram for the offering.

In 1989, while I was working in Afghanistan, I also had an experience when God tested me through altering his guidance. I had only been there for four months when the Soviets announced their intention to withdraw their forces from the country. Anticipating the ensuing civil unrest between the various local factions, many of the foreigners working in the country began to evacuate. The organization I was working for decided officially to support the evacuation of foreigners, though they allowed each worker to make his or her own decision. We were asked only to let them know by a certain date what we had decided.

I will never forget the struggle that I went through trying to reach a decision. Why would I leave the Afghans whom I had just come to serve? But why would I stay in this troubled place if most of my team was leaving? It was only after many intense hours of struggle that I decided I would stay.

However, the very next day the American embassy announced that they would be closing their doors, and they strongly encouraged all Americans within the country to leave. This pushed me again to prayer, and I asked the Lord for confirmation regarding my decision. Without any delay and as clear as I have ever heard God, he said, *Dan, I want you to leave.*

Immediately I asked, "But Lord, I thought that you wanted me to stay?"

My son, he answered, *I want you to go. I did ask you to stay, to see to what extent you would be willing to obey me, but now that I know I have your heart, you can go. I don't want you to experience the hardships that you will experience if you stay.* Tears welled up in my eyes as God's love flooded my heart. Oh, how he loved me and cared for me in the deepest of ways.

Whatever means God is using to speak guidance into our lives, it is a unique opportunity for God to deepen our trust in him. This is especially evident when there is a change in guidance—our trust is put to the test, as well as our ability to hear from God.

Although we have identified a wide variety of ways that God speaks to us in the area of guidance, sometimes we still struggle to hear from God. And sometimes God may not be speaking to us in the way we want to hear him. Again, we need to be reminded that God is the one who chooses when and how he will speak. We cannot force him to speak to us in a certain way or at a certain time. Sometimes we may go through times of silence when God is testing us.

When this happens in your life, I would encourage you not to give up hope but to stay focused on God. Honor and glorify him with all your heart. Even in the silence, he is worthy of our worship and our complete surrender. Spend time in the Scriptures and recommit yourself to obey all that is revealed to you. Also, commit yourself to be involved in the last thing you knew for sure that God was leading you to do. Don't be quick to move on to something else until it's clear that God is asking you to move on. Recently I had a sense that God was leading me to move away from Colorado, but as I began to walk toward it, nothing came together. So I simply went back to what I was already doing, in the place that I was doing it.

In times of silence, we need to be reminded that one of the main ways God leads us is through our desires. Psalms 37:4 says, "Delight yourself in the LORD and he will give you the desires of your heart." When our hearts are surrendered to God, then increasingly our desires conform to his will; we begin to desire what God desires for us, and it pleases God to bless us with what we want. Of course, sometimes we need to die to our own selfish desires and dedicate ourselves afresh to the purposes and plans of God. But more often than not our decision-making process as Christians is very practical. We ask God to guide us, and we commit our ways to him. Then, with a keen awareness of God's peace upon us, we do what is in our hearts to do.

Moreover, God remains faithful to us whether or not we are conscious of hearing his voice. God is gracious, and he works with us even when we don't understand his leading in our lives. Even when we are completely unaware of it, he is faithfully and gently leading us. It's not all up to us. We need a revelation of God's sovereignty, that he is watching over our affairs and orchestrating our lives according to his good purpose. As the Hebrew proverb affirms, "In his heart a man plans his course, but the LORD determines his steps" (Prov. 16:9). Ultimately God is in control. Man's responsibility finds its limits within God's sovereignty.

> If our hearts are for God, then it's virtually impossible to miss his will for our lives.

I sincerely hope that these insights put our minds at ease somewhat as we seek understanding of God's will for our lives. This is certainly a big question among Christians today, and in some ways we're often too preoccupied with the prospect of missing God's will. If our hearts are for God, then it's virtually impossible to miss his will for our lives. A leader once told me, "The only way to miss the will of God is to know it without a doubt, then go in the other direction." If we are not walking in blatant disobedience, then we probably just need to relax in the arms of God and live our lives for him.

When uncertainty persists as we pray for guidance from God, I have found it helpful to ask three simple questions concerning our options:

1. What would be the most honoring to God?
2. What would Jesus do?
3. What would be the most loving to the other people involved?

These questions won't necessarily lead us to specific answers in every difficult situation, but it is amazing to me how often they have helped me make decisions when I wasn't sure what to do.

Remember, most of all God desires friendship with us, and guidance is something that flows from a place of intimacy with him. Sometimes, when we are desperate for guidance, we can actually become self-absorbed in our effort to hear from God. We can become so fixated on making the right decision that we actually push God aside. At times like that, we need to be careful that our desire for guidance doesn't distract us from the simple pleasures of our relationship with God.

In closing, I just want to emphasize that all who follow God will hear his voice in some way or another. Hearing from God is not just for the missionary or the pastor. God wants to speak to his people whatever their vocation, whether they are in business, in school, or at home. God is committed to having his voice heard by us. I sincerely hope that as you finish this chapter, you will be refreshed and excited about the prospect of hearing from God. Again, as the metaphor of sheep with a shepherd affirms, hearing God's voice comes from spending time with him. As we invest in our relationship with God, our trust in him will be deepened and we will be inspired to give ourselves wholeheartedly to him. From that place of intimate trust, then, we will also be ready to give ourselves genuinely to others.

Part Three

Serving

The final two chapters of this book focus on *serving*. Service is the natural overflow of a life surrendered to God. As we give ourselves to God, he delights in using us to positively affect the lives of others around us. When we align our hearts with this godly purpose, through believing and trusting in him, we find ourselves serving. In chapter 7 we will look at the most important and basic way we serve, loving people, and in chapter 8 we will look at our availability and readiness to serve.

Chapter Six

Loving People

And now these three remain: faith,
hope and love. But the greatest of
these is love.

—1 Corinthians 13:13

Dear friends, let us love one another,
for love comes from God.

—1 John 4:7

Jesus calls us not only into relationship with him but also into relationship with others. Loving God inevitably leads us to loving people. The apostle Paul was a man who loved God, and it was that love that compelled him to spend his life in service to others. In his letter to the Philippians, Paul takes an honest look at his own life, and he explains that, in one way, he would rather die so that he could be united with Christ; but if God chose to allow him to remain alive, then Paul would live not for himself but for the sake of others (1:22–26). Paul loved people.

This is exactly what Jesus modeled as well. In Mark 10:45, Jesus explains that he "did not come to be served, but to serve, and to give his life as a ransom for many." Jesus knew exactly what his mission in life was. He lived, and died, for the benefit of others. We ourselves have no better example to follow. The more secure we are in ourselves and in our relationship with God, the freer we are to serve others. True spiritual maturity is tested in our relationships with others.

> *When you wake up in the morning and don't know what to do, just ask yourself how you can love God and love people.*

This is very much in line with how Jesus defined the chief responsibilities in life. One day, when he was being questioned by the Pharisees, a lawyer from among them asked him,

> "Teacher, which is the greatest commandment in the Law?"
> Jesus replied: "'Love the Lord your God with all your heart and with all your soul and with all your mind.' This is the first and greatest commandment. And the second is like it: 'Love your neighbor as yourself.' All the Law and the Prophets hang on these two commandments." (Matt. 22:34–40)

These two commandments summarize what God has required of us. They get to the heart of what life is all about: loving God and loving people. What a beautiful thing Jesus has done to clarify our lives. Can it really be that simple? Yes, it can.

When you wake up in the morning and don't know what to do, just ask yourself how you can love God and love people.

It isn't always easy to know exactly *how* to love, but these two simple responsibilities certainly give us the right focus. They require us to continually return to God and ask, "How can I show love in this situation, toward you and toward others?" This is the life that Jesus lived. This is the life that he calls us to live.

While I was in college, God challenged me through this scripture to get outside of myself and into the lives of others. I tended to be quiet and reserved, and sometimes I would use that as an excuse to be self-centered. But I decided to make a commitment to ask a simple question in prayer every morning, "God, how can I love people today?" It was difficult, especially at first, but week by week it became easier, and slowly I learned how to love the people that God brought into my life. After six months I took some time to evaluate. First, I had found that the more I focused on loving others, the more joy I had in my life. Second, I realized how much I had grown in certain areas of my character without even focusing on them. I found that I had more patience for people and that my mind was no longer filled with worries about my future, my finances, and my reputation. It was just as Jesus explained in the Beatitudes: "You're blessed when you care. At the moment of being 'care-full,' you find yourselves cared for" (Matt. 5:7 MSG). It was so refreshing for me to focus on the simple responsibility of loving others and to allow God to work on other areas of personal growth in my life.

One of the realities of this lifestyle is that our time and energies become more and more focused on "the now." We learn to embrace the present moment. We learn to pay attention to what God is doing in each and every situation, especially in the lives of those around us. This goes against the grain. So often we live our lives either in the future or in the past. We are consumed with what we should have done or what we should do. We are plagued with guilt and worry, and we end up being distracted, unable to engage what is before us in the present. How often do we miss an opportunity to really pay attention to someone or to listen to what God may be speaking to us through someone else? We are so preoccupied with our own concerns that we miss out on real life.

As usual, the example of Jesus is inspiring and instructive for us. Look at the way in which he was able to be *with* people. He gave them his undivided attention. Consider the Samaritan woman at the well (John 4) or the belligerent blind man (Mark 10:46–52) or the thief on the cross (Luke 23:39–43) or the many, many others who wanted his attention. Jesus graciously gave it, and in most cases he granted their requests. He met people where they were. Jesus loved people.

Think about how two lovers interact. They cherish every moment with each other. They are consumed with each other. Nothing else matters. The moment is everything. They pay attention to each other with everything that is within them. Though we cannot expect the same level of emotion to infuse every encounter with others, we can learn to love in a way that communicates sincere respect and appreciation. We need to ask ourselves if we have a genuine interest in people. Do people matter to us? How do people feel when they're with us? Do they feel loved and accepted?

When someone really pays attention to me in a one-on-one encounter, it makes me feel very good and means a lot to me. One man that has modeled this to me very effectively has been Floyd McClung. He is serving as a pastor now, but formerly he was one of my leaders in YWAM. Although he was a very busy man with much responsibility, whenever I met with him, he gave me his undivided attention. He made me feel important and loved, as if our conversation was all that mattered to him at that moment.

One of the greatest ways to show love to others is to listen to them. We all need people in our lives who listen to us, people with whom we can share our hearts. But we also need to be this kind of person for others. We need the grace to love in this way. We need to put others first and trust that Jesus will provide for our own needs. Jesus says, "Give, and it will be given to you" (Luke 6:38), and this is true in relationships. We may often feel like we don't have much to give. We may feel that we need the attention ourselves. But as we reach out to others and serve them, we will discover that God is also caring for us and meeting our needs.

> We need to put others first and trust that Jesus will provide for our own needs.

Sometimes when we meet lots of people, we are tempted to shut some of them out. We think we cannot handle any more. The demands seem to be too much. We feel that there are natural limits on our ability to love. I, too, have found at times that I just couldn't love any more than I already was. In those times I thought that I had only so much love to give. I imagined that my capacity to love was like a pie—if I was loving four people and God brought me four more, then my love was divided into eight portions, each one now receiving only half the love that the original four had received. This caused me much frustration, and I struggled to understand God's perspective on it. Then one day God shed some light on the issue for me. He helped me see that God, rather than simply accepting my limitations in loving, wanted to *expand* my capacity to love. Then I would be able to love all eight people to the same extent as I had loved the original four. Of course it didn't mean that I was able to spend as much time with each one, but it did mean that in my heart I was able to find room for more people and love them in the way that God wanted.

> **God wants to expand our capacity to love.**

It is important for us to value each and every person God brings into our lives and to make an investment in each one, whoever he or she is, whatever the situation. As I have had the opportunity to travel, God has allowed me to meet many people, some for as short as a minute, others for a much longer time. Even though sometimes it's been hard for me to say goodbye to old friends, and equally hard sometimes to give myself wholeheartedly to new people in my life, God has challenged me to reach out in love to others, whether or not I will ever see them again. The fact is, as people step out of our lives, we never know if we will get another opportunity to see them. But if we have made an investment in a relationship, then we are able to pick up right where we left off when we get the chance to meet them again. I have found this to be a great blessing in my life. I left my full-time post in Kabul, Afghanistan, in 1993, but ever since then I have taken every opportunity to return there. God has allowed me numerous opportunities, and I have been able to deepen existing relationships and build new ones there. Kabul and its people will always be a part of my life.

Sometimes people's ability to love others is restricted because of past hurts. Often, when we get hurt in relationships, we try to protect ourselves the next time we face a similar situation. We aren't quite as willing to make ourselves vulnerable.

We guard our hearts. I have struggled with this and have often allowed my hurt to diminish my capacity to love others. What should we do when we get hurt? Jesus invites us to run to him. The more I run to him in these situations, the more he is able to meet my deepest needs and restore my capacity to love. Jesus commands us to love our neighbor, no matter how difficult that may be. It is a command without conditions. When we find it hard to reach out to others with love, let us remember both the commands of Jesus and his example. He will give us the grace to obey.

> *What should we do when we get hurt? Jesus invites us to run to him.*

When I have been hurt and tempted to withhold my love from others, I have often recalled the wise words of my youth pastor. He said, "It is better to love and get hurt than not love at all." This is just another area in our lives in which we are called to die to ourselves and to choose Jesus above our own insecurities. Even though it has been tough, I have experienced God's blessing time and again as I have made myself vulnerable and made the choice to love. It has brought great joy to my heart, and it has kept me open and tender not only before God but before others as well. As I have become more involved in the lives of others, I have learned so much about the character of Jesus through these relationships. Oh, that we would understand the tragedy of closing ourselves off from others due to past hurts. It leads only to isolation and further pain.

Our commitment to relationships is frequently tested. One of the greatest challenges in loving others is in seeking to restore relationships that have been damaged or even broken off. God's heart is always to repair and restore, and we need to believe that God is able to do this with the difficult relationships in our lives. I have had such relationships in my own life, even with family members, but I have experienced God's commitment to reconciliation and restoration in all relationships that have somewhere gone wrong.

> *Even in the midst of personal crisis, Jesus modeled servanthood for us, and he calls us to follow.*

Jesus has shown us his commitment to relationships through servanthood. He modeled it for us over and over again, but perhaps nowhere else was it displayed so beautifully as at the Last Supper, when he washed the feet of his disciples. During the evening meal Jesus got up and dressed himself as a typical servant, taking off his outer clothing and wrapping a towel around his waist. Then he poured water into a basin, and kneeling before each disciple one by one, he washed their feet. This was Jesus' final opportunity to be with his friends in such an intimate setting. He was in great need himself. His heart was heavy with what lay ahead, and yet he reached out to serve. He displayed his great love for his disciples through active and humble service. Even in the midst of personal crisis, Jesus modeled servanthood for us, and he calls us to follow: "Now that I, your Lord and Teacher, have washed your feet, you also should wash one another's feet. I have set you an example that you should do as I have done for you" (John 13:14–15).

We see this also stated clearly in Paul's letter to the Philippians, where Paul exhorts, "Your attitude should be the same as that of Christ Jesus: Who, being in very nature God, did not consider equality with God something to be grasped, but made himself nothing, taking the very nature of a servant, being made in human likeness" (2:5–7). Jesus laid it all down for us. He lowered himself for us.

How do we love our neighbor? We become servants. We give up our own rights and desires for the sake of others. We humble ourselves and give our lives in service. If that's what Jesus did for us, should we do any less for others? If we follow his example, we will find ways to serve—to honor others and put their desires above our own.

Jesus teaches us that loving our neighbor also includes loving our enemies. Jesus makes this very clear in the Sermon on the Mount:

> But I tell you who hear me: Love your enemies, do good to those who hate you, bless those who curse you, pray for those who mistreat you. . . . If you love those who love you, what credit is that to you? Even "sinners" love those who love them. And if you do good to those who are good to you, what credit is that to you? Even "sinners" do that. . . . But love your enemies, do good to them, and lend to them without expecting to get anything back. Then your reward will be great, and you will be sons of the Most High, because he is kind to the ungrateful and wicked. Be merciful, just as your Father is merciful. (Luke 6:27–36; see also Matt. 5:43–47)

Loving our enemies is not easy. Jesus explains in these verses that it requires something beyond what is natural. It's easier to love those who love us, but to love those who hate us is quite unnatural and definitely difficult. Because of this, it seems that many Christians today fail to obey this command. We want this simple command to mean something other than what it plainly says. We want to justify our hatred and prejudice. But the real problem with this command is not so much in the understanding but in the obeying.

Jesus calls us to embrace not only the easy to love, the obvious objects of our affection, but the difficult people in our lives as well—even our enemies. This takes loving our neighbor to the farthest limits, in what is truly a test of Christian love. We all have such people in our lives—people we avoid or against whom we hold a grudge. It may be someone at work or perhaps someone at church. Or it may be an extended-family member, perhaps the individual who is, for you, the downside of attending the annual family reunion. Of course, it may be helpful, when considering this challenge to love, to remember that we ourselves may be the "difficult person" in someone else's life! Whatever our personal situation, we are all challenged to deal with such relationships in the way that Jesus calls us to: with simple, supernatural love.

The apostle Paul echoes the words of Jesus when he instructs his readers to "bless those who persecute you; bless and do not curse" (Rom. 12:14). He goes on to underscore his point by quoting Proverbs 25:21: "If your enemy is hungry, feed him; if he is thirsty, give him something to drink" (v. 20).

I saw this kind of love in action one day during Afghanistan's civil war, when I was working in a hospital in Kabul. Intense fighting had broken out on the city streets. As was our custom on such days, some of us at the hospital who were foreigners gave the national workers rides home, as most public transport had stopped. On this occasion, Bill, a coworker of mine from New York, and I were dropping off an Afghan coworker when we found ourselves amidst a violent skirmish.

As we began to retreat, we saw our Afghan friend being accosted by a local soldier. Immediately Bill and I recognized that the soldier was a member of the ethnic group within the country that had been responsible for recent kidnappings and killings, an effort to cleanse the nation of a rival group. Our friend was from that rival group, and this soldier appeared intent on dealing cruelly with him. We also saw the fear in our friend's eyes. Realizing that this situation would most likely end in the execution of our friend and coworker, Bill and I chose to intervene. We got out of our car and attempted to retrieve our friend, but the soldier held on to him firmly. He then turned his RPG (rocket-propelled grenade) directly at us and commanded us to leave at once. With the RPG pointed right at our heads, Bill looked the soldier in the eye and noticed that it was bloodshot. Realizing that he had some eye drops from the hospital in his pocket, Bill asked the soldier, "Does your eye itch?"

> *Jesus calls us to embrace not only the easy to love, the obvious objects of our affection, but the difficult people in our lives as well.*

With a look of bewilderment, the soldier answered, "Yes." Bill pulled the medication out of his pocket and offered it to the soldier. Setting his gun aside, the soldier reached out his hand to receive the eye drops. Other soldiers, looking on with envy, gathered around to receive medication also. Right there on the street, Bill and I were hosting an eye clinic. Only moments before we had been face to face with an angry and armed soldier. We distributed eye medication to five soldiers, and all of them immediately began to feel better. Not only that, of course, but their moods had been completely transformed. They apologized profusely to us, released our friend, and then invited us for tea. We declined the invitation and, with a great sigh of relief, went on our way, amazed at the power of a love that reaches out to serve.

Jesus not only commanded us to love our enemies; he gave us an example to follow. He himself loved those who hated him. He endured all manner of evil and corruption at the hands of his enemies. Even as Jesus was dying on the cross, he was loving his enemies, asking God to forgive those responsible for his death (Luke 23:34).

> *Jesus not only commanded us to love our enemies, he gave us an example to follow. He himself loved those who hated him.*

In my case, it was during my unjust imprisonment in Iran that I learned more than I ever could have imagined about loving my enemies. From the very first day that I began to be interrogated, God challenged me to love my interrogators. The more hostile they became, the harder the challenge became. On the second day of interrogation, they began to use physical force to persuade me to speak. As they slapped me in the face, I heard the Lord speak to me: *Dan, ask me what I think of this man.*

Initially I thought to myself, *I don't want to know.* But after a few minutes I prayed to heaven and asked, *Lord, what do you think of this man?* As soon as I asked that question, I began to have an overwhelming compassion for my interrogator. My heart broke for him. God gave me a glimpse of his love for this man. This change in my own heart was not of my own doing but truly a miracle. I began to pray for the man and to bless him in whatever way I could. The compassion grew in my heart.

The actions of my interrogator didn't change, but I continued to love him, hoping that God was working in his heart. One day, during the sixth week of my imprisonment, the guards came and led me out of my cell. I was terrified, thinking that I was being led to another session of interrogation. This time, however, instead of going downstairs, they led me into a small office. I walked into the office and was given permission to take my blindfold off, and there sat my interrogator behind a desk. As usual the very sight of him struck fear in my heart. He was my enemy. He was the one who had hit me repeatedly and yelled at me over and over again. But this time, as I sat across from him, something began to happen within me. I was supplied with a supernatural boldness. I looked at him and said, "Sir, if I'm going to see you for the rest of my life, why don't we become friends?"

"What?" he said, shaking his head.

I continued, "Sir, I know it's in your heart to become my friend. It's just your job that stops you. You can start by telling me your name." As I said that, I stretched out my hand to shake his. Expecting to get hit or be ridiculed, I was truly amazed at what happened next. It was far more beautiful than I could have imagined. My interrogator did not move, but tears started to well up in his eyes. I watched as the hardness in his face melted away before me. I waited, my hand still outstretched across his desk. His tears continued to flow. Finally he stretched out his hand, grasping mine, and said, "My name is Razaq, Mr. Baumann."

Up to that point I had never heard this man call me by my name; I had simply been "Number 58," the number of my cell.

Razaq continued. "I can't help you get out of here. It's not in my jurisdiction, but maybe I can help you within the prison. I have some influence over the guards. Is there anything you need? Perhaps a better cell?"

I thought for a second, hardly believing what I had just been offered. "Sure, I would like that."

"Then I will see what I can do," he replied.

We continued to talk for fifteen minutes, no longer as enemies but as friends. I was amazed at what was happening right before my eyes. God's love had won Razaq's heart, and he was changed. My interrogator had become my friend. Later that night the guards came and moved me to a better cell.

We believe in a God who makes friends out of enemies. Love will always win in the end. Never give up loving. God can change the hardest of hearts. I had the privilege of seeing God at work that day in prison.

> We believe in a God who makes friends out of enemies. Never give up loving.

Around the same time during my imprisonment, I also saw the love of God at work in the lives of my guards. One day I overheard the guards talking at the end of the corridor. They were speaking in Farsi, a language that I had learned in Afghanistan, so I listened carefully as they began to talk about Glenn and me, the foreign prisoners. They began to ask questions among themselves: "Why? Why did they come here, knowing that we kill Christians? And why are they praying prayers of blessing upon those who could kill them?" (I didn't know it, but they had hidden a microphone in my room and had been listening to everything I had been saying, and praying.)

> **When we truly love God, the lives of those around us will also experience that love.**

Then one of the guards spoke up and said, "Well, I know what Christians believe." He began to tell the others that he had heard the whole gospel story many years before. He began to tell them about Jesus and why he came. I sat in my room amazed as the guard shared about the love of God.

After three or four days of discussing these things, three of them agreed and said, "These foreigners have a reason for living. They have purpose—a reason to live and a reason to die. They talk about a God of love, and that seems so right. I want to have this same reason and purpose for living."

I sat in my cell as these three guards gave their lives to Jesus in the corridor. Again God had challenged me to love my enemies, and now I was privileged to see how his love had won their hearts.

I saw the same amazing love at work in another man as well, none other than the judge who had all but condemned me to death. I will never forget the day of my release from prison, when that judge read aloud a letter that stated I could be set free. As I turned to walk away from the judge, God showed me yet another incident where his love was victorious. This time the judge approached me, reached out his arms, and drew me close. Then he gave me three kisses, cheek to cheek to cheek, which I knew was a customary greeting between Iranian men but only practiced between good friends. I was stunned. The man who had hated me most, who had been my foremost accuser, and who I had thought of as my greatest enemy in Iran, now had had a change of heart and wanted to become my friend. Again the love of God prevailed.

As we continue to discover the depths of God's love for us, we will be set free to be channels of that love to others. When we truly love God, the lives of those around us will also experience that love. This should be the trademark of the followers of Jesus—our love for others. As God calls you to love, he will give you the grace to love, whatever the circumstance.

Chapter Seven

Ready to Serve

Then I heard the voice of the Lord saying,
"Whom shall I send? And who will go for us?"
And I said, "Here am I. Send me!"
—*The prophet Isaiah, Isaiah 6:8*

My grace is sufficient for you, for my power is
made perfect in weakness.
—*God's word to Paul, 2 Corinthians 12:9*

There is no higher calling in this life than to serve the
High King of Heaven, the Lord Jesus Christ. As we
break free from the various obligations and requirements that
we put on ourselves, or that we receive from others, we are set
free to respond to our Lord in wholehearted service. We are
able to offer ourselves out of inspiration rather than obligation.
We are able to say, "Here I am, Lord; I'm ready to serve."

It is not so much my concern in this final chapter to
describe the different ways we serve. The previous chapter has
identified the most important and basic way—love. Here I
want to do all that I can to encourage you to make yourself
available to God—to help you remove the obstacles that get

in your way and to persuade you to lay down your life for the service of your King.

God has blessed each and every one of us with various abilities. We all have something to offer, something to benefit and further the kingdom of God. As we submit ourselves to Jesus and seek to do his will, we will discover that he is using us. And when you discover that, your life takes on new meaning. What an amazing thing that is: the God of all creation finds people like you and me *useful* for his purpose and for the glory of his name!

> Our service to God is the natural outworking of his life within us.

Service is, in some ways, the ultimate act of surrender. It's not so much what we *do*, but rather what we *allow*. We are allowing God to live through us. It brings to mind again the powerful image from John 15 of a branch bearing fruit—it does so only because of its connection to the vine. It is the vine that gives life to the branch and actually causes the fruit to grow. In the same way, our service to God is the natural outworking of his life within us.

As we think about serving God, then, what could possibly hinder us? One of the statements that I hear again and again as I travel and talk to many Christians is, "Well, I don't feel ready." The importance of *being* ready, or *feeling* ready, is an idea with a strong hold on our culture. This keeps so many Christians from stepping out and making themselves available to God. Yet we have no right to give this excuse of not being ready. We have no right to disqualify ourselves in this way. Jesus said, "Come, follow me, *and I will make you* fishers of men" (Mark 1:17, emphasis added). Jesus will do what is necessary to qualify us and equip us for service. Unless we are walking in blatant disobedience, according to Jesus we are ready to serve.

It is a terrible lie that we must achieve greater levels of holiness and readiness *before* we are able to offer ourselves in service. Jesus is willing to accept us now. We must not put requirements upon ourselves that are not from God. He knows how weak and frail we are, but still he calls us to serve him. He invites us to abandon ourselves to him and to go for it! The apostle Paul agrees: "Not that we are competent in ourselves to claim anything for ourselves, but our competence comes from God. He has made us competent as ministers of a new covenant" (2 Cor. 3:5–6). If we are willing, we will see God do amazing things around us, through us, and in us. We need to allow God to use us even when we don't feel ready. Jesus didn't necessarily feel ready in the Garden of Gethsemane, but he obeyed anyway, saying to the Father, "Not what I will, but what you will" (Mark 14:36). Jesus was willing to trust, and willing to act upon that trust, whatever the consequences.

It is important to remember that God is both our loving Father and our sovereign Lord and Master. We are his children, but we are also his servants, awaiting his instruction, willing to do whatever he asks. We must submit to his wisdom and authority, trusting him to decide when and where he will use us. He will commission us—it is our responsibility to obey.

Sadly enough, because of our insecurities and lack of trust, we are not always ready to obey. Sometimes we even allow our understanding of personal giftedness to distract us from what Jesus is calling us to do at that moment. As we discover our gifts, sometimes we become preoccupied with a particular gift, and then we neglect opportunities to serve that don't immediately seem to fit that gift category. We say, "I'm a teacher, so

I won't take this opportunity in evangelism." Or we think, "I have leadership gifts, so that task is below me." All the while we are resisting the prompting of Jesus and missing out on an opportunity to serve. We need to remember that we are servants of Jesus and obedience to his call is always our immediate priority.

> We are servants of Jesus, and obedience to his call is always our immediate priority.

Sometimes people use other excuses for not being ready. One is education: "I need a college degree before I'll serve God." Another is the great delay: "Give me a couple years, and then I'll be ready." Desperately we give excuses, often to cover up our fears and anxieties. Whatever our reasons, we are unwilling to obey the call of God. We forget that he has chosen us to accomplish his will in the world. Whatever our issues, whatever we are struggling with, God has chosen to work with us. God is longing to give away his life and love to a hurting world, and he wants to do that through us. He wants to use you.

Now, of course, God may lead us to attend college or to spend a year or more doing this or that. But we should do so only in obedience to his leading, not as an excuse to avoid or delay obedience. I spent four years in college to earn a degree in business administration, and afterward I went off to Afghanistan to work in hospital administration. Was serving in Afghanistan the goal and going to college the preparation? No, I didn't see it that way. Both tasks were, for me, steps of obedience. I was simply doing the next thing that I felt Jesus had asked me to do. If he had asked me to go to college, then that's where I would live for him and serve him until he called me elsewhere. I had a rich spiritual life at college. I had many opportunities to serve people, to build friendships, and to grow in my relationship with Jesus. I wouldn't trade that time for anything. If I had been preoccupied during those years with going overseas, I might have missed out on all that. When I finally did get the opportunity to go to Afghanistan, I received it from God simply as another opportunity to love him and serve others. It was the next thing I felt called to do. All along our journey, wherever we are, whatever we are doing, we need to have a sense of calling, that we are being obedient to God's will, eager and ready to serve.

> God is longing to give away his life and love to a hurting world, and he wants to do that through us.

The apostle Paul didn't always feel ready. We sometimes imagine him as a man of great skill and confidence. But in his first letter to the Corinthians he admits to something quite different: "When I came to you, brothers, I did not come with eloquence or superior wisdom as I proclaimed to you the testimony about God. . . . I came to you in weakness and fear, and with much trembling" (1 Cor. 2:1–3). Paul was nervous. He felt insecure. He wasn't confident in his speaking abilities. He had issues just like you and I. But he doesn't appear to be hindered by some notion of readiness. Despite his insecurities, he served wholeheartedly. And in Paul's mind, his weaknesses helped to clarify the divine origin of his message: "My message and my preaching were not with wise and persuasive words, but with a demonstration of the Spirit's power, so that your faith might not rest on men's wisdom, but on God's power" (vv. 4–5).

What if Paul had waited until he felt ready before he brought the gospel to Corinth? Would he ever have gone? In the same way, the world waits for us to come to them even in our weakness. Like Paul, we need to offer ourselves in wholehearted service despite our fears and insecurities. God's grace will be sufficient for us.

However, many of us allow our feelings to rule our lives, even when it comes to decisions about serving God. Sometimes we give in to apathy. We don't fully give ourselves to God's service, simply because we don't want to, we don't feel like it. As petty as it sounds, it hinders our service, not to mention our relationship with God.

> We need to offer ourselves in wholehearted service despite our fears and insecurities.

I have struggled with these feelings in my own life. When I first arrived in Afghanistan I didn't feel like being there. I was confident that God had led me there, but I was lacking a sense of purpose and passion. Instead I felt hesitant and inadequate. My early days there were difficult, but as I began to settle in to my situation, a sense of urgency came over me to pray for the people of Kabul and the work there. I began to walk through the city streets and to pray as I walked. I did this every day for at least an hour, and within weeks I was beginning to experience a miracle within me. Slowly but surely God was giving me a heart for the people of Kabul and a passion for the work of his kingdom there. After three months my heart was completely there, and there was no other place that I would rather have been. I spent the next several years there, excited about the opportunity that God had given me to serve him.

That love for Afghanistan continues to grow even today. I am so thankful to God that he not only allowed me to live in Afghanistan for those years but also gave me a piece of his heart for the Afghan people. And to think that I could have missed out on all that if I had chosen to follow my feelings from the beginning rather than the call of God.

As Christians we are constantly faced with decisions like this. Our feelings often scream out to us and plead with us to choose what feels better, which can often be against the way of God. But we don't have to give in to our feelings. It's never easy to choose against them, but the more we do it, the easier it becomes. It is a constant challenge, but as we walk with God day by day, we can learn to choose his ways over our feelings. I have also found that the more I choose God's ways, the more I begin to see God's goodness and love in those ways. I begin to see how unreliable my feelings actually are and how they are able to distract me from choosing what is God's best for my life. When we do give in to our feelings, which I have often done, we end up forfeiting the freedom and joy that God wants to bless us with. We only need to trust in him.

It is important that we are able to see the difference between these personal feelings that distract us and the desires of our hearts that guide us. Both come from within us, yet they have a very different effect on us. Those feelings that distract us from obedience will grate on us. They pull us down, and when we give in to them, we know we are settling for something less. They align themselves easily with fears and insecurities, and they are dealt with only as we face them honestly and choose to rise above them. In contrast, as discussed in chapter 5, the godly desires of our hearts speak within us as viable options for our path. They present themselves clearly, and instead of bringing confusion, they help us to discern a certain direction. Ultimately, instead of distracting us from obedience, these desires in our hearts express precisely what it is that God is calling us to do at the moment. In them, we have aligned our hearts with God's heart.

I learned a lot from Glenn, my friend and fellow prisoner in Iran, about living by faith and not by feelings. Although we were imprisoned together, we were immediately separated, and it was only on the day of his release, some five weeks later, that we were able to spend a couple of hours together. During that time Glenn shared with me about how God had led him to meditate on Philippians 4:8 during his imprisonment: "Finally, brothers, whatever is true, whatever is noble, whatever is right, whatever is pure, whatever is lovely, whatever is admirable—if anything is excellent or praiseworthy—think about such things." Any time that thoughts and feelings caused Glenn to dwell on something other than what fit into this verse, he chose to put it out of his mind and to focus only on good things. At first this was very difficult, but as he practiced it, slowly he was able to discipline his mind in this direction. He found that as he persevered in this, his mind was being renewed. He experienced the truth of Paul's challenge in Romans 12:2, "Do not conform any longer to the pattern of this world, but be transformed by the renewing of your mind." As Glenn experienced this transformation in his mind, his feelings followed and came under his control. For him it was one of the most important things he learned in prison.

What about when we fail miserably and feel unworthy to be called a servant of Jesus? What about when we fall into sin in the midst of serving? At that moment our greatest need is to repent. We confess our sins to God and receive his forgiveness. For many of us, it is difficult to move on. We tend to grovel in our guilt. For example, if I sin in the area of lust, I usually feel guilty about it and not worthy of serving God for at least a day or two. I feel dirty. And often, by the time I start feeling on top of things, I stumble again—and the cycle continues. In these situations, it's almost as if we feel we need to pay the price for our own mistakes. Somehow we think we can earn God's forgiveness. But we are very wrong—we cannot earn this gift.

> *[God] does not treat us as our sins deserve or repay us according to our iniquities.*
> *—Psalm 103:10*

David was a great man of God who fell into sexual sin while he was serving God as king of Israel. In Psalm 103 David delights in the grace of God when he affirms that "[God] does not treat us as our sins deserve or repay us according to our iniquities" (v. 10). So often, when things don't go well for us, we imagine that God is somehow getting back at us for what we have done wrong. God is not like that. He does not treat us as our sins deserve. When we become aware of our sinful state, we naturally feel that we deserve to be treated like lousy sinners. But God loves to forgive us. He loves to accept us, even though we don't deserve it. God wants desperately to take away the very thing that keeps us in our guilt and separates us from him. It is as David explains two verses later in the same psalm: "As far as the east is from the west, so far has he removed our transgressions from us" (Ps. 103:12). God has removed our sin from the picture. He wants us to enjoy unhindered fellowship with him. He wants us to enjoy the freedom that he has accomplished for us on the cross: "So if the Son sets you free, you will be free indeed" (John 8:36).

This is the kind of freedom that is available to all who follow Jesus. In Matthew 11:28–30, Jesus says, "Are you tired? Worn out? Burned out on religion? Come to me. Get away with me and you'll recover your life. I'll show you how to take a real rest. Walk with me and work with me—watch how I do it. Learn the unforced rhythms of grace. I won't lay anything heavy or ill-fitting on you. Keep company with me and you'll learn to live freely and lightly" (MSG). When Jesus says, "work with me," he is inviting us to serve. When we choose to follow Jesus and to serve him, we are embarking on *a beautiful way.* It is a life that is full of refreshing fellowship and learning.

> *Keep company with me and you'll learn to live freely and lightly.*
> —Jesus in Matthew 11:30 (MSG)

God never meant for our obedience and service to be a chore. It is meant to be the natural overflow of enjoying our relationship with him. As I was once told, "Everything we do for God will be the overflow of intimacy with God." More than anything else, love is what motivates service. The more I understand God's love for me, the more I want to love him back, the more I want to offer my life in service. The deeper the love, the deeper the commitment and the less our feelings will work against us. In other words, as we become more and more focused on Jesus, our desire to please him takes precedence over our other desires. As a result, feelings that once distracted us from our obedience to Jesus now have less and less of an effect on our hearts. There is victory for each one of us over our feelings but only in the context of relationship, only as we accept the invitation that Jesus extends to us.

Are you ready to serve? If Christ lives within you, then nothing can stop you. It doesn't matter whether you are young or old, whether you are working in a career or going to school or staying at home, God wants to use you for his glory, and he will give you opportunities to serve. If you understand his personal love for you and believe in your heart that he is good, then what could possibly stand in your way? Center your life on him, and your choices will reflect his priorities. Learn to trust in him as you encounter fears. Spend time listening to his voice and walk in obedience to it. As your life becomes consumed with Jesus, let his life and love flow through you to the people around you. If you do this, the world will never be the same again. You will see God's kingdom come here on earth as it is in heaven.

> *Are you ready to serve? If Christ lives within you, then nothing can stop you.*

What is our reward? Is it happiness? Fulfillment? Success? No, even though we may experience these, none of these is guaranteed to those who serve Jesus. The reward *is* Jesus— Jesus himself and our relationship with him. If that doesn't seem like it's enough, then you don't know him. You don't yet understand the true value of knowing Jesus. You have not yet found a beautiful way. You have not yet found the treasure in the field that you would joyfully give up everything else to acquire (Matt. 13:44). Everything else comes and goes, but Jesus is always with us. The more you know Jesus, the more you know that nothing else compares. The encouragement for each one of us is that the invitation to experience more of Jesus is still being given. We need only to accept it.

What happens within us as we stand before a beautiful sunset? Do we strive to enjoy it? No, we just relax and enjoy the beauty. When we stand before Jesus, do we strive to enjoy him? No, again we need only to embrace the beauty and enjoy it. We're already there before Jesus. In striving we are only giving in to distractions. We become restless. We are trying to change something to make the moment better, to put something else in order before we can enjoy it. Instead we need to stop and simply enjoy. It is finished. All is ready. The door is open. Come and enjoy. Jesus is more beautiful than anything else you have ever seen or heard or experienced. He waits for you to embrace him. He invites you now to enjoy him forever.

About the Authors

Dan Baumann is presently serving with Youth With A Mission in Kona, Hawaii. YWAM Kona, led by founder Loren Cunningham, is the mission's largest training center in North America. For more information on Dan's ministry and YWAM, please visit his website at danbaumann.com. If you would like to learn more about Dan's harrowing experiences in Iran, his book *Cell 58: Imprisoned in Iran* tells the story.

Mark Klassen is a personal friend of Dan Baumann. He served for several years with Youth With A Mission and was involved with YWAM's School of Biblical Studies in various locations around the Pacific and Asia. Mark has a bachelor's degree in Biblical Studies from YWAM's University of the Nations and a master's degree in Old Testament from Regent College in Vancouver, BC, Canada. He presently lives in Yarrow, BC, with his wife, Amy, and their two daughters, Alexis and Dania.

Doug Knutson

HÉCTOR TOBAR has been a weekly columnist and a foreign correspondent for the *Los Angeles Times* and is a Pulitzer Prize–winning journalist and a novelist. The author of *Translation Nation* and *The Tattooed Soldier,* he is a native of Los Angeles, where he lives with his wife and three children.

www.hectortobar.com

Also by Héctor Tobar

Additional Praise for *The Barbarian Nurseries*

THE
BARBARIAN
NURSERIES

Héctor Tobar

PICADOR   FARRAR, STRAUS AND GIROUX   NEW YORK

www.picadorusa.com
www.twitter.com/picadorusa • www.facebook.com/picadorusa
www.picadorbookroom.tumblr.com

Picador® is a U.S. registered trademark and is used by Farrar, Straus and Giroux
under license from Pan Books Limited.

For book club information, please visit www.facebook.com/picadorbookclub
or e-mail marketing@picadorusa.com.

Designed by Jonathan D. Lippincott

The Library of Congress has cataloged
the Farrar, Straus and Giroux edition as follows:

Tobar, Héctor, 1963–
    The barbarian nurseries / Héctor Tobar. — 1st ed.
    p. cm.
    ISBN 978-0-374-10899-1
    1. California, Southern—Fiction. I. Title.

PS3570.O22B37 2011
813'.54—dc22

2011010703

Picador ISBN 978-1-250-01379-8

First published in the United States by Farrar, Straus and Giroux

First Picador Edition: September 2012

10 9 8 7 6 5 4 3 2

For Dante, Diego, and Luna

BOOK ONE
The Succulent Garden

The American mystery deepens.
　　　　　　　　—Don DeLillo, *White Noise*

1

Scott Torres was upset because the lawn mower wouldn't start, because no matter how hard he pulled at the cord, it didn't begin to roar. His exertions produced only a brief flutter of the engine, like the cough of a sick child, and then an extended silence filled by the buzzing of two dragonflies doing figure eights over the uncut St. Augustine grass. The lawn was precocious, ambitious, eight inches tall, and for the moment it could entertain jungle dreams of one day shading the house from the sun. The blades would rise as long as he pulled at the cord and the lawn mower coughed. He gripped the cord's plastic handle, paused and leaned forward to gather breath and momentum, and tried again. The lawn mower roared for an instant, spit a clump of grass from its jutting black mouth, and stopped. Scott stepped back from the machine and gave it the angry everyman stare of fatherliness frustrated, of a handyman being unhandy.

Araceli, his Mexican maid, watched him from the kitchen window, her hands covered with a white bubble-skin of dishwater. She wondered if she should tell *el señor* Scott the secret that made the lawn mower roar. When you turned a knob on the side of the engine, it made starting the machine as easy as pulling a loose thread from a sweater. She

had seen Pepe play with this knob several times. But no, she decided to let *el señor* Scott figure it out himself. Scott Torres had let Pepe and his chunky gardener's muscles go: she would allow this struggle with the machine to be her boss's punishment.

El señor Scott opened the little cap on the mower where the gas goes in, just to check. *Yes, it has gas.* Araceli had seen Pepe fill it up that last time he was here, on that Thursday two weeks ago when she almost wanted to cry because she knew she would never see him again.

Pepe never had any problems getting the lawn mower started. When he reached down to pull the cord it caused his bicep to escape his sleeve, revealing a mass of taut copper skin that hinted at other patches of skin and muscle beneath the old cotton shirts he wore. Araceli thought there was art in the stains on Pepe's shirts; they were an abstract expressionist whirlwind of greens, clayish ocher, and blacks made by grass, soil, and sweat. A handful of times she had rather boldly brought her lonely fingertips to these canvases. When Pepe arrived on Thursdays, Araceli would open the curtains in the living room and spray and wipe the squeaky clean windows just so she could watch him sweat over the lawn and imagine herself nestled in the protective cinnamon cradle of his skin: and then she would laugh at herself for doing so. *I am still a girl with silly daydreams.* Pepe's disorderly masculinity broke the spell of working and living in the house and when she saw him in the frame of the kitchen window she could imagine living in the world outside, in a home with dishes of her own to wash, a desk of her own to polish and fret over, in a room that wasn't borrowed from someone else.

Araceli enjoyed her solitude, her apartness from the world, and she liked to think of working for the Torres-Thompson family as a kind of self-imposed exile from her previous, directionless life in Mexico City. But every now and then she wanted to share the pleasures of this solitude with someone and step outside her silent California existence, into one of her alternate daydream lives: she might be a midlevel Mexican government functionary, one of those tough, big women with a mean sense of humor and a leonine, rust-tinted coiffure, ruling a little fiefdom in a Mexico City neighborhood; or she might be a successful artist—or maybe an art critic. Pepe figured in many of her fantasies as the quiet and patient father of their children, who had chic Aztec names such as Cuitláhuac and Xóchitl. In these extended daydreams Pepe was a land-

scape architect, a sculptor, and Araceli herself was ten kilos thinner, about the weight she had been before coming to the United States, because her years in California had not been kind to her waistline.

All of her Pepe reveries were over now. They were preposterous but they were hers, and their sudden absence felt like a kind of theft. Instead of Pepe she had *el señor* Scott to look at, wrestling with the lawn mower and the cord that made it start. At last, Scott discovered the little knob. He began to make adjustments and he pulled at it again. His arms were thin and oatmeal-colored; he was what they called here "half Mexican," and after twenty minutes in the June sun his forearms, forehead, and cheeks were the glowing crimson of McIntosh apples. Once, twice, and a third time *el señor* Scott pulled at the cord, turning the knob a little more each time, until the engine began to kick, sputter, and roar. Soon the air was green with flying grass, and Araceli watched the corner of her boss's lips rise in quiet satisfaction. Then the engine stopped, the sound muffled in an instant, because the blade choked on too much lawn.

Neither of her bosses informed Araceli beforehand of the momentous news that she would be the last Mexican working in this house. Araceli had two bosses, whose surnames were hyphenated into an odd, bilingual concoction: Torres-Thompson. Oddly, *la señora* Maureen never called herself "Mrs. Torres," though she and *el señor* Scott were indeed married, as Araceli had discerned on her first day on the job from the wedding pictures in the living room and the identical gold bands on their fingers. Araceli was not one to ask questions, or to allow herself to be pulled into conversation or small talk, and her dialogues with her *jefes* were often austere affairs dominated by the monosyllabic "Yes," "*Sí*," and, occasionally, "No." She lived in their home twelve days out of every fourteen, but was often in the dark when new chapters opened in the Torres-Thompson family saga: for example, Maureen's pregnancy with the couple's third child, which Araceli found out about only because of her *jefa*'s repeated vomiting one afternoon.

"*Señora*, you are sick. I think my enchiladas *verdes* are too strong for you. *¿Qué no?*"

"No, Araceli. It's not the green sauce. I'm going to have a baby. Didn't you know?"

Money was supposedly the reason why Pepe and Guadalupe departed. Araceli found out late one Wednesday morning two weeks earlier, following an animated conversation in the backyard between *la señora* Maureen and Guadalupe that Araceli witnessed through the sliding glass doors of the living room. When their conversation ended, Guadalupe walked into the living room to announce to Araceli curtly, "I'm going to look for some *chinos* to work for. They can afford to pay me something decent, not the *centavos* these gringos want to give me." Guadalupe was a fey *mexicana* with long braids and a taste for embroidered Oaxacan blouses and overwrought indigenous jewelry, and also a former university student like Araceli. Now her eyes were reddened from crying, and her small mouth twisted with a sense of betrayal. "After five years, they should be giving me a raise. But instead they want to cut my pay; that's how they reward my loyalty." Araceli looked out the living room windows to see *la señora* Maureen also wiping tears from her eyes. "*La señora* knows I was like a mother to her boys," Guadalupe said, and it was one of the last things Araceli heard from her.

So now there was only Araceli, alone with *el señor* Scott, *la señora* Maureen, and their three children, in this house on a hill high above the ocean, on a cul-de-sac absent of pedestrians or playing children, absent of traffic, absent of the banter of vendors and policemen. It was a street of long silences. When the Torres-Thompsons and their children left on their daily excursions, Araceli would commune alone with the home and its sounds, with the kick and purr of the refrigerator motor, and the faint whistle of the fans hidden in the ceiling. It was a home of steel washbasins and exotic bathroom perfumes, and a kitchen that Araceli had come to think of as her office, her command center, where she prepared several meals each day: breakfast, lunch, dinner, and assorted snacks and baby "feedings." A single row of Talavera tiles ran along the peach-colored walls, daisies with blue petals and bronze centers. After she'd dried the last copper-tinged saucepan and placed it on a hook next to its brothers and sisters, Araceli performed the daily ritual of running her hand over the tiles. Her fingertips transported her, fleetingly, to Mexico City, where these porcelain squares would be weatherbeaten and cracked, decorating gazebos and doorways. She remembered her long walks through the old seventeenth-, eighteenth-, and nineteenth-century streets, a city built of ancient lava stone and mirrored glass, a colonial city and an Art Deco city and a Modernist city all at once. In

her solitude her thoughts would wander from Mexico City to the various other stops on her life journey, a string of encounters and misfortunes that would eventually and inevitably circle back to the present. Now she lived in an American neighborhood where everything was new, a landscape vacant of the meanings and shadings of time, each home painted eggshell-white by association rule, like featureless architect models plopped down by human hands on a stretch of empty savanna. Araceli could see the yellow clumps of vanquished meadows hiding in the unseen spaces around the Torres-Thompson home, blades sprouting up by the trash cans and the massive air-conditioning plant, and in the rectangles cut into the sidewalk where young, man-sized trees grew.

When Araceli stood before the living room picture window and stared out at the expanse of the ocean a mile or two in the distance, she could imagine herself on that unspoiled hillside of wild grasses. Several times each day, she walked out of the kitchen and into the living room to study the horizon, a hazy line where the gray-blue of the sea seeped into a cloudless sky. Then the shouts and screams of the two Torres-Thompson boys and the intermittent crying of their baby sister returned her to the here and now.

When there were three *mexicanos* working in this house they could fill the workday hours with banter and gossip. They made fun of *el señor* Scott and his very bad *pocho* accent when he tried to speak Spanish and tried to guess how it was that such an awkward and poorly groomed man had found himself paired with an ambitious North American wife. Guadalupe, the nanny, cooed over the baby, Samantha, and played with Keenan and the older boy, Brandon. It was Guadalupe who taught the boys to say things like *buenas tardes* and *muchas gracias*. Araceli, the housekeeper and cook, was in charge of the bathrooms and kitchen, the vacuum cleaners and dishrags, the laundry and the living room. And Pepe, with the hands that kept the huge leaves of the elephant plant erect, that made the cream-colored ears of the calla lilies bloom, and the muscles that kept the lawn respectably short. They filled the house with Spanish repartee, Guadalupe teasing Araceli about how handsome Pepe was, Araceli responding with double entendres that always seemed to go right over Pepe's head.

"Your machine is so powerful, it can cut anything!"

"*Es que tiene mucho* horsepower."

"Yes, I can see how much *power* there is in all those horses of yours."

Pepe was a magician, a da Vinci of gardeners, worth twice what they paid him. How long would the orange beaks of the heliconias in the backyard open to the sky without Pepe's thick, smart fingers to bring them to life? The money situation must be very bad. Why else would *el señor* Scott be outside in this white sun, burning his fair skin? The idea that these people would be short of money made little sense to her. But why else would Maureen be changing the baby's diapers herself, and looking exasperated at the boys because they were playing on their electronic toys too long? Guadalupe, the aspiring schoolteacher, was no longer there to distract them with those games they played, outside on the grass with soap bubbles, or inside the house with Mexican lottery cards, the boys calling out "*El corazón,*" "*El catrín,*" and "*¡Lotería!*" in Spanish. Through the picture window in the living room, Araceli studied *el señor* Scott as he struggled to push the mower over the far edge of the lawn where it dropped off into a steep slope. TORO said the bag on the side of the lawn mower. No wonder *el señor* Scott was having so much trouble: the lawn mower was a bull! Only Pepe, in a gleaming bullfighter's uniform, with golden epaulets, could tease the Toro forward.

Araceli made *el señor* Scott a lemonade and walked out into the searing light to give it to him, as much to inspect his work as anything else.

"*¿Limonada?*" she asked.

"Thanks," he said, taking the wet glass. Beads of water dripped down the glass, like the beads of sweat on *el señor* Scott's face. He looked away from her, inspecting the blades of grass, how they were sprayed across the concrete path that ran through the middle of the lawn.

"The work. It is very hard," Araceli offered. "*El césped.* The grass. It is very thick."

"Yeah," he said, looking at her warily, because this was more conversation than he was used to hearing from his surly but dependable maid. "This mower is too old."

But it was good enough for Pepe! Araceli glanced at the grass, saw the brown crescents *el señor* Scott had inadvertently carved into the green carpet, and tried not to look displeased. Pepe used to stop there

to adjust the height of the mower, and Araceli would come out and give him lemonade just like she was giving *el señor* Scott now. Pepe would say *"Gracias"* and give her a raffish smile in that instant when his eyes met hers before quickly turning away.

El señor Scott swallowed the lemonade and returned the glass to Araceli without another word.

As she walked back to the house, the lingering smell of the cut grass sent her into a depression. Exactly how bad was the money situation? she wondered. How much longer would *el señor* Scott mow the lawn himself and wrestle with the Toro? What was going on in the lives of these people? They had let Guadalupe go, and from Guadalupe's anger she imagined that it was without the two months' severance pay that was standard practice in the good houses of Mexico City, unless they caught you stealing the jewelry or abusing the children. Araceli was beginning to see that it was necessary to take a greater interest in the lives of her employers. She sensed developments that might soon impact the life of an unknowing and otherwise trusting *mexicana*. Back in the kitchen, she looked at *el señor* Scott through the window again. He tugged at the cut grass with a rake and made green mounds, and then embraced each mound with his arms and dumped it into a trash bag, blades sticking to his sweaty arms and hands. She watched him brush the grass off his arms and suddenly there was an unexpected pathos about him: *el señor* Scott, the unlikely lord of this tidy and affluent mansion, reduced to a tiller's role, harvesting the undisciplined product of the soil, when he should be inside, in the shade, away from the sun.

A moment after Araceli stepped away from the picture window, Maureen Thompson took her place, taking a good, long minute to inspect her husband's work. The mistress of the house was a petite, elegant woman of thirty-eight, with creamy skin and a perpetually serious air. This summer morning she was wearing Audrey Hepburn capri pants, and she strode about the house with a confident, relaxed, but purposeful gait. She ran this household like the disciplined midlevel corporate executive she had once been, with an eye on the clock and on the frayed edges of her daily household life, vigilant for scattered toys and half-full trash cans and unfinished homework. The sight of her

husband struggling with the lawn mower caused her to briefly chew at the ends of her ginger-brown hair. Could *la señora* see the yellow crescents at the beginning of the slope, Araceli wondered, or was she just put off to see her husband dripping sweat onto the concrete? Araceli examined *la señora* Maureen examining *el señor* Scott and thought it was interesting that when you worked or lived with someone long enough you could allow your eyes to linger on that person for a while without being noticed: Pepe, a stranger, always caught Araceli when she stared at him.

Much like her Mexican maid, Maureen Thompson had also sensed the disturbing non sequitur playing itself out on the other side of the glass: her theoretician, her distracted man of big ideas, the man she had once proclaimed, in a postcoital whisper, "the King of the Twenty-first Century," frustrated this Saturday afternoon by a technological relic from the previous millennium. They had been married for twelve years of professional triumphs and corporate humiliations, of cash windfalls and nights of infant illnesses, but nothing quite like this particular comedy. *He's having trouble just keeping the thing running. It uses gasoline: how complicated can it be?* Her eyes shifted to the drawn curtains of the neighbors' houses, the blank windows that reflected the blank California sky, and she wondered who else might be watching. She had not agreed with the calculus her husband had made, the scratched-out set of figures whose bottom line was the departure of the more-than-competent and reliable gardener, a man of silent nobility who, she sensed, had tended the soil in a distant tropical village. Scott was a software kind of guy—both in the literal sense of being a writer of computer programs, and also in the more figurative sense of being someone for whom the physical world was a confusing array of unpredictable biological and mechanical phenomena, like the miraculous process of photosynthesis and the arcane varieties of Southern California weed species, or the subtle, practiced gestures that were required, apparently, to maneuver a lawn mower over an uneven surface. *Later on he'll look back at this and laugh.* Her husband was a witty man, with a sharp eye for irony, though that quality had deserted him now, judging from the sweaty scowl on his face. *Hard labor will cleanse you of irony*: it was a lesson from her own childhood and young womanhood that returned to her now, unexpectedly.

It was a short walk across the living room to a second picture window, this one looking out to the backyard tropical garden, which was suffering a subtle degradation that was, in its own way, more advanced than the overgrowth of the front lawn had been. They had planted this garden not long after moving in five years earlier, to fill up the empty quarter acre at the rear of their property, and until now it glistened and shimmered like a single dark and moist organism, cooling the air that rushed through it. With the flip of a switch, a foot-wide creek ran through the garden, its waters collecting in a small pond behind the banana tree. Now the leaves of that banana tree were cracking and the nearby ferns were turning golden. Not long after Scott dropped the little bomb about Pepe, Maureen had made a halfhearted attempt at weeding "*la petite* rain forest," as she and Scott called it, making an initial foray into the section of the garage where she had seen Pepe store some chemicals. She had no green thumb but guessed that keeping a tropical garden alive in this dry climate took some sort of petrochemical intervention: pest and weed control, fertilizers. Unfortunately, she had been frightened off by the bottles and their warning labels: Maureen had stopped breast-feeding only a few weeks earlier and was not yet ready to surrender the purity of body and mind that breast-feeding engendered. If she hadn't yet given in to the temptation of a shot of tequila—though she suspected she soon would—why was she going to open a bottle marked with a skull and crossbones and the even more ominous corporate logo of a major oil company?

A downpour of dust and dirt was killing their patch of rain forest; she would have to step in and care for it or it would wither up in the dry air, and as she thought this she felt a pang of anxiousness, a very brief shortness of breath. *It isn't just the garden and the lawn, is it?* Maureen Thompson had spent her teens and her twenties shedding herself of certain memories forged in a very ordinary Missouri street lined with shady sugar maple trees, where the leaves turned in October and it snowed a few days every winter, and the weather aged the things people left on their porches and no one seemed to care. Those days seemed distant now: they fit into two boxes at the bottom of one of her closets, outnumbered by many other boxes filled with the mementos of her arrival in California and life with Scott. Here on their hillside, on this street called Paseo Linda Bonita, one day followed the next with a comfortable

and predictable rhythm: meals were cooked, children were dressed in the morning and put to bed at night, and in between the flaming sun set over the Pacific in a daily and almost ridiculously overwrought display of nature's grandeur. All was well in her universe and then suddenly, and often without any discernible reason, she felt this vague but penetrating sense of impending darkness and loss. Most often it happened when her two boys were away at school, when she stood in their bedroom and sensed an absence that could, from one moment to the next, grow permanent; or when she stood naked in the bathroom, her wet hair in a towel, and she caught a glimpse of her body in the mirror, and sensed its vulnerability, her mortality, and wondered if she had asked too much of it by bringing three children into the world.

But no, now it passed. She returned to the living room and the picture window, where the drama on the front lawn had reached a kind of conclusion and the King of the Twenty-first Century was sweeping up the grass on the walkway.

When Scott Torres was a kid living in South Whittier he cut the lawn himself, and as he pushed the machine over the slope of his bloated home in the Laguna Rancho Estates, he tried to draw on those lessons his father had passed down two decades earlier, on a cul-de-sac called Safari Drive, where all the lawns were about a quarter the size of the one he was cutting right now. *Try to get the thing moving smoothly, check the height of the wheels, watch out for any foreign object on the grass because the blades will catch it, send it flying like a bullet.* His father paid him five dollars a week, the first money Scott ever earned. Like the other two adults in this home, Scott had been put in a reflective mood by the unusual events of the past few days, by the departure of two members of their team of hired help, and by the June shift in domestic seasons. Summer vacation was upon them and yesterday had been filled with the summing-up celebration of their two boys' return from the final day of third and fifth grade with large folders filled with a semester's worth of completed homework and oversized art projects that their mother oohed and aahed over. Now he brought the mower over the last patch of uncut grass and gave it a haircut too.

Scott stopped the engine and breathed in the scent of freshly

cut grass and lawn mower exhaust, the pungent bouquet a powerful memory-trigger of his days of teenage chores. He remembered the olive tree in front of the Torres family home in South Whittier, and many other things that had nothing to do with lawns or lawn mowers, like working on his Volkswagen—his first car—in the driveway, and the feathered chestnut hair and the Ditto jeans of the somewhat chunky girl who lived across the street. What was her name? *Nadine*. The olive tree dropped black fruit onto the sidewalk and one of Scott's jobs back then was to take a hose and wash away the stains. The neighborhood of his youth was a collection of flimsy boxes held together by wallpaper and epoxy, plopped down on a cow pasture. The Laguna Rancho Estates were something altogether different. When Scott had first come to this house the lawn had not yet been planted, there was a patch of raw dirt with stakes and string pounded into it, and he had watched the Mexican work crews arrive with trays of St. Augustine grass to plant. In five years, the roots created a dense living weave in the soil, and he had struggled to make his haircut of it look even; in fact, he failed. After he raked up the grass he noticed the blades that stuck to his sweaty arms, and as he wiped them off he thought that each was like a penny when you added up how much you saved by cutting the lawn yourself.

Two weeks earlier, he had quickly calculated what he paid the gardener over the course of a year and had come to a surprisingly large four-figure number. The problem with these Mexican gardeners was that you had to pay them in cash; you had to slap actual greenbacks into their callused hands at the end of the day. The only way around it was to go out there in the sun and do it yourself, because bringing these hardworking Mexicans into your home was expensive, and in the end all those hours the Mexicans worked without complaint added up. That was also the problem with Guadalupe: too many hours.

Scott's parents were frugal people, much like Pepe the gardener: Scott could see this in his methodical, cautious count of the bills Scott gave him. Pepe scratched out the amount with a stubby golf course pencil he kept in his wallet along with a piece of invariably soiled paper. Scott's father was Mexican, which in the California of Scott's youth was synonymous with poverty, and his mother was a square-jawed rebel from Maine, a place where good discipline in the use of funds was standard Protestant practice. *Use it up, wear it out, make it do, or do without.*

Scott remembered his late mother standing in the doorway of that South Whittier home under the canopy of the olive tree, watching him earn his five dollars with her frugal eyes, and felt like a man waking up from a long drinking binge as he looked back at the white house with the ocher-tile roof that rose before him. His home had become a sun-drenched vault filled with an astonishing variety of purchased objects: the coffee table handmade by a Pasadena artist from distressed Mexican pine and several thick, bubbling panes of hand-blown glass; the wrought-iron wall grilles shipped in from Provence and the Chesterfield sofa of moss-green leather; a handcrafted crib from the Czech Republic.

We have behaved and spent very badly. Scott held on to this idea as he rolled the creaking, cooling mower into the garage, feeling a meek, half-defeated self-satisfaction. *I cut the goddamn grass myself. It wasn't rocket science.* He reentered the house and his Mexican maid gave him an odd smile with some sort of secondary meaning he could not discern. This woman was more likely to ignore you when you said hello in the morning, or to turn down her lips in disapproval if you made a suggestion. Still, they were lucky to have her as their last domestic employee. Araceli was the only person in this house besides Scott who understood frugality: she never failed to save the leftovers in Tupperware; she reused the plastic bags from the supermarket and spent the day turning off lights Maureen and the children left on. Scott had never been to the deeper reaches of Mexico where Araceli hailed from, and he had only once been to his maternal homeland in the upper reaches of Maine, but he sensed they were both places that produced sober people with tiny abacuses in their heads.

A few moments later Scott had slipped out of the kitchen and looked through the sliding glass doors that led out to the backyard and felt like an idiot. He had forgotten about the garden, the so-called, mis-named "tropical" garden, which was actually a "subtropical" garden, according to the good people at the nursery who had planted the thing. For the first time Scott contemplated its verdant hollows and shadows with the eye of a workingman, a blister or two having formed on his palms thanks to his efforts on the front lawn. He remembered Pepe wading into this semi-jungle with a machete, and the crude noise of his blade striking fleshy plants, emerging with old palm fronds or withering flowers. Scott wasn't ready to enter into that jungle today, although he

would soon have to. It seemed to him it would take a village of Mexicans to keep that thing alive, a platoon of men in straw hats, wading
with bare feet into the faux stream that ran through the middle of it.
Pepe did it all on his own. He was a village unto himself, apparently.
Scott wasn't a village and he decided to forget about the tropical garden
for the time being because it was in the backyard, after all, and who
was going to notice?

2

In the Torres-Thompson family, every child's birthday was an elaborately staged celebration built around a unique theme, with *la señora* Maureen purchasing specially ordered napkins and paper plates, and sometimes hiring actors for various fanciful roles. She made HAPPY BIRTHDAY banners with her own art supplies; she scoured the five-and-dime stores for old scarves and suits to make into costumes, and ordered special wigs and props over the Internet. Maureen hung streamers over the doorways, and drafted Guadalupe to create big balloon flowers, while Araceli labored in the kitchen to make cookies in the shapes of witches and dinosaurs. Keenan, the younger boy and middle child, would be turning eight in two weeks, and at the moment the preparations required that Araceli mix the paste for a papier-mâché project. Araceli did not mind doing this, because she appreciated the idea of a birthday as a family event organized by women in kitchens, and celebrated by large groups of people in places open to the sun and air, as they were in the parks of her hometown on the weekends. This birthday, like all the others, would be celebrated in the Torres-Thompson family backyard, in a setting filled with *la señora*'s uncomplicated and appropriately child-like decorations, most in the primary colors also favored in Mexican

folk art. Araceli believed that if you had transplanted this woman to Oaxaca she would have made very fine pottery, or *papel picado*, or been an excellent stage manager for a theater group wandering through the suburbs of El Distrito Federal.

Araceli took the bowl of completed paste to *la señora* Maureen in the playroom. She found her *jefa* kneeling on the floor over a piece of yellow construction paper with a red pencil grasped between her fingers, wearing an artist's smock over her brown yoga pants.

"*Señora, aquí está su* paste," Araceli said.

"Thanks." After a few seconds passed without Araceli walking away, Maureen looked up and found Araceli examining her work with that neutral expression of hers, a half stare with passive-aggressive overtones. Maureen had seen Araceli's wide, flat face assume this inscrutable look too often to be unsettled by it, and instead she gave her maid a half shrug and quick eye-roll of ironic semi-exasperation, as if to say, *Yes, here I am again, on my knees, scratching away at an art project like some preschooler.* Araceli broke her trance by raising one eyebrow and nodding that she understood: it was the sort of exchange that took place several times each day between these two women, a wordless acknowledgment of shared responsibilities as exacting women in a home dominated by the disorderly exertions of two boys, a baby girl, and one man. Maureen was writing HAPPY BIRTHDAY KEENAN in the classic, serif-heavy font of Roman buildings and monuments. Below these letters, *la señora* was trying to draw what looked like a Roman helmet, a birthday theme inspired by Keenan's recent fixation with a certain European comic strip. Maureen drew one more line with Araceli watching, and then they were both startled by the cry of a baby, seemingly just behind *la señora*'s shoulder. Turning around quickly, Araceli saw a burst of red lights on the baby monitor as Maureen calmly rose to her feet and headed for the nursery.

A few moments later Maureen appeared in the hallway with Samantha, a baby girl of fifteen months with hazel eyes still moist from crying to escape from her crib. She had her mother's milky complexion and fine hair, though the baby's locks were a deeper chestnut. *La señora* held her daughter, bounced and made kissing noises until she stopped her crying, and then did something she had never done before: she handed Samantha to Araceli. In the Torres-Thompson household, this

baby girl carried the aura of a sacred and delicate object, like a Japanese vase on two teetering legs. In the last few weeks, she had started to walk, entering a world of possibility and danger, stumbling across the room to her mother's embrace with a precarious Frankenstein step. Guadalupe carried the baby for hours every day, but now that Guadalupe was gone it appeared that some of this responsibility would fall to Araceli, who wasn't sure if she was ready or willing to help take care of a baby. In fifteen months, Araceli had disposed of several hundred soiled diapers, but she had changed Samantha herself not more than three times, and always at the behest of Guadalupe. The truth was Araceli had never been close to children; they were a mystery she had no desire to solve, especially the Torres-Thompson boys, with their screams of battle and the electric sound effects they produced with their lips and cheeks.

But a little girl was different. This one led the life any Mexican mother would want for her baby, with an astonishing variety of pinks and purples in her wardrobe of onesies, bibs, T-shirts, nightshirts, her closet in the nursery overflowing with Tinker Bell Halloween costumes and miniature sundresses, and outfits like this casual track suit of velvety ruby-colored cotton she was wearing today. In El Distrito Federal, these clothes would cost a fortune; if you could find them at all it would be in the marble-floored malls in the affluent satellite fringes where there was valet parking at the front doors and perfume piped into the air ducts. Araceli gently touched one of the lavender barrettes in Samantha's thin strands of hair, and the baby wrapped her small hand around one of Araceli's fingers. In an instant, Araceli found herself cooing, making infantile noises. "*¡Qué linda! ¡Qué bonita la niña!*" Samantha smiled at her, which was so unexpected that it made Araceli lean over and kiss the baby on the cheek. *Maybe that is not something I should do.*

Araceli carried the baby and walked in circles as Maureen built a small collection of papier-mâché helmets, using a bowl as a frame, until she had enough to outfit a platoon of child Romans. Her *jefa* left the helmets to dry and gave a stealthy peek through the playroom's window at the backyard. Pepe was gone and the plants in the tropical garden were mourning his absence even more than Araceli. The translucent stems of the begonia 'Ricinifolia' were performing a deep bow in Pepe's honor, reaching down to kiss the drying soil at their feet, while their asterisk bursts of flowers, each pale pink petal the size of Samantha's

thumbnail, were drying and withering and being plucked off by the breeze. Like flakes of ash, the paper-thin petals caught hot drafts and floated magically upward and away from the garden and the window, where two women and a baby girl stood watching.

Later that afternoon Maureen changed out of her smock and yoga pants into jeans and a loose-fitting STANFORD T-shirt of Scott's. She put on a wide-brimmed straw hat and walked purposefully back into the garage, deciding to ignore the bottles of chemicals for the moment as she retrieved a stiff pair of garden gloves and some rusty tools. Then she marched up to *la petite* rain forest and got a good look at the crabgrass weeds that were filling up the dry soil at the base of the calla lilies and the banana tree. These could be removed rather simply, with a hoe, and Maureen began to do so, with a rhythmic and therapeutic hacking. *Hurry, hurry, before the baby starts to cry.* Maureen felt a pang of guilt when she remembered Guadalupe's departure, and she regretted not having told her sons that their babysitter would never be coming back. Samantha would forget about Guadalupe quickly, but the boys would not, because after five years she had truly become "part of the family," a phrase that for all its triteness still meant something. Her boys deserved some sort of explanation, but the thought of giving them one squeezed Maureen's throat into silence: how much longer could she keep up the fiction about Guadalupe's "vacation"?

Moving more quickly, Maureen retrieved a hose from the side of the house and sent streams of water over the ribbed banana leaves: a tree like this was worth having just for the wide sweep and silhouette of the leaves. That had been the impulse of planting *la petite* rain forest in the first place: to hide the adobe-colored wall behind it and create the illusion that these banana trees and tropical flowers were the beginning of a jungle plain where savage tribes lived and vines swallowed the metal shells of downed airplanes. With a quick spray the stand of Mexican weeping bamboo looked healthier, though Maureen didn't have time to rake up the dead leaves clustering at their base. With regular watering and maybe a bag of organic mulch—tropical gardens needed mulch, didn't they?—she might get *la petite* rain forest looking fit and trim again in time for Keenan's birthday.

With Araceli's help they would make it to the day of the party without any major embarrassments. It was to be both a birthday party and the annual, informal reunion of the old crew from MindWare, the company her husband-to-be had cofounded a decade earlier in the living room of Sasha "the Big Man" Avakian, a garrulous charmer and pitchman from Glendale. Maureen had joined them eighteen months later as their first-ever "director of human resources," which in those undisciplined and freethinking early days made her a kind of company den mother. Mind-Ware had since been sold to people who did not wear canvas tennis shoes to work, and the twenty or so pioneers who were its core had been dispersed to the winds of entrepreneurial folly and corporate servitude. Scott came out of his shell when "the Duo of Destiny and Their Devoted Disciples" were reunited and drank too much sangria, which was another reason why Maureen went to the trouble of making each party a small exercise in perfection.

Maureen stepped back inside and found Samantha resting her cheek against Araceli's shoulder in the living room, looking out the big picture window in a somnolent daze while beads of sweat dripped from Araceli's forehead. *She's been holding the baby this entire time.* "Thank you, Araceli," Maureen said as she relieved her maid of Samantha's weight.

Maureen was carrying Samantha to the playroom when a flash of green on the floor caught her eye: her husband had left a trail of cut grass on the Saltillo tiles in the living room. She followed the blades to the hallway that led to the bedrooms and his "gaming" room, and touched them with the tips of her toe-loop leather sandals. Before she could call out to Araceli, the Mexican woman had arrived with broom and dustpan, quickly corralling the stray blades into a palm-sized pile. When it came to the upkeep of the house, Maureen's and Araceli's minds were one. Keeping Araceli and letting Guadalupe go was the better outcome of the we're-going-broke saga Scott had foisted upon them, though she was not entirely convinced they were indeed flirting with bankruptcy. Guadalupe and Pepe were ill-timed and too-sudden losses. But as she watched Araceli sweep up the grass from the floor, Maureen felt less alone before the enormous responsibility of home and family, and somehow stronger. *You pay to have someone in your home, and if it works out, they become an extension of your eyes and your muscles, and sometimes*

your brain. This protected feeling stayed with her as she watched Samantha try to take a step in the playroom and listened to the distant and soothing growl of the vacuum cleaner: Araceli was busy erasing the last traces of Scott's footsteps from the carpeted hallways.

Scott entered his sons' bedroom and found his progeny with heads bowed and eyes fixed on tiny screens. Their fingers made muted clicks and summoned zaps and zips and tinny accordion music from the devices in their hands. He considered them for a moment, two boys transported by semiconductors into a series of challenges designed by programmers in a Kyoto high-rise. Keenan, his younger boy, with his black madman wig of uncombed and pillow-pressed hair, was opening his hazel eyes wide with manic intensity; Brandon, his older son, with the long russet rock-star hair, sat slumped with a bored half frown, as if he were waiting for someone to rescue him from his proto-addiction, which was precisely what Scott had come here to do. Maureen had told him to get them out of the house and "run them a bit," because without Guadalupe to get them outdoors and away from their insidious, pixilated gadgets, the first week of summer had failed to add much color to their skin. "Why don't you play football with them?" Maureen had said, and of course Scott resented being told this, because like every other good parent he lived for his children. When he grabbed a book from their library to read or when he watched them swimming in the backyard pool, the money spent on this hilltop palace felt less like money lost. That was the idea behind the home in the first place, to give their boys, and now Samantha too, a place to run and splash, with a big yard and rooms filled with books and toys of undeniably educational value, such as the seldom-used Young Explorers telescope, or the softball-sized planetarium that projected constellations onto the walls and the ceilings.

"Why is your game barking?" Scott asked his older son.

"I'm taking Max for a walk," Brandon said.

After a few perplexed seconds, Scott remembered that his oldest son was raising virtual puppies. He walked, shampooed, and trained his dogs, and the animated animals grew on the screen during the course of an hour or two, soiling the rug and doing other dog things. *We don't own a real dog, because my wife can't stand the mess.*

"Okay, guys, that's enough of that. Games off . . . please."

Brandon quickly folded shut his game, but Keenan kept clicking. "Let me just save this one," he said.

"Go ahead and save it, then." Scott was a programmer and a bit of a gamer himself: he understood that his son was holding a toy that told a story, and that he could lose his place by the flipping of the OFF switch. Scott walked over to see precisely which gaming world his son had entered and saw the familiar figure of a plumber in overalls. "Ah, Mr. Miyamoto," Scott said out loud. The alter ego of the game's Japanese creator jumped from one floating platform to the next, fell to the ground, was electrocuted and then miraculously resurrected, and eventually entered passageways that led to virtual representations of forests and mountain lakes. In this palm-sized version, the game retained an old, arcade simplicity, and to Scott the programmer, the mathematics and algorithms that produced its two-dimensional graphics were palpable and nostalgia-enducing: the movement along the x- and y-axes, the logical sequences written in C++ code: *insert, rotate, position.*

"You're doing pretty well," he told his son. "But I really think you should get off now."

"Okay," Keenan said, and kept on playing.

Scott looked up and surveyed the books and the toys in the real space around them, the oversized volumes stacked unevenly in pine bookcases purchased in New Mexico, the plastic buckets filled with blocks and miniature cars. Here too he felt the mania of overspending, although in this room much of the excess was of his own doing. How many times had he entered a toy emporium or bookstore with modest intentions, only to leave with a German-designed junior electronics set, or a children's encyclopedia, or an "innovative" and overpriced block game for Samantha meant to kindle her future recognition of letters and numbers? But for the gradual diminishing of their cash on hand, and the upwardly floating interest rates of credit cards and mortgages, he might now be conspiring to take them to their local high-end toy store, the Wizard's Closet, where he had purchased toys that satisfied unfulfilled childhood desires, such as the set of miniature and historically accurate Civil War soldiers that at this moment were besieging two dinosaurs in the space underneath the bunk beds. The bookshelves were stacked with multiplication flash cards, a geography quiz set, a

do-it-yourself rock polisher, and a box of classical architecture blocks. Scott's parents had sacrificed to make his life better than theirs; they had saved and done without luxuries: but Scott spent lavishly to ensure the same result for his own children. He remembered the childhood lesson of his father's hands, with their curling scars three decades old, earned in farm and factory work, hands the father urged the son to inspect more than once, to consider and commune with the suffering that was buried in Scott's prehistory, unspoken and forgotten before the clean and sweat-free promise of the present and future.

"Dad, Keenan hasn't quit his game yet," said Brandon, who had gone back up to his bunk to pick up the book he was reading the night before.

"Keenan, turn off the game, please," Scott said, in a faraway voice his boys might have found disturbing if they were a few years older and more attuned to adult emotions like reflection and remorse. He had felt this way, also, the night Samantha entered the world, during those three hours he spent overwhelmed by the fear that he and his wife might be tempting fate by having their third child when they were pushing forty. His God, part penny-pinching Protestant and part vengeful Catholic, would wreak a holy retribution against him and his wife for wanting too much and trying for the girl that would give their family a "perfect" balance. But Samantha had entered the world easier than her brothers, after a frantic but short labor, and was a healthy and alert child. No, the reckoning came from the most likely and obvious place: the private spreadsheet disaster of his bad investments. *I thought I was being prudent. Everyone told me, "Don't let your money get left behind, don't let it sit—that's stupid. Get in the game."* The absurdity that a six-figure investment in a financial instrument called a "security" could shrink so quickly and definitively into pocket change still did not compute. He worried about the two geniuses in this room, if he was about to set them on a tumultuous journey that would begin with the sale of this home and a move to less spacious quarters. Scott considered the precocious reader sitting on the top bunk, and his younger brother, who appeared to have a preternatural gift for logical challenges, judging by his swift advancement through the levels of this game, and wondered if he might soon be forced to subtract something essential from their lives.

3

The first guests arrived and rang the doorbell ten minutes early, a terribly rude North American habit, in Araceli's opinion. Rolling her eyes in exasperation, she left a stack of *sopes* waiting to be garnished with Oaxaca cheese in the kitchen and walked toward the finger that had set off the electric chimes, but stopped when two midget centurions with papier-mâché swords ran past her. Brandon and Keenan raced to the door, holding their helmets atop their heads as they ran, and Araceli listened, unamused, as they stumbled over the lines Maureen had told them to recite: "Friends, Romans, countries . . ." Keenan began, and then faltered, until Brandon finished with, "Give us your ears!"

"How cute," the early guests called out. "Little Romans!"

When the second and third guests arrived at precisely the appointed hour, the boys were off playing with the children of the first guests, while Maureen and Scott were busy in the back, which left Araceli to open the door for the *invitados*.

"We're here for Keenan's party?" An American woman with vaguely Asian features and a child and husband in tow tried to look past Araceli into the interior of the house, her expression suggesting she expected to see wondrous and magical things there.

"*Sí, adelante.*" What Araceli really wanted to say was, *Why do you people insist on treating an informal social gathering as if it were the launching of a rocket ship? Why do you arrive with a clock ticking in your head? How am I supposed to finish these* sopes la señora *Maureen wants if you keep ringing the doorbell?* In Mexico it was understood that when you invited people to a party at one o'clock, that meant the host would be *almost* ready at one, and therefore the guests should arrive at their leisure at least an hour later. *Here they do things differently.* The punctual guests walked past her, oohing and aahing at the decorations in the living room, at the Roman-lettered cardboard signs declaring HAPPY BIRTHDAY KEENAN and VIII on either side of the Chesterfield sofa, and the Doric Styrofoam columns topped with plastic replica helmets. Araceli recognized this couple, and the other guests that followed, from parties past. They were people she saw frequently back in the days when she first started with the Torres-Thompsons, when *el señor* Scott had his own company. They arrived dressed in the assertively casual attire Southern Californians wore at their weekend parties: in cotton shorts and leather sandals, in jeans faded to the whitish blue of the Orange County sky in summer, and in T-shirts that had gone through the washer a few times too often. Her *jefa* wanted everything "just right," and now these early arrivers in their unironed natural fabrics were preventing Araceli from finishing her appointed task. The way some of these people dressed was the flip side of their punctuality: they were like children who cling to a favorite blanket or shirt, they valued comfort over presentation, they were unaware or unconcerned about the spectacle they inflicted upon the eyes of the overworked *mexicana* who must greet them. How disappointing to work so hard preparing a home for an elegant event, only to have such unkempt guests.

"Hello, I brought some cookies for the party," the next early arriver said. "Can I leave them with you?"

The woman with the chocolate chip cookies was Carla Wallace-Zuberi, chief publicist of the defunct MindWare Digital Solutions. She was a roundish white woman of Eastern European stock with box-shaped sunglasses and a matriarchal air, and she lingered near the doorway as her husband advanced into the Torres-Thompson home with their daughter, Carla's gaze settling on Araceli as the Mexican woman took a few impertinent moments to assess the cookies. Carla Wallace-Zuberi prided

herself on having an eye for strong personalities and here was one that clearly could fill a room, and not just because she was a tad larger than most other Mexican servants. Araceli wore her hair pulled tightly and gathered in two fist-sized nubs just over her ears, an absurd style that suggested a disoriented German peasant. *The only thing this Mexican woman accomplishes by pulling her hair back is to establish a look of severity: maybe that's the point.* A small spray of hair, just a few bangs, jutted forth from Araceli's forehead like the curled plume of a quail, a halfhearted concession to femininity. On this as on all other workdays, Araceli wore the boxy, nurselike uniform called a *filipina* that was standard for domestics in Mexico City. Araceli had five such uniforms and today she wore the pale yellow one because it was the newest. She took the cookies from the publicist with a frown that said: since you insist on giving these to me . . . The publicist suppressed a surprised chuckle. *This is one tough woman, a no-nonsense mom. Look at those hips: this woman has given birth. Of course she is irritated, because she is separated from her child, or children.* Carla Wallace-Zuberi was a self-described "progressive," and a few days before this party she had spent twenty minutes in her neighborhood bookstore perusing the back cover, jacket flap material, and opening paragraphs of a book called *María's Choice*, which related the journey of a Guatemalan woman forced to leave her children behind for years while she worked in California: *How terrible*, Carla Wallace-Zuberi thought, *how disconcerting to know that there are people like this living among us.* This bit of knowledge was disturbing enough to keep her from buying the book, and for the rest of the party, whenever Carla Wallace-Zuberi caught a glance of Araceli, guilt and pity caused her to turn her head and look the other way.

When Sasha "the Big Man" Avakian appeared at the door five minutes later, his eyes caught Araceli's directly in a way that was at once irritating to her and familiar. He was a tall, bulky man with curly chestnut-blond hair, and much darker eyebrows that were shaped like railroad boxcars. Now he raised both boxcars spryly as he made eye contact with the Mexican maid. The Big Man was the partner of *el señor* Scott in that business of theirs, and there was a time when he made frequent visits to this home, assaulting Araceli with this same impish look. A self-described "professional bullshitter," the Big Man saw in Araceli an authenticity lacking in ninety-nine percent of the people who crossed

his path. He had no line, no clever riposte with which he could amuse and beguile this woman, the way he could with people who came from his own, English-speaking, California software entrepreneur circle. He had seen Araceli out of uniform and with her hair much longer and not tied back like it was today, and had once managed to make her laugh with a bilingual pun. The memory of her laughter, of her round face brightening and the ivory sparkle of her teeth, had stayed with him. She worked with another girl, Guadalupe, who was too petite and too fake-cheerful to hold his attention, and today he barely noticed her absence. The Big Man also knew, because he had made a point of finding out over the years, that Araceli had no children, no boyfriend that Scott or Maureen knew about (on this side of the border, at least), and that Scott considered her something of a sphinx. Scott and his wife had coined nicknames for her such as "Madame Weirdness," "Sergeant Araceli," and the ironic "Little Miss Sunshine," but she was also extremely dependable, trustworthy, and a dazzling cook. The Big Man's stomach rumbled as he contemplated the Mexican hors d'oeuvres that would be on offer at this party, as at all the others the Torres-Thompsons hosted. He entered the home ahead of his long-suffering wife, and son, without saying any other word to Araceli than a mumbled "*Hola.*"

The lingering resentment in the chocolate swirl of Araceli's eyes confronted all the other guests too as they passed through the front door and followed the sounds of screaming children and chattering adults to the backyard. None of the mothers invited to the party had a full-time, live-in maid, and to them Araceli's subservient Latin American presence provoked feelings of envy and inadequacy. They knew of Araceli's cooking and her reputation as a tireless worker, and they wondered, briefly, what it would be like to have a stranger living with them, taking away all the unpleasantness from the porcelain surfaces of their homes. *Does she do anything and everything?* Some associated Maureen and her summer fitness and frail beauty with this Mexican woman and the other one, Guadalupe, who for reasons unknown was not present today. *Give me two extra sets of hands to do the housework and carry the baby and I'd look good too.* For most of the husbands, however, Araceli blended into the domestic scenery as if she were a frumpy, bad-humored usher guarding the entrance to a glittering theater. The memory of her faded quickly before the birthday decorations in the living room and

the eye-catching colors and textures of the furniture and ornamental touches to be found there—the mud-colored Bolivian tapestry thrown over the sofa, or the shimmering stone skin of the floor, which Araceli had mopped and polished the night before, and the bookcases and armoires of artificially aged pine where two dozen pictures framed in pewter and cherrywood documented a century of the Torres and Thompson family histories. The guests passed through the impeccable prologue of the living room, thence through an open sliding glass door to the backyard, a semicircle of grass the size of a basketball court framed by the restrained jungle of *la petite* rain forest, which was starting to look dry and wilted because the automatic sprinkler system had stopped working a week earlier. A humming engine accompanied a large inflated castle on the lawn, the swimming pool shimmered with ultramarine highlights in the sun, and a small tent covered a table stacked with toy swords and shields and papier-mâché helmets. Another VIII made from cardboard and painted marble-white dangled from the roof of the tent.

The guests found Maureen standing near the center of the lawn, with the baby Samantha on her hip, looking as elegant as ever in a powder-blue camisole and a taupe chiffon skirt printed with orchids. She gave each adult guest a peck on the cheek, taking a bit of pleasure in the gentility of this gesture, which was foreign to people in the river town of her Missouri youth. "Maureen, you look great!" the guests called out. "How did you lose all the weight so quickly?" "Look at Sam: she's so big now!" "Look at all this stuff for the party! How do you do it? Where do you find the time?" She gave an aw-shucks shrug and guided the guests' children toward the table with the faux-Roman outfits. "We've got helmets and swords for you guys to try out. But no hitting, please!"

By 2:00 p.m. there were two dozen adult guests in the backyard, squinting before the sun-drenched grass as if the onset of summer had caught them by surprise, even though some were holding bathing suits for their children, none of whom had yet shown any interest in the pool. They were in their thirties and forties and had programming degrees and MBAs; they were young enough to have started new careers, and old enough to begin to grow nostalgic for the adventure they had shared with one another first on the single floor of an Orange County business park, and then in MindWare's own, commissioned headquarters, an architectural gem in downtown Santa Ana that now belonged to

the county's largest real estate brokerage. They had been plucked from staid jobs in accounting and marketing departments, from the IT bowels of corporate towers, for an undertaking the Big Man had likened, repeatedly, to leading a wagon train across the Oregon Trail. The final months of MindWare's meteoric rise and fall had been filled with a series of competitive enmities and clashes over business strategy, and in the company's last days of independent existence, before the responsible investors had arrived to purge all but two of the original employees, several of the people today present in the Torres-Thompson backyard were not speaking to one another. But time had a way of making those bad feelings a mere seasoning floating atop the sweeter narrative of possibility that had once bound them all together.

"Hey, it's the head of research!"

Tyler Smith had arrived, with his three children and his wife, an immigrant from Taiwan who was telling her charges, in Mandarin, to behave themselves and not jump in the pool without their mother.

"Are they reading yet in Sierra Leone?" the Big Man called out, in an oft-repeated ribbing of the head of research, who had once traveled to West Africa to test MindWare software that was supposed to wipe out illiteracy.

"You're not taking those dialysis treatments anymore, are you, Tyler?" Maureen asked, because the project had left the head of research with a life-threatening kidney infection.

"Stopped two years ago."

"Oh, thank God."

MindWare had been held together by Maureen's concern for their daily well-being, and by Scott's technical creativity and grounded common sense. Everyone liked Scott and Maureen, and the MindWare alumni who had moved away from California timed their annual summer vacations so they could be present at Keenan's parties. Now Carla Wallace-Zuberi drew the group's attention to Scott, who was standing by the humming pump that kept the castle filled with air, wearing khaki shorts, sandals, and an oxford shirt with the sleeves rolled up.

"Scott, the house looks great. The kids are so big."

"Yes, they don't seem to stop growing, no matter what we do." *Each birthday finds us a little heavier*, Scott observed, *a bit saggier, our eyes less bright*. The Big Man was the one member of their crew who looked

exactly the same: Sasha Avakian, a onetime fund-raiser for Armenian independence, who in his reincarnation as California entrepreneur had sweet-talked a trio of venture capitalists into funding MindWare and its many offshoots, including Virtual Classroom Solutions and Anytime Anywhere Gaming, some of which were still in business, though no longer under the control or guidance of the people gathering this afternoon in the Torres-Thompson backyard.

"So, it's a Roman theme, huh, Scott?" Avakian said. "A kid army of centurions—and their parents, the Huns!"

"There's always a theme. The party cannot be themeless."

"You had the wizard thing going on the last time I was here. And the astronaut thing a while back. My favorite was the safari theme, the explorer bit. That was a couple of years ago, right?"

"Right," Maureen interjected. She said this without looking at her guest—she was holding the baby Samantha over her shoulder, trying to get her to take her afternoon nap, and was at the same time keeping an eye on the still-empty swimming pool and the inflated castle, where two small centurions were trying to hit each other with their swords in between trampoline jumps.

"How do you find the time to do these things, Maureen?" the wife of the Big Man said. "With three kids?"

"Araceli," Maureen said, turning to look back at her guests. "She's a godsend."

Maureen watched Araceli walk toward her guests with a tray of drinks, and not for the first time felt comfort in her employee's dependability. True, Guadalupe would be laughing and chatting up the guests in bad English if she were here, not scowling at them. But Maureen never needed to tell Araceli what to do more than once.

Araceli's tray contained a collection of blue glass tumblers filled with a sangria concoction that Maureen made for summer parties. Each drink was chilled with ice cubes Araceli had pried from a dozen trays, because Maureen wanted moon-crescent ice in her tumblers. Araceli watched each guest take a glass with the soon-to-melt crescents and went back to the kitchen with the empty drink tray to retrieve more hors d'oeuvres. When she returned to serve the guests she refused to acknowledge those few who were courteous enough to say thank you, and gave a sidelong glare to Mrs. Tyler Smith when she dared to say

"Gracias." I speak English, Araceli wanted to say. *Not much, but "Thank you" has been in my vocabulary since the fourth grade.* On one of these trips she crossed paths with *la señora* Maureen, who was walking back into the yard with a baby monitor in hand. Araceli began to lose track of the number of trips she had made with drinks and hors d'oeuvres. Finally came the culinary climax, her *sopes,* which were a California variation on a recipe of her aunt's. The *sopes* had begun their existence as balls of corn *masa* in Araceli's palms last night. Each was fried and garnished with Haas avocados, shredded cilantro, vine-ripened tomatoes, and white Oaxaca cheese, so that as she walked into the crowd of partiers she was presenting the colors of the Mexican flag. *I could eat five of these all by myself,* Araceli thought. Maybe if I go through here quickly enough I can keep them from getting all the *sopes.*

The Big Man began to gather an audience around him, regaling the group with tales from his new "mercenary" work as a consultant/lobbyist. He came to Scott and Maureen's parties because he respected them for their work ethic and loyalty, qualities he did not possess in large quantities himself, and once he was in their home his "gift" to them was to keep their guests amused and entertained. "So there I am, all of a sudden, shuffled into the mayor's office. The mayor of Los Angeles. He's saying goodbye to some people in Spanish. That guy, let me tell you, he's got a thankless job. Because there's a whole city filled with Mexicans who elected him to office—they think their day has come. And that's going to be a problem: because he can't keep them all happy. There's too many Mexicans. It's mathematically impossible."

The Big Man lived in Los Angeles, on its Westside, but to the rest of the partygoers that city and its overpopulated unpleasantness were far away, and the reference to the ethnic divisions in Los Angeles led to a moment of awkward silence filled by the laughs and squeals of children inside the inflated castle. In the circle of Maureen and Scott's friends, discussing any topic related to ethnicity was on the fringe of what was considered polite. Many now had interracial children, and all believed themselves to be cultural sophisticates, and had given their progeny names like Anazazi, Coltrane, and Miró that reflected their worldly curiosity. They avoided discussing race, as if the mere mention of the subject might cause their fragile alliances to come apart. "Mexican" was a word that sounded harsh, somehow, and it caused a few of them to look at Araceli.

Maureen's maid was a woman with the light copper skin of a newly minted penny, and cheeks that were populated with a handful of summer freckles. Araceli's Mexican forebears included dark Zapotecs and redheaded Prussians, and in her family she was on the paler side of the spectrum. But in California, and at this party, she stood out unmistakably as an ambassador of the Latino race. Still, she appeared oblivious to the Big Man's comments as she walked past. Others glanced briefly at Scott: he didn't have any of the qualities associated with "Mexicans" by those in the metropolis who were not Mexican, but his surname was Torres, after all. Scott was sipping his sangria and had just closed his eyes and wasn't listening either. He was, instead, trying to discern all the different fruits in this beverage: grapes from the wine, of course, and also orange and apple. *And is that pomegranate? Pomegranate? That takes me back.*

"Still, I guess they really do deserve a share of the pie," the Big Man said, renewing his monologue with a conciliatory tone, as if there might be a closeted Mexican in his audience. "But this mayor guy, he's a real piece of work," the Big Man continued, and he began to pronounce on the swirl of rumors surrounding the personal life of the city leader. Suddenly his son ran through the cluster of his audience: he was a boy of eight with the same curly hair and round belly as his father, and was wearing one of the papier-mâché helmets, along with plastic breast armor and a skirt of cardboard scraps painted to resemble leather. "Hey, it's the Little Big Man!" someone called out, and the ensuing laughter finally brought the Big Man's monologue to an end.

The adults scanned the backyard for their children and saw how their swords and other homemade Roman paraphernalia were starting to fall apart, littering the lawn with scraps of cardboard and paper. They bit into their taquitos and tasted bits of shredded chicken in a red sauce that was boldly spiced with organic *chile de árbol*. Now Araceli was weaving between them with two *sopes* on her tray: they were the last two, she had just realized, and she was going to try to make it back to the kitchen and impertinently devour them. But just as she broke free of the main cluster of guests, she walked into a patch of open grass to discover the Big Man standing alone and suddenly staring straight at her, and then at her tray and the *sopes*. The Big Man raised his boxcar eyebrows jauntily and extended his hands, using one to take the last two *sopes*, and the other to place his empty drink on Araceli's tray. "Thanks, kid."

"¡*Cabrón!*" Araceli muttered under her breath, but the Big Man did not hear her because he was circling back to the conversation, which had taken the lamenting, retrospective tone that eventually came to dominate the reunions of the MindWare alumni, once the alcohol started to set in.

"We should have set up in India," Tyler Smith was saying. "Everyone is doing that now. Bombay."

"Mumbai," Carla Wallace-Zuberi corrected.

"Yeah. Or Bangalore. Everyone was telling us to do that."

"The stockholders," Tyler Smith said, repeating a word whose connotations only further darkened their shared mood. "The guy from that hedge fund. What an asshole!"

"Shahe!" the Big Man's wife shouted toward the inflated castle. "Shahe Avakian! Take your foot off that boy's neck now!"

"Those bouncy houses always bring out the aggressive behavior," Carla Wallace-Zuberi said.

"The stockholders! The sacred stockholders!" interjected the Big Man, as his molars crushed what was left of Araceli's last *sope*. "The first thing we should have done is killed all the stockholders."

"Uh, that would have included all of us too."

"And the board members too. Where did we find those people?" said the Big Man, who knew perfectly well.

"They actually expected us to make money," Scott said.

"Remember that letter from that stockholder in Tennessee?" the head of research said. "The guy who said he was sticking with us even though he'd lost half of his investment."

"And all those stupid suggestions he made," Scott said. "That we should move our headquarters to Nashville."

"Toyota moved there," Carla Wallace-Zuberi said dryly. "At least the guy was loyal."

"I'm sure he sold what he had pretty soon after."

"I'm still living under the dictatorship of the stockholders," Scott said. He was a midlevel executive at a new company, supervising programmers. "The stockholders measure and quantify everything you do. Most of them you never see, but they seem to know everything you do. Like God, I guess. They'll turn their backs on you if your numbers aren't right, and then go off running in the direction of another guy who does have the right numbers. Like a herd."

This observation caused a pause of agreement and knowing nods. "If you think about it," Carla Wallace-Zuberi offered, "the whole system is like mob rule."

"Woe to the land that's ruled by a child!" the Big Man shouted suddenly, and for no discernible reason. They turned to find his flush face staring at the grass, at nothing, and at that point they all shared the same thought: *He's getting drunk again.*

"He's on a Shakespeare kick," the Big Man's wife explained laconically. "He's saying that one a lot. Because with his new work, he's getting to know a lot of politicians."

"That was from one of the Richards," the Big Man said, holding back a burp, but otherwise recovering himself. "Richard the Second. The Third, maybe. No, the Second." He was feeling the wine in the sangria, and what a pleasant sensation it was.

"This is what we do for recreation now," the Big Man's wife said. "We look for Shakespeare festivals. Sasha says he likes the bard for his speeches. Says he's studying how they're put together—so we get to write off all the trips. We saw a *Tempest* in the redwoods in Santa Cruz. That was memorable. We'll do Ashland this month and maybe Stratford next year, right, hon?" The Big Man gave an approximation of a nod and started to drift away. He wanted to find that Araceli kid and see if she had any more of that silver-dollar-sized tortilla dish—and maybe talk to her. His wife stood there for a moment, her question unanswered, and now she abruptly left the group too, to look for their son. The others in the group watched them leave in opposite directions, and for a moment the Big Man's drunken shuffle and his wife's distracted scanning of the backyard was like a snippet of conversation all by itself, a piece of gossip to mull over.

A few moments later the first of the children jumped into the water with a splash and most of the adults drifted over to the fence that circled the pool. Tyler Smith's wife took off her blouse and shorts to reveal a one-piece bathing suit underneath, folded her clothes and left them on the grass, and followed her sons into the water. Having exhausted the conversation topics of business, politics, and property values, the guests watched her silently as she took a few moments to touch the water with her palms before plunging gracefully below the surface. In a few minutes there were a dozen children in the pool, water glistening on their buff and khaki skins. With their mixed Asian, African, and European

features, their epicanthic folds and proud Armenian noses, their Chinese cheekbones and Irish foreheads that were turning deep saffron in the sun, they resembled a group of children Marco Polo might have encountered on the steppes of the Silk Road, at a crossroads where spices and incense and brass pots were traded at the edge of a river.

The Big Man stood alone by the garden and picked up one of the helmets that had been tossed on the lawn and tried it on: the papier-mâché shell wrapped itself around his curls but refused to reach his ears, so he pulled it off and let it fall to the grass. Next he took a few steps toward *la petite* rain forest and examined the azaleas, before turning back to study Araceli, who was standing in the middle of the lawn distributing the last plate of finger foods. *That woman looks miserable and lonely, like someone forced to sit in a stranger's room and listen to the silence for days, weeks, years.* He again remembered her laughter, all those years ago, and wondered what he could say to make her smile again. *How do you make a Mexican woman chuckle? What causes her to let go of her worries and show the sparkle of her teeth like a burst of white fireworks?*

Araceli nearly dropped her tray when she caught the Big Man gawking at her again, his lips rising slowly into an idiotic grin of mischievousness and craving. This was a more direct and prolonged stare than he had ever given her and she quickly realized that he was drunk. Yes, drunk, as confirmed by the fact that he was now stumbling into the garden and trying to kiss one of the flowers.

The Big Man found himself embraced by the banana tree, then escaped its grasp to stand over the azaleas and the calla lilies. Every time he came to the house he spent some time admiring the tropical garden, but today something wasn't right. *These birds-of-paradise need work.* The calla lilies were shriveling and a few snakes of crabgrass were starting to climb up their stalks from below. *What are these little things growing down here? Sow thistles, interlopers from the desert, pale green and drought-resistant, with paper-dry flowers. And look at these tiny holes in these otherwise pretty leaves of the banana tree.* The garden was dying, and in its decay the Big Man felt a slow-moving but irresistible force at work; something as simple as the passing of time, perhaps, or some profound and unseen truth about the family that owned it. The Big Man remembered one of his favorite lines from *Hamlet*: ". . . 'tis an un-

weeded garden that grows to seed, and things rank and gross in nature possess it merely." *What beautiful poetry, those lines.* His voice rose as he repeated the phrase out loud several times, his poor approximation of a British accent growing more affected each time, especially when he said "merely." He turned to face the other partygoers, and addressed them with full thespian voice.

"'Tis an unweeded garden and things rank and gross in nature possess it merely! An unweeded garden that grows to seed! That it should come to this!"

Maureen was a dozen or so paces away, handing a towel to the Little Big Man at the gate to the pool, when she heard the boy's father yelling. "An unweeded garden! Fie on it! Rank nature possesses it! An unweeded garden! Fie! Fie! Fie!" *What is that lunatic saying about my garden?* She had slaved on those azaleas for an hour, to have Sasha Avakian throw his insulting verbiage at them. Reexamining the garden as the party chatter sounded around her, she could see, even from a distance, that the fat drunk had a point. "An unweeded garden!" Her *la petite* rain forest was dry and exhausted, it lacked water and an application of pesticides. In the middle of the week she had asked Scott to fix the broken sprinklers, but he had either forgotten or decided to ignore her. The Big Man was opening his arms wide as if to embrace the decay of her tropical garden, turning to address the partygoers and reaching up to grab one of the drooping banana leaves for dramatic effect. His circular, repetitive soliloquy had drawn the attention of the children, who paused in their water-diving, mock sword battles, and bouncing games to look at the Big Man with the perplexed and furrowed brows of boys and girls working their brains to understand an adult truth just beyond their comprehension. The adults were ready to laugh off his drunken speech, but for the reaction of Maureen, who had left the pool and taken several steps toward the Big Man with full, jaw-tightened fury. Then they turned to the garden and saw what the Big Man and Maureen had seen: a living thing that was aging, suddenly, a green corner of this perfect home that had become stricken with a deadly disease.

"That it should come to this! But two months dead!" the Big Man shouted. "This unweeded garden grows to seed. And things gross and rank in nature possess it. Merely!"

Maureen heard one of her male guests give a chuckle that seemed

laced with knowing. She turned to find the party responsible, but instead caught Carla Wallace-Zuberi studying her with a mixture of puzzlement and pity. In an instant the rage left Maureen's face, and she unwittingly presented an image of wan surrender as she folded her bare and sunscreen-protected arms across her camisole and turned away, shaken. All of her cutting, drawing, gluing, weeding, and arranging had been for naught. *What a farce.* Her papier-mâché creations were splitting apart too, and her sons were hitting each other inside that stupid castle, and she had forgotten to clean the pool, and her guests were swimming in filthy water. *It's all tumbling around me, but do I even care?*

Later in the afternoon, long after the Big Man had sobered up and left with his embarrassed wife, Maureen said goodbye to the last guests filing out the front door: Tyler Smith and his wife and sons. Mrs. Tyler Smith stopped on her progress toward their car, startled by the spectacle of the flaming ball of the sun as it raced toward the ocean horizon, the purple wisps in the stratosphere, and the blood-orange pastel glistening in the water. "What an amazing view," the wife of the erstwhile head of research said, trying to convey sympathy and solidarity. "This is an amazing house, Maureen. You're so lucky to live here." Maureen gave a distracted thank you: she was still thinking about the Big Man and *la petite* rain forest and how the weeds and wilting flowers had ruined everything. After two weeks of driving herself to the point of exhaustion in pursuit of a liberating confab with their friends, the Big Man's booming voice had drawn the eyes of all of their friends to the telling flaw in their home. Damn him. Damn that fat jester, and damn Scott for letting Pepe the gardener go.

4

Night had fallen and the kitchen window had become a mirror once again, leaving Araceli to catch glimpses of herself as she listened to the dishwasher, to its timed sprays and its rhythmic swishes, and the click-clack of cycles beginning and ending. One more load and she would retire for the evening, out the kitchen's back door, past the trash cans, into the guesthouse. The last three glass bowls, two pots, and assorted serving spoons and spatulas were soaking in the sink, where steaming water and detergent worked to dissolve the final vegetable, olive oil, and fruit-fiber memories of the party concluded hours earlier. If this were her own home, and not the home of *la señora* Maureen, Araceli would simply take a sponge and scrubber to these dishes and be done in ten minutes, but *la señora* insisted on running everything through the searing, sterilizing water of the dishwasher. Still, Araceli could have ignored her *jefa* this evening, because *la señora* Maureen was fighting with *el señor* Scott and thus too busy to wander over to the kitchen and check on Araceli. The argument had been going on intermittently for three hours, with long and toxic silences in between, having started just moments after Maureen's final goodbye, and it had filled several rooms with recriminations and miscellaneous shouting, with descriptions of

the flaws in the tropical garden, passing on, through an odd and not entirely logical chain, to events deep in the couple's shared past. Araceli wondered how it was that her *jefa*, clearly simmering with outrage after the departure of the last guest, had been placed so quickly on the defensive. "You said the same thing in Barcelona!" Maureen yelled from the living room. Araceli had missed what it was Scott had said that reminded Maureen of Barcelona, a city that came up in their conversation from time to time, most often in sensuous and nostalgic tones that suggested, to Araceli, the romantic postcard images of embracing middle-aged couples in certain magazine and television advertisements common to both English- and Spanish-language media. Araceli would like to visit Barcelona and the Gaudí towers, and if she had a passport with the stamps and stickers that would allow her to come and go from the United States, she would take the several thousand dollars she had saved and buy an Iberia ticket and be out the door with not more than a week's notice.

"Jesus, I was twenty-five!" Scott insisted from another room, his voice muffled because he was deeper in the house. Araceli could only hear Scott intermittently, when the dishwasher paused, or when he wandered into the living room to parry one of Maureen's assertions with a weepy, prepubescent voice one moment, and a husky old-man's rant the next. "You're so totally pathetic!" he said, following up with uniquely raw English vulgarity, which Maureen shouted back at him with a "you too" added for punctuation's sake. Araceli guessed that if she were to leave the kitchen and burst into the living room and step in the acoustic line of fire, they would stop. She had done this before, entering to the scene of Maureen's reddish eyes and Scott's straining temples, one party or the other halting in midsentence at the sight of their underpaid Mexican employee. Other immigrant servants might be made uncomfortable by being forced to hear their employers baring intimate and apparently irreconcilable grievances, they might even shed a tear at the sense that "their family" was spinning apart—Araceli did not. She felt distant from their dysfunction. But it was annoying, all this shouting, so she quickly and without much hope for success took some basil leaves from the refrigerator and placed them inside a glass jar filled with water. This was an old Mexican folk remedy against angry spouses, one her mother used frequently. Fifteen minutes later, the arguing had stopped and the dish-

washer too. She threw in the last of the bowls and serving spoons like the good employee she was, and snuck out the side door of the kitchen, across the lawn, empty and quiet under the yellow bug light, and into her room, her sanctuary.

When the argument finally exhausted itself, Maureen withdrew to her bedroom and slipped inside the cotton and wool cocoon of her quilted comforter, alone. On any other day she wouldn't have been able to go to bed before restoring order in the rooms beyond the closed pine door, without forcing her two sons to help recover the scattered toys around the home and backyard, returning them to storage bins and shelves, but the boys had retreated to their room hours ago. Now she took comfort in the silence and order in this one room, where a vintage clock gave a steady and reassuring click and an incandescent bulb glowed through the maroon fabric of the lampshade, its light suggesting a hearth in a mountain cabin. Once again, she'd take the lamp's companionship over her husband's. He was sleeping on the couch, or in his beloved game room, and in his absence this shared niche of theirs had a feminine pulse, it was an organism of finely spun fibers, wood grain, and old metal. Scott sullied it daily with his discarded clothing, the stacks of memos and the electronic toys masquerading as office tools that she gathered up and placed in the drawer of his nightstand. How many computer chips did a man need to order his life? This gadget man, this collector of ring tones and black plastic slabs with glowing green lights, had wounded her with viciousness and sarcasm for daring to express her hurt and humiliation over the garden fiasco.

All that was left was to surrender before the weight of sleep, a mass made heavier by the torture-memory of many nights of sleep interrupted by Samantha's crying in the predawn darkness. Would the baby have a nightmare as she remembered her father's straining eyes and gritted teeth, like the toothy goblins that populate a child's scary story? *Maybe we would be better off alone, my daughter and boys and I.* She pulled the comforter up to her chin, and was aware how childlike that gesture was, to seek solace in the softness of fabric. *Nothing looks right when you haven't slept.* Sleeplessness made them both slaves to their reptilian brains and brought them to the brink of shouting. *That is why he is less*

forgiving, why he is less willing to bury what I said on La Rambla. In the morning, when they were rested, they would see the abundance of blessings in their lives, the sharp and clear voices of their boys, the flower-bud mouth of their daughter, the powerful sense of nurturing purpose she felt when the five of them traveled and ate together, when they assembled before breakfast tables with pancakes, orange juice, and chocolate milk.

There was still so much to do in this house, but it was getting late. Araceli would take care of it all in the morning.

Stepping out of her room the next morning, Araceli noticed bits of trash in the backyard that had escaped her attention in the fading light at the end of the party the day before, shredded pieces of papier-mâché armor that gave a light dusting of newspaper snow to the grass. The vanquished shell of the piñata, a traditional Mexican ball with seven spikes representing the seven deadly sins, had been split into several pieces, with one spike at the base of the banana tree. She moved quickly to pick up what she could and resolved to return later with a rake, then opened the door to the kitchen, where the white-tile sparkle and faint scent of detergent told a story of order and calm. There was nothing left to do here. She was about to walk out to survey the damage in the living room when she noticed a note in Maureen's handwriting on the tile counter of the kitchen's center island: *Araceli: We went to The Strand for breakfast. Be back around noon. Sorry about the house.* Ah, the warring couple made up this morning. *Qué bueno.*

In the living room she found a few tossed red fabric capes Maureen had made, along with toys and dolls the guests' children had looted from the boys' and Samantha's rooms and left scattered on the furniture and floors. She gathered plastic board-game pieces in her palm, a foam ball, and a book entitled *Airplanes*, and proceeded to the boys' room. Harvesting toys and placing them in the appropriate receptacle was another element of Araceli's daily routine and it could be said she knew the children's play and reading habits better than Maureen did. Araceli visited the boys' room at least three times a day and had given it her own, private nickname: *El Cuarto de las Mil Maravillas,* the Room of a Thousand Wonders, because it was filled with objects designed to

amaze and delight, from the colored-glass Art Deco mobile of planets and comets hanging from the ceiling, to the Viking ship made of interlocking Danish blocks and the collection of two or three hundred books of widely varying sizes. When she was in this room alone, Araceli sometimes spent several minutes with the books, especially the series of twelve hardcovers designed to introduce young children to Michelangelo, Rembrandt, van Gogh, Picasso, and other great masters of art. There were other books that produced three-dimensional dragons and castles when opened, or that made cricket sounds, jungle hoots, and whistles. Any child anywhere in the world would kill to have such a room, and to have a mother whose chief preoccupation was to "stimulate" her progeny, though of course these boys didn't appreciate it. *If I had grown up with a mother like* la señora *Maureen . . .* The mental comparisons between Araceli's own austere childhood and the abundance that enveloped the Torres-Thompson boys were inevitable when she entered this room—it was the only time in her workday Araceli felt self-pity and resentment at the absences and inequalities that were the core injustice of her existence. *It is a big world, divided between rich and poor, just like those humorless lefties at the university said. What would I have become with a mother like Maureen and a room like this?*

Next Araceli made all the beds in the house, picked up the pillows and blankets from the couch where *el señor* Scott appeared to have slept, and folded them up and put them away. She returned to the living room, to run a duster over the furniture, turning its feathers lightly as she touched the tall, distressed-pine bookcases and the vases, as if applying a touch of invisible rouge on everything. She lingered a bit longer, as she usually did, over the family photographs arranged inside one of the bookcases, including a sepia-toned picture of *el señor* Scott's father: in the photograph, the elder Torres was a boy only slightly larger than Brandon was now, but scrawnier-looking, his eyes an expression of startled confusion as he leaned against an adobe wall in ill-fitting corduroy jeans. Northern Mexico, Araceli guessed, a dry village where nopals offer the rare green touches to a khaki landscape. Araceli never lost the momentary feeling of paradox that came with finding this relic of a Mexican family history in the home of a wealthy California family. Next to it was a second photograph of the same boy as a teenager, in front of a bungalow in a city that Araceli guessed was Los Angeles in

the 1940s or 1950s. A few times the person depicted in these two photographs had come to this house to visit, transformed into a senior citizen with a penchant for irritating remarks. "*El abuelo Torres,*" Araceli called him, with mordant irony, since the old man never spoke a word of Spanish, despite the faint accent that flavored his English and suggested a tongue that was secretly hoping to pronounce an *eñe* or an *erre* or two every time he opened his mouth. He never answered Araceli's "*Buenas tardes*" with a "*Buenas tardes*" of his own. Araceli had the impression that he had been banned from the home, since it had been about two years since she had seen him, and what Mexican grandfather doesn't want to see his grandchildren every chance he gets?

Araceli allowed the feathers to tickle the poor Mexican boy in the photographs a few times more than necessary, then went to the laundry to begin sorting through the clothes. The few things to be ironed she left for last, then stacked the rest in piles according to family member, from Scott's sweatshirts and pajamas, to the tiniest stack of onesies and little skirts for Samantha. One o'clock and the Torres-Thompsons were still away. *¿A dónde habrán ido?* The clothes were destined for the orderly backstage of the Torres-Thompson home, the walk-in closets in each bedroom, spaces organized with design-magazine minimalism. The shelves were thin white wafers of metal that floated in the air, sweaters and towels and blue jeans forming rectangular clouds above Araceli's head. She derived a good deal of satisfaction from the uniformity of these stacked clothes, from the way the folds rose in neat, multicolored waves from the shelves, and from the light scent of mothballs that she had strategically placed here and there after Maureen discovered some telltale holes in a sweater.

When Araceli finished with the ironing she was done for the day—and it was only two o'clock. There was still no sign of the Torres-Thompsons as she closed the kitchen door behind her and stepped into the backyard for the short walk to the guesthouse, which was a baby clone of the main home, with the same cream-colored paint scheme, the same window moldings, the same black wooden door, the same brass doorknob. Opening this door was the small triumph at the end of Araceli's workday, her principal North American achievement, to have a room of her own for the first time in her life. It contained the baroque collection of recycled objects that constituted her possessions: posters that

had been salvaged from *la señora* Maureen's "spring cleanings," various art pieces Araceli had assembled (including a mobile hanging from the ceiling), and a spare table with a particleboard top that she used as a work space. One of the room's two windows opened to the backyard, where the adobe-colored wall that defined the Torres-Thompson property was visible through the retreating foliage, and for a moment she imagined Pepe walking through his old garden, shaking his head knowingly. She took off her uniform, purging herself of her servant identity as the big blouse and pants fell into her hamper. Probably she wore the uniform precisely for this moment when she could put on her own clothes, a pair of leggings or jeans that transformed her into the Araceli who once haunted galleries and clubs in Condesa, Roma, and other Mexico City neighborhoods. *Thank you, family, for these uniforms. I send you thousands of dollars earned with my sweat and you send me five* filipinas. Then into the shower, and away with the smell of cleaning agents and fabric softener and into a nimble wakefulness in which she was fully herself.

She went to her worktable and reached inside and pulled out a piece of construction paper on which she was assembling a collage. The half-started project before her was taking form, in this early phase, with pictures cut out from the magazines Maureen discarded every month: *International Artist, Real Simple, American Home, Smithsonian, Elle.* Reaching under the table, she picked up a handful of magazines and then opened the table's small drawer and took out an envelope. A collection of hands fell out. Araceli couldn't draw hands very well, and she had begun gathering them as a kind of study, a communion with the anatomy of fingers, cuticles, and lifelines. There were hands from a Rembrandt, hands from an ad for skin lotion, hands wearing gardening gloves, a hand reaching out to shake another hand. There were just two hands glued to her construction-paper canvas so far, and she had placed them at the center of the composition-to-be. Painted in oil and open in a pleading expression, they were from Caravaggio's painting *Supper at Emmaus,* a favorite of one of her art history instructors at the Instituto Nacional de Bellas Artes; for some reason they had popped up in an insurance advertisement.

After an hour of trying out various hand arrangements, searching for more hands in the magazines, and attaching a few to her collage,

Araceli stopped, rubbed her eyes, and tossed herself onto her bed for a nap. She looked at the framed picture of her four-year-old nephew, the only family picture in a gallery dominated by shots of old friends from Bellas Artes. All had been scattered to the winds of employment and migration, to jobs in restaurants in the Polanco district of Mexico City, and to American cities and towns with exotic names she had collected on a handful of envelopes and postcards: DURHAM, NC; INDIANAPOLIS, IN; GETTYSBURG, PA. At moments like this, when she was alone to encounter the lonely contradictions of her American adventure, the natural thing to do was to turn on the television and forget. Instead, she threw her arm over her face and closed her eyes, embracing the exhausted darkness and the acoustic panoply it contained: a singing bird whose call was three short notes and a fourth long one that sounded like a question mark. The very distant bass of an engine, and then the much sharper and high-pitched vibrations of a car pulling into the cul-de-sac of Paseo Linda Bonita, the motor puttering to a stop, the driver setting the brake. Now the voice of a woman talking in the next home, less than five feet from her second window, which opened to the narrow space between the two properties. She heard a girl responding to the woman, and though the words were indiscernible, it was clearly a mother-and-child dialogue, a series of questions and observations perhaps, moving forward at an unrushed rhythm. Each time Araceli heard these feminine voices she remembered the room in Mexico City she'd shared with her older sister, and their whispered conversations in the post-bedtime darkness. In the dry winters they awoke to the sound of their mother sweeping away the daily film of grainy soot that settled down from the atmosphere and built up in the courtyard her family shared with five others. The broom was made of thin tree branches tied together and made a scratchy, percussive sound as it struck any surface, leading Araceli the girl to think of it as a musical instrument that produced a rhythmic song many hours in length: clean-clean, clean-clean, clean-clean. During the day, her mother, aunt, and cousins gathered on the courtyard's concrete to sort beans, hang clothes, and tend to a bathtub-sized planter filled with herbs and roses. Araceli had run away from that home, but sometimes in a restful moment she returned to the cold skin of its cement walls, to the steel front door that popped like the top of a can when opened, and to the rough, pebble-covered floor of the courtyard outside.

Araceli missed Mexico City's unevenness, its asymmetry and its impro-vised spaces. She missed those women and those voices, and her mother's observations about tomatoes and men, and the aroma of sliced onions and marinated beef in industrial pots floating about the courtyard when they gathered outside on a good-weather Sunday, a table and conversa-tion squeezed in between parked cars.

When she woke up, some twenty minutes later, Araceli expected for an instant to see her mother, and for an instant longer she felt the faint sensation that there was a household chore for her mother she had left undone.

5

Over the years, Maureen had developed the habit of keeping her eyes lowered and focused on the driveway when she pulled her sport-utility vehicle out of the garage, so as to avoid eye contact that might draw her into chitchat with her cul-de-sac neighbors. Exchanging pleasantries would force her to remember certain unpleasant encounters. The family next door was a very even-tempered aeronautical engineer and his wife, slightly younger than Scott and Maureen, with a lone daughter who was about Keenan's age. A single "playdate" in which Keenan accidentally ripped off the arm of one of little Anika's treasured imitation-antique dolls and left her weeping uncontrollably had embarrassed Maureen so thoroughly, she had not knocked on their door since. The boy-girl divide was too wide, you had to keep them in separate worlds, which would be a problem when Samantha got older. Opposite the Torres-Thompsons was the Smith-Marshall family, whose two boys were about the same ages as Brandon and Keenan, but who were so thoroughly medicated for aggressive behavior and general weirdness that Maureen shuddered when she remembered stepping into their home. "Something not good is going on in that family," she had told her husband. "The mom is in a place you get to by taking

pills that come in pretty pastel colors." In general, Maureen was put off by the undeniable superficiality of the Laguna Rancho Estates, by the plastic surgery fad that had swept through the place in the same way Astroturf porches had once swept through the small-town Missouri neighborhood where she had grown up. Her encounters with the remade women of the Laguna Rancho Estates made Maureen self-conscious enough about her middle-aged looks that, after having three children by natural methods (excepting the epidurals, of course), she had briefly contemplated a tummy tuck of her own. But in the end the idea of submitting the imperfections of her midriff to a surgeon's blade put her off: she wouldn't become one of those silicone Californians the people back home would sneer at. High-priced real estate in a new subdivision attracted the kind of people who could throw money at their insecurities, a description that Maureen would apply to herself in the occasionally candid moment. The difference was that she didn't mind, too much, looking at the mirror and seeing a slightly older version of herself than the one in her memory, the odd silver strand in the rusty sweep of her hair, and the crow's-feet advancing from the very slight folds in the corners of her eyes, an odd Gaelic mutation that suggested squinting in the face of a powerful Atlantic breeze. She preferred the look of distinction and experience to the scrubbed and washed-out look of one eye and cheek job too many, or the unreal orange hue produced by electric suns. *I'm not any less superficial than they are. I just have a different aesthetic. I'll take a weather-beaten chair or table with character over a brand-new but flavorless piece of furniture.* Maureen wanted to age as gracefully as humanly possible in a climate where each day was a battle to defend her complexion against the dry air; she wanted to raise her children without the aid of prescriptions for psychotropic compounds, and without a game console like the one their father played with. What Maureen wanted, the only thing she could say with certainty she wanted, was to bring goodness and beauty to the life of her family.

For that reason she was headed to her local nursery to research some clever, cheap, and elegant solution to the problem of the dying rain forest in her backyard.

Through the smoky glass of the sport-utility vehicle, Araceli watched freeway destination signs pass overhead. SAN DIEGO. LOS

ANGELES. NEWPORT BEACH. Being the car-trip escort to *la señora* Maureen used to be one of Guadalupe's responsibilities. *Other people go to work in factories. I have to squeeze into this automobile, with this woman and her children. All for that moment at the end of the week when they give me an envelope with two pictures of Benjamin Franklin and one of a man called Grant.*

No one talked, but Araceli could hear Brandon and Keenan tapping away at their electronic toys in the backseat. Brandon's hair was auburn, darker than his mother's, though he had the same smart, wide-apart eyes that to Araceli suggested ancestors in some rough-hewn European village, like those peasants of Daumier and Millet in Araceli's art history textbook, the largest of the handful of books in her personal library: gleaners, sowers, potato eaters. Brandon's fingers moved over the buttons of his little machine with artistic precision and for a moment it occurred to Araceli that he might do well with piano or guitar lessons, but *la señora* Maureen never pushed him. Sometimes you had to push children to do things that were good for them: if she ever found a partner to share her dreams, they would raise their offspring with that piece of Mexican wisdom. Maureen had the air conditioner on high and the cold made Araceli's nose run, and she gave a theatrically loud sniffle and feigned a cough, but her *jefa* didn't seem to notice.

The idea had come to Maureen after her perusal, at a local bookstore, of various gardening guides. She had begun with a handbook or two on tropical gardens, but was quickly intimidated by their instructions for elaborate irrigation systems and complex recipes for organic fertilizers, and tips for keeping alive fragile species. The authors lectured her on keeping the air and soil humidity above seventy percent, and insisted she install various electric sensors, then teased her with shots of couples standing next to their Balinese jungle gardens, and stone paths lined with breadfruit trees and palm fronds dripping water. A tropical garden, she decided, was like a "special needs" child: you could make him bloom if you made him the center of your universe, but she had three children already, thank you very much.

Wandering deeper into the stacks, she came upon a book titled *The Wonders of the Desert Garden*. Its cacti and assorted succulents caught her interest, as did a chapter called "Southern California: the

Sonoran Possibilities" that carried several photographs of the agave, aloe, and the Golden Barrel cacti in the Huntington Gardens in San Marino. In another she found a map that showed the Sonoran Desert reaching to a mountain range in California: on a clear day, you could see these mountains, the Palomars, from the toll road that cut through the hills behind her home. *We're practically on the fringes of the Sonoran and the Mojave.* It made so much more sense to try to re-create an ecosystem that was native to this part of California, rather than one native to Southeast Asia or the Amazon. Desert gardens, by definition, needed very little water. The moisture that came from the occasional ocean breeze or from the fog bank that climbed up from the sea into their hillside cul-de-sac was more than enough.

They arrived at a nursery, Maureen leading the way with Samantha in her arms, Araceli and the boys trailing after, walking through the narrow spaces between the tables with plants.

"Yeah, your tropicals are high-maintenance, no doubt about it," the nursery manager concluded, after hearing Maureen describe her garden's decline. "Probably your succulents are something you wanna look at." The nursery manager was a sun-blanched woman of about thirty in jeans and a wide-brimmed straw hat, and she led Maureen and her retinue through aisles of potted vincas and roses underneath a canopy of translucent fabric, to a section at the back of the nursery where the sun blazed down on a crowd of mini yucca plants and other succulents filling several tables, alongside some potted cacti that were as tall as Samantha. "Over at our Desert Landscaping location in Riverside we've got a spectacular saguaro, five feet tall. A majestic plant, really, a centerpiece to an entire garden. With your succulents, drainage is key. Of course, it's all low-maintenance once you get it in . . . For a small fee, we'll do the landscape design for you." When you first encountered them, Maureen thought, these plants possessed a menacing aura: the armor of their spines, the short hair of barbs. But their architecture was graceful and sturdy, especially the baby saguaros, with their interlocking arches. Pastel-green was the predominant color, but when you spent time looking at them you noticed subtle variations in hue. Maureen examined a plant that looked something like a desert sea urchin, and detected orange-red highlights in the tips of its spiky arms. They soaked up the noonday rays with the same gusto with which the banana trees

soaked up water. "You're gonna save a ton on your water bill, no doubt about that," the nursery manager said, as if reading Maureen's thoughts. "And you'll save on labor too, because these things practically take care of themselves."

"Brandon, *cuidado*," Araceli said.

Maureen turned to see her oldest shaking his finger and mouthing the word *Ouch*, and then laughing. "Didn't hurt," he said. Yes, Maureen would have to build some small barrier to discourage the boys and Samantha from wandering into the desert garden—if she decided to go ahead and follow her instinct, which told her that replacing the water-starved tropicals with a succulent garden was the perfect solution to her problem. Their thick, sunproof skins would forever remove from her property the humiliation of the Big Man reciting lines about weeds and "gross nature."

Walking up alongside Maureen, getting a glimpse of her from the side while trying not to stare, Araceli saw her employer's eyes focusing. Clearly her *patrona* was planning some big, dramatic statement with these plants. The nursery manager was explaining things and studying Maureen, examining her reactions. The nursery manager could see *la señora* was a moneyed person: Araceli's Mexican presence trailing behind the children was equivalent to that of a German luxury vehicle, or a piece of gaudy jewelry hanging from Maureen's neck. Add to the picture Maureen's regal bearing, the long languorous crescents of her recently styled hair, and her air of pampered distraction, and it came as no surprise to Araceli that the nursery manager was giving her that special treatment *norteamericanos* reserved for people with serious money to spend. She answered Maureen's questions with "Sure," "Of course," and "We could probably do that." For a moment the unctuous manager added to Araceli's lingering, growing, and not entirely explicable sense of dread. She didn't like walking between these armored plants, every one of which was designed to inflict injury, and she didn't like the anxious and impatient look on the face of her *patrona*. Maureen was pulling at the crescents of her hair again, biting the ends.

"Well, we'll be in touch, then," Maureen said to the nursery manager. After looking absentmindedly at the collection of small succulents arranged haphazardly on the table before her, she turned to Araceli and announced, "Let's go to the mall."

6

The park consisted of a rubber mat and the requisite slides and swings, resting at the bottom of a slope of irrigated fescue overlooking the beach and the ocean. Midmorning dew covered the grass and the park was deserted, a fact that Araceli found disappointing somehow. She expected crowds, children running, the smoke of barbecues drifting skyward, but here the only movement was from the empty swings being tapped forward by the invisible hand of the ocean breeze, their plastic seats garnished with mist. In the distance, the roar of the surf, and sometimes the whine or purr of a car gliding down the street that curved around the park. The overcast was a whitish gray roof, as it was most summer mornings before the sun came to burn off everything to blue. The tableau was quiet, oceanic, meditation-inducing, but for the sound of Maureen berating her two sons inside their idling car.

Thirty minutes earlier, alerted by a series of screams and shouts, Maureen had discovered her two sons gripped in a pretzel headlock on the living room floor underneath the bookcases with their picture frames and two glass vases from Andalusia that rattled when, in their wrestling, Keenan had managed to push his brother backward into the furniture. "You're going to break something!" Maureen had shouted, referring

simultaneously to their bodies and the objects in her bookcase. They grunted and yelped and Maureen had struggled to separate them as Keenan tried to dig his teeth into his older brother's wrist, while Brandon screamed "Get off me" and tried to free himself with a kick. *I order them off the television an hour ago, and without the pacifying power of that screen, they are trying to draw blood.* There was no play in this, they were like two drunks on the sawdust-covered floor of a bar. Once or twice a week this happened, a testosterone brawl born suddenly from a moment of peaceful brotherly play. Maureen believed a mother had to eradicate the disease of Y-chromosome violence during childhood, lest her family one day be consumed by the gunplay horrors broadcast on the television news. She had decided to whisk them out of the house, into the punishment of open space and an afternoon spent with Araceli as their caretaker.

Inside the car, with Keenan still in tears and Brandon glaring defiantly out the window, Maureen launched into a familiar monologue of threats that revolved around the loss of "privileges." "Boys!" she said by way of conclusion. "Sometimes I wish I could just leave you with your father and take Samantha and just go. Go someplace far away." Then, turning to face the boys directly, she said, "I wish I could just leave you with your father!" It was an unforgivably mean thing to say and Maureen would regret it later, after she had driven off with Samantha and seen the defiant expression of proto-adolescent withdrawal on Brandon's face, a narrowing of the eyes that suggested a future rebellion with sweaty and disheveled male textures. But in her frustration Maureen told herself she didn't care, because there was only so much boy craziness a woman could put up with.

"Listen to Araceli," Maureen told her sons after opening the door and lining them up on the sidewalk next to their housekeeper. "She's in charge. And if I hear from her that you didn't behave, you're going to lose your Game Boy privileges for the rest of the summer." Turning to Araceli, she announced, "I'll be back about one." Araceli was standing with her arms folded across her chest, dressed from head to toe in a pink *filipina*, looking back at her *jefa* with bemused irritation. Maureen thought briefly that perhaps this was not such a good idea, suddenly leaving her boys at a park with this ill-tempered Mexican woman of unproven child-rearing skills. Araceli was allergic to her boys; she would just as well limit her contact with them to making their meals and pick-

ing up their scattered toys, but in Araceli's severe disposition there was an air of ample responsibility, the sense that she wouldn't panic in an emergency. Maureen looked around the park and saw a pay phone: she gave her maid a handful of quarters. "You should really get a cell phone," she said, provoking no response from Araceli. "I'll be at home with Samantha. Call me if there's a problem. I can be here in fifteen minutes."

Araceli tugged at her uniform, wishing she'd had a chance to change. She had been plucked by Maureen from the laundry room as she folded a stack of *el señor* Scott's boxer shorts and in the chaotic evacuation of the boys from the home she had carried that underwear into the dining room and left it on the table, and it annoyed her to think it would still be there when she got back.

When the car turned a corner and disappeared, the boys and Araceli shared a few moments of contemplative silence. *She's really gone*, Brandon thought, *our mother left us here on the sidewalk*. Even though it had been announced with that angry speech, his mother's absence felt stark and sudden, and for a moment he imagined that he had been dumped into the plot of a melodramatic novel, like the parentless hero of a multivolume series of books he recently finished reading, the adventures of an adolescent boy unwittingly thrust into an adult world of crime and magic. He was alone out here in public, without even Guadalupe to take care of him. Araceli did not yet register in Brandon's mind as a protective force, and he quickly scanned the park like a young warrior about to enter a dark and threatening forest. He imagined a "strike force" suddenly descending on the park, a hooded army of armed underworld types, the machine-gun-toting villains in one of the books he was reading.

"Do you think the Russian mafia would ever come to Orange County?" he asked his brother.

"What?"

Keenan believed that his big brother read entirely too much and knew him to be an incessant confabulator, prone to confusing and scaring his younger brother with fantastic thoughts. At their very expensive private school, Brandon's big imagination caused him to run afoul of the otherwise laid-back teachers there, primarily because he had freaked out many of the girls with new and ever more elaborate versions of the Bloody Mary myth, causing them to avoid the girls' bathroom, with a handful of peeing-in-the-hallway incidents the result.

"You know," Brandon insisted. "Like in *Artemis Fowl*."

"Nah," Keenan said. "It's too sunny here for the Russian mafia."

Brandon was still only eleven years old, and the morbid and fantastic imagery from his middle-reader novels did not linger in his mind's eye for long; in less than a minute he was running down the grass with his brother chasing after him, the reasons for their living room fight forgotten. Araceli followed them down the slope of the park toward the rubber play mat and swings and took a seat on a bench facing the ocean. Brandon watched her as she looked off in the distance at a lone surfer tossing himself into the waves, the charcoal skin of his wet suit swallowed up by water the color of the backwash in her mop bucket. Araceli was a major planet in Brandon's universe, and he studied her often as she shuffled around the Paseo Linda Bonita house. Sometimes he wondered if she was angry at him, if he had done something to upset her, because why else would someone be so quiet in his presence for so long? But after careful consideration of his actions—he was, in his own estimation, despite a few flaws, a "good boy"—Brandon arrived at the conclusion that Araceli was just lonely. And when he thought about her loneliness, he concluded that she should read more, because anyone who read was never alone. In books there were limitless worlds, there was truth, sometimes brutal and ugly, and sometimes happy and soothing.

Brandon considered giving her the book he had managed to bring with him, but then he thought better of this, and instead left it on a bench and joined his little brother on the plastic body of the play structure and its short hanging bridge, and began to playact with battle sounds formed by trilling tongues and popping cheeks. Araceli listened to them and slunk down on the bench, looking up at the gray sky and wondering why it was that here along the beach the sun seemed to come out less during the summer than it did during any other season. The blankness of the sky reminded her, for some reason, of Scott's underwear left on the table, and of other things left undone at the house up on the hill, where Maureen was probably just now arriving to the quiet of a house without boys. Araceli would give anything to be back in Mexico City on one of those summer days when balls of white drift across the blue canvas of the sky and you can follow them on their march across the valley of the city, and know that they will soon drop a cooling rain shower on your face. She wanted to feel something cold or warm, be-

cause in this uniform, in the amphitheater of this park, she felt like a stiff pink box and not like a human being. Looking down at the beach, she saw the surfer climbing out of the water, a brown-haired teenager in a black wet suit, and in an instant she imagined he was Pepe the gardener, dripping water from his bare chest. She imagined herself sitting on the beach on a towel, Pepe walking toward her with beads of water clinging erotically to his pecs, climbing up the sand to reach her, leaning over her, dripping salt water over her dry and lonely skin.

Ten miles away from the Laguna Rancho Estates, on the third floor of an office building in a business park on a wide and sparsely traveled boulevard, in a corner of the city of Irvine, itself sparsely populated by various medium-sized corporations with generic and quickly forgettable names, Scott Torres toiled at work, sitting before a flat-panel computer screen displaying five different images of the perimeter fence at the Cincinnati/Northern Kentucky National Airport. He waited with a dulled sense of anticipation for the knee-high grass at the base of the fence to be whipped back and forth by a gust of wind or the backdraft of a passing airplane, a confirmation that the image was, in fact, "live." Over the course of the morning, Scott had opened windows on his screen that revealed various locales in the United States, noting that it was raining at Minot Air Force Base in North Dakota, and watching the long, Arctic-summer shadows stretch underneath the Alaska Pipeline. The pipeline to the Bering Sea was a favorite summer place to spend time at the Elysian Systems office because there was a chance you might see an elk or deer scurrying across the tundra. All day long the computers on the third floor of the Elysian corporate headquarters were open to windows showing lonely stretches of fencing that seemed static and frozen in time, like the peopleless backdrops to a deep and disturbing dream, with only the effects of the weather and the moving of the shadows to prove they were objects in a real, living world.

Scott and his programmers at Elysian Systems were drawn to the images for their clandestine, remote allure and for the rare pleasure of officially sanctioned voyeurism. They had been given access to this government system to develop software, a contract that happened to be the only source of positive cash flow in the Elysian Systems corporate spreadsheet. When Scott thought about his responsibility to enforce

this contract by telling his seven programmers never to discuss their project "with any individual outside our direct work group," or when he was forced to ask them to sign numerous promises of confidentiality and loyalty to the United States of America, he could not help but feel silly, because such admonitions ran counter to the iconoclastic programming ethic of his youth, and even the essential élan of his initial foray into entrepreneurship. This was the central contradiction of Scott's professional life, to be the enforcer and organizer of a project that did not fire his imagination, and to be the oddball in a moneymaking culture that as of yet generated little money. He was a relic, an aging survivor from that clan of "robust" programmers who came of age in the interregnum between the slide-rule epoch and the Ethernet era. There were moments during the workday when he felt this characterization growing among his underlings and Elysian's executives; it was a fleeting sensation, a truth just beyond his grasp, like knowing the meaning of a word but not remembering the word itself, the syllables that described the idea unwilling to gather on your tongue. *No one here admires me, no one looks up to me*, Scott thought, except maybe Charlotte Harris-Hayasaki, a young and as yet unsuccessful game designer who was as misplaced at Elysian Systems as Scott was, and who often stole glances at him through the glass of his office.

The executives running Elysian Systems were serious, middle-aged, and worked on a separate floor, the fourth, as if to immunize themselves from the eccentricities of the programmers: the executives wore suits and ties, and decorated their walls with plaques earned during their days as mid-grade managers at detergent and soft-drink companies. They had charged this government contract to Scott, the "vice president of programming," even though any first-year graduate student in computer science could have managed to write the essential code. The contract was for the "accountability software" of the "Citizen Anti-Terrorist Sentry System," CATSS, by which the Department of Homeland Security, the Department of Defense, the Department of Energy, and other agencies farmed out guard duty at airports, nuclear power plants, and military bases to thousands of Americans sitting at home staring at their computer screens.

Scott's programming mission was to find ways to make sure the "citizen sentries" were actually monitoring the 12,538 cameras in the sys-

tem, instead of using their computers to play solitaire or shop for shoes. His programs gave these people, like rats in a laboratory experiment, meaningless tasks to do while watching the camera images on their computers, then rated them on those tasks and produced a waterfall of statistics that was especially pleasing to Washington. Scott clicked through fence images from a half dozen more places, including a perimeter fence in a piñon forest in Los Alamos, New Mexico, then went back to the work he was supposed to be doing: analyzing his programmers' progress on a project to design animated fake "intruders" who would "walk" and "dig" and perform other suspicious acts alongside the fences and gates, frightening the citizen sentries into pushing the ALERT! button on their computer screens and causing an Elysian Systems server to register another entry in the VIGILANT column. He tried out "turban man," an image of a swarthy fellow with a towel wrapped around his head running and ducking: the actor was his lead programmer, Jeremy Zaragoza, and the clip had been filmed at a rented studio along with others of "binocular lady" and "shovel man," all played by various programmers in this office. Scott made turban man run along various fences: the challenge was to create animations in correct proportions to the various barriers on the screen as they ran and shoveled alongside them, which was proving to be trickier than anyone had anticipated. After watching turban man pass improbably back and forth through the steel mesh fence at the San Onofre power plant, like some superhero possessed of special powers, Scott absentmindedly clicked open the latest numbers from NASDAQ, which had been especially bad all morning.

No one in Elysian Systems bothered to hide the fact that they were using their computers throughout the workday to watch their stocks and mutual funds and 401(k) accounts, not even the executives up on the fourth floor. *Before, we played Nerf football in the hallways, and practiced tango dancing in the cafeteria. Now we watch our retirement shrink in multicolored graphs. Football and tango were better for the soul.* This morning, as on most mornings in recent months, Scott squinted at his screen in frustration at the dynamic displays, updated at five-minute intervals, that confirmed his poor financial judgment, his bad bets. For several years the market had risen dependably, and people started to think of it as a machine that made money, but that wasn't its true nature.

The market did not behave according to any pattern Scott had been able to discern. Turning the market into the graphs and charts of the type filling Scott's flat-panel display created the illusion that it was a mathematical equation, that it obeyed rules like those hidden inside the core of computer games, where players spent hours exploring and prodding to uncover the underlying logic, the key that opened the jewelry box. The equations that ran the market were, in fact, too vast for any computer to decipher: they were the sum of the desires and fears of millions of people, divided and multiplied by the ostensibly rational but really quite subjective calculations of "analysts." The math was twisted further by the fiscal legerdemain of accountants who could be as creatively fuzzy as impressionist painters. The numbers their spreadsheets spit out, Scott now knew, were inflated by narrative inventions like those Sasha "the Big Man" Avakian used to confabulate at meetings with venture capitalists. Scott had learned these lessons while watching the Big Man run their company, but unfortunately he had no way to apply them to his own investment decisions, and he had spent several frustrating years moving the "go-away" money from MindWare around the market and into various "instruments." Five years ago the charts and graphs pointed, unmistakably, toward exotic new fields being tested in Research Triangle laboratories, and if they had continued to follow that logic Scott would not be working at Elysian Systems today, he would not have a mortgage to worry about, and Pepe the gardener would still be cutting the lawn and tending to the backyard garden and Scott would be liberated of his wife's complaining to him about it.

As was their custom, the regulars at Laguna Municipal Park South began arriving around noon. They brought packed lunches, strollers stuffed with extra diapers and moist towelets, and carried pay-as-you-go cell phones to talk to the barrio relatives who were watching over their own children as they earned dollars caring for their *patrones'* boys and girls. The weekday routine of the park was broken this morning by the appearance of a new woman, a fellow *latinoamericana* who occupied the bench by the play structure, and who instantly reminded the regulars of locales deep to the south, and not because of her broad face and caramel skin, or the way she slumped on the bench and

sneered at the play structures. No, it was the uniform that reminded them of their home countries, the excessive professional formality of matching pink pants and the wide, pocketed blouse that was known back home as a *filipina*. It was the uniform of the high-society domestic back home, though hardly anyone wore one in California, where most employers preferred their domestics in the sporty and practical attire of jeans and tennis shoes, complemented with the odd gift garment from the boss: a quality hoodie from Old Navy, or a sturdy cotton blouse from Target. The new woman in the park was sitting with her arms folded defiantly across her chest, as if she were a prisoner taking some fresh air in the recreation yard, watching over two boys who themselves were very familiar because they used to come here with Guadalupe, a favorite of the group.

"*¡Buenas tardes!*" announced a perky older woman in sweatpants and a loose-fitting blouse as she took a seat next to Araceli. "Those are Guadalupe's kids."

"*Así es,*" Araceli said.

The woman introduced herself as María Isabel and pointed out that she had brought a girl to the park who was about Keenan's age. Araceli watched as the girl and Keenan stood on opposite sides of the elaborate play structure, as if contemplating the gender divide and the walkways of plastic and compressed rubber that stood between them, until Keenan made another mouth explosion and returned to the game with his older brother.

"I heard that Guadalupe might quit," María Isabel announced. "So, you took her place?"

Before Araceli could answer, María Isabel rose to her feet to push the girl, who had run over to the swing, and then turned toward Araceli in anticipation of an answer.

"No, we used to work together."

"That Guadalupe was a funny girl. Always telling jokes. Did she ever tell you the story about the little boy getting lost in the women's section in the mall?"

"Yes."

María Isabel gave the girl another push, the wide fan of her charge's blond hair catching the air and billowing in the moist morning air, her pendulum movement and the creaking of the apparatus keeping a kind

of harried time. "Push me higher, María," the girl yelled, and María Isabel obeyed and gave another heave. María Isabel was a woman of oakbark hue with freshly dyed and aerosol-sprayed short hair, and she was wearing smart matching accessories of gold earrings and a thin gold chain on her wrist that were mismatched with the bleach-burned T-shirt draped over her short frame. *This woman arrives at work dressed as if she were a secretary, and then strips down into janitor clothes.* "You tell a few good stories and the time just flashes by," María Isabel continued. "A lot of us come here every day. Later on we'll probably see Juana. And Modesta and Carmelita. Carmelita is from Peru and the nicest woman you'll ever meet. Maybe we'll see Fanny, though I hope not. Fanny is a mess."

Araceli said nothing and for a moment they watched Brandon chase Keenan over a bridge of plastic slats, until Brandon lost his footing and fell over the edge, headfirst onto the black mat below. Keenan laughed as his brother climbed up and rubbed his head, unhurt.

"*Niños traviesos,*" María Isabel said with a tone of mild exasperation that she intended as a gesture of sympathy with Araceli. "But I'd rather take care of children. If you've got a girl, it isn't any work at all. A boy is a little more work, but I'll take even three boys over an old lady. That was my last job, taking care of a *viejita* on her deathbed."

"Really?" Araceli said, unable to mask her complete lack of interest.

María Isabel lauched into a story about *la señora* Bloom "wrestling with death" and "trying to keep him from taking my old lady away." Araceli was going to speak up and say, *I really don't want to hear this story*, but at that instant María Isabel shifted her gaze to an object or person behind Araceli and began to wave.

"Juana! *¡Aquí estoy!* Over here."

Within a few minutes Araceli was sitting in a circle of Spanish chatter, with three more women greeting Araceli with smiles and *holas* and polite kisses on the cheek.

"You're taking care of Guadalupe's kids," said Carmelita, a stubby-legged woman from Peru. "Those are good boys. She loved them."

"This is one of the nicer parks around here," said Juana, who had oily, uneven bangs, and the coffee-colored skin of her ancestors in the mountains of Veracruz. "They clean it every night. And the police patrol past here, so you hardly ever see any vagrants."

As the women gathered in the play area, Araceli had a fleeting sense of nostalgia for the company of colleagues, the banter of coworkers,

the space that Guadalupe and Pepe had filled in her life. The women told her about their families and the American homes they worked and lived in, while simultaneously keeping an eye on their charges, who were swarming over the play structure and filling the air around it with the squeals their parents called "outside voices." Carmelita sat on the mat a few feet from Araceli and allowed the boy in her care to stand in his leather shoes and overalls, walk toward her, and then fall into her embrace. Modesta, a freckled and green-eyed *mexicana*, raised a finger at a girl climbing the roof of the structure's plastic cube, and the girl immediately clambered down to safety. They were all parents themselves (and María Isabel a grandparent), and their motherly self-assurance fell over and calmed the children around them like a rain of warm milk. Once they'd finished greeting Araceli, their conversation drifted, as it often did, to the practical problems of child-rearing.

"This is a good place to practice walking. If he falls, he can't hurt himself."

"If you don't let them fall, they don't learn to walk."

"I remember when Kylie was that age. *Es una edad de peligros*: they fall as much as they talk. She still has that scar on her forehead, underneath her hair."

"I finally got Jackson to eat the squash, after I tried that recipe with the food machine. *Un milagro*. But it didn't work with his sister."

"Each one is different. God makes them that way."

Araceli watched and listened, saw the children on the play structure casting glances at their paid caregivers, and the caregivers looking back as if to say, *You are okay, I am here.* They knew that each child was his or her own shifting landscape because the estrogen that ran through their veins, and their own histories as mothers, allowed them to see these things: Araceli sensed that North American employers and Latin American relatives alike revered them for this power. *They all seem to possess it—and to know that I do not.*

After a while their attention returned to Araceli, the quiet, awkward woman in their midst, and the small mystery and break in the park routine she represented. What, they now asked directly, had happened to Guadalupe?

"I guess they didn't have enough money to pay her what she wanted," Araceli told them. "Or to keep her."

"Or she didn't want to stay," María Isabel said knowingly.

"No sé."

"Yes, I remember her saying something about the money," María Isabel said. "First they asked her to work for less. Then her *patrón* said they were going to need just one person to cook and clean and take care of the kids too. To do everything. Guadalupe said she thought it was too much work for one person. And that she wouldn't do it, even if they asked her . . . So I guess they hired you."

Araceli said nothing.

"Do you know where she went?" Carmelita asked.

"No."

Suddenly the newcomer looked perplexed and agitated. Araceli could see now that all the scenery at Paseo Linda Bonita had been shifting around her, even before Guadalupe left: calculations were being made, consultations undertaken. Araceli worked harder than Guadalupe, she was infinitely more reliable, but she didn't chat with her bosses, or make friendly with them, and so they had revealed their crisis to Guadalupe, the flighty and talkative one. But they hadn't even bothered asking Araceli what she thought, and had instead simply foisted more work upon her. Araceli saw her standing in the world with a new and startling clarity. She lived with English-speaking strangers, high on a hill alone with the huge windows and the smell of solvents, and lacked the will to escape what she had become. She quietly accepted the Torres-Thompsons' money and the room they gave her, and they felt free to make her do anything they asked, expecting her to adapt to their habits and idiosyncrasies, holding babies, supervising boys at the park, and probably more things that she could not yet imagine.

"Sometimes, you just have to pack your things and go to the next job," María Isabel said. "That's how it was when *la señora* Bloom died . . ."

"Again with *la viejita*," Carmelita said. Juana and Modesta rolled their eyes.

"I was telling the story to Araceli when you all got here. And I never finished."

"The Day of the Dead isn't until November," Carmelita said with a wry smile. Already Juana and Modesta were starting to drift away, walking closer toward their charges. "Why don't you wait until nighttime to start telling your scary stories?"

"There's nothing scary about it. It's a story about a human being. About two human beings. Me and *la señora* Bloom."

"Araceli doesn't want to hear that story," Carmelita said.

"No, no, it's not a problem," Araceli said. Already, this woman's rambling had revealed one unexpected truth, and if she allowed her to go on, she might reveal another.

"Like I was saying, *la señora* Bloom lived by herself, with only me to keep her company. None of her kids even lived nearby. The one daughter who called to check in every week, she lived in New York. So one day, finally, *la señora* Bloom gave up and let go. I was talking to her, just like I'm talking to you right now, about my ungrateful children in Nicaragua. Then I looked at the bed and I saw her with her eyes open. I waited for them to close, but they never did. So I crossed myself about twenty times, and called the ambulance. Two very nice young men came, and they said, 'She's dead.' And I said, 'I know that.' And then they said, 'There's nothing we can do.' They said I had to wait for the coroner. And they left her with me. So here I am all alone with a body in the house! I call the daughter in New York and there's no answer. Just the machine. I keep trying, all day long, and I'm thinking, I can't say that into the machine, *Your mother is dead.* So finally I tell the machine, 'Please call your mother's house.' But she never did. I was all alone with that body for fifteen hours, until the brown van came and they took my *viejita* away."

María Isabel stopped and saw Araceli looking off at the ocean, but plowed on. "The house smelled like death to me: so I cleaned all night long, until all the disinfectant was gone. Finally the coroner called: they wanted to know what to do with the body. 'I don't know,' I said. 'I can't reach the family.' So they tell me, 'If we don't hear from someone in forty-eight hours, we're going to cremate her.' *Así de frío.* So I started yelling at them, saying, 'Don't you have a mother? Would you burn your own mother?'"

"*Increíble,*" Araceli said flatly.

"By the time I finally heard from the daughter, my *viejita* was just a box of ashes. After I got the box, *then* they all show up at the house. The daughter, the son-in-law, the other daughter, the long-lost brother, who I had never met before. *Todos.* And they start asking me questions as if it were all my fault. One of them wanted to search my things when I moved out, but when I started crying they let me go."

"I've never taken care of an old lady," Araceli said distractedly. "And I've never taken care of children until now."

Araceli stood up, gave a perfunctory *"Con permiso"* to María Isabel, then walked over to the play structure, where Keenan was now running across the bridge with the girl María Isabel had brought. At the other end of the play structure, Brandon was sitting on a step, reading a book. *Where did he get a book? Is he always carrying one, the way other boys hold toy trucks or security blankets?*

"What are you reading?" Araceli asked him. In four years of living with the Torres-Thompsons, it was the first time she had ever asked this boy that question: it felt like a correct, motherly thing to do.

"El revolución," Brandon answered, holding up the book to show her the title, *American Revolution.*

"La *revolución*," Araceli corrected.

She sat next to him, another thing she had not done before, and looked at the pages as he read them. The book contained short snippets of text and pictures of long muskets, reproductions of old paintings of battles, studio shots of museum artifacts like rusting buttons and uniforms. There was something sad about a young boy sitting in a park reading about men in white wigs who were dead. She wanted to tell him that he should put down his book and play, but of course that wasn't her business, to talk to him like his mother.

"What happened to Guadalupe?" Brandon asked suddenly.

"Yeah," Keenan chimed in from the play structure. "Where's Lupita?"

Araceli was momentarily taken aback. Guadalupe had taken care of these boys for five years, she was like a big sister to them, and no one had explained her absence.

"¿Tu mamá no te dijo nada?"

"No. Nothing."

"I don't know why, but she is gone," Araceli said, hoping to forestall any further questions.

"She's gone? You mean she's not coming back?"

"Is she working somewhere else?" Brandon asked in a distracted voice that suggested he already had an inkling that Guadalupe had quit. "Is she mad at Mommy? Is she getting married?" Brandon was continuously peppering the adults around him, including Araceli, with questions,

and these queries about Guadalupe seemed more like the casually curious questions he posed to Araceli from time to time: "Why can't we have turkey dogs two days in a row? . . . Why do you say '*buenos días*' in Spanish but not '*buenos tardes*'? . . ." In the Torres-Thompson family, doing your best to answer Brandon's questions was a house rule. *La señora* Maureen was proud of her inquisitive oldest boy and liked to brag about the very first "brilliant" question he had asked when he was four years old: "Why do moths always fly around the lightbulbs?" Neither of his parents knew the answer and they scrambled to reference books and the Internet before giving their incipient genius the information his young brain demanded: moths use the moon to navigate at night, and the lights confuse them, so that "they think they're circling the moon."

When a boy got answers as satisfying as that one, they only fed his desire to ask more questions. "An atomic bomb? Why? How does that work? How do bald eagles see fish in the water from way up in the sky? Who is Malcolm X, and why is his last name X?" The boy was destined to be either a brilliant scientist or an irritating attorney.

"Did Lupita go back to Mexico?" Brandon asked his temporary caregiver. "What part of Mexico is she from? Is it the same time there as it is here? Can we call her?"

"*No sé*," Araceli said, giving an annoyed looked to make it clear that this answer applied to all of Brandon's questions. "*No sé nada.*"

Araceli felt a sudden warmness on her face: looking up, she saw a shimmering white disk of phosphorus eating through the clouds. *The sun will come out*, Araceli hoped, and then she said it out loud and Brandon looked up and nodded and returned to his book, lingering over a picture of two armies gathered at opposite sides of a bridge, engaged in a standoff of martial posturing. As he read the accompanying text, running his fingers over it, Araceli gave out a loud sigh.

The nursery manager paid a quick visit to Paseo Linda Bonita and left Maureen three pieces of paper. First there was a schematic drawing on a sheet from her sketchpad in which small symbols represented the various succulents the consultant proposed planting in the Torres-Thompson backyard. Second, there was a form in which the price of creating this desert garden was laid out, with separate quotes

for "labor," "flora," and "base material," and the alarmingly high figure of the sum total. The third and final piece of paper was a drawing that depicted the succulent garden as it would look from the perspective of the sliding glass doors of her home. The cylinders of a miniature organ pipe cactus would rise to the right, creating an anchor to the composition that would draw the eye leftward, toward the cluster of barrel cacti, mesquite shrubs, and large yuccas with arms blooming like human-sized flowers. When Maureen looked at the numbers on the smallest piece of paper she winced, and felt the dream of the drawing slipping away, becoming so many grains of pencil graphite dissolving into the white blankness of the paper. Then she remembered the argument that she would present to her husband, the logic that would make the garden real, the words the nursery manager had said in a matter-of-fact tone, because the truth of it was so self-evident: "I know it looks a little high. But in the final analysis you're gonna save a good chunk of money each year off your water bill, and even more off your gardening bill. Because this is the sort of garden you just put in and forget about. Maybe two or three times a year you go in and weed the thing, but otherwise you just stand there and watch it look pretty."

The drawing of the garden looked like a desert diorama, and Maureen imagined the dreamlike effect you got at an old-fashioned natural history museum, the sense of standing in a darkened room before a window that looks into another, brightly lit world. The succulent garden would create the illusion that their house was a portal into the unspoiled landscape of old California. Only Scott and his calculator stood between Maureen and the diorama coming to life. Against this obstacle, there was the accelerating decay of the current garden: in time, it would resemble a dried-out mulch heap, or one of those corners of Brazil ravaged by cattle ranchers. She could make this argument to her husband, or she could simply take control of the situation—as she did with every other problem in this home—and present him with a rather costly fait accompli. He'd be angry, but he'd pay the bill, because he always had before.

7

Every other weekend the Torres-Thompson family engaged in a ritual of austerity, a temporary purging of the primary luxury that smoothed over their lives. It had been Maureen's idea, years back when hired help in the home was still a novelty. They would reconnect with their self-reliant past and spend forty-eight hours cooking their own meals, doing their own dishes, making their own beds. This act of self-abnegation required getting their full-time live-in off the property. Maureen had dreamed up the maid-free weekends after realizing that Araceli didn't expect to have days off, that she was content to spend her weekends in the guesthouse in the back, entering the main home to cook meals and wash dishes on Saturday and Sunday with only slightly less energy than on the weekdays. "If you want to, it might be good if you took a couple of days off every couple of weeks," Maureen told Araceli. "Leave the house, you know. But only if you want to." In Mexico bosses did not give their employees choices, and ambiguous statements like Maureen's were a common way around the unpleasantness of a direct command: so Araceli took the suggestion as an order.

Araceli's biweekly excursions took her to the home of a friend in Santa Ana, an hour away by foot and bus. After a while, Araceli had

grown to appreciate the routine that got her out of the Torres-Thompson universe and into the Mexican-flavored neighborhoods of Santa Ana's barrio, squeezed in between the railroad tracks and the bargain shopping of the city's Main Street. On this particular Saturday, she swung by the dining room to say goodbye to Maureen and discovered her *patrona* on her hands and knees, with several sheets of newspaper spread over the tile floor of the dining room, trying to interest her two sons in a Saturday morning art project using three fist-sized blocks of sculptor's clay. Keenan was kneading a lump, and the baby Samantha had ocher-colored fingers after sticking them in a bowl of clayish water, while Brandon was on the couch reading a book. Maureen looked up at Araceli with a smile of parental pride—*We are doing something educational, my children and I*—and if Araceli had a slightly more cynical bent she might have concluded the scene had been arranged for her benefit. *Yes, Mexican woman, you are leaving us to fend for ourselves, but as you can see we Americans can manage okay.*

"*Adiós,* I am leaving now," Araceli said, tapping at the small travel bag hanging over her shoulder.

Maureen looked up from the table and said, "Okay. See you Monday," and then added a gentle reminder. "Morning. See you Monday morning."

"*Sí, señora.*"

With that Araceli was through the door and free from work, relishing those first few, very light and liberating steps down to the sidewalk, a happy reencounter with the person she once was, the woman who lived in a true city, with crowds, art, subways, and beggars. The twenty-minute walk to the bus stop took her downhill along the curving streets of the Laguna Rancho Estates, past one block where, for reasons Araceli never understood, all the houses were exactly alike, each a copy of a tile-roofed home from a white Andalusian village, each with the aesthetically misguided and culturally inappropriate addition of garages with tiny arched windows in their tin skins. The garages were as Spanish-phony as the made-up names on the street signs, which still brought a smile to Araceli's lips. Mostly variations on the words "*vía*" and "*paseo,*" the street names had lots of pretty vowels that, when put together, meant absolutely nothing. Paseo Vista Anda. Via Lindo Vita. Her *jefes* lived on Paseo Linda Bonita, which was not only grammatically incorrect, Araceli noted, but also a redundancy.

Paseo Linda Bonita and all the other *paseos* and *vías* in the Laguna Rancho Estates bent and twisted in arbitrary ways, as if the designers had intended to frustrate impatient motorists, unpunctual deliverymen, novice mail carriers. When Araceli first came to work here she too had been disoriented by the anti-linear geography of the place, more than once finding herself turning into an unfamiliar dead end, having to retrace her steps back out of the maze. Now she reached the front gate, a stone portal with a guard shack and two big black iron gates with the letters L, R, and E superimposed in polished steel. A man of chocolate skin and cornrow braids was posted there, and he gave a distracted half wave back as she walked past, headed to the bus stop marked by a fiberglass sign, ORANGE COUNTY TRANSPORTATION AUTHORITY. Only the maids and construction workers used this bus stop, so there was no sidewalk, just the dust and pebbles of the shoulder and a post driven into the undeveloped meadow that ran down to the beach. Araceli turned her back to the road and gate and faced the rolling expanse of yellow grass that mamboed in the breeze, the remnant of the "*rancho*" the Laguna Rancho Estates were named for, the millennial silence interrupted only infrequently by the sound of a vehicle moving behind her with a low purr. Looking past the meadows at the blue ocean beyond, she saw a large vessel many miles offshore, a black box drifting northward across the horizon, like a flat cutout in an arcade game. It was routine to spot ships as she waited at the bus stop, and seeing another evoked a fleeting sense of hopelessness: their slow, industrial drift seemed free of any romantic purpose, and their presence somehow tamed the Pacific and robbed it of openness and adventure.

Araceli waited. She had spent her formative years in Mexico City lines standing before elevator doors and cash registers, in buses stranded before stoplights, and in constipated thoroughfares, but it seemed illogical to find herself waiting in this open, empty stretch of California. Making a Mexican woman stand under this bus sign for thirty minutes was a final subtraction from all that was supposed to be relaxing, leisurely, and languorous about these neighborhoods by the sea. When her time became her own again, when she was a woman with a party outfit stuffed into a travel bag, Araceli reverted to the city dweller she was by birth; she was in more of a hurry, restless. *Ya, vámonos, ándale,* let's get moving. *¡Ya!* In Nezahualcóyotl, you didn't have to walk twenty minutes to get to the bus stop, all you had to do was walk half a block, and there

would be two or three buses waiting for you, double-parked, the drivers honking at one another and all the taxis and shuttle vans around them. No one complained: that was life in Mexico City, you waited as the multitudes shuffled around you, jabbing elbows into your chest, pushing grocery bags into your stomach. Araceli never would have imagined herself also waiting in the United States, so pathetically alone on a winding road.

Not long after Araceli walked out the door, Maureen noticed that Samantha had worked bits of clay into the zipper of her yellow pajama jumpsuit, a discovery that caused Maureen to feel the sudden weight of motherly sleeplessness behind her pupils. Looking up at the clock, she noticed her morning sense of being fully awake and alert had not lasted past nine-thirty. As soon as a baby entered the world, you were sentenced to two years of interrupted sleep, unless genetic probability favored you with the rare "easy baby," the ones fated to become grown-ups with the gentle dispositions of Buddhist priests. In three tries Maureen had never been so blessed; each child had sapped a bit of her youth with nights similar to the last one, which had been interrupted by Samantha's cries at 12:04 a.m., 2:35 a.m., and 4:36 a.m. The years of infant and toddler helplessness took a toll on a mother's body too; they were an unexpected extension of those nine months of gestation that a mother endured not in her womb and hips, but rather in the muscles around her eyes, and in her arms and spine. This Saturday would begin with the cleaning of this clay-covered baby and move later to the harried cooking of lunch and dinner, all the while keeping an eye on the boys so that they didn't spend too much time on their electronic toys, and on Samantha to make sure she didn't injure herself, and would end with the washing of the dishes in the evening after she had put her children to bed.

On most days Maureen didn't mind the responsibility; she felt the purpose and nobility of motherhood flowing through her body like warm blood, and saw those exalted notions alive in the healthy, glowing skin of her children and in the nurturing home she had built around them. Today would not be one of those days. Today she would see only the frayed ends of a family project that was subtly coming apart, with

two boys of growing muscle mass and bad attitude, and little time for the arranging, sorting, and creating that made up Maureen's notion of what family life should look like. In the back of the closet a year of the boys' schoolwork and art projects were gathering dust because Maureen didn't have the time to catalogue them as was her wont, nor had she filed away the pictures from Samantha's first birthday. If Samantha napped and Scott did the dishes she might get to those things today. He was probably hiding in that carpeted nook of his, with a game, and thinking of this she felt the sense of petty injustice that overcomes a slave upon learning she is carrying the heaviest rocks of all.

All the disciplined orderliness and empty lawns of the Laguna Rancho Estates disappeared in the barrio where Araceli's friend Marisela lived. The Santa Ana neighborhood was cluttered and improvised, and the homes stucco and clapboard, ash-gray and flaky fuchsia. There were palm trees and olive trees and avocado trees and jacarandas, some overgrown and older than any of the homes, with tree roots buckling the sidewalks into waves. Some lawns were green squares of watered perfection, and others were eaten up with patches of dust upon which lawn chairs and frayed couches rested, and clusters of people sat talking with wide sweeping gestures, while women and children stood on the porches behind them and examined the landscape like mariners on the prow of a ship.

The bus stopped on Maple Street and Araceli stepped off and walked a few blocks to the white wood-frame house where Marisela lived with a family from Zacatecas. She climbed onto the porch, which was covered with a worn carpet of plastic grass, opened the screen door, and entered the uniquely Mexican set of cultural contradictions that was the home of Octavio Covarrubias, a longtime friend of Marisela's family and the owner of this house. She found him in a torso-swallowing blue lounge chair: he was reading, in a rather conspicuous display of his lefty bona fides, the Sunday edition of the Mexico City daily newspaper *La Jornada*, which he received by mail every week, devouring its star-studded lineup of radical Mexican literary and political commentators. Covarrubias was a semiretired carpenter and one of the thousands of proletarian, Spanish-speaking autodidact intellectuals scattered across

the Southern California metropolis, and he had two large moles above his left eye that he called Io and Europa, after the moons of Jupiter. His wife and adolescent progeny, meanwhile, were sitting semierect on a couch as they absorbed the pings, sizzles, and cheers of a television broadcasting a Mexico City–based variety show hosted by a garrulous man whose vulgar shtick annoyed thoughtful people on both sides of the border. The living room décor further echoed the contrasts between high and low culture, with the velvet painting of tongue-wagging dogs on one wall looking across the space at the bowed, dignified heads of the mother and child in a Siqueiros woodcut on the other. Even on the bookshelf, the gravitas of Elena Poniatowska and José Emilio Pacheco were pushing up against the pulp crime of *Los secretos del cartel del Golfo* and *The True Story of Los Zetas*, announcing to Araceli her arrival at the home of a workingman grappling for ideas, arguments, and facts to understand his world.

Octavio lowered his newspaper to say "*Hola, Araceli, ¿qué tal?*"

Araceli returned the greeting and asked if Marisela was in.

"She's waiting for you."

Araceli zigzagged around the children in the living room and made her way to the last bedroom in the back, where she found Marisela lying on her back on a bed, pushing buttons on her cell phone.

"No one ever calls me," Marisela said without looking at Araceli. She was a short and roundish young woman who always wore jeans that were a size too small. Araceli liked Marisela because she was blunt and often unaware of the fact that she was offending people, and because she was a *chilanga*, a Mexico City native. They had met in a Santa Ana thrift store, two Latinas sorting through the same rack of men's vests, and weeks later it was Marisela who introduced Araceli to the friend who knew a gringa in Laguna Rancho who in turn knew another gringa, named Maureen Thompson, who was looking for a new maid.

"The only call I got today was from *el viejo*," Marisela said, turning on her side to look at her friend now. "He didn't even ask how I was doing before telling me he needed money."

"Is your brother still sick?"

"No, he got better. Now they need one hundred dollars because there's a hole in the roof."

Once it had been taboo to complain about their families and the

demands they made. A Mexican daughter in exile was supposed to place individual ambitions aside and make ample cash transfers in the name of younger siblings and nephews. So their money flowed southward, every month without fail, even as the months and years passed and the voices on the other end of the telephone became older and more distant. Their U.S. wages fertilized a tree of family narratives that had grown many new and gnarly branches that no longer involved them directly. Now Araceli and Marisela complained openly and without guilt, because it had become painfully clear that their families didn't understand the complications of life in the supposedly affluent United States of America, and because their relatives were using their telephones as probes to discover how deep the well of dollars went, as if they sensed, correctly, that the faraway daughters in exile were squirreling away money for their own selfish use.

"I'm going to send them fifty instead of one hundred," Marisela said.

"They need to learn to take care of their own problems," Araceli said, the phrase having become a refrain in their conversations.

"Exactly. I'm going to keep that extra fifty dollars to buy another hat like this one I'm going to wear tonight. I got it at that new place on Main Street. Let me show you."

Marisela went to the closet and emerged with a cowboy hat made of black jute straw, its brim bent up saucily on two sides, like a bird about to thrust its wings downward. "*Qué bonito*," Araceli said through half-gritted teeth, because they had an unspoken agreement not to speak ill of each other's party clothes, what with Marisela's having adopted the rural, denim-centered tastes of the Zacatecas people who dominated this neighborhood, while Araceli stuck stubbornly to the pop-inspired trends of Mexico City.

"And it hardly cost me anything at all."

Several hours later, after watching a bit of television in the living room, and then getting themselves dressed and primped in Marisela's bedroom and bathroom, they were out on the street and walking down Maple Street, headed to a *quinceañera* party. Marisela wore her new hat and a pair of jeans with arabesque-patterned rhinestones swaying on the back pockets. Araceli had let her hair down so that it reached halfway to her waist, brushing it out for a good long while. The effect of this

liberated mane on her appearance was striking to anyone who knew Araceli the maid: all the tension of her workday face disappeared, and with her temples freed of the pulling strain of the buns in which she imprisoned her hair, her face took on the relaxed expression of a young woman without children to take care of or meals to prepare. She was wearing her "Saturday night *chilanga* uniform": short black leggings with flamingo-colored trim that reached halfway down her calves, a black miniskirt with a few sequins, and a T-shirt with the word LOVE across the front, a peace symbol filling the O. Three strands of necklaces made of raspberry-colored plastic rocks, and a few matching bracelets, were her chief accessories. It was a bold statement of where she came from. Similar versions of her *uniforme de chilanga* had previously earned Araceli a derisive comment or two from Marisela. "You know that people here think you look ridiculous. This isn't the Condesa district."

"That, my dear, is precisely the point."

But today Marisela also kept to their pact and said nothing as they walked to the party, her teeth gleaming in their ruby lipstick frame, the most expressive part of her face, given the large, wraparound sunglasses she was wearing, another example of *norteño* chic, with encrusted "diamonds" on each side, eyewear that possessed an aeronautical quality, as if Marisela were preparing to be the first Zacatecas astronaut blasted into space.

"I don't really know the people at this party that well," Marisela was saying. "The girl who is having the *quinceañera*, her name is Nicolasa. She's very tall, very pretty. I know her aunt, Lourdes is her name, because I used to work with her at that clothes factory."

"I remember you telling me about Lourdes."

"Actually, I do know some *chisme* about these people." It was more tragedy than gossip, a story with dark, nausea-inducing contours, complete with psychopathic border smugglers and a father who disappeared once the family was safely ensconced in California. Abandoned with two children, Nicolasa's mother had soldiered on until illness struck. "She got too sick to work, and too sick to even take care of the kids. So some people from the government came by and took the kids. They put them in something called Foster Care."

"Foster" was one of those words than never quite found a home in Araceli's mental arrangement of the English language. She'd heard it

before and sometimes confused it with "faster"—much in the same way some English speakers themselves confused words like "gorilla" and "guerrilla," or "pretext" and "pretense"—and she'd wondered if the American fix to broken families known as Foster Care somehow involved finding the quickest solution possible: instant guardians for the parentless, quick meals for the unfed.

"In Foster Care they separate siblings," Marisela continued. "So this girl and her brother lived in different places for, like, three or four years."

"What about the mother?"

"She died."

"*Dios mío.*"

"I wish I could remember what she had."

"AIDS?"

"No, it was something more like cancer. But anyways, my friend Lourdes tried for a long time to get them out of Foster Care. They tried looking for the father too. Finally Lourdes's sister and brother-in-law tried to adopt them, but of course it took forever, because they were stuck in Foster Care and once they're in that I guess it's really hard to get them out."

The story stayed with Araceli as she walked with Marisela past old bungalows whose windows and doors were open to catch a breeze in the final hours of a dying summer afternoon. Araceli saw kitchen walls shimmering in stark incandescent light, and heard a radio tuned to a Spanish-language broadcast of a baseball game, and a murmur of voices followed by a chorus of laughter, and she wondered about the voices she could not hear, and the tales of betrayal and loss they might tell. Araceli knew she could knock on any door, ask a question or two, and find herself inside a melodrama about a family forced to endure separation and travel great distances, and to struggle with the authorities and with their own self-destructive foibles.

They arrived at a bungalow decorated with a string of lights gathering in luminance in the twilight, its unseen backyard pulsating with accordions, trumpets, and clarinets. Marisela and Araceli had missed the actual *quinceañera* ceremony, because it had started on schedule, in violation of the Mexican social conventions Marisela and Araceli still followed, although they had arrived in plenty of time for the party that

followed. After pushing in a splintery wooden gate, the two women stepped onto a concrete patio thick with more spectacled recruits to the Zacatecas space program who were shuffling about in cowboy boots and swaying inside jeans, while streamers dangled over their heads, brushing against the tops of their ten-gallon hats.

Following Marisela, Araceli cut through the dancers and found her way to a corner, against a wooden fence, where the nondancers held plastic cups and studied the patterns of the shifting feet on the dance floor with serious eyes, as if trying to decipher the meaning of the interlocking circles. Three pairs of women were dancing together, which was not unusual at these parties, the men of northern Mexico being a shy bunch, and when the music stopped and another song started, Marisela turned to Araceli to ask, "¿Bailamos?" In an instant they were dancing on the patio, Araceli laughing loudly as she led her friend in a merry-go-round waltz, their legs intertwined and arms around each other's waists. "Just watch," Marisela shouted into Araceli's ear above the music. "We dance like this once, and all these guys will be all over us." Soon enough, several *paisanos* holding beers were trying very hard to look unimpressed by the sight of a tall woman with thick polyester legs protruding from her miniskirt, spinning deftly in her checkerboard flats and dancing cheek-to-cheek with her short friend in the persimmon-colored blouse.

When Araceli and Marisela stopped dancing, a young man in a baseball cap stepped out of the crowd and grinned and squinted into Marisela's sunglasses, as if studying himself in the reflection there. He spoke words Araceli did not hear, and when the music started again he pulled Marisela into the center of the patio, and soon they were swallowed up in the mass of moving bodies like rocks plopping into a lake.

Araceli walked to the fence on the edge of the patio and prepared herself for the possibility that none of the brass-buckled astronauts would step forward and lead her back out onto the concrete floor to spin around. *When Marisela finishes with that little guy she doesn't seem to like so much, maybe we can dance again.* At that instant, Araceli felt a tap on the shoulder and turned to see a lofty mass of flesh and denim standing before her. He was a man of about her own age, but significantly taller, with a head that was sprouting a full fountain of sexy, moist black curls. "¿Quieres bailar?" he asked. *Where did you come from?* she wanted to say, and soon found one of her hands rising for the nameless man to

guide her onto the patio. Her partner was husky but moved well, clasping her hands with confidence and with the slightly callused, blackish bronze hands of a man who earns his living outdoors. As they spun to the repetitive swirl of the trumpet and clarinets, Araceli took in the motion of his slacks, the churn of his shirt. Little miracles like this happened to people like Marisela all the time, but only very rarely to Araceli: to meet a stranger and, in an instant, to find herself moving in synchronicity with him.

Halfway through that first song, he leaned over as they danced, pressed his cheek against hers, and said, loud enough to be heard against the blaring music, "Hey, you dance well!"

"I know," she shouted back.

The music stopped. People around them wiped perspiration from their foreheads and headed for the edge of the patio dance floor. Before Araceli could prepare herself for the inevitable *Thank you and goodbye*, the music had started again and the curly-headed man was asking, "*¿Otra?*"

"*¡Sí!*"

During the second song he said his name was Felipe and after the third he asked her name. When the music stopped after the fourth song she asked him where he was from, just so he wouldn't go away. "Sonora," he said. "A little town called Imuris. It's near Cananea. *¿Y tú?*"

"El De Efe."

When it became clear he did not want to run away, she asked Felipe if he knew anyone else at the party. A few people, he said.

"I don't know anyone."

"Look, over there," he said. "It's the girl who is having the *quinceañera*."

Araceli turned to see a tall young woman with mahogany skin who wore a tight white dress covered in constellations of beads. Nicolasa had the confident look of a young woman enjoying her day of neighborhood celebrity, and was listening to an older man and studying him with smart, dark eyes that occasionally darted away from him to the landscape of the backyard party: the crowd, and the strings of lights, and a large white sign attached to the fence that read FELIZ 15 NICA. Her black hair was parted in the middle and long braids ran down over her shoulders: a girl's hairstyle and a woman's face and body. Next to

her was a boy with the same complexion but a foot shorter: her brother, apparently. He looked small and vulnerable, and possessed all the tragic aura that his sister lacked: without the black suit he was wearing, he might be one of those boys you see weaving between the cars in Mexico City, raising their palms to catch coins and raindrops from the sky. Now the big, beefy man talking to them raised a bicep to show them a tattoo, a portrait of a cigarette-smoking soldier in a steel helmet, with SGT. RAY, R.I.P. written inside a scroll underneath.

"They've been through a lot," Felipe said.

"So you know that story?"

"You mean about their mother dying and being adopted and all that? Yeah. Everybody does. Everybody in the neighborhood, at least."

"I'm not from the neighborhood."

"Yeah, I know. I think I would have remembered you," he said, naturally and simply, without any secondary meanings.

"You see that guy next to them? He got back a few months ago from the war. His name is José. He's a cousin of the lady who owns this house."

"What about you? What's your story?"

"I paint houses. And some construction. But mostly I paint houses."

"That pays well, *qué no?*"

"It's okay. But I like to paint other things besides walls. *¿Entiendes?* The other day I was painting at this family's house and I heard *la señora* asking my boss if he knew anyone who could paint a design on a table for her. I stepped in and said I could do it, because I like to draw. She wanted a dragon for her son's room, so I made her one. A big red dragon. She liked it and the boy did too. That was fun."

"You're an artist!"

"No, I wouldn't call myself that. But I like to draw. The dragon turned out okay."

"I studied art," Araceli offered, making a conscious effort not to speak breathlessly: a dancing artist had fallen into her lap, and she wanted to tell him everything, all at once. "I was at the Instituto Nacional de Bellas Artes in El De Efe, but only for a year. Then I had to quit." Araceli thought she should explain why, but stopped herself: among *mexicanos* of their status, in this place called California, no explanations were necessary when describing dreams that died.

"I could tell by looking at you that you're really smart. You look like one of those girls from the show *Rebelde*. A student. I could tell. That's why I asked you to dance."

At the end of the evening, the two of them having danced for two hours, Felipe said he had to leave because he had to be up early the next morning. *Tomorrow is a Sunday, why would you have to be up early?* Araceli wanted to ask, but she resisted the temptation. He asked for her phone number, which she wrote on a slip of paper he tucked into the front pocket of his shirt.

"I work in a house," she told him. *Trabajo en una casa.* It meant, *Yes, you can call me, but a gringo will answer, and be polite, please, and don't call me in the middle of the night because my jefes won't appreciate that.* He appeared to understand and smiled as he turned away, and Araceli got one last good look at the backside of his slacks as he left: he was husky when you looked at him from the front, but from the back he was much better proportioned, the width of his shoulders stood out, suggesting a certain musculature. He was a sensitive *mexicano* trapped, like her, in a too-big body.

On Sunday afternoon, some thirty-six hours after the departure of her only domestic help, Maureen found herself sitting on the floor of her walk-in closet, listening to the steady static that came from the baby monitor, and to the distant sounds of heads being smashed, flesh being pierced, and stone walls crashing to the ground. Allowing the boys the pleasures of movie-made warfare was the only way she was going to get a little time to herself, to sort through her box of family pictures and to arrange the photographs of Samantha's first birthday in the album she had purchased months ago. Maureen did this to calm herself, and as an affirmation of the nurturing progress of her family. She took a picture of Scott holding Samantha at the party and placed it next to another that showed the baby sitting before her cake, with Brandon and Keenan on either side, helping her blow out a wick that burned atop a wax number one. The blending of features in the faces of their children was plain to see: there was Ireland in the specks of emerald in Keenan's eyes, Maine in her daughter's prominent jaw, and Mexico in the way Brandon's long nose stretched. Her children blended the

features of many branches of the human tree. In their faces she saw the hands of an eccentric creator, an artist who surprises his audience with the unexpected.

On the other end of the Paseo Linda Bonita home, Scott was gripping a console control with two hands, playing a football simulation of cutting-edge visual complexity. He had purchased the newest release two days earlier, thinking that he could justify the cost as a professional, tax-deductible expense, because he had designed a game or two in his day and might again. But the unadorned truth was that a bestselling game like this was beyond his talents, which had been honed in the days of "real programming." You had to manage and inspire large groups of people to bring a game like this to market: artists, teams of technicians conducting motion studies, and brain trusts of football mavens to work out the strategy book. This game was a big Hollywood production: the credits were buried deep in the disk for true geeks like Scott to find, and ran on for several pages, as if for a David Lean epic.

A man needed to play, to feel the exhilaration and escape of sports, even if he was sitting down while doing it, so Scott returned to the task at hand: leading his team of animated San Francisco players to victory over a Pittsburgh team. The glossy realism of the animation more than made up for the lack of exertion, and as he completed a third-and-long backed up against his own goal line, Scott thought that a virtual triumph was the most ephemeral source of adrenaline out there, but it did make it easier to do the dishes afterward. Maureen expected Scott to leave the kitchen spotless, to attack the stacks of bowls and oily pans in the sink, wipe the counters, and sweep the floor. It was an absurd rule of Maureen's that the house had to look "presentable" when Araceli walked in the door on Monday morning. Unfortunately, the disarray built rather quickly in Araceli's absence, with dishes filling the sink and loose laundry invading the hallways and bedrooms, while children's shoes walked midstride on the living room floor and plastic warriors massed for battle on the dining room table, surrounded by a toast-crumb snowfall.

Maureen had decided to aggressively ignore this growing disorder, and was still in the closet, retreating deeper into family nostalgia, remembering the gentle, funny, and neglected but handsome man her husband was. Back then, she had thought of his surname, Torres, as a signpost announcing her arrival at a remote, exotic village.

After all these years what had seemed like silent strength had been revealed to be a deeply rooted stoicism, a disconnectedness from people. The promise of a Latin journey seemed closer to fruition after their marriage, when her new mother-in-law had graciously presented her with an album of Torres family pictures, including some bleak photographs of her father-in-law as a boy, and others of him as a cocky young man. She had framed a couple of these sturdy old images and placed them in the living room for guests to see, but they were artifacts in a historical vacuum, since in her few conversations with the old man he refused to talk much about his life in the black-and-white, Spanish-speaking past. "We had a raw deal when we were kids, but we never complained about it. And I sure as hell ain't going to complain about it now." The old man had dedicated his life to the erasure of the language and rituals he associated with short hoes and lettuce fields, with the transience of old Ford trucks and night arrivals at labor camps and menacing urban ghettos. The old man confused amnesia with reinvention, and thus the only trace of Mexican in her husband was that very faint brownish red she saw when he allowed himself to stand under the sun for an hour, and perhaps his Julius Caesar nose, which may or may not be Indian. Everything else about Scott was as pale and severe as the Maine winters her late mother-in-law used to talk about, though Maureen never would have dared to say such a thing out loud, to anyone, because as an American "white" woman it wasn't her place to make such judgments.

Her journey through the albums having failed to transport her away from the messy and complicated present, Maureen put her family memories back in their shoe boxes and decided to start cleaning the house. As she picked up dirty pajamas and towels, she marveled, not for the first time, at how much work Araceli did. This home, even when you thought of it in the most abstract sense, as a place of security, order, and happiness, depended on the Mexican woman as much as it did on Maureen. Allowing Araceli to leave for two days was, Maureen realized, a way of claiming it as her own.

She was in the kitchen, holding Samantha and heating up a bottle of milk, when her oldest son entered the kitchen to ask for something to eat.

"How about a sandwich? Turkey and cheese?"

"Okay."

"Is the movie over? Did you turn off the TV?"

"Yes," Brandon said. "And yes."

She looked at the dishes in the sink, remembered to scan the backyard for toys, and thought about what she would make for dinner and what she could get the boys to do this afternoon: perhaps a game of Scrabble Junior. *It takes concentration to do all these things at once.* Already today she had played Risk with her boys and had set them to work with aprons and paintbrushes and butcher paper. Later she would wade into her boxes of colored scrap paper and fabric strips and assemble another art project. There was an element of performance to being a good mom, but no one gave you executive bonuses for getting through the day, for keeping three kids fed, entertained, and stimulated without doing the easy thing and leaving them in front of the television. It took stamina and a certain optimistic and demanding outlook.

Maureen had the baby on her hip and was walking to the bedroom to retrieve her children and call them to an early dinner when she caught a glimpse of her husband, sitting on that boomerang-shaped chair before the mirage of a high-definition television monitor, a series of color images quick-flashing in response to the movement of his fingers. *Again? What is the fascination? I am carrying the baby and he is playing.* She took in his frantic fingers, and the intense look of excited concentration she could see in profile, and decided the moment presented an opportunity.

"Honey, I wanted to ask you something."

"Uh-huh," he said, giving a quarter turn in her direction without taking his eyes off the screen. "Sorry, I'm in my two-minute offense here."

"Okaaaay. Well, I came up with a plan for the garden. Something that will save us some money in the long run. But it's gonna require a big expense to get started."

"Uh-huh."

"I'm going to have them put in some desert plants."

"Cool."

"I'll go ahead and do that, then."

"What?"

"The desert garden."

"But how much is it going to cost?" he said, giving a half turn in her direction while the screen behind him replayed the last running play.

"Not too much. Honest."

"Really," he said, and then the pull of the game caused him to turn fully to the screen.

"Honest, I promise," she said to the back of his head.

"Cool," he said, and Maureen thought that at any other moment she would have been angered by his failure to pay full attention to her.

"So I'll just charge it, then," she said.

He did not answer, but instead leaned his body forward in his chair. On the screen the animated representation of a football quarterback threw a very long pass, and through a mesmerizing miracle of technology the game's eye followed the ball through the air and into the hands of an animated receiver, though Maureen had already turned away and was in the hallway when that very masculine corner of her home filled with a semiconductor-produced simulation of a multitude, a sizzle of voices and cheers celebrating a touchdown.

8

The kitchen window offered only a partial view of the sidewalk at the bottom of the sloping lawn, and when the work crew rolled up to the cul-de-sac at Paseo Linda Bonita, Araceli saw only the top half of their truck. Three men of Mesoamerican heritage stood in the back, peering over a side panel of rough-cut plywood with the startled look of Aztecs about to enter a town filled with conquistadores. They looked around at their alien, affluent surroundings for a few moments, and began talking to a person invisible to Araceli, and she could lip-read them saying "¿aquí?" and "¿bajamos?" The answer to both questions was yes, apparently, and soon they were jumping off their perch to the street below. Two more men who had been sitting on the floor of the truck rose to their feet, one of whom was holding a long machete, which he proceeded to strike once against the truck's plywood panels, as if to test the blade. Both the eager-to-work peasant expressions of the workers and what Araceli could see of the truck itself seemed like anachronisms, and Araceli half expected them to admit they were lost and turn around and drive away. The presence of these roustabouts in their used clothing inspired in Araceli a familiar and comforting burst of sarcastic thoughts: *I'm sorry, but there is no farm here. There are no cabbages to*

pick, as you can see! Put your machetes away: we have no bananas to harvest! To her surprise, another man, an older Mexican-American type dressed in a freshly ironed plaid shirt, came walking up the path.

Araceli was headed for the door, preparing the polite words by which she would inform this man that he and his poorly fed day laborers had obviously come to the wrong place, when she saw her *jefa* reach the door first and open it.

"You're late," Maureen said abruptly.

"I'm really, really sorry, lady, but my usual guys didn't show up. So I had to pick up some new guys." The raffish "guys," five in all, were now standing near the bottom of the walkway behind their foreman, hands in their pockets and silent.

"Day laborers?" Maureen asked in a tone that suggested concern.

"Yeah, but these guys are cool. I've hired them all before."

"As long as you finish in time. You need to be done by eleven. You know that, right?"

"We'll be outta here by ten-thirty, I promise. I got another job at eleven anyway over at Newport. I brought a couple more guys than usual to get done in time. Trust me."

What is going on? Araceli wondered as she watched Maureen show the contractor the gate where his crew could enter the backyard without tramping through Araceli's freshly cleaned living room. *These men have come to do some serious labor,* Araceli concluded, *something involving plants and soil, and of course I am the last to know, because my* patrona *doesn't feel the slightest need to inform me.* Araceli felt mildly insulted, an emotion that had become familiar in the days since she had discovered that she was now the do-everything *doméstica,* her workload doubled without a corresponding raise.

She walked across the living room to the glass doors that opened to the backyard and watched as the contractor and Maureen gathered before the withering tropical garden. Half the calla lilies were tan and irrevocably dead, the banana tree would never again produce the tiny fruit that it used to give each spring, and the ferns were as dry as Egyptian parchment. The river boulders inside the little stream had lost their rich black texture and turned a brittle, pale gray because the small pump that fed the stream stopped working days ago, which Araceli could now see in retrospect was a final, unmistakable sign of what was about to happen.

Having finished their conference, the workers and their boss made for the side gate and their truck, while Maureen contemplated *la petite* rain forest for the last time. A few minutes later the contractor was back with his laborers, each of whom was holding a machete and studying the boss as he consulted with Maureen. He gave the workers a set of instructions with wide sweeps of his hands and pointing fingers. Not one of these workers, Araceli guessed, had been in this country for longer than a year. The one with the droopy mustache and the sweatshirt that said LOUDON COUNTY HIGH WRESTLING TEAM was likely a grandfather. The stringy young guy next to him was wearing a Banamex giveaway T-shirt and appeared to be the newest one in this country. The grandfather looked intently at the boss, suggesting he was anxious to prove himself, and they all seemed to have a need to get a good day's work out of their systems, having just won the lottery and wrestling match back at the hiring site.

The boss was addressing the workers, and through the window Araceli could make out his bad, shouted Spanish. "*¡Comienzan con estos! ¡Con puro machete!*" At the sound of the first machete whacks Araceli felt the briefest pang of nostalgia. *Adiós to Pepe's garden, to the green leaves and flowers that carry the memory of his hands.* The hacking machetes reverberated loud enough to be heard even when Araceli retreated to the kitchen and turned on the water in the sink. She heard them too in the laundry room, the messy, sickening sound of blades cutting into fleshly stalks. A whack, whack, whack filled the house, punctuated by the long, rising whistles of the men calling back and forth to one another. "*¿Qué hago con esto?*" "*¿Todo?*" "*¡Está bien duro el bambú!*" Each time she wandered past the sliding glass doors of the living room, she turned to catch glimpses of the day laborers raising their machetes and slashing, stalks and branches falling to the ground starkly and suddenly, as if murdered. These roustabouts were machete experts and each of their blows sent a living thing flying into the air: they worked in a line, advancing into *la petite* rain forest like men assigned to clear a cane field.

"They're chopping down the garden!" Brandon said as he came running into the living room, drawn by the sounds. "Keenan, look! They're chopping it down! The bamboo! Look!"

Brandon watched them work and remembered the British children in *Lord of the Flies*, on a tropical island armed with spears and a knife,

behaving like savages—and he thought he'd like to pick up a blade and join them.

"They're taking away our jungle," Keenan said. Once the boys ran through shady caves formed by the healthy branches and jumped over the tiny stream, and arranged toy soldiers between the stalks of bamboo. They hadn't played there in ages, not since Pepe left, as if they too were put off by the garden's slow death in the dry, Pepe-less air.

After forty minutes of chopping, nothing in the garden was left standing and the plants were an organic heap the men walked over like soldiers in a battlefield, checking to see if any of the vanquished were still living. For the first time, Araceli could see the entirety of the curving, adobe-colored cement wall that marked the boundary of the Torres-Thompson property. Like an empty canvas, it assaulted the eyes with its blankness: she could understand why Maureen and Scott had gone to the trouble of planting a big tropical garden to cover it.

Maureen reappeared to examine the work, and tapped at some of the fallen stalks with her sandaled foot. The roustabouts began grabbing armfuls of chopped-up plants and carrying them back to the truck, and two of the workers appeared with rusty pickaxes and shovels, and started hacking away at roots. The men were covered in dust, soil, and a sprinkling of shredded bamboo leaves, ferns, and flower petals. Araceli heard an engine start on the street, and then a series of high-pitched, banshee screams. Following the sound, she stepped away from the glass doors facing the backyard and drifted to the picture window in the living room, but could still not see the source of this deathly wail until she walked out the front door. The roustabouts were tossing the remains of *la petite* rain forest into a machine attached to their truck, which was spitting a verdant cloud into the back. Pepe's garden was being turned into green dust and Araceli watched, entranced, as the machine covered the workers' arms and faces with a dappled chlorophyll skin that affixed itself to the sweat and soil on their faces and arms. Soon they resembled science fiction creatures, or maybe just the poorest of the poor castes of Mexico City, the people who scavenged through the trash all day until they were wearing the gooey black contents of discarded plastic cartons and boxes on their faces and arms.

By 10:30 a.m., the workers and their foreman were smoothing out the empty black soil with heavy iron rakes. They picked up their equip-

ment and were gone, the truck pulling away as Araceli watched from her post in the kitchen. *I should have offered them something to drink. But they were in such a hurry.*

Forty-five minutes later Araceli was mopping one of the bath-rooms when she was surprised, again, by the rumble of a truck and the squeal of brakes, followed moments later by a second rumble and squeal, and the opening and closing of doors. Once again she approached the picture window in the living room. An American woman of light com-plexion with oval-shaped sunglasses emerged from the first truck, fol-lowed by two mestizo-skinned men in identical forest-green uniforms. Four more men in green uniforms emerged from the second truck, and soon they were all walking up the path toward Araceli.

The doorbell rang and this time Araceli beat Maureen to the door.

"Hi, good morning!" the American woman said. "We're from the landscape company."

"*¿Cómo?*" Maureen quickly reached the door behind her and Araceli was forced to step aside before she could ask the many questions she wanted answered: *What have you come to do to my backyard? Why didn't anyone tell me you were coming? How long will you be here? Did you bring your own lunch?* Araceli could only watch through the glass as this new crew of workers traipsed around the side of the house, led by Maureen to the backyard and the fallow plot where the tropical garden had once stood. Araceli opened the sliding glass door to hear what the woman was saying to her *patrona* and watched as the stranger opened a scroll to show a large schematic drawing to Maureen, who beamed giddily in the scroll's creative glow. Then the stranger began to talk, in English, to one of her crew members.

"Fernando, did we bring enough base?"

"*Es un espacio grande,*" he answered in Spanish, surveying the space before them. "*Pero sí. Creo que nos alcanza.*"

"I guess we start with the willow, right?"

"*Es lo que nos va a tomar más tiempo,*" Fernando answered. "*Y tam-bién el ocotillo. Eso va a ser todo un* project."

"I had forgotten about that one. Let's start with the ocotillo, then."

Fernando wore a white oval patch on his uniform that read FERNANDO, and all the other workers had name patches too. These uniformed men didn't whistle or shout as they walked around the backyard. Instead

they examined the turned-up earth of the backyard with considered glances, sometimes kicking at a clump of soil, or picking up a stray leaf or flower stem. They worked with efficient and practiced movements, consulting with one another and their boss in short bilingual conversations like the one Araceli had just overheard. In this strange country that Araceli now called home, the market for labor in the soil was stratified, and these men were jokingly known at Desert Landscaping as "high-end Mexicans." Most of them were natives of Guanajuato and Jalisco who had known one another for half of their adult lives; in many loyal years of work for Desert Landscaping they had developed an artisan familiarity with the root systems of the ocotillo, the saguaro, and the assorted Sonoran and African succulents that made up the Desert Landscaping catalogue. They earned triple the wages of their untrained, subcontracted morning counterparts, had some limited medical benefits, and, though Araceli did not yet know it, they had brought their own lunches, sandwiches, and burritos made by their wives and girlfriends and stored in black metal lunch boxes each had hauled to hundreds of work sites over the years.

As the men carried bags of sand from the truck to the backyard, Maureen sat on the grass, holding on to Samantha while admiring the schematic drawing, thinking that the money involved would be well spent. The nervousness of the last few days lifted away, a hair-chewing anxiety heightened by the anarchic chopping, hacking, and slicing of the first crew of the morning. *What am I doing, allowing these sweaty barbarians into my home?* But no, she was taking charge of her little domestic empire again, and now there was this crew of handsome if somewhat older Mexican men, and this woman nursery manager/landscape designer who was the kind of desert bohemian you encountered in the inner Southwest. When Scott saw the finished product he'd say they should have done this years ago. She watched the uniformed workers bring a few plants that were growing inside wooden crates and plastic pots, including a specimen that resembled a tree in miniature; its thick branches had a taupe skin that looked like bark, and its fleshy petals seemed to be made of emerald clay, and the entire plant had the heaviness and simplicity of a work of sculpture.

"Isn't this the biggest jade plant you've ever seen?" said the nursery manager, who had caught Maureen's perplexed examination of the

specimen, which spread out some four feet and stood about three feet tall. "In the late fall, or the early winter, whenever you get the first good rain, it's going to give off hundreds of tiny white flowers. Most of these plants are going to flower at one time or another. Some in the spring, others in the fall."

"It just makes so much more sense, from an ecological point of view," Maureen said. "Down on the beach, it's misty and cloudy right now. But up here, the sun is beating down on us—over time, it kills anything that needs water."

"You've got your own little microclimate here," the nursery manager said. "I could feel the weather changing as I came up the hill. You're getting a hot counter-draft to the ocean breeze from those mountains. That makes this like an African savanna. You can fool the plants in the garden, you can make them think they're really somewhere else, but it takes a lot of work."

"I love this one too," Maureen said. It was some sort of agave, an arrangement of concentric rosettes, one stacked inside the other, painted pale green and crimson, and all the colors in between. "It's like a flower without being a flower."

"It's called Morning Light. I've got a whole bunch more like that for you. We're going to do a little section of Morning Light, surrounded by some nonthreatening succulents, like this one over here, *Cheiridopsis africanus*, which is from South Africa, of course. In general, I'm going to put your more barbed and spiny plants away from the edges and from the path, so it won't be so dangerous for your kids."

"Excellent."

"*¡Con cuidado!*" the nursery manager called out suddenly, and unexpectedly, in Spanish.

A group of men were entering the backyard with a ten-foot-long plant wrapped in white canvas, rolling it on two platforms, but they had gotten the wheels stuck at the spot where the cement of the driveway ended and the lawn of the backyard began. They carried the package sideways into the backyard, straining under its weight, and stood it on its end; then they began to unwrap it slowly and its branches opened up and stretched out like a man waking from a long sleep. "This, to me, is the pièce de résistance," the nursery manager said. "It's the compositional anchor to the whole garden."

"Oh, my God, it's huge. Is that the . . . what is it called?"

"It's an ocotillo. I call it 'the burning bush' because it looks like something from the Ten Commandments. It must be a good twenty years old. This one isn't from the nursery, of course, it's a transplant. We rescued it from the Palm Springs area, from Rancho Mirage, to be exact. It was on some land that was being cleared for a subdivision, a stunning stretch of desert. I got five of these from those developer gangsters, and half a dozen amazing willows too, one of which is over in the truck. They didn't just give them to me, of course. They sold them to me. Really nice of them. They destroy a bunch of native habitat for all kinds of desert animals, they're chasing the roadrunners into the hills, literally, but they make a little extra selling off the flora. But I only paid them a fraction of what they were worth. I got them for a song." The nursery manager gave the quick, sly laugh of a woman claiming winnings at a poker table. "Speaking of money," she added with a congenial, gently pleading smile.

"Yes, I have something for you," Maureen said, reaching into her pocket. "You said credit was okay."

"No problem. Let me just phone this in."

As the nursery manager took a few steps toward the edge of the backyard to use her cellular phone, Maureen worried about the stack of bills that little plastic rectangle would have to produce, and swallowed. She wondered, for the first time in ages, whether the charge would clear. When the nursery manager got off the phone, the transaction apparently complete, Maureen felt a bit like a shoplifter. *This ocotillo now belongs to me.* The exotic arms of the "burning bush" rose above her from a rough-hewn planter box, each decorated with black barbs arranged in a swirling, candy-cane pattern; it was a beautiful creation from a land with a harsh but practical aesthetic. *I would like to think of myself as being pretty and barbed like this plant, a survivor of three-digit temperatures, rescued from greed by muscled Mexicans in freshly starched uniforms.* The workers brought in more succulents, including one with cone-shaped bursts of saffron petals, a desert equivalent to Maureen's departed birds-of-paradise, and a tiny shrub with pastel turquoise branches as delicate as coral. A succulent garden played more to the sunlight than her subtropical garden ever could; *la petite* rain forest was dark and colorless by comparison.

The workers brought in bags of sand, walking in a line from the truck to the backyard with the bags slung over their shoulders, like Egyptians toiling in some pharaonic project. They took pocketknives from their belts—each one of them had a tool belt—and soon they were ripping the bags open and spreading orange sand and rocks through the backyard, and for a moment longer the patch of ground looked as bleak and barren as Mars.

At the offices of Elysian Systems, Scott Torres was moving the mouse of his computer in subconscious circles, making the white arrow on his screen flutter until he finally clicked and dispatched four words that bounced at the speed of light from his desk to the company mainframe in the basement, and back up to the programmers' cubicles he could see through the glass and half-open shades of his office. As expected, Charlotte Harris-Hayasaki broke into a smile at the sight of the box that popped up in the lower right-hand corner of her screen, asking, *Wanna have lunch???—Robustus.* "Robustus" and variations thereof (Robustus65, Scotus Robustus) was his screen name on several email and message systems, a Latin nod to his roots in "robust" programming. Charlotte turned away from her screen and looked straight at him through the glass and gave him a groupie-girl smile and a thumbs-up. He discreetly raised his own thumb, then sent her another IM that read, *Meet you outside at 1 p.m.* This would be his third lunch with Charlotte Harris-Hayasaki in the past month, each beginning with a furtive meeting in the parking lot, because even though programmers were the employees least likely to spend time imagining the secret lives of coworkers, they could not fail to notice the evolving "special friendship" between the boss and his female underling. Scott did not find the round, fashion-challenged Charlotte attractive in any sinful way; he was drawn instead to her callow programmer enthusiasm, her youthful appetite for his old dot-com stories. During her interview she had made it known that she was aware of his small contribution to the early history of the dot-com boom: he was mentioned in the short Wikipedia entry on Sasha "the Big Man" Avakian, and in one or two others. In the last few weeks Scott had taken to plugging his name in several search engines, feeling narcissistic as he did so, and had been somewhat dismayed that the Scott

Torres Ford dealership of Salinas, California, generated twenty search hits for every one about Scott Torres the programmer.

Scott had been raised not to worry about leaving a mark on the world. Both his mother and father limited their ambitions to their private universe, to the steaks whose fat sizzled and crackled over charcoal briquettes, a beagle panting on a concrete patio, and the unassailable moral rewards of family safety and health. Escape from work in the strawberry and cabbage fields of California, or from the horizonless hamlets of Maine to the modest affluence of South Whittier, was accomplishment enough. Scott followed this path and was thus content to dedicate himself to solving the mathematical and logical challenges that make computers do magic, and took his greatest pleasures in the wide-eyed astonishment that greeted his creations when they came to life. Back in the day, the Big Man responded to Scott's programming feats with manic bursts of verbal excess that usually began with "This is going to change everything!" Scott's professional success changed his image of himself, as did a mysterious shift in the culture at large, which had caused Scott to lose his geekiness, though now he seemed to be getting it back again.

Two and a half hours after surreptitiously meeting in the parking lot, Scott was sitting opposite Charlotte at the Islands Restaurant in Irvine, working on his second mango margarita and winding up his long story about the development of MindWare's "virtual university" software, having taken special delight in describing the poor skills of the first group of hackers who tried to defeat Scott's security and cheat on a medieval history test. He looked down at his watch and noticed the time. "Holy shit, it's almost four." They rushed back to the office, with Scott registering only briefly the way Charlotte squeezed his hand for two seconds when they said goodbye in the parking lot, Charlotte taking the elevator while Scott took the stairs. *How incredibly lame of me*, Scott thought as he walked into the office. *Like they're not going to notice we were gone for three hours.*

He stayed late at the office for appearance's sake, and it was nearly sunset as he meandered out of the building. By the time he reached home, the long summer dusk was almost over, the last glowing embers of daylight had dropped below the silver blue Pacific, and in the half light he didn't notice the clods of dirt in the driveway, the scrapes in the cement left by the second gardening crew as they rolled in the willow

and a bush of desert lavender. When his field of vision passed the sliding glass doors, he failed to focus on the strange silhouettes in the backyard cast by the new flora. The significance of his wife's announcing "Honey, they put in the new garden today" escaped him as he worked to corral his two boys into the bathroom for their nightly shower, and for a half hour of reading in their bedroom. What a relief to have these familial tasks to throw himself into after an agonizingly slow and pointless day at the office. Here, in these neat and orderly rooms with his sons and his daughter, he was king, provider, and executive rolled into one. Not for the first time Scott thought that the private satisfaction of reading to his sons in this bedroom with the Art Deco solar system floating over his head was a very good exchange for the adulation of the past. When he spotted his daughter walking in the hallway in her pajamas, smiling up at him and raising her arms in a wordless request to be lifted, and when she wrapped her small arms around his neck and tucked her head against his cheek, the sensation that Scott the Geek had miraculously found his place in the world only increased. "I can never be mad at you, Samantha, even if you wake up ten times at night." Fatherhood was a medal and a slap every ten minutes: you could be a persecuted pygmy holding back a scream of surrender at one moment, and then an immortal hero and prince the next. Scott forgot about the snide executives and the money evaporating from his bank account, and tucked his children into bed and kissed them good night.

9

Go away, go away. In his sleep, Scott flailed at the loose pillow tickling his nose, but in his dream he was pushing Charlotte Harris-Hayasaki away. Her hands were cold and sweaty, they were gripping at his cheeks and eyelids, and he was afraid Maureen would see Charlotte holding him and get the wrong idea, and that a horrible argument would ensue. He was sitting at his desk at work, in a cluttered office lined with stacks of boxes, and Charlotte was standing behind him as he tried to type something on his keyboard, and Maureen was in the next room and might walk in any minute. He felt an apocalyptic dread of his wife's power to banish him from family and home, and could hear Maureen breathing in the next room as Charlotte moved her hands down to his chest and began unbuttoning his shirt. He wanted to break Charlotte's grip, but she wouldn't let him go, and finally he turned to grab his young employee by the shoulders and give her a good strong shove, but when he did this he heard a screaming that brought the fuzzy movie running in his head to an abrupt halt and transported him in an instant to his darkened bedroom and the sound of his daughter's voice crying from the baby monitor.

"Wah! Wah! Wah!"

Maureen, a comforter and a pillow thrown over her head, gave a murmur that sounded like the word "yes" but showed no signs of waking up as Scott stood up from the bed and made his way to the nursery. His wife had built up so much sleep debt that she was immune to Samantha's screams, and Scott felt a strange combination of sympathy for her and annoyance at the general situation as he walked through the darkened hallways. When they went to bed there was always the hope that this night would be different from the others over the past fifteen months, that this might be the night when their youngest progeny released her grip on their biological clocks, bringing forth a morning in which the California sunlight returned to its normal soothing hues, losing the stark whiteness that had assaulted their eyes since Samantha's birth. But no, here Scott was again, awake at 2:06 a.m., according to his watch—*I fell asleep with my watch on, Jesus.* He noticed that he was still wearing his button-down shirt from the workday, though he had managed to get his pajama bottoms on. He reached the nursery and found his daughter, as usual, standing up in her crib with her favorite yellow blanket, looking disoriented and confused, her rust-colored locks in a sweaty disorder. *Come to me, my little girl, while I get you your milk. One day soon you'll be a big girl and this torture will stop.*

While Scott tended to their daughter, waiting in the kitchen for the microwave to warm her milk, Maureen slipped in and out of various episodic dreams, and then into the longest one, whose images would linger in her consciousness after she woke up. Mexican day laborers were tramping about her home, eating her food, sitting on the tables, playing with Samantha. A man with stringy and shiny hair that resembled black hay was trying to take apart her coffee table with the point of his machete, using it like a screwdriver. *What are you doing here? Please leave. Please.* Dirt encrusted their faces and their fingernails, and they bumped into one another and into the furniture as they walked about the house. They were leaving small piles of red sand on the living room floor and she pleaded with them again, but they answered her in Spanish, or rather in a jumble of words that resembled Spanish: *la cosa mosa; la llaga es una plaga; waga, waga, waga.* After she woke up, Maureen would think, *I've never dreamed in Spanish before.* The men were filling their mouths with salad greens and big gulps from plastic milk jugs, and she started to look for Scott because maybe he could get

them to leave, but she couldn't find him. She walked into the kitchen, where someone had turned on a garden hose that was spraying water into the air, causing her to run back into another room lined with closet doors, which she opened, looking for her husband in between the brooms and boxes until Samantha's cries sounded in her dream and she opened her eyes.

The baby monitor was flashing red lights as it broadcast Samantha's wailing. The clock on her nightstand said 4:29 a.m. and Scott was snoring almost as loud as Samantha was crying. *Thank you, Scott. It would be nice if my husband could get up at one of these middle-of-the-night feedings and tend to the baby and allow me to get a full night's sleep.* When she reached the nursery and saw the empty bottle on the floor she realized that he must have been up earlier. *I slept through the baby crying again.* It was always a somewhat disturbing realization, that you could sleep through the ambulance-siren blasts of a baby girl.

While Maureen carried Samantha and tried to soothe her back to sleep with a lullaby, "turban man" and "binocular lady" were running inside Scott's final dream. He was trying to force his software creations to take a seat in the back of his car, but they were busy running through the fences and climbing the play structure in his backyard, and now Samantha was running after turban man. In his dream Scott began to laugh at their antics, and the laughter shook him out of the dream and into the light of day. "Whoa, that was wild," Scott said out loud, but there was no one to hear him: Maureen was in the shower and the first light of morning was squeezing through the blinds. As he rose to get dressed, something caught his eye, a series of odd shapes squeezing through the narrow spaces between the blinds: a collection of green tubes and triangles, and some sort of brown cloud. What could it be?

He pulled open the blinds to a strange apparition that, for a few moments, seemed to be a continuation of one of the dreams he had been having. The succulent garden, lit from behind by the first rays of morning light, pulsated in turquoise. The ocotillo stood proud just a few yards from his window, the exotic barbs of its branches leaving Scott with a nagging sense of dislocation, as if he were standing in a place that was not his bedroom, looking through the window into a backyard that belonged to someone else. He searched his bedroom for the familiar visual clues that indicated this was indeed the same room he had gone

to sleep in—the bed with its wooden frame, the faux-vintage windup clock, which actually ran on batteries—then looked back at the succulent garden again. He gawked at the plants a few seconds longer until the phrase his wife had uttered the night before suddenly popped into his head and put everything into its proper place: yes, she had said something about the garden, hadn't she?

"Hey," he said to Maureen a minute or so later, as she stepped back into the bedroom, dressed and with a towel wrapped around her head. "We've got a new garden."

"Pretty awesome, isn't it?" Maureen said with a muted cheerfulness that masked her anxiety.

"Uh, yeah. But it's huge."

"I think there's twenty or so different species of plants."

"Really?"

"Uh-huh."

"And how did you get all that stuff in here?"

"The landscapers did it."

"Landscapers?"

"From the nursery."

"Didn't that cost a lot of money?"

"Yeah, it cost a bit, but we talked about that," Maureen said, draping the towel over the doorknob, leaving it for Araceli to pick up later.

"We did?"

"Yes."

Maureen casually walked toward the door. "But we won't have to work on it anymore," she said. "In the long run we'll save money . . . I have to check on the baby."

She left Scott alone in the room with this information, and after a few moments he decided to file it away in the archive of unexpected and unexplainable things that happen to a guy when he gets married: like coming home to discover your new wife has tossed out your old clothes; or suffering her jealousy when, after ten years of marriage, the name of an old girlfriend of yours comes up; or her suddenly insisting one day that you no longer eat red meat, and then a week later coming home to find she has prepared you steak fajitas for dinner. *So now we have a desert in our backyard. First she wanted a jungle, now she wants a desert. "In the long run we'll save money," she says. Maybe we should dig*

*up the front lawn and make that like the Mojave too. It must have taken
a helluva lot of work to get that in here. How much could it cost?* He
should probably ask her, but was certain the question would provoke
another argument. And it did look pretty, in a gnarly and harsh sort of
way, once you got used to it.

The boys were in the pool and Maureen sat in a chair playing
lifeguard, while at the same time making sure Samantha didn't stray
into the desert garden. As she rubbed sunscreen on the back of the
baby's neck, she studied the barrel cactus and told herself not to worry
so much about it, even though the ankle-high fence that surrounded
it wasn't a barrier that could keep Samantha away. Already the boys
had tossed a ball into the garden, though they were sufficiently put off
by the menacing barbs of the plants not to wander inside. Overall, she
was pleased with herself for having removed that dying tropical blight
from her home and bringing this property back in concert with the
desert.

"Araceli, we have a new garden," Maureen said with a smile to her
employee. "*¿Te gusta?*"

Araceli placed a large jug of *agua de limón* on the squat folding tray
next to Maureen and used the glass stirring rod to make the cloud of
lemon pulp inside swirl, and then finally looked up at the garden.

Well, there was certainly something exotic about this patch of desert her *jefa* had purchased. Standing this close to it, Araceli got the
sense of being transported to a place of mystery and timelessness even
as the boys screamed from the pool a few yards away, and as Maureen
sat in her folding chair, sunscreen glistening from her bare legs, a floppy
canvas hat protecting her against the sun. But no, Araceli couldn't say
she liked it. There was a certain minimalism to this new garden with its
red volcanic rocks and expanses of scarlet and mustard-colored sand
filling the space between the plants—Araceli's aesthetic, however, had
always leaned toward the ornate and complex. She remembered her startling first impression of the tropical garden on the day she interviewed
for this job at the Torres-Thompson household: she had emerged from
the house on a hot day like this one to encounter a jungle of defiant wet-
ness fighting back against daylight. Later she had studied the garden for

hundreds of hours while working in the kitchen, laundry, and master bedroom, and from the window of her *casita* in the back. She liked the way the leaves of the elephant plant caught the slightest breeze, the way the calla lilies changed their shape from early morning to noon, and the movement of the false stream. This new desert garden was a static construction, while the tropical garden was a work of performance art, with Pepe as its star, stepping inside its verdant stage to send streams of water that cascaded over the tops of the plants, catching the sun's rays and making rainbows.

"Well, what do you think?" Maureen insisted. "You don't like it. I can sense you don't like it."

What could Araceli say? She really didn't possess the words in English to communicate what the tropical garden and this new desert garden made her feel. How did you say in English that something was too still, that you preferred plants that you could feel breathing around you?

"*Me gustaba más como era antes,*" she said in Spanish, and then in English, "I like it before . . . But this is very pretty too, *señora*. Very pretty, *muy bonito*. Very different." Empty words, Araceli thought, but they seemed to be what Maureen wanted to hear.

"Yes, it is very *bonito*, isn't it?" Maureen said with satisfaction. "And *muy diferente* too."

That morning at the headquarters of Elysian Systems, Scott invited his staff out to lunch to celebrate shipping the final version of the CATSS "accountability" program to the government. The corporate guys on the fourth floor had suggested he do these sorts of things, because even a bunch of loner programmers expected the occasional perk. "You take them to a nice place, you blow off half a day of work, and you pick up the tab," said the executive, as Scott tried not to frown at the paperweight on the executive's teak desk awarded for "outstanding leadership" by a lumber trade group in the Pacific Northwest. "Then you expense it. You go back to the office and everyone works just a little harder the next few days."

They gathered in the nearest chain restaurant that served decent mojitos and margaritas and plodded through two hours talking about

sports, video games, celebrities, and other banalities. His programmers were five men and two women, the oldest about five years younger than him. They had bounced around various software companies in search of the place that offered the most pay with the least work expected and they all considered the drudgery of programming at Elysian Systems to be a necessary compromise with their free-spirited, late-hacker ethos. *That's why I hired them: because I saw a little bit of myself in each of them. I wanted to surround myself with me.* You could get them going if you talked about open sourcing, and the fences big companies were putting around their code. "There's all kinds of languages out there, but they're not accessible," said Jeremy Zaragoza, who was a thin twenty-eight-year-old of indeterminate ethnicity. "So your average kid in suburbia can't just open a machine and start playing with the code." Scott had grown tired of these conversations—he'd been listening to them, in one form or another, for two decades—and he said nothing, and eventually their talk exhausted itself, until their silent gathering was overwhelmed by the sounds of a lacrosse game on the cable television in the bar, as the programmers quietly fingered scattered french fries and rattled glasses of iced tea while the play-by-play man screamed, "Spinning! Shooting! Score!"

"Hey, my nine-year-old said something really funny the other day," Mary Dickerson said suddenly, startling everyone to attention. She was a frumpy, raspy-voiced woman and the underling closest in age to her boss.

"And what was that?" said Scott, who was the only other person at the table with children.

"Well, I guess he's been listening to me and his dad talk a lot, because he asked me, 'Mommy, which is worse: a fool, or an idiot?'"

"Good question!"

"I've often wondered that myself!"

"So what did you tell him?"

"'Well, Patrick,' I said, 'a fool is someone who is aware that they're stupid, sort of, and doesn't care. You know, like a court jester. At least that's how I understand the word "fool." And an idiot is someone with, how should I say, a medical condition. They just can't help being stupid. Which one is worse is, I guess, in the eye of the beholder.'"

"Good answer!"

"We aren't allowed to use the word 'stupid' in my household," Scott said, rolling his eyes.

"So what did your little boy say?"

"He said he thought it was worse to be an idiot. And then he went back to playing his Game Boy."

Moments later, the check arrived, setting off a round of programmer stretches, sighs, and yawns. By the time the waitress returned with Scott's credit card in a leather holder, Mary Dickerson was already on her feet and ready to leave.

"I'm sorry, but the system is rejecting this card," the waitress said with a no-nonsense directness that contrasted markedly with her cheeriness when she first took their order more than two hours earlier. She was a tall black woman in her forties, her safari uniform covered midway through her shift with salsa and coffee stains: her suddenly stern demeanor caused the procession of programmers toward the front door to stop.

"What's going on, Scott?" Mary Dickerson said, more as a rebuke than a question.

"Are you sure?" Scott asked the waitress.

"Yes, honey. I am. Shall we try another one?"

Scott opened his wallet, quickly surveyed the various plastic representations of creditworthiness and family photographs contained therein, and concluded that rather than taking a chance on a second card, the best course of action would be to make a run to the nearest automated teller machine. He looked at his now-standing employees, who were all staring at him as one does a second-rate substitute teacher in junior high school, and remembered that there was a dispenser of cash about three or four hundred yards away, at the other end of the asphalt lake upon which this restaurant, an armada of automobiles, and a dozen commercial establishments floated. Scott would hop into his car and drive to the machine and the round trip would take less than two minutes. "I'll be right back," he said to the waitress.

"What?"

"Just gotta get some cash." He could feel the discomfort of his employees' forced gathering propelling them toward the door. "Sit down. Don't leave. Please." Mary Dickerson glared at him with her mouth agape as he rushed out the door.

When he returned, six minutes and forty-five seconds later according to the timer function on his watch, a Mexican busboy was wiping off the empty table, whistling the melody of a reggaeton song, and all of Scott's employees were gone except for Charlotte Harris-Hayasaki, who greeted him by the cash register with a sympathetic grin.

"We all just paid it, split it eight ways," she said. "Everyone really wanted to go. So I paid your share."

Which am I now? Scott wondered. *A fool or an idiot?*

Back at the office, it took sixty seconds at his computer terminal for Scott to uncover his wife's latest credit-card betrayal. At the top of his online statement there was a charge from a company called Desert Landscaping for an astonishing four-figure amount, as much as he would have paid Pepe the gardener for two years of work, if not more. The cactus garden, he could now see, was another obnoxious vanity foisted upon him by his wife, equivalent to three months of their inflated, adjustable-rate mortgage payments, which were the chief obstacle to Scott getting their finances back into the black again, along with the several thousand dollars he spent on private school for his two sons every month. In fact, thanks to his spendthrift wife, they were going to have to struggle to round up the cash to pay for the boys' "facilities and activities" fee at the start of the next semester. He squeezed his face in a half wince as he scrolled through the page in search of the interest rate he would pay on said credit card. *Twenty-six-point-four percent, compounded!* There were formulas taught in finance classes that calculated how quickly the "force of interest" could destroy a family with the slow but powerful engine of exponential calculus. Now he scrambled to grab a memo pad, and scratched out a worst-case scenario.

$$x = \$9,250\left(1 + \frac{.264}{12}\right)^{12 \times 3}$$

The result was a five-figure catastrophe: he would be a servant to that borrowed money for the foreseeable future. Its preposterous largeness made him feel bullied and violated, as if his wife had grabbed him

by the shirt collar and tossed him into a locked room whose walls were plastered with receipts, bills of sale, service contracts, and warranties, each a mocking reminder of her relentless and happy assault on their disposable income. His three kids were trapped in that room with him too, prisoners to the debt as much as he was. Scott stood up from his chair and grabbed at the air around his temples, and began pacing in his claustrophobic work space, fighting the desire to kick at his chair, or pick up everything on his desk and hurl it against the glass. Finally he flung a pencil at his computer screen with the violent windup of a rioter throwing a rock at a liquor store; the pencil snapped in two but failed to do any damage to the screen itself. "Fuck!" He looked out through the glass and noticed that Jeremy Zaragoza, Mary Dickerson, Charlotte, and all his other employees were staring at him with expressions that combined various degrees of glee, concern, and puzzlement. *Yes, here I am in my cage, the boss who lives at the mercy of his wife's weaknesses and wants.* Soon he would be wandering away from his post as corporate laughingstock, to spend a day searching for neighborhoods with affordable homes and half-decent public schools.

When Araceli cooked and cleaned, she daydreamed, and when she daydreamed, her train of thought often ended at the Instituto Nacional de Bellas Artes, just off the Periférico Highway in the western part of Mexico City. She had opened her eyes in the morning remembering Felipe, and how he painted dragons, and thought that at the National School of Fine Arts painting dragons would have invited contempt and ridicule. Only a narrow strip of park, with jacaranda trees and walkways where dogs sniffed and pulled at leashes, separated Araceli's temple of artistic knowledge from the boorish city that surrounded it, buses and microbuses congregating nearby and nudging against one another like cattle in a slaughterhouse pen. At the Instituto Nacional de Bellas Artes all the first-year students were too somber of disposition to paint or draw anything but abstract representations of their inner demons, or starkly detailed studies of the overcrowded, exhausted city. *That was my problem: I was too serious.* If she had contented herself with painting dragons and fairies for her nieces and nephews, Araceli concluded, she wouldn't be the miserable migrant she was now. Those first,

few light days of art school she would walk into the main lobby and study the board announcing various exhibitions and gallery openings, watch the students march back and forth in their creative torment across the patios, holding brushes and portfolios, and feel she was standing at the center of the artistic universe—or considerably closer, at least, than she had been at her home in Nezahualcóyotl.

Araceli felt especially attuned to the visual world then, and as she crossed the sooty metropolis her eye was constantly searching for compositions. On the Metro she studied the tangle of wires between the tracks, the contorted faces of passengers squeezing through doors, and the rivers of scampering feet that flowed up and down the wide stairways linking one Metro line to another, and the improvised geometry of the underground passageways that intersected at odd angles. One of her instructors had looked at these first-year sketches and pronounced, "You will make a first-rate cartoonist," and even Araceli knew that was a slight. Then her classmate Rafaela Bolaño told her she too had been declared a "cartoonist," and it became their running joke. "We are starting a new movement, Rafaela, you and I. We are the Visceral Cartoonists!"

In the end Araceli was done in not by the snobby teachers, but by the long journey across the city from home to school and back again, east to west to east, and by the lists of required materials submitted at the beginning of each term. At the art supply store the clerk gave a satirical grin as he laid the required oils on the counter before her, each an import from England: quinacridone red, raw umber, terra rosa, titanium white, 150 pesos a tube. And then the brushes whose supple bristles suggested the hides of large mammals migrating across the Mongolian steppes; the collection of flesh-toned pastels from Germany, the entire human spectrum in a pine box; and finally the textbook tomes with prices as flashy and exorbitant as their glossy pages of illustrations. "They come from Spain, so it's all in euros, which is really bad for us Indians here in Mexico," the clerk said. Beyond the cost of these accoutrements, there was the simple question of having enough money to buy a *torta* for lunch, and the exhaustion that overcame her after the final, hour-long journey home on the Metro and on the bus as it inched forward the last three miles along the main drag of Nezahualcóyotl with its littered sidewalks, the multitudes of factory workers fighting

the gridlock on Ignacio Zaragoza Boulevard, pushing against the domestics and the peddlers of pirated CDs. She would rise up before dawn to finish assignments she'd been too tired to complete the night before. "Araceli, why are you killing yourself like this?" her mother said one morning, her words heavy with a sense of futility and absurdity. "¿Para qué?" The decision to go to art school was, for her mother, a superfluous act of filial betrayal, because daughters, unlike shiftless boys, were expected to place family first. A wayward daughter counted as much as six wayward sons on the scale of neighborhood shame. When Araceli gave up art school after a year and started working, handing over half of her earnings to pay for her baby brother's future college education, her parents stopped assaulting her with their prolonged silences.

Probably Felipe had an artist's soul and had also been forced to surrender his ambitions. "You look smart, that's why I asked you to dance," he'd said. Felipe, she sensed, had long ago made the accommodation Araceli still struggled to live with; he could make art without feeling the sense of injustice that ate away at Araceli whenever she thought about her mother and the Escuela Nacional de Bellas Artes.

In the late afternoon, when Araceli was finishing cooking dinner and was getting ready to set the table, she noticed that she had absentmindedly arranged Maureen's silver forks, knives, and spoons into patterns on the kitchen counter while polishing them earlier in the day: an asterisk, a series of overlapping triangles, an arrow. Araceli imagined, for a moment, a sculpture that would make an ironic statement about the fine curlicue designs on their handles: she imagined taking a blowtorch and welding forks, knives, and spoons into tangled sculptures of machetes and plows. *That would be fun, but expensive.* She was rubbing a spot on the last spoon that had somehow escaped her cleaning when she heard the front door slam, hard enough to provoke a faint rattle of the dishes in the cupboard. *What was that? One of the boys again?*

After a minute or so Araceli began to hear raised voices, *el señor* and *la señora* yelling at each other. The usual back-and-forth barking and pleading, their voices pushing through the closed door as an irritating and genderless vibration. She considered the basil remedy again, but then thought better of it: their fighting was part of a natural rhythm, a kind of release; they would fight and a day or two later Araceli would

see Scott rubbing his wife's back, or Maureen clasping his hand as they watched their children play in the backyard. After observing the Torres-Thompsons for several years she could begin to see their arguments as a kind of marriage fertilizer: they were ugly, one recoiled before their nasty smell, but they appeared to be necessary. She listened as the shouting continued, rising in volume so that she could begin to make out clear phrases: "Because you have to be more responsible!" "Don't humiliate me," and finally a laughing shout of "Pepe? Pepe?" Well, Araceli's curiosity was piqued now, she had to see what was going on, so she opened the door to the living room but pushed it too hard, bringing forth a moment of unintended theatricality in which the yelling instantly stopped and both Scott and Maureen turned to face her, their foreheads and cheeks burning with an identical angry hue. No, Araceli hadn't intended to do that; she wanted to hear more clearly what they were saying, not to stop the fight altogether. One glance at her *jefe* and *jefa* told her that this argument was significantly more serious than any that had come before, that the words passed between them were dangerously close to finding a physical expression in the exercise of limbs and muscles. Scott was standing in the center of the living room with his arms tensed at his sides, and as he turned to look at Araceli she saw a man with an expression she barely recognized: here was a man who felt his power slipping from him, who strained to open his eyes wide to take in the room and the woman before him, as if he had never really seen her before this moment. A few feet away, Maureen sat on the couch, before the coffee table and its plane of blown glass, legs crossed and arms folded, in that tenuous state of mind that exists between being amused and being afraid. Araceli sensed she was trying very hard to convince herself that her husband's yelling was nothing more dangerous than the grumbling of an eight-year-old.

Araceli raised her eyebrows and prepared to turn away, but then something happened that had never happened before: they resumed their argument, without caring that Araceli was still in the room. Scott raised his finger and declared, "Don't you dare, don't you dare say another fucking thing." *I didn't think he could do that. He screams while I watch.* Maureen rose to her feet and began to walk toward Scott, causing Araceli to immediately turn around and close the door with the same speed and sense of repulsion that one uses to change the

television channel upon encountering a gory, tasteless scene from a horror movie.

Inside the kitchen Araceli removed her apron: she would leave the dinner ready, in covered bowls on the marble counter, and then leave the kitchen and seek shelter in her room for the time being. When men raised their voices in imitation of carnivorous mammals, smart women made for the exits; that's how it was in her home, in many other homes, in too many homes to count in the stacked cubes of the Nezahualcóyotl neighborhood where women conspired during the day to undo the tangles men made with their words at night. *Sometimes you just have to run away. You have to close the window, close the door, and seal off your ears from the sounds people make when the dogs inside them decide to come out and snarl.* Araceli made a conscious effort not to listen to the back-and-forth coming from behind the pine door, not to hear what words were being said as she finished putting clear plastic wrap over the bowls filled with pasta and fish sticks.

Araceli was reaching for the back door when she heard a half-grunted "Be quiet!" followed by an unmistakably female scream and a high-pitched crash that sounded like fifty porcelain plates striking the floor and shattering all at once. Instinctively she ran back across the kitchen, pushed open the swinging door, and found Maureen on the floor, half sitting and half prone upon the ruins of the coffee table, raising her arms in an attempt to steady herself without getting cut on the pool of shattered glass around her. She looked to Araceli like a woman who had been dropped from an airplane, or who had fallen from a cloud, landing on a spot of the earth she did not recognize, and who was surprised to see she had survived. Scott stood above her, raising his hands to his temples as he looked down at his wife.

"Oh, my God, I didn't mean it, I didn't mean it," he said, and he reached out to help her.

"Get away from me!" Maureen shouted, and he instantly stepped back. "Araceli, help me. Please."

The Mexican woman froze. *What have they done to each other, these people?* Araceli felt the need to restore order and understood that the violence in this room might spin into something unspeakable were it not for her presence. *Today I am the civilized one and they are the savages. They have taken the living room I have worked so hard to give the*

sparkle of a museum and they have transformed it into a wrestling ring. Lucha libre. *If I hadn't come in they would be grabbing the chairs from the dining room and throwing them at each other.* Stepping gingerly around the ruins of the table she had cleaned that morning, and too many other mornings to count, with blue ammonia spray, Araceli reached out and took the hand of her *jefa* and helped her to her feet.

BOOK TWO

Fourth of July

"You know, Bigger, I've long wanted to go
into these houses . . . and just *see* how your
people live."

—Richard Wright, *Native Son*

10

Waaaaaaaaaa!

The alarm startled Araceli awake at the lazy hour of 7:30 a.m., the summer sun already blasting through the curtains. On most mornings she would have been long awake, but the memory of the powerful matriarch of the mansion momentarily helpless on the floor had kept her from sleeping well. During the summer the Torres-Thompson household got a later start to the day and Araceli could often spend some time in the morning with the hosts of the Univision morning show as she got dressed, half listening to their interviews with diet experts, the celebrity gossip, the reports on the latest drug murders in Guerrero and Nuevo Laredo, the videos of the dead being pulled from overturned buses, and the like. Now she had witnessed a kind of news event in this home, too close and too raw to be entertainment. The crash and scream had invaded her dreams, causing her to sleep right up to the deadline announced by her digital clock. By now, *el señor* Scott would have made himself some toast and be out the door—on this morning, perhaps more than any other, he would have wanted to avoid contact with his servant. Araceli took her time getting dressed and put on her white *filipina*, dreading the stony mood that awaited as soon as she entered the

main home; a day of silences from Maureen, followed by the tense sharing of the domestic space in the evening when Scott returned from work. When a man tosses his wife to the ground, there can be no easy forgiveness.

With some trepidation Araceli opened the door to the kitchen, and then the door from the kitchen to the living room. No one, nothing, all quiet, as orderly as she had left it the night before, when she swept up the glass and steel ruins of the coffee table and collected them in two boxes she placed next to the plastic trash barrels outside. Only the conspicuously empty space in the living room hinted at what had happened the night before. Perhaps she should examine the floor for any traces of glass, lest the baby Samantha pick one up and place it in her mouth. Leaning down, Araceli examined the ocher surface of the Saltillo tile floors and found two slivers, each smaller than a child's fingernail. She held them in her palm to examine them, meditating not so much on the shards as on the unexpected violence that had produced them. *This house will not return to normal so quickly.* Suddenly Araceli the artist, the Araceli who didn't care, longed for the ordinary. She was the strange one, the *mexicana* they couldn't comprehend, but it would fall to her to bring the Torres-Thompson household back to a calm center by restoring the broken routines: the comfort of served breakfasts, lunches, and dinners, the tonic of a sparkling kitchen and smartly made beds at the end of the day. She tossed the shards into the trash and started breakfast, following the rotation *la señora* had established on a refrigerator calendar. Friday: Cream of Wheat.

Brandon wandered into the kitchen first, at 8:36, followed by his brother a few minutes later. They sat at the kitchen table, eating silently, their spoons hitting the bottom of their bowls with a comforting clank-clank, Brandon reading a thick book with a dragon on the cover as he ate. Araceli wondered how much they knew about their parents' altercation the night before. Probably they heard everything, she thought, and this was almost true: they had retreated to the television room and the comfort of cartoon warfare just as the shouting had reached a peak, but before their father had shoved their mother backward into the coffee table. Brandon had guided his softly weeping younger brother away with a "Hey, Keenan, let's go watch a movie," and the crash and their mother's short scream had been lost behind a closed door of sound-

swallowing Mexican pine, and in the swirling orchestral theme music that accompanied a boy on his animated martial-arts adventures through a world inhabited by dueling tribes of warriors. When Maureen had shown up sometime later to tell them to get ready for bed, they had assumed everything was normal because they were too young to pick up the muted exhaustion in her voice, too unknowing of the cruelties that adults could inflict upon one another to recognize the meaning in the puffy droop in their mother's eyes.

Maureen awoke atop a cushion of comforters on the floor of the nursery, next to her daughter's crib. With its lavender walls, Samantha's incipient doll collection, and the stuffed purple pony in the corner, the nursery was a safe room, its femininity a shield against the masculine harshness outside. He didn't follow her there; he didn't hit her or yell at her with her baby girl by her side. Having failed to injure Maureen with his words, Scott had infected the household with fear and unpredictability and the silencing power of his muscle. He unleashed a monster, to ravage her body and violate unspoken codes, to inflict the injuries his words could not. At first the argument about Maureen's spending on the desert garden had played out as the mirror image of the argument about Scott's neglect of *la petite* rain forest. In this case it was Scott who was the aggrieved party, having been humiliated before his employees, but somehow Maureen had wrested the upper hand, shifting the discussion to Scott's failings as husband and parent, and their roots in his emotional distance. She had taken the argument back to South Whittier, to that sad little two-story home of thin drywall and crabgrass lawns, with the box rooms that had mirrors along the walls to create the illusion of space. It had been her misfortune to visit this property as their courtship reached its climax, to see the Torres family home in all its faded, lower-middle-class glory, and last night she had allowed herself to blurt out certain truths he refused to see, long-held but never-spoken observations that focused on that brittle woman whose admonitions were the font of her husband's ambition and also much of his self-doubt. It occurred to Maureen now, in the morning, that bringing her late mother-in-law to the conversation was not a good idea: the rage she provoked by doing so was entirely predictable, but not what

happened next. He had taken two purposeful and irrational steps toward her, and attacked her with the muscles of his forearms and hands, sending her sprawling backward across the room and into the table. There was the moment of stunned helplessness as she lost her balance and the table collapsed and shattered underneath her, followed, seconds later, by a moment of clarity, the sudden understanding of a long-suppressed fear.

I always expected him to do this.

Maybe from the first time they dated she sensed that the nervous, faded-cotton exterior of Scott Torres concealed a roiling core. That was the attraction to him in the first place, wasn't it? Before she had seen the home in South Whittier, before she had lived with the man, she saw the anguished exertions of an artist searching for perfection, though he possessed only some of the language and social gifts that oozed from painters, actors, and writers. He suffered to bring his creations into the world, and when they did not come he could turn sullen and angry in a disturbingly adolescent kind of way. His daydreams and his projects were his best friends and companions, and often they caused his face to brighten with a mischievous sparkle. There was something charming, she decided, about a man whose brilliance lay in solving problems that could not be easily explained in words. *I will make you* my *project, Scott Torres.* She had taken this shy man and, like a wizardess, had given him at least some charm, and a surplus of family riches. And now he had rewarded her with the same common violence that sent women to shelters. Hours later she could still feel his assault just below her collarbone, and see the two bruises that seemed to float on the surface of her skin like jellyfish.

Fatherhood did this to men. They weren't prepared for it. After the boys were born there were days when Scott glared at the clutter of baby paraphernalia in their home, the spit-up stains scattered on the rugs and their clothing, with the resentful eyes of a prison convict. *What? Did you expect it to be easy? This sagging you feel around your eyes, the ache in your arms, that is called parenthood, and it is no longer the exclusive province of women.* Then came the scattered moments of aggression when his toddlers committed minor sins, when Brandon was a two-year-old just learning the power of felt-tip pens to deface freshly painted walls, or when Keenan tossed a wineglass on the floor, and

Scott blared a too-loud "No!" When she was halfway into carrying Samantha, he punched the wall, leaving a crater for a week before fixing it, never bothering to explain what had set him off. *It's true what my mother said. You can think you know someone as intimately as they can be known, you can commune happily with their odors and their idiosyncrasies for years, but then they show you something distasteful, something frightening precisely at the moment when you're too far in to get out.* Maureen's father was old Missouri Irish and the hurtful memory of his living room explosions had led her to adopt her mother's maiden name when she was eighteen. Now the neighbors had likely heard Scott too, they knew that his wife and children were inside cowering. They all knew.

Maureen felt the curtains of an ancient, unerasable shame being drawn across the windows of this bright home. *I have to flee. Again.* When she was eleven Maureen walked out and no one heard the slap of the screen door because her older sister and her mother were in full-throated battle with her father. On that day she ran out in her spring sundress and sandals, jumping down the steps, running to the corner, and then walking when she looked over her shoulder and saw no one was following, past other small houses like hers in that Missouri river town, underneath the impossible pinks of the flowering dogwoods, past the lonely Baptist church and the venerable, abandoned gas station and its gravel bays. Past the fields at the edge of town, with pebbles in her sandals, she walked slowly toward the unfettered horizon that loomed over the stubs of early corn, feeling comfort in the promise of other fields fallow and freshly plowed, and then to the hills where tractors cut plow lines that flowed around the undulating contours of the landscape, until she finally stood alone at the entrance to a solitary farm. Two silos stood guard there, each looking like a man with steel-pipe arms and a tin-roof hat, and she thought how much better it would be to have a father who was as tall and stately and silent. She thought these things until tires rolled on the dirt path behind her, and she turned and saw the police car that would take her home.

Now Maureen would leave and stay gone for a few days, and her absence would teach Scott a lesson. She would leave and decide later whether, and under what conditions, she would come back. But how would she cope on the road with three children, driving on the interstate?

How long could she even control her boys in a claustrophobic hotel room? She envisioned herself with her three children at a nearby hotel suite, the boys pushing each other backward into the fold-out couch, the minibar, in subconscious imitation of their father. Did she really want to be around that boy energy, their unpredictable physicality? A woman alone with two boys and a baby girl would not work. Her mother was in St. Louis, and if Scott was right about the credit cards Maureen wouldn't be able to buy plane tickets to get there. Maureen went over her options during a mostly sleepless night and in the last hour before dawn she knew exactly what she would do: she would raid the emergency cash that the ever-cautious Scott kept in a washroom drawer next to the earthquake kit. And then she would leave with Samantha for a few days, allowing Scott to contemplate her absence and take care of the boys. Araceli would be there to keep the household from falling apart and the boys from going hungry. It was what she had always wanted to do anyway, to take off with Samantha for a few days, for a "girls' vacation."

As she carried a half-asleep Samantha through the house and to the car, she thought, *It's going to be another hot day*. For the moment, however, there would be the chill of early morning, and she tossed a blanket over her daughter. She wanted to be out the door before Scott woke up, to avoid any further, unpleasant confrontations and present him with a fait accompli, but when she entered the garage at 7:45 a.m. she discovered his car was already gone; he was off to work about an hour earlier than usual. This did not surprise her, though it did cause her to pause in her escape plan: if she left now, her two boys would be alone in the house, because Araceli was still in the guesthouse, and not yet at work, separated from Brandon and Keenan by two walls and the five paces or so it took to walk to the kitchen's back door. *Damn it!* To leave now would violate a taboo of motherhood: she would have to carry Samantha back into the house and start her escape all over again. *If I go back in, I might not leave at all, I might lose my nerve*. She opened the garage door to confirm his car was also absent from the driveway, then stepped outside into the morning air. Now the light came on in the kitchen, and from the driveway Maureen could see, through the window, the sleepy rebellion on the face of her Mexican employee as she began the breakfast routine. Araceli was in the house, and the sight

of her was enough to set Maureen on her journey again, to surrender to the momentum and sense of emancipatory purpose that had brought her to the driveway in the first place. She opened the car door and gave a faint sigh as she freed herself of her sleeping daughter's weight and strapped her into the car seat. She had a vague idea of where she was headed: to that spa in the high desert mountains above Joshua Tree she had read about in the arts section of the newspaper, the one said to be relatively cool even in the heat of summer, the one with the babysitters who took care of your child while they pampered you in steam and lavender.

Maureen was outside the gates of the Estates, turning onto the road that skirted through the meadows, when she realized she had forgotten her cell phone. It was too late to go back home, if she did so she might cancel her expedition altogether, so she directed her car to the first gas station and a public phone and called directory assistance, and reached a half-awake clerk at the spa-hotel and made a reservation. Minutes later, mother and daughter were on the unencumbered early morning highway, heading out of the city, sprinting eastward in the face of an incoming bumper-to-bumper, heading toward the dry foothills at the edge of the metropolis.

Inside the game room, beneath the flat-screen and the game console, Scott Torres awoke on the floor at 5:35 a.m. after a night of surprisingly uninterrupted sleep, six hours in which the memory of what had happened in the living room disappeared in the inky cube of a lightless room and he lived in blissful nothingness. Within three seconds of opening his eyes, the series of events of the night before replayed itself in his memory with the stark simplicity of those PowerPoint presentations the executives concocted on the fourth floor at Elysian Systems. He remembered the staccato dialogue of exchanged insults, each slightly more crude than the next, and then his attempt to get away while Maureen followed him around the room, yelling at the back of his shoulders. *That's what happens when you call a woman that word you should never use: they either sulk away or come at you with newfound ferocity.* She had counterattacked with a spiteful commentary about Scott's being unable to see a horizon beyond "the stupid stucco coffin"

in which his mother, separated from his father, had lived her final days
alone; it was a remark so stunningly cold that it had caused the argument
to stop while Scott took in the realization that he had married a woman
who could insult the dead. His thoughts had turned to the many ways
he might impose his will with his hands at precisely the moment Maureen took a step toward him to renew the argument: he pushed her
away with the full, furious strength a man in his early forties could
muster, a half-defensive shove that had sent her sprawling backward
into the coffee table.

For an instant before she lost her balance he felt a strange and
childlike gratification. *At last!* When she hit the table—such a fragile
construction, that piece of Mexican craftwork—and Araceli entered
the room, it all disappeared. Now a hollow numbness occupied the space
between his eyes. Maureen had violated a trust by spending that money,
she had damaged their family, but of course he had lost the moral high
ground when he pushed her. Would she ever forgive him for her fall, see
the full picture of events, and apologize for what she had done and
said? *There is a less than fifty percent probability.* Or would she believe
that her fall and the broken table had absolved her of any need to acknowledge how vicious she had been? *The much more likely outcome.* If
she'd managed to get a full night's sleep she might feel something other
than the outraged sense of victimhood of the night before, when he
feared, for a moment, that she would call the police. By the feminist
calculus that followed these events, he was an abuser, a male inflictor
of bodily harm, and therefore would be permanently expelled from the
garden of family love, into the purgatory inhabited by the alcoholics, the
goons, and the serial adulterers. Perhaps, after the erasures a few hours
of sleep could bring, Maureen would see the crash and fall for what
they really were: an accident, an act of mutual stupidity and clumsi-
ness, like a pratfall in a comedy skit. *This is what happens,* he would tell
her, *when two middle-aged people push their sleep-deprived bodies to
raise small children, a task we should leave for twentysomething decath-
letes, ballerinas, and other spry and limber people.*

Scott would tell her these things in due time, but after just a few
minutes awake, he had decided that for the moment a full retreat was
in order, an escape from his wife's sense of entitlement, from her new
fascination with rare desert flora, which appeared to have replaced

earlier fascinations with rustic Italian furniture and abstract California art. Let her figure it out on her own: or rather, with Araceli, who did the bulk of the work, who kept the house livable and the children fed and gave Maureen time to dream up schemes that would empty their bank accounts—now, as many times before, he thought of Araceli as a kind of subtraction from his wife. In Maine's "Down East," where his mother was from, and in the unknown Mexican places his father had lived, they understood about respect and responsibility. He was still the son of scrappers and survivors.

I have to get the hell out of here. It was what he told himself those last days at MindWare, when he longed to work with adults again. Living with Maureen was looking like the final act at his roller-coaster start-up, when the Big Man spent an extravagance on five-star hotels, dinners at restaurants on the Strip, and a thousand dollars in golf lessons in a quixotic campaign to seduce the venture capitalists, raise cash, and fend off the board. At some point you had to say, *Stop, it's over.* Suddenly, those old sayings of his Mexican father didn't sound so silly and quaint: *Live cheap and smell sweet. Never hang your hat where you can't reach it.* After grabbing a few clothes, he was out the door and in his car, gliding down toward the ocean with only the red eye of Scorpio watching him.

Such was the domestic discipline in the home on Paseo Linda Bonita that several hours passed before either Araceli or the two boys noticed that Maureen and Scott were gone. Having been conditioned by a half summer's worth of their mother's anti-television, anti-computer exhortations, Brandon and Keenan began their day with appropriately mind-nurturing and solitary activities. It was a quiet, sisterless morning, and through the open summer windows and the screens the house filled with the squeaky *chee-deep chee-deep* of the tree swallows that were acquainting themselves with the ocotillo in the backyard. Samantha's usual prespeech utterances and screams were not there to ring in the ears of her brothers, though the boys were not yet conscious of her absence. The boys did not know that their sister was already halfway to the Sonoran Desert with their mother just as they were finishing their Cream of Wheat with Araceli. Keenan drifted over to the Room of a

Thousand Wonders and began assembling a three-level spacecraft with Danish plastic mini-bricks, while Brandon climbed onto the couch in the living room and lost himself in the fourth volume of a detective-fantasy thriller for "middle readers" that involved teams of elves capable of time-bending magic. So gripping was the escape of the boy-detective protagonist from yet another band of machine-gun-toting criminals, that Brandon failed to notice that the coffee table was missing.

After the usual and easy post-breakfast cleanup in the kitchen, Araceli wandered about the house picking up dirty laundry, starting with the pajamas in the boys' room, and then moving to the nursery. She was preoccupied, once again, with Felipe, because after putting away the saucepan she had used to prepare the Cream of Wheat, she had a sudden premonition that he would call her today—perhaps it was some sort of psychic displacement produced by having witnessed the fight between Scott and Maureen the night before. In the presence of violent disagreement, a germ of happiness might take root. *Hoy el gordito me va a llamar.* Araceli was daydream-dancing with her "little fat man" when she entered the nursery and noticed the comforter on the floor and quickly surmised that Maureen had slept there. A few minutes later the conclusion was confirmed when Araceli entered the master bedroom and found the bed exactly as she had left it yesterday afternoon. Clearly, *el señor* Scott had not slept here either; he had probably bedded down with the big television set, and indeed, on her final stop on the laundry search Araceli found a sleeping bag and pillow tossed on the floor there. Well, of course they didn't make up before going to bed, that was no surprise. Araceli made her way to the laundry room, got the first load of Maureen's clothes into the washer after checking for and failing to see any blood: *It appears they did not kill themselves.* Finally, she circled back to the kitchen, unsurprised that in her wanderings through the house her path did not cross with that of *la señora* Maureen. It was a big house and on many days Maureen wandered in and out, unannounced, quite often.

At 12:15 p.m. the boys came back to the kitchen table for lunch, and it was only after they had devoured the last of the chicken tenders Araceli had prepared that Keenan, who was always slightly more attuned to any change in his surroundings than his older brother, finally asked Araceli casually, "Where's my mom?"

Araceli turned from the sink, where she had a saucepan soaking in lightly soaped water, and faced Keenan.

"¿No está en la casa?"

"No, she's not here."

"That is strange," Araceli said. It occurred to Araceli, for a second, that she should utter something to *disimular*, one of those verbal misdirections that Mexicans are especially good at, a fiction such as, *Oh, now I remember, she went to the market*, that would lift the look of mild concern that had suddenly affixed itself to Keenan's hazel eyes. Instead she said nothing and thought how on any other day Maureen exiting the house unannounced without the two boys for an hour or two or three wouldn't cause her any concern, but after the events of the night before . . . ? Given the swirling cloud of disorder and emotional collapse gathering around this household, anything was possible. One day a crew of men hacking the garden with machetes, the next her *patrones* wrestling in the living room. What next? *Maybe my crazy jefa left the baby with me too and didn't tell me.* In the time it took to scrub the saucepan the idea morphed from preposterous to credible. *The baby is wandering somewhere alone in the house! I have to find the baby!* Araceli bolted from the kitchen, her hands dripping with dishwater, leaving Keenan's unanswered "What's wrong?" in her wake as she moved in big, loping strides to the living room, and to the nursery and through the hallways, into the walk-in closet, calling out, "Samanta! Samanta!" eating the "th" in much the same way the baby herself would in six months' time when she tried, for the first time, to pronounce her own name. Finally, Araceli sprinted out of the house and into the backyard, across the lawn, and toward the cool, still blue plane of the swimming pool. *No, please, no, not here, aquí no, in the name of* Nuestra Señora Purísima, *no.* The baby was not in the pool, nor in the desert garden, nor anywhere else within the confines of 107 Paseo Linda Bonita, because Maureen had taken the baby with her, of course. Araceli could see that the baby was with *la señora* Maureen. There was no need to panic.

Back in the living room, Araceli tried to regain her breath and her sense of composure. She stood at the empty section of tiled floor where the coffee table had once stood and tried to sort out what exactly was happening in this household.

•

After the last of the lunch dishes had been put away, at about the time Araceli had removed the ground turkey from the freezer to begin to defrost for dinner, she began contemplating calling Maureen on her cell phone. This presented a small problem of etiquette. For all her feistiness and independence of spirit, Araceli was still a slave to certain customs and habits, and her undeniably inferior social standing prevented Araceli from immediately picking up the phone and demanding of her *jefa: Where are you and when are you coming back?* That wasn't Araceli's place; she had to come up with a pretext for calling, something related to her professional duties, such as they were. The better part of an hour passed, with Araceli distractedly wiping off counters and tabletops and sweeping floors that were already as spotless and shimmering as they were ever going to be, before she thought of something plausible to say: she would simply ask Maureen if the children would eat Spanish rice for dinner. This would be an exceedingly thin and probably somewhat transparent reason for calling, although *la señora* had mentioned before the onset of summer something about forcing the boys to broaden their palates and working a few vegetables into their diet of processed meats and cheeses. Araceli would now suggest that Latin American staple, asking if she should throw in some peas and carrots. She moved to the refrigerator and the list of "emergency phone numbers" located there, a typed list Maureen had prepared on Scott's computer more than a year earlier, in one of her last acts of domesticity before she went into labor with Samantha. The list had been made for Araceli and for Guadalupe, neither of whom found the need to consult it, and it had not been updated since.

Maureen, cell was at the top of the list and Araceli quickly punched the numbers into the kitchen phone, anticipating her boss's voice on the other end and the calming effect it would have not just on Araceli, but also on the children once Araceli could provide information about their mother's whereabouts and expected hour of return. It was 2:29 p.m., according to the oven clock, and the boys were now ensconced in front of the television set, aware that they had done so without permission for the simple reason that their mother wasn't around to be asked. Araceli listened with her ear on the receiver and began to worry after the fourth

ring, surprised and a bit angry at the sixth and seventh rings. The ringing stopped and the voice mail message began. "Hi, you've reached Maureen Thompson . . ."

Araceli found herself answering, "*Señora*," until she realized it was a recorded voice. She tried again with the same result. *Something strange is going on*, Araceli decided, looking at the clock again. 2:34 p.m. For the first time, Araceli wondered if Maureen would be home by the time *el señor* Scott arrived home from work at 5:45, and Araceli pessimistically concluded that the answer was no. *She leaves me with her two boys all day without telling me. ¡Qué barbaridad!* Up to now, her boss had been the epitome of responsibility and what Mexicans call *empeño*, the putting of effort and thought into one's actions. Maureen was precisely the kind of person hundreds of thousands of Mexicans came to the United States hoping to work for, a smart and civilized employer who never needed to be reminded it was payday, and who with her daily conduct taught you some of the small secrets of North American success, such as the monthly calendar of events posted on the refrigerator and in the boys' bedroom. June 2: *School is out.* June 22: *Keenan's day!* August 17: *Ob-gyn.* August 24: *Brandon's day!* September 5: *School begins!* ☺ Planning, organization, compartmentalization. Respect and awareness for the advance of the clock, the ritual and efficient squeezing of events and chores into each day and hour. These were the hallmarks of daily life with Maureen Thompson.

These thoughts occupied Araceli as she stood in the living room before the picture window, absentmindedly staring at the lawn, which was returning, again, to a state of unevenness and unkemptness, when she heard a faint electronic tone. After much circular wandering through the house, she traced the sound to the backyard and the ocotillo: at the very top of the tallest arm of the desert plant, a mockingbird was imitating the tone emitted by Maureen's cell phone, a series of four marimba notes. A few seconds later Araceli heard the sound repeated, this time clearly coming from the master bedroom, and she rushed back inside. In the half darkness of the late afternoon a light glowed near one of the lamps on the nightstand. Araceli moved to pick up the device, something she never would have imagined herself doing just that morning, because there were certain personal objects in the home she never touched—wallets, jewelry, and loose bills left lying about.

On this day, however, the unexplained absence of her boss caused such objects to begin to lose their radioactivity, and Araceli picked up the phone with the tips of her fingers, like the detectives in those American television dramas, and read the message on the display: 7 MISSED CALLS.

Araceli had left Mexico City just as the cell phone craze had taken off, and had never owned such a device. She did not know that pressing two or three buttons would reveal the identity of the callers, in this case herself (HOME) and SCOTT, who had just phoned five times in the past hour from his office in an attempt to talk to his wife directly.

Scott usually arrived, punctually, at 5:45 p.m., an hour that Araceli knew well because it marked the beginning of the winding-down phase of her workday: *el señor* Scott would come in through the door that led to the garage, and his sons would bother him about playing in the backyard or starting a game of chess, and Samantha might teeter-run to him with her arms raised. This was the signal for Araceli to leave dinner in a handful of covered Pyrex dishes ready to be served, ask Maureen if she needed anything more, and then retire to her room with her own dinner, to return later for the final cleanup. Such were the work routines carved into Araceli's day during four years of service. Rarely were these rhythms broken: the light and weather in the outside world shifted, with dinner served in darkness in the winter, with white sunshine outside in the summer, and once with a rain of ash visible through the windows. Awaiting the arrival of this hour now became Araceli's quiet obsession. She watched the clock on the oven advance past five, and then walked into the living room to check on the Scandinavian timepiece on the dresser to see if it had the same time. The boys were taking care of themselves. After a motherless lunch, they could feel their mother's authority in the home waning further, and they had switched on their handheld video games.

Her putative hour of emancipation came and went without Scott coming through the door. The pasta and *albóndigas* were ready. She'd finished her work for the day. *Where is this man?* At 6:45 p.m. Araceli impulsively walked out the front door, down the path that led through the lawn, to the sidewalk of Paseo Linda Bonita and its silent and peopleless cul-de-sac. She stood with her arms folded and looked down the street, hoping to see *el señor* Scott's car coming around the corner, but

the vista never changed from the blank-page sweep of wide roadway. *He's not coming home either.* No lo puedo creer. *They've abandoned me.* The sun was just beginning its rush toward the daily ocean splashdown and Brandon and Keenan were in the house without a parent in sight. She could hear the air-conditioning turn off suddenly in the home next door, and then in another, leaving a disconcerting silence that soon took on an idiotic, satirical quality, as if she were standing not in a real neighborhood, but rather on a stage set crafted to represent vacant American suburbia. *Why is it that you almost never see anyone out here? What goes on in these luxurious boxes that keeps people inside?* There was no human witness on Paseo Linda Bonita to see Araceli in her moment of distress, no nosy neighbor to take note of the anomaly of a servant in her *filipina* waiting impatiently for her bosses to arrive, gritting her teeth at the darkening street. Araceli began to contemplate various scenarios that might explain this new and strangest turn of events. Perhaps the violent encounter in the living room had been followed by others, with Maureen finally deciding to leave her husband for good. Or maybe she was in the hospital, while Scott had taken flight lest he be arrested. Or he might have killed her and buried her in the backyard. One saw these news reports about American couples bringing the narrative of their relationships to a demented end with kitchen knives and shovels: Araceli had expanded her knowledge of U.S. geography from the maps in Univision stories that showed the places where North American men murdered their pregnant wives and fiancées, places with names like Nebraska, Utah, and New Hampshire.

Araceli would like to leave too, but she could not, thanks to the chain that ran back to the house and those two boys anchoring her to this piece of California real estate. She could not run away, or stray too far, because there were children in the home and to leave them alone would be an abdication of responsibility, even if they had been left in Araceli's care against her will. *¿Qué diría mi querida madre?* Subconsciously, Araceli began to pace the sidewalk, reaching the boundaries of the next property and turning back, because anything might happen to those boys, unsupervised: they might even start a fire. She could not therefore simply continue walking down the hill, and this realization caused her to stamp her foot into the concrete like à child forced back inside for supper.

Araceli was still outside, about twenty-five yards beyond the closed front door, when the phone rang inside the Torres-Thompson home. She did not hear it. Anticipating that the person calling was his mother, Keenan interrupted his game play at the second ring and ran from the living room to the kitchen, stood on his tiptoes, and grabbed the dangling cord of the receiver from its perch five feet off the ground on the kitchen wall on the fourth ring.

"Hello? Mommy?"

"Hi, sweetie."

"Mommy, where are you?"

"I'm just taking a little break."

"A break?"

"Yes, honey. A little vacation."

"Why?"

"Because I'm angry with your father."

"Oh."

The pause that followed lasted long enough for even young Keenan to feel the need to fill it, though he couldn't think of anything to say.

"Mommy loves you," Maureen said finally. She was in a hotel room with musty old Navajo rugs and sage burning on an incense tray, watching her baby girl devour a banana. The squeaky tones of her younger son's voice evoked images of domestic routine: *Araceli must have the situation in hand*, Maureen thought; *she is helping Scott*, and Maureen felt her concerns about the boys and home she had left behind lift quickly. "Mommy's just a little angry with your father."

"When are you coming back?"

"Soon, honey. Soon."

These words comforted Keenan sufficiently that he started thinking about getting back to his game. It had been ages since he'd played it as long as he had today.

"What have you been doing today?"

"We're playing on our Game Boys," he said. "I got to the top of Cookie Mountain. Brandon showed me how to do it. It was really cool."

Maureen winced. *Scott gets home and the first thing he does is let them play those mindless games.*

"Did you eat?"

Keenan looked across the kitchen and noticed the dishes Araceli

had left on the counter. "We're having spaghetti and meatballs," he said. Maureen heard the "we" and assumed it included Scott. Satisfied that her boys were being taken care of by Araceli, and that Scott was hovering nearby, she said goodbye to her son and hung up the phone quickly, the better to avoid any awkward conversations with her husband.

Years of being married and raising children had brought Scott's and Maureen's parental clocks into sync. Thus, a minute or so after Keenan had replaced the phone in its cradle, the phone rang again. Keenan had returned to the living room and turned his Game Boy back on, and now he circled back to the kitchen, picking up the phone on the eighth ring.

"Hello?"

"Hi! Keenan?"

"Dad?"

"Yeah, it's me."

"Where are *you*?" Keenan said. Scott was sufficiently distracted by his surroundings and the circumstances under which he was making the call—he was standing in the patch of grass by the street outside Charlotte Harris-Hayasaki's apartment building—that he failed to notice the subtle verbal clue that perhaps not everything was right in his home.

"I'm taking a little break from being home."

"A vacation?" Keenan asked.

"Yeah, like a vacation."

Keenan was less interested in this conversation than the one he had just had with his mother. Hearing their two voices within minutes of each other had returned to him a sense of normality, and he wanted to get back to his game, and also start eating the spaghetti and meatballs on the counter.

"How's Mommy doing?"

"She says she's really angry at you."

His wife had spent the day filling his sons' ears with soliloquies about what a horrible man he was, the completely predictable sequel to the pratfalls and crashes of the night before.

"I know she's angry at me," Scott said, the words coming out with a sad sense of finality. In an instant, his mood changed. *How dare she try to turn the children against me.* "I'm angry at her too," he said. He imagined his wife hovering nearby, and that she might take the phone away

from Keenan and start to harass him about where he was, so he said his goodbyes quickly, telling his son to listen to what his mother told him to do.

"Okay, Dad," Keenan said, even though his mother wasn't there, because like his father, he was in a hurry to get off the phone too.

11

"I'm scared. Araceli, can you sleep with us?"

Keenan asked this with the comforter pulled up to his chin, in bed after forty-five minutes of crying and confusion Araceli would not soon forget. It seemed to Araceli that getting the boys into their room with their teeth brushed and under the covers, in her best approximation of what their mother would have done, was a Herculean task in itself, and that asking her to throw herself on the floor next to them was asking one thing too many. She needed a moment alone, to step back and think what to do next. The boys had begun to panic an hour or so after dusk, when the windows turned into black planes broadcasting images of parentless rooms. "Where's Mommy?" "Where's Dad?" They had peppered her with these questions and had grown increasingly insistent on receiving some answer other than "I don't know," "Soon," or the Spanish "*Ya mero.*" Araceli told them they had to go to bed, and this had set off a round of silent tears from Brandon, and a strange, high-pitched grunt-growl from Keenan. They were going to bed with neither their mother nor their father in the home, with only the surly Mexican maid in the house, and suddenly they felt as lost as two boys separated from their parents on a busy city street. Brushing their teeth and changing into

pajamas had calmed them to the point that they could wipe the tears from their faces; the nightly routines their mother had inculcated in them became, for a moment, a soothing substitute for her presence.

"Will you sleep with us, please?" Keenan repeated.

Araceli desperately wanted to return to her room, but of course that wasn't possible: if she retired to her *casita* in the back she would be leaving the children alone in the house.

You shouldn't just give in to children. You shouldn't just give them anything they ask for.

In Araceli's family home in Nezahualcóyotl children were obedient, quiet, and nondemanding: girls, especially, were expected to occupy quiet, scrubbed spaces that adults were free to ignore. Her own childhood equivalent to the bedtime routine in the Room of a Thousand Wonders took place in the spare room of tile floors she shared with her sister, floors both sisters had been required to mop from the age of ten onward. At bedtime the only good night was a quick look-in from their mother, a check of their obedience. They feared their mother's disapproval and the idea that they might delay her from that final reward of her workday: the climb to the roof, where pennants of denim and polyester caught the breeze and, in their cool evening stiffness, announced, *En esta casa, yo mando*: In this house, I am love, a river of order and sustenance that flows steady in all seasons.

"I won't sleep here next to you, no," Araceli said. "But I will sleep close. Over here, in the hallway. Okay?"

"In the hallway?"

"Yes. *Aquí.*"

She opened the door to their room and in a few moments she had taken two comforters from one of Maureen's closets and tossed them on the floor, along with a pillow.

"*Aquí voy a dormir. Aquí voy a estar.*"

"Okay."

Araceli, for the first time in her life, bedded down in her *filipina.*

Araceli awoke before dawn with the children asleep, the chorus of morning birds yet to begin outside the windows, and walked through the empty house as if in a trance. There seemed to Araceli a

slight chance that either Scott or Maureen had returned during the night, but each flick of a light switch revealed only a stark tableau of dust-free furniture: the comforter was still taut on the bed in the master bedroom, there were no blankets on the floor to indicate anyone had slept in Scott's game and television room, and the kitchen showed no signs of anyone having been there since Araceli gave the last wipe to the counters as the boys prepared for bed the night before. She circled back to the master bathroom, the space Araceli most strongly associated with Maureen's physical presence, and surveyed the objects as if one of them might tell her when *la señora* would return. *¿Dónde estás, mi jefa?* A paddle brush resting in a wicker basket on the marble slab of the sink drew Araceli's eye. This inelegant piece of black plastic did the daily hard work of Maureen's morning and bedtime grooming, and a thick weave of Maureen's russet hair had built up between the nylon bristles, and for an instant Araceli imagined the strands rising from the brush and taking form, and then Maureen herself emerging magically underneath, calming her children with her motherly exhortations.

There's nothing I can do but wait. It occurred to Araceli, momentarily, that she had been spoiled by life with these people, that she had been conditioned to a crisis-free life, above all by Maureen's relentless attention to daily routines, and the comfort of schedules assiduously kept. Over the last four years the two women had built many wordless understandings between them, so that, among other things, towels and dirty clothes circulated through the house as efficiently as the traffic on the empty streets of the Laguna Rancho Estates, from wet bodies to hampers to washing machines to shelves, touching the hands of both women in their circuit. Disposable diapers moved from plastic packages on store shelves to babies' bottoms to special trash cans with deodorizers, and finally to the master trash cans in the back of the house, only briefly tainting the aroma of a country retreat that emanated from the pine and oak furniture, and from a handful of strategically placed bowls of potpourri and lavender.

Maureen was the center of gravity of this home, and with each hour her unexplained absence became harder to fathom. *Why would she leave, where is she?* If there were an explanation it might be easier to cope, and Araceli decided that she would call Scott and demand one: *What did you do to* la señora? *Did you hurt her?*

It was 8:30 a.m. and the boys were still asleep when Araceli marched to the refrigerator and called the second number on the list: *Scott, cell.* In four years of working for the Torres-Thompson family, Araceli had not once called Scott. This morning she would call him and simply demand to know why she had been left alone with two boys when since the beginning it had been made clear she was not to be a babysitter. After a night of being forced to be a mother and father to two boys, after sleeping on the floor in her clothes, Araceli was beyond politeness or deference. *¿Dónde estás?* she would ask, in the familiar "*tú*" instead of the formal "*usted,*" in violation of ingrained Mexican class conventions, as if she were the boss and he were the employee, though of course the monolingual Scott would never pick up on her sassiness.

The phone rang once and moved to voice mail. She called again, with the same response.

Scott's phone was in Charlotte Harris-Hayasaki's apartment, which was on the second floor and inside one of those signal shadows that bedevil cell-phone engineers. He was sleeping, after staying up late into the night telling Charlotte about his fight with Maureen, and then falling asleep on her couch. By the time he awoke, just before noon, his phone would be dead because in the harried flight from his home he had neglected to pack the charger.

Araceli called a half dozen times in succession, the final attempt coming as Keenan came into the kitchen and demanded, "I'm hungry! I want something to eat!"

The sight of his thin eyebrows squeezed in irritation and the corners of his mouth drooping plaintively set Araceli off. A missing mother, a missing father, children expecting to be fed: it was all too much. *The pots and pans, the salads and the sauces—that is my work. I am the woman who cleans. I am not the mother.*

"I am not your mother!" Araceli shouted, and realized instantly her mistake, because Keenan turned and ran away, screaming, "Mommy! Mommy! Mommy!" His shouts filled the living room and became fainter as he ran deeper into the house. Araceli chased after him, cursing herself and the situation and calling out "Keenan, Keenan" until she found him sitting with his arms wrapped around his knees on the floor of the bathroom, the one he shared with Brandon, with shower curtains de-

picting a coral reef teeming with tropical fish, and decorative rubber jellyfish affixed to the mirror, a tile-lined annex to the Room of a Thousand Wonders. Tears and mucus cascaded over his cheeks and lips and into his mouth. A very faint, motherly impulse to reach down and wipe his tears and clean his nose gathered in Araceli's chest, but she resisted it. Instead, she picked up a bar of amber-colored soap and said, "Keenan, *mira*."

She held the soap delicately between thumb and forefinger and drew lines on the mirror, making quick, sweeping movements to capture and hold his attention, like those clowns in Chapultepec Park who squeezed and stretched balloons into dogs and swords. In less than a minute she had produced a creature on the glass. It floated in the multidimensional space between Keenan and his reflection, ghostly and amber, and he stopped crying the moment he realized what it was.

"A dragon," he said.

"Yes. A dragon," Araceli said, her mouth bursting open into a rare display of happy teeth. "For you, Keenan."

The boy wiped the tears from his face and considered the fanciful animal, which had been rendered in half flight, seemingly ready to pounce.

"That's really tight," he said.

"I'm going to make you pancakes," Araceli said. "Pancakes with bananas. You like that, no? Nice?"

He nodded. After she had coaxed the boy back to the kitchen and served him chocolate milk, after she had prepared the banana pancakes and served them with generous portions of Grade AA authentic Canadian maple syrup, and after the boys had left the kitchen for the entertainments of Saturday morning television, Araceli was once again alone with the telephone list on the refrigerator.

Below Scott's cell phone on the list of emergency numbers there was *Scott, office*, which she called even though it was Saturday. "We are currently closed. Our office hours are . . ." Next was *Mother*, meaning Maureen's mother, a woman with cascading ash-colored hair who had visited this home three times since Araceli began working here, most recently in the days after Samantha was born. She was a reserved

woman whose main form of communication was the lingering, considered stare, and she had rarely spoken more than a few curt words at a time to Araceli. There had been one unguarded moment, though, during the older woman's first visit to this house, when she had encountered Araceli in the kitchen and said, "You're lucky to have this job. You know that, right?" The house on Paseo Linda Bonita was a freshly minted masterpiece then, the virgin furniture was free of child-inflicted scratches, the walls were freshly painted, and *la petite* rain forest still resembled a small, transplanted corner of Brazil. "Working with my daughter and grandchildren, in this amazing house. I hope you appreciate it." The words contained an odd patina of regret and envy: as absurd as it sounded, Maureen's mother resented Araceli for working in this home in daily proximity to her daughter, for the perceived intimacy of their relationship. *I could cook and clean too*, the old woman was saying without saying it, *as good as, if not better than, you, Mexican woman. I could live in the small house in the back and see my grandchildren every day, but of course my daughter won't have me.*

For Araceli to call this *gringa acomplejada* and ask to be rescued was a measure of the desperation of the moment.

Araceli punched in the number. "The area code for this number has changed," said a recorded voice. *¿Cómo?* She tried the number again and heard the same message, then tried it again with the new area code but this time heard three loud tones, ascending in frequency, followed by the message "The number you have reached has been disconnected or is no longer in use . . ."

¡Caramba!

Next on this list was *Goldman-Arbegasts*, the family that was the Torres-Thompsons' best friends, although they had missed, for some reason, the most recent birthday party. Yes, these Goldman-Arbegasts were responsible people, the mother was a somewhat taller and more even-tempered version of Maureen, another matriarch of schedules and smartly dressed children.

"Hi, you've reached the Goldman-Arbegast residence," said a woman's voice. "We're not here right now because we're in Italy."

"No, we're in Greece!" said a boy's voice.

"No, we're in Paris!" interrupted the voice of a man.

"No, we're in London!" said a second boy's voice.

And then in chorus all four voices said, "We're in Europe! On our dream vacation!"

Araceli put the phone back in its wall cradle and looked at the remaining two numbers on the list: they were both for the doctors who had treated Maureen during her pregnancy and delivery, and thus useless for the crisis Araceli now faced.

Who could she call now? No one immediately came to mind. She did not know the neighbors, not their names or anything about their relative trustworthiness, and it would be dangerous, she sensed, to share the secret of their isolation with strangers. She had no phone numbers for any uncles or aunts that might exist in the Torres-Thompson universe: Scott was an only child and Maureen had a sister that Araceli had never met. As the hours passed and Scott and Maureen did not return, the strangeness of her predicament only grew. Araceli sensed, for the first time, a larger malaise, the consequences of one or more hidden family traumas at work, as in the convoluted narratives of a *telenovela*. The woman whose hair filled the brush, whose voice kept the boys bright-eyed, eager, and well behaved, could not and should not have abandoned them. Araceli expected to hear the long-gaited slapping of Maureen's sandals on the Saltillo tiles at any moment, but until then there was no place she could walk to where Brandon and Keenan might be welcomed as relatives or friends. Nor was the phone ringing with calls from the outside world, with compadres and acquaintances calling in to chat: in fact, the phone didn't ring very often at all. It seemed impossible to Araceli that a family and a home could become something akin to an island surrounded by vast stretches of salt water, and that its young inhabitants and their innocent housekeeper might become castaways. The peninsulas that linked this island to a continent of annoying relatives and nosy neighbors had been quickly and definitively washed away. Araceli realized now that the daily solitude she felt in this home, the oppression of the droning appliances and the peopleless views from the picture window, was not hers alone. This American family whose home she inhabited had come to this hill above the ocean to live apart from the world. *They are runaways, like me.* It was an obvious truth, but one Araceli had never fully pondered before. Among Mexicans the peculiar coldness of the *norteamericanos* was legendary because it came to infect the many *paisanos* who lived among them. One heard how

individualism and the cult of work swallowed up the hours of the American day, their sunsets and their springtimes, causing their family gatherings, their friendships, and their old people to disappear. But it was quite another thing to be thrust directly into an American family's lonely drama, to find your *mexicana* self a player in their game of secrets and silences, their separation from one another by long stretches of freeway, by time zones and airline hubs and long-distance phone rates. And what about the absent family patriarchs? Not once had she heard Maureen speak of her father, there were no pictures of the man anywhere. Was he dead too, like Scott's mother? And if so, why was he not mourned with photographs? Or was he simply banished from the home like the boys' Mexican grandfather? It seemed to Araceli that *el viejo* Torres should have his number on the refrigerator. Why wasn't it there?

Maureen's room at the High Desert Radiance Spa was a two-room suite in which both rooms opened to a strand of Joshua trees, their twisted limbs arranged on a gently sloping hillside in the poses of a modern dance troupe. Just after sunrise, she stepped outside and sat in a plastic chair on the small cement patio, while Samantha slept inside the room, curled up under her favorite blanket in a fold-up crib that housekeeping put away every afternoon. The evening chill would be baked away soon, but for the moment wisps of freezer air whispered to the Joshua trees and nudged the tumbleweeds forward. Yesterday morning she and Samantha had walked the spa's hiking trail ("difficulty: low"), following it to the opening of a scrub canyon, where Samantha climbed up a small sandstone rock shaped like the belly of a very pregnant woman. *Oh, to have brought a camera to capture my little mountaineer!* The hours here passed with few thoughts of shouting men or broken tables. A mother and daughter on their own had a mellow symmetry, and since arriving at this oasis Samantha had not had a single tantrum: obviously this girl needed more time alone with her mother; she relished not having to compete for attention with two older boys. Maureen herself felt replenished. There was an essence of herself that she had neglected, a part of her soul that was attached to this dry, austere, and harsh place. A California equivalent to the Missouri grasslands, to the places where her homesteader ancestors stood on the blank slate of the

land. *I am a woman of open spaces.* The only male presence in her get-away was the kneading hands of a man named Philip, who applied oils scented with sage and chamomile to her skin, and who left only the few, forbidden centers of her body untouched. *Now I know all the things I haven't allowed myself to feel for years.*

The plan had been to return home Monday morning, to face Scott again and perhaps to forgive him. Perhaps. But then the good people at the front desk had mentioned their Monday discount. She would have just enough of the emergency cash left to stay one more night and take one more session on that table.

On Saturday night, Araceli put the boys to bed with none of the drama and screaming of the night before. They had spent the after-noon in various illicit pursuits, chief among them an hour-long gun battle with plastic pistols that fired foam bullets, the boys laughing as the projectiles bounced harmlessly off the furniture and their bodies. Araceli had forced the boys to clean up the house, and they had simply acquiesced when she declared, "*Ya es tarde,* time for sleep." Once they were in bed, she pulled back the blankets to cover them, in imitation of the mothers she had seen in movies, because she couldn't remember her own mother doing such a thing. These boys seemed to appreciate and need the gesture, and Araceli even touched Brandon on the fore-head when she noticed the tears welling in his eyes.

"Do you think Mom and Dad will ever come back, Araceli?" he asked.

"*No te preocupes.* Your mommy will be back soon. And Araceli is taking care of you now." Araceli spoke these words more soothingly than any she had ever addressed to these boys, or to any other children, and she felt a sudden and unexpected welling of altruism coursing through her veins, a drug that straightened your back and made you feel taller. *What else can you tell two lost boys but that you will take care of them?* "Araceli will take care of you," she repeated. "I will sleep here, on the floor, again. *¿Está bien?* A little later. After I wash the dishes."

Araceli pulled herself from the hallway floor just outside the door of the Room of a Thousand Wonders the next morning with the

boys still sleeping. They were sweating inside their brightly colored pajamas, shirts and pants with superheroes imprinted on them, men of rippling muscles in various flying poses whose courage offered protection against such evil threats as temporary parental abandonment. Their wet hair was matted against their foreheads, strands clinging to beads of perspiration. Keenan was curled up in a fetal position, clutching a pillow and a stuffed lion between his arms. *If I am still taking care of them tonight, I will tell them to go to bed in shorts.*

She wandered through the house again, quickly peeking into the garage to see if Maureen's or Scott's car was there, and then to the living room and the gallery of faces inside teak and cherrywood on the bookshelves. These pictures, Araceli realized, were the only clues that could untangle this family mess. The portraits of the grandfather, *el viejo* Torres, called out to her most loudly, smiling wryly from the final decades of black-and-white photography, a teenager standing before a Los Angeles bungalow, his swarthy skin rendered in tones of gray and darker gray, hands on his hips and an irresistible twinkle in his eye. This relic had been here since Araceli had started working for the Torres-Thompsons, when the old man was still coming to the house regularly, before he uttered the words that caused his banishment. *What did you say,* viejo? *And where might I find you?* Araceli remembered the looks of exasperation on the faces of Maureen and Scott when they discussed *el viejo* Torres in the kitchen one Saturday afternoon, and snippets of conversation: "What a jerk." "What a dinosaur."

Probably Maureen had not yet gotten around to removing *el dinosaurio* from this family gallery because he was on the bottom shelf, in a lesser spot in relation to the recent school pictures of the boys with eager smiles and moussed hair, and of Maureen herself holding the newborn and slippery Samantha while sitting up with exhausted ecstasy on a hospital bed. Maureen in the delivery room was on the shelf next to a recent shot of Samantha with a red bow in her thin hair and to the bronze-toned image of a woman with pinned-up hair and a giant curtain of a dress staring back from the Victorian era, the folds in the corners of her eyes suggesting she was Maureen's grandmother or great-grandmother. Next there was a recent shot of Maureen's mother, taken in a pine forest, a gray-haired woman in khaki shorts and hiking books, with a faint and uncharacteristic smile. *This is the woman's shelf: there are four generations of girls from Maureen's family here.* Araceli consid-

ered too, on the second shelf from the top, the wedding pictures of Scott and Maureen, including a shot of the couple laughing and bending their bodies in an expression of the kind of uncontainable hilarity that hadn't been seen in the Torres-Thompson household for quite some time.

Of all these people, Araceli concluded, old man Torres was the only adult still alive and likely to live in a place reachable from Paseo Linda Bonita. They hadn't yet purged the old man from the family, not completely—he was a resilient *mexicano*, apparently. *If their parents don't come back, I'll take them to this old man's house.* Araceli would have to prepare herself for the worst contingency. She had been used to thinking this way once, her naturally pessimistic outlook had served her well in her single-woman bus journey to the border, and then through the sprint, hike, and crawl into California, and in the first few harrowing and lonely weeks in the United States. Those were days of important lessons, though the subsequent four years in this household on Paseo Linda Bonita had led her to the false belief that the world might still have sanctuaries where prosperity and predictability reigned. Standing here now in front of pictures of the absent and departed members of the Torres and Thompson clans, she realized she might soon have to start thinking like an immigrant, like a desperate woman on the highway uncertain where the asphalt and the invisible trails of carbon monoxide might take her.

Scott awoke on Charlotte Harris-Hayasaki's couch, following a forty-eight-hour bacchanalia of popcorn, nachos, pizza, diet soft drinks, and power beverages consumed in front of Charlotte's flat-screen TV and game console, fighting Persian armies and completing post routes to sinewy wide receivers. Charlotte listened to his complaints about his wife, she fed him munchies he consumed compulsively and without joy, and she nestled into a spot on her vinyl couch next to him, her leg and sometimes her shoulder touching his. She tried rubbing his neck: "You have to watch out for the carpal tunnel with these game controllers." But she wasn't able to stir those passions that begin below a man's waist and reach, through circuits of nerve and muscle and irrationality, to moist lips and tongue. Instead, she had set free an inner boy.

To steal a few minutes of play here and there was one thing, Scott

thought: to fully indulge your inner gamer was another. These games were meant to be played by the hour, the better to appreciate their narrative mazes, the overwrought art of their virtual stages. Now, in his second morning here, Scott continued his playing tour of Charlotte's impressive and diverse collection, chipping onto the green at Pebble Beach to the sound of the roaring surf nearby, negotiating with Don Corleone in his study, forging blades of steel in a medieval foundry, and carrying his new weapons into battle against hordes of bearded Vikings on a Scandinavian beach.

"They'll probably put them in the Foster Care. Until they can find their parents. What else are they going to do?" That was Marisela's considered opinion, rendered by phone, and it matched Araceli's own assessment of what would happen if she called the police. "And of course they'll start asking you questions. The police have to ask you questions."

"That's not good."

"No, not for you."

"And the boys?" Araceli asked.

"They'll probably put them in the police car, take them to the station, and then to Foster Care."

"What else could they do?"

Children who spent their nights under blankets decorated with moons and stars in the Room of a Thousand Wonders should not have to spend a single night in the Foster Care. Araceli imagined communal sleeping arrangements, bullying twelve-year-old proto-psychopaths, and cold macaroni and cheese without salt. Children raised in the recirculated air and steady temperatures of the Paseo Linda Bonita would not last long in the drafty warehouses of Foster Care. She imagined the boys cuddling under unlaundered blankets, and suffering the cruel admonitions of caretakers who did not realize how special and smart they were, how they read books about history, how they had learned to identify Orion and Gemini, quartzite and silica, from the library in the Room of a Thousand Wonders. Children with the sensitive intelligence of these boys—qualities their mother did not sufficiently appreciate, because she saw only their boisterous and disorderly masculinity—should not and could not be exposed to the caprices of Foster Care.

Araceli did not want to be responsible for that loss of innocence. There was a finite amount of innocence in the world and it should be preserved: like Arctic wilderness and elephant tusks, it was a precious creation of nature. And what would the police say or do to her? Probably they would report her to the immigration agents in the blue Windbreakers, the ICE people—it was difficult to imagine that a Mexican woman without a green card could call the police and present them with two unaccompanied and guardianless American children without herself being drawn into a web that would eventually lead to her deportation.

Perhaps she was getting ahead of herself. If by Monday morning neither Scott nor Maureen had returned, she would call Scott's office and demand that her boss return home immediately.

Araceli was in a deep sleep on the floor in the Room of a Thousand Wonders, dreaming that she was walking through the corridors of her art school in Mexico City, which did not resemble her art school at all, but rather a factory in a desolate corner of an American city, when she was awakened by a series of screams.

"Mommy! Mommy! Mommy!"

She sat up, startled, and in the yellow glow of the night-light saw Keenan yelling at the wall next to his bed.

"Keenan, *qué te pasa?*"

"Mommy!"

"Keenan. *¡Despiértate!* You're having a night mirror!"

"Mommy!"

"It's just a night mirror!" Araceli insisted, and with that Keenan stopped, turned, and searched for his Mexican caretaker. To his young eyes his room had become a small submarine in a deep ocean of darkness, a bubble of light and security in a frightening world without his mother and father. The captain of this craft was the Mexican woman with the wide face now looking up at him from the door to the hallway with startled and irritated eyes.

"What?" Keenan asked in a high, perplexed voice suddenly stripped of his fear.

"You said he's having a what?" Brandon said from the perch of his bunk above Keenan.

"A night mirror."

"What?"

"A night mirror," Araceli repeated. "You know, when you see ugly things when you're sleeping."

After a pause to digest her faulty pronunciation, Brandon said in a scholarly voice, "No, in English we say *nightmare.*"

"*Pues, una pesadilla entonces,*" Araceli said angrily. "Nightmare," like many other expressions with Old English origins, was a word she would never be able to wrap her tongue around, especially since it bore no resemblance to the Spanish equivalent.

"Yeah, a *pesadilla* is what you say in Spanish," Brandon said diplomatically. With that he and his brother put their heads back on their pillows, and both boys thought that "night mirror" was in many ways a more apt description than "nightmare": Keenan looked at the wall and thought of it as a reflection of his motherless room and a window into a parallel world, and within a few minutes he was asleep again, as was his brother.

Araceli listened to their boy-sized puffs become rhythmic, the quiet song of children at rest. *This is the third night I am spending alone with these boys. I should be the one crying out in my sleep. I should be the one screaming for my mother. ¡Mamá, ayúdame!*

Unable to fall back asleep, she decided to get up and make herself tea. She took her steaming cup of *manzanilla* to the silent living room, lit one of the lavender-scented candles there, and sat on the couch. Maureen never brought a match to these candles—why buy something and never use it? Araceli sipped her tea and watched the yellow flame flicker and cast long shadows throughout the room, the soft, dancing light falling upon the pictures in the Torres-Thompson gallery, coloring the faces with nostalgia and loss. *Here are people related by blood, but distant from one another.* Pobrecitos. The photograph of the younger version of *el abuelo* Torres was the one most closely related to her own experience: the urban setting was familiar, along with the mestizo smile. Had he run across the desert to reach the United States as Araceli had? Araceli had a photograph like this of her mother in Mexico City, a snapshot taken by one of those men with the big Polaroids in the Zócalo, when her mother was a young woman recently arrived from provincial Hidalgo. *My mother still felt like a tourist in Mexico City then, and so*

does the young man in this picture—he is a young man in the first days of his Los Angeles adventure. In this picture too there was a just-arrived feeling, the brow raised in something between astonishment and self-assurance. Now something behind the young man caught her eye. Three numbers could be seen floating above his slicked-back hair, attached to a wall behind him: 232. A street address. She remembered how her mother carefully wrote dates and other information on the back of family photographs. On a hunch, she picked up the frame, turned it around, and moved the tabs that held the photograph in place and pulled it out. She found words and numbers written on the back in the elegant, masculine script of another era, the florid penmanship of a teenager educated according to the standardized rules of Mexican public education, the looping letters teachers of the Secretaría de Educación Pública had tried to force upon Araceli too, until she rebelled.

West 39th Street, L.A., Julio 1954.

On Monday morning, Araceli approached the preparation of the oatmeal with a sense of finality. After breakfast was cooked and served she would be free, because *el señor* Scott was sure to be at his office, the desk altar where he never missed a weekday prayer. When they finished eating, the boys went directly to the game room and within a minute or so the sound effects of steel striking steel were wafting toward the kitchen, where Araceli stood before the refrigerator, a tremor of anticipation in her hands as she picked up the telephone and began to punch in the number.

"You've reached Scott Torres, vice president of programming at Elysian Systems. I'm currently on the phone or away from my desk. Please leave a message or press zero to talk to the operator."

Startled to hear another recorded voice, she pressed zero. After a single ring, an actual human voice answered, a woman.

"Elysian Systems."

"*Con* Scott Torres, please. Mr. Scott Torres."

"I'm sorry, he called in sick today."

"*¿Qué?*"

"Excuse me?"

"He called sick?"

"Yes," the operator said, speaking slower now, because the person on the other end of this call was obviously English-challenged. "He called *in* sick."

"*¿Cómo que* sick?"

Now the operator was amused by the incongruity of a woman with a thick accent and poor telephone skills calling a cutting-edge, if somewhat small, software company, and asking for a midrange executive in the same tone of voice these people probably used to order their spicy food.

"Sick, yes. Ill. Unwell. Would you like me to transfer you to his voice mail so you can leave him a message?"

"A message? Yes. Please."

Araceli thought quickly about what she should say while Scott's message unfurled again over the phone, her pulse racing anew.

"*Señor Scott. Estoy sola con los niños.* I am alone with the boys." She stopped and seconds passed as she thought how she should elaborate on that central fact. "*¡Sola! Por tres días ya. Se nos está acabando la comida.* The food is gone almost. *No sé qué hacer. La señora Maureen se fue.* I don't know where she is . . ."

A loud tone sounded on the receiver and the call went dead.

Scott Torres was not at his desk because he was recovering Monday morning in a hotel room, alone, having fled Charlotte Harris-Hayasaki's apartment after two nights, his marital fidelity more or less unblemished. Thanks to the hotel minibar, he was hung over and had awakened at 8:45 in a bright, sun-drenched room with open curtains, stumbling over to the phone to report in sick to the office switchboard some ten minutes later, having forgotten, in his unsettled state, that he'd given the entire programming department, including himself, the day off for a four-day weekend. He showered, dressed, and paid the hotel bill in cash. It was time to go home and face Maureen.

After hanging up the phone, Araceli lingered by it for several minutes, because it seemed within the realm of possibility that Scott could receive her message immediately and call her back. She had al-

ready decided that she would not spend another night sleeping on the floor of El Cuarto de las Mil Maravillas. Before the day was out either she would have reached one of her *patrones* with the message of her plight, or she would head out for the Los Angeles address of the Torres family patriarch, the clapboard building depicted in the glossy photograph. During her first few weeks in California, Araceli had lived at a similar address, a 107 East Twenty-third Street, and she believed that if the address corresponded to the logical system one expected from an American city, a 232 West Thirty-ninth Street must not be far away. It was not within Araceli's experience, or that of most people who had been born and raised into adulthood in Mexico, that families picked up and moved themselves and abandoned their old properties every few years, in the same way one might discard a dress that had been worn once or twice too often. Property in Mexico stood as a constant. Once in possession of a deed, and sometimes without a deed at all, a family would plant itself on a patch of topsoil and allow themselves to become as rooted as noble old oak trees, their branches of children and grandchildren a canopy blossoming over the land. Either old man Torres himself or someone related to him would certainly be living at this West Thirty-ninth Street address, just as one could find twenty to thirty people connected by blood, marriage, and poor judgment to Araceli at Monte Líbano 210 in Nezahualcóyotl and the adjoining houses.

This escape plan liberated Araceli's mind of the mocking ticks of the clock, of her dependence on absent bosses. She had taken control of the situation.

At 10:45 a.m. she entered the gaming room and found the two boys sitting on the couch amid the ambient noise of a cheering crowd. There was a football game taking place on the flat screen in front of them, only the players were frozen in their positions, several stopped in midstride, an image that seemed unnatural precisely because the players looked so lifelike. The virtual football teams were waiting for one or both of the boys to set them in motion with controllers that had been tossed on the rug and forgotten. Having grown bored, finally, with the pleasures of computer-generated fantasy, the boys were both reading, Brandon immersed in a Bible-sized tome, Keenan with a book of brightly colored cartoons depicting the adventures of a journalist mouse, the text rendered in a crazy pasticcio of changing fonts.

"When are Mom and Dad coming home?" Brandon asked.

"Get ready," Araceli announced, ignoring the question. "After lunch, we go to your grandfather's house."

"To Grandpa John's?" Brandon asked.

"Yes."

"Excellent!" Keenan said. They had not seen their paternal grandfather in two years, a time at the very limit of young Keenan's pool of memories, though the old man had left a lasting impression on both of them because he was a bit of a libertine, a dispenser of large quantities of hard candy who didn't care if a movie was rated PG-13, and who often handed over meaningful sums of cash that raised the eyebrows of their parents. The boys associated him, most strongly, with visits to a soda fountain in his neighborhood, a place where a certain dish of chocolate in excess was served. They remembered their grandfather sitting in a booth across from them, wringing his hands in delight as they devoured their dessert and turning down their offers of, "Wanna try some, Grandpa?" Brandon and Keenan packed their rolling suitcases and backpacks with extra speed, anticipating another visit to that temple of sugar, and the condominium with the expansive recreation facilities where the elder Torres lived alone in a long-dashed hope that his grandchildren might visit him and use the kidney-shaped swimming pool. They packed their bathing suits and Game Boys too, until Araceli told them to leave all toys behind and to bring more underwear instead.

12

Brandon and Keenan led the way, rolling small suitcases that click-clacked along the cement walkway, backpacks filled with books and a few small toys hanging from their shoulders. Araceli locked the door behind them and crossed herself, against her secular inclinations: she would be traveling with two children and one never knew what one might encounter on the road. At the corner and the first turn that led away from the Paseo Linda Bonita cul-de-sac, Brandon stopped to look back at Araceli, his eleven-year-old eyes finding reassurance in the plump image of improvised motherhood she presented. She wore jeans and a billowing cotton blouse, and over her shoulder she carried one of his mother's old backpacks (used, in its day, to transport Keenan's diapers and bottles) and a floppy khaki safari hat Maureen liked to wear on all-day summer excursions to theme parks. Minutes earlier, she'd packed the very minimum for herself—two changes of clothes, the unspent and unbanked cash she had on hand, tucking away her savings passbook in a drawer. In the backpack's front pocket she placed the photograph of their destination, along with a package of the moist wipes Maureen used to clean the baby's bottom, and the only piece of identification in her possession: a Mexican voter registration card. Then she'd announced to

the boys the route they would be taking, speaking with a voice of confident authority and in clipped clauses that wedded English nouns with
Spanish verbs. *"Primero bajamos al* front gate, *y luego al* bus stop, *y
después* al train station *que nos lleva* a downtown Los Angeles, *y final-
mente tomamos* the bus *a la* house *de tu* grandfather." The boys were
eager to leave, imagining their grandfather's conspiratorial whispers, his
aftershave aroma, and his swimming pool at the end of their journey.
But before taking his next step forward, Brandon waited until Araceli's
eyes caught his one more time, because after less than a minute walking under the July sun, he was struck by the strangeness of what he was
doing: undertaking an expedition through streets he knew only from
the windows of his parents' automobiles. From the edge of the sidewalk
he looked up at Araceli and then once again at the street: heat waves
shimmered up from the asphalt in imitation of a lake, as if they were
standing at the edge of a pier, in a skiff about to push off into roiling
waters.

"*Vámonos,*" Araceli said, and Brandon resumed the march, Keenan
and Araceli behind him in single file. Brandon listened to the barking
of unseen dogs that marked their advance down the hill, the animals
communicating through what Brandon concluded must be a language:
Humans! Alert! Unknown humans! Alert! Until they reached the front
gate the only people they encountered were two Spanish-speaking gardeners trimming the edges of a freshly cut fescue lawn who were too
engaged in their work to take notice of a countrywoman leading two
North American children down the street on foot. When Araceli and
her charges reached the gate of the Estates, they failed to capture the
attention of the pregnant young woman on duty at the guard kiosk that
morning: she was on the phone and was simultaneously inspecting the
credentials of a battered moving van and its Mexican driver. They walked
another block down the sidewalk-free public access road, Araceli leading them now, trying to get the boys to walk on the grass shoulder, which
required them to grab their suitcases by the handles and carry them.
Then, for the first time in their young lives, Brandon and Keenan waited
for a city bus. "What color is the bus?" Brandon asked. "Will it have seat
belts?"

·

Seat belts on a bus would be a good idea, Araceli thought as the grinding bus climbed and coasted toward the Metro Center transportation hub. The boys sat next to each other in the row in front of Araceli, grabbing on to the rubber safety bar attached to the seat in front of them, leaning forward with the wide eyes of boys taking a ride at the amusement park, and for a moment Araceli was struck by their smallness and fragility, and worried about the bruises and broken bones an accident could bring. These boys never traveled without the protection of seat belts and the crash-tested engineering of American family vehicles. A bus crash could send bodies flying against metal and glass. Araceli had learned this in Mexico City; she knew the dangers first-hand. True, this American bus driver did not bob and weave through traffic like his Mexico City counterparts, who plied their routes with homicidal aggressiveness in rattling and rusty vehicles. Once she had stumbled upon the scene of a bus accident, during her final visit to the art fair in Coyoacán, moments after purchasing a small oil painting rendered on a piece of wood that depicted a suited and masked *lucha libre* wrestler standing stiffly with his bride. The tableau of stupidity and suffering she encountered that day finally convinced her it was time to leave Mexico. The bus passengers had suffered no visible injuries, though a few were sitting on the edge of the sidewalk theatrically rubbing their necks while a taxi driver remonstrated with them. A few paces away a skinny teenager with chocolate skin and oily hair was gasping for breath as he lay on his back in the gutter, his eyes blazing open to the dirty blue sky as two dozen of his fellow citizens gathered around him, studying him with the distant, emotionless stare *chilangos* are famous for. *Look. A young man is dying right here in front of us. This is something we don't normally see. It's all so more real than what's on television, isn't it? This isn't an actor. He is a poor man like us, just trying to make a few more pesos like the ones he is still clutching in his hand. We can't help him; we can only look and thank the Virgin that it isn't us down there.*

"Is he dying, Mommy?" a child's voice asked.

"*¿Y la pinche ambulancia?*" shouted an irritated voice from the back of the cluster.

The young crash victim was a street vendor: a few paces away his bicycle lay bent, while a passerby gathered his scattered load of loofah sponges and stacked them in a small pyramid next to the bicycle. *Yes,*

the boy is dying, but they might need his loofahs in heaven. Araceli was standing at the edge of Coyoacán's seventeenth-century plaza, in sight of the domed church and the gazebo, next to a line of trees whose trunks were painted white to discourage drivers from crashing into them. She felt bile rising in her throat as the other bystanders pushed their elbows against hers. A red trickle flowed from the young victim's nostrils, and when he stopped blinking the crowd started to thin, people walking away in a silence as yet unbroken by the wailing of an ambulance. At that moment Araceli fully and finally comprehended the cruelty of her native city, the precariousness of life in the presence of so much un-regulated traffic and unfulfilled need, a city where people born farmers and fishermen sprinted before cars faster than any horse or sailing ship. The crash cured her of any lingering procrastinator's malaise and set in motion her oft-delayed plans to leave for the United States. That night she made a fateful phone call to a friend in downtown Los Angeles, and believed she heard in her friend's upbeat voice a place where cars, bi-cycles, and pedestrians each occupied their own byways, sensibly and safely moving through the city.

Scott's route from the Irvine Hampton Inn to his hillside home took him along the five northbound lanes of Interstate 5, a high-way that was considerably thinner and less traveled in Scott's youth, when it had been known as the Golden State Freeway. The highway was an immense channel of metal and heated air, and at forty miles an hour or seventy-five, its straightness and width exercised a hypnotic power over drivers. As he navigated through the thinly populated fringes of Orange County, at a late-morning post-commute hour with only moder-ate traffic, Scott found his thoughts about the coming reencounter with Maureen intermingling with the running dots and dashes of the white lines that demarcated the lanes. The lines were a siren speaking in murmurs of rushing air that bade him to *follow-me, follow-me, follow-me,* to mountain passes, meadows, and interchanges as yet unknown, to places where no one would know he had pushed his wife into a table. When this trance of happy forgetfulness ended, Scott found himself just one hundred yards from his turnoff, but still in the number-one lane, too late to cross the three lanes of traffic to reach the exit for the freeway

that led to the coast and the Laguna Rancho Estates. Damn! Scott gritted his teeth and gave a second half curse as his usual exit and overpass
grew smaller in the rearview mirror. He was speeding toward the met-
ropolitan center of Orange County and the course correction back home
required shifting lanes and taking the next exit, but Scott's hands resisted moving: instead, they allowed the car's momentum to continue
carrying him forward and away from Maureen. *Maybe I'm not ready to go
home yet.* The car stream was like a data stream and maybe he needed
to see where the information took him, so to speak. He passed Disneyland, left Orange County and entered Los Angeles County at La Habra,
and a short while later approached the Telegraph Road exit to his old
South Whittier neighborhood. Now, at last, he exited, and headed for
the inelegant, weed-happy patch of suburban sprawl where Scott the
adolescent and teenager had been introduced to the joys of FORTRAN
and masturbation.

He entered the late twentieth century industrial parks of an old
oil patch called Santa Fe Springs, onto surface streets plied, at this
hour, by fleets of tractor-trailers, then past a baseball field and a high
school with soccer goalposts, where a single, middle-aged Latino man
was sprinting with a ball at his feet. Scott followed the splintering posts
that carried telephone voices, antiquated analog signals pushed through
copper, toward the horizon and the Whittier hills beyond. He reached
the first neighborhoods, where the homes boasted miniature gabled
roofs, and jumbo vans and pickup trucks in the driveways of mini–
Spanish cottages and mini-ranches, their humble size a kind of camou-
flage. *South Whittier does not want you to remember it; it wants to pass
unnoticed.*

When he reached the intersection of Carmelita Road and Painter
Avenue, the vista changed abruptly, shifting Scott's mood along with it,
because everything at that familiar crossroads was laden with painful
memories from the predigital, pre-Internet era. The homes here were
taller, and yet flimsier than those he had just passed, and were more uniform, each having been built by the same developer from the same
"Ponderosa ranchette" kit. He hadn't been to his old neighborhood since
his mother's death, and for a moment the weathered, fairy-tale pastels of
the two-story homes glimmered as strangely as they had on the August
day of her funeral. He slowed the car to the speed of a brisk walk as he

turned the final corner and saw the old Torres family homestead and its watered-down mustard stucco with a flavoring of avocado trim, hiding behind an overgrown olive tree. He had expected to feel a superior satisfaction returning to this place, because he had become bigger and more worldly in the decades since, conquering the nodes and networks that united the world. Instead, he felt smaller. *We were still fucking poor and I didn't even realize it.* He looked for a place to park his car on the dead-end street, but found all the available spaces taken up with sedans of dated styling, pickup trucks abused by their loads, and a station wagon. Did they even make station wagons anymore? There were never this many cars when he played baseball here.

Scott parked a half block away and stepped out of his car, surveying the workday quiet as he walked toward his old home, but he stopped when something in the backyard of the next-door property caught his eye. The Newberrys had once lived here, with their Ozark cheeks and corduroy jeans. Peering down the end of the driveway, he noticed something that was foreign to his memory: a large glass and metal box with a pitched roof and a small crucifix on top, plastic party streamers flowing out from the roof to the adjacent garage. Stepping closer, he saw a statue of a suntanned Virgin Mary inside the box, her clasped hands and powder-blue mantle rendered in painted plaster, a garland of fresh white roses draped around her neck, votive candles aflame at her feet. *This is so strange, so Mexican.* These people had taken his old neighborhood, once connected to the rest of modern America by AM radio and VHF television signals broadcast from zinc towers, back into history, to a rural age, a time of angels and miracles.

"*Buenas tardes,*" a woman's voice called, startling him. "*¿Le puedo ayudar en algo?*"

Scott looked to his right and saw a woman of about fifty in sweatpants: she held a broom, and judging from her otherworldly smile she believed he was in need of spiritual direction.

"No, nothing, nada," he sputtered. "I used to live in the house next door. I came to see, sorry . . ."

"Isn't she beautiful?" the woman said in accented English, and Scott sensed a religious speech about to begin and backed away. "*No tengas miedo,*" the woman said, trancelike, as Scott scurried away. He *was* afraid: of her statue, her Spanish, her weird religiosity, and the power of

all those things to chase away his old neighbors. What had they done to the Newberrys? The Newberrys weren't rich. They were from Little Rock. "She wants to help you," the woman continued in English, and Scott wondered how many years ago the Newberrys had left and if they knew there was a Mexican lady praying to a statue in their old backyard.

The Laguna Niguel train station was a typical example of the soulless functionality of late twentieth century American public architecture, and as such it deeply disappointed Brandon, who expected the "station" to be an actual building, with schedules posted on the wall and long wooden benches inside a high-walled waiting room. When Araceli had told them they would take a train, it had conjured images in Brandon's head of locomotives spitting steam, and passengers and baggage handlers scrambling on covered platforms underneath vaulted glass ceilings. Instead the station consisted of two bare concrete runways, a short metal awning where six or seven people might squeeze together to find shelter from the rain, and four refrigerator-sized ticket machines. Brandon thought of train stations as theatrical stages where people acted out momentous shifts in their lives, an idea shaped by a trilogy of novels he had read in the fifth grade, a series in which each book's final scene unfolded inside the Gare du Nord in Paris. His only previous train ride had come some years back on the Travel Town kiddie train at Griffith Park, and there too the station consisted of a kid-sized replica of an actual building, complete with a ticket booth and a swinging LOS ANGELES sign. The small steel rectangle that announced LAGUNA NIGUEL in the spare, sans-serif font of the Metrolink commuter rail network didn't rise to the occasion, and Brandon frowned at the recognition that actual life did not always match the drama and sweep of literature or film. Nor were there the large crowds of people one associated with trains in the movies. In fact, Brandon, his brother, and Araceli were the only people on either side of the platform.

As the boys projected hopeful eyes at the rusty sinews of the tracks that stretched away from the station, Araceli scanned the space that immediately surrounded them. Until she got them to their grandfather, these were her boys. It was one thing to be in charge of children inside the shelter of a home, protected by locked doors, or in the fenced

boundaries of a park—it was quite another to be herding them about a city. She wanted to cover them with sheets of protective steel. The thought that an accident of man or machine might hurt them filtered into her consciousness and caused brief and irrational pangs of loss, followed by the manic darting of her eyes at each of their stops on the journey from the gate of the Laguna Rancho Estates to the empty platform and the stairways leading to the street and the bus stop and parking structures beyond.

"Hey, here it comes."

A double-decked white commuter train with periwinkle stripes moved toward them as a snake would, the locomotive yawing back and forth on uneven tracks.

"*Atrás,*" Araceli commanded. "Back until the train stops."

The boys opened their mouths as the cars rolled slowly before them, their massive weight causing the ground beneath them to shift and rise.

"Tight!"

"Awesome!"

"*¡Cuidado!*"

The train stopped and two sliding doors opened before them, the boys entering ahead of Araceli, rolling their suitcases straight into the car, whose floor was conveniently level with the platform. With a quick turn of their heads the boys found the stairway leading to the upper deck and began to climb, Araceli scrambling after them, muttering "*¡Esperen!*" at the backs of their feet. They found two pairs of empty seats arranged before a table.

"Hey, we're moving."

The train began its advance away from the station, and Brandon and Keenan were briefly mesmerized by the illusion of flight that came from looking through the railcar's large windows and watching their enclosed space move against the low skyline of the transit center's false downtown, a Potemkin village of parking garages masquerading as office buildings. As the train rolled away from the station, past gates with flashing red lights and waiting cars with daydreaming drivers, Araceli threw herself back into her seat and let out a sigh. *Halfway there, more or less.* The train itself was a clean comfort, with its white walls and stainless steel poles and vinyl seats with aerodynamic shaping and the

plaque by the door that proclaimed its provenance: BOMBARDIER, MON-
TREAL. After dropping off the boys and the briefest of stays at the old
man's house, she would set off south again for Marisela's and await news
of Scott and Maureen. She imagined different outcomes for their family
debacle, including a divorce that ended with an empty house and Araceli
vacuuming after the movers had left, or a tearful family reunion and
ample thanks from Scott and Maureen to Araceli for seeing their boys
through the crisis.

Through the window, the boys saw a landscape of shrinking backyards shuffle past: the repetition of laundry lines and old furniture did
not hold Brandon's attention for long, and he finally looked across at
Araceli and asked, "Can you draw me a picture? Here in my notebook?
Like the dragon you drew for Keenan. That was cool."

"Yeah, it was tight," Keenan said.

"I didn't know you could draw," Brandon said.

"*¿Qué quieres?* What do you want I draw for you?"

"How about a soldier?"

"*¿Un soldado? Fácil.*"

She took his lined notebook and pencil and looked for a blank page,
glancing quickly at his crude war scenes, little stick-figure Brueghels in
which one army of stick men set off cannons and laid siege to rectangular forts and pummeled enemies who raised up stick hands and ran
from scribbled explosions. *This boy is very smart but he does not know art.*
Brandon watched, intently, as she traced some initial lines and a man in
uniform with a weapon held across his chest took form on paper. It was
a musket like the ones in his book *American Revolution* and Araceli
drew it from memory, though she gave her soldier a modern uniform,
with a row of medals and a steel helmet. Then she worked on the face,
choosing features that were deeply familiar to her, and made it stare
straight back at the viewer.

"Wow," Brandon said when she finished. "That guy's face—he looks
really tough."

"Really mean," Keenan added.

The face belonged to Araceli's mother.

Her art session was interrupted, suddenly, by the jolt of the train's
arrival in Fullerton, the last station before Los Angeles. Four people waiting on the platform quickly stepped on board and the train lurched

forward anew. Soon the train was entering the industrial districts south-east of Los Angeles, one windowless warehouse followed by another as the train accelerated and began to vibrate slightly. The buildings began to age, the neutered, primary-colored plaster of the late twentieth century giving way to the earth-toned constructions of brick and cement of earlier eons. Suddenly the warehouses had windows, many dark and frosted over with dust and cobwebs so that they resembled thousands of cataract-infested eyes. The train went faster still and vibrated violently, causing Keenan to squeeze Araceli's hand. Brandon held on to the armrest and felt his head strike the window, and wondered if the train might disintegrate, or if the forces of acceleration might transform this rolling steel box into a time machine that would transport them from the archaic era of brick now visible outside the window, to even simpler ages of wood, smoke, and stone.

The train slowed suddenly as it entered a switching yard with at least twenty parallel tracks. They rolled slowly past rusting hopper cars that had made hundreds of journeys from Kansas with wheat and corn, past tank cars oozing black tar, and container cars with German and Chinese names and bar codes stamped incongruously on their sides. The train made a long, sweeping turn under a freeway bridge and Araceli watched the haphazard cables and wires that followed the tracks moving like a black, horizontal rain. She noted too the random dispersal of trash on the embankment, the plastic bags and food containers sprinkled over the track gravel, the rusting iron overpasses, the graffiti-covered switching boxes, and a lone, stubby brick control tower with wooden doors chained shut. There was a spare beauty to all this decay, it was the empty and harsh landscape of an unsettling dream; these were spaces you were not meant to see, like the hidden air ducts and trash chutes of a glittering mansion, where cobwebs and dust and rat droppings collected freely and concerned no one. Her aesthetic lived in barren places like this, and she missed them. *Here the wind, rain, and sun are free to shape and cook the steel and cement into sculptures that celebrate forgetfulness.* She took a small notebook from her backpack and tried to quickly capture the manic, twisted essence of electrical lines, the bounce of the trash in the wind, the fluid shape of the rust patterns, until Keenan proclaimed, "Everything is really dirty here," and her reverie and her concentration were broken.

The train slowed to a walking pace and a valley of smooth concrete walls suddenly opened alongside the tracks, stretching more than a mile in the distance, with several bridges vaulting over it. "What's that?" Keenan asked.

"It's the river," Araceli said.

"That's a river?" Brandon said, perplexed, until he noticed the bottom of the chasm held a narrow channel of flowing water with perfectly straight edges. "What's it called? Why is it made out of cement? It hasn't rained, so where does the water come from?"

"Too many questions," Araceli said.

"Too many?" No one had ever told Brandon such a thing.

"Yes."

Brandon looked at the river and saw that a giant with a paint can had covered the top of the valley with a mosaic of sparkling elephant-sized letters, spelling words in mongrel greens and tainted yellows that pulsated inside a pool of gray-blue swirls. Or at least it seemed a giant had painted them. He wondered if he should ask Araceli, then decided against it. Probably it was a giant.

"Hey, look, there's people down there," Keenan shouted, loud enough to get the attention of the four or five other adults in the car, who looked up from their newspapers and laptops just long enough to glance at and quickly forget the familiar sight of the soiled caste who lived by this stretch of track.

"*Los* homeless," Araceli said.

Brandon pressed his nose against the glass and looked downward, spotting a line of shelters between the train tracks and the river, teetering house-tents of oil-stained plywood, sun-bleached blue tarpaulin, frayed nylon rope, and aluminum foil. They looked like ground-hugging tree houses, improvised assemblages built by children and taken over by tubercular adults. A few humans sat on chairs in between their creations in this village as it followed the curve in the tracks, their roofs a quilt of tarpaulin and wood forming a long crescent dotted with the occasional column of smoke. Brandon searched for the sources of these fires, and spotted a gangly man in aviator glasses tending to a kettle on a grill. The train rolled slowly toward the man, and for a few seconds Brandon was directly above him. He bore a long scar on his cheek oozing red and black liquids. A battle wound? Brandon wondered. A cut

inflicted by a knife or a sword? A month earlier Brandon had finished the last volume in a four-book series of novels, *The Saga of the Fire-Swallowers*, and as he sat in the train with his nose pressed to the glass, the violent and disturbing denouement of that epic narrative seemed the only plausible explanation for the existence of this village of suffering passing below him. *These people are refugees; they are the defeated soldiers and the displaced citizens of the City of Vardur.* The novels were a fantasy tale for young-adult readers set in a world of preindustrial stone villages. His father had bought the entire set and read them some years earlier, leaving them forgotten on a shelf for his oldest son to discover, Brandon's fascination growing with each chapter he spent in the company of its villains, a cult of rugged men and boys who engaged in the ritual eating of flames before and after battle. There was something about this homeless camp that seemed to belong to the ancient times described in those books, a way of life untroubled by electricity, or modernity in general. In truth, Brandon never should have been allowed to read the Fire-Swallower books, given their graphic descriptions of scorched-earth warfare, including the slaughter of entire villages and their children with blades forged from various metals, real and fanciful, and the antagonists who filled their speeches with fascistic rationalizations about "the weak," "the strong," and "the pure." It was all meant to be an allegory about the cruelty and demagoguery of the modern age, and its imagery drew heavily from the outrages of the twentieth century, so much so, and so realistically, that the sharp-eyed Brandon had long ago concluded that the story was not entirely the product of a writer's imagination. Long before this train journey Brandon had begun to warm to the idea that the Fire-Swallower saga was, in fact, a thinly veiled, detailed account of a real but primitive corner of the actual world. Entire cities emptied of good people, civilians tortured, their homes and their books set to the torch. How could such injustice exist, how could humanity live with it? He knew he should speak of what he read to his mother, who obviously had no idea about the taboos being broken in the works of literature he carried about the house: "You're such a good little reader," was all she said. It was stunning to be confronted with such adult naïveté, though it was undeniably cool to possess knowledge forbidden to eleven-year-olds who were not as precocious readers as he. Still, the stories told in the saga caused him to lose sleep some nights, until he finally convinced himself that what he was reading was indeed

fantasy. And now this, a wounded man, an actual victim of the Fire-Swallowers' wrath, driven to seek shelter by the concrete river with his fellow Vardurians.

"Those flame-swallowing bastards!" Brandon cried out, in imitation of the hero of the saga, the noble Prince Goo-han.

"*¿Qué dices?*" Araceli said. "*¿Bastardos?*" Suddenly the eleven-year-old was saying swear words. *He's only been out of the house and into the world a few hours and already he's being corrupted.*

"It's the Fire-Swallowers," Brandon said in a tone of patient explanation, having realized quickly that Araceli had never read those books: they were in English, after all. "The Fire-Swallowers made these people refugees. They destroyed their towns and houses. They fled and they've come to live here by the river. I read about it in *Revenge of the River-walkers*. The Fire-Swallowers burned down their village, Vardur, because they wouldn't swear loyalty to the evil king. So they had to seek shelter on the riverbanks, but I never thought . . ."

"*Estás loco*," Araceli said. "You read too much."

No one had ever told Brandon such a thing: in the Torres-Thompson home reading was a sacred act; it was the one activity the children were allowed without time limits or parental supervision. Books were powerful and good, they told truths, and Brandon decided he should ignore his temporary caretaker's remarks and study the Vardurian camp and see what secrets it might reveal. Brandon's memory stretched back only a few years beyond the time they moved into the Laguna Rancho Estates, and his idea of what homes looked like was deeply influenced by the repetitive conformity of his neighborhood, with its association-approved paint schemes and standard-sized driveways. Below him, now, was a place where every shelter was entirely different from its neighbor, many with tiny yards fenced in with loops of electrical wire and plastic bags tied together to form a kind of rope. Before the train made one final turn and headed into the station he spotted one last Vardurian: a woman with a fountain of silvery hair who was sweeping out her shelter with a broom.

Maureen stood over the portable crib in her hotel room and studied her daughter as she took an afternoon nap. Samantha slept on her back, clutching the yellow blanket that accompanied her day and

night, her closed eyes peaceful hemispheres, with her rusty eyelashes as delicate equators. With her eyes closed Samantha's oval face was nearly identical to her oldest brother when he was the same age, the boy's sleeping face recorded in a photograph framed in mahogany in their living room gallery: Maureen's separation from Brandon for more than seventy-two hours only heightened the sense that she was looking down at her son and not her daughter, and she began to feel the deepening absence of her boys from her life. *When you see your children sleeping you understand the full glory and beauty of being a mother; you stand tall and awake before their silent need, before their purity and vulnerability.* She looked up at where she was, in a hotel room of slightly overdone southwestern décor, with a Navajo rug nailed to the wall opposite the bed and an authentic, desert-baked ram's skull hanging on the door, and could hear the startled voice of her conscience screaming out, *What have I done? My son! My sons!* She picked up the phone and called home.

At that moment, Maureen's boys were walking dutifully behind their Mexican caretaker, taking their first steps off the train at Union Station. They walked along one of several parallel platforms between locomotive behemoths, one of which was ringing a bell as it rolled away, roughly at the pace of a walking man, into open tracks toward the city beyond. Brandon and Keenan saw porters wearing stiff caps, and seniors defeated by the stacks of luggage on steel carts, and heard a speaker pronounce, "Last call for the Sunset Limited . . . all aboard!" and thought that at last they'd arrived at a real train station. The boys wanted to linger out on the open-air platform, in the meaningful presence of all that rolling stock and those travelers, but Araceli was telling them to follow her, with an impatient *"Órale, por aquí,"* and they descended down a long, sloping ramp, going underground.

They entered a long and wide hallway with low ceilings that reminded Keenan of airports he had visited. Araceli had passed through here during her first days in Los Angeles, and the sight of the crowds of people with huge duffel bags and boxes tucked under their arms reminded her of that other, more innocent Araceli. *Sola.* With a hard-shell suitcase the smuggler had mocked for its patent impracticality, dazzled

by the city's alien and sleek feel, suffering a kind of weird agoraphobia because she was in a vast plain of unknown things. The reencounter with her recent past only made Araceli more uncomfortable, more anxious to reach her destination. She looked left and then right and decided to go right, beginning to walk very quickly, navigating smartly between the crosscurrents of passengers, like a *chilanga* again, almost losing Brandon and Keenan because she was in such a hurry.

"Hey, Araceli, wait up," Brandon shouted, and Araceli turned back and gave him a mildly exasperated look identical to the one she showed him two or three times a day in his own living room, bedroom, and kitchen.

Walking side by side now, they passed an electronic sign announcing destinations and departure times, LAS VEGAS BUS, TEXAS EAGLE, SURFLINER NORTH, and then suddenly entered a room where the low ceilings disappeared and the space above them opened up, causing Brandon and Keenan to crane their necks skyward. They marveled at the vaulted ceiling, which was covered with tiles of vaguely Mediterranean or Arabic styling, exuding both warmth and largeness. Chandeliers resembling baroque spacecraft hung from the rafters and both boys silently mouthed the word *Whoa* as they walked underneath them. There were rows of high-backed, upholstered benches where boys in baseball uniforms and weary, sunburned Dutch and Italian travelers sat with clusters of nylon backpacks at their feet. A crew that was in the second day of a music-video shoot was packing up in the unused and locked wing of the station where tickets had once been sold, where the oak-paneled ticket windows served as permanent and oft-used sets.

"I've seen this place in the movies," Keenan said. "I thought it was pretend."

They passed through an arch high enough for the tallest troll or giant to fit through, and then walked out the main door of the station, where they were confronted by the summer sunlight, and cars and pedestrians all moving purposefully northward and southward on streets and walkways. Behind this shifting tableau stood the imposing backdrop of the downtown Los Angeles skyline, the glass skyscrapers of the Financial District, and the stubby stone tower of City Hall, which had a ziggurat pyramid on top, so that it resembled a Mesopotamian rocket ready for launch.

"*No, por aquí no es,*" Araceli said, and she circled back into the waiting room again, the boys scrambling behind her.

She walked up to the information booth and the tall, lean, sclerotic man standing there, the name tag on his jacket announcing him to be GUS DIMITRI, VOLUNTEER.

"We are looking for the buses," Araceli said.

Gus Dimitri was a spry octogenarian and a native of South Los Angeles, old enough to remember when that black and brown ghetto of today was a whites-only haven for Greeks, Jews, Italians, Poles. He had seen more L.A. history than any other employee or volunteer at this transit hub, and when he looked at Araceli and her charges he understood, immediately, that this was a servant woman from Mexico hired to care for the two children that accompanied her.

"Well, where are you headed, exactly, ma'am?"

As the woman fumbled in her backpack for an address, Gus Dimitri took time to think that California had really pushed this immigrant-servant fad to the extreme. *Is it really wise,* he'd like to ask the parents of these boys, *to have a Mexican woman guiding your precious children across the metropolis like this? To have them in the care of a woman lost at Union Station?* At about the time Gus Dimitri had retired from the workforce, California had gone mad with immigrant-hiring—from front yards to fast-food joints, these people did everything now. They were good workers, yes, real old-fashioned nose-to-the-grindstone types. But jeez: Didn't Americans want to do anything for themselves anymore? When he was about the age of this older boy here, he'd sold newspapers on the street himself, making a killing hawking extras on Crenshaw Boulevard for the Max Schmeling–Joe Louis fights. But did American kids even have paper routes anymore? His own paper was delivered via pickup truck by a Mexican guy (he assumed) named Roberto Lizardi, according to the Christmas card that arrived with his paper once a year.

"To Thirty-ninth Street," Araceli said. "In Los Angeles."

"That's back, the other way," he said. "Patsaouras Plaza."

"Thank you."

Araceli quickly circled back into the long, low-ceilinged passageway.

"Where are we going?" Keenan asked. "Why are we going underground again?"

"We are going to take the bus," Araceli explained. "*Tenemos que ir a la otra estación.* Another station, not this one." They reached a wide cement staircase and climbed into a sunlit atrium with several exits. This was the transit center where the buses departed, but Araceli could not remember which gate led to the buses serving the neighborhood in Los Angeles where *el viejo* Torres lived. She approached another information booth and the boys' attention was drawn upward again, this time to the mural on the wall behind the desk: an old steam engine rushed toward a village set amid verdant fields, advancing through a series of orchards, leaving a column of black smoke in its wake. To the left, there was a second mural in which the steam engine ran alongside a blue ribbon of river, which itself snaked past a city thick with squat buildings; in a third panel to the right the same city gleamed with skyscrapers and the river had morphed into a concrete channel.

"Is that what was here before?" Brandon asked, before Araceli could get her own question in.

"Yeah," said the man behind the counter, an MTA employee. "And let me tell you something else—this'll really blow your mind. Where we're standing, right now—it used to be Chinatown. There's all sorts of archaeological stuff they found buried underneath here. Chinese stuff."

"So what happened to the Chinese?"

"Ah, they knocked all that down ages ago. Flattened it."

"Well, that's disturbing," Brandon said, parroting a phrase his mother used quite often.

Brandon pondered the revelation about Chinatown as the man explained to Araceli where she could catch the bus they needed to take. The ground he and his brother were standing on was older than the oldest person he knew, and probably older than the oldest Vardurian, which was a horizon-opening realization for an eleven-year-old boy. Probably if you dug down deep you could find not just Chinatown, but also the ruins of many other cities and villages of the past, just like in that picture book on his shelf where you see the Stone Age, the Roman Age, the Middle Ages, and the Modern Age all inhabit the same stretch of earth beside a river, with battles fought and buildings burned and people buried and cities rebuilt and torn down and rebuilt again as you turn from one page to the next.

"*Ya, vámonos,*" Araceli called out. "*Es por aquí.*"

The boys followed her to one of several parallel sidewalks and within seconds an empty bus had pulled up and Araceli and the boys climbed in. This bus, Brandon noted immediately, was a battle-worn version of the first bus they had taken in the Laguna Rancho Estates earlier in the day. It appeared to have traveled through a few hailstorms, given the scratches on the plastic windows, and as it headed out of the shady transit center and into the sun of the Los Angeles streets and the light shone inside, Brandon noted the worn seats and the assorted scribbling in the interior. "It stinks in here," Keenan declared. A sweaty, vaguely fecal aroma seeped out of the seats, and the sour sweetness of spilled sugar beverages attached itself to the humid air molecules in the aisles, the smells riding the bus up and down and across the city all day for free.

They rolled slowly away from the transit center, to streets that brought them closer to the glass towers of the Financial District. Brandon and Keenan had seen this stretch of the city many times before, in the company of their parents, from the high perch of a car speeding along elevated freeways. That was the Los Angeles they had always known, the city center that was home to the Dodgers and the Lakers. On those trips they had glided over the heart of Los Angeles, traveling near the tops of its palm trees, driving to museums and parks that were somewhere on the other side of a vast grid of stucco buildings and asphalt strips that stretched as far as one could see into the haze. Studying this landscape from the ground level for the first time, Brandon noticed how every object appeared to be built from bare metal, brick, and concrete, arranged into simple geometric forms: the right angles formed by the traffic lights welded to poles, the open rectangular mouths of the storm drains, the strange tower on the roof of one building assembled entirely from triangles. It was all more linear and rough-edged and interesting, to his young eyes, than the curvy contours of Paseo Linda Bonita.

Sitting next to his brother, in an aisle seat, Keenan was closer to the clusters of passengers who began to fill the aisle after a few stops, grabbing the bar above them. Keenan didn't know it was possible to stand up in a moving bus. An older woman towered above him, carrying a plastic bag filled with documents and envelopes, the heavy contents swaying about as the bus lurched forward. Directly across from Keenan,

a seated middle-aged man with green eyes held another plastic bag, his weathered hands covered with small cuts, and through the bag's translucent skin Keenan could make out folded clothes, two thick books, and a pair of pliers. The man held the bag close to his body, inside the vessel formed by his legs and the metal back of the seat in front of him, and Keenan sensed that whatever was inside was very important to him. *These people are carrying the things they own inside the plastic bags my mother and Araceli use to bring things from the market.* Keenan was eight years old, but the poignancy of poor people clutching their valuables in plastic bags close to their weary bodies was not lost on him and for the first time in his young life he felt an abstract sense of compassion for the strangers in his midst. "There are a lot of needy, hungry people in this world," his mother would say, usually when he wouldn't finish his dinner, but it was like hearing about Santa Claus, because one saw them only fleetingly. He believed "the poor" and "the hungry" were gnomelike creatures who lived on the fringes of mini-malls and other public places, sorting through the trash. Now he understood what his mother meant, and thought that next time he was presented with a plate of fish sticks, he would eat every last one. Two passengers in front of him were speaking Spanish, and this drew his attention because he thought he might make out what they were saying, since he understood nearly all of what Araceli said to him in that language. But their speech was an indefinable jumble of new nouns, oddly conjugated verbs, and figurative expressions, and he only understood the odd word or phrase: *"es muy grande," "domingo," "fútbol,"* and *"el cuatro de julio."*

"Nos bajamos en la próxima," Araceli said as she rose to her feet. "Next stop. We get off."

They stepped from the bus to the sidewalk and the door closed behind them with a clank and a hydraulic sigh. Araceli took in the yellow-gray heat and the low sun screaming through the soiled screen of the center-city atmosphere. *Goodbye blue skies and sea breezes of Laguna Rancho,* Araceli thought. This was more like the bowl of machine-baked air of her hometown: she had forgotten the feeling of standing in the still and ugly oxygen of a real city. "We walk. That way," Araceli said, pointing south down a long thoroughfare that ran perpendicular to the street the bus had left them on, the four lanes running straight

toward a line of distant palm trees that grew shorter until they were toothpicks swallowed up by the haze.

"This doesn't look like the place my grandfather lives," Brandon said.

"Is it close?" Keenan asked.

"*Sí*. Just a few blocks."

They stood alone, housekeeper and young charges, on a block where only the bus bench and shelter interrupted the empty sweep of the sidewalk. So strange, Araceli observed, a block without people, just as on Paseo Linda Bonita, but this time in the middle of an aging city with buildings from the previous century. All the storefronts were shuttered and locks as big as oranges dangled from their steel doors, while swarthy men struck poses for the passing motorists from rooftop billboards, their fingers enviously wrapped around light-skinned women and bottles of beer and hard liquor. For a moment Araceli thought that Brandon might be right, that *el viejo* Torres could not live near here. Then again, you never knew in Los Angeles what you might find around the next corner. You could be in the quiet, sunny, and gritty desolation of a block like this at one moment, and find yourself on a tree-lined, shady, and glimmering block of apartments the next. Mexico City was like that too.

Once again, the wheels of the boys' suitcases clack-clacked on the sidewalk as they marched southward. "This doesn't look like where he lives," Brandon repeated, annoying Araceli. "In fact, I'm pretty sure this isn't the place."

"It's just a few blocks," she insisted. In a few minutes she would be free of the care of these two boys and the pressure would be lifted from her temples. Their grandfather would emerge from his door, she would tell him the story of the table and the empty house, and he would make them an early dinner and she would be free of them. They advanced southward, witnessed only by the passing motorists, who were all accelerating on this stretch of relatively open roadway, going too fast to take much note of the caravan of pedestrians headed southward in single file, a boy with rock-star-long hair leading the way, his brow wrinkled skeptically, a smaller child behind him, and a big-boned Mexican woman bringing up the rear and studying the street signs. These were the final minutes before the clock struck five, and the driv-

ers were eager to cover as much ground as possible before the skyline to the north began to empty of clerks, analysts, corporate vice presidents, cafeteria workers, public relations specialists, sales wizards, and assorted other salaried slaves. On this midsummer day, most of these automobiles proceeded with windows sealed and artificial alpine breezes blowing inside, but the air-conditioning was not working inside the Toyota Cressida of Judge Robert Adalian, a jurist at the nearby concrete bunker known as Los Angeles Municipal Traffic Court—Central District. Judge Adalian was driving with the windows open when Araceli, Brandon, and Keenan passed before him at the crosswalk on Thirty-seventh Street and South Broadway, thanks to the rare red light on his drive northward along Broadway, his daily detour of choice to avoid the Harbor Freeway. These pedestrians pushed the button to cross and broke the sequence of the lights, the judge thought as he took in the odd spectacle of a woman who was clearly Mexican with two boys who were clearly not. *It's not their skin tone that gives the boys away, it's their hair and the way they're walking and studying everything around them like tourists. Those boys don't belong here.* Through his open window he caught a snippet of their talk.

"I think we're lost," the taller boy said.

"*No seas ridículo, no estamos* lost," the Mexican woman answered, irritated, and the judge chuckled, because he'd grown up in Hollywood with some Guatemalans and Salvadorans, and the Mexican woman's brief use of Spanglish transported him to that time and place, twenty years ago, when Spanish could still be heard in his old neighborhood, before that final exodus from the old Soviet Union had filled up the neighborhood with so many refugees from the old country (including his future wife) that the city had put up signs around it announcing LITTLE ARMENIA. The light turned green and the judge quickly filed away the Mexican woman and the American boys in the back of his memory, alongside the other unusual event of the afternoon: the sentencing of a onetime sitcom actor whose career had been so brief and distant in time, only the judge recalled it. It had depressed the judge to think that, at forty-four, he was older than his bailiff, his clerk, and his stenographer, older also than the defense attorney and the representative from the city attorney's office. Only the accused surpassed him in age, and when Judge Adalian finally realized that no one in the court

was aware of the defendant's contribution to television history, the fifty-two-year-old drunk driving defendant had looked at the judge and raised his eyebrows in an expression of shared generational weariness. "Time passes," the defendant said, and this too struck a chord in the judge's memory, because it wasn't often that the alcoholics who passed through his court imparted any wisdom. The light turned green and the judge glided northward, unaware that in a few weeks' time his memory of crossing paths with the faded actor and the Mexican woman with the two "white" boys on the same ordinary day would win him an appearance on cable television.

Araceli reached the curb on the other side of Broadway and turned right, Brandon now bringing up the rear, because he felt the need to protect his younger brother by walking behind him, lest some monster or Fire-Swallower emerge from one of the shuttered storefronts.

"Don't look at anyone in the eye, Keenan," Brandon said.

"What?"

"This is a dangerous place."

"You can't tell me what to do."

"There might be bad guys inside these buildings," Brandon insisted. "Look at the markings. That's a bad number. Thirteen."

"Really?" Keenan said, and for a moment he saw the world as his brother did, thinking that xiii had to be some warrior code.

Logic told Araceli she was just two blocks away from the address on the back of the old photograph, but now she too was beginning to have serious doubts, given the ominous, spray-painted repetitions of the number 13 on the walls and the sidewalk. She sensed, for the first time, that her naïveté about the city might be leading them to the place where graffiti scribblers and gang members were nurtured under the opaque roof of the smoggy sky, a kind of greenhouse nursery of mannish dysfunction. Now they walked past a large vacant lot, a rectangle filled with knee-high milkweed and trash, which in the glory days of *el abuelo* Torres had been the Lido Broadway movie theater. As a young man *el abuelo* Torres had seen *High School Confidential* screened here, lusted after the curvy starlet Cleo Moore, and been pummeled by a couple of African-American guys who didn't appreciate his comments during a midweek matinee of *Blackboard Jungle*. Juan Torres and his parents were still in the city-to-farm circuit then, forced with a number

of other Mexican-American families to live among blacks. Juan fought the black guys over girls too. Living here and tasting blood in his mouth had shaped his sense of racial hierarchy, and his ideas about where he fit in the pigmented pyramid of privilege that he understood the United States to be. *As dark as we are, we ain't at the bottom.* When he had a glass of sangria or a shot of whiskey too many, the brawling, proud, and prejudiced Johnny Torres of Thirty-ninth Street and the Lido Broadway was resurrected: as during Keenan's sixth birthday party, when he remarked very loudly on how fair-skinned and "good looking" his younger grandson was—"a real white boy, that one"—a remark that led his progressive daughter-in-law to banish him from her home.

If Araceli had not been trailing two children, if she had not been anxious to reach the place that would liberate her from her unwanted role as caretaker of two boys, she might have stopped and taken the time to study the rubble of the Lido Broadway, a half dozen pipes rising from a cracking cement floor like raised hands in a classroom. Time worked more aggressively in the heart of an American city than in a Mexican city, where colonial structures breezed through the centuries without much difficulty. Here, cement, steel, and brick began to surrender after just a decade or two of abandonment. *The people who lived and worked here ran away. But from what?* It was best to keep moving, quickly. She spotted a woman pushing a stroller on the next block and a young child walking beside her, two hundred yards away, next to a liquor store with a painted mural of the Virgin of Guadalupe on its side.

Araceli walked toward the store and the Virgin, and soon she and the boys were entering a neighborhood with houses and apartment buildings that were occupied, clapboard structures, mostly, some with iron fences enclosing rosebushes. They saw a woman flinging a carpet against the stairs of a porch that led to a two-story building with four doors. Brandon noted the strange numbers above each entrance—3754¼, 3754½, 3764¾—and was reminded of the fanciful numbered railroad platform from a famous children's book; he wondered if these doors too might be a portal to a secret world. They passed a two-story clapboard bungalow with the rusted steel bars of a prison, and both boys wondered if some bad guy was being held inside, but a few doors down, they saw an identical structure, with no bars and freshly painted coral-colored walls, an organ pipe cactus rising ten feet high in the garden,

alongside a small terra-cotta fountain with running water and a cherub on top. "That's a nice house," Keenan said. *"Muy bonito,"* he added, and Araceli thought, yes, they must be on the right track, because the houses were suddenly getting prettier. But half a block farther along they encountered a square-shaped rooming house whose doors and windows had been boarded up, the plywood rectangles forming the eyes and mouth of a blindfolded and muzzled creature. "I really don't think my grandfather lives around here," Brandon said again, and this time Araceli didn't bother answering him.

Two blocks later they arrived at a street sign announcing Thirty-ninth Street and the final confirmation of Araceli's folly: on this block, where the photograph and the street name on the back had led her, there was a collection of powder-blue duplex bungalows, apartments in a two-story clapboard building surrounded by snowflakes of white paint, and two windowless stucco industrial cubes. The address corresponded to one of the bungalows, which faced the street, with side doors opening to a narrow courtyard. Araceli reached into Maureen's backpack, retrieved the old photograph, and matched the bungalow behind the young *abuelo* Torres to the structure before her: the windows were covered with steel bars now and the old screen door had given way to a fortress shield of perforated steel, but it was the same building. Together, the two images, past and present, were a commentary on the cruelty of time and its passage, and of Araceli's chronological illiteracy, her ignorance of the forces of local history. After a day of walking and bus and train rides she had arrived at her destination, and it was clear that *el abuelo* Torres did not live here, and could not live here, because everything about the place screamed poverty and Latin America, from the wheeled office chair someone had left in the middle of the courtyard amid a pool of cigarette butts, to the strains of reggaeton music pulsating from inside one of the bungalows.

"La fregué," Araceli muttered to herself, which caused both boys to look up at her in confusion.

"Is this it?" Brandon said. "Is this the address?"

"Sí. Y aquí no vive tu abuelo."

"No, he doesn't," Brandon said. "His house is in a big apartment complex, with a big lawn in front. It's yellow. And there aren't any ugly buildings like those over there."

"Now what?" asked Keenan.

Behind the security door of the bungalow directly before them, Araceli could hear a second, inner door opening. "*¿Se le ofrece algo?*" a female voice asked through the perforated steel shield.

Araceli walked to the door and held up the photograph. "*Estoy buscando a este hombre,*" she said. "*Vivía aquí.*"

Seeing no danger in a *mexicana* with two young boys, the woman opened the steel door and reached out to take the picture, revealing herself to Araceli as a world-weary woman of about thirty whose smooth skin and long, swept-back eyes appeared to have been carved from soapstone. Her nails were painted pumpkin and her hair seemed oddly stiff and perky, given the circles under her eyes, but those same eyes quickly brightened as she took in the photograph.

"*¡Pero esta foto tiene años y años!*" the woman declared, and chuckled after recognizing the black-and-white porch and arriving at the realization that the little shotgun house with the sagging floors and peeling faux linoleum in which she lived had been standing so long, and that once it had been possible to live there without metal barriers to keep out predators: she wouldn't live there now without bars on the windows. She returned the photograph and gave Araceli and the boys the same dismissive look she gave the impossibly earnest young men with narrow ties who visited her earlier in the day searching for the family of Salvadoran Mormons that had once occupied this same bungalow. "*Ni idea,*" the woman said.

Araceli stomped on the wooden porch in frustration. A day on foot, in trains, and buses, from station to station, neighborhood to neighborhood: for this? In the time they had walked from the bus stop the sun had dipped below the buildings on the horizon, the western sky had begun its transformation into the colors of a smoldering hearth. She looked down at the boys and wondered if they would be able to make it all the way back to Paseo Linda Bonita and how much trouble they would become once she told them they would have to start walking again.

The woman at the door sensed Araceli's predicament, which was centered on the presence of the two boys behind her, both of whom seemed to be English speakers. "I think someone I know can help you," she said, switching languages for the benefit of the boys. "*El negro.* He

lives right here behind me. Apartment B. I think he's the oldest person who lives here. They say he's been here forever."

A minute or so later Araceli was knocking on the steel door with the B next to it.

"Who the hell is it? What are ya knockin' so loud for, goddamnit!" Behind the perforated steel sheet, an inner door of wood opened, and Araceli saw the silhouette of a large man with thick arms and a slightly curvy posture. "Oh, shit. Didn't know you had the kids with you," the voice said. "What? What you need?"

"I am looking for this person," Araceli said.

"Huh?"

"I am looking for the man in this picture. His name is Torres."

The man opened the door, slowly, and stretched out a weather-worn hand to take the picture, examining it behind his screen. "Whoa! This takes me back!" the man shouted. Now the door opened fully and the man looked down the three steps of his porch to examine the woman who had given him this artifact. He was a bald black man, inexplicably wearing a sweater on this late afternoon in July, and when he fully opened his door the sound of a television baseball announcer filtered out, causing Brandon to stand up on his tiptoes and try to look inside. The man from Apartment B was easily in his seventies, and still tall despite the stoop in his back. The spaces under his eyes were covered with small polyps, and his cheeks with white stubble.

"What are you? His relative? His daughter?"

"No. They are his, how do you say . . . ?"

"He's our grandfather," Keenan offered.

"You know, there's been a lot of people in and out of this place since I moved here." James "Sweet Hands" Washington had arrived on Thirty-ninth Street as a single man in the middle of the last century, picking out these bungalows because they reminded him of the old shotgun houses in his native Louisiana. The spot at the end of the block occupied by the garment factory had been the site of a car-repair shop back then, and Sweet Hands had worked there for a number of years, dismantling carburetors with the hands dubbed "sweet" first for his exploits on the football field, and later for his exploits with the ladies. Sweet Hands examined the picture, the way the Mexican subject wore his khaki pants with a distinctive mid-1950s swagger, and then the

bungalow in the background, and was momentarily transported to that time, when the Southern California sky was dirtier than it was today, and when Sweet Hands himself was a young man recently liberated from Southern strictures. This young man in the photograph looked like he had been liberated too: or maybe he was just feeling what Los Angeles was back then, in that era of hairspray and starched clothes, when the city had a proper stiffness to it, and also a certain glimmer, like the shine of those freshly waxed V8 cruisers that rolled along Central Avenue at a parade pace of fifteen miles per hour. Sweet Hands held the picture a long time, and finally let out a short grunt that was his bodily summation of all the emotions this unexpected encounter with the distant past had brought him. "Johnny. That's his name. Johnny something."

"Torres."

"Oh, yeah. Johnny. Johnny Torres. I remember the Torres people." They were one of the first Mexican families to move into these bungalows, way back when Mexico was a novelty Sweet Hands associated with sombreros, donkeys, and dark-eyed beauties with braids and long skirts that reached down to white socks and patent leather shoes. After the Torres people had left—four of them, he seemed to remember, including khaki-pants Johnny here—there hadn't been many other Mexicans around until well after the Watts troubles. They started to show up in large numbers in the years before the Rodney King mess, in fact. It was quite a thing to be able to measure the passing of time by the conflagrations one had seen, by the looting crowds and the fire-makers. Bad times chased away his "people" in all the senses of the word: his relatives, his fellow Louisiana exiles, and most of the other sons of Africa who once lived here. His people had gone off to live in the desert, leaving the place to the Mexicans. Sweet Hands understood, from the way they carried themselves and from the singsong cadences he detected in their speech (without understanding precisely what it was that they were saying), that they came from a verdant place like his own Marion, a place of unrelenting greenness and tangled branches where the rain made songs on the tin roofs. The Mexicans brought with them that slow, boisterous, and tropical feel of rural Louisiana, and he liked having them around, especially since all his relatives had moved out to Lancaster. The few times his daughter and grandchildren came back in

their clean and ironed clothes and told him "This place stinks" were enough for him to ask that they not come back—and to resist their entreaties that he move out to the desert. Here on Thirty-ninth Street, Sweet Hands could still take a couple of buses and find the last place in South Los Angeles that served Louisiana buffalo fish, and he might find two or three other old-timers there to talk about baseball and Duke Snider and Roy Campanella, and watching the Yankees play the Los Angeles Angels in 1961 at the old Wrigley Field, just a short walk away on Forty-second Place. There wasn't any buffalo fish in Lancaster, it was dry as all hell out there, not a place for a man from Louisiana to live. Whereas on certain moist summer mornings the seagulls came to Thirty-ninth Street and circled over the trash cans behind the garment factory, where the taco trucks tossed the tortillas they didn't sell. When Sweet Hands closed his eyes and listened to the caw-caw of the seagulls, he could see the ocean.

"Yeah, I remember this guy," Sweet Hands said finally. "He used to live right there. Where Isabel and her kids live now. Moved out ages and ages ago. I think he moved to the desert. Or to Huntington Park. Used to be that Huntington Park was all the rage. A lot of people from here moved to HP, especially after they opened up that Ford plant . . ." With that he returned the photograph to Araceli, who looked crestfallen. "Sorry." He gently closed the door and got back to his Dodgers, even as Brandon and Keenan stood up on their tiptoes to get a glimpse of the television inside.

"Now what do we do, Araceli?" Keenan asked as they walked back toward the street. The question echoed in Araceli's mind in Spanish: *¿Y ahora qué hacemos?* Araceli looked down Thirty-ninth Street and the end of the path she had followed to get to this place. It would be dark by the time they reached the bus stop and she sensed that walking through these neighborhoods at dusk could be worse than putting the boys into Foster Care, and that the best course of action might be to simply pick up the nearest pay phone and call 911. "Maybe we should go to this Huntington Park place," Brandon offered. "That sounds like the kind of place my grandfather would live . . . by a park." This absurd suggestion only made Araceli feel more trapped and desperate. *I am the woman who cleans!* She pulled down angrily at her blouse, which had been bunching up on her since they had left the house, then plopped herself

down on the edge of the sidewalk. The boys followed, their Velcro-strapped tennis shoes next to her white, scuffed-up nurse's shoes in the gutter.

The unwanted closeness caused the muscles of her legs and back to tense. *Why are you so spoiled and helpless? Why can't you have one nosy aunt or uncle or cousin nearby like all the other children on earth?* She was going to have to make a decision about them. Was $250 stuffed in an envelope every week enough to justify this march across the city? Looking across the street and to her right, she saw a phone booth. If she just picked up the line and called, then maybe she could get the Foster Care people without summoning the police. *And then I would be free.* Down the block to Araceli's left, a group of squat men and women with round faces gathered around a taco truck, in a chatty cluster before the swing shift began at what she guessed was a garment factory. Behind them she could see a loading dock with a large opening to a vast interior space with low ceilings and a bluish glow, engines groaning and puffing metallically. The boys from the Room of a Thousand Wonders did not know that there was a world of dangerous machines and a city of dark alleys all around them. Having been thrown together with these two boys, in the inescapably intimate situation of being their sole care-taker, Araceli suddenly felt the great distance that separated her life from theirs. *I am a member of the tribe of chemical cleansers, of brooms, of machetes and shovels, and they are the people of pens and keyboards. We are people whose skin bakes in the sun, while they labor and live in fluorescent shadows, covering their skins with protective creams when they venture outside.* Deeper and farther away to the south, beyond the mean city, there were rocky landscapes where men dug tunnels under steel fences, and deserts where children begged for water and asked their fathers if the next ridge was the last one, and cried when the answer was no. Brandon and Keenan did not know of such horrors, but Araceli did, and had survived them, and she wondered how many scars the boys might have after a night or two, or perhaps a week or a month, in Foster Care, which she imagined to be an anteroom to that dark and dangerous world. Maybe she couldn't and shouldn't protect them, maybe it was better for them to see and know. *Maybe innocence is a skin you must shed to build layers more resistant to the caustic truths of the world.* She wondered if she was living at the beginning of a new era, when the

pale and protected began to live among the dark and the sorrowful, the angry multitudes of the south.

Behind them a door opened and Araceli and the boys turned around to see the woman from the first bungalow heading down the steps and walking toward them, with three giggling children trailing behind her.

13

Isabel Aguilar peeled back the curtain and spied on the lost strangers through the window of her small living room, which also doubled as the bedroom of her son and the Other Boy who lived with her. The three strangers sat on the curb, two white boys and a *mexicana* in a foul mood. Encounters with disoriented travelers were not unusual on Thirty-ninth Street, where Isabel's rented bungalow stood at the edge of a district of hurricane fencing and barbed wire, of HELP WANTED signs in Korean, Spanish, and Cantonese, where cloth was transformed into boutique T-shirts and steel was cut and solvents were mixed. When lost pedestrians reached Isabel's front step and contemplated the industrial horizon that began on her street, they realized they were in the wrong place and knocked on her door, twisting their faces into question marks: "¿Y la Main, dónde está?" "You know where my homie Ruben lives?" "Have any idea, honey, where I might find the United States Post Office?" Isabel answered the door for all of them, and sometimes opened the outer metal barrier, the better to hear their questions, even though she was a single mother living with her two children and the Other Boy who was not her son. She had been born in a town in the municipality of Sonsonate, El Salvador, a place of rusting railroad tracks where the

green mushroom-cloud canopy of a single ceiba tree billowed over the central plaza and where neighbors knocked on your door expecting to be invited in.

The big Mexican woman sitting on the curb stood out among the parade of the lost on Thirty-ninth Street first for the startling photograph she presented as a calling card, an image of Isabel's bungalow before the floors sagged and the doors and windows were encased in steel, and second because the children she had with her were obviously not hers. Isabel detected a faint coloring of Oaxaca or Guatemala in their skin—perhaps she was their aunt or cousin. But there was something decidedly non–Latin American in the air of pampered curiosity with which they sized up Isabel and the bungalow. They reminded Isabel of the children she had cared for in Pasadena when she worked there one summer, boys who knew the abundance of expansive homes with un-locked doors and clutter-free stretches of hardwood floor that were swept and polished by women like her. Why was the Mexican woman dragging them around these parts, where the only white people she saw regularly were the policemen and the old man who collected the rent?

"What are you looking at?" asked the Other Boy behind her. "Why are you on my bed?" His name was Tomás, he was eleven, and he had lived with Isabel and her son and daughter for two years. The Other Boy was an orphan, and under strict orders to be quiet and grateful, and to bother her as little as possible, though he was constantly forget-ting that last commandment. Isabel turned and gave him a scowl that involved a slight baring of her pewter-lined teeth.

"¡*Callate!*" she snapped.

Tomás raised his eyebrows, smiled, and turned away, unfazed, return-ing to the movie he was watching with Héctor, Isabel's son and Tomás's best friend on earth, and with María Antonieta, Isabel's daughter.

Isabel found her natural provincial generosity once again pulling her toward the front door and down the stairs. These small-town in-stincts had gotten her into trouble before—the Other Boy being the principal reminder of this. But she sensed that outside on the curb there was a woman in a situation much like her own: alone with two children and the Other Boy and only the twice-monthly visits of the father of her children, Wandering-Eye Man, and his cash stipend to make the situa-tion livable. Her ex had visited the previous weekend, which was why

Isabel had had her nails and hair done, but all she had accomplished with that was to make his eyes fix on her for a heartbeat or two longer than usual.

When Isabel opened the door, Héctor, María Antonieta, and the Other Boy paused the movie they had been watching on their DVD player and the three of them followed her out the door and down the stairs.

Isabel leaned down and asked a question softly of Araceli. *"¿Tienen hambre? Tenemos* hot dogs."

"Hot dogs?" Keenan shouted. Before Araceli could answer, her charges were rising to their feet and following the three children into the bungalow. Araceli mumbled a *"Gracias"* as she scrambled after the children and up the three stairs through a doorway whose wood moldings had been painted and repainted so many times over the course of eight decades they seemed to be made of clay. They entered a room where the floor nearly disappeared in the impossible clutter of furniture: a secondhand sofa of coarse fabric, a dresser, two beds, a television, and assorted shelves squeezed between walls of much-abused plaster that held the memories of the dozens of families that had lived there, including a clan of worn-out farmworkers named Torres.

When Keenan and Brandon stepped into this space, their eyes were drawn to the alabaster face of a motionless woman on the television screen. She was holding a large white scepter and wearing a crown of crystals, while riding a chariot pulled by a panther. "Hey, this is a cool movie," Brandon said as he and his brother dropped themselves to the carpet, to watch the image atop the dresser spring into movement, while the three children in Isabel's care positioned themselves around their guests, all five children craning their necks upward to watch an elaborately staged battle unfold between the stacks of folded clothes and towels that framed the television on either side. Brandon's eyes were momentarily drawn to the tall votive candle burning on one edge of the dresser: the flicking flame illuminated Saint James the vanquisher of the Moors, a sword-wielding man on horseback trampling people underfoot, an image that suggested that the memory of warfare and conquest was alive among the inhabitants of this home.

Araceli followed Isabel to the kitchen, which occupied the transitional space between the room where the children were watching television and a third room in the back where there were two more beds and a dresser covered with cold creams, rouges, eyeliner, and perfume bottles and makeup containers that filled the air with a bouquet of ethanol and coconut oil. From this spot, Araceli could keep an eye on the children, and also watch as Isabel drew water from the tap and filled a pot to boil the hot dogs. *La señora* Maureen would be scandalized: she insisted that all cooking in her home be done with bottled water.

"And the kids?" Isabel asked Araceli in a conspiratorial Spanish half whisper. "What's going on with them?"

"They belong to the family I work for," Araceli said in a matter-of-fact voice. "Their parents disappeared on me. And I came looking for their grandfather. I thought he lived here."

"Maybe he lived here once. But I've been here two years and haven't seen any other *viejos* other than Mr. Washington." Isabel opened a cabinet and removed a small, flat package from a space where boxes, loaves of bread, cans, and plastic bags were packed in as tight as passengers on a Mexico City subway, then threw the package into a microwave, and the room was soon filled with the sound of corn popping. Araceli looked over and saw that Brandon was talking to the children who lived here, their heads leaning forward, Isabel's boy nodding, his eyes narrowed in an expression of serious contemplation. She wondered in which language they were conversing.

When the movie ended, Brandon and the Other Boy renewed their discussion of the plot and characters, talking in a bilingual mix of English and Spanish that leaned heavily toward the former. "I think the *bruja blanca* has to come back in the next movie," the Other Boy, Tomás, was saying. "There's lots of movies where people come back from the dead."

"Who are they going to do battle with if not the witch?" Héctor offered, and then he and Tomás looked at Brandon, because in the twenty minutes they had been watching the movie together Brandon had, with a few comments and observations, already established himself as an authority on the subject.

Brandon moved his head back and forth in a gesture that meant *Yes and no*. The movie was based on another series of books Brandon had read and finished, over the course of Thanksgiving and Christmas vacations and many school nights in between during his fourth-grade year. More than a year had passed since he had completed the seventh volume in the series, but he remembered all the books in great detail. "The witch is really dead and she's not coming back. But she's in another book that comes before this one."

"Really?"

"Yeah."

Brandon began a patient, detailed recitation of the long, winding series of adventures of the characters portrayed in the movie, an epic narrative that involved an apple core, the tree that blossomed from it, a piece of furniture built from the tree, and various magicians, professors, and animals with visionary powers, all unfolding in the City of London and other places in the real world, and in a magical, parallel realm. Brandon had also read about the historical war that took place in the background of the seven-volume fantasy saga, in a big picture book called *Eyewitness: World War II*, and he wove a few events from that conflict into the story that he told Tomás and Héctor, who were shocked to hear that German planes had bombed British cities and transformed entire neighborhoods into flaming rubble. "How could they do that to the kids down there?" Tomás asked, and Brandon replied, "Don't know. That's just the way war is, I guess."

"It happened to my grandpa in the war, in Chalatenango," Héctor interjected, causing the other boys to stop and look at him and await more details, though he had none. Héctor was a shy boy and not a natural storyteller, and El Salvador was a place that might as well have been a place from a fantasy novel, because he had never been there and he knew the country only from the stories his father told him during his twice-monthly visits.

Returning to the fantasy saga depicted in the movie, Brandon told them how, over the course of seven books, it had become clear that the magical and the real inhabited the same physical space—"not like in the movie, where they have to go into that closet to get to the other world." Brandon shared this revelation with Tomás and Héctor with special relish, because it matched his growing sense of the weird urban

districts in which he and his brother were traveling. The train had brought them to this place called Los Angeles, where the magical and the real, the world of fantasy books and history, seemed to coexist on the same extended stage of streets, rivers, and railroad tracks. "Did you know that there are Vardurians living close by?" he told his new friends. "The Fire-Swallowers chased them to the railroad tracks and the river. Did you know that?" Tomás and Héctor looked perplexed: *They haven't read those books either*, Brandon realized.

"There are many things happening in this city, but I haven't heard of any Fire-Swallowers," Tomás said, giving a philosopher's rub to his chin. Tomás knew more about the real Los Angeles and its vagaries than other boys his age, and he had never imagined it to be anything other than a harsh kingdom ruled by adult realism and caprice. He was a semi-orphan (that's what Isabel called him sometimes, *"un semi-huérfano"*), a wily survivor whose parents were slaves to a Colombian drug recipe, and each had dragged him separately through some of the filthiest single-room-occupancy hotels in the city. He had a four-inch-thick file in the Los Angeles County Department of Children and Family Services, a set of folders marked with red tabs in the cabinet of the social worker who had lost track of him at about the time he fell to Isabel. He had ridden on top of trains in southern Mexico, snuck into the backs of buses in Calexico, and had once called the Los Angeles City Fire Department's 911 emergency line when his father's eyes rolled back and he had stopped breathing on a bus bench on Main Street, an act of heroism that had later earned the boy belt lashes from his recovered father: "Don't let me fall asleep like that again! You hear me?" Tomás knew his alphabet and went to school now that he lived with Isabel, and he was lucky enough to have a teacher who could see how bright he was despite the fact that he could not read more than a few words at a time. Tomás had learned to place himself in the path of generous and educated people from outside the calculating and cruel milieu that dominated his life—a patient teacher's aide, an alert produce vendor willing to give a poor boy a banana or an orange or two. The well-read, English-speaking boy before him now struck Tomás as another one of those people, and he concentrated on every word the boy was saying, telling himself that he would one day learn to read books so he could study these stories himself. Tomás did not know books could

contain dramatic and violent tales rooted in real life. As Brandon wrapped up the final fate of the characters in the movie, the boys were still dipping their hands into the bowl, and starting to chew at the few unpopped and salty kernels at the bottom of the bowl Isabel had set out for them.

"A train crash? No way!" Tomás shouted in disbelief.

Brandon gave a nod of solemnity. "It was a surprise to me too."

"*¡Tomás!*" Isabel cried from the kitchen. "*¡Venite para acá!*" His exclamation had alerted Isabel to his presence at the moment she and Araceli were discussing what else to feed the children. Isabel was short of milk and other foodstuffs, and now she summoned Tomás for a quick run to the market. She believed that running errands was the one thing the Other Boy was good for, and when she saw him coming back with groceries, or hunched over the sink washing the dishes, or at the table chopping carrots, she felt less stupid for having been tricked into becoming his guardian. "*Andate a la tienda y comprame leche y un poco de ese queso que le gusta a mi hijo,*" she commanded. "*Y pan también. ¡Apurate!*"

Isabel slipped two bills into his palm, money supplied by her Mexican visitor. Tomás was a lithe boy with luminous, summer-burned cherrywood skin, and was an inch or two shorter than Brandon, but when he moved through the house and street it was with the confidence and gracefulness of an adult athlete. He winked one of his smart brown eyes at Brandon as he stepped out the door.

Brandon and Keenan jumped on the bed and watched through the window as Tomás walked away. *He's going down the street by himself! Without any grown-up! And now he's jaywalking across the highway!* Nearby South Broadway resembled a highway to Brandon, and seeing Tomás sprint across its four lanes of asphalt was like watching a diver jump off a rocky cliff into a narrow pool of water. Tomás slipped into a gray stucco prison labeled LIQUOR MARKET and emerged a few minutes later carrying one white plastic bag in his right hand and two in his left. Now he executed a return sprint across South Broadway, running with a scurrying gait thanks to the weight of the bag, and in less than a minute he was climbing up the stairs to the bungalow.

"*Esta vez no aplastaste el pan,*" Isabel said at the top of the stairs in Spanish that was too fast for Brandon to understand, though he judged from the harsh tone that Isabel had given him a reprimand, or perhaps

another command. Sure enough, a moment later Tomás was in the kitchen, slipping the jugs of milk into the refrigerator. Isabel snapped at him again in Spanish and the boy climbed up on the counter in the kitchen to retrieve a box from a cabinet near the ceiling. From these interactions Brandon was able to intuit that Tomás was not Isabel's son, and that, in fact, he was a slave.

Slavery was another of those vicious human institutions depicted again and again in the various fantasy and history books Brandon pored through. In the prologue to *Eyewitness: Civil War* there were photographs of chains that wrapped around the necks and ankles of slaves, and etchings that showed slaves being whipped, and these images gave greater weight to the tales of slavery in *Revenge of the Riverwalkers* and other works of fiction he'd read. Clearly, Tomás wasn't that kind of slave, since there were no chains to be seen in the house, but he wasn't a free boy either, free to play and shout and read. Rather, Tomás was at the mercy of the pretty but angry woman who ran this household. Now she was making Tomás do something Brandon would never have imagined another boy their age doing: he was serving everyone dinner.

What was left of Scott's anger melted away in the early afternoon drive back from South Whittier to the coast, and when he made the final turn onto Paseo Linda Bonita, he realized Maureen had every right to hate him. He had behaved poorly the night of their argument, and aggravated his sins to higher orders of shame by leaving his home and his post as patriarch for seventy-two hours. The absence of his family's voices and faces from his direct orbit had brought him a sense of clarity about his own failings, if not necessarily the courage to face the consequences of his actions. He parked the car in the driveway, not wanting to open the garage and set off the grinding motor and door slam that would announce his arrival to the interior of the house. Instead, he performed a quiet sidle into the living room through the front door, sensing that the element of surprise would work in his favor during the reencounter with his wife. He listened for the sounds that would give away the location of his children and Maureen, but heard nothing.

He peeked into the kitchen and found the basins and marble counters in silent repose: the stainless steel sink was bone-dry, and the science

geek in him kicked in and deduced it had not been used for several hours, at least. Now he noticed the stuffy air: the air-conditioning was off. This realization led him to begin moving through the house more aggressively and purposefully. When he opened the door to the garage, he was not surprised to find Maureen's car missing, final confirmation that none of his family members were here, because his children would have to be with their mother. Unless . . .

"Araceli!" he called out from the kitchen. "Araceli!" he called out again in the living room. Finally, he opened the sliding door and stepped into the backyard, walking up to the edge of the new desert garden, looking past the alien form of the ocotillo and into the garden's deeper recesses, which were populated by shorter succulents and sandy paths. He turned away from the cacti and returned to the kitchen, and used the phone there to call his wife, but the call went directly to voice mail. Next he moved to the guesthouse, and gave the door to Araceli's room three blows of his closed fist. "Araceli," he shouted again, and then listened for movement in her room, but heard only the very distant whir of a leaf blower, and the taps of a hammer coming from another corner of the undulating hillside subdivision. "Araceli!" The absence of the Mexican employee in the middle of the week was more disturbing than all the other absences; it was a dramatic break in the routine that signaled, in Scott's mind, that a kind of crisis, a deliberate flight, had played itself out here, as if word had come of an impending tsunami, a landslide, a fire. He stepped in a slow daze back through the interior of the house, wondering if he might discover a clue to his family's whereabouts. In the bathroom he found a soap dragon on the mirror, pouncing. *That's weird.* It suggested boredom, like the scratching a castaway might leave in his cave while waiting to be rescued. In the boys' room the beds were made, there were no toys on the floor, and this orderliness also felt unnatural. He opened the closet doors and noticed a conspicuously empty space on the top shelf, and after a few moments remembered that the boys' suitcases were usually stored there.

They've gone.

They've run away.

He felt his wife's anger at work in the empty stillness. After twelve years, could this be the long-feared final break, the end of their family

project? *This is what happens when you strike and injure your wife. She leaves, of course. What else did I expect?* A bland, numb, and lonely future loomed, the silence and emptiness of this child- and wife-free moment stretched out into a future of carpeted and sparsely furnished bachelor apartments. What is a father without his family? A lonely object of scorn or pity. He would be transported back to the directionless, passionless days of his adolescence and young adulthood, when algorithms were his only progeny. Daydreaming about his children, about the daily routines that would no longer be his pleasure to share, he unconsciously followed the same path his sons and Araceli had taken some hours earlier: out the door, into the cul-de-sac, and downhill toward the front gate, accompanied by the same canine protest. He drew the stares of the Mexican landscaping crew that had failed to take notice of Araceli nine lawns and gardens earlier, his distant eyes suggesting to them the sorrow of a wealthy man. *You see: even a big house in a flawless neighborhood like this one cannot guarantee happiness.* At the front gate, the pregnant attendant watched him approach and asked, "Sir, is there something I can help you . . . ?" but he was soon past her, headed toward the bus stop and then into the meadow behind it, following a ghost trail through the grass that led down toward the Pacific.

We Californians drift to the sea. I will fall asleep on the beach and the rising tides will pick me up and carry me westward, like those Mexican fishermen who left their village chasing sharks, only to find themselves with cracked lips and sunburns weeks later on an island in the South Pacific.

After they had finished their meal, the four boys and Isabel's daughter sat on the front stairs of the bungalow, with Araceli and Isabel behind them in the living room, Araceli making sure she didn't allow more than thirty seconds or so to go by without glancing at Brandon and Keenan as she listened to Isabel recount in great detail her romance, pregnancies, and eventual falling-out with Wandering-Eye Man. Isabel had opened the inner door to catch an evening breeze after a day in which the sun had beat down on her little structure, and the children had gravitated to the steel security door, and had been drawn outside by the air molecules that squeezed through the pinholes. In between pauses in Isabel's monologue, Araceli heard the occasional passing car on Broad-

way, a whistling firecracker exploding several blocks away, and a merengue from the building next door that was going on about lips and kisses, and more kisses, in a chorus of *Bésame, bésame, bésame.*

On the porch just past the open door, Tomás was telling the newly arrived visitors the story of the neighborhood he, Héctor, and María Antonieta lived in, as Tomás understood it from two years of observations made from the doorway and his bed, which was under the window that faced out onto the street. Many a night he had crawled out from under the covers and peeked out the window to investigate the source of a noise, relaying whispered descriptions to Héctor, who was usually too frightened to get out from under his covers and look for himself: "It's the police. They've got a guy, I haven't seen him before. He's sitting on the curb. They're pulling back his hands." "It's just some drunk guy." "She's crying and she's hitting him on the chest and now he's hugging her again . . ."

In Tomás's mind the window and the doorway were like a television of constantly switching channels, with new actors and dramas arriving to perform on the Thirty-ninth Street set before departing for new lives in other neighborhoods offstage. Having himself survived a transient existence, this did not strike Tomás as an abnormal state of affairs. He watched people pull up to the neighborhood in Chevy Novas brimming with boxes and towels pressed against the curving glass of rear windows, or jumping off the backs of pickup trucks, or on foot carrying their belongings in big duffel bags they dragged forward on the sidewalk like stubborn farm animals. They came chatting and laughing in large family groups, or quiet and alone with flight bags tucked under their arms, squinting up at the street names on the sign poles to make sure they hadn't taken a wrong turn. Tomás secretly took in their stories with his eyes, and now he tried his best to relate what he had seen, to show his new friends that he could tell tales too, even though he had never read a book. Thirty-ninth Street was a book-story, Tomás now realized, although one with characters more varied and fleeting than those in Brandon's readings.

Many of the events in the neighborhood book-story took place underneath the four streetlamps visible from the front porch, Tomás said. They were nocturnal machines that came to life with a snap and a buzz an hour after sundown, and their yellow glow had the curious property

of subtracting the color from the street, so that the events of the night played out like a black-and-white movie. For many months the neighborhood story was dominated by events that took place at the far edge of what could be seen from Tomás's window, at the corner of Calvino Street, underneath a streetlamp recently repaired by a crew of city workers with a truck that had a stretching bucket that lifted a man into the air. A group of young men used to gather underneath the lamppost on Calvino Street, not for its light (which they repeatedly broke with rocks) but for the markings they had painted on the post's metal skin, a tangle of letters and swirls that made the post resemble a stiff, tattooed arm. The young men gathered for conferences, listening with their hands in their pockets as the members of their group took turns making speeches, and then they would wrestle one another and shadowbox, and sometimes they would pick one boy and pummel him while they counted to thirteen. The lamppost was no longer covered with graffiti, and the cluster of young men no longer gathered there because they had gone off to battle in another neighborhood, Tomás had heard, and afterward their spot under the lamppost was occupied for several weeks by police cruisers staffed by bored officers with leaden eyelids.

With the young men gone, other people spilled out onto the streets, Tomás said. On some nights the male workers from the factories played soccer using the no-longer-tattooed lamppost to mark the goal, and their shouts, whistles, and laughter echoed against the buildings. There was a teenage girl who sat in a doorway of the apartment directly behind the lamppost, and for several months a teenage boy had come to court her. They talked for an hour or two each night at the open door, the girl's awkward silhouette framed by a kaleidoscope television light flickering through the doorway. Once the girl came down and sat on the steps next to the boy, pulling down her skirt and adjusting the straps on her blouse, her leg touching the boy's, until the bulky shadow of the girl's mother appeared in the doorway. Tomás said he watched the couple talk for eight nights until the boy stopped coming, leaving the girl on the front steps with her elbows resting on her knees, waiting. After two nights she slipped inside the room with the television, leaving Tomás with a peculiar and enduring desire to see her again, though he never did.

Over here, to the right, on the sidewalk underneath the lamppost near the corner of Thirty-ninth and Broadway, a street vendor had come

one Saturday evening to sell toys, Transformers, at a price that lured buyers from distant places. As the crowd of milling people around his wares grew, the vendor gave both Héctor and Tomás a Transformer. The next week more peddlers appeared, men and women selling toy cars made of steel, balloons, dolls, and other objects made of plastic or wrapped in plastic, and the crowds grew even further, enticing vendors of churros and hot dogs to come and sell also. These vendors laughed and chanted the names of their wares, and drew other strangers, who came to glue posters on the lampposts, and finally the crowds on the narrow street grew so large that people were blocking the Saturday traffic. Then the police cruisers returned, their lights strobe-flashing rosy light against the factory buildings, the apartments, and the bungalows, and the vendors disappeared. Today the only reminders of that noisy marketplace, Tomás said, were the broken Transformers that he and Héctor still had and the two or three layers of posters glued to the lamppost a few feet from the bungalow, the paper slowly bending and peeling with age. Tomás pointed out the old posters to the visitors and Brandon rose to his feet and briefly examined the lamppost from the front steps of the bungalow, seeing words and pictures half exposed by weathering.

"Los Tu-ca-neys de-el Nor-tay," he enunciated slowly, taking delight at the phonetically exotic sounds emanating from his lips, foreign words that appeared to derive a meaning from the black leather vests and tiger-print shirts worn by Los Tucanes, a group of troubadours who traveled, apparently, in the tractor-trailer depicted behind them. He imagined them rolling into this neighborhood, which was clearly a crossroads, an outpost, an oasis of some kind. Brandon's books were filled with accounts of such places, gathering-spots in jungles and deserts, in caves and on mountaintops, market towns where the protagonists rested before important battles and other plot shifts. Some secret force drew people to this place. How else to explain all the comings and goings of travelers, warriors, and traders, and then his own arrival with his brother and Araceli on their long trek from the Laguna Rancho Estates?

Some nights, sitting on these steps, Tomás continued, he would see a man walking down South Broadway and imagined he might be his father, especially if the man advanced with the uneven, slumped-over walk of people whose heads were swimming with what Isabel called *estupefecantes*. Tomás wasn't especially eager to see his father, and the sight

of these drugged and drunk men often caused him to retreat back into the bungalow, lest the old man come and claim him and renew their hotel-hopping adventures. But Tomás quickly realized it was silly to think this, because his father and mother were almost certainly dead: if they were alive they would have come looking for him long ago, because they needed him to help feed them, and to call the ambulance when they lost consciousness, even if they said they didn't want to be rescued.

"Maybe our parents are dead too," Brandon said absentmindedly. "Maybe that's why they left us alone with Araceli."

"No, they're not," Keenan said. "I talked to them."

Before Keenan could explain further, Araceli was hovering over them, telling them it was time to go to bed. They changed into their pajamas and giggled a bit with Tomás and Héctor in the darkness, until Araceli stretched out on the floor alongside Brandon and Keenan and told them all to be quiet. The weariness of a day spent walking and traveling soon caught up with the boys, and they slipped effortlessly into a sleep that was black and complete, devoid of dreams, fantasies, and illusions.

"Nah, I wouldn't recommend setting out on those freeways, I really wouldn't at this particular moment." The hotel clerk was a smart, cosmopolitan-looking young Iranian-American man of about twenty-five, and he offered his advice with a relaxed confidence that made it just a bit harder on Maureen to leave and rush home to her children, so that she could solve the mystery of the unanswered fifty rings of the telephone at her home. She was several hours past checkout time, apparently; there was no way around that, which was unfortunate, because after the fight over the new garden Maureen had a newfound appreciation of the buying power of the money she would be throwing down the drain by leaving. But more serious than wasted cash was this new fact about the traffic. "Look, I just came in off the Ten, and it isn't pretty in either direction. It could take you five hours to get into the city. It's the Fourth of July tomorrow." Maureen contemplated five bumper-to-bumper hours with a volatile, well-rested baby girl in the backseat. "But if you leave first thing in the morning, it'll be free and clear. And you can have the breakfast buffet you already paid for. We'll have fresh croissants!"

When she balanced the traffic and the croissants against the unanswered phone, the idea that her boys were probably out with their father on some "boys-only" adventure seemed more plausible. They were out, running away from the shut-in fever that gripped the residents of 107 Paseo Linda Bonita on long weekends. She imagined them camping in a forest, the boys snuggled next to their father after sunset, asleep in their underused nylon sleeping bags on a bed of pine needles, underneath the darkening summer sky.

Araceli awoke to the feel of the stiff floor beneath rising and falling with a wavelike motion, and opened her eyes to see the unilluminated, bare lightbulb above her in a pendulum swing. *¿Un temblor?* Unmistakably, yes. And then it was over. Now she took note of the white summer-morning light streaming through the gaps in the thick rubber skin of the curtains, dust dancing in the shafts. She propped herself up from her position on the floor in the center of the living room, and saw Keenan asleep on Tomás's bed, and Brandon on the floor between her and Tomás, resting upon billowing rafts of polyester comforters imprinted with parrots, Japanese action figures, and the logo of a Mexican soccer team. Brandon lay with an open mouth and craned neck that suggested to Araceli a tortured, uneven sleep, and Keenan with a wet hitchhiker's thumb before his mouth. They had slept through the morning street cacophony that seeped past the iron bars and through the curtains: a motorcycle sans muffler, a truck whose passing weight caused the wooden floor to shift, a wino's squealing call to prayer: "Wooooo ooohhh! Motherfuuuuuuuckers! Earthquake! Come an' get it! Come on!" Araceli considered the pathos of the well-fed and long-haired Torres-Thompson boys amid the exterior noises of poverty and addiction, asleep inside the cramped nest of the bungalow living room, with its particle-board dressers and walls whose gray paint seemed to be perspiring. The boys' thin hair was moist with sweat and they gave boy-sized puffs of breath that floated upward toward the bare glass bulb, now still again. What would Maureen say and do if she were to suddenly appear and see her two princes sleeping in a room with a Salvadoran and a Mexican boy? Her *jefa* would lower her thin, lightly sculpted eyebrows into an aggressive prow of disapproval, she would make assorted English half-word noises

of outrage. *Humph! You brought my children here? To this disgusting little bungalow tenement? To sleep next to an orphan boy?*

Yes, señora, Araceli would say. *You were gone.* And that would be the end of the argument.

Araceli stepped carefully over the boys on the floor, opened the front door, and walked out into the street, toward the liquor-grocery and its public telephone.

14

Their bus headed eastward, deeper into the modern industrial heart of the metropolis, over the north-south thoroughfares and railroad tracks that carried cargo and commerce, into districts of barbed wire and sidewalks blooming with fist-sized weeds, past stainless-steel salt-water tanks excreting briny crystals, past industrial parking lots with shrubbery baked amber by drought and neglect, past storage lots filled with stacked PVC pipes, past stunted tree saplings and buildings marked CHOY'S IMPORT and VERNON GRAPHIC SERVICES and COMAK TRADING, and through one intersection where a single tractor-trailer loomed and groaned and waited. The setting triggered no new reveries in Brandon's overactive imagination, because he was too sleepy to think, having stayed up late into the night thinking about Tomás and his stories about the crossroads on Thirty-ninth Street, and then being forced to get up early by Araceli for the departure to their next destination. They were headed for a park where it was said his grandfather might live.

"I don't know where," Araceli said. "But I know who to ask." She told them about her friend Marisela, and the uncle of hers by marriage who lived in Huntington Park, *su tío político*, a man said to occupy an orderly American suburban house in a neighborhood that was also

the one *el abuelo* had moved to, according to Mr. Washington back on Thirty-ninth Street.

"This uncle of my friend can help us," she said.

"You have a friend?" Keenan asked, and wasn't surprised when Araceli didn't answer.

Already, it seemed to Araceli, things were going more smoothly than she expected, the bus was advancing quickly through streets with little resistance from the usual weekday morning traffic. For a moment Araceli was struck by the emptiness, and the sense that she might be missing a key piece of information that explained this strangely quiet Tuesday.

They switched lines on California Street and headed southward, now inside a bus in which they were the only passengers, alone with the driver's unauthorized personal radio. "That was a four-point-eight, centered in Barstow," the radio declared. "L.A. County Fire Chief Bill Abrams asks that we all use fireworks safely . . . There's a red-flag warning in the canyons of Los Angeles and Orange counties, which means acute fire danger . . . It's clear sailing on the freeways for all you holiday travelers . . ." The bus entered a neighborhood of cream-colored mini-Mission cottages with arched doorways, and unadorned apartment buildings that resembled Monopoly hotels, the skyline behind them dominated by the steel monsters of twin power trunk lines, and a half-dozen parallel strings that drew the boys' gazes upward to watch their arcs descend and rise from one tower to the next.

"We're following the electricity," Keenan said.

"Yeah," Brandon said. "We're like electrons or something."

They reached their final stop and moved to the door at the front of the bus, Araceli taking a moment to ask the mustachioed driver, who looked Mexican, "*¿Qué se hizo toda la gente?*"

"*Es el* Fourth of July. *¿No sabías?*" the driver said, the English coming out as harsh as a native's, the Spanish flat and unused. "Wake up, girl. Haven't you been listening? It's a holiday!"

Maureen rolled her car out of the spa at the early but sane hour of eight-fifteen in the morning. She arrived at Paseo Linda Bonita without stopping three hours and twenty-six minutes later, according to

the onboard computer in her automobile. By then, the sun was noon-high and July-strong, and for some reason her husband's automobile was baking in the driveway instead of the garage, an incongruity that nevertheless lifted the anxiety that had overtaken Maureen the night before. *Scott is here.* She opened the garage door, parked her car, and took pleasure in the feeling of having returned to take charge of the home she had built. With her daughter on her arm, Maureen walked purposefully to the door that led from the garage to the kitchen, stepping inside with a shout of "I'm home!" Her eyes settled on the familiar and spotless kitchen, each square of clean tile, each gleaming plane of marble a musical note of order. "I'm home!" Maureen shouted again, putting a little rasp into it this time. The sound echoed through the home without an answer, and for a second or two Maureen concluded this must be a silence of resentment, and that her sons and husband would soon emerge from one of the rooms glowering at her because she had left them for four days.

They debarked from the bus onto a wide avenue that seemed very new to Brandon and very old at the same time. A line of storefronts rose over the street, each edifice a bold, rectangular robot emblazoned with the names of commercial concerns: SOMBREROS EL CHARRO, KID'S LOVE, SPRINT MOBILE. The multitudes that filled this shopping district on most days were absent, and in the soft light of that holiday morning there was only an eight-foot-tall teenage girl with braces and a billowing white dress to greet Araceli and her charges. She was frozen giddily in two dimensions behind a curtain of black steel bars, and when Brandon peeked into her darkened storefront prison at the merchandise that surrounded her, he saw glittering, child-sized crowns and pictures of chariot limousines. This was a place, he concluded, where girls came to be transformed, by dollar and by ritual, into princesses. But Brandon didn't like princess stories and his attention quickly returned to the street and to his brother and Araceli, who were both turning their heads north and south and back again.

"Which way do we go?" Keenan said.

"*Tengo que preguntar,*" Araceli said, but there was no one around to ask, and they began to walk down the sidewalk, past parking meters

and empty diagonal parking spaces, underneath the fluted tower of a shuttered Deco movie palace, Keenan craning his head to admire the melting green skin of a nonfunctioning bronze clock affixed to the top. After half a block, they found one store with an open door and lights on behind the display windows.

"Not open," said the Korean woman inside. She was kneeling on the floor with a clipboard, surrounded by boxes and racks of rayon blouses. "*Cerrado.*"

"I am not looking for clothes," Araceli said. "I am looking for a street." She showed the woman a slip of paper with the address Marisela had given her.

Myung Lee rose to her feet, took the address, and then sized up the child-accompanied woman who had given it to her. In the four months since opening her business, every day seemed to bring another oddity, another riddle, like this Mexican woman and her handsome children. Myung Lee was a native of Seoul, single, thirty-eight years old, and fluent in the language of local fashions: rayon with tropical flowers and leopard prints and bold décolletages, free-flowing polyesters to drape over bodies of any shape or size. "Maybe I know this street," she said. Geography was easy: what she didn't understand was the stealthy methodology of the shoplifters, or the pricing logic of the wholesalers in the garment-factory district, or why her uncle would lend her $40,000 to open a business, while expecting her to fail. This Fourth of July morning brought more lonely hours of inventory, and more obsessive daydreaming about her uncle and his haughty California millionaire confidence and his thin teenage daughter with her size-two dresses and their mansion in that Asian Beverly Hills called Bradbury. The longer Myung remembered her debt to her skeptical *samchon*, the more she hated rayon and tropical flowers and leopard patterns. Oddly, however, she still liked being in the presence of American women, or Mexican women, or whatever most of her clients were, and as she moved to the door to show Araceli which way to go, she felt the irritation on her face slipping into the pleasantness that was always good retail practice.

"This is over there," Myung Lee said, pointing to the east. "Not far. Two blocks." She placed a hand on Keenan's shoulder and said, "Your boys are very nice," leaving Araceli too stunned to offer any clarification. *Their father must be very fair,* Myung Lee thought, and she imagined

this missing white partner as the strangers walked away down Pacific Boulevard. *I am a single woman, yes, but I haven't allowed a man to leave me with two boys to feed and clothe. No.*

"She thought you were our mother," Keenan said. "That was weird."

"*Estaba muy confundida,*" Araceli said, and they headed away from empty Pacific Boulevard into a neighborhood of houses with sandpaper skins painted blue-violet and carnation-pink, with little patches of stiff crabgrass enclosed behind painted brick pillars and iron bars welded in feather and fan patterns. A canopy of intersecting utility wires drew Brandon's eye upward again, while Keenan looked across the street and saw a man leaning against a fence with his hips thrust out in the style of Latin American *campesinos*, a pose that reminded Keenan of the hand-ful of childhood photographs he'd seen of his grandfather. "Maybe this *is* where Grandpa John lives," Keenan said.

"I guess," Brandon said. "It's not as poor as Los Angeles."

They advanced two blocks more and the street name still did not materialize on any of the signs, and Araceli stopped again, and the roll-ing wheels of the suitcases ceased their noise, and for a moment she and her charges stood in an unexpectedly deep silence. The thorough-fares and the freeways that surrounded the neighborhood were empty in those first hours of a holiday morning, no trucks or forklifts were at work in the nearby industrial districts, and in the absence of the usual noise there was a natural stillness that seemed somehow unnatural. Every Huntington Park resident who was up and about that morning noticed the quiet too; it hit them first through the windows left open on a summer night, and later when they stepped outside. They heard the calls of the birds for the first time in months, the *keek-keek* of high-flying, black-necked stilts heading for the nearby Los Angeles River, the three-note carols of American robins, and the Morse-code tapping of woodpeckers hunting for acorns stored inside the utility poles. As their ears adjusted to the quiet, they heard fainter sounds still: the whistling of air through the wings of the mourning doves, and the creak and rustle of tree branches moved by the weak flow of the July wind. They were small-town sounds, country sounds, and they had the effect of making those who heard them more aware of the charms of their time and place, and of all that was comforting and homey in the cluttered workingman's paradise that Huntington Park wanted to be.

The quiet caused Victorino Alamillo, the only man awake and out-doors on his block, to pause in the unfurling of his American flag, con-templating for a moment his 1972 Chevy truck and camper shell in repose in the driveway, until his eye was drawn skyward by the sight of a crow bullet-gliding one hundred feet in the air. After climbing to the top of his ladder, he stopped again, flag in hand, because from that perch the spread of the quiet across the neighborhood was all the more apparent. He could scan the roofs of his neighbors' houses, see their satellite dishes and kitchen vents and the nearby district of salvage shops, and hear a few distant but sharp sounds: the *fee-bee? fee-bee?* question posed by a black phoebe, and then, most improbably, the braying of an invisible goat. *¿Un chivo?*

Suddenly, the spell was broken by a clack-clack coming from the sidewalk.

"Excuse me," Araceli said. "Excuse! Me!"

Araceli and her charges had stopped at their first encounter with a person who seemed capable of helping them—a man whose flag seemed to imbue him with authority. They had been watching him for several seconds, beginning with his climb up the ladder, flag in hand, looking to Brandon and Keenan like a man claiming a piece of real estate for his country at the end of a battle.

Victorino Alamillo looked down at Araceli, and hearing her marked accent answered, "*Espérate allí un momentito.*" Seeing this lost trio, ob-viously in flight from some familial mash-up, brought him fully back to the real Huntington Park, reminding him of the transient, unsettled place this really was. Suddenly, the flag and the hammer he was hold-ing both fell from his hand.

"I think the star means he has a kid who's in the war," Brandon said, pointing to a rectangle with a single blue star that was affixed mys-teriously to the inside of the home's living room window.

"Correct," Victorino said, as he descended to retrieve the flag. "My son is in Kandahar. *En* Afghanistan. He is a medic." He pronounced this last word in a way that conveyed pacifist fatherly pride.

"That's cool," Keenan said.

"*Estamos buscando esta calle,*" Araceli said. "*La calle* Rugby."

"*Está del otro lado de* Pacific," Victorino said, pointing westward. "*Regrésate por allá.*"

"*¿Está seguro?*" Araceli asked, rather impertinently. "*Porque una coreana nos dijo que era por aquí.*"

"*Sí, señorita,*" Victorino said. Switching to the authoritative sound of English, he added, "I've lived here fifteen years. It's that way."

Araceli grave a curt "*Gracias*" and without further ceremony headed west, with Brandon and Keenan trailing after. They had entered a landscape of very old American dreams. Huntington Park was a collection of truck farms subdivided a century ago into a grid of homes, and inhabited ever since by men and women lured in by affordable mortgages, by a shared belief in the value of square footage in a U.S. city, the nearby factories, warehouses, and freight trains be damned. For the first third of its history Huntington Park had been homesteaded by English-speakers with Oklahoma and Iowa and other flat American places in their pasts, and for the next third of its history those proud but paranoid people had fought to keep various dark-skinned others out, until finally evacuating in favor of those who dominated Huntington Park in the most recent third of its history: transplants from South Texas, Jalisco, Zacatecas, and East Los Angeles, and other places filled with Spanish-surnamed people. All these home owners, in all these epochs, came and found comfort in the perpendicular streets, in the surveyor's patient construction of uniformity and efficient use of space, in the stop signals, and in the city workers who cleaned the parks. A red-and-white-striped flag and its blue field with white stars had long been a symbol of that nurturing and protective order, and it remained so for many in Huntington Park, even those who still preferred the colors of other flags and the other kinds of order those banners represented.

With the clack-clack of Keenan's suitcase resuming behind him, Victorino Alamillo took his Stars and Stripes and began to hammer, unaware that the sounds were rousing his neighbor Jack Salazar from his bed, causing him to pull back a curtain. *Alamillo is putting up his flag. Finally! He waits until the actual Fourth!* Jack Salazar also had a blue star in the window, and a son in Ramadi, Iraq, and two American flags that hung from the eaves 365 days a year. He noted that with the addition of Alamillo's flag there were now three houses on the block that were bold enough to show their patriotism on Independence Day—*a whole three!*—though one of those belonged to a Pakistani family, and they almost didn't count in Salazar's right-leaning, fourth-generation

Mexican-American opinion. The Pakistani family's flag was plastic, and Salazar sensed they'd put it up so he would stop looking at them suspiciously, or so that he would come over and chat with them as if they were normal Americans, though the truth was that the Pakistani family put up that flag because their daughter Nadia had purchased it during an immigration-rights march in downtown Los Angeles. Nadia Bashir, a twenty-year-old UCLA biochemistry undergrad, had decided that hanging it over the front door would make for a personal and somewhat ironic statement about her family's ongoing state of cultural evolution. On the day she put up the flag, she remembered her uncle Faisal and his tales of his first, carefree travels through middle Canada and middle America in a Volkswagen Beetle in the 1980s, selling bongs from the trunk. The U.S., he liked to say, was still the feel-good country he had known then.

"There are no clans here," he'd say. "That is why the Americans prosper. They don't have these silly, inbred resentments like we do. We are too clannish. It's always held us back."

To which Nadia very often answered, in the sassy and slightly nasal tones of a Los Angeles accent that sounded charmingly provincial to her Pakistani-born, London-educated uncle, "No clans? Gimme a break! Even in this tiny city, all we have is clans!" In Huntington Park there was a large Spanish-speaking Mexican clan, and the shrinking but still influential Mexican-American clan that never spoke Spanish, and a small clan of people who still called themselves white, and the scattered and reserved Koreans and Chinese, and now a very quickly growing Muslim clan, which was the newest in this part of the metropolis and thus the most feared and misunderstood by all the others. Add to this the warring clans of the street gangs with their baroque entanglements, and the caustic comedy delivered by the two political clans viciously facing off every other Tuesday at the meetings of the City Council, and it all looked as messy as anything on the subcontinent. There was an undercurrent of psychic violence to Huntington Park, Nadia thought, alive underneath a façade of coexistence that was as fragile as the quiet that had miraculously enveloped the neighborhood this morning, interrupted only by the clack-clack of three outsiders walking past her bedroom window.

"Maybe we should show someone the picture of our grandpa, to see if he lives around here," Keenan said.

The same idea had occurred to Araceli, until she remembered how ancient the photograph was—she would only make a fool of herself. This neighborhood they were in now, Araceli noted, was clearly newer than the one that housed the shack where *el abuelo* Torres had lived a half century ago, and most of the people she could see stirring behind screen doors and windows were much younger than he was. They seemed unabashedly Mexican to her, despite the occasional U.S. flag. Araceli sensed they were, like her, relatively recent beneficiaries of the American cash boom, that they were housekeepers and laborers just a decade or so ahead of her in filling their dollar-bill piggy banks. No, they would not know John, Johnny, or Juan Torres, so she wouldn't waste any energy asking. Instead, she would find Marisela's uncle and ask him to tap into those rivers of American information that were still a bit of a mystery to Araceli, the lists of names and numbers that smart fingers could make appear on computer screens, and he would make a phone call, and liberate her from her charges and this journey.

Huntington Park more fully awakened in the half hour it took Araceli and the boys to return to Pacific Avenue and cross to the other side, into a neighborhood where they were greeted by the creaking springs of two sets of garage doors opening. Freshly showered patriarchs began to retrieve oil-barrel grills, lawn chairs, and other Fourth of July accoutrements, while behind kitchen curtains stoves sizzled with cholesterol-spiking breakfasts. Brandon felt an order in these sounds and their growing volume, the power of routines repeated behind fences and inside homes, while Keenan grew more convinced they were closer to his grandfather, because these were noises he made with his clumsy, old-man hands. As the day progressed further the neighborhood noises would grow louder and more varied: they would become electric and gas-powered, amplified and transmitted far beyond property lines, with pirated MP3 melodies and power-tool percussion jams ruining the quiet inside next-door living rooms where old men were trying to read, goddamnit, to bedrooms a block away where adolescents were trying to sleep past noon. The growing holiday din reminded every resident of the existence of their many neighbors and all their irritating habits, of their penchant to shout for Mom and their poorly maintained toilets, their excessive hair-drying, and how they badgered their sons and daughters and disrespected their parents. With each hour the noise

grew, and it grated, serving as further proof, if any were needed, of the central, inescapable fact that subtracted from Huntington Park's pleasantness: the existence of too many people, too close to one another, in too little space.

The residents of Huntington Park were going to try to forget these many irritations during a Fourth of July they planned to fill with hamburgers and *carne preparada* with cilantro, and mesquite charcoal and the not-necessarily-patriotic acts of crabgrass-lounging and beer-can-lifting. It was a time of down-market plenty in Huntington Park, thanks to second mortgages and their illusory windfalls, and the extra cash on hand from copious overtime working at ports and railyards and warehouses unloading goods from an Industrial Revolution taking place on the other side of the Pacific. *Les va bien,* Araceli observed, *because the Americans still have plenty of money to spend on the things that people like me and these people can do for them.* Araceli did not know, however, that the flow of containers marked with Asian logograms had begun to slow, imperceptibly, and that the burden of mortgages here had begun to grow, as it had elsewhere, leaving the working people of Huntington Park worried about all the purchased pleasures of second cars and debt incurred when garages were converted to playrooms, and thus a bit relieved, relaxed, and decompressed by the prospect of enjoying a free pleasure this evening. For the Fourth of July there would be no tickets to buy, no parking to pay for, no lines to form, but simply the joy of resting and having the show brought to them when the inky curtain of the post-sunset sky fell over the horizon. At that hour they would turn their lawn chairs and their necks toward Salt Lake Park and the municipal fireworks show, and all the neighborhoods across the city grid would be joined together by the light and the explosions of Chinese powder, louder than any other noise on that noisy day. They were sounds of simulated battle meant to unite the respectfully quiet families of Huntington Park and their dysfunctionally loud neighbors in place and purpose, reminding them all of the name of the sovereign land upon which they were standing: Los Estados Unidos de América, the USA. It was a land held together by paychecks with tax deductions and standardized forms available in just about any language, and police cruisers that sometimes stopped late at night at the homes of the most serious violators of aural tranquillity, to tell them to keep it down, if you would,

please. And it was home to a suburb where two boys wandered with their caretaker, scanning the doors and windows for a grandfather who had never lived there.

The rest of the home was as perfect as the kitchen. Maureen found no truant dishes wandering about the house, no bowls filled with cereal and curdling milk in the living room. No dirty clothes marred the hallways, none of the small Danish building blocks were tossed about, the windows were free of smudges. In Araceli's orderliness Maureen sensed an explanation for the emptiness. *They've gone off to do something, it seems, and Scott has taken Araceli with him, which would be the sensible thing to do, and Araceli cleaned before they left, because Araceli is like me and cannot step away from a disorderly home.* But what about Scott's car? Had they left on foot, on an expedition to the park, almost a mile away? Or a picnic in the meadows?

Maureen decided she would wait for them to return, and made lunch for her daughter, leaving the pan and dirty dishes in the sink for Araceli to clean. When they had finished, she said: "Come on, Sam, let's go find your brothers . . . and your father." They were probably walking back from the park. "Let's go rescue them, because that's a long walk uphill. Wonder if poor Araceli can make it."

Five minutes later Maureen and Samantha had pulled up to the same park where she had deposited Araceli and the boys in a fit of pique two weeks earlier, but it was empty, all the maids who usually gathered there absent because it was the Fourth of July. She accelerated away quickly, drove back toward the Estates, and stopped at the bus stop, and from the front seat of the car she looked into the knee-high grass of the meadow, which had been bleached golden-green by the sun, remembering that she actually picnicked there with Scott and the boys a few years back, to take in the unobstructed view of the ocean. They would have returned, but for the cow chips that littered the field and ruined the taste of her sandwiches and of the Pinot Noir. Now she searched the shifting surface of the windblown grass for her husband, or her children, or the tall, thick shape of her Mexican employee.

"Where are they, Samantha?"

Wherever they are, they have to pass by here. On foot, or in a car, they

have to enter through this gate. She had turned off the engine, wondering how long she would have to wait, when she saw a figure emerge on the horizon, a man walking where the meadow dropped steeply, struggling to keep his footing, as if working against an unseen tide.

Araceli unlatched the front gate, followed a straight path through a crabgrass lawn, climbed up to a porch, and rang the doorbell. Her long journey to reach this address was rewarded, delightfully, by the sudden appearance at the door of a ruggedly handsome man in his forties who greeted her with a chivalrous *"Buenos días"* and the same pencil-thin mustache and jaunty smile that had broken hearts when he left Mexico City two decades earlier. Salomón Luján was expecting Araceli and her charges, because an hour earlier he had half listened to his niece's explanation of the Torres-Thompson family saga, while simultaneously watching two work crews install a canopy tent and trampoline in his backyard for the big Luján family Fourth of July fiesta.

Now Mr. Luján stood at his door and heard Araceli tell the story of the absent parents herself. *"Estás haciendo lo que debes hacer, y tus jefes te lo van a agradecer,"* he said. Once a common laborer, Salomón Luján believed that being loyal to your gringo employers was the secret to *mexicano* success on this side of the border, his barrel-chested exertions on behalf of various warehouse owners and construction contractors having lifted him through many layers of North American achievement, including the purchase of this home, his triumphant entry into the water-heater business, and his oath-taking as an American citizen and his recent election to the Huntington Park City Council. He sized up Araceli and decided she too was destined for something better, and, judging from the free-flowing hair styles and leather-sandaled feet of her charges, she was the one who kept order in the hippie household where she worked.

"Stay with us today and tonight if you like, and tomorrow I will find the grandfather," he said, switching to English for the benefit of the two boys. "Today is impossible, because it's the Fourth of July and all the city offices are closed. But first thing in the morning I'll call the city clerk and check voter registration and we'll find him. For the moment, come to the backyard. Our party is just getting started."

He led Araceli and the boys through his living room, which was decorated in a style Salomón's smart-aleck Ivy League daughter called "Zacatecas Soap Opera Chic," with an oil painting of Don Quixote and Sancho Panza on one wall. The Knight-Errant of La Mancha stood for the idea that the Lujáns were descended from a place of nobility and history, where men stood tall on horses and looked proudly over the dry, yellow hills of their patrimony. Don Quixote shared the living room with assorted horseshoes, mounted vintage revolvers, and a sofa-bench and love seat with fragile, wood-carved legs and cream velvet cushions embroidered with gold swirls, both pieces shipped in from "the best kitschy furniture maker in Durango," as his daughter put it. Scattered among these symbols of his romantic outlook were family pictures, including one portrait of the aforementioned daughter in cap and gown, and another of the family patriarch raising a clasped hand on election night with the mayor of Huntington Park. Brandon and Keenan looked at that picture a second or two without knowing what its precise meaning might be, though Brandon surmised from both the image and the air of steadiness and authority of Mr. Luján that he had recently been named president of Huntington Park.

They moved to the backyard, where six rented white tables had been arranged under the mustard-colored light that seeped through the tarpaulin skin of the tent. Salomón led Araceli and the boys past a cluster of half-awake young people gathered at the tables, to the edge of the backyard, where two men with shovels were standing and conversing around a mound of beige dirt that seemed to have bubbled up from the lawn.

"We're having *carnitas*, the way they do it in the ranchos," Salomón told the boys. "There's a pig buried in there."

"Underground?" Brandon asked.

"Yeah, we got hot rocks down there. And the pig, wrapped in foil, cooking. We let it cook for some hours. When it finish, you have very juicy meat. *Sabrosísima*."

Brandon gave the mound a look of innocent puzzlement, causing Mr. Luján and the two sweaty, stubbly-faced men with the shovels to grin: he was, in fact, deeply troubled by the idea that combustion was taking place in the unseen hollows beneath his feet. "I thought fire needed oxygen to burn," he said, but Mr. Luján had turned his attention

elsewhere and did not answer, and his two cousins with the shovels didn't speak English well enough to explain the simple physics of their *carnitas* barbecue. After thinking about it for a few seconds, Brandon came to the disturbing conclusion that he was standing over a pit of buried flames, as in the underworlds often depicted in the books he read: souls trapped in subterranean passages, evildoers building infernal machines in caves. He considered, for a moment, running away, until Mr. Luján returned and put his arm on his shoulder.

"Let me introduce you to the people here," he said to the boys. And then he turned to Araceli and said in collegial Spanish, "*Y tú también.*"

For the moment, the only guests were the four young adults sitting half asleep at the table, seemingly hypnotized by the piano resonating from two transistor-radio-sized speakers. A single piano note repeated inside the swirl of a flute, and then a tenor began to sing, pushing into falsetto, and Araceli found it odd that these people with their obvious Mesoamerican features were listening to a rather effete voice singing words in English.

> *History involved itself,*
> *mysterious shade that took its form.*
> *Or what it was, incarnation,*
> *three stars,*
> *delivering signs and dusting from their eyes.*

"*¡Buenos días!*" Councilman Luján said, causing his daughter, Lucía, to startle and sit up straight, and her three friends to emit wake-up groans and coughs.

"This is Araceli," he said to Lucía. "She's a friend of your cousin Marisela. And she's visiting us for Fourth of July with the two boys she takes care of. *¿Cómo se llaman?*"

"Brandon."

"Keenan."

"Look, they just finished with the trampoline," Councilman Luján said. "*Vayan a jugar.* Go play."

The boys ran off, while Araceli joined the four young adults. Lucía Luján was nineteen, and Araceli recognized her immediately as the girl in the cap and gown in the living room, even though the thick

braids into which she had woven her hair for summer had the curious effect of making her look younger than in the photograph. Her friends wore jewels and studs in the crooks of their noses, and loops inside their earlobes, and presented Araceli with the realization that she was losing touch with urban fashions. Probably they were already wearing these things in Mexico City, or would soon be, Araceli thought. "*Hola, ¿qué tal?*" Lucía said, after rubbing the sleepiness out of her eyes. "I think my cousin told me about you once."

Lucía was wearing the same clothes she had put on the night before, but even in this wrinkled and weary state, she presented a picture of hip and fashionable *mexicana* femininity. She wore a vintage pin-tucked blouse of caramel silk, its shimmering skin playing an odd light-game with the copper tone of her skin and the half dozen friendship bracelets on her wrist. That blouse looked one hundred years old to Araceli and brand-new at the same time. Lucía was two weeks back from Princeton and still suffering from the cruel cultural whiplash caused by her return to Huntington Park: she had lived nine months among assorted geniuses and trust-fund children from across the United States, none of whom understood the contradictions of being a young expatriate from her own, wire-crossed corner of *mexicano* California. A week before finals she had split up with a young man who hailed from a moneyed Long Island suburb, in part because he had talked about coming to Huntington Park this summer, and the thought of him entering her home in his Tommy Hilfiger summer-wear was too much to bear. She imagined him reciting to her friends those Lorca poems he had memorized—*¡verde que te quiero verde!*—and thought, *No, that won't go over well in HP.* She was still trying to figure out where she stood after a nine-month waking dream of calcified eastern tradition and unadorned American ambition. *I am not the same Lucía.* She was trying to figure out too how to tell her father that she had already dropped the premed classes in favor of Walt Whitman, Jack Kerouac, and James Baldwin. Lucía the Ivy Leaguer did not smile or laugh as easily as before, and sometimes she laughed harder and louder and with a kind of cynical meanness her friends did not recognize. Both Lucía's father and her friends had been giving her strange looks as if to say, *Is it possible you think you are better than us now?* It was, therefore, a pleasure for Lucía to fall into conversation with an educated Latina from outside her

Huntington Park and Princeton orbits. After just a few minutes of casual conversation, she had learned a lot about Araceli, the Instituto Nacional de Bellas Artes, and what it was like to clean houses in Orange County.

Araceli said she wasn't sure if she'd ever go back to school, but that she wasn't going to be doing *"esto"* much longer, gesturing rather coldly in the direction of Brandon and Keenan on the trampoline. She had a little money saved up, and the *"aventura"* with the boys would be her last.

Lucía understood everything Araceli said, although her own *castellano* came out slowly and with the simple vocabulary of a much younger person—she had studied French in high school and never been formally educated in Spanish—and she often fell back to English.

"Go with what your heart tells you," Lucía said, and then repeated the phrase in Spanish, *"Haz lo que te diga tu corazón."* She gave a sidelong glance to her friends, who had drifted into semi-sleep again, their heads resting on the table. "I'm studying history and American literature. I don't know why. Just because I like stories, I guess. My dad's got a good story. Maybe I'll write it someday."

Scott had stayed up late into the night on the beach, watching the march of the constellations along the ecliptic, his dark-adjusted eyes making out the oval smudge of the Andromeda Galaxy. He had watched the flight of low-flying birds along the purple-blue twilight waters, the black featureless forms of two helicopters headed southward to Mexico, and the silent, slow drift of lighted ships, and then he had fallen asleep sometime deep into the night, his head resting near the top of the sloping sand that rose from the water. He had been awakened after dawn by the simultaneous assault of the first rays of morning sun on his face and the first wave splashing the balls of his feet. He stretched out, then took a long, slow walk along the beach, listening to screaming seagulls. When he reached a tide pool he'd once visited with the boys, he held back tears at the not entirely rational thought that he might never enjoy such a life-affirming paternal moment again, until finally his rumbling stomach cured him of such melodrama and he decided to begin the long climb back to his house. He would launch

a search for his wife and children, who had likely left for Missouri to spend a week, or perhaps a month or two in recreation and exile from their abusive paterfamilias, and perhaps he would go there to plead his case.

He was surprised to spot, halfway through his quarter-mile trek through the meadow, the familiar high silhouette of his wife's car. For a moment he felt a sense of relief and reprieve—they had not left him after all—and then once again a sense of foreboding when he realized he would have to add an explanation for this night out on the beach to his apology for the fiasco in the living room and his absence over the past four days. *She'll think I've gone totally nuts.* He got closer to the car and imagined his unhappy sons inside, and the daughter who would wrap her arms around him no matter what. When he reached the car, smiling despite himself, the electric-driven window lowered theatrically, revealing Maureen's sunglasses, which she quickly lowered to study him and his surroundings with unshaded eyes.

"Where are the boys?" she asked quickly.

"What?"

Maureen had seen Scott appear on the horizon, and she too felt her apprehensions lifting, a motherly reunion just moments away. She too imagined an embrace, or several, dropping to her knees as one did when children were smaller. But no, Scott was alone.

"Where are the boys?" she insisted.

"You don't have them?"

"I have Samantha! I left with Samantha and left you with Brandon and Keenan."

"No, you didn't. I wasn't home."

"What are you talking about?"

"I don't have any of the kids. I left. I thought they were all with you."

"I left on Friday with Samantha."

"You didn't take the boys?"

"Obviously not!"

"Where are they?"

By dusk the Lujáns' ample backyard was filled with a hundred people chewing pork whose succulent juices pooled at the bottoms of

paper plates, and triggered memories of summer barbecues in provincial Mexican cities with gazebos and stone churches. Araceli noted that they were significantly better dressed than the summer partygoers at the Torres-Thompson residence. They were all immigrants linked to Mr. Luján by blood, marriage, and business ties, and several were compadres of Mr. Luján and his wife. Not having lost the sense of formality attached to family gatherings in their native country, the men were dressed in freshly ironed shirts tucked into jeans and polished snakeskin boots, and the women wore big jewelry and ran wet combs through their sons' hair, and teased and pulled their daughters' hair into buns, braids, ponytails, and little black fountains held in place with barrettes that bore butterflies and flowers. The men showed off new brass belt buckles with Mexican flags and the names of towns in Jalisco and Durango, and the women moved about in newly purchased jeans or stiff dresses whose wide linen cones resembled the style worn in U.S. movies during the Eisenhower era.

Alongside this older, largely Mexican-born and Spanish-speaking group, there was a younger circle of partygoers, speakers of English and Spanglish, teenagers and sedate twentysomethings who equated good taste with understated flair and the ironic embrace of fashions past. They wore porkpie hats and baseball caps, jeans with narrow legs, canvas tennis shoes and mauve T-shirts of high-quality cotton, and campy links of faux-gold chains. A couple were dressed in baseball jerseys as wide as capes, and the shorts and knee-high white socks that a goofy midwestern suburban dad might wear, their cottoned feet stuffed into *guarache* sandals, a style Lucía liked to call "retro summer gangster casual." They were all people of understated ambitions too, most having graduated to new jobs at hardware stores and composition-writing classes at community colleges, or to long drives across the metropolis to the waiting lists and crowded parking lots of underfunded state universities.

Both groups of guests, young and old, looked at Mr. Luján and his daughter, Lucía, with varying degrees of respect and envy, because in their own way father and daughter were the most successful people they knew. The compadres entered Mr. Luján's home and found its knight-errant furnishings tasteful and elegant, and they saw in Lucía and the famous university attached to her name a shiny specialness that made them sick to their stomachs with worry about their own progeny and

how studious and dedicated those children might or might not be. Among her friends too, Lucía was the subject of awe, esteem, and suspicion, because she had gone farther away from Huntington Park than anyone else they knew, and because she had come back from this distant and wealthy place to stand underneath the power wires and sip beer as if she were an ordinary HP girl, even though she knew she would never be an ordinary HP girl again.

Among all these people, young and old, Mexican-born and California-born, the presence at the party of two Orange County boys went largely unnoticed, with Brandon and Keenan slipping easily into the mostly English-speaking orbit of the children, and only a few parents noticing their long bohemian locks, or the ease with which they glided across the backyard in their bare feet and untrimmed toenails. But after just a few minutes no one failed to notice the *paisana* with Germanic height and bronze freckles, dressed like some explorer in a canvas hat, presenting them all with the mystery of her person. She was too old and not casually stylish enough to be one of Lucía's friends, but too young and not formal enough to be one of the compadres.

"*¿A quién llevas en la camisa?*" Araceli asked one of Lucía Luján's friends, switching to English when he didn't seem to understand her right away. "On your shirt. *Ese hombre.* He looks like Jesus, but he is smoking. *Y tengo entendido que Jesucristo Nuestro Señor no fumaba.* Jesus does not smoke."

Griselda Pulido, Lucía Luján's best-friend-forever, heard Araceli's *chilanga* accent, and began to pepper her with questions about Mexico City. Griselda had long thought of Mexico's capital as a kind of Paris, a destination she would visit one day in solemn pilgrimage, a place where a woman with Mexican roots might escape her fraught American existence and find her true self. She wanted to know where the *chilangos* went out at night, what rock bands they listened to, and at which nightclubs they danced. "What is the Palacio de Bellas Artes like?" Griselda Pulido asked. Switching to Spanglish, she asked, "*Tienen las pinturas de Frida allí*, or do you have to go to her house in Coyoacán?"

To Araceli, this woman Griselda seemed as intelligent and curious as Lucía, but with a tragic air that was only heightened by the velvet eye shadow she wore, and cross-combed hair that ran down her forehead and crashed upon the eyebrows. "I got into Brown, which is in Rhode Is-

land, and I thought I'd hang out over there on the East Coast with Lucía, but I couldn't go," Griselda said, and Araceli looked her straight in the eye to say, *I understand completely.* Going to school for as long as they wanted was one of those things *latinoamericana* girls couldn't do, and hadn't been able to do for centuries, the same inequity having kept at least one of Araceli's grandmothers illiterate her entire life. *Our feminine emancipation is incomplete: maybe our daughters, if we ever have any, will be free.* Araceli tried to answer Griselda's questions about Mexico's capital city as best she could, even though she was a bit thrown by the way Griselda weaved English and Spanish together, so freely and without care.

"Lucía and I are going to go there," Griselda said. "*Un día. Tal vez.*"

Araceli wanted to suggest some museums Griselda might not have heard of, but before she could the small man with the smoking Jesus asked her if she'd been to Huntington Park before.

"No," Araceli said. She twisted her mouth into English so Smoking-Jesus Boy would understand her. "But this is a place you can forget easily. So maybe I was here before and I just don't remember." Hearing this, the two homeboys among Lucía's friends stuck their hands deeper in their pockets and squinted approvingly at Araceli through dilated pupils and gave weak and wicked cannabis grins and wondered briefly if this lady had ever been in The Life, over there in Mexico, because she looked like a girl who could handle herself in a fight. A moment later they forgot about her, and looked up at the sickle moon and the first stars of dusk and listened intently to the pulsating bass of the music and how deeply it inhabited infinite space, and then they smelled the fat-laden air coming from the barbecue pit and their stomachs suddenly ached with hollowness, and they decided it was time to get something to eat again.

Araceli was the deepest mystery to all the parents and older relatives present, some of whom were a bit put off when she entered their circle—they were all standing by the tables and their pyramids of pork and side dishes. She was about to plunge her fork into a serving of *carnitas* when she noticed she had inadvertently brought the conversation between the compadres to a sudden halt. "*Buenas tardes,*" she said, eliciting a round of not-especially-friendly "*Buenas tardes*" in return. These mothers and fathers were put off too by Araceli's failure to pay much attention to the boys she was apparently assigned to look after, even

when the older of the two approached and said with a stricken plea, "I think someone should tell all these kids to stop playing with firecrackers because it's so dangerous."

"*¿Qué quieres que haga?*" Araceli asked rhetorically, because there was nothing she could do, and the boy snuck away, leaving all those who observed the exchange to wonder what exactly was going on here with this child-unfriendly woman and those American boys.

"It's true what *el niño* says," one of the moms said in Spanish. "Those things are too dangerous. Someone is going to get burned."

"They see more dangerous things at school, believe me," said another mom dismissively, and with this all the mothers and fathers in the circle nodded. "The other day, I go to pick up my son and the entire school is surrounded by police cars and police officers, and there is what they call a 'lockdown.' My son is in the sixth grade, believe it or not, and one of the kids is running down the hallway with a knife. I think he stabbed a teacher in the leg with it."

"*Qué barbaridad.*"

"The things that go on in those schools."

"My son is in sixth grade too, and he doesn't know his times tables past three," one of the fathers said. "'What's six times eight?' I ask him, and he looks at me all confused. So I tell him, 'What are they teaching you there?' and he says, 'I don't know.' In my pueblo, they taught us that in the second year."

"What are we supposed to do?" one of the mothers said.

"You're supposed to go to the teacher and complain," Lucía Luján interjected in English, having just entered the circle on the hunt for her own plate of food. "You're supposed to get in the face of that teacher and say, '*What's up with the times tables?*'"

"*¿Podemos hacer eso?*"

"Of course you can. That's how this country works. Get a classroom full of white kids, and that's what their parents do all the time. They treat every teacher like a worker."

"*Tiene razón,*" Araceli said. "*La señora Maureen, mi jefa, siempre está peleando con los maestros.*"

"But if we go, they don't take us seriously," one of the mothers said, speaking directly to Lucía. "You go to the office and they tell us, 'What are you doing here? Go away. We're busy.'"

They all paused, middle-aged and young, Mexican-born and U.S.-born, and considered the betrayal of the schools, and the steel mesh that covered every window, the security cameras in the hallways, the posted warnings aimed at student and adult alike, and a few of them very self-consciously allowed their eyes to drift over to those young girls and boys who were their blood and their responsibility, running and bouncing in the backyard, each child gleaming and full of promise, and each poor and stripped of it. Boy and girl screams filled the silence that followed, which was heavy with hurt and powerlessness and a certain unfocused sense of workingman's defiance that found no words in which it could be expressed.

Araceli broke the wordlessness suddenly, to say that the kids she cared for seemed to be getting an excellent education.

"Where are they from?"

"*Los* Laguna Rancho Estates. *Por la playa. En los cerros.*"

"The public schools are good down there, I bet," Lucía Luján said.

"*No van a la escuela pública,*" Araceli said. "Private school. *Todo pagado. Y muy caro.* Very expensive. I see the bills."

"How much?" Lucía Luján asked quickly.

Araceli spoke the figure in slow and deliberate Spanish, allowing its mathematical obscenity, its thousands and thousands, to hover over the assembled hardworking, cash-strapped, taxpaying adults and scholarship-funded college students like a blinding glow of fake sunshine. There were one or two gasps, though Lucía Luján's eyebrows rose with only moderate surprise—the tuition for those two boys, together, was a bit more than her tuition at Princeton, before all the financial aid kicked in.

"*Imposible,*" one of the parents said.

"*Estás loca,*" said another.

"*No sea chismosa. Por favor.*"

It was preposterous, and suddenly everyone in the circle except Lucía was angry at Araceli for revealing a figure that, were they to accept it as truth, would temporarily strip them of some of their own moderately elevated sense of accomplishment, by revealing just how small their achievements were relative to true American success and affluence. The compadres with kids in parochial school imagined they were paying top dollar, but in fact it was a small fraction of the sum Araceli had just divulged, even though those gringo boys didn't look so

much different than theirs, not especially special, and certainly not that rich.

"*Es lo que cuesta,*" Araceli insisted. She explained that she knew this startling fact not because she'd made any effort to find out, but rather because her employers were exceedingly casual with their paperwork and left letters and bills lying around. And with a dollar figure that big screaming from the kitchen countertop, even a normally circumspect housekeeper like Araceli had to take a look.

"You're pretty sure about that number?" Lucía asked.

"*Claro que sí,*" Araceli said.

"No," one of the compadres insisted. "*Estás confundida.*"

I might be just a housekeeper and a chilanga, Araceli wanted to say, *but I know basic English and math and the meaning of commas and decimal points and dollar signs.* But instead she gave a long glance at her disbelieving audience, then shook her head with a dismissive chuckle that was instantly recognizable to Lucía for its thick layering of intellectual condescension. With that all the compadres and Lucía drifted away, leaving Araceli amused and finally able to take a first real bite of the *carnitas,* which were quite juicy. She searched for the boys and spotted them, and then decided she could forget about them again, because here in this big backyard they would be safe.

Brandon and Keenan were running about the backyard with the children of the extended Luján clan. Having watched the men with the shovels remove their dirt and then the foil-wrapped meat, and a few hot rocks, Brandon had persuaded himself that he was no longer in danger from the fires in the earth, though now there were various firecrackers and flames and explosions going off in the air around him. Salomón's brother Pedro had brought three large boxes' worth of assorted hand-held pyrotechnics from Tijuana, and the children were playing with them, the most popular being small silver balls that burst into sparks when the children flung them against the patio's concrete floor.

"I got you! I got you!" a girl yelled as one of her "fire rocks" exploded at Keenan's feet, and Keenan replied by throwing one back at her, and laughing as she squealed.

"Be careful!" Brandon shouted at his brother and anyone else in earshot, though no one listened. A boy was lighting firecrackers and throwing them into the now-empty pig pit and there were no adults

stopping him. Gunpowder tickled Brandon's nose, and bits of paper and cardboard from the firecrackers were littering the patio floor and the lawn, and there were other kids igniting sticks that spit fire and whistled, holding them too close to their eyes, and they wouldn't stop even when Brandon shouted out "*¡Cuidado!*" in Spanish. He looked for Araceli, but she had drifted away into the crowd of people tearing at meat from the buried pig with their teeth, and for the first time since leaving his home on Paseo Linda Bonita, Brandon felt truly alone and afraid. The firecracker explosions pinched his eardrums and the neighborhood dogs were suffering too, filling the air with their wailing and barking on this block and all the others surrounding it, begging the humans to cease fire. It was one thing to play war when all the sounds came from your mouth or your imagination, and quite another to be standing in a cloud of gunpowder. Now he heard a powerful explosion, felt the thumping vibration in his chest, and then the echo of the boom. "An M-80!" a boy shouted, and Brandon wondered why no one in the backyard was ducking for cover when there were bombs exploding out on the street.

A flash of light on the horizon caught his eye, and he turned to see three fire bursts growing in the shape of dandelions against the dark gray sky, followed by the muffled sound a few seconds later of distant cannons.

"*¡Son los* fireworks *de la ciudad!*" someone shouted, just as more burning dandelions emerged, their light shining on the distant transmission lines and the towers. "The city fireworks show!" someone else said, and now everyone was turning and watching as more bursts followed, some in the shape of flying saucers, in green and crimson and yellow, some drooping like jellyfish, others slithering through the sky like serpents, and finally one forming a large orb that loomed over the towers and the neighborhood like a small planet, causing many oohs and ahhs from the people gathered in the Luján backyard.

The planet fell from the sky and the explosions stopped, suddenly. For ten, twenty, thirty seconds the adults and children looked up at the blank sky and waited for the next burst of light. They saw only a large cloud of smoke, drifting slowly eastward like a white Rorschach test across the dark sky. From beginning to end the sixty-third annual Huntington Park Fireworks Extravaganza was the shortest in city history,

having lasted just four minutes and thirty-five seconds, the city having failed to take note of the nationwide fireworks shortage caused by a warehouse explosion in China's Guangdong Province some months earlier.

"That's it?" someone said in English.

"¿*Se acabó?*"

"What a rip-off!"

Standing by the table where the *carnitas* were being carved, City Councilman Salomón Luján stood with a large serving fork, took in the empty horizon, and uttered a useful English exclamation that had been one of the first to drift into his vocabulary:

"Oh, shit."

After a harried exchange of shouted questions and answers during their five-minute drive up the hill to Paseo Linda Bonita, Maureen and Scott realized that Brandon and Keenan had been alone with Araceli since Friday morning, and that neither had talked to the boys since calling home on Friday evening. The length of their absence stretched out to unseemly numbers: four days, more than ninety-six hours of blank and unknown chapters in their sons' lives, ninety-six hours in which they had abdicated their parental responsibilities. *When they are small, you are vigilant at the playground, you never allow your eye to stray from them for more than a few seconds,* Maureen thought. *And if you lose sight of them, for twenty seconds, for a minute, you are transported suddenly into an abyss of guilt and panic, and you scan the surroundings against the idea that your loss will endure forever, until you spot them and your heart returns to that calm place where parents most seek to live.* Maureen drove past the guard shack without bothering to acknowledge the pregnant woman on duty, and violated the 25 MPH speed limit signs, flying over speed bumps and making several squealing turns up the sinuous streets of the Laguna Rancho Estates. She pulled into the garage and ran into the house, leaving Samantha still strapped in the car with her father.

Although Maureen had been in the house thirty minutes earlier, and recognized the improbability that her sons might have returned in that short time, she called out their names again: "Brandon! Keenan!

Mommy and Daddy are home! Brandon! Keenan!" This maternal reflex became more of a plea and lament with each repetition, until Scott said, "They're not here," which caused Maureen to turn and snap at him, "I can see that!"

Scott began looking for a note from Araceli, and for clues about her departure and destination. There was nothing in the kitchen, the place where one might have expected her to leave a message. In the living room he was distracted by the great open space where the shattered coffee table had once been, and thus failed to notice that one of the picture frames on the bookshelves was empty. He moved back to the kitchen, where he informed Maureen of the undeniable conclusion that their children had not been home for a while. "If you look closely you can tell the bathrooms haven't been used for at least twenty-four hours, if not longer," he said. "And no one used the kitchen until you got here and made that meal for Samantha. Right?" Before Maureen could answer, Scott headed toward the door that led from the kitchen to the backyard and the guesthouse, and stepped across the open space to Araceli's door again, and tried turning the handle.

"Do we have a key for this door?"

For the next ten minutes, Maureen and Scott searched their home for a spare guesthouse key, until they found a plastic sandwich bag filled with keys in a drawer in the laundry room. They rushed back to Araceli's room: neither had set foot in this locked corner of their property for the four years Araceli been their employee, respecting the Mexican woman's privacy and trusting her to keep it clean. They opened the door and entered a space of unexpected clutter and mystery. Their eyes were drawn immediately upward, to an object hanging from the ceiling of the small living room. It hovered over a small drafting table and many drawings taped to the walls, along with pictures cut from magazines, a floating sculpture that drifted very slowly in the faint, hot breeze that seeped through the room's lone, partially opened window.

Maureen stepped back to the doorway so that she could focus on the object in its entirety. It was a bird of prey, assembled from one hundred or more blue, white, red, orange, and yellow disposable forks, knives, and spoons that Maureen had purchased for the last few birthday parties. The utensils had been fused together into a bird about three feet long, its clawed feet made from broken fork prongs, while

many serrated knives were layered together to form the teeth, and two layers or more of utensils formed the body and wings, the smooth plastic covered, haphazardly, with ripped-up strips of discarded clothing and dishrags, the various textures creating an especially meaty-looking representation of flesh and feather. The sculpture had the crude quality of an object formed by a series of haphazard and violent collisions, and in a letter to one of her friends Araceli had called it *El Fénix de la Basura*, the Garbage Phoenix. Araceli liked it both for its disturbing, otherworldly quality and as a commentary on her situation in the United States: she dusted it once a month, but had recently considered taking it down, because in the one-woman artistic circle that followed her work, the Garbage Phoenix was becoming passé. Maureen studied this creation and then examined the drawings on the walls. There was a eight-by-eleven-inch self-portrait in which Araceli had enlarged the size of her own nostrils, and rendered the rest of her face in a Picasso-inspired abstract geometry, but without the master's sense of balance and composition. There were several pencil and charcoal sketches of shoes and sandals ascending and descending the steps in the Tacubaya Metro station, their rotting laces and heels melting into concrete steps covered with swampy moss and dripping water. And there was a collage of hands, assembled from magazines that were stacked on the floor: *My magazines, the ones I threw in the recycling bin.* Maureen studied the hanging sculpture and the drawings, and felt she was looking into the mind of a woman upon whom various psyche-smashing torments had been inflicted. *Is this the same woman who has lived in my house for four years and fed my children and cleaned my clothes? No. This is a stranger. She sulks while she cooks for us, and then she sits here in her free time and creates monstrosities with the broken fragments and discarded objects of our home.* The grim aesthetic of the utensil bird, the cavernous nostrils, and the melting shoes suggested, to Maureen, self-hatred and a suppressed desire toward destruction. Understood in the light of her art, Araceli's surly everyday nature took on new meanings, and this sudden, unexpected insight was all the more unsettling in the light of Scott's announcement that "I looked and there's nothing here, no note, no clue." Araceli had taken the two boys someplace without giving word of where she might be.

Still holding Samantha, who had reached up to try to touch the

mobile, Maureen returned to the kitchen and wondered what they should do next.

Forty minutes after the fiasco of the fireworks, Brandon and Keenan stood on the front porch of the Luján home on Rugby Avenue, having been drawn there, along with much of the Luján family and their guests, by the shouting and chanting coming from the street. With Araceli at their side, the Torres-Thompson boys cast a disoriented squint at a crowd of about one hundred people, all of Latin American descent, gathered in the middle of the roadway, under the flickering light of a streetlamp. Some carried beer bottles in foam sleeves, and others held folded lawn chairs, but all shared the disheveled, sun-burned, and offended look of Fourth of July recreation interrupted and unfulfilled. They had come from the park, and they had come from their lawns, confused by the empty sky, the missing explosions, and the very ordinary, very unpleasant sounds of car alarms and car stereos and crying children left in the truncated show's wake. The vacuum caused by the sudden lack of explosive noise was filled by their own voices telling them to be angry, telling them to remember where they lived. It was a holiday insult added to all the usual, daily HP insults—the dirty tap water, the aggressive parking cops, and the annual surprise of supplemental property-tax fees. "Those fucking council incompetents! Again!" "*¡Pinche ciudad de la chingada!*" And when a certain, very *metiche* woman at the park suggested Luján was to blame, they began to head off in a group to his home, gathering more people on the way.

Councilman Luján appeared on the porch, hanging both thumbs on his belt, and even the children in the crowd seemed enraged, their high-pitched voices adding a feminine squeal to the crowd's collective chant.

"*¡Afuera los Tres! ¡Afuera los Tres! ¡Afuera los Tres!*"

"Out with the three?" Brandon asked no one in particular. "What's that about?"

"They mean my dad and Councilwoman María and Councilman Vicente," said Lucía, who was standing behind him. Sensing the boy was smart enough to understand, she quickly explained the political dispute that pitted her father and two allies against a corrupt mayor. "So when-

ever anything goes wrong, the mayor blames my dad. And his Special Friend, that lady in the back over there, she gets her rabble from *el movimiento* to come out and harass us because we want to reform things." With that, Lucía stepped to the front of the porch and down the steps to the concrete path that ran through the front lawn, and leaned forward into a screaming shout: "Go home, losers!"

"*¡Rateros!*" someone in the crowd shouted back, starting a new chant with the Mexican Spanish idiom meaning "bandit" or "crook." "*¡Ra-te-ros! ¡Ra-te-ros!*"

"You stole the money for the fireworks!"

"Get out here and defend yourself like a man, Salomón. We see how you spent the money for the fireworks on your own party. *¡Ratero!*"

Having heard Lucía's explanations, Araceli scanned the back of the crowd and spotted the mayor's Special Friend, a woman with a black head of hair-sprayed raccoon quills, her temples sporting identical white wings. She was light-skinned and small inside her wide summer paisley dress, and she held at her side a cell phone, which Araceli understood to be the instrument by which the Special Friend rounded up crowds and exerted her will. The Special Friend spotted Mr. Luján on the porch and gave him a long, self-satisfied stare, like a half-deranged chess master sizing up the effect of a game-changing move on her opponent. Finally she raised her eyebrows quickly, as if to summon a reply from her rival—but Mr. Luján seemed unfazed. "*No hay que hacerles caso,*" he said to his daughter and anyone else who would listen. Mr. Luján said this with calm conviction, a deepness of thought that hinted at reserves of belief and self-awareness. Now the Special Friend was back on the phone, summoning additional troops. Araceli could see the Special Friend and Mr. Luján were locked in a familiar struggle, the same one played out in village councils and big-city demonstrations in their native country, at inquests and in courtrooms, between those who understood that wielding power meant being a paternalistic shepherd to the stupid flock and those who dreamed of an Empire of Reason and a literate citizenry. Araceli could see the Special Friend and Councilman Luján were standing on opposite sides of Mexican history, even as they stood in the United States.

A man in the crowd wearing a backward baseball cap and an incipient beard stepped forward to stand on the edge of the lawn and send a glob of spit toward Lucía, causing Councilman Luján to remon-

strate with the spitter and then to pull back his daughter to the safety of
the porch.

Keenan, who had never seen an adult use his saliva as a weapon,
grabbed Brandon's hand for security. "What is this?" he asked his brother.

"I think it's a lynch mob," Brandon said with the amused detachment of an anthropologist describing some primitive rite. He took a
weird comfort in the idea that he had stumbled upon another case
where life clearly and obviously imitated literature. He had believed
lynch mobs were creations of novelists and filmmakers, but here was
one before him, with real people showing their canine teeth and twisting their faces into other expressions that suggested incipient revenge.
"I've read about them in books. In this lynch mob, no one is carrying
torches. But I guess torches are not, like, required for it to be a lynch
mob."

"What are they going to do?" Keenan asked. "Are they going to
hurt us?"

"Well, I don't see them carrying any rocks, so I guess they can't
stone us. I predict they'll start throwing those bottles and cans. Unless
the police get here first. In a situation like this, it helps if the police
show up. They call that 'restoring order.'"

A minute later two police cruisers slowly wheeled up to the
block, each painted white with slanted steel-blue letters proclaiming
POLICE, and progressively smaller letters declaring HUNTINGTON PARK,
and the department's wordy motto: DEDICATED TO SERVICE THROUGH
EXCELLENCE IN PERFORMANCE. Police Chief Mike Mueller emerged
from one of the vehicles, standing tall and thick and midwestern in
navy wool, and strode into the space between the contending parties,
raising his hands like an announcer in a boxing ring. "I'm sorry, but
I'm going to have to remind all of you, once again, that we have a whole
new city ordinance related to so-called political gatherings on residential streets."

He kept his arms raised and turned his beef-fed torso 360 degrees,
his preferred method for ending these "Mexican standoffs." "Okay,
all right, everyone go home now." The crowd in the street obeyed, as
did the members of the Luján family on the porch, until Lucía stood
alone on the front steps and started a chant directed at the retreating
lynch mob.

"¡Re-for-ma! ¡Re-for-ma! ¡Re-for-ma!"

Brandon soon joined the chant too, his voice squeaking as he tried to match Lucía's. "Ray-for-mah! Ray-for-mah!"

Keenan stood on tiptoe and joined them too, trying to mimic the Spanish sounds, as his brother was. When the last of the lynch mob was gone and the chanting had stopped, Keenan turned to his big brother and asked, "Who's Ray Forma?"

"*No sé*," the boy answered.

Maureen and Scott stood in the kitchen looking at each other, studying the main work area of their servant, the unwashed plastic tumbler and bowl in the sink the only objects out of place: the leopard skin of the marble countertops gleamed, spotless, even the windows suggested they might squeak if you put a cloth to them. The perfect kitchen and the disturbing art were both the work of the same Mexican woman, and Maureen felt blind and ignorant in the face of this newly revealed proof of human complexity: *I took her for granted, allowed her to seep into the white noise around me.* It was not immediately obvious what Maureen and Scott should do next, and they wandered about the house, hoping that the ring of the phone or chime of the front door would liberate them from waiting for something to happen. For the moment, it seemed likely, or at least probable, that their two sons and their employee might appear at the door at any moment. It was Maureen and Scott's experience as parents that all crises eventually ended and their home returned to its placid normality. Fevers dropped, cuts were stitched up, X-rays were taken, and doctors pronounced the children resilient and fated to healthy lives, and when it was all over the home's routine comforts—the hum of television sets, the salty smell of cheese and prepared meats cooking in the kitchen—confirmed their faith that good parenting values and vigilance would protect them.

But very quickly the passing time and the empty home and all its objects and boyless silence became an excruciating judgment on their own actions, a slow ticking punishment. "Where could they be?" Maureen asked as she wandered into the boys' bedroom and studied the modular plastic boxes that contained their toys. "Where did she take them?" Maureen repeated the questions out loud several times as she

moved from the boys' room to the media room and the kitchen, carrying Samantha through the house on her shoulder, trying to get her baby girl to take the noon nap that was now two hours overdue. *The time is all wrong for her to go to sleep now. She will be awake late into the evening. She can sense something is wrong; she can sense her parents are panicked.*

Maureen ran through her mind what she knew about Araceli, wondering if she could summon a fact or name that might provide an answer or clue to the question of where she had taken the boys. The mother who had given Maureen Araceli's name was in South America as of three years ago, having become an expatriate for a U.S. company in São Paolo, Brazil, and Maureen had no number for her. Araceli was from Mexico City, if Maureen remembered correctly. It took some effort of memory to produce Araceli's last name: Ramirez, a name confirmed moments later when Scott found, in Araceli's bedroom, a stack of postcards addressed to her and also the bank book for the savings account Scott had set up for her four years ago. The savings book revealed the last name Ramirez too, but the address was their own. "We have a full name, but that's it. What else do we know?" Maureen had no idea what Araceli's parents' names might be. How many people lived in Mexico City? Ten million? Twenty? And how many Ramirezes might there be in such a metropolis? Such a common last name offered these Mexican people a kind of anonymity. *They're all Ramirez, or Garcia, or Sanchez.*

"Where does she go on the weekend?" Maureen asked Scott.

"I think she said to Santa Ana. I'm pretty sure I heard her say that once."

Scott decided he would go through the old phone bills and check for any unfamiliar numbers. He returned from the office with a stack of paper, began scanning, and soon realized he would find nothing. "I think I've seen her use a card or something when she calls Mexico," he said. "And Santa Ana is a local call." The toll-free access numbers for the long-distance services left no trace on the bill, which was precisely what Araceli had intended—she didn't want to owe the Torres-Thompsons any money for the phone bill, and felt the details of her Mexican life were hers alone to possess: they were not for others to see, or study, or to be amused by. Araceli was "very private," as Maureen put

it to her friends, and until this moment Maureen didn't mind, because she equated Araceli's reserve with an efficient and serious approach to her job. For a year before Araceli joined them the Torres-Thompsons had a Guatemalan housekeeper, Lourdes, who kept a continual lament about the daughter she had left behind in a place called Totonicapán, often weeping as she did so. After one tearful soliloquy set off by the sight of children her daughter's age celebrating Brandon's seventh birthday in the Torres-Thompson backyard, Maureen had decided to let Lourdes go. Madame Weirdness, the childless woman from Mexico City, came to take her place. *I have allowed this person to live in my home for four years without once having a substantial conversation about where she is from, about her brothers and sisters, or about how she got here. I have allowed this foreign mystery to float from one room of my home to the next, leaning into the vacuum cleaner, flexing forearms as she mops with that look that often goes far away. I have allowed this state of affairs to persist, and may have placed my sons in danger, in exchange for her chicken mole, for the light and tart seasoning of her black beans, and for the passion we share for the sanitizing power of chlorine.*

Maureen's ignorance about Araceli's life beyond Paseo Linda Bonita meant she had no information on which to base even an educated guess about where the Mexican woman might have taken Brandon and Keenan. "Where did she go? What is she *doing* with them?" If Scott was right and they hadn't been in this house in two days, at least, then the situation became even more inexplicable: Why would a woman who had shown so little interest in her sons suddenly take an overnight excursion with them? As the light shining through the windows lost its white sheen and aged into a faint yellow, and the shadows in the succulent garden turned longer, and the memory and guilt over her own absence from the home grew fainter, Maureen's thoughts took on a darker and increasingly suspicious hue, leading her to declare, just a few minutes before sunset:

"I think we're going to have to call the police."

15

Not long after the lynch mob dispersed, Keenan put his thumb in his mouth and wandered to the backyard and slumped down in a lawn chair. Araceli found him there, and realized her charges needed to go to bed. She approached Lucía, who offered her bedroom, saying, "I'm going to be out late." The boys could sleep on her bed, and Araceli in a sleeping bag on the floor, she said, and soon Brandon and Keenan were dozing off underneath a poster of Frederick Douglass, a photograph of a teenage Spanish matador clipped from a magazine, and the orange and silver tassel from Lucía's high school graduation cap. Araceli dozed off quickly too, studying the image of the bullfighter in the dim light projected by a streetlamp through the sunflowers on Lucía's curtains, and wondering what her *gordito* Felipe would look like in a bullfighter's tights: comical, most likely. She wondered if he had tried to call in her absence.

"My children are missing. My two sons."
"What is your name?"
"Maureen Thompson."

"And you are their mother?"

"Yes."

"Are you calling me from your home?"

"Yes."

Maureen had punched 911 into the kitchen phone, and had reached a female voice that was following the passionless protocol of emergency operators, establishing essential facts in a weirdly detached voice.

"What are their names?"

"Brandon and Keenan. Torres. Torres-Thompson."

"How old are they?"

"Brandon is eleven. Keenan is eight."

"And when did you last see them?"

"Yesterday," Maureen said quickly.

"Yesterday?"

Maureen paused at the operator's tone of surprise, and in the brief silence she could hear a roomful of voices in the background. "No, no, I mean day before yesterday."

"Sunday?"

"Yes, Sunday morning." Maureen could not bring herself to say four days ago. Had she been slightly less panicked she might have felt the need to unburden herself of the full, complicated truth. But it would have taken a very calm, rational frame of mind to untangle for a stranger how a mother and father could abandon their sons for four days, and how it all went back to a dying garden and an argument in their living room. "My husband and I. We went to a spa." She looked up at Scott, who was shaking his head, but this only strengthened her conviction that taking the time to explain their fight in the living room and the events that followed would only slow the search for their sons. *This is not the time to revisit our little episode with the table.* And what did it matter anyway? The important thing was to find the boys, to bring them back to the shelter of this home. "We left them with the maid. Sunday. With their nanny." Two tones sounded, an automated notification that the conversation was being recorded. "We told her we would be back this morning, but we were a little late. And we've been waiting all day for her to come back with the kids. We don't know where she is."

"We?"

"My husband."

"He's there with you?"

"Yes."

"His name?"

"Scott Torres."

At the Orange County Emergency Communications Center, the operator considered the choices on her screen, which required her to classify the urgency of the dozens of dramas, mundane and bloody, that were whispered and screamed at her through her headset each day. Satisfied that the two children in this case were in the presence of an approved guardian (the nanny) and that the usual perpetrator in missing children cases (the father) was present, she reached the correct conclusion that this was probably not an abduction in which the children were in imminent danger, but rather some sort of household miscommunication. The caller was clearly lying about the last time she saw her sons: *Probably she's trying to get us to move quicker*, the operator thought, *probably she saw them just a few hours ago*. Emergency Operator II Melinda Nabor was a Mexican-American single mom with two young boys at home who were being looked after by their grandmother while she worked, and it was her experience that parents and "caregivers" got their signals crossed all the time. The "caller location" flashing on her screen was an address in one of the ritziest neighborhoods in the county, and she imagined herself saying, *Get a grip, lady. I'm sure your expensive Mexican nanny has everything under control*. Sometimes the operators let slip words of wisdom to the confused people on the other line, but Emergency Operator Nabor never did so, she always stuck to the call scripts and protocols, with their comforting sense of logic and professionalism, and their ability to channel events of all kinds into a machinery that translated human folly into codes and correct "unit deployments" from the twenty-eight overlapping law-enforcement jurisdictions in her calling area. In this case, it would be the county sheriff, to a community so rich it collectively preferred to be unincorporated rather than pay for its own city government.

"We're sending a patrol car out there."

"Thank you," Maureen said meekly.

"Orange County sheriffs. They should be out there shortly."

"Thank you."

•

Deputy Ernie Suarez was taken by the incongruity of the setting, a red-eyed mother lost to a mourning lament in her perfectly appointed living room, the father holding the baby girl because the mother was so distraught. "My beautiful boys. I left them and now they're gone," the mother cried. "They're gone!" He had entered the Laguna Rancho Estates only once before, on a domestic violence call that was coincidentally in a home on this very same block, an old sailor beating up on his Vietnamese wife, who didn't cry or scream about pressing charges, but just looked out the window at the ocean, dazed, most likely thinking about the continent on the other side of that curving blue hemisphere. Otherwise this part of his patrol area was a dead zone. He'd drive his Chevy Caprice past the front gate, wave at the guard, and accept a thumbs-up as the signal to execute an accelerating U-turn back down to the real city and the real work.

"We left them with their nanny. With our housekeeper," the husband said, repeating the story the mother had told before she started weeping.

"Araceli is her name, right?" the deputy said, looking at his small notepad.

"Yeah."

"And a last name."

"Ramirez."

"Age?"

"Late twenties. I think."

"Where's she from?"

"Mexico."

"Immigration status?" Deputy Suarez knew he really wasn't supposed to ask that question, but the word "immigration" was out there in the air, in the television news chorus, the talk radio banter: immigration, immigrant, illegal, illegals. You heard "Mexico" and you thought of one of those *i*-words, and you thought of a crime. And when you heard a Spanish surname that ended with a *z*, like his, you thought of Mexicans and the various federal codes they violated when they jumped over a steel fence into the United States. Other than that *z*, Deputy Suarez had no connection to Mexico himself, and saw no contradiction between

his growing concern about Mexico and *i*-words and his Texas Gulf Coast family history.

"I have no idea whether she's legal or not."

"But you're pretty sure she's from over there? From Mexico."

"Yes."

Deputy Suarez bit his lip with concern. A few weeks back he had traveled down to the Border Patrol station in San Ysidro, to have lunch with an old sheriff's deputy pal and to get a closer look at a potential career move into federal law enforcement. As a result of this conversation Deputy Suarez's vision of Mexico had undergone a rapid devolution. Up to then, he'd thought of the Border Patrol gig as a chasing-chickens kind of job, a human roundup in the desert, and Mexico as a colorful haven of booze and cheap handicrafts. But to hear his old pal tell it, there was a terrorist army growing on the other side of that fence, flush with cash from cocaine and crystal meth. These lawbreakers lorded over Baja with their automatic weapons and their fleet of luxury SUVs stolen from law-abiding Californians, and they had weird nicknames like "Mister Three Letters" and "The Crutches." They controlled the smuggling rings that brought people through the desert and sometimes right through the checkpoints because there were customs agents on the take: "You can smell it," his friend said. It disturbed Deputy Suarez to think that there were places where the waters of corruption ran so deep and wide that even the well-paid agents of the U.S. government could be swept in. The drug gangs ran kidnapping rings that snared doctors and schoolteachers and the children of the Tijuana rich, and they tortured their enemies and tossed their bodies onto highways with notes attached and severed fingers stuffed into their mouths. "There's some scary fucking shit going on down here, bro." Deputy Suarez had gone to TJ as a child, and he remembered holding his mother's hand as she weaved between the teeming market stalls, worrying that he might get lost. Now there were these new, real-life demons set loose in that city behind the fence.

"You think she might have taken them to Mexico?" the deputy asked Scott.

"No. No. I mean, no, I don't think so. But I'm not sure. What? Do *you* think she might have taken them to Mexico? Does that happen?"

"Hey, it's what doesn't happen that surprises me."

Scott led him to Araceli's room, thinking the deputy's professional eyes might see something there he could not. "This is some weird stuff," the deputy said out loud. His eye was drawn to one of the cutout magazine pages stuck to the wall with tape: it showed an oil painting of a woman prone on a bed, her face shrouded by a white sheet, legs spread open. A baby with the face of an adult woman bearing a single eyebrow emerged from the woman's vagina. Deputy Suarez said, "Jeez, that's really sick," and took a subconscious step backward. He had managed to complete four years of high school and two years at Rio Hondo College without studying a single work of modern art, and he was also in the minority of people of Latino descent in Southern California who had never heard of Frida Kahlo. *This is what they call "pathology." I remember that from my criminology class.* He next looked at Araceli's cubist self-portrait and mistook it for a drawing of one of the two missing boys. *What is the word for this? "Dismembered." The face is dismembered.* He started to wonder if perhaps the children were being harmed by this person in some hidden place.

Having seen enough, the deputy left the room and asked the father for photographs of the two boys and the nanny, and the man and his wife disappeared into other rooms deeper in the house to search for them. Once he was alone, the deputy called his station. There were two or three kidnap-to-Mexico cases every year in the county, though they always involved immigrant families and domestic disputes. A cross-border kidnap case in the Estates involving a nonrelative screamed urgency. At any rate, it was the usual procedure in cases of suspected child abuse and missing children to speak directly with the watch commander.

"Hey, Sarge, I'm up in the Estates and I think this is pretty serious. I've got two missing children. Possible kidnapping situation."

"Huh?"

"I said I got a child kidnapping situation. Possible. Up here in the Estates."

"In the Estates?"

"Yeah."

"Aw, fuck."

"Yeah, that's what I'm talking about. I got two missing kids from the Estates. Looks like the nanny took 'em. Mexico, maybe."

"She took 'em to Mexico?"

"Maybe. Don't know. Looks like a line of investigation."

"You got a ransom note?"

"No. But she didn't have permission to take them anywhere either."

"How long they been missing?"

"Since Sunday," the deputy said, but then checked his notes and saw the parents had told him two different times. "Or yesterday, I guess."

"Yesterday? Are you sure they're not just late coming back from Knott's Berry Farm or something?"

"Negative."

There was a long pause on the other end of the phone, and Deputy Suarez understood why: among other things, when a peace officer declared a child missing, a county child-abuse file was opened, and an elaborate system of reports and notifications was triggered. The case entered a federal database, and county social workers were notified. It was a big bureaucratic to-do, and if the nanny suddenly walked up to the door in half an hour, it would all be just jerking off.

"So that's your call, on scene there? Two missing kids in the Estates?"

"Yes."

"How old?"

"Eight. Eleven."

"Possible two-oh-seven kidnap to Mexico?"

"Yep."

"Fuck."

"Yeah, exactly."

Over the course of the next several hours, the story of the Mexican housekeeper and the two missing boys from one of the richest neighborhoods in Orange County gathered mass and momentum in the digital flows of the news stream, pushed along with a flotsam of facts and half facts and speculations. It began with a stilted, bare-bones Sheriff's Department press release: "missing since Sunday . . . ages 11 and 8 . . . in care of Mexican national . . . Border Patrol advised . . ." This information was delivered to various news organizations by the

hopelessly archaic method of fax, and first landed in the hands of a reporter at the Sunset Boulevard headquarters of the news-tip agency City News Service. Working without any supervisor present at the cash-strapped company, a twenty-three-year-old scribe at the agency called the South County sheriff's station at 1:45 a.m., eliciting from the half-alert deputy manning the phone that the case might be a kidnapping. "The deputy who rolled out on the first call says it's a possible two-oh-seven to Mexico." The CNS reporter then tagged the item for the agency's 2:00 a.m. news roundup with the keywords "Child Kidnapping—Illegal Immigrant," an act of journalistic carelessness that would take up an entire chapter in a PhD dissertation in the Communications Department at the University of Southern California two years later. "I boiled it down to the most exciting part," said the former reporter, who was by then in law school. The City News Service bulletin appeared on a list of "break-ing stories" dispatched by old-fashioned wire transmission to morning assignment editors at every newspaper and television and radio station in Southern California, and by six in the morning Pacific Daylight Time the story was on the websites of the CBS affiliates in Los Angeles and San Diego, the latter reporting the "enhanced surveillance" at the border. That San Diego television report, accompanied by the first officially is-sued photographs of Brandon and Keenan, caught the attention of the midday editor at a Miami Beach–based news aggregation website, who made the story his lead item, with a headline in the usual all-caps, tabloid-inspired, thirty-six point font. CLOSE THE BORDER! CALIFORNIA BOYS IN ALIEN KIDNAP DRAMA. Perusing this website's unique blend of celebrity gossip, political news, and weird animal and weather stories was a guilty pleasure in office cubicles and on laptops and smart phones across the country, and its fans included millions of American mothers whose children were in the care of women named María, Lupe, and Soledad.

The morning after the Fourth of July, Brandon and Keenan wandered over to the backyard of the Luján home alone and listened to the roof of the tent pop as it caught the occasional breeze. They had left Araceli behind in Lucía's room, snoring as she slept off four consecutive restless nights, next to a nightstand and a bubbling lava lamp that Bran-

don had turned on in the morning to read. They had moved quietly around their temporary guardian and through the silent house, past the bedroom door that vibrated with an older man's tectonic snore, through the living room, where a pair of empty plastic cups with cigarette butts sat on the coffee table, and finally to the empty backyard. At the pit they used splintering pieces of discarded and weathered lumber they had found nearby to poke at the stones inside, wondering if they might get in trouble for doing so. They discovered scattered pieces of foil and bits of charcoal, and a few scattered bones that had been chewed and tossed inside and basted with ashes and dirt, but failed to discover flames, or melting rocks, or any other sources of combustion.

"It's only rocks," Keenan said, and looked at his older brother, aware of his disappointment.

"Maybe, maybe not. Just because you don't see something doesn't mean it isn't there."

They wandered around the backyard, kicking at the paper cylinders that once held firecrackers and picking up the sticks of bottle rockets. Brandon gathered some scattered beer cans and stacked them into pyramids and arranged them into small forts that he bombarded with the spent firecracker casings, and they collapsed with a realistic clank. Once they finished, they plopped themselves down on the rented picnic benches, resting their elbows and their heads on the tables like students struggling to stay awake in an afternoon class.

"I wanna go to Grandpa's," Keenan said.

"Yeah, me too."

Keenan wondered if crying would help, even if it was not the spontaneous bawling that came from scraping your elbow or being called a nasty name by your brother, but rather the self-conscious, manipulative weeping he sometimes heard from his younger sister, Samantha, who cried for any reason, and who always seemed to get her way. He told himself he would employ this strategy with the next adult that came into view, and then he heard a screen door being pushed open and slamming shut, and saw Lucía Luján run toward him and his brother. Griselda Pulido trailed after her, both women wearing stylish evening clothes that suggested they had been up all night, their faces wide awake with strange expressions that merged surprise, delight, and concern.

"We just saw you guys on TV," Lucía said. "You're missing."

"What?"

"The TV says you're missing children. On the news."

"We're missing?"

"That's what they said."

"But I'm right here," Brandon said. "How can I be missing?"

The boys followed Lucía and Griselda to the Luján family living room and the glowing television screen. They were disappointed to see images of a brush fire racing up a hillside. "Hey, you were on just a second ago," Lucía said, and she picked up the remote control and began switching channels.

"*¿Qué pasó?*" Araceli said behind them, having been awakened by the sound of doors opening and slamming shut.

"We saw the boys on TV," Griselda said.

"*¿Qué?*"

"On the news."

Several images and voices cycled through the screen: a blond starlet on a red carpet, waving to a crowd; the green-clad members of Mexico's national soccer team tackling and embracing a goal-scorer during a game from the night before; a supermarket with empty shelves and a floor covered with boxes and cans, the words BARSTOW EARTHQUAKE underneath; two Spanish news anchors in a studio, engaged in a chatty, light back-and-forth with the pregnant weather woman, who rubbed her belly and stuck out her tongue cartoonishly, causing the two anchors to slap the table, laughing.

"I saw you guys," Lucía said. "I swear."

"You're crazy," Araceli said. "You're just like this boy here. Imagining things."

"They said they were lost," Griselda said in English. "*Perdidos.*"

"There we are!"

"Cool!"

Brandon and Keenan were suddenly grinning broadly on the television screen, the imperfections in their front teeth frozen in the high-definition transmission for several seconds, causing Brandon to subconsciously raise his hand to his mouth and then close it shut and to think, *My mom is right, I am going to need braces soon.* Maureen had retrieved this image from her digital camera some eight hours earlier, as the first of many detectives stood in her living room. It was a cropped

close-up from a picture taken at Keenan's eighth birthday party, a late afternoon image that showed the boys standing over the cake in the gathering's final, exhausted hour, because in all the others from earlier in the day they were wearing papier-mâché helmets.

"Police are asking for your help this morning in finding these two young boys, little Brandon and Keenan Torres-Thompson, of the Laguna Rancho Estates," a male voice was saying gravely. "They've been missing two days, Nancy, and their parents are frantic to see them."

"Oh, my God, they're so cute!" The screen cut back momentarily to the news studio, where Nancy, the female co-anchor, had brought her hand to her mouth and twisted her eyebrows into a face that was too theatrically mawkish given the subject matter, and the screen quickly moved to another still image.

"They are believed to be in the custody of their housekeeper, a Mexican immigrant. Araceli Ramirez is her name." Maureen had searched frantically for thirty-five minutes through her boxes of family pictures before finding a photograph in which Araceli appeared. It was a fleeting image, also taken in the dim light of a late afternoon, but at another birthday party a year ago, Brandon's tenth. Araceli stood fuzzily in the background of a larger photograph that had been cropped out, save for the ear of the main subject—Maureen, who was posing in the missing portion with a newborn Samantha in a chest-hugging sling. Out of the range of the flash, Araceli appeared in a blurred gray profile, walking quickly in her *filipina* across the backyard lawn, passing behind her boss with a stack of dirty dishes, following the quail-bangs that popped from her forehead. It was not an image that flattered. Removed of its context, its fuzzy quality suggested something furtive about its subject, as if she were already in flight when it was taken. "The boys' parents apparently left the boys in the care of the housekeeper, and the housekeeper disappeared—with the boys."

"She disappeared with them?"

"That's what the police say."

"God, let's just pray that they're safe."

"Their mom and dad are obviously anxious to see them."

The report ended, leaving Araceli and the boys in the living room with the unsettling sensation that they occupied bodies and faces that had just been transmitted, via airwaves, cables, and satellite dishes,

into many more living rooms besides this one across the metropolis. Araceli was confused over the meaning of the phrase "disappeared with the boys," and wondered if "disappear" carried exactly the same mysterious and nefarious definitions as *desaparecer*: and then Lucía spoke the English word out loud and Araceli realized, from her tone of surprise and restrained disgust, that there was no difference at all.

"They say you disappeared with them. That you took them. Didn't you have permission?"

"*¿Permiso?*" Araceli spat back. "*Me dejaron sola con dos niños. Me abandonaron.*"

"But now they're looking for them."

"Yes, I know," Araceli said, switching languages because Lucía didn't seem to fully comprehend. "But they left four days ago and never told me anything. I was all alone."

Griselda retook the remote and waded anew into the selection of channels, until she reached a shot taken from a helicopter, a plugged-up flow of automobiles on one side of a freeway. The words at the bottom of the screen had caused her to stop—MISSING CHILDREN—and now Griselda raised the volume to better hear the repartee between another studio anchor and a man who seemed to be speaking from inside a blender.

"We've got Captain Joe McDonnell in Sky Five over San Ysidro, over the U.S.-Mexico border . . . And whoa, look at that line."

"That's right, Patrick. We've got a two-mile backup, and from what I can see now . . . it stretches far beyond the last San Ysidro off-ramp. And it's all due to the case of those two missing children. They're eleven and eight years old, and they may have been abducted by their Mexican nanny. Apparently the detectives in this case have reason to believe she may be taking them to Mexico."

"That's right, Joe. Brandon and Keenan Thompson of Orange County. Here they are. And here's their nanny, Araceli Ramirez. She is from there, apparently, allegedly, so they're checking all the cars crossing the border. We understand. They haven't closed the border completely, now, have they, Captain?"

"No, Patrick. As you can see, if we zoom in here . . . there is some traffic going past the checkpoint, but it's at a real snail's pace. A snail's pace, because in a case like this, in this kind of Amber Alert involving

a suspect, a possible Mexican national as the suspect, they don't want to take any chances."

The camera's eye zoomed back, briefly taking in the U.S. and Mexican flags at opposite ends of a twenty-lane stretch of concrete, and the inspection booths, and then the long, curving, interlocking-puzzle pieces of cars on the southbound roadway in the United States, simmering and stationary between shoulder and center divider, the boxes of tractor-trailers, pickup trucks, and taxis, and a car hauling a boat. The camera then turned back on itself and showed how the parallel lines of vehicles climbed and banked northward, toward the San Diego downtown skyline, a hazy Oz many miles distant. Finally the broadcast switched to a taped shot, taken on the ground, of a U.S. customs agent holding a piece of paper printed with Brandon and Keenan's picture as he peered into a van.

Araceli grabbed the remote from Lucía's hand and turned off the television, hoping to stop the delusional machine's madness, which would spread if she allowed it to keep flashing its images and its lies. *In the news I am a fuzzy criminal. Officers are looking, agents are checking.* They were searching for the boys, to rescue them, and they were looking for Araceli, so that they could arrest her. *Maureen did this. Because she came home and found no boys, because she wants to punish me for acting like their mother, even though I never asked to be their mother. I never wanted that.* Her instinct to keep away from her *jefes'* children had been right after all. She had crossed a boundary by thinking she was their guardian. And they would arrest her, because she dared to save those parentless children from Foster Care.

Now she caught Griselda and Lucía staring at her. *Could it be true?* they seemed to be asking themselves. *Do we have a child abductor among us?*

"*Están locos,*" Araceli said dismissively in Spanish, referring to the newsmen and newswomen, Maureen and Scott, and the two young women in the living room with their doubts all at once. She turned and repeated this in English to the boys, who knew the truth, hoping they might say something in Araceli's defense. "They are crazy. They say I took you."

"I wanna go home," Keenan said. The television news had unsettled him further, because seeing a television report that said you were missing

seemed to be a step closer to actually being missing. He didn't want to be "disappeared," a state which he imagined to be something like sitting in a white room in another dimension while you waited to return to the world of the known and definite. "I don't want to be missing. I want to be home."

Brandon was worried about being missing too, but at the sound of Keenan's pleading whine, the older brother in him kicked in. "We should call home and tell them where we are," he said, his voice rising with the discovery of a simple and quick solution to their dilemma. "Then they'll pick us up!"

"Good idea," Lucía said.

"Then I should go," Griselda interjected quickly. "Before the police get here." She gave Lucía a knowing look that turned pained when she realized her friend didn't get her meaning right away. "Because they'll start asking everyone questions."

Lucía's eyes shifted in confusion, then fixed on her friend until she understood. "Oh, yeah, right. Of course. You should go."

"What?" Araceli demanded, suddenly irritated by the mysterious dialogue between friends. "The police are looking for you too?"

Griselda Pulido shook her head and said bluntly, in English, "I don't have papers."

It seemed impossible. Here was a young woman who spoke about music and boyfriends in English, who was obviously educated in the freewheeling, free-girl-thinking of U.S. schools, a privilege imparted to the country's brightest daughters, announcing solemnly that she was an *indocumentada*. This predicament didn't match, somehow, with the thin silver bracelets on her wrist, her slender and confident bearing, her gentle, even voice of the academically inclined. Nor did it match with her puckish party outfit, a billowing spinach-green dress with forest-green leggings and elfin slippers, all of which suggested an actress fresh off the set of *A Midsummer Night's Dream*.

"*Pero eres gringa*," Araceli said.

"No I'm not. I'm *mexicana*."

"*¿De veras?*" Araceli insisted. "*Pero ni hablas bien el español.*"

"I could speak Spanish a little better, yes," Griselda said calmly, and suddenly she radiated a youthful, black-haired confidence and inescapable meekness all at once. "But I've never really lived in Mexico, so it's understandable." After a pause to consider the paradox of her status,

Griselda lowered her voice and said, "I came when I was two. And I've never been back, because I can't go back. Brown was going to let me in anyway, but they couldn't give me any financial aid."

This was a shock to Araceli. Griselda had been an *indocumentada* when she was still in diapers; it seemed a country would have to be excessively cruel and cold to place such a label on a baby girl, and keep it on her even as she grew into an English-speaking woman.

Lucía placed a hand on Griselda's shoulder. "You should leave, then. When the boy calls, leave right away." She turned to Araceli, and spoke with a sternness that she would later regret. "And maybe you should go too."

"*¿Qué?*"

"*¿Tienes documentos?*" Griselda asked, and quickly discerned the answer in Araceli's sudden silence and discomfort. Griselda knew that wordlessness too; it came from carrying a secret so long you forgot you were carrying it, until someone or something reminded you of its existence and you felt the pressure of the words against your skin, and you realized the words were always there.

"Hi, Dad," Brandon said into the phone. "We're here." He paused to listen to his father's voice. "Yeah, we just saw ourselves on TV. But I'm not missing. I'm right here." Now an excited shouting could be heard, miniature adults celebrating inside the earpiece, clapping, screaming in joy. "We ate tacos last night," Brandon continued. "They cooked a pig. With a fire in the ground. But I don't think it's burning anymore . . . What? The address?"

"It's 2626 Rugby Street," Lucía said, and looked at Griselda. "In Huntington Park."

Brandon repeated the address to his father. "Yeah, Araceli is here with us. She's been taking care of us. We rode on a train, and on some buses too. We saw a river, but it didn't have water in it." Suddenly he narrowed his eyes to a look of irritation. "And where did *you* go? Is Mommy there?" He listened to the answer, and turned to Keenan. "He says Mommy can't talk right now, but she's okay."

Keenan took the phone and announced flatly to his father that he was okay too. "I love you too," he said, and immediately hung up, because he thought of a phone I-love-you as meaning more or less the same as goodbye.

The clatter of the phone on the receiver was the cue for Griselda to

reach over and give Lucía a kiss on the cheek. Without any more drama
Griselda moved calmly to the front door, turned, and smiled and waved
to the boys and to Araceli, mouthing the Spanish word for luck as she
did so. *Suerte.* The screen door closed behind Griselda with a slap and
Araceli watched through the living room window as she walked across
the lawn, onto the sidewalk, gliding in her slippers and wide dress
past parked cars and other lawns, a green fairy *indocumentada* walking
without worry, her unhurried air causing her to melt into the surroundings, another Mexican-American, another *mexicana* on these streets
with so many other people with stories and faces like hers. That's how
you did it. You acted as if the city belonged to you. You walked with the
pace of a limber woman taking her daily stroll. *I can do that too, and slip
back across the city, and maybe back to Mexico, with a little stop at the
bank to get my money.* Araceli liked the idea of thumbing her nose at
the police and the immigration authorities with the simple fact of her
absence, her unwillingness to answer questions or offer explanations,
even though she had no reason to run away, no reason to hide from
anything, except for the inconvenient matter of her Mexican citizen-
ship. They would arrest her and sort out the truth later. *But I don't want
to be a prisoner, not even for a few hours.* Araceli had digested, over
the years, a regular diet of stories from across the U.S., fed to her by
Spanish-language radio and television, all offering ample evidence that
those who arrived on this side of the border without permission were
returned home via a series of humiliating punishments. Meat packers,
garment workers, mothers with babies in swaddling clothes: Araceli
had seen them on the television, rounded up in vans, into buses with
steel mesh over the windows, gathered up in camps behind fences, onto
airplanes that landed on the tropical runways of San Salvador and Tegucigalpa and other places, far away from those other places they had
learned to call home—Iowa, Chicago, Massachusetts. *Pobrecitos.* When
this saga was on television you could dismiss it as the bad luck of others. She was too busy to worry, and too much at peace with the risky
life choices she had taken. But now that her name and her face had
been fed into that tragic stream of the wanted, the apprehended, and
the deported, she felt the need to resist. *My words and my true story will
not buy me my freedom, not right away.* Araceli would speak her story in
Spanish and *la señora* Maureen would tell hers in English: it was obvious to her that the two languages did not carry equal weight.

"*Me voy*," Araceli announced happily. "Good luck, boys. I'm glad you didn't go into Faster Care. Lucía and her father will take care of you until the police come."

After returning to Lucía's bedroom to retrieve the backpack she had been carrying, Araceli passed through to the living room one last time, patted Keenan on the head, and placed a hand on Brandon's shoulder.

"I leave them with you," she said to Lucía, and to Mr. Luján, who had just entered the living room. "*Cuídenlos, porfis.*"

Araceli took a moment longer to consider the surroundings, the grown-up man and his daughter, giving them the kind of cursory, self-assuring once-over a hurried mother might before leaving her children in a familiar day-care center. Then, remembering the police were on their way, she stepped toward the front door. "*Adiós, niños,*" she said, adding an unnecessary "Stay here," as she stepped into the furnace of July daylight and down the Luján family steps, across the lawn and the patch of street where the lynch mob had gathered the night before, following a path that would lead her back to the bus stop, where she would begin a journey to some new place unknown to her.

Among the tribe of sheriff's deputies, detectives, social workers, and assorted county officials gathered in the Torres-Thompson living room, it was the presence of the representative of Orange County Child Protective Services that Maureen found most threatening. Olivia Garza was 220 pounds of Mexican-American woman on a five-foot ten-inch frame whose labored breathing and loud exhales of exasperation filled the silences in the room. This rotund stranger had spent quite a lot of time inspecting the pictures on the bookshelf, and Maureen sensed that she was looking for clues in the faces she saw there, in the body language of her wedding pictures, the grooming of her boys in their school portraits.

Alone among the assembled members of the Endangered Child Emergency Intervention Team, Olivia Garza did not feel the need to hide her skepticism. She had a unique gift for untangling family dysfunction and had worked her way up from Case Worker I in the Santa Ana office with the files of 127 children whose parents and guardians were raccoon-eyed heroin addicts, pugilistic plumbers, wannabe street-corner

kingpins, and shoplifting Chicana versions of Scarlett O'Hara waiting in Fullerton subdivisions for their tattooed heroes to slam the door in their faces. She was especially adept at spotting the custody-fight manipulations, the Halloween-scary fictions mothers and fathers made up about their exes, but had also rescued babies dying from malnutrition, plucking them from their cribs and from the sticky kitchen floors of Santa Ana apartments. She had cornered the thirteen-year-old sons of Newport Beach glitterati in Anaheim crack houses too: *de todo un poco*.

Olivia Garza did not believe a Mexican nanny would take off with her two charges in a kidnapping adventure with two boys the ages of the Torres-Thompson children. Or, rather, she had not yet been presented with any facts that would allow her to believe such an unlikely scenario. What is she going to do? Sell them in Tijuana? Make them her own children, teach them Spanish, and raise them in a tiny village in the mountains? None of this had she expressed to the other members of the intervention team. She didn't need to, because the two sheriff's detectives sent out to the scene had reached the same conclusion, more or less, though they were trying hard to be deferential to the weeping mother and the worried father.

After hearing the basic outline of the story from the father, Olivia Garza had wandered about the house. Too clean, she observed, too perfect. She looked into the Room of a Thousand Wonders and was unimpressed. If you saw too many toys, it implied distance, parents who substituted objects for intimacy, though the presence of so many books, and the variety of their sizes and subjects, was reassuring. Olivia Garza picked up a handful and examined the dog-eared pages of a novel, and then the worn cover of a picture book on medieval armor and decided, *These kids are going to turn up by the end of the day*. The members of Olivia Garza's elite team had been precipitously assembled here simply because the family lived in the zip code with the highest per capita income in their district, and because the photogenic boys had attracted the news crews gathered outside. *Some things are so obvious you just want to force them out like a wad of spit*.

She encountered the two detectives back in the living room, off by the windows that looked out to the succulent garden.

"Is there anything else here I should see?"

"Have you seen the nanny's room? It's a little house in the back."

They entered the guesthouse, which wasn't much smaller, truth

be told, than the condominium in Laguna Beach where the childless Olivia Garza lived with her two cats. One of the detectives reached up and tapped at the mobile, watching it spin and bounce.

"Interesting," Olivia Garza said.

"Art," Detective Harkness said.

"Yeah, that's what they call it," Detective Blake said.

"This is what got our responding deputy all worked up," Detective Harkness said, waving his hand at the drawings, the collages, and the mobile, which didn't bother him at all.

The intervention team had been called up just before dawn, roused from their beds, and in the full light of midmorning there was an everyday clarity to the situation that had eluded the first responders the night before.

"My theory: the nanny took them to Disneyland or something and got lost or delayed on the way back," Detective Blake said.

"Yeah, they're probably sleeping in a hotel someplace, dreaming about the apple pie they had for dinner last night," Detective Harkness said.

"I predict, after the all-points," Detective Blake said, "that they turn up around lunchtime."

"Nah, earlier," Detective Harkness said. "Ten, ten forty-five at the latest."

"What do *you* think, Garza?"

She looked about the room, shuffled the papers and envelopes on Araceli's table-desk, and finally said, "These parents have lied to me. And I don't like it when people lie to me."

"And how many years have you been in Child Protective Services?" Detective Harkness said.

"That's what we do, Garza," Detective Blake said. "We go places, and people lie to us. And then we catch them in their big lies, and we make them feel bad, and then they cry and tell us smaller lies."

"I don't like it when people lie and force me out of bed early," Olivia Garza said. "And I don't like it when they make me walk past the TV crews without having had a chance to put my makeup on."

"You mean you can look even more beautiful than you do already?" Both detectives chuckled. "You're funny, Garza."

Olivia Garza brought her bad temper back to the living room, refusing to sit on the couch or at the table in the dining room, and decided to continue her self-consciously insolent pacing instead, as if daring the

other members of the team to put up with her. After listening to Scott again recite, without much conviction, the story Maureen had first told the 911 operator, she addressed the parents for the first time.

"How much do you pay this woman?"

"Two hundred and fifty dollars a week," Scott said.

"Under the table. Right?"

There was no answer, but Olivia Garza pressed ahead. "Do you leave your kids alone with her often?"

"No," Maureen said, breaking a long silence. "We never have. Before. We had another person . . ."

"You've never left her alone with them and then you go away for two days and leave two boys with her?"

"That's what they've been telling us," interrupted the representative of the district attorney's office, who was sitting on the sofa seat at a right angle from Maureen.

Olivia allowed the silence to stand there and make her point. The two detectives had been doing the same thing, off and on, for an hour, walking up the story to the parts that were not quite believable, and then stepping back because the representative of the DA's office had placed himself next to Scott and Maureen and was, with his repeated words of support for the alleged victims, preventing the detectives from probing any further. Olivia Garza and the detectives both wondered the same thing: *What are these people hiding?* Something small and insignificant, Olivia Garza concluded, a fact not completely essential to the recovery of their children: some family embarrassment, or petty crime. Probably she and the detectives could pry the truth from this couple, but for the presence of the representative of the district attorney's office, who was leaning forward in his seat, over the space where the coffee table used to stand. He was conspicuously overdressed in glossy Brooks Brothers sharkskin, and looked intently at Maureen and Scott, his clothes and demeanor suggesting a corporate-minded Catholic priest.

Ian Goller was the third-ranking member of the district attorney's office and his official title was Senior Assistant District Attorney for Operations, but unofficially he was the district attorney's fixer and protégé. Goller had mobilized the Endangered Child Emergency Intervention Team at 5:25 a.m., after sitting down to his morning news and coffee ritual, and seeing the faces of the boys flashing next to the words

ORANGE COUNTY MISSING CHILDREN. Ian Goller was thirty-eight years old and, like Olivia Garza, he lived alone, though in a much more spacious condominium with a view of the harbor in Newport Beach. He had turned up the volume and heard the outline of the story, and in two deep breaths and two heartbeats he felt the great swell of popular indignation it might provoke. A nanny who was, more than likely, an illegal immigrant: absconding with two Orange County children with All-American looks. It would make the good people and voters of Orange County angrier than a dozen Mexican gangbanger murders, or twenty homicidal drunk drivers with Spanish surnames and no driver's licenses, and, as such, it was precisely the sort of high-profile case for which the emergency-response team had been created.

Ian Goller was a native of the Orange County suburb of Fullerton who liked to tell people that his otherwise plain and unassuming hometown had once been home to the science fiction writer Philip K. Dick. "You know, *Blade Runner?*" Fullerton had produced no other greatness, as far as he knew, other than a perennially excellent college baseball team, and Goller himself was a graduate of San Diego State University and the middle-of-the-pack Chapman University School of Law. At the DA's office he put in long hours, unlike many of his colleagues, and quickly worked his way up from traffic court and DUIs, his rise aided by a few idiosyncrasies that identified him as an Orange County local, and thus made him a favorite of the OC-born DA. Goller still allowed his blond hair to reach his collar, wore a braided leather Hawaiian surf bracelet over the French cuffs of his dress shirts, and in his youth had flirted with a career as a professional surfer—which had led to a recent profile in *California Lawyer* as "the surfing prosecutor."

Now, sitting with these two parents in their well-appointed living room in the Laguna Rancho Estates, he could see that he was in the presence of an Orange County mother who cared. He could feel it in the dust-free air, the good and life-giving scent of the nearby ocean, in the baby dictionaries and well-worn swing set, and see it in the way she stroked her baby girl's back, as if to comfort the child when she was really comforting herself. As he contemplated the fate of the boys this OC mom had left in the care of a Mexican nanny, Goller saw everything that was at once satisfying and frustrating about being a prosecutor.

Protecting children and prosecuting abuse was the purest thing a

lawyer could do: the victims were sinless, and the defendants were invariably transparent scumbags, convicted by juries with great speed and relish. And in the suspect's copper-tinged face and nationality, he saw the math of the multitudes that would one day drive him out of the profession altogether, because naïve Latin American immigrants like her were filling up his courtrooms. This was a painful realization for the son of an old-line Democratic family to make, and one he'd arrived at after years of observation, and despite his steadfastly liberal outlook on most other issues, from abortion rights to preserving the local wetlands. Ian Goller's meta-knowledge of how foreign nationals clogged his superior court flowcharts, matrices, and spreadsheets, along with the victim-centered culture at the DA's office, with its victim's rights manifestos and procedures, tilted his view of the case decisively in favor of Maureen—despite her nervous and not-entirely-consistent recounting of events.

Ian Goller thought of this woman's children, and about other children he had not been able to rescue, and he bowed his head in silent, private prayer.

Seeing the prosecutor lower his head and clasp his hands suddenly and without explanation only filled Maureen with more dread. She did not understand the source of the prosecutor's intense stares, nor of the obvious irritation of the big woman who represented Child Protective Services. *These are the people who take children away from parents.* The arrival of the obese Mexican-American woman, especially, with her large nose and ruddy skin with a strange Indian-ebony mixing, and the plastic ID badge with the county seal, was nearly as frightening to her as the idea that Brandon and Keenan were wandering the city somewhere. Maureen entertained the prospect that the police might find her children, listen to Araceli's true and entirely plausible story, and then decide to take her children away. *Maybe I should tell them now what really happened: that it's been four days, not two, and that Araceli had no idea we were leaving.* How much trouble had she gotten her family into with that small lie? Maureen decided she would reveal the complexity of the situation, how she and Scott had played a part in its unfolding, and perhaps this small truth would bring her children to her quicker, and loosen the surly mask of the representative from Child Protective Services, the only other woman in the room besides Maureen, and the

only one of the strangers who seemed to sense the hidden and juvenile chain of events that had brought them all here.

Maureen was about to launch into her confession when the phone rang.

Araceli walked through the neighborhood at a leisurely pace, past aging front-yard cacti and blooming rosebushes, and the unpainted gray skins of newly built cement homes with gabled roofs and dangling wires for light fixtures. She walked past pickup trucks with gold wings painted on their sides, three-toned pickups with mismatching doors and hoods, and pickups with the color schemes of Mexican soccer teams, and then squeezed between two more pickups after jaywalking across California Street. Despite her deliberately unhurried pace, she decided it might be better not to walk in a straight line, but rather to make large zigzags through the grid of streets, especially now that a helicopter had appeared overhead.

The aircraft was chop-chopping like a lawn mower in the airspace above the Luján home, and it did not take much imagination to conclude that the police were at that moment engaged in the "rescue" of Brandon and Keenan. Araceli marveled at the fact that in this country police could emerge from the empty sky in the time it took to walk five blocks. The police would now return Brandon and Keenan to the Room of a Thousand Wonders and the two-dimensional superheroes of their bedsheets. The helicopter was loud enough to bring a scattering of people to their front doors, to look up and wonder who or what the machine was looking for.

Now the helicopter began to move, making circles concentric to the point where it had started, banking and turning in ever larger circles until its spinning blades and green body dipped over Araceli's head, a giant mechanical dragonfly whose beating squeal announced crisis and urgency. Araceli began to walk faster as more people came out of their homes and stood on their lawns, craning their necks upward. An accelerating automobile drew their eyes back to the ground, a Huntington Park police patrol car zooming past with exaggerated masculine purpose. Araceli halted her sidewalk march and watched the flashing lights of the patrol car reach the end of the block, cross the intersection, and

then accelerate into the next block with another throttle burst and thought, *They're trying to scare me out into the open. They think that if they zoom through here I will begin to run, and give myself away.*

She began walking again, but was aware that by stopping and starting with the passing of the patrol car she had drawn attention to herself.

"Hey, that's her!" shouted the voice of an adolescent boy standing behind her on the sidewalk. She continued walking without looking back. "That's the lady! From the TV!"

Araceli took a few more steps until a second voice shouted from one of the doorways, "*¡La secuestradora!*" She turned and saw a woman with dimpled cheeks pointing at her from a cement porch, with the glee of a person who has scratched the skin of a lottery card and discovered a twenty-dollar prize. Araceli stumbled away, walking faster, frightened as much by the voyeurism of the people around her as by the idea that they might hand her over to the police. "*¡Es ella! La vi en el canal 52. ¿A dónde vas?*" She began a light jog, thinking that she might be safe as soon as she turned the corner and escaped this block and its Greek chorus of television watchers, people who believed she was the *secuestradora* in the news montages, a villainous taker of children.

"*¡Córrele!*" a man shouted with a gusto usually reserved for horse races and cattle roundups.

"*¿Y los niños?*" a woman's voice pleaded as she turned the corner, and Araceli was tempted to turn and say, *I don't have them, I never took them.* She reached a block where narrow bungalows were lined like railroad boxcars in parallel rows, their square lawns transformed by drought into flat and featureless dust squares. Plastic curls of Christmas lights hung from the eaves, and all the residents were inside, glued to their televisions, she guessed, looking at Araceli's fuzzy picture on their screens. A block later she found herself standing underneath the enormous zinc torso of a power transmission tower, eight lines attached to four arms that stretched out like a woman having herself measured for a dress. The lines loomed above a corridor of vacant land that ran several straight miles through residential neighborhoods, one tower following another until they gradually disappeared into the midday ozone bake of dirty-blue haze and nothingness. Araceli took a second or two to contemplate the hugeness of the tower above her, and the oddity of the notch that

had been cut into the grid of homes. She jumped over the short fence that proclaimed NO TRESPASSING and began to walk under the trunk lines, thinking there would be no nosy television watchers to bother her as she walked here, and that she might be able to follow the lines north-ward to the peopleless heart of the metropolis, and the safety of factory buildings and warehouses. Her legs labored against the uneven, weed-covered ground, because she was entering a kind of urban wilderness, a nursery of odd flora sprouting up through the mustard grass. A cypress tree, its canopy shaped like a large wing. Sickly rosebushes without buds. Strawberry plants clinging to a patch of loam. Bamboo grasses and a stunted palm with thin leaves that sprouted, fountainlike, from its trunk, and the wide, tall bouquet of a nopal cactus. She had stumbled into the back closet of California gardens, the place where seedlings of plants discarded and abandoned came to scratch their roots into the dry native soil. If she hadn't been on the run, she might have stopped to admire this freakish landscape, and she might have noticed too the cluster of cameras and lights in the distance.

Instead, the film crew saw her first, when, about eight hundred yards to the north, an Estonian cinematographer peered into the viewfinder of his camera. Araceli was under the second tower in the distance, a woman stumbling forward in the dancing waves of rising heat, lifting her legs over the weedy land like a woman wading through snowdrifts. "Someone is in my shot," the cinematographer said, his neck bent and face attached to the eyepiece. "They are coming into the shot."

"Again?" the director called out. "Where?"

A dozen or so members of the small film crew began squinting at the horizon. They were shooting the coda of an indie feature with a modest $3.1 million budget, and they had already been bedeviled by the appearance of the helicopters, which were driving the sound guy loopy. At the director's behest the cinematographer had filmed the cir-cling craft for two minutes and forty-five seconds, capturing their lead actor looking up at the machines circling over the wires, the expression of foreboding and curiosity on his tanned face completely in line with the themes of the screenplay. Electrical towers appeared at the end of each of the film's three acts, and the cinematographer had shot other towers and wires in the San Bernardino Mountains, and in the plain of tumbleweeds outside Henderson, Nevada, and the Cimarron Grasslands

of southwestern Kansas. The Huntington Park shoot was intended for the epilogue, the towers and the barren channel of weeds at the actor's feet symbols of the protagonist's failed search for self in Las Vegas casinos and a Kansas beef-processing town.

"I told you these Eastside locations were a bitch," the key grip said. "I told you." Most of the local residents had behaved themselves: they were used to being put out by film crews drawn to the grim and epic backdrop, and only the appearance of an A-list actor or Mexican television star really got them very excited. Every few minutes, however, there was the straggling homeless person, or a gangbanger on his bicycle, people who hadn't read the letter: *Sorry for the inconvenience: We're bringing a little bit of Hollywood to your neighborhood!*

"Now I see him," the director said.

"Her. It's a she."

At that instant a helicopter swooped in close to the trunk line and a police car emerged with a squeaky skid on one of the streets that cut through the corridor. Two officers jumped out of the car and the figure of the woman began to run toward the crew.

"Whoa, they're chasing her."

"They've got their sticks out."

"Is this real?"

"Batons. You call them batons, not sticks."

"Are you getting this?" the director yelled to the cinematographer. He called out the name of the lead actor, a bright young prospect whose presence in the film had assured its funding—he was a twenty-four-year-old Australian with a sparse chestnut beard that matched his eyes, and a Gary Cooper everyman quality that screamed out he was destined for big-budget greatness. "In character," the director said. "Stay in character." The actor took a breath and a moment to remember his drama-school improvisation training and stretched his arms down at his sides. He relaxed his facial muscles into a look of genuine puzzlement and muted pleading captured in profile as he watched the foot chase that was now headed in his direction, a Mexican woman towing a cloud of dust and two running men in black, a spectacle now about one hundred yards distant.

"They're going to beat her," a crew member said breathlessly. "They're going to beat her to a pulp."

"Take a step toward them. Just one step."

The actor moved hesitatingly toward the running woman, as if he wanted to help her but was not sure he could.

"Good. Now one more. Just one. Are we still getting this?"

"Yes, I'm on a tiny f-stop," the cinematographer said. "The depth of field is magnificent."

"Beautiful."

Weeks later in the editing room, the director and his editor would incorporate about seventy-five seconds of this footage into the final version of the film. Araceli never saw the camera, or the actor, or the film crew. She was focused on the men trailing behind her and the idea that she might elude them. They had come to grab her and bind her hands in plastic strings, but she still found herself suppressing a laugh as she ran, even with brambles scratching at her ankles, because there was the quality of a schoolyard game to being chased around like this. *There are other, easier ways of returning to Mexico. They will grab me and drag me across the dirt like a calf in the rodeo, and then cage me. We must endure these rituals of humiliation: this is our Mexican glory, to be pursued and apprehended in public places for bystanders to see.*

If you let me go, señores, I will merely walk to the bus station and buy a ticket back to my country. No les molesto más. They were far behind her, at first, and for a moment she entertained the thought that if she could reach the next street, or slip into an alleyway or a backyard, she might elude them and find her own route home. But she was not a good runner. The first police officer quickly closed the gap, sprinting with a determined, middle-aged ferocity that surprised and frightened her, his face turning crimson and sweat bursting from his face and chest. When he reached her he was still running much too fast, and stumbled on top of her while trying to apprehend her, his body crushing hers as they both fell to the soil, their mouths filled with dirt and sticky weeds.

BOOK THREE

Circus Californianus

I would take up wickedness again . . . And
for a starter I would go to work and steal Jim
out of slavery again . . .
　　　　　—Mark Twain, *Huckleberry Finn*

16

Araceli refused to speak for the first two hours she spent in custody. She did not complain after being covered with dust by the police officer's clumsy collision tackle, or offer a retort to the taunt of the second officer, who said, "Back to Meh-hee-coe for you, buh-bye," as he escorted her to the patrol car. She said nothing as they walked past the cluster of residents who repeated in whispers the accusation they had heard on their Spanish-talking televisions: *la secuestradora*. She resisted the temptation to sling back a riposte when one of the more ignorant members of the crowd spat at her in English, "What did you do to those kids, bitch?" She merely squinted up into the midday glare and the fleet of circling television helicopters, which had joined the police helicopters in an aerial hyena prowl, and then at the crowd, recognizing a face or two from the lynch mob that had gathered outside the Luján residence the night before: they were looking at her with the same mixture of morbid fascination and inch-deep pity with which a *chilango* crowd greeted a corpse on the sidewalk, and she thought of all the sarcastic things she might say if she had the nerve. *Look, and look closely, because any one of you might be next.* But of course she said nothing, and she kept to her mute act as another set of officers took her

fingerprints and escorted her to a holding cell at the Huntington Park
Police Station. Nor did she speak as a third set of officers drove her
across many suburbs and freeways and interchanges, through city air
heavy and opaque with the gray haze and smoky aroma spewed by a
distant and massive brush fire. When she arrived at another holding
cell, at the South County Operations station, she told herself she would
remain silent until they escorted her across the border, or until she
landed at the airport in Mexico City. *Obviously, I would prefer to take
the plane back.* She'd watch the route she took to this country pass beneath her feet, backward: the American highways, the desert passes,
the Sonoran cities, the toll roads through arid landscapes dotted with
oak trees and adobe walls painted with the slogans of presidential can-
didates, and finally the mouse-maze sprawl of that last metropolis she
had once called home and would call home again soon, that city of
museums and galleries and monuments that Griselda wanted to visit,
but could not.

They brought her to an interrogation room and told her to sit down
and she began to think about what she would say to her mother when
they saw each other, and how much time would pass before she found
herself working in that cramped kitchen next to the old woman again.
She wondered if there might still be a way to get to that money she had
in the bank in Santa Ana. Saving that money had been a "bad girl"
thing to do, but now it might emancipate her from her mother's kitchen
and open the path to a new, radical Mexican self. There were rebellious
things a woman could do in Mexico if she didn't care what people said,
bohemian gathering spots that awaited the free spirit: Huatulco and the
hippies on the Oaxacan coast, Palenque and incense-burning shamans
of Veracruz.

Now three men entered the room: a police officer in a stiff wool
uniform and a brass badge; a green-eyed police detective of about fifty
in gray blended slacks, emitting an air of slovenly boredom; and a smartly
dressed man of about thirty-five, with a narrow face that sprouted like
a tree stump from his stiff collar, and blond hair that swooshed across
the top of his head like a golden wave frozen at midcrest. Alone among
these three, the last man was not perspiring, and he took a seat at the
table where Araceli was sitting, the older police detective squeezing
next to him, and after an elbow collision or two it was clear the room

was too small to accommodate them all. The room was about the size of the walk-in closet off the master bedroom in Paseo Linda Bonita, and the three men bumped chests and shoulders as they tried to sit down at once on the empty chairs, until the officer in uniform finally stood up and took a place in the open doorway.

"Damn. Couldn't we get something bigger?" the younger man in the suit said.

"Budgets," said the man with the gray slacks. "We asked for more rooms. So they took the ones we had and split 'em in half." Settling into his chair, he now introduced himself as Detective Mike Blake, and said the younger man in the suit was Assistant District Attorney Ian Goller.

"And your name, according to this card we have here, is Araceli N. Ramirez," the police detective said, speaking with a weary congeniality that caught Araceli by surprise. He placed a manila envelope on the table, removed her Mexican election card, and studied it, as if he were trying to discern the meaning of the words Instituto Mexicano Electoral, which circled an eagle clutching a serpent. "Interesting. I guess you need this to vote in Mexico."

Araceli remained silent, remembering the little speech given by the officer who'd put her in the patrol car, reading in Spanish from a card that he drew from his back pocket: *Usted tiene el derecho a guardar silencio. That's another thing I really like about this country,* she thought. *The right to keep your lips pursed together like a chaste nun in a convent is enshrined in their Constitution, and there is no officer or judge who can force you to open your mouth.*

"Had lunch yet?" Detective Blake asked. "Because I can get you something to eat. But I need you to start talking to me."

"Or we can send you back down to that little cell without lunch," Goller said.

"Look, I'm sure it was just some misunderstanding, right?" Detective Blake said. "Explain it to us."

Araceli looked firmly into their English-speaking eyes and wondered if she should trust them.

"Listen, we know you speak English perfectly well," the representative of the district attorney's office said brusquely. Ian Goller had received this essential bit of information from Maureen back at Paseo

Linda Bonita, and he now believed that Araceli was deliberately pretending not to understand, which only added to his frustration. He had seen this behavior many times before: criminal suspects from foreign countries who believed their non-English-speaking tongues gave them additional immunity from speaking the truth. "So why did you run away?"

Araceli almost replied to this question, because of its transparent stupidity. *Why does the rabbit run from the fox?* she wanted to say. *Why does the hen run from the woman with the knife in her hand?* Instead, she narrowed her eyes and glared back in approximate imitation of an irritated Mexican schoolteacher.

"Wanna go back to the cell?" Goller barked. "We'll send you back now. Without lunch. Or you can just tell us what you were up to. Why would you take those two boys on a little jaunt? To what purpose? Where did you go?" It had been ages since Ian Goller found himself sitting across a table from an uncharged criminal suspect—he was, almost exclusively, an administrator now—and he was quickly falling back to a bad habit from his early days as a prosecutor: losing his professional detachment. "Here's what I see. You took these children without permission to a dangerous corner of the city. You left two good parents worried sick inside the house, without a clue to where you might be." The detective sitting next to him was looking irritated, but Goller didn't notice and wouldn't have cared if he did. "You never expressed any interest in the welfare of these boys and suddenly, when you're alone with them, you go off. Why?"

The assistant district attorney did not fully appreciate the bewilderment that had suddenly taken hold of Araceli's face, though the detective did. Detective Blake decided he should try and take back control of the interrogation. But before he could, Goller blurted out, "What did you think? That you were their mother? Or was it money you were after? Because, obviously, you weren't being paid enough for all the work you did. Right? So you wanted more money."

Araceli took a few seconds to digest the insinuations and to study the man making them. She was struck by the embittered outrage with which the assistant district attorney embraced his vision of her. He seemed to believe that she lacked basic human morality and intelligence; at the same time, he thought her capable of great criminal cunning. Certain backward men in Mexico looked at all women this way

and Araceli was momentarily reminded of a few ugly encounters in her past. "You just couldn't stand working for this family," Ian Goller continued, and fell back in his chair with a satisfied lean, as if he had figured it all out, striking the flimsy wall of the interrogation room as he did so and causing the tiny room to shake. "They trust you with their kids and you want to make them suffer? I don't get it. Or are you just incredibly irresponsible?" Araceli tried to see the events of the past week as this excellently dressed and coiffed gentleman imagined them. She formed a mental picture of herself taking Brandon and Keenan to a bank, exchanging them for their weight in gold; or to some mustachioed broker of stolen children, for a stack of pesos. In the prosecutor's vision, Araceli was doing those things, while Maureen and Scott were two parents who dutifully entrusted Brandon and Keenan to her, maybe even kissing them goodbye as they left them in her care. These absurd thoughts, and the prosecutor's look of deepening revulsion, caused her mouth to explode suddenly with a loud and sustained guffaw, what Spanish speakers call a *carcajada*, an onomatopoeia that suggests a cackling bird. Araceli's laugh, however, was a deeper mammalian sound, born below the esophagus, a laugh she associated in her youth with certain mean-spirited street vendors in Nezahualcóyotl, and with her own *hidalguense* grandmother. She laughed and felt the lifting of the day's sum of tension, a release that gave her mirth its own momentum, and she leaned forward in her chair with a true burst of joyfulness that showed the three men in the room the grinning teeth that had seduced Sasha "the Big Man" Avakian so long ago. She kept on laughing as her eyes caught those of the detective and the police officer, who were both raising their lips in subtle smiles that suggested they got the joke too. Her laughter pinged off the steel table and the glass of the two-way mirror that dominated the room, for thirty seconds in all, until she finally stopped and let out a satisfied half sigh.

The detective thought, *That's definitely not a perp laugh.*

The police officer lifted the Kevlar shell underneath his uniform and concluded, *Naw, this lady ain't a kidnapper. Too bad we gotta hand her over to the immigration people.*

The assistant district attorney had precisely the opposite reaction: *All but an admission of guilt. With her aggressive laughter she mocks and challenges us.*

"I was taking them to their grandfather!" Araceli said suddenly at the top of her voice in English. "Because those people you put on the TV, that mother and father, *los responsables*, left me with Brandon *y* Keenan for four days! *¡Sola!* Since Saturday morning! I had no more food to give them."

"They told us they were gone for two days," the detective said.

"*¡Mentira!*"

"That means 'lie,' in Spanish," said the police officer in the doorway, whose name tag identified him as CASTILLO.

"By the grandfather, you mean who?"

"*El abuelo* Torres."

"John Torres?"

"Yes."

"Is that who this is?" the police detective asked, producing the black-and-white photograph of *el abuelo* Torres that Araceli had left in her backpack.

"*Sí.* I mean, yes. That is him."

In short order the police detective established Araceli's story, which began with the fight between Maureen and Scott and the broken table, and led to her own, ill-advised journey to the center of Los Angeles, and finally to Huntington Park, and her flight after seeing herself on television. "I see the television say I am a kidnapper. What am I thinking?" she said. "That is why I run. As fast as I can, which is not very fast, I am sorry." Goller remained silent, seemingly disoriented by the detective's sudden burst of questions and Araceli's unhesitating answers.

"I did not wanna see Brandon and Keenan in Faster Care," Araceli said.

"What?" the detective said.

"In Faster Care. *Porque no estaban sus padres.* Because they no had parents! I didn't want them to go."

"To go where?"

"To Faster Care."

"She means Foster Care," Officer Castillo interjected from the doorway. "Not 'Faster Care,'" he added with a roll of his eyes. "Foster Care."

Detective Blake studied the old photograph and the address scrawled on the back and slumped in his chair, feeling exasperated by the small comedy he had been drawn into. After a month in which he had crossed paths with a Taiwanese child-smuggling ring and a meth-

addict grandmother whose idea of discipline was a lighted cigarette, and after three trips with preschoolers to emergency rooms for examinations and photograph sessions for that grim and perverse task known as evidence collection, he was more annoyed than relieved by the harmless stupidity of this case. There was no crime here to investigate, but there were others awaiting him. *Serious shit follows bullshit—it always works that way.* A few seconds later, he rose to his feet and left the interrogation room, with the assistant district attorney following behind him, and they began an argument that continued during the twenty minutes it took them to drive back to Paseo Linda Bonita.

Deputy Castillo escorted Araceli to the holding cell, where she had three hours alone to study the art on the walls, which consisted of five representations of a unicorn with bulbous legs, three crucifixes tipped with arrowheads, and an exquisite rosebud, all drawn in pencil lines that had faded into ghost images in a fog of glossy, waterproof yellow paint. She thought she might ask one of the guards to lend her a writing instrument, because once they did set her free her time would be her own again, forever, and why not use this time to get started? Perhaps she would add a Picasso bull or an El Greco horse to the gallery.

"Sir, a pencil, please, is it possible?" she asked Deputy Castillo when he returned. Unexpectedly, he unlocked the door and held it open.

The news-aggregator website kept a flashing police-car light on its home page, along with a series of rapidly rewritten headlines, as the news of Brandon and Keenan's alleged kidnapping and rescue unfolded, scoring three-point-four million "hits" over the course of the first three hours, with the traffic doubling for the next two hours, when the site linked to footage obtained by an ABC news affiliate: forty-five seconds of Araceli running and being tackled by a police officer, as captured by the film crew in Huntington Park, and sold by the director for one thousand dollars—worth two days of on-location catering, the director would later tell his friends. Soon the footage began circulating on national cable shows, and by midafternoon assignment editors and managing editors across Southern California were dispatching a battalion of wiseass reporters to stake out the south county sheriff's station and Paseo Linda Bonita.

At the front gate of the Laguna Rancho Estates, the guards let

through anyone carrying the Day-Glo-green rectangle of a laminated plastic press card issued by the sheriff's department. Outside the Paseo Linda Bonita home the reporters pestered the sheriff's department patrolmen and lower-level public information officials on the perimeter for details of the boys' "drama," and set up tripods and light reflectors on the lawn. A second media cluster laid siege to the Luján family home in Huntington Park, where the councilman had sealed all the doors and windows, leaving the reporters to hound the neighbors for some throwaway speculation about possible kidnappings and flights to the border.

"Police sources say that Councilman Sal Luján is not a suspect in the case," went the report on KFWB all-news radio, delivered by a baritone-voiced veteran of riots, celebrity trials, and airplane crashes, big and small, a macho reporter-gumshoe who was on a first-name basis with mid- and high-ranking police officials in most of the dozens of jurisdictions in Los Angeles and Orange counties. "Seems he's just a Good Samaritan who got caught up in the drama of the two boys. But authorities say they're still trying to figure out what this lady Araceli Noeh-my Ramirez was up to. But, once again, the children she absconded with are said to be safe . . . Reporting from Huntington Park, this is Pete . . ."

The case was a "troubling mystery," said the NBC television affiliate reporter, a portrait of gray-haired youthfulness well known to Southern Californians for the calm urgency of his reporting on the edge of brush fires, mudslides, and assorted gangland crime scenes. "We really don't know what shape those boys are in or what they went through. We don't know if this Mexican nanny will be charged with anything. We don't know what, exactly, her intentions were," the reporter said, summarizing all he didn't know when his affiliate patched him into the network's national cable feed. For several hours the repeated transmissions of Araceli's blurred backyard photograph were juxtaposed with the footage of the searches and lines at the border, and of Araceli being tackled, and of the gleaming white home in a neighborhood most often described with the adjectives "exclusive," "hillside," and "gated." As interest in the story deepened in the early Eastern Daylight Time evening on national cable news, the class of professional tragedy-pundits chimed in. They were former prosecutors and defense attorneys who specialized in taking small bites of nebulous information and

chewing them until they became opinions and insights based on "what my gut tells me" and "what we know and what we don't know." Some opined, why not, on what they believed they knew about Mexican women and the well-off families that could afford to place their children in the care of foreigners. These comments intermingled with those of faceless callers to nationwide toll-free lines, for whom Araceli grew into a figure of menace and dread, while Maureen and Scott became objects of pity splashed with a touch of envy and populist scorn. "There's a good reason to stay at home and be a mom, and not leave your kids with a Mexican girl, even if you can get one for ten bucks a day," a caller opined in Gaithersburg, Maryland, speaking to the woman of the flaring nostrils, who nodded gravely.

In those American homes where Mexican, Guatemalan, and Peruvian women actually worked, mothers and fathers digested the news, and looked across their freshly dusted living rooms and tautly made beds and gave their hired help a closer look. They asked themselves questions that they usually suppressed, because the answers were, in practice, unknowable. *Where is this woman from, and how much do I really know about her?* Many of them were familiar with the superficial details of their employees' lives. The most empathetic among them had studied the photographs that arrived in the mail from places south, little faraway images with KODAK imprinted anachronistically on the back, of wrinkled parents in village gardens of prickly pear cacti and drought-bleached corn, of children in used American clothing celebrating exotic holidays involving the burning of incense and parades with religious icons. The knowledge of that distant poverty provoked feelings of admiration, guilt, and mild revulsion in varying degrees, and also a sense of confusion. *How can we live in such a big world, where hooded sweatshirts and baby ballerina dresses circulate from north to south, from new to old, from those who pay retail to those who pay for their clothes by the pound?* Now toss into this mystery a villain, and the possibility of hidden peccadilloes and secret motives of revenge, and the result was a slight but noticeable uptick in the volume of phone calls in the greater Southern California region, as mothers in cubicles, mothers leaving yoga sessions, mothers leaving staff meetings, mothers at the Getty and the Huntington, at the Beverly Center and the Sherman Oaks Galleria, looked away from their monitors and turned off their car radios, and picked up office

phones and cell phones and called home, just to check, just to listen to the accented voices of their hired help, to see if they might hear an intonation suggesting deception, the verbal slip of the schemer. "Everything okay? *¿Todo bien? Sí?* Yes? Okay, then." When they returned home they counted the items in their jewelry boxes and some examined the arms and necks of their children for bruises, and a very few even asked their toddlers, for the first time in weeks, if Lupe and María and Soledad were really "nice" or if they were ever "mean," to which the most common responses were, "What?" and "*¿Qué*, Mommy?"

17

Brandon sat with his legs crossed on the floor of the living room, telling the story of the journey he and his brother had taken to a distant land called Los Angeles. For the first time in his young life he had an audience of strangers listening to him with the same expression of urgent concentration that adults put on their faces when they talked and argued among themselves. The grown-ups sat on the edge of the couch and the love seat, and on a chair from the dining room, four adult men and two women in various states of formal dress, and with assorted metal and plastic badges and communication devices attached to their garments, accessories that, in Brandon's eyes, established their membership in officialdom. None of this made Brandon nervous. Rather, he saw in the presence of people introduced to him as "the officers" and "the social workers" a confirmation of the fact that he had survived an adventure tinged with danger. He had gone to a place far from the warm security and predictability of his home, and had returned to tell the tale.

"And then we got on this train that had two levels, and we left for another place. In Los Angeles," he said, his younger brother nodding alongside him. "This other place was made of bricks, mostly."

"And wood," Keenan added.

"Yeah, and wood, I think. And we went by a river," Brandon continued. "Or was it a canyon?"

"Yeah, a really big canyon," Keenan said.

"With bridges over it. And there were these people living there. Refugees from the Fire-Swallowers."

"The Fire-Swallowers?" Olivia Garza asked.

"Yeah, those are the people who came and destroyed the village of Vardur at the end of *Revenge of the Riverwalkers*."

"It's one of his books that he reads," Keenan said. Seeing the adults confused, he felt compelled to inject some explanation. "When Mom and Dad left, and Araceli said she would take care of us, she really didn't take care of us—I mean, she didn't tell us what to do like Mom does. So Brandon started reading more than he usually does. And when he reads—"

"Yeah, but these people I saw were real people," Brandon interrupted. "They had scars on their faces, from their battles with the Fire-Swallowers. Then we went to a big train station. And then we got into a bus, and we were looking for Grandpa's house, because Araceli said we should look for him. But we found this other place instead, where there are houses that are like jails, I guess. And then we found other houses that had half doors and quarter doors, and three-quarter doors, and other things I thought only existed in books. But they were real. And then we found a shack, which was in this place that's kind of like an oasis in the desert, where people come from all over to meet and sell things. We met this boy, who's a slave. I have a book about slavery, and he didn't look like any of the slaves in that book, but he was still a slave. We stayed with him in his shack. And he told us about the warriors who used to live across the street, and the battles they had, which always lasted thirteen seconds. The lady who lived there, she was really mean to this boy, and she made him work."

"That's true," Keenan said. "He really was a slave."

"Right. He was like my age, but he was a slave. So we slept there one night, until we woke up in the morning and heard some guy screaming outside."

"I didn't hear anybody screaming," Keenan said.

"You were still asleep, but I heard it. It was right after the earthquake."

"There was an earthquake?" Keenan said.

"Yeah. So this guy, he was like in pain, or something. He was yelling like he was hurting in his guts. And then everybody got up and we went to another place, which is called a park even though there isn't any park there. We went there because we thought Grandpa lived there, I guess, but he didn't live there either. At this park place they had a fire burning in the ground, to take a pig and turn him into bones. And the fire was burning hot, even though it was buried, because later we touched the rocks that were under the ground and they were still hot. But before that, everything started exploding around us. A bomb exploded in the street. And Keenan was holding some fire in his hand, and I told him to drop it, but he wouldn't listen to me."

"No, I didn't."

"Yes, you did. Don't lie. I saw you. You were holding fire, it was sparking from your palm, and then the bomb went off in the street. That's when I wanted to cry. After that a lynch mob came to the front porch, and they started yelling at us, because they were against the guy who lived there, and we started yelling back the name of Ray Forma, who is against them. Ray Forma is like some sort of hero that protects people against lynch mobs. These people yelling at us, they didn't have torches, but it was a lynch mob, I'm pretty sure, and they were really angry at the guy who lived there, because he's a president. But then the police came and chased away the lynch mob and we went to sleep and when we woke up the next morning we were on television so I got on the phone and called Dad."

The assembled audience of adults stared at Brandon with perplexed mouths agape and brows wrinkled, each mystified by the nonsensical details of Brandon's story and his straightforward and sincere way of recounting them, and the way Keenan sometimes nodded in confirmation of what his brother said. Adults and children had been momentarily transported into a shared state of mystery and innocence, a kind of mental blankness where anything was possible, and the adults allowed themselves to entertain, for the briefest instant of grown-up time, the possibility that these two well-spoken boys had actually returned from a magical land. Even Olivia Garza, who believed she had heard every kind of story a child could tell, did not know precisely what she should make of Brandon's monologue, so she simply looked at her digital recorder and turned it off.

Detective Blake and Assistant District Attorney Goller rose to their feet simultaneously, while a second detective named Harkness patted both Brandon and Keenan on the head and said, "Thanks guys." Detective Blake called back the parents from their temporary exile in the kitchen and left the boys with them, and the committee retired to the backyard for a tête-à-tête. For a few moments, they stood in a circle and looked at one another with now-what expressions.

"I don't know what to make of that," Detective Blake said finally. "That kid's got quite an imagination."

"This is what happens when you leave them alone too much, in my opinion," Olivia Garza said. "Whether it's TV, or books, or computer games. There are drawbacks. They slip into their own world."

"God knows what really happened to them," Assistant District Attorney Goller said. "I'm not a psychologist, but maybe this is some sort of emotional fantasy response to severe trauma."

The eyes of everyone present turned to the staff psychologist from Child Protective Services, a twenty-nine-year-old recently minted PhD from UCLA named Jennifer Gelfand-Peña. This was Dr. Gelfand-Peña's first time with the so-called emergency intervention team and she had overdressed for the occasion in her best, virgin-wool business skirt, and now she thought it strange that they were meeting with a representative of the district attorney's office and two detectives, given the manifest innocuousness of the case.

"What do I think?" she said with a pretty-woman cheerfulness that made everyone else in the group deepen their growing irritation with her. "I think the view up here is spectacular. I'm sort of bummed because I think we're missing the sunset. I also think this desert garden is really beautiful, but it's kind of over the top." Her colleagues shot her stony glances, but she seemed unconcerned. "And in my professional opinion, this kid Brandon is a fascinating case. He's got the verbal and reading skills of an eighteen-year-old. And the socialization of a seven-year-old, which isn't surprising, since he's very sheltered up here, and since he goes to the most expensive, touchy-feely private school in the county. So I think what's probably going on is that he's just read too many books."

"Well, the way I see it, the boy basically confirmed what the maid told our detective here," Olivia Garza said. "She said she was taking

them to the grandfather. Right, Detective? And that's what the boy said. He said they were alone in the house with the maid and they left to look for the grandfather."

"But he didn't know since when," Detective Blake offered.

"Yeah, kids are terrible with time," the staff psychologist said.

"No harm, no foul, as far as I'm concerned," Detective Blake said. "I don't see what we can hold this Mexican lady on."

"So we're going to throw the parents' statement out the window?" Goller said. "Shouldn't we be investigating, at least, for child endangerment?"

"Eleven one sixty-five-point-two?" Blake said. "By the parents? Or the maid?"

"No, not the parents, because they left the boys with an adult guardian," Goller said. "But I wasn't thinking about that so much as a two-seventy-three-A."

"Interesting," said Dr. Gelfand-Peña, which was her ironic way of saying a child abuse charge seemed far-fetched.

"Really?" Olivia Garza said.

"Do we have evidence of either of those crimes?" Detective Blake asked.

"Remember that address our victims appear to have visited first?" Goller said. "I called the LAPD. It's smack in the middle of the gang-infested garment-factory district of L.A. If taking two Orange County kids to that hellhole isn't two seventy-three-A, then I don't know what is."

"Felony two seventy-three-A?" Detective Blake said. "I don't see it. Misdemeanor two seventy-three-A? Maybe."

"Do we go back and question the parents again?" Olivia Garza asked.

"We've got their statement," Goller said.

"Can't we just drop the whole thing?" Jennifer Gelfand-Peña asked.

There was a collective silence in which the three senior members of the emergency intervention team—Goller, Blake, and Garza—looked at one another and waited like *pistoleros* in a western for one to blink. The truth was, once you amassed as many resources as they had, it took a bit of courage to simply cry out, *Sorry! False Alarm!* After all, K-9 units had been assembled to search the hills, Explorer deputies had marched through the meadows, and a suspect had been named, with her alleged crime denounced. They had called an Amber Alert and semi-sealed-off

the border for a few hours, all in the name of protecting two Orange County children. Some grown-up had to be held responsible for this mess.

"From what I can tell," Goller said finally, "and from what I can see of this family, and from having questioned this woman, I think it's pretty obvious Ms. Ramirez didn't like her employers. So she conspired to dump their kids someplace. Just leave 'em somewhere god-awful. If she 'willfully' placed those boys in a situation where they might be endangered, then that's two seventy-three-A. That's the law."

Detective Blake was unconvinced. He sensed familiar political-theatric motives at work, the usual DA baloney. "Well, you go ahead and make your phone call, Mr. Goller. And I'll make mine."

"You know Goller, sometimes things really *are* what they seem to be," Olivia Garza said. "It's pretty obvious we should just call it a ten-forty and go home."

"No, I don't think that I'll be able to do that," the assistant district attorney said, raising his chin and directing the group to look up at the sky and its spreading wash of ultramarine ink. The beating engines of two television helicopters had slipped into the airspace above them as they were debating the case. "They pulled those choppers away from the fire to cover this," Goller said. "That's huge. My guess is that we're live on national cable right now." The assistant district attorney allowed the members of the emergency intervention team to ponder the meaning of the hovering crafts, and the small globes attached to their undercarriages. "Unfortunately, we're in America's living room now," he said. "Therefore, we must proceed with an abundance of caution."

They were smack in the middle of that great spectacle Goller had foreseen in his condo during the first hours of the morning, when Brandon's and Keenan's faces first flashed on his television. And already he sensed where its pressures might take them.

"So go ahead and release your suspect if you have to, Detective," Goller said. "But in a few days you might have to pick her up again."

After a first kiss of his daughter's forehead, after looking at his two sons, embracing them, and confirming, with a scan of his eyes and a few minutes in their untroubled presence, that they had suffered no

harm, Scott found himself stepping back and away. "We missed you, Dad," Keenan said, and the simple statement brought a rush of water to his eyes. He turned to his wife, seeking a glance, a shared moment of understanding and forgiveness, but she was aggressively not looking at him, so he drifted off into a state of shocked silence, in which he listened to his wife repeat, again and again, "Are you okay? Are you okay?" Then, after the police and the social workers and the psychologist had finished their "talk" alone with Brandon and Keenan, and after he and Maureen had a second reunion with their sons that was a shorter and less emotional version of the first, he drifted away from the room entirely, leaving his wife to assuage her guilt by reading to the boys and Samantha from a large picture book, in a kind of forced imitation of domestic bliss that, Scott guessed, was intended for the police and social services officials still huddled in their yard. Scott looked at Brandon rolling his eyes because *Ladybug Girl* was not exactly his idea of compelling literature. *My son is eleven, but he's already a book snob.* Eventually Scott drifted to the television room, to the high-tech masculinity of objects plugged into the wall, and reached for the television's power switch with a Pavlovian purposelessness, flipping through the cable channels. He stopped when he reached an aerial news shot of a structure on a dead-end circle that looked familiar. When he saw the graphic that read MISSING CHILDREN FOUND he knew it was his home, and he considered the size of the crescent-shaped backyard, and how much of it was filled by the desert garden. From the air, and in the fading illumination of dusk, the garden looked like a herd of small spiked animals escorted by tall cacti shepherds. He thought that it all made for an aesthetically pleasing composition of circles and lines when you saw it from the sky, before the little commentator in his head finally woke up and he realized, *Holy shit, there's a helicopter floating above my house.*

Before he could rise to his feet to go to the window to look for the helicopter, the television switched to a video clip shot from the ground, footage that showed Scott himself talking with a sheriff's deputy at his door several hours earlier, a few minutes after Scott had received that phone call from Brandon. The deputy was smiling and patting him on the back, and Scott guessed that this image was supposed to convey the idea that the drama had been resolved happily, and sure enough seconds later there was a shot of his two sons walking up the driveway,

escorted very quickly by a deputy to the front door. The television cut
to a studio shot, of a woman with flaring nostrils and stiff blond hair
that sprayed forth, fountainlike, from her head, and a band of gold coins
around her neck, and she was speaking to a camera with a kind of vehemence that Scott found unappealing, until she stopped suddenly and
just stared at the camera for several seconds and began nodding. This
caused Scott to reach for the volume and turn it up. The woman on the
television was listening to a caller with an accent that Scott recognized
as upper New England.

"... and I just look at those two precious little boys, Nancy, and I
wonder, what did that Mexican lady want with them? What was she
thinking she was gonna do with them? I just wonder."

"That's what we're all thinking," the blond host said, which led
Scott to change the channel, inadvertently causing Araceli to appear on
the screen. She was being escorted to the police car, earlier in the day,
with her wrists clasped together with plastic strings. *Oh, my God*, Scott
thought. *What have we done to this poor Mexican woman?* The screen
cut to another shot tagged LIVE: ORANGE COUNTY, CALIFORNIA, which
showed his $250-per-week housemaid emerging from a police station,
winding her way through concrete obstacles meant to fend off terrorist
attacks. "Araceli Noemi Ramirez, kidnapping suspect, has now been set
free, with investigators saying . . ." Araceli was walking away from the
cameras, studying the news-gatherers filming her from a distance with
the same quizzical and annoyed look she gave Scott when he asked for
catsup to apply to her turkey sandwiches. Now she stopped, to listen
to a shouted question, apparently, and the camera zoomed and shook,
with his large domestic employee bouncing at the center of the frame
as she turned and walked away with long and loping strides, an image
that reminded Scott of that footage of Bigfoot supposedly walking through
a clearing in a California forest, a video moment halfway between the
real and the simulated, like those shots of turban man and binocular
lady Elysian Systems sold to the government.

Scott was changing the channel again when Maureen appeared at
the door behind him.

"Scott. The police say the reporters outside won't leave," she said,
and there was something startling in hearing her address him. "They
say they're going to wait until we make a statement." She had not slept

in two days and she was fading quickly, her voice dreamy and far-away.

"I'll go out there and talk to them."

"No, I have to go with you. You can't be out there alone."

"Why?"

"Because they need to see both of us. We both need to be there. To defend ourselves."

"What?"

"People are talking about our family. All over the city. Didn't you know? Stephanie Goldman-Arbegast just called. They were driving in from the airport and heard people talking about us on the radio. About the boys and Araceli and me and you. For an entire hour. People are saying we're bad parents. We have to show ourselves. Because people are saying things about us. Didn't you know?"

The news of the "kidnapping" had circulated in Spanish too, in a flow of words only slightly less robust than in English, beginning in the morning, when a popular FM radio talk/variety jock interrupted his usual series of bawdy jokes and barnyard animal noises to reflect on *el caso*, lowering his voice an octave into what he called, off the air, his "citizen voice." "Friends," he said in Spanish, "this is a case that might impact each and every one of us. I don't know what this lady is doing with these boys, but if you're listening to me, *señora*, or *señorita*, take them home. Let's remember that our relationship with these people is built on trust. Because I know there's thousands of *nuestra gente* out there taking care of these little *mocosos* with blond hair and blue eyes. And if just one of us messes up like they say this lady is, a big load of you know what is going to fall on top of all our heads." In kitchens where meals were being prepared by women named Lupe and María and Soledad, the anxiety level rose significantly after listening to this lecture, and rose further after Lupe and María and Soledad saw the reports on the city's three Spanish-language television stations, and the footage of Araceli in flight. So by the end of that fifth of July, the floors gleamed brighter, the food was prepared with extra care and fewer spices, until, in the evening when Lupe and María and Soledad arrived home to the cluttered hominess of their apartments in South-Central

and Compton, or when they settled into their cramped servant quarters in Beverly Hills homes, and they turned on their televisions and their radios to hear the happy news that Araceli Noemí Ramírez had been set free and that she had been *exonerada* of all charges.

On Spanish-language television, the images of Araceli walking free were broadcast with commentary that took on a thinly veiled tone of the celebratory, the rising voices of a soccer victory, or the birth of a celebrity baby. "*Salió una mujer libre, con la cabeza alta, y digna.*" It had all been a misunderstanding, they reported in voices a half breath short of a sigh. The charges against Araceli, now dropped, were a false wrinkle in the freshly starched blanket of responsibility for which *latinoamericana* nannies were famous. *Una mala comunicación.* On the telephone, "*la soltaron*" became the refrain: They let her go, they let her slip away. It was an observation dropped into conversations that soon swung back to the mundane quotidian chatter and melodramatic gossip about school meetings and *comadres* who were pregnant again and jobs opening up in "*casas buenas,*" and the irritating behavior of employers in "*casas malas.*" They let Araceli go and everything was back to normal until the next morning, when the workday began in the early morning darkness, and Lupe and María and Soledad entered kitchens and bedrooms and looked for the faces of the women who paid them, their *jefas,* and saw the upturned corners of pert lips, the flaxen caterpillar eyebrows that rose in recognition and comfort: *Yes, I know you, you are my Lupe, my María, my Soledad. You are here again, on time, and you will wave your chestnut hands and return these sheets and comforters to order, and you will erase the grease from the kitchen surfaces and keep the ants away, and you will change my baby boy's diaper, and I will leave you here alone in my nest, alone with my child and my possessions, because of that moment of faith and calculus when I close my eyes and feel that thing called trust.*

Maureen led Scott back to the living room, where Assistant District Attorney Goller was standing alone by the front door with the attentive look of a best man awaiting the bride and groom at a wedding. When Maureen reached the door, he gave her a comforting smile, put his arm around her shoulder, and lowered his chin to speak sotto voce, even though no one else but Scott was listening.

"There's about a dozen reporters out there. Don't let that scare you." He guided Maureen gently to the picture window and pulled back a corner of the drapes, revealing the spectacle of lights and telescoping microwave antennas outside; they felt to Maureen like an alien force, gathered on her lawn with nefarious cinematic intent, fed by the electricity generated by their humming vans. "The sheriff department's PIO was just out there fifteen minutes ago. The public information officer, I mean. And he gave a statement, saying they were releasing your employee, and not charging her with anything. He said this was all a, quote, 'misunderstanding.'"

"Right," Scott said quickly.

"But when they pressed him for details, he got off his script," Goller continued. "He started saying some things that weren't on the release. He said some things that our friend Detective Blake told him, apparently. He said your employee was trying to, quote, 'rescue' your children because you had, quote, 'abandoned' them."

"Fuck," Scott said, which earned him a pointed look from his wife.

"That's what he said. 'Rescue.' Which, of course, implies that you two placed your children in danger."

"Jesus," Scott said.

"Why would he say that?" Maureen asked. "Why would anyone care? We got our boys back."

"He said that because he needed to explain how it was that a sheriff, an American sheriff, could simply release an illegal immigrant onto the streets, especially one that was just a suspect in a child abduction case."

"Child abduction?" Scott said. "But is that really—"

"The PIO had to give them something," Goller continued. "So he gave them you, in so many words."

"Us?" Maureen said.

"And as soon as he made that suggestion, well, it got the reporters excited. They started throwing around phrases like 'irresponsible' and 'negligence' and asking if we're going to 'press charges.' Being reporters, they don't really understand what those words mean. But when they start asking those kinds of questions, Child Protective Services will eventually get their noses in the case." Goller quickly explained the competing bureaucratic imperatives that would soon envelope Maureen, Scott,

and their children, and how it was that two good parents could easily end up before a skeptical judge in family court. It shouldn't be that a mother and father who called the police in search of their boys ended up under the scrutiny of Child Protective Services, that crude, cheaply staffed machinery, as Goller saw it, where parents were studied under a lens of maximum disbelief. But it happened all the time.

"So what do we do?" Maureen asked finally.

"Number one, you go out there and speak very calmly and show these people who you are," Goller said. "You're the very picture of a happy California family. Just you standing up there will do a lot to calm the waters, so to speak. You don't answer any questions. But you do say that you're thankful to the sheriff's department and the Huntington Park police and the media—it's important that you remember the media—that you're thankful to all of them for helping to find your two sons. If they shout any questions, you don't answer. You just say thanks and walk away. Okay?"

Scott digested this information as he walked down the lawn, Maureen following after him with Samantha over her shoulder, having left the boys inside their room with the assistant district attorney. Like a family condemned to the guillotine, they walked with heads bowed toward the spot where the lawn dropped off and sloped downward. A cluster of microphones attached to two poles stood waiting there, their steel silhouettes glinting against a cloud of white light from the television lamps. Scott felt the heat of the lights on his skin, and a kind of nakedness he had not felt since he was an adolescent. *Here we stand before you, my American family and I: have pity on me, their bumbling provider and protector, and on them, because they aren't to blame.* He approached the microphone to speak, though before he could open his mouth someone yelled out, "Is that Torres with an *s* or with a *z*?"

"An *s*," he said, and smiled, because the question calmed him and brought him to the moment.

"I, we, my wife and I . . . we just want to say thank you to everybody," Scott began. "To the sheriff's department, to the Child Protective Services people, to everyone. And to the media too, for getting the word out. Brandon and Keenan are home safe now. They're going to be okay." In ten seconds, he had reached the end of all he could say.

"Were they kidnapped?" a male voice asked in a tone that suggested irony and disbelief. "Was there a note?"

Scott could see the wisdom of Ian Goller's advice: unwrapping the full and complicated truth for this assembled rabble of news-gatherers would be an act of suicide. "And we're glad this is over," he continued, ignoring the question. "Thanks for coming." He sensed, in an instant, that his attempt at expressing finality had fallen flat. In the time-swallowing silence that followed, he became aware that he, Maureen, and Samantha were on live television, because he could see their family portrait, animated and mirrorlike in miniature, on five monitors that rested at the feet of the reporters, each with the words LIVE: LAGUNA RANCHO ESTATES in various fonts. "So good night, everyone. And thank you."

Maureen mouthed the words *Thank you* silently, with perhaps a bit too much wan affectation. They were just turning to leave when a voice boomed from behind the blinding lights.

"I have a police source that says you, quote, 'abandoned' your children. For four days. You just disappeared, apparently. Why?" Scott and Maureen were caught off guard by the questioner's bluntness. The voice belonged to the veteran KFWB reporter, who had arrived at the scene just a few minutes earlier, after a gear-grinding race from the south county sheriff's station, where an off-the-record conversation with the chief of detectives before Araceli's release had tilted his view of the case toward the Mexican woman.

"Why did you leave them alone in this house for four days?" None of his colleagues were surprised by the radio reporter's directness. His gadfly irritability with interview subjects was legendary, and included a live television dress down of the chief spokesman for the United States Army Central Command in Riyadh during the first Gulf War. "It's a simple question. Did you abandon your children to this illegal immigrant?"

Maureen could not see the questioner, a stranger who was standing on her property and slandering her before a live television audience. He was yelling from behind the pack of cameras, beyond the white aura of light bursting behind the reporters' heads. "That's a lie!" she snapped. She had a moment to think, *This is the most desperate thing I've done in my entire life,* but failed to notice the surprised and mildly disgusted expression on the woman in the first row of reporters, which might have given her a clue to the response of her viewing audience. "How dare you!" After thirty-six hours without sleeping, her eyes were amnesiac

droopy, but she could not accept a total stranger saying she was a bad mother. Her hair was flat and stringy, and she was wearing the same dress she had put on the morning she left the desert spa, a spaghetti-strap pullover whose patterned sunflowers now hung forlornly from her shoulders. Her fuming shout only made her look more haggard, poor and harried, as if she'd stepped off some trashy tabloid-reality stage. Later, Maureen would see this moment replayed on television and understand what she had done as an act of self defense, more desperate, even, than being nineteen years old and trying to escape from underneath the sweaty grip of a drunken college friend, the only time in her life she'd actually used her fists and teeth to inflict injury. "I did *not* neglect my children. That's a vicious, vicious lie!"

"Yeah, we got it!" the reporter said sarcastically.

"Pete, gather yourself," one of the other reporters said.

"C'mon. Tell us what happened."

Maureen squinted and searched the silhouettes of the reporters one last time, and turned and walked away, Scott mumbling a thank-you at the microphones and then scurrying after her.

Araceli thought the cameras outside the sheriff's station might follow her, but they did not. She walked quickly around the corner, through the station's parking lot and its fleet of patrol cars, and into the empty center of Aliso Viejo, where the streets were free of pedestrians after four-thirty in the afternoon. The police had returned her money, and in her first moments of freedom she was momentarily fixated on that act of honesty. *Transparencia*, they called that in Mexico, an idea symbolized by the clear, large plastic bag in which her belongings had been gathered and catalogued. *Now, that's an example of* el primer mundo *if there ever was one.* In Mexico, you paid cash for your freedom, and the police made sure you left custody with nothing but your wrinkled clothes and all the stains you acquired during a night or two in jail: it had happened to a couple of her alcoholic uncles. A bribe and it was all forgotten. If your car was stolen, you paid the police to get it back for you, which had happened to her father, in the *comisaría* in Nezahual-cóyotl. Here at the sheriff's station, by contrast, Araceli had been set free not by monetary payment, but rather with truth and laughter, and

this realization made her chuckle again, all by herself on the street corner, and reminded her of that folk saying: *La que sola ríe, en sus maldades piensa*. She who laughs alone is remembering her sins. "That's
dumb: I haven't committed any *maldades*. I'm just a poor *mexicana* trying to find her way." The detective had asked her, simply, for a phone
number at which she might be reached—"in case we need some help
with the investigation"—and had then handed her the plastic bag. She
advanced one block down the street before she realized she didn't know
where to go next. Returning to the home of the Torres-Thompsons was
out of the question. *No los quiero ver.* She did have the money in the
plastic bag, and briefly considered buying a bus ticket to the border:
she had enough for a ticket to Tijuana, and for a *torta* and taco once she
got there, but not enough to go any farther. And getting her money out
of the bank was impossible without returning to Paseo Linda Bonita.
So she called Marisela, with a quarter dropped into the last pay phone
left in the center of Aliso Viejo, and asked her friend for *posada* for a
night.

"You were on TV," Marisela said. "You're still on TV."

"*Estoy cansada.* I think I'll sleep for two days."

"Did they hurt you? When I saw them grabbing you on the news,
when you were running, I told Mr. Covarrubias, 'Oh, my God. They're
going to break her arm!' And then we saw you walk out and you looked
fine."

"They were polite. Once they realized I am not a *secuestradora* . . .
So can I stay with you?"

"Let me ask my Mr. Covarrubias and see what he says." Araceli
heard the sounds of dishes being moved about the kitchen, and the
formless chatter from the television, and then the very clear jingle of a
beer commercial, followed by an exchange of voices.

"He says he's going to drive out there to pick you up," Marisela said
with a cheer. "He's really angry about what he saw on the TV. He says
we have to help you. He's running out the door right now. Expect him
there in about twenty-five minutes."

In her home on Calmada Avenue in South Whittier, Janet Bryson was angry too, though for entirely different reasons. She watched

television dumbfounded as Araceli Ramirez walked to freedom, perched on the edge of her old but homey and recently reupholstered couch, in a big house with a faulty air conditioner. The heat and the events on the television put her in a foul mood. She'd begun to follow the drama of Brandon and Keenan before dawn, in the final hours of her hospital swing shift, catching the first images of the boys on the television in the empty reception area. Later, at home, she searched for details on the Internet and then sat down in her living room to watch the final, insulting denouement of the day's events live on Channel 9.

"They're letting her go? What is this?"

Janet Bryson did not personally know any of the protagonists, of course, although her home happened to be eight blocks from Scott Torres's old home on Safari Drive. She was a nurse technician, and a divorced single mom raising a teenage boy in a two-story ranchette with a layout identical to the former Torres residence, a home plopped like his on the flat surface of forgotten cow pastures, alongside a concrete drainage channel called Coyote Creek. A small thread of brackish liquid ran in Coyote Creek during the summer, fed mostly by the runoff from storm drains that collected the water wasted by neighbors who babied their lawns, rose gardens, and low riders with twice and thrice-weekly deluges. That thread of brackish water attracted crows and cats and, occasionally, a flock of feral parrots with emerald and saffron plumage, and now, as Janet slumped back into the newly stiff cushions of her couch to fully absorb the release of yet another illegal alien criminal suspect into American freedom, one of the parrots gave a loud, humanoid squawk just beyond her backyard fence.

"Oh, shut up, you stupid bird!"

Janet Bryson felt roughly the same about Araceli Ramirez, the nanny kidnapper, and all the other Mexicans invading her space, as she did about the untamed parrots. Like the Spanish-speaking families in her subdivision, the parrots were intruders from the south. They were the descendants of escaped pets and, in a landscape that was the natural home of gray-brown house sparrows and black crows, they were disturbing for the ostentatious display of their exotic colors. Five years earlier she had written to the SPCA, the Sierra Club, and the Audubon Club about how disturbing it was, what a violation of natural rhythms and habitats, to have these tropical birds gathering on the telephone wires and

bathing in the creek. Only the Audubon people had written back, with a polite and oft-circulated letter decrying the "invasive species" but lamenting the expense and impracticality of rounding up all the birds, which were in fact six different species of the genus *Amazona*.

The Mexicans came after the parrots. There had always been a few, but they were English-speaking and generally decent folk back in the day when Janet Bryson was a newlywed and lived in this same home with her former husband. She could talk to those Mexicans because they were Americans, and she could even see a bit of herself in the family comings and goings she witnessed on their driveways and in their garages, the household routines shaped around automobiles, football, and the holidays. Their cousins and grandparents concentrated for Thanksgiving and their lights went up every Christmas. But then came the slow drip of Spanish speakers, the inexorable filling of her block with actual nationals of that other country. She'd knocked on the door of one of the first of these Spanish-speaking families when they moved in next door, offering a plate of brownies because it was the neighborly thing to do. A man of about thirty with a head of black Brillo-pad hair had greeted her, seemingly perplexed by the gesture and also delighted by the appearance of a still-hot white woman on his doorstep. Moments later, this man's wife had joined him at the door and had given Janet Bryson a reluctant "thank you"—or, rather, "tank you"—and then a dismissive up-and-down, as if to say, *No, my husband won't go after this one.* And they still hadn't returned her plate several years later! Janet Bryson didn't forget a slight, which was why she hadn't spoken to her ex-husband for several years, not since an incident at a Super Bowl party involving one of his girlfriends. She remembered the missing plate as more Mexicans arrived, with one family on her block raising a Mexican flag on an actual flagpole they planted on their front lawn, in violation of a building code no one bothered to enforce.

The parrots squawked and waddled in the wash, and thrived and multiplied on a diet of oranges and lemons, and their sudden bursts of noise, their early morning squawk-chorus, often startled Mrs. Bryson awake, as did the Mexicans who revved up their old cars at six or seven to get them going. The parrots flew in groups of about twenty, in large, diamond-shaped formations, and the Mexicans moved in clusters, pairs of men standing over engines, groups of women and girls carrying

pots. The Mexicans always seemed to be plotting, with the men putting arms around one another, speaking in lowered voices. Most ominously, she heard, several times a week, one of them make a seven-tone whistle. It was a kind of signal, a summoning, the last note trailing off in plaintive demand. What was the meaning?

Janet Bryson had begun to study the Mexicans in the same way she had studied the parrots, by plugging keywords into Internet search engines, and then by writing letters and emails in which her sense of dislocation found voice. She had come to see herself as part of an under-the-radar network of concerned citizens, isolated voices scattered about suburbs like El Monte and Lancaster, fighting the evils of bilingual education and the bad habits of these people, such as using their front lawns to park their cars and dry their laundry. From her Internet friends, she learned about the conspiracies hatched at the highest levels of government and finance to join together the United States, Canada, and Mexico into a single country, with a single currency called the Amero. She had seen schematic drawings that were said to represent the superhighway that would link the interior of Mexico to Kansas City, and thus accelerate the country's plunge into foreignness. Watching the Mexicans on Calmada Avenue plot, and reading about the much larger scheme to transform her country, was like living in a dream: the events were strange, menacing, and out of her control.

Janet Bryson worked, sacrificed, and kept an eye on the Mexicans for her only son, an ungrateful sixteen-year-old who was beginning to talk English like a Mexican: she could hear it in the way he stretched out the vowels into a long whine in words like "really" and "guy," and the gangster intonations with which he pronounced phrases like "so what." "Why are you talking that way?" she would demand, but he would just shoot back that annoyed sneer that had taken over his face since he turned thirteen. Before he met Mexicans, Carter was a boy who understood they were a mother and son against the world. She had recently given him the keys to his first car and he had rewarded her by working on it in the driveway with one of the Mexicans, and then disappearing every afternoon and most evenings in that old Toyota Celica, leaving her alone in the house to think about her Mexican neighbors and to watch television, where the news was filled with Mexicans. If you looked closely, you saw them everywhere: on the edges of fires, at basketball

games, in mug shots. And now in the face of that running woman, the stealer of children who, for mysterious reasons, was now walking free.

On the day that Araceli Ramírez became a national celebrity, Janet Bryson stood on the front porch of her home and called out to her son, "Carter! Where are you going?" He waved but didn't answer. She had been planted in front of her television set for most of the day, and her obsession with the story had caused her to consume, all on her own, a family-size bag of cheese curls. *It's not good to eat that way.* But what else could she do? Those boys looked like her boy, in the old grade school picture with the brown fixer stains in the hallway, Carter before hormones swelled his arms and thickened his neck. Two American boys spirited away southward into Mexico. Unprotected. She found herself actually weeping when word of their rescue had flashed on *Headline News*. "Thank God!" She slipped into the kitchen and made herself a late lunch, and allowed the television to fill the house with noise as she waited for whatever epilogue the news might bring. And then she had heard the announcement of the Mexican woman's release, and the scurrilous insinuations against the American parents.

When Maureen shouted, "That's a lie," Janet Bryson shared her sense of motherly indignation, and felt herself instantly freed from the state of vibrating meaninglessness that seemed to settle over her mind and home during those long hours when her son was away. *We should all shout like that.* Janet Bryson wanted to shout at the next-door neighbor with the string of Christmas lights circling a backyard shrine, whose nighttime glow filled her bedroom 365 days a year, to shout at the unseen young Mexicans who had taught her son to whine at the end of his words. She had to do something; she had to join her shout to the shout of that American mother who had been wronged. She had to rally the troops. She returned to her computer and started writing.

18

In thirty minutes, Maureen told Stephanie Goldman-Arbegast the entire story, beginning with the fiasco of the birthday party and the drunken ramblings of Sasha "the Big Man" Avakian and the planting of the desert garden. They were sitting in the kitchen, with Samantha's somewhat plump, pre-toddler body squeezed into a now-stationary hand-crank rocker. Samantha was about three months and fifteen pounds past the appropriate age and size for this contraption, Stephanie Goldman-Arbegast observed, and it disturbed her, mildly, to see her old friend subject her baby to this uncharacteristic and extended moment of in-attention. Stephanie Goldman-Arbegast was used to seeing Maureen in elegant control of just about any situation that presented itself, moving slowly and deliberately and in good cheer in the face of poolside scrapes and wine-glass mishaps. Stephanie admired and in many ways sought to emulate her old playgroup friend, even though, in a few, select en-counters over the past few months, she'd noticed how the old, even-tempered Maureen was being slowly ground down by the demands of two growing boys and a baby girl. But never had Stephanie Goldman-Arbegast seen Maureen in the sleep-deprived and disoriented state in

which she found her today, circling aimlessly about the kitchen as she spoke, and finally wiping the tears from her face as she brought the strange and accidental tale forward to the argument that ended with the broken living room coffee table, and her journey with Samantha into the desert, and her return to the spotless and empty rooms of this home.

"And that's how we got into this mess," Maureen said, and as she looked up through her swollen eyes at her old friend the phone rang once more. Peter Goldman picked it up after the second ring in the dining room, where he was drinking wine with Scott.

"The reporters," Maureen said. "We're living this media plague. They've made us into a story."

"It was big on the morning shows," said Stephanie Goldman-Arbegast, who had black hair cut man-short for the summer. She was a lean woman of forty with the no-nonsense air and taste for embroidered blouses of her Wyoming forebears.

"They called here last night, before we took the phone off the hook so we could sleep. The *Today* show. Scott talked to them and told them to leave us alone."

"And then there's the stuff in the papers. And in the blogs."

"The blogs? I can only imagine."

Stephanie removed three printed pages of blog posts from her purse, and held them so that Maureen could see them, a sampling of the 316 postings on the *L.A. Times* website as of late morning. She did this simply so Maureen would know, because that was the job of friends, to be both loyal and alert, and to bring knowledge that might be uncomfortable and unwanted but also necessary. Almost exactly half the postings expressed sympathy with Scott and Maureen: of those, half cited the clip of Maureen shouting back at the reporter in expressing their own outrage at the "liberal" and "immigrant-loving" media for refusing to believe that Brandon and Keenan had been kidnapped. These posters and their paranoid rhetoric held Maureen's attention only momentarily. The other half, however, made various snide observations about the Torres-Thompsons and the Laguna Rancho Estates, about Maureen's "rant" and how "spoiled" she and her husband were, and the obvious "heroism" of the Mexican woman who'd been briefly jailed for "the crime" of trying to save two children who'd been abandoned by their parents.

"Don't take that stuff too seriously," Stephanie said. "I just thought you should know. Maybe I shouldn't have shown you."

"No. I need to see this."

"There was this one guy on the radio. KABC. Some guy from an immigrant association, talking about how Mexican women are the 'salt of the earth,' how they raise our children and do heroic things every day, and how Araceli is, what's the word, 'emblematic' of this big 'font of mothering' these Latina nannies provide. I tried calling in to defend you, to say something, but—"

"A font of mothering? Araceli?"

"Yeah. It was some really overwrought expression like that."

"Unbelievable." Maureen scanned a few of the English postings, then stopped and returned them to her friend. "Araceli is the real mother, I guess," she said with sarcastic resignation. "I'm just the rich parasite."

"Ignore them. You know who you are. You're a great mom. To three kids. And now with Guadalupe gone? All by yourself you're raising them. None of those people know how hard you work. And who cares, frankly?"

Above all, Maureen was offended simply by the idea that distant strangers would offer their glib and automatic opinions about her home and family. They peered into her household and made a wicked sport of her, Scott, and their children, extrapolating conclusions based on a few photographs released to the public, their own prejudices about people "like her," and the recorded moment when she chose to defend herself before the intrusive white light of the television cameras gathered on her front lawn. These faceless strangers could type insults and collectively craft the big falsehood of Araceli's lionization, without knowing that the Mexican woman disliked Maureen's children and frowned at them as she served them dinner, and that she had once had the gall to tell Maureen, "These boys have too many toys to keep in order. They are not organized in their brains to have this many toys." *Araceli questioned my sons' intelligence, she sat for hours in her room playing artist with our trash, she recoiled at the sight of my baby girl's spit-up. But now she is a Mexican Joan of Arc.*

"It's true that I left, that we left her alone in the house," she told Stephanie finally. "But that doesn't give her the right to take our children on some bizarre journey to the city, for God knows what purpose."

"No, it doesn't."

Maureen thought of the daily vigilance necessary to keep domestic order and to stay true to her values and raise children who would be good citizens and thinkers. It was all a private, selfless act, and now she was being mocked as precisely the opposite. Araceli was responsible for this chorus of snarky and misspelled voices against her.

"How could she not believe we were coming back? That doesn't make sense to me. She doesn't even leave a note. That woman was always off. And why take them into Los Angeles, of all places?"

"She was wrong to do that."

"She placed them in danger."

Stephanie Goldman-Arbegast kept silent and gave her friend a weak nod of solidarity. She sensed that Maureen would eventually add her voice to those seeking to punish Araceli, and she did not approve. *I will not hold this against my friend.* Here before her was a good woman in an impossible situation. She lived for her children. Her children were her art. And now the city belittled her as a bad mother. *Would I act any different? If my jaw tightens in anger when my New York in-laws criticize my parenting, how would I act if an entire city were sitting in judgment?* Stephanie watched as her friend bit her lip and turned to look at her sleeping baby girl.

"This rocker is too small for Samantha, isn't it?" Maureen said finally, as if she had stepped out of a fog and found her daughter, unexpectedly. "I can't put her in this thing anymore. She's all squeezed into it. What was I thinking?"

In the space Araceli knew as the Room of a Thousand Wonders, Brandon and Keenan huddled with their friends, Max and Riley Goldman-Arbegast. For once they had not drifted immediately to the pleasures of interlocking plastic blocks arranged as imaginary parapets, forts, and bunkers, or the distractions of handheld electronic games. Instead, they talked about their recent adventures: the Goldman-Arbegasts' trip to Europe, and the train journey that Brandon and Keenan had taken out of their home and into another world in the center of Los Angeles.

"We saw the Parthenon in Athens," Max said.

"Is that where Zeus lived?" Keenan asked.

"No, that's Mount Olympus," Brandon corrected. Both he and Max, the older of the Goldman-Arbegast brothers, were great fans of Greek mythology.

"And then later we went to London and saw the marbles the English took from the Greeks."

"The Greeks played with marbles?" Keenan asked.

"No. They're these big flat pictures carved out of marble," Max said. "And we saw the Rosetta Stone."

"When we went to L.A., everybody spoke in Spanish, mostly," Keenan said. "We saw *el cuatro de julio.*"

"I learned how to say 'thanks' in Italian," Riley countered. "It's '*grazie.*'"

"And we saw you and Keenan on television," Max said.

"Yeah," Brandon said flatly. "We were on lots of TV stations."

"Lots and lots. Like every one, I think," Riley said.

"Were you scared when that lady kidnapped you?" Max asked, rushing in the question, as if he had been waiting to ask.

"Nah, I don't think she kidnapped us," Brandon said. "We were looking for our grandfather. But we got all mixed up. We saw some cool things, though."

"We saw the Colosseum," Riley said.

"Were there gladiators?" Keenan asked.

"Nah," Max said. "It's all ruins now."

"Parts of L.A. are ruins too," Brandon said. He began to share a few more details of his journey to Los Angeles, and his encounters with war refugees and lynch mobs, though this time with less gusto than before. He had already tried telling the story to his parents, only to be interrupted by so many of his mother's questions that the story didn't sound like his anymore. *Why is it*, he wondered later, *that stories begin to turn old the first time you tell them? Why won't a story allow itself to be told over and over?*

"I think L.A. sounds cooler than Europe," Max pronounced once Brandon had finished.

"I guess," Brandon said. "I really wanna go to Greece, though. And Rome too."

The four slumping boys remained sitting in a circle; the older boys felt their bodies slip into an unease, a too-bigness that hinted at their

coming adolescence. Finally, Brandon noticed a book sticking out of Max's back pocket.

"Whatcha reading?"

"It's an old book I found on my grandpa's bookshelf when we stopped to visit him in New York," Max said. "He said I probably should be older to read it. Because there's stuff in it I shouldn't read 'cause I'm only twelve. But then he gave it to me anyway when my mom wasn't looking. It's got some bad parts. Some parts that are really bad, actually."

"What? Like murders and stuff?"

"Nah. I can't describe it. There's no dragons or warriors or elves like in all the other books I read before. But it's really, really cool. And bad. There's kids smoking in it."

"Smoking?"

"Yeah. Cigarettes. It's, like, the best book I've ever read."

Max gave a conspiratorial scan, and then took the old paperback from his pocket and handed it to Brandon, who examined its timeworn cover, and a title whose meaning he could not immediately decipher.

"You can keep it," Max said. "I finished it in the car."

Brandon opened the first page and began to read. When the narrator promised to describe "what my lousy childhood was like," Brandon was hooked.

"You know, eventually, they're going to prosecute that poor woman because of me." It was one of the few comments Scott had allowed himself to make about the situation, and Peter Goldman decided he would try and ignore it. "It's either her or me. Or us, I mean. I guess we deserve to be punished more." They were near the bottom of the bottle and had been talking baseball and football, for the most part. Having bared his guilt for a moment, Scott caught himself, took another gulp of wine, and looked up at his old friend, who seemed more amused than outraged by Scott's situation. *Here's one person*, Scott thought, *who won't sit in judgment*. Scott was trying to think of something witty to say to chase away the unwanted pathos of the moment, when the phone on the dining room table before them rang again and Peter Goldman picked it up.

"No, he's not interested," Peter Goldman said. "That's right. Thank you. Bye-bye, now . . . bye."

"Thanks for doing that, buddy," Scott said. "I really owe you."

"Every good quarterback needs a good offensive line. Especially when the pass rush is as murderous as the one surrounding this household, let me tell you." They had a camaraderie forged during five years of school meetings, birthdays, and excursions to amusement parks, a brotherhood born of their marriages to women who dragged them all over the city and erased many hours of potential sports viewing, all in the name of family obligation.

There was a knock on the door. Three evenly spaced and polite taps, followed by a pause, and three more evenly spaced but louder taps. Peter Goldman rose to his feet and said, "I'm on it." A moment later Scott felt a shaft of warm light enter his home through the half-open door and heard the mumble of a voice from outside. After a quick back-and-forth, Peter came walking back to the table.

"It's a guy from the district attorney's office."

"Not again. Fuck."

"Should I tell him to go?"

"No. I have to talk to him."

Scott stood up and walked to the front door and swung it open.

"Mr. Torres, we haven't been able to get through on the phone," said Ian Goller. He wore a light-swallowing charcoal suit and a thin red tie over a starched white shirt, and to Peter Goldman, who had never met him before, he radiated the unrealness of an actor who'd wandered off the soundstage of a Technicolor spy flick. Goller had been shot back to Paseo Linda Bonita, quickly, by the dizzying spin of the news cycle, and the clamor of a vociferous segment of the voting public inside Orange County, and an influential segment of watchers and commentators beyond the county's borders. These voices were demanding, via various forms of digital and analog media, that Ian Goller and his colleagues in the district attorney's office apply the "rule of law" in the case of Araceli Ramirez, alleged childnapper.

Goller had arrived at the district attorney's office, off the beach and with his hair still wet (figuratively speaking and maybe literally too), with certain idealistic notions firmly rooted in his brain—specifically, the belief that criminal law was a scientific pursuit in which American and European traditions of jurisprudence were applied to the dispassionate weighing of facts and the protection of the public. During his ascent to the upper layers of the agency, and with his eventual

admission to the walnut-paneled sanctuary of the district attorney himself, this idealism had aged and matured into a more realistic understanding of the job and its responsibilities. Above all, he had come to learn it simply wasn't possible for a public servant to ignore public opinion—completely—when defining right and wrong. The perceptions of the people counted, their collective fears and wants, what outraged them and what did not. In this case, the law-abiding sensibilities of many an Orange County resident had been offended by the suspect's unauthorized arrival in the United States of America. It made them skeptical and suspicious of her actions with the boys, and eager for punishment. In nonlegal terms: they would not cut her any slack. So he couldn't either. Goller found himself more or less obliged, therefore, to dive into the unpredictable waters of a politically necessary but potentially tricky prosecution.

Once he took such a plunge, however, Goller needed to make sure he could reach the other side. In other words, he needed to make sure he didn't lose. And for that, he needed to clean up the image and stiffen the resolve of the victims.

"Have you read the newspaper this morning?" Goller asked Scott.

"This has been a really trying time for my family," Scott said slowly, pinching the space between his eyes, while resisting the temptation to reach across the table and serve himself another glass of wine.

"I understand. But you should see this." Goller placed the local news section of the *Orange County Register* on the dining room table. The headline in question ran on the lower half of the page, incongruously below a photograph of children at a public swimming pool in Santa Ana.

CHILD PROTECTIVE SERVICES TO INVESTIGATE PARENTS IN MISSING BOYS SAGA

Goller allowed this piece of unpleasant information to settle in as Scott slumped back in his chair, pushing it away from the table as he did so, adopting a pose of aggressive nonchalance in which the sky-blue fade of his jeans stretched out into view. Peter Goldman thought that Scott looked just like his son Brandon when he did this.

"What happened to you and your sons is being twisted by certain

people," Goller said, with an expression of fatherly concern. Maybe it was the wine, or maybe just the pressure: whatever it was, Scott was having trouble paying attention.

"Scott. Can I call you Scott?"

"Sure."

"I take it you're a native Californian, Scott. Right?" Goller said, though he already knew the answer.

"Uh-huh."

"Where did you go to school?"

"South Whittier. St. Paul High."

"Ah, I went to Mater Dei, in Santa Ana. And I think we're about the same age."

"Probably. But what does that have—"

"I want you to understand what's happening around you," Goller interrupted. "Let's be blunt: there's a lot of people taking a certain perverse pleasure in what's happening to you."

Scott had no answer to this statement, no observation. He wanted to say he didn't care what people thought, he didn't care about Araceli or the newspapers or the television. But he did.

"So why is it happening?" Scott asked with a teenager's skeptical insolence.

"It's because California's changed. Because it's not the same place it was when we were growing up."

"It's not?"

"No. Think of the way people respected certain things. In the past, no one would have questioned the good intentions of two good American parents like you and your wife."

"Probably not."

"Now they do. And why? Because you're being accused by a woman with thousands of defenders. Fine: it's their right to stand up for her, to say she's being victimized by the system. But these people, they see me, and you, as their enemy. It's totally whacked that they think that way, but that's how it is. And now they see in this case a chance to make all of us look silly."

"I really don't mind looking silly," Scott said, without completely meaning it. He was confused by the direction Goller had taken their conversation.

"Well, it's more than looking silly, isn't it?" Goller continued. "Really,

these people want to humiliate you, so that they can make the Mexican woman the hero. And why? For an idea." Goller was going to go abstract, and back in time, because he had learned that Scott was a programmer, and sensed the man needed to see a robust architecture of ideas before he took any action. An outline for this talk had come to Goller as he drove to the Laguna Rancho Estates, through undeveloped marshes and hill country, past towering eucalyptus trees and the bare breasts of yellow hills. In general, being a DA in his hometown was a daily assault on Goller's childhood memories, but this place by the sea, with its open vistas and untainted, orderly neighborhoods, transported him back in time, to his Orange County youth of puka shells and Op summer shirts. Certain things were clearer to him when he came here, and now he would explain these essential truths to Scott, show him the larger picture.

"Think of this moment we're living in, this craziness, from the perspective of history. California history," Goller began. "We grew up in the same kind of places, really. Me in Fullerton, and you in Whittier." Their homes had been parked on the same plain of scattered orchards and cow patches southeast of Los Angeles, and they had gone to schools that were big rivals back when there were "still enough big German and American kids around to make up a good football team." California was a paradise of open land and sea breezes, the sliver of Eden between the desert and the sea. This was the California of Scott's and Ian Goller's birth, a place of quiet, neat settlements separated by the geometry of melons and cabbages growing in fields, by the repetition of citrus groves, the scent of orange trees blooming. "That beautiful place was our playground. It was a place where anything was possible, where the open spaces matched how we felt about ourselves. How we saw the future." This paradise was gone, Goller said; the orchards had been plowed over to make room for new neighborhoods, rows of houses that became more ramshackle, more faded from one decade to the next. In the years since he'd been a DA, Ian Goller had been forced to see the decay of his hometown up close. There were too many people here now, a crush of bodies on the sidewalks and too many cars on the highways, people crowded into houses and apartment buildings in Santa Ana, in Anaheim, cities that used to be *good* places to live. The landmarks of Scott's youth, the burger stands and the diners, were now covered with the

grimy stains of time and something else, an alien presence. There was more trash on the streets than ever. Who threw trash on the streets when Scott and Ian were boys? No one. Everything had been corrupted and despoiled. But most people simply didn't care. They allowed these multitudes to fill the state. Outsiders, most of them uneducated, people without prospects in their own country. And when those multitudes produced, with a kind of mathematical inevitability, the inmates that filled the jails and prisons, too many Californians averted their eyes and pretended it wasn't happening. Worse, the defenders of these people twisted everything, and demonized American families like Scott's for having the good sense to live behind the gates that protected them from the criminal anarchy outside. These people were now cheering the idea that his family would be investigated.

Scott had been looking at the oak surface of the table, and at times directly into the eyes of Ian Goller as he spoke, and had failed to notice that at some point in Goller's talk Maureen had entered the room with Stephanie Goldman-Arbegast, who was holding a sleeping Samantha. They had been drawn in by the sound of the stranger's voice, with Maureen at first amused by the incongruity of Goller's black suit on a hot July day, and by the way he slipped into a geeky trance as he spoke. His motives soon became perfectly clear to Maureen, and in another set of circumstances she would have asked him to leave. *I don't like to hear that meanness, that intolerance,* she might have said. But these were not normal times, and she found herself a bit taken in by the emotional pull of his argument. *I don't really understand anything anymore. I am surrounded by mysteries and apparitions: like the presence of this man in black. This man is telling me what to feel as much as he's telling me what to think.* It was not the immigrants she thought of as alien, as much as the L.A. reporters who had parked themselves on her lawn, and who now staked out the front gate to the Estates. They were a disorderly and insistent clan of microphone men and women, of camera-holders and question-shouters, and they reminded her of the City of Los Angeles proper, and her first days in the metropolis. She had come to California expecting something altogether different than what she had first encountered, as a single woman in her twenties in an L.A. neighborhood called Mid-City, an ugly place of wide thoroughfares and gray liquor stores and bunkered apartment buildings with underground garages

that were rape traps. She carried Mace in her purse back then, and put a steel lock over the steering wheel of her parked, single-girl Honda Civic with its Show-Me State license plates. Quickly she had found a way to escape southward. *That's why I'm living here, on this hillside overlooking the ocean, instead of in some condo off La Cienega, or in Brentwood. Here I have found a purer version of California.*

"There are people who believe that this change in our hometown is a natural and inevitable thing," Goller continued. He watched as Maureen stepped forward and picked up the newspaper on the table, and saw the indignation that filled her eyes when she saw the headline. "It's in their interest to treat this Mexican woman as the victim, and you as her victimizers. And that's the way everyone will see it, unless you tell them differently."

Maureen looked at him with equal measures of skepticism and curiosity. He was a strange, elegant little man; it was not every day you met someone who could make a harsh and angry line of argument sound gentle and reasonable. "I don't quite get what you're telling us," Maureen said. "We're supposed to start talking about immigration and the undocumented, or the illegals, or whatever, and that's going to get the media off our backs? Isn't that just going to get us deeper in a mess?"

"No. You don't talk about those things. Definitely not. Your part is very simple. You just tell your story to someone with a sympathetic ear. You tell them your story, and you erase the idea that you're just this crazy family." He had them now, Scott especially: he was daydream-listening, processing truths. "There's a reporter I know. He's actually the local guy for one of the cable news networks. He'll guide you through an interview, I believe, without compromising you on anything."

Stephanie Goldman-Arbegast watched Maureen take a piece of paper with two phone numbers from Goller and give the faintest nod of assent. *No, Maureen, don't.* In a short while, Stephanie would politely round up her husband and children and they would leave, and not return. Maureen was going to link her fate to the kidnapping story circulating among the nativists and rightists on talk radio, when instead she should be telling the story of the broken coffee table. That's how Stephanie saw things. People would understand a woman's desire to escape an angry husband. But Maureen had too much pride to do such a thing. Maureen wanted, with the stoic resolve of a British monarch, to

protect the family image: she did not want the world to think of her sprawled helpless on her back.

For a moment, Stephanie felt more connected to the Mexican woman who had worked in this house, the hardworking oddball and perfectionist who had been Maureen's shadow since Stephanie had first come for a playdate. *The sad thing is that Araceli and Maureen are really so much alike.*

Goller shook everyone's hand and left. Stephanie followed her husband to the window, where he studied Goller walking down the path and to his car.

"He's got a surfboard on top of his car," Peter Goldman said, laughing at the incongruity as Stephanie looked at his parked BMW and saw it was true. "Look, he's starting to take off his jacket. He's like Batman or something."

About a mile down the coast, there was a surf break called Cotton's that was one of the best-kept secrets on the coast this summer. A little slice of Orange County goodness, known only to the locals, a place where, after a terrain-shifting winter storm, long walls of water now moved left over sand and rocks, large and steady at middle tide. Ian Goller thought that he might, with a little luck, have it to himself late on a quiet weekday afternoon like this one.

19

In his small kitchen-dining room in Santa Ana, Octavio Covarrubias made Araceli a breakfast of eggs with chorizo, fresh-squeezed juice from oranges plucked from the tree in the backyard, and a side dish of fried nopals, from the petals of an enormous cactus plant that grew in a vacant lot down the street. With every serving he raised the eyebrow that was hovering between his Jupiter eye and his moles Io and Europa, and asked if she wanted more coffee. Araceli grinned widely at the sight of this unshaven family patriarch of about fifty-five, a semiretired truck driver dressed in faded green work pants, holding a pan and making breakfast for her when, to her knowledge, he never even made breakfast for himself. "Ay, Octavio," his wife, Luz, said, after she noted the irony too, "*a mí nunca me haces* breakfast. *Qué bonito sería* if you brought me breakfast in bed one morning." Since Araceli's arrival at his home last night, Octavio Covarrubias had a sudden and strange need to dote over her, a woman whose presence on earth had only faintly registered in his consciousness before.

Octavio Covarrubias was impressed that an ordinary *mexicana* could be put through an arrest and a symbolic flogging by the machinery of the English-language media, survive with her *mexicana* dignity

más o menos intact, and then enter his living room, of all places. He was an avid reader and a faithful consumer of cable television news in two languages, and almost always this made him nothing more than a passive witness to the way his people were crushed, time and again, in American courtrooms, on desert smuggling trails, and in Arizona detention centers. He read and pontificated so much on these issues to his neighbors on Maple Street that they called him *licenciado* behind his back, because his outrage and verbosity reminded them of a certain kind of annoying politico-bureaucrat back home.

When Araceli was on her last mouthful of eggs, Octavio Covarrubias began to speak. "*Proceso* has a correspondent here in Los Angeles," he said. "Maybe we should call him, because *Proceso* will want to write something about you, I'm sure." Octavio Covarrubias was a *Proceso* subscriber, receiving the Mexican investigative magazine by mail from Tijuana every week. Before Araceli could respond, he began describing a report by this same *Proceso* correspondent about a facility for the detention of immigrant children in San Diego County, and a Televisa report on the same story, and then later more reports on CNN en Español, and finally on CNN in English. Octavio's news appetite was such that he could explain to his wife and neighbors why the U.S. Army was to blame for the flooding of the Mississippi and the conspiracies behind the assassination of the Mexican presidential candidate Luis Donaldo Colosio, and the links between drug cartels and former President Salinas de Gotari. Having been forced to drop out of his final year of high school in Durango, his dream of a degree in political science unrealized, he studied the news instead, in the belief that he might understand the seemingly unpredictable events of the world, which were obviously orchestrated to keep his people poor, ignorant, and enslaved.

Araceli ignored the passing question about the *Proceso* reporter, and helped Octavio and his wife clean up. Her hosts obviously wanted her to fill in the silence with an insider's account of her arrest and the news they had seen on TV. But she couldn't think of where to begin.

"So, it looks like they treated you okay?" Luz Covarrubias said, as Araceli dried a plate with a cloth and handed it to her to put away. "*No te veo traumada. Te veo tranquila.*"

"*No me imaginaba,*" Araceli said suddenly. Octavio and his wife thought she meant she never imagined she'd be pulled into the depths

of the machinery of hate, that she never imagined being tackled and having the humiliation broadcast on the airwaves, that she never imagined a million televisions would defame her as a criminal. But no. She meant she never believed she could be pulled so quickly and definitively from her stasis, from her comfortable but boring existence, from the cycles of meals and laundry, into the full mad circus of a life lived without a schedule or rhythm. For this reason, her face brightened with a strange, bemused expression as she said *"No me imaginaba . . ."* a second time. The break had begun with the arrival of that first rabble of barbarian gardeners, the men who took the machetes to Pepe's tropical forest. Those men had ripped her from her roots too and tossed her from a shady jungle into the full California sunlight. Liberated now from jail and from the worry of the fate of Brandon and Keenan, she could appreciate the journey away from Paseo Linda Bonita and into Los Angeles for its carnivalesque qualities. The decaying art of the railroad tracks, the startling dream-sense that came from being in a jail one moment, and then in the silent, spooky glory of the nighttime streets of Aliso Viejo the next. Out here, in the world away from the paradise of the Laguna Rancho Estates, there was the silver skin of taco trucks on Thirty-ninth Street, and the fat tortillas the hungry men and women workers raised to their mouths, and the deep-sea purple of the dying daylight over their heads. Those images belonged in her sketchbook, and then later on a canvas as big as she imagined Picasso's *Guernica* to be. She imagined a composition with orange and red explosions of fireworks in the background, and in the foreground the rabid teeth of a mob that marched and shouted. And why not the horizontal march of the electric transmission towers, and that corridor of feral grasses and palms, a road to unseen American provinces beyond? An artist needs to be out and about: Araceli understood that now. The study of the visual world while on her feet had informed her life in Mexico City, but in the defeat of her creative ambitions she had gone into a kind of retreat, she had accepted the little room the Torres-Thompsons gave her and the bills in the envelope at the end of each week. She felt like Brandon, who saw fantasy and wonderment in everything new. She wanted to find her *gordito*, the dancing painter Felipe, and tell him what she had seen.

"I never imagined," Araceli said after a brief silence, "that I could see things the way a little boy saw them."

"*¿Cómo?*"

"Brandon. He's the older boy. He loves to read. He thought the things he saw in Los Angeles were like the things in his books. He was funny. You see things differently when you open your eyes the way a child does." There were children in this house too, Octavio and Luz's kids, hovering nearby and listening for story details they might share with others.

"Well, it's good to see you calm," Luz said.

"*Sí, me siento calmada,*" Araceli said. Octavio looked a little thrown, a little disappointed by her light mood.

"Next time, Señor Covarrubias," she said, "I am going to make breakfast for you."

The lights came on and Maureen and the television reporter looked at each other through the layers of makeup that covered their faces, and Maureen had one last moment to think, *Ah, this is really show businesses, isn't it?* before listening to the reporter's first question. It had taken forty minutes to transform her living room into a studio. The point of this interview, as she understood it, was to make a public defense of her own motherhood. But as the crew ran black cables as thick as garden snakes along her tiled floor and raised a half dozen lamp stands to varied heights, her stage fright and anxiety had been replaced, momentarily, with a kind of morbid fascination at this glimpse of the inner workings of television news. The crew shielded their portable four-hundred-watt beams with transparent fabric squares until all shadows disappeared and an eerie, even light settled over her living room. They rearranged photographs on the bookcase and produced fresh-cut roses and a vase, and opened the sliding glass doors to the succulent garden and taped L's onto the floor where a high folding chair was later placed, so that Maureen could be photographed with the roses, a family portrait, and a mini-landscape of cacti and the ocotillo plant all looming behind her. The producer, a woman of about twenty-five, had punched a message into one of those handheld devices that required much use of the right thumb, and waited a few minutes for a reply, and had looked up from the screen to announce that Maureen alone would be interviewed, with the boys, Samantha, and Scott making

silent cameos in the "B" footage to be shot around the house afterward, in a simulation of their daily living, sans Araceli. Of course, Maureen thought, *I'm the one they want on camera.* Her twelve-second "rant" had been repeated enough in its thirty-six-hour existence for an observer or two on the motherhood blogs to call it "iconic." *Why is it,* Maureen wondered, *that in any walk of life, from corporate CEO, to U.S. senator, to harried flower vendor and distraught Orange County mother, an angry woman provokes such intense feelings? Why is it considered such a remarkable and noteworthy thing for a mother to raise her voice?*

"Maureen Thompson, how are you doing? How is your family?" the reporter asked.

"We're fine. We had a little scare. For two days and one very long night that seemed like an eternity. I mean, to come home to this house and find it empty, to expect to see our boys here, and then, well, to find them missing." She was aware that her voice had begun to tremble, that she sounded tenuous and frail, and as soon as she became aware of this, she realized that this was not necessarily a bad thing. "And then to find out they were all the way on the other side of the city."

"And they're okay?"

"Yes, yes. They've got a story to tell, a wild story, but it appears nothing happened to them."

"A wild story?"

"Yes. It seems our employee, Araceli, took them on a train ride. For what purpose, God knows. They were among the homeless at some point, or so it seems."

"The homeless?"

"Yes. Which is very disturbing, of course."

"But they're okay?"

"Yes."

"Tell us a little about yourself."

"My husband, he's a programmer. I teach art at my sons' school. I'm an art teacher there. Well, a volunteer art teacher, I should say, because they don't pay me anything, but I do get to be close to the boys and their school." Her voice had lost its quaver suddenly. "And we've lived in this beautiful house for five years now."

"Now, explain to us exactly how it was that you found your children missing," the newsman said, and then looked her directly in the eye and

added in a markedly more friendly voice, as if he were an actor speaking an aside to the groundlings, "And please, feel relaxed. We can do this more than once if we need to."

"We left on a little trip, my husband and I," Maureen began, and she resisted the temptation to say *separately*, which would have kept her closer to the truth. "You know, when you have three kids, you need a break." *No, I shouldn't have said that. I sound spoiled.* "And our boys are bigger now, and they're easier to take care of, so we thought we could leave them overnight with their nanny and just take Samantha with us. Because Samantha is so little, we thought we should take her with us." She paused, and inhaled fully, because she was stepping closer to blatant untruth than she wanted to go, and she made the mistake of looking down at her floor and away from the camera. Quickly she recovered herself, and felt strangely aware and alert. "Then we came home. And it was so quiet. So incredibly and unnaturally quiet here." Now that she had returned to a full, solid truth she could see its power and how it made the newsman's eyes sharpen their focus with anticipation. "Something didn't seem right. And we went from room to room and didn't see the boys. And I thought, This is so strange. How can Araceli not be here in the house with the boys? I mean, she doesn't have a car, or permission to take the boys anywhere. At first I thought, Oh, maybe she got bored and took them walking to the park or something. It sort of didn't make sense, because she doesn't have a car. But you know how it is: you have in your mind this little voice that tells you not to think the worst. And then it started to sink in that they were gone. And this house started to feel so empty. So horribly empty. And I started to think about where they might be, and what they might be suffering, and how I wasn't there to protect them. And I just couldn't stand it." Yes, this was true: she loved her boys and had lost them for an afternoon, a night, and then a morning, and had spent that time living with the deepest fears a mother can know, an ache she felt in those parts of her body where her boys had once lived and kicked and slithered into the world.

Maureen was burying her subtle falsehoods in a larger truth unknown, until now, to the millions who had followed the story. Their Internet commentary would soon be peppered with sympathetic descriptions: "the screamer" was, in fact, a woman who sounded "quite reasonable." She was an "educated and articulate" mother who "obviously loved

her children," had suffered "every parent's nightmare," and who was "clearly telling the truth" about discovering her sons missing.

"Did you ever authorize this woman, your employee, to take your children to East Los Angeles?"

"No. Absolutely not."

"So they were kidnapped?" the interviewer said, making it sound as much suggestion as question.

"Well, they were taken on . . . this bizarre journey. They set off for L.A. And the hills there were on fire that day. So when we got them back, I swear they smelled like smoke."

"Uh-huh," the interviewer said, and Maureen knew she had answered poorly.

"But we did find some strange things in her room."

"What things?"

"Strange art. Trash that she had played with. It's strange. Because this is someone we thought of as part of our family. She lived with us. We trusted her implicitly. And then I realized I didn't even know who she was."

"Now, tell us about this," the interviewer continued. "There's this clip I want to play for you. It's become sort of famous now." On a small monitor at the interviewer's feet, her twelve-second rant played again, and she cringed at the way her nostrils flared and her jaw tightened as she shot back at the reporter, as if she were a suburban mother bear snapping at the camera-toting naturalist threatening her cubs, an effect heightened by the way she searched behind the cameras for the man who had insulted her.

"Really, why were you so angry?"

"I had just been reunited with my sons, and I hadn't slept for two days. I was just incredibly stressed out. I mean, to go through all that: first, the worry of not knowing where the boys were, if they were okay. And then, you know, the joy of having them with us again. I was completely wiped out. Plus, I couldn't even see this guy, because he was standing near the back. And here I am, the mom of these two kids who've been taken away, and he's accusing me. But I shouldn't have yelled like that. Like I said, I was just incredibly exhausted."

"Of course," the interviewer said. "We can only imagine."

They wrapped up and when the four-minute, twenty-five second

segment aired later that evening near the top of the 8:00 p.m. cablecast, Janet Bryson turned on her TiVo and watched it three times.

In Santa Ana, Octavio Covarrubias missed the interview because he was preparing and serving a marinated *carne de res* barbecue in Araceli's honor. An hour or so later, with the main course served to the small party of family and neighbors, he slipped into the empty living room for a moment to feed his news fix, and caught a few seconds of Maureen's interview when it was replayed on the cable news station as an introduction to the show hosted by a very conservative man who Octavio Covarrubias watched, occasionally, with the same sense of stealthy intent that Janet Bryson felt when she studied the Mexicans in her neighborhood. Octavio needed to get back to the party, and told himself he shouldn't watch this man tonight, but he allowed himself to listen as the man began to talk about "the illegal who was set free." This television man was always well dressed, Octavio noted, and tonight he was wearing a black suit with rather bright white stripes, and Octavio thought that, if he ever bought a suit, it would be one like that, because it had a certain big-city, old-time gangster movie look to it, though the way he moved in his chair and talked to his guests suggested to Octavio a policeman: a man who runs his small fiefdom with aggressive self-assurance, who intimidates with a crackling diction and an unflagging faith in his right to do so.

"Do we really want to entrust our children to these people from this essentially backward society?" the man was saying. He was in New York, but was talking, via satellite link, to the reporter who had sat down with Maureen Thompson. "Isn't it a sign of weakness in our social fabric that we do this? It's the most important job we have. It's the foundation of our civilization, for chrissakes. Motherhood. Why should we sell it off, to the most desperate and least educated people, as if we were hiring a day laborer to dig a ditch? I'm telling ya, and I know a lot of people aren't going to agree with me, but it just sounds to me like an essentially stupid thing to do."

Luz Covarrubias entered, with Araceli trailing behind her.

"Octavio!" Luz snapped reprovingly. "*¿Por qué estás mirando a ese hombre feo, ese hombre que nos odia?*" his wife asked, not for the first time.

"*Porque hay que saber lo que piensa el enemigo,*" he said.

"*Basta,*" his wife said, and she grabbed the remote control from the

front table and punched the mute button, because she knew from prior experience that he wouldn't let her turn it off completely.

Octavio Covarrubias turned to Araceli and put his hand on her shoulder. *"Ese hombre te quiere encarcelar."* On the TV, the man who wanted to send Araceli back to jail peered into the camera without speaking for a few seconds, then gave a dismissive nod, followed by a playful bobbing of his head that, Araceli guessed, was meant to convey incredulity. His hair, she noted, was the color and thickness of a weak mountain stream during a summer drought, and his lips were arranged in a crawling half smile with the geometry of a roller coaster. *Ese hombre*, all by himself, Octavio added, might have the power to lock her up again. Millions watched him. *"No lo entiendo."*

Octavio drifted away, leaving Araceli with a plate of leftover barbecued beef she had brought in from the backyard, alone before the television. She had seen this commentator flicker past during the nighttime page-turning of channels on her television, but she had never stopped to watch him. Now she saw that his eyebrows and mouth, in close-up, were a theater all to themselves. He played to the camera with his eyebrows, which moved like elaborate stage machinery above the radiant blue crystals of his eyes. His eyebrows rose, fell, twisted, and contorted themselves in ways that appeared to defy the limits of human facial musculature. The camera pulled back as he brought his body into the show by leaning back in his chair, and he puffed his cheeks quickly with a suppressed laugh, and finally shook his head, and gave a forty-five-degree turn to face another camera.

It was frightening to think that the brain behind that face could somehow shape her fate, and Araceli quickly reached over and turned off the television, the image of the man shrinking to a point and going dark with an electric pop. What other eyebrows, mouths, and brains were out there, conspiring to put her behind bars again, and what did they see in her, that they would want to punish her so? The thought made her want to put on running shoes, to see if she could outsprint the men in uniform this time. But no, she was tired of running. *No voy a correr.* She would wait and prepare herself. For starters, she would get another tortilla and make herself a taco out of the beef on this plate, because when a man is as good a cook as Octavio Covarrubias, you really shouldn't let his food go to waste.

20

A pretty and tiny Latina woman of about twenty-five arrived at the Covarrubias residence first, with a long, thin notebook in her hand. She had swept-back eyes with chestnut irises and strands of thin coal-black hair; a significantly older and taller man of rugged features who smelled of cigarettes accompanied her. They were an odd, English-speaking couple in a Spanish-speaking neighborhood, and a decidedly bad omen for a Mexican woman who expected to be arrested at any moment. Araceli might have taken the man for a retired cowboy, but for the camera in his hand and the nylon bag on his shoulder. *These people have probably not come to arrest me,* Araceli thought, and after they introduced themselves as journalists, she stepped outside onto the porch, and then onto the lawn, to see if there was a police cruiser lurking nearby. After a few moments of conversation on the grass it became clear that these two *periodistas* had not expected to find Araceli alone. "There's no cops here," the photographer said in a half question and half observation, after glancing inside the living room.

"¿*Cómo que* cops? ¿*Entonces sí me vienen a arrestar?*"

"Uh, I think that I, that we . . ." the reporter began, and she gave a guilty, girlish smile that was inappropriate to the moment. "*Disculparme,*

por favor, no sabía," the reporter began in Spanish, but stopped, because that language was obviously not her first, and was barely her second. She handed Araceli a business card, a stiff little rectangle with glossy letters that rose from the paper, inviting one's fingers to linger over them, claiming the title *Staff Writer* for its owner, a *Cynthia Villarreal*.

"Well, this is awkward," the photographer said, and he reached inside the pants of his jeans and grabbed a cigarette and put it in his mouth but did not light it. "The captain will not be pleased to see us, I think."

"Well, they told me ten-fifteen."

"It's ten-oh-five, my dear."

"Dang. I thought we were late. But we're early."

The photographer shook his head and, having determined that the young scribe with him was going to take a while to figure out what to do next, he began to shoot, capturing Araceli as she stood on the lawn, looking up at the sky. She searched for prowling helicopters, and then scanned the cars on the block and the distant intersections. The first frame the photographer shot, of Araceli's worried squint searching the street for the authorities, would be on the web in an hour and on the front page of the newspaper the next day, a haunting and lonely close-up of a notorious woman in limbo, waiting for her abductors to arrive.

"Um, Kyle . . . ," the reporter said, but Kyle ignored her and held down his finger, the camera shutter opening and closing six times with the staccato beat of a flamenco song.

"*¡No les tengo miedo!*" Araceli shouted suddenly, turning to face the journalists. "I am not afraid! No. Why I be afraid? For nothing!" The photographer let off another burst of shutter openings as Araceli spoke, and those images too would appear on the web, in an essay of eleven images that his Los Angeles newspaper would headline "Arrest, Anger, and Drama in Santa Ana," accompanied by the breathless audio narration of Cynthia Villarreal: "Araceli Ramírez knew that she would soon be taken into custody, but her response was a defiant one." The second shot in that series featured Araceli looking directly into the camera, her mouth open and index finger pointing skyward at the moment she was repeating, "*¡No les tengo miedo!,*" an image with echoes of Latin American protest marches, as if Araceli were a market woman in a Mexican square, among tens of thousands of other women with open mouths joined in an outraged chorus over the price of onions, or the torture and murder of a comrade.

Now the rising pitch of accelerating engines announced the arrival of four sheriff's cruisers: two parked in front of the Covarrubias home with red and blue lights flashing, the others taking position at either end of the block, sideways, as if to seal off the street. A burly but handsome sheriff's captain emerged from the first cruiser. He was freshly shaved, with three bloody nicks on each cheek and an expression of wounded befuddlement that overcame him as it sank in that his "little reporter friend," as she was known at the station, had tipped off the suspect to his arrival. He gave a plaintive opening of his arms and shouted at the reporter, "What's going on?"

"I'm so sorry, Captain. Sorry!"

"Get that lens off me, jerko!"

"Negative, Captain," the photographer said. "You're on a public street."

"Shit," the captain said, and at that moment he decided that this was the last time he'd try to impress Ms. Villarreal, who was fifteen years younger and almost two feet shorter than him. He turned to Araceli, who now stood before him on the lawn, her arms folded across her chest. "You obviously know what I'm here for."

Araceli said nothing and in the few heartbeats of silent standoff that followed, shouts could be heard coming from the homes and backyards around them. "¡La migra!" An invisible but audible panic was unfolding around them, with the percussion of slamming doors and windows opening so that people could stare down at the police cruisers from second-floor windows, followed by more, indecipherable yelling from the next block, and the scratchy and hurried tennis-shoe strides on the cement sidewalk of a young man in a CLUB AMÉRICA *fútbol* jersey. The soccer fan walked with his hands in his pockets across the street, and then glanced once over his shoulder at the officers, and finally broke into a trot as he reached the corner. *Get away, get away.* The residents of Maple Street had been sitting snugly in their homes for two days, watching Araceli's short sprint and capture looping on their televisions, listening to secondhand reports in Spanish detailing the English chorus of *los medios norteamericanos* for her rearrest. Word had spread that the subject of this broadcast frenzy was living among them, but now the arrival of the deputies' brass badges and their dangling batons and the flashing lights of their cruisers transformed this novelty into a threat, and brought to life the goblins that haunted their daily consciousness. *The* paisana *from the television has brought* las autoridades *to our*

neighborhood, and now they will take us all away before we can finish our breakfasts and wash the dishes. Córrele, córrele.

"For some reason, these people think we've come to enforce the immigration laws," the captain said. "It's because of you, little lady," he said to Araceli. He cupped his hands and gave a halfhearted megaphone shout: "Attention, neighbors! I am not the *migra.* I am not here for any of you."

In a building down at the end of the block, a woman from rural Guanajuato grabbed her infant son and executed a panicked climb into the attic of her two-story duplex, then crawled into a nook of stacked boxes and took her cell phone to call *el licenciado* Octavio Covarrubias. The self-educated, self-appointed conscience of Maple Street often gave out his number to the new arrivals, presenting himself as a levelheaded, semiretired family man who might be able to help people in trouble. The ring tone on his phone sounded as he stood on the porch, and its burst of trumpets and accordions from a song by Los Temerarios broke the trance of the standoff on the front lawn, where the sheriff's captain was trying to think of a way to persuade the woman named in the arrest warrant to get into his patrol car quickly, the better to calm everyone around them.

"*Sí, quédate allí escondida,*" Octavio said into the phone, which caught the attention of all the Spanish-speakers around them, including one of the deputies.

"Hey, Captain," the deputy said. "There's people hiding in these houses."

"Probably in the closets and the attics again," said another deputy.

"God, I hate that."

The captain ignored his underlings and turned to Araceli. "The quicker you come with us, young lady, the sooner the good people of this neighborhood will be able to come out of their closets." Araceli was standing ten feet away from him on the lawn, but he didn't want to step toward her and simply grab her, because if she tried to run away she might spread the panic to other blocks, and if she resisted and his deputies had to restrain her, they could have a minor disturbance on their hands, in full view of the press.

"*¿Y para qué me vienes a piscar?*" she asked.

"For child abuse," said the captain, whose encounters with Orange

County suspects had familiarized him with some of the basic Spanish idioms used in such cases, though he had no idea of the full range of uses of the verb *"piscar,"* a California-Spanish mongrel of the English "pick" that had managed to sneak into Araceli's speech through the daily drip of Los Angeles television and radio. He looked down at the warrant and repeated three words he saw there: *"Felony* child abuse. Child endangerment, to be precise."

"I don't understand," Araceli said.

"It means you put the children in danger. *Peligro, los niños.*"

Araceli shook her head and gave the captain a murderous look. He was trying to be gracious, but he was an extension of the eyebrows on the television, and now it was clear that the eyebrows and the other faces on the news had persuaded the authorities to invent any reason to detain her. What's more, the *norteamericanos* were at war with themselves over whether they should throw her in jail or allow her to live free, with the sheriff's captain standing before her obviously in the latter camp, even as duty forced him to arrest her.

This is like living with el señor *Scott and* la señora *Maureen: they cannot decide what they want for dinner, or if they want dessert, so they have me going two ways at once.*

"That's a good girl," the captain said, and did not notice as Araceli gave him another penetrating stare for that unnecessary bit of condescension.

Janet Bryson's contribution to the campaign to return Araceli Ramirez to jail, and eventually back to Mexico, began at the southernmost point on her big fold-out map of Orange County, in the community formerly known as Leisure World. She was out collecting handwritten and signed letters, having been rallied to do so by the One California activist organization, and her first stop placed her underneath the hanging ferns inside a Leisure World veranda of breeze blocks, where a woman held a dog in her purse, and stroked its long hair and compliant head. "God bless you for doing this," the woman told Janet, recounting how her Shih Tzu had been frightened by the firecrackers on the Fourth of July, set off a mile away in the uncontrolled neighborhoods where "those people" lived. "It was so unfair, because Ginger had just had surgery, the

poor thing." They were united, Janet Bryson and the woman with the dog, by their sympathy for Maureen Thompson and their contempt for illegal immigrants and lawbreakers of all stripes, but when she drove away Janet Bryson could only think about how lonely the woman seemed, and how unnatural it was to carry a dog that way. Next she drove her son's Toyota Celica northward into the suburbs of central Orange County—her own Chevy Caprice having again failed to start this morning—and wondered about the meaning of the pink dice hanging from the rearview mirror. Was that a gang thing? This worrying possibility stayed with her as she advanced along Main Streets and First Streets lined with the rusting steel and broken glass tubes of the neon signs of their heyday. Once people drove their rumbling Ramblers and El Caminos down and across these overlapping grids, along Beach Boulevard and Katella Avenue, the thoroughfares that carried people of her father's generation past malt shops and burger joints, to the tower marquees announcing double features at drive-in theaters. The drive-ins were all Swap Meets now frequented by the illegals and the Vietnamese. She remembered sitting in the backseat of her father's Ford Falcon, unbuckled and unworried, behind his parted and moist hair, and feeling her bare legs sticking to the vinyl seats. Janet Bryson knew she could never make those old days come back. Instead, in this work of letter-gathering, this volunteer activism, she felt like a woman weather-stripping her windows and basement in September: it was something she did not so much with the hope of making things better, as much as to keep them from getting worse.

The letters Janet Bryson carried were filled with warnings of the impending criminal and budgetary doom wrought by the legions of illegal crossers; she was retrieving these missives personally for afternoon delivery to the Orange County Board of Supervisors. The One California group had emailed and faxed its members talking points to be included in the letters, and a separate list of individual crimes and crime-types attributable to illegals, including: the "epidemic" of identity theft; the murder of a sixteen-year-old boy outside a beach park the previous August by members of a Los Angeles street gang; a sudden spike in DUIs in Anaheim; and the rape and murder of a twelve-year-old girl in Fullerton. Each writer chose from this felonious buffet and plopped phrases into one of five different form letters written by One California. They wrote in the creaky cursive of a septuagenarian, or squeezed

five hundred words of all capitals onto a single page of notebook paper, or typed on old IBMs and Olivettis. The writers had been encouraged to fill their letters with their own observations about the larger problems of illegal immigration, and at red lights Janet stopped to peruse these sections.

> Araceli N. Ramirez should be arrested and deported no matter what the outcome of the criminal proceedings the County undertakes against her. Illegal Mexican labor lowers wages while demanding entitlements. Examples: Title One schools, WIC, Medical Care, Bilingual education. Not to mention they breed like there's no tomorrow, regardless of whether they can support their children because they know the state will subsidize them.

> The Latino movement backing this woman is AGGRESSIVE. The pressure and the outright numbers of people moving into this country, the outright force of the Spanish language is a clear statement of revolution. I am shocked by this Latino movement which is now supporting this woman despite her obvious crimes against two innocent American children.

> To those who want to point out how much these illegal immigrants like Araceli N. Ramirez contribute to their society because they like their housekeeper and their gardener, and because they like paying less for tomatoes, spend some time looking at the real California around us. Look at our full prisons, our higher insurance rates, our lowering education standards, the new diseases spreading in our cities. For me, I'll pay more for my tomatoes.

Janet Bryson's journey took her next to a Garden Grove apartment block the color of overripe avocado flesh, where a too-thin woman of about forty with bony, sunburned shoulders handed her a letter through a security gate and said, "Don't go yet, hon. Want some iced tea?" Janet climbed up briefly to the woman's apartment and living room and sipped and listened to the woman describe "the unraveling of my life." Her husband had succumbed to liver problems three years earlier, "and my mom died a year ago this week in Kenosha." She too complained

about the Fourth of July noise and smoke, but also about the disability bureaucrats and her glaucoma, and the neighbors who stole her newspaper, and how she heard her dead husband speaking in the hallways on certain warm summer nights, until Janet finally said, "I'm so, so sorry. But I really have to go." It pained Janet Bryson that she could not listen more. She picked up the last letter at 3:45 p.m. on Citrus Avenue in Yorba Linda, four blocks from the Richard Nixon Library and Museum, and made her away southward on the State Highway 57 freeway to Santa Ana. By 4:55 p.m., she had managed to deliver one copy of each letter by hand to the five offices of the members of the Orange County Board of Supervisors.

At 5:30 p.m. she was back on Interstate 5, heading north toward South Whittier in heavy traffic, but feeling light and free of the congestion of red lights braking and cars inching forward. She touched the passenger seat, where the letters had lain, and gave a sigh of satisfaction, thinking how she would type *Mission Accomplished* in the subject line of the email she would send to the One California office when she got home. And then she remembered the woman with the dog, and the woman who heard ghosts, and thought she had helped them that day simply by listening. *Owe no man anything, but to love one another, for he that loveth another hath fulfilled the law.* She felt attached to something larger than herself. Not just the story of the wronged American family, but also to other homes and automobiles where women looked out their windows and into the city and tried to make sense of what they saw. She turned on the radio and found it tuned, by her son, to some Spanish hip-hop monstrosity: so she changed the station, finding some rock-and-roll songs from her father's era. Those joyous anthems with their ascendant guitars and big soul choruses matched the way she felt. Her reverie lasted through forty more minutes of bumper-to-bumper, until she reached her exit at Carmenita Road and she turned northward home.

John Torres was well inside the house on Paseo Linda Bonita before Maureen became aware of his presence. He had talked his way past the useless guards at the front gate easily enough: they were quickly persuaded that a seventy-year-old man was harmless, and Maureen was sweeping in the kitchen when he opened and stepped through the un-

locked front door. He quickly found his grandsons in their bedroom—
"You guys are reading? In the middle of a summer day?"—and was hugging
them and bribing them with twenty-dollar bills by the time Maureen
could rush into their room. She glared at the old man with a *how dare
you!* affixed to her lips that died, undelivered, when she saw Brandon
and Keenan waving greenbacks ecstatically before her.

"Look! Grandpa gave us money!"

"Hello, daughter," John Torres said with a stiff cheerfulness, and
Maureen wondered if he knew how much she hated hearing him call
her that. He was dressed like an angry workingman forced to play a
round of golf against his will, copper jowls resting over the collar of his
polo shirt, khaki pants affixed to his bony frame by a belt that was
about six inches too long. Now he grabbed at its flapping leather tongue
as he waited for her to reply, because he sensed that she was studying it
and judging him and his simplicity. She was, in fact, looking at his fingers and hands, and thought that the contrast of the wounded digits at
the end of arms stuffed into a teal shirt summed up all his contradictions, and for that reason she resisted the temptation to say, *Hello, Juan*,
which was his birth name, after all. Scott had discovered this a few
years back, when helping the old man with some Social Security paperwork, and Maureen had rather spitefully called him that on that last
time he had come to this home, two years ago. It was during Keenan's
sixth birthday, in a moment of high dudgeon following his outrageous,
bigoted, and incorrect observation that Keenan was "the white boy" and
Brandon was "the Mexican." It was the sort of thing he said when he
had too much alcohol, which was nearly every time he arrived for a
family gathering, and she had resolved at that moment to banish him
from Paseo Linda Bonita for at least a dozen birthdays.

"Hello, Grandfather Torres. To what do we owe the pleasure?"

He seemed a bit taken aback by the polite greeting, having failed to
notice the sarcasm in it. "Well, I have a television," he began. "And I've
been watching my grandsons on it for a couple of days now, and the one
time I called here I got some stranger who hung up on me when he
heard me say, 'What's going on over there?' So I figured I'd have to come
over here and see for myself."

"As you can see, everything is under control."

"Is it?" He looked around the room, at his grandsons, who were now

busy putting away the two twenties he had given each of them in little plastic safes with numbered combinations. "The newspaper said they were going to investigate you."

"No, Scott just . . ." Maureen stopped and gestured with her palms in the direction of the boys. "Should we be having this discussion here?" But John Torres was looking straight into her eyes, demanding an answer to soothe a kind of skeptical parental concern she recognized. "Scott just called," she lied. "He went to talk to those people at the county. And they dropped it."

"Because they arrested that Mexican girl you had here. Right?"

"What, they arrested Araceli?" Brandon shouted. "They're going to put her in jail?"

"No, no, they're just asking her questions," Maureen said, and would think later that it had been a long time since she had deceived her children.

"Someone needs to cut the grass," the elder Torres said abruptly.

"Scott will do it."

"No. I will." The old man touched each of his grandsons on the head, and left the room with the air of a man eager to get started on a new job. Ten minutes later she heard a grinding roar from the front yard, and she looked out to see a septuagenarian in a polo shirt digging his leather Top-Sider shoes into the overgrown, spongy grass. The old man pushed the machine over the sloped lawn with surprising efficiency, though after less than thirty seconds he was already covered with beads of sweat, and she wondered if he might have a stroke. *He tackles this physical task with the same gusto Scott attacks a programming problem.* After an hour of grinding, whizzing, and sweeping with various implements, motorized and muscle-driven, he was done. When Samantha woke up from her nap Maureen wandered out with her daughter to inspect his work. He had cut the lawn with a perfection that made the living thing look plastic, or painted, an evenness that was unnatural but also pleasing to the eye.

"Your grandfather knows how to cut a lawn," Maureen said.

21

First came the excitement of rushing through the jail, after being told she would face the judge, and then finding there was an anteroom before you got to the court. The guards guided Araceli into a cube-shaped room and directed her to wait alongside two other women on a bench bolted to the floor, one a Latina with eyebrows that looked like they were drawn with a 0.5-millimeter drafting pencil; the other an African-American woman with a head covered with parallel rows of hair and skin, as if plowed by a miniature farmer. The old cement walls of the cube-cell were freshly painted, and in their bone-colored blankness Araceli sensed hundreds of existential agonies, endured by people in much worse situations than hers. Araceli knew that her fate ended in Mexico, that at the end of her current visit to purgatory she would step into the disorderly but familiar sunshine of a Mexican border town, and that afterward she would walk to a bus station or a telephone booth and decide what to do next. It might happen in a year, or two, or maybe even in a few days, but eventually that would be her fate, and it calmed her to know this with certainty. The Latina woman to Araceli's right apparently did not have such knowledge to settle her nerves, because she was repeatedly folding and unfolding a piece of paper. Finally she looked up

at Araceli and showed her a row of crooked teeth, as if to say hello. She was gaunt and sallow-faced, with the nervous energy of a twenty-year-old, though she seemed a decade older than that, at least. She also seemed battered and confused, but not especially worried about being that way.

"I'm going to make a run for it," the woman whispered into Araceli's ear. Seeing Araceli's confusion, she switched to thickly accented Spanish: "*Voy a correr. Para ser libre.*"

"*¿Qué?*"

"When we get into the court, there's just a little fence. *Chiquito.*" The woman glanced at the other inmate on the bench, who seemed to be nodding off, and then raised her voice well above a whisper. "It's a tiny fence about as high as your waist. I'm going to jump over. And I'm gonna book it for the back, and into the hallway, and down the stairs if I'm lucky. If I'm lucky I'll get to the front steps and out the door. Now I can do it, because I'm still in my own clothes. Later, they'll have me in jail blues, and I won't make it. I have to do it now, because if I don't, I'll be locked away forever."

Araceli gave the woman a glance that said, *Please stop bothering me with your lunacies.*

"I ain't lying. Because this is my *tercer* strike. *Uno, dos, tres* strikes. *¿Entiendes?* I got my first two strikes with my crazy *novios*. Armed robbery and ADW. Assault with a deadly weapon. Now they got me because I was making eyes at an undercover cop over on Pico. They got me good. And for looking at that cop, and asking him for fifty bucks, I'm looking at twenty-five to life, believe it or not. I said, 'Okay, honey, if you ain't got fifty, forty'll do,' and that's when he showed me his badge, the tiny, ugly little fuck. So I told him, 'Don't do me that way, Officer. I'm begging you. I got two strikes. I'll do you for free, just let me go.' But he was a real tight-ass, and that's why I'm here, and that's why I gotta run." She gave Araceli a wild-eyed look of desperation and mischief. "You're not understanding me, are you?"

"You're going to run?"

"Yes."

"Don't tell me," Araceli said. "I don't want trouble for me."

The door opened and the paper-folder left, giving Araceli one last ugly smile. Araceli listened to the closed door for a minute or so, in anticipation of the noises of anarchy the inmate's attempted escape would

set off, but heard only mumbling vibrations of calmly spoken words. Five minutes later, the paper-folder returned with her head bowed, and a palm filled with paper shreds. She averted her eyes from Araceli, sniffled, and began weeping loudly. Before Araceli could ask what had happened, the bailiff called out, "Ramirez and Jones," and Araceli stood up with the other inmate and followed her braided head into the courtroom.

Unlike Araceli, Jones wore a thin chain around her arms and legs, and a blue jumpsuit. The bailiff directed Jones to a chair in front of the judge, and Araceli to a steel folding chair next to the door they had just passed through. "You're next," the bailiff said to her. Forms were shuffled before Jones, an attorney sat next to her and whispered in her ear, and she was asked over and over again if she understood a statement about rights and procedures. Jones nodded several times, and looked impassively at forms that were placed before her, and at the finger of a man who was either a clerk or an attorney and who indicated places she should look. Then he gave her a pen, and whispered into her ear, and she began to sign her name. Araceli had never been in an American court before and wondered if most legal business was conducted this way, with gestures, mumbles, and whispers. Nearly everyone drifted through the proceedings with heavy, tired eyes, even the bailiff, who spent most of his time at his desk. What could be producing this drowsiness? Was it the early hour, the long banks of fluorescent lights, was it something in the air-conditioning? Was it all the paperwork, the forms in triplicate, the stacking of so many manila files? Araceli sensed that the bad-teeth, *tres*-strikes girl had entered this room determined to run, but had been anesthetized by the lights and the drone of bored voices. Now the judge began to speak. He looked like a schoolteacher, and sounded as if he was reading to the defendant from a prepared text, but he wasn't looking at any papers before him and for a second it seemed as if he was reading words that were suspended in the air. *What a strange trick!* When the inmate stood up to leave, Araceli saw that her wrists and ankles were still shackled and linked together, even though she looked too lethargic to be a threat.

Finally, the judge said, "We're ready for Ramirez, Araceli."

She walked to the bench, and a skinny, older man with thick glasses stood next to her. "We're ready, Your Honor," the older man said,

and Araceli was puzzled by his use of the first-person plural, which seemed to join him to her for some purpose. "I'm your public defender," the man whispered into her ear suddenly. "But just for today. For your arraignment. Later, you get someone else."

She nodded and looked back over her shoulder at the courtroom: there was, indeed, just a very short barrier separating the place where Araceli sat from the public gallery and the doors at the back of the courtroom. The only guard present, the bailiff, stood near the judge, and in the gallery there was a single witness, a man in business attire with a Mexican flag pin on his lapel. He gave her a twinkling-finger wave, and Araceli wondered if he was there to take her back to Mexico.

"Are they going to deport me?" she asked the public defender in a whisper. Resigned as she was to returning to Mexico, she did not like the idea of having other people decide for her what she should do. A woman should be able to pick the road on which she traveled, and it riled her to think the men gathered in this room—because there were no other women present now, besides her—would decide for her. She looked up at the judge, a kind of anti-angel in his black robes and white hair, holding the keys to the gates of freedom.

"I asked you a question," she repeated to the public defender in full voice, loud enough to cause the other attorney, standing above a table next to hers, to look across. "Are they going to deport me?"

"No, not for the moment," the public defender whispered back from the corner of his mouth, and before Araceli could ask him to elaborate, he, the judge, and other people in the court began to speak in another language she only vaguely recognized as English, a torrent of numbers and terms that she did not understand, with roots that seemed to be in Latin, except for some of the very last words the judge spoke before she was directed back into the cube and the jail beyond.

"Ten thousand dollars."

Assistant District Attorney Ian Goller monitored the routine arraignment of Araceli N. Ramirez from his fourteenth-floor office, in a room adjacent to the office rarely occupied these days by the district attorney, because the boss was on the road, testing the political waters in preparation for a long-shot run for the Republican nomination to the

U.S. Senate. Ian Goller was, at that moment, a worried man, though not for the reasons that should have preoccupied him. The matrices and spreadsheets that mapped and tallied the flow of cases through the courtrooms in the lower floors of his building, and in five satellite courthouses across the county, were arranged on his antiquated, smudged computer screen, and they pointed to a rising flood of drug trials that would eventually lead to a breakdown in the ability of the district attorney's office to meet its legal mandates. But the slow drip toward judicial chaos did not concern him this morning, as much as the simple contents of a clear plastic bag, and a single piece of paper in a manila folder. Through the skin of plastic he could see the train and bus tickets retrieved from Araceli's backpack, while the manila folder contained a copy of a hotel sign-in sheet retrieved by a sheriff's detective who had just returned from a trip to the desert. The tickets confirmed, with those stamped digital codes that juries loved, the truth of the time frame of the defendant's version of events, and the document from the hotel-spa, along with a statement from one of the clerks, offered a disturbing contradiction to the statement of his primary witness.

One day and it's already falling apart. He hadn't handled a case himself in a while, and it had been a long time since he'd been confronted with the elemental messiness of a criminal prosecution seen in its prosaic details, with prospective arguments and "facts" tainted by the poor memory and moral fallibility of human beings. *This is why I'll never go back to litigating. Because people are idiots and they lie even when, no, especially when you put your faith in them.*

If his boss were there, Ian Goller would walk into his office, past the door with the seal of the district attorney and its scales of justice. The Sage of Santa Ana, with his undeniable trial and political skills would then tell him how to handle this conundrum casually and effortlessly, but there were only pictures of his boss's children in that office, and diplomas, and various photo-trophies of the district attorney's encounters with national politicians and conservative celebrities, including a snapshot with a distracted and now-deceased President of the United States. Ian Goller could look at those pictures and the district attorney's confident grin, and intuit what he should do next, and he could even hear the district attorney saying it: *Just kick the can down the road and see what happens. Fifty-fifty, it'll go our way.*

The trial attorney he eventually assigned to the case would likely protest his inability to lift *The People v. Araceli N. Ramirez* over the low bar of proof required for a successful preliminary hearing. But a natural outcome already suggested itself, an obvious deal resting like a jewel box inside the charges the district attorney's office had just filed. Simply negotiate the charges down from felony to misdemeanor in exchange for a guilty plea, give the defendant credit for time served and hand her ass forthwith to the Immigration and Customs Enforcement representatives at the county jail. She would then be swiftly deported, as were the legions of other foreign nationals without papers who landed there. News of the defendant's erasure from the American justice system and media orbit would satisfy the constituents clamoring for punishment, and the defendant, in turn, would receive her freedom—in Mexico. Basic fairness to the people of California dictated such a result. After all, the defendant was one of two million residents of the state living every day in violation of Section 8, Title 1325 of the U.S. Code. It fell to county prosecutors to enforce this statute, indirectly, by waiting for each of those two million people to run afoul of some state law, be it a homicide or a DUI. Goller still saw in Araceli N. Ramirez's actions a basic ignorance of American ways, and the recklessness and bad choices that characterized the existence of so many other, unambiguously guilty defendants. He believed the public defender would find the plea offer appealing, as long as the public defender did not see these train and bus receipts, and the hotel clerk's statement, and realize just how weak the prosecution's case really was. Thankfully, the rules and practices of discovery were such that the DA could plausibly delay releasing this information to the defense until after an expedited preliminary hearing. Given the nonviolent nature of the charges, the administrator at the public defender's office would likely assign the case to a Deputy Public Defender II who would see the plea down to a misdemeanor as an easy and fair resolution, a quick deal that would allow him or her to bank a little extra time to work on the thirty or forty other cases on his or her plate. Deportation was, at any rate, a federal matter beyond the purview of mere county officials: every attorney in the two concrete buildings on the opposite sides of Civic Center Drive accepted such outcomes as a matter of course. There was a door at the end of the maze of jail cells and courtrooms into which a fifth of all the defendants in the county

disappeared; the door opened to a vortex of weeping Spanish souls that drained into Tijuana and Mexicali and other forsaken places. Goller told his lawyers that each case that ended in deportation was, in its way, a victory for the rule of law. Even the most liberal member of the public defender's office long ago accepted this state of affairs without effective complaint, and it fell to the PDs in courtrooms to explain to defendants again and again that they were about to be deported. Very often this information was relayed at ostensibly happy hearings during which sentences were reduced and probation granted, the news given by twenty-five-year-old PDs in quick murmurs relayed by whispering interpreters, which caused the oft-repeated paradox of defendants weeping inconsolably even as the judge was telling them to behave themselves after being "released." They cried because they knew their American lives were coming to an end, and in the galleries their sons and daughters and wives wept too, once the truth set in. It was a cruel thing to watch, but it was as it should be, Goller thought. Soon, inevitably, his defendant and her problems would pass through the door that led to Mexico.

As he contemplated the quarter-inch-thin newborn baby of paperwork called *The People of the State of California v. Araceli N. Ramirez*, Ian Goller could already see its final fate on that day when, as an inch-thick folder, it would be rolled away into that mausoleum called Archives.

For the first few days without Araceli, the disorder at the home on Paseo Linda Bonita began to gather momentum at first light with the unmade beds, whose comforters and sheets endured in the shape of lumpy cotton corpses until late in the afternoon. Only Maureen tackled that essential household task, until she finally scolded Scott into action: "If you could make *our* bed, at least, before you leave in the morning." He grumbled and complied, but left it all uneven. Was it that he didn't care that the comforter was drooping on her side of the bed, or was it some kind of eye condition that prevented him from seeing it? She was going to have to teach the boys to make their own beds, and give them some incentive to do so, perhaps an allowance. *They're old enough to do chores now. I swept floors and folded clothes when I was a girl.* Then

there was the kitchen, whose crowded sink soon evoked the dishwashing station of a cheap diner, with sticky pots and pans beginning to climb upward and over the edge of the sink by 10:00 a.m., their leftover contents becoming encrusted as noon approached. All three bedrooms, the hallways, and the living room were littered with the sweaty fabric of shirts, socks, and underwear of every size but her own. She found Samantha's soiled socks hiding under the couch, and pajama tops in the backyard, and children's picture books on the floor underneath the dining room table. And then there was Samantha herself. Though the smallest member of the family, she tossed more objects into the splatter of disarray than everyone else put together. No one could tell her to pick up her hand puppets, her dolls, her stuffed lions, her rubber blocks, her Tinker Bell wand. Apparently, Araceli had spent a good amount of her day picking up after Samantha, who required a pair of eyes on her at all times and thus subtracted from Maureen's ability to be in all the corners of the home where she needed to be. *Samantha, you came to this world to make your mother's life more beautiful, and feminine, but you've also made it infinitely more complicated.*

The only solution was to spur gadget-man into action.

"Scott. The dishes. Could you, please?"

He studied the spread of steel bowls and plastic plates across the kitchen's marble counters, three complete sets associated with the preparation and serving of breakfast, lunch, and dinner. "Why didn't you use the dishwasher?"

Maureen didn't answer this question, and allowed the aggression in her silence to linger until she heard the water start to run in the sink.

When the school year began and Maureen started volunteering three days a week at the boys' school it was going to be very difficult. She was going to have to find day care for Samantha because they could never again hire a stranger to work in their home.

The consequences of their years of comfort, their pampering by Mexican hands, were there to live with. Voices of judgment continued to occupy the space beyond the pine, glass, and tile cocoon of Paseo Linda Bonita, and she sensed they were growing in volume and meanness. The need to escape that noise gave a greater focus and purpose to her cooking, scrubbing, folding, and other domestic pursuits, as if each muscle exercised in domesticity were building walls that sealed her off

from those profane outsiders. But how long could you transform your home into a monastery, with all the televisions and radios permanently off, and the phone off the hook, before you went crazy? She tried calling Stephanie Goldman-Arbegast, but the awkward silence and transparent excuses that followed her invitation for Max and Riley to come and play in the backyard and swim in the pool dissuaded her from calling again. *What have I done for my friend to treat my family with the frigid distance the uninfected have for the diseased?* For the rest of that day, Maureen understood that she had lost a part of herself when she stepped out the door with Samantha that fateful morning. *Goodbye, happy innocence.* She suppressed the recurring thought that she should call her mother. *No, that would be much worse.* Instead, she turned on NPR because she knew she would find dispassionate, adult voices, and for forty-five minutes she allowed the reasoned cadences of its afternoon news report to fill the living room and kitchen. She listened to a Prague coffee machine, the musical speaking-voice of a Louisiana shrimp fisherman. It was all very eclectic and relaxing, until she heard the sudden teaser: "Next, from California, a story that many people say defines the social divide in that sunny place. It's a case involving two children, their parents, and a Mexican woman . . ." Maureen took three leaping strides across the room and hit the OFF button. *Social divide? My home is a social divide?*

Her "social divide" was, at any rate, erased now because Araceli was gone and in jail again. This knowledge caused Maureen to feel a pang of guilt every time she did something in the house that Araceli would have done. When she picked up a sponge at the kitchen sink, or emptied out the dishwasher, or took out the trash, she felt she was standing in Araceli's footsteps. *Is there a special place of torment, down there in the circles of hell, for those women who betray their sisters? I can speak the words that will set her free: but if I do, will I lose my children?* The anger that she felt toward Araceli in the first days of her sons' disappearance had dissipated. *It's a natural, motherly thing, to seethe at the person who took your sons.* Now her guilt was assuaged only by the information provided by the assistant district attorney at her front door this morning—he had come to "warn" her that the "alleged abductor" of her children would likely go free in a plea bargain. He seemed to think this would make her bitter, that she would spew motherly recrimination, and she

pursed her lips in a kind of simulated grimace, but in fact she was relieved. *We worked on this house together, Araceli and I, it was our joint
project. The orbit of men, of news and jurisprudence, has driven a wedge
between us.* Then the prosecutor had added that Araceli would be likely
deported, and this had caused Maureen to ask her only question: "Deported? For a misdemeanor?" Araceli probably would have been deported
anyway; it was inevitable once the police descended on her home. *I am
responsible for the exile of the woman who worked in my home. Or rather,
Scott is. And me. We are.* She thought these things as she prepared and
poured her daughter's milk, and in her distraction the white liquid spilled
over the top of the bottle and onto the table where Samantha was sitting.

"Milk!" the baby screamed.

"Oh, my God, Sam, you talked! Your first word!"

"Milk!" her baby girl repeated.

Maureen gave her daughter a kiss on the forehead and reached for
a rag to clean the spill. When she knelt down to wipe the white drops
on the floor, a small moving object at the foot of the table caught her
eye. It was an ant, and she watched it join the flow of one of two serpentine threads that converged on the tile underneath her daughter's high
chair. The ants were bumping, circling, and shifting around a spot of
spilled and dried Cream of Wheat. Maureen followed their highway
across the dining room to the kitchen, and found it led out into the
backyard, passing underneath the door that Araceli once opened every
morning to begin work.

While Maureen studied the ants and remembered Araceli, the
story of the seemingly soon-to-be-deported *doméstica* caused the mayor
of Los Angeles to daydream while ostensibly perusing the menu at his
favorite downtown eatery. "The filet mignon here is so tender," the may-
or's political consultant said, "you can cut it with a spoon." The mayor of
Los Angeles glanced across the white cloth of the table and the sweating goblets of water and gave the consultant a listless and distracted
shake of the head.

"I'm thinking the Asian tuna salad," the mayor mumbled. "Lost my
appetite."

The mayor had slipped into a brooding funk, a rare twenty minutes

of reflective silence, causing his consultant and even the regular customers at the Pacific Dining Car to take notice. He was a man who spent
most of his waking day in conversation and monologue—on the phone,
in his City Hall office, in parking lots and passageways, in elementary
school auditoriums, at doughnut shops, in Westside receptions, in his official Lincoln Town Car. The mayor was a self-described pathological
talker who liked to brag that he'd been talking nonstop since the age of
four; he knew his consultant had two small children and that he could
call and find him awake at dawn. Six hours earlier, he had done just
that, after catching the appearance of an up-and-coming state senator
from Fremont, California, on Univision's ¡Despierta América! talk show.
"Hey, I just saw Escalante talking about that Mexican nanny again," the
mayor had said, without preamble. "He's going to town on this. He was
on Telemundo yesterday. And someone told me they heard him on the
radio a couple of times."

"Really," the consultant had said wearily into his kitchen phone,
while watching his eight-year-old son and six-year-old daughter eat
Cream of Wheat and simultaneously twirl their chestnut ringlets. The
consultant was a New Jersey transplant of Italian heritage with a wild
shock of gray Beethoven curls, a lefty pamphleteer who had risen from
1980s rent-control battles to become the master tactician of the progressive wing of the state Democratic Party, helping a variety of principled and competent leaders win election to office. "I think it's obvious
why Escalante's doing this," the consultant began. "He's not on anyone's
radar, because he's never done anything. A Latino politician who has to
wave his arms like crazy to get the attention of Latino voters isn't going
anywhere. He's got no shot at winning any statewide primary. None."

Araceli Ramirez was a cause célèbre and a deepening obsession
among the mayor's core Latino supporters, but the consultant's position
on what the mayor's position should be in her case had not changed. It
was the same at 6:45 a.m. in the kitchen of his Northeast L.A. bungalow as it had been in two previous conversations on the subject: keep
closed lips and fight the temptation to opine. "You're the mayor of Los
Angeles—this is in Orange County. Leave it alone. Because if you don't,
this crazy family and their nanny could blow up in your face."

At 6:45 in the morning, the mayor had accepted this counsel as
wise and obviously true. He had forgotten about Escalante and the

proto-martyr languishing in a Santa Ana jail cell. Then, in the waning moments of his third and final public appearance of the morning, at the Bonaventure Hotel, he had been given another rude reminder of Araceli's existence. The mayor was paying a courtesy call to a group of striking hotel workers, and had just finished up with a few words in his thick-accented but steadily improving Spanish, when one of the striking maids reached over and squeezed his wrist. She was a short woman with the angular face and short hair of a female prize-fighter, and she had pulled the mayor close to her. "*No tengas miedo,*" she said, in a tone that recalled the mayor's late mother. "*Ponte los pantalones. Di algo para apoyar a Araceli. Me enoja que no hayas dicho nada sobre esa pobre mujer.*" The mayor gave a grimace-smile and pulled away, startled a bit by the strength of the woman's grip.

"She told me to put my pants on," the mayor said suddenly to his consultant as his salad arrived. "That last woman in the hotel. The short one. Did you see her? I actually recognized her once I was forced to take a look. Die-hard shop steward. Walked precincts in each of my campaigns. She told me she was angry I hadn't said anything about the Mexican maid. 'Put your pants on,' she said. 'And say something to support Araceli.'"

"What is that, some sort of Mexican thing? Not having pants?"

"Yeah. Precisely."

"Well, that's emasculating. Is that why you ordered a salad?"

"Very funny," the mayor said, and with that he gave his famous, world-conquering grin—it was the flash of erect porcelain that had gotten him elected mayor, and that got him into trouble, sometimes, when he directed it in private at petite, single young women in their thirties. He dug into his salad, took a few bites, and began to talk. "But she has a point."

"She does?"

"The way she sees it, she didn't vote for me just to run the City of L.A."

"Right. The whole icon thing. The long-oppressed people thing."

Legions of people expected the mayor of Los Angeles to opine on the case of a wronged Orange County nanny simply because they shared an ethnic heritage. They saw in his election the fulfillment of his people's long-held aspirations for power and respect. Never mind that most of

the voters who had elected the mayor to office were white: he was expected to speak out in favor of immigration reform and amnesty and other subjects far beyond the influence of his actual, quite meager powers, as outlined in the city charter. When he spoke out for immigrant legalization, like these people expected him to, it caused another kind of voter to focus on the seeming threat of his Mexicanness, and a few to harden their belief that he was the leader of a Chicano conspiracy to enslave white people. His Mexican heritage was, at once, his greatest political asset and his heaviest albatross.

"Not saying anything at all makes me look weak," the mayor said. He did not use that word often in referring to himself, it was a sort of taboo in the mayor's circle, and hearing the mayor say it caused the consultant to sit forward in his seat. "People are starting to think I'm running away from it." The mayor's career, from a rough-and-tumble Eastside childhood, to UC Berkeley and a quixotic minor crusade or two as a civil-rights lawyer, to the state legislature, and finally to election as the mayor of the second largest city in the United States, was a dance between affability and toughness, charm and ruthlessness. He understood that "weak" was poison in politics, just like it was on the streets of his youth. The early chapters of his biography were set in a preppy Chicano Catholic school, where the mayor-to-be wore cardigan sweaters and played Black Panther dress-up games, and finally got into the fistfights that led to his expulsion. When the mayor heard the word "weak" and its many synonyms he felt a twinge of the old aggression, and his silence for the past twenty minutes had come from having suppressed a powerful desire to tell that hotel maid to go fuck herself.

It was a rare moment of self-doubt from a politician on an incredible winning streak, a man who spent his day subjecting his consultant and everyone in his circle to his constantly shifting enthusiasms, his volatile self-belief. He was going to plant a hundred thousand trees, hire a thousand police officers, and lay a cute TV reporter or two—all by Christmas. Now the imprisoned nanny was mucking it all up, and threatening to detract from his brilliance, and she was doing it all the way from Orange County. The mayor sensed that the pro-Araceli grumbling would eventually spread to his old civil-libertarian circles and to the unofficial club of well-to-do Westside liberals who funded his campaigns. A few of these people had already written letters to the editor,

emails, op-ed pieces, and Internet postings that commented on Araceli's "railroading" as emblematic of the "marginalization" of immigrants in the justice system and the workforce, and the "power relations of narrative and belief" in the city between immigrants and nonimmigrants, and other nonsense like that. The mayor understood that these people measured his silence in such matters, it was a running tally they kept in their heads. They kept expecting him to break out in a rash of cowardice.

"I'm going to have to say something," the mayor said.

The consultant brought his hands together in concentration. He was a wordsmith, an avid reader of history, and a dedicated student of marketing and message. Quickly he arrived at a broad outline of what the mayor might say—the trick, as always, was to make an essentially moderate and cautious position sound bold, principled, and eloquent, a skill all great American politicians possessed going back to Lincoln. He shared his ideas with the mayor and once he was done the mayor smiled at him and said, "Brilliant."

"The key thing is the tone," the consultant said. "You want to sound measured. Like an adult. Above the fray."

Several hours later the mayor was in East Hollywood, at a memorial service for one of the last remaining survivors in Southern California of the Armenian genocide. When the event was over he addressed the four television reporters outside, who were expecting a few innocuous Armenian-centered remarks. "I'm going to take pity on you guys today, and make a little bit of news," the mayor whispered into the ear of a female reporter. "I'm going to say something about that Mexican nanny. Get ready." There was a brief scramble, a hooking up of microphones, a positioning of cables and cameras, and when it had settled, the mayor began:

"Like a lot of people, I've been following the arrest, and now the prosecution, of Araceli Ramirez. It's a case that has a lot of people concerned. And while it isn't appropriate for me to comment on the facts of an ongoing criminal case, I'd like to make just one observation. One of the beautiful things about this country is that everyone, no matter if rich or poor, immigrant or citizen, is entitled to a fair trial. To be judged on the facts, and not on passions or prejudice. I'm concerned about the passions surrounding this case. I think everyone needs to take a step

back, and allow the facts, and only the facts, to determine the outcome. We grant our prosecutors a lot of power to protect us—and that's good. But we also trust them to use their power with discretion. I am confident that that will be the case here."

Two hours later, Ian Goller sent a transcript of this statement via BlackBerry to his boss, who was traveling in Bakersfield that afternoon. The district attorney of Orange County sent back a one-word answer: "Surprising." Goller's feelings were stronger. *It's outrageous. This isn't even in his jurisdiction.* The assistant district attorney felt a few pangs of wounded local pride, until he stepped back to think about what would lead such an ambitious and savvy politico to comment on *The People v. Araceli N. Ramirez.* Clearly, the mayor believed that Los Angeles and the Laguna Rancho Estates rested atop the same shifting tectonic plates, and he spoke cautiously to keep his footing as the ground beneath him rumbled. Goller's own Republican boss might soon feel the same political tremors and decide that pursuing a weak *Ramirez* case wasn't worth the risk. In "serious" California political circles both the right and left feared ethnic earthquakes, which was one reason why the immigration problem lingered and deepened.

The longer Araceli Ramirez stuck around Orange County's courtrooms and jail cells, Goller concluded, the bigger the political problems she presented. The mayor of Los Angeles had spoken, ostensibly, to temper a rush toward final judgment. But his brief remarks only strengthened Goller's resolve to shuffle her off U.S. soil and on her way to Mexico as soon as possible.

22

Araceli's back ached because she spent much of the waking day turning and twisting on a thin mattress, feeling it slide back and forth over the steel sheet her jailers called a bed frame. She waited for night to fall and day to come back again. When the thin rectangle of her cell window briefly glowed orange in the morning, she could imagine she was somewhere else. Back in colonia San Cosme in Mexico City, where her last *chilango* boyfriend lived, the sun warming their faces, rows of fault-shaken buildings leaning over the sidewalks; or on the subway train when it climbed up out of the ground and ran in the open air, the passengers squinting in the sudden pulses of light. What a mistake it had been to leave Mexico City. Her step north had brought her to a cell in Santa Ana, to become familiar with the angles in the walls, the sounds of the corridors, among inmates hypnotized by the collective need to sleep. The ritual dispensing of pills caused a powerful drift of inmate will toward the recreation room at the end of the corridor, where a television set filled the jail with a perpetual stream of canned laughter and commercial jingles and their tin echoes. Her fellow inmates stayed in this neutral, half-conscious state even at three in the afternoon, when the natural sun was bearing down on people in the world. They were all in

a kind of frozen storage, these women in their blue jumpsuits, sitting on their beds, some with charcoal blankets thrown over them, a hundred grungy little dolls in their cells stacked up like toy blocks, reminding her of a Diego Rivera piece from his red-star Marxist didactic days, a painting depicting bodies filling a bank vault. *Frozen Assets.*

On his first day back at work, Scott was chased away from his office by too many "Are you okays?" and too many hugs, and by not getting a single IM from Charlotte, who turned her head away with a snap when he caught her studying him through the glass. At home it was Maureen who averted her eyes, even as she handed him a shopping list for the grocery store. But at the market, with the list in hand, it was all stares. First, the Latino guy at the end of the line of carts, who gave Scott a good long look that passed quickly from initial surprise to irritated aggression. This guy was, what, thirty, thirty-five? His bald-headed look transported Scott back to South Whittier and to the first recruits to a lifestyle his father told him was "for losers who don't want to learn good English." He had a goatee and the unanchored expression of a man about to enter middle age unawares and unprepared. Five, ten seconds passed, and Scott gave him a what's-up? raising of his chin, but the guy didn't blink. Scott pushed forward into the grocery store and began to fill his cart dutifully, but when he reached the checkstand he endured another, shorter glare of recognition from the Latina cashier, followed by a frown and then a look of deliberate indifference. He had seen this cashier perhaps a half dozen times but never engaged in conversation with her, and he now sensed she was disappointed with him somehow, and that his surname had something to do with her reaction. *I'm supposed to be one of them.* This explained too the stare from the shopping-cart *vato.* Scott Torres was being judged by a set of rules of tribal loyalty, simply because he possessed a Mexican surname. *So strange, the clannishness of these people.* Scott, with his one Mexican name, was responsible for the jailing of a woman with three: Araceli Noemi Ramirez. She was just a face and a name on the television, and he their customer, a familiar face—and yet they scorned him. Scott's presence here at the checkstand, his basket filled with jars of baby food and diapers for his daughter, and juice boxes for his sons, meant less to this

cashier than the abstract construction of Araceli, a Latina martyr in a jail cell.

"Is there something wrong?" Scott asked the cashier, whose name tag announced EVANGELINE.

"Is there?" Evangeline asked cryptically, and he was left to think about the question as he wheeled out from the store with his purchases in the cart, grasping a receipt between his fingers that was nearly a yard long.

The representative of the public defender's office was a tall, elegant woman with a low-key demeanor, a Filipino surname, and a button nose that suggested a heritage that owed as much to the *Mayflower* as to Manila. Ruth "Ruthy" Bacalan-Howland was about thirty years old, and she paused to think for a second or two whenever it was her turn to speak, looking down at her hands and then using them to pull idiosyncratically at the batik fabric of her long skirt. "Of course, you should not plead guilty to a crime you did not commit, no matter how good a deal it seems," she said to Araceli. "*Mucha gente lo hace, supongo*, but really that's not the way the system is supposed to work."

They were in the attorney conference room, which they had all to themselves. Ruthy Bacalan, a deputy public defender, had listened to Araceli explain the series of events that had landed her in "a very strange North American circus," as Araceli put it in her accented but clear English. The attorney had then laid out the government's offer, speaking the occasional confident if somewhat accented Spanish. She translated "misdemeanor" into the closest Spanish equivalent she knew: "*delito menor*," a phrase that didn't quite carry the innocuous shadings of the English original. "So if you plead guilty to this *delito menor* they will release you from jail—but directly into the hands of *migración*. To the American legal system, it's considered a crime as serious as going through a red traffic light. But it does mean that you will never be able to return here again—legally—since they will hand you over to the immigration people that work inside the county jail even when they are, technically, 'releasing' you from jail. Of course, even if you fought the case and won, you still might get deported." Ruthy Bacalan sat perpendicular to Araceli at a square table, with her long legs crossed one over the

other, exposing her leather hiking boots, which had pink trim and pink shoelaces. The deputy public defender wore these shoes because she was seven months pregnant, with swollen feet that kept her perpetually off balance. "If you fight it, you get a chance to call witnesses. I would be your attorney, and the government would pay for everything. Gratis. But, once again, if you lost," the public defender continued, "you could go to a prison for five years. Then you would certainly be deported." Araceli forgot, momentarily, what the attorney was saying, and remained fixated on her footwear. *These are shoes for an active outdoor woman,* Araceli thought. *Girlie-pink and rugged leather. With those, you can climb a mountain in feminine style. I'm pretty sure I've never seen shoes like that in Mexico City, not even at the Santa Fe Mall.*

"Can I ask you, señorita, where did you buy those boots?"

Ruthy Bacalan was momentarily taken aback—apparently, people whose futures hung in the balance did not often interrupt the conversation to ask about her shoes.

"Oh, these. At the Sport Chalet."

"If I am ever released from this place and allowed to live in the United States," Araceli said, "I will go to this chalet and buy a pair of those shoes. In fact, I will tell you that I want to stay here, and not accept the very generous offer to be deported directly to Mexico, because Los Estados Unidos de América is a country where women can wear boots like that."

"So you're not going to accept the government's offer?"

"No. *¿Para qué?*"

"*Fantástico*," Ruthy Bacalan said, her face erupting into youthful brightness, as if an undergraduate had suddenly arrived to chase the gloomy attorney away. Ruthy Bacalan had been preparing to resign from the public defender's office, and not because she was pregnant and carrying forty-seven cases as a Deputy Public Defender II. Her recent conversion to Buddhism helped her with the stress, and she felt quite prepared to be a working mother. No, what was causing Ruthy Bacalan to doubt her commitment to the public defender's office was the lack of fight and purpose in the work, her servitude to the assembly line of advancing manila folders, and the flow charts that established all the hearings and procedures through which a soul had to be squeezed before emerging either guilty, exonerated, or in various legal limbos on

the other side. She had come to this job out of a sense of civic duty and compassion, a belief that she might be able to reduce the suffering of the defendants who passed before her and imbue them with at least some constitutional dignity. In the cramped office she shared with two other deputy public defenders, she had sat down to meditate for ten minutes before leaving for this interview, and realized immediately afterward that she needed to place herself in a job where she might more directly confront the inequities of her time. Maybe as a teacher in an "inner city" school, or as a union organizer, or perhaps simply as a stay-at-home mom raising future citizens with good Buddhist values. And now this defendant had appeared before her, prepared to take a defiant stance in a case that might attract some media notoriety and send a small message to the city and the nation beyond.

"I think you can win this case," Ruthy Bacalan said quickly and eagerly. "Everyone in the office was expecting you to take the guilty plea."

"Why would anyone plead guilty if they did not commit the crime?" Araceli asked. "That makes no sense."

"A lot of people do it. There are a lot of things about the law and the courts that don't make any sense."

"What you were saying before, *licenciada*? Let me make sure I understand correctly," Araceli said. "You were saying I might be punished for trying to tell the truth. I mean, if I lose the case. Because I would be telling the truth—that I am not guilty—but they could send me to prison for a longer time because I tried to tell the truth."

"Yes." Any layperson could see it, Ruthy Bacalan thought. The shock of seeing principles of the law sullied and mocked—it was the expression on the face of every idealistic attorney after a week or two inhabiting a deputy public defender's skin. "There is this beautiful idea. A word with Latin roots: 'justice.' Of course, it's the same word in both our languages. *Justicia*." These were the opening words to a little speech Ruthy Bacalan sometimes gave to undergraduate classes in the law, but never before to a client. "The justice system is like plumbing. In cases like yours, the basic problem is that there are too many defendants to fit in the system—so we lawyers use tricks to squeeze you through. Against this there is a tradition in the law that says everyone should be treated fairly. My job exists, for example, because a poor man from Florida sat down and wrote a letter to the Supreme Court, with paper and pencil.

From his jail cell. Thanks to him the laws were changed so now every-one gets a public defender, gratis. A fighter like that can change the law. United States history is filled with people like that."

"Mexican history is the same," Araceli said.

"I imagine it is."

"But I am not a fighter."

"Neither am I. Not truly."

"But I think I want to be respected. *Merezco respeto*. And I want to respect the rules too. The rules say you should not lie."

Above all, the thought of pleading guilty to a *delito menor* and ac-cepting the convenience of a "deal" offended Araceli's sense of order and decorum. It only added to the sense of unraveling about her: that she was living in a metropolis where all the objects, once arranged in order, had been shuffled out of place. *When you live far away, you never associate California with clutter.* When Araceli was in a messy home, when the beds were not made and the dishes were left unscrubbed, she invariably felt pangs of disappointment and loss. She had been this way as a girl in Nezahualcóyotl, when her mother slipped into those sea-sonal depressions that kept her from working for several days at a time, once or twice a year. And she was that way as a woman living in the guesthouse on Paseo Linda Bonita. Now Araceli could see that this place called California was like a home that had fallen into a state of obsolescence and neglect, a conclusion confirmed by the fact that this idealistic woman with the pink-trimmed boots had been forced to make an absurd offer: tell a lie and you can go free. The truth had been build-ing for a long time now—it had been there for her to see intimately in the Paseo Linda Bonita home, in the increasingly frayed interactions between Scott and Maureen, the sense that she was living with two people confused and angry with the familial roles assigned to them. She felt this same unsettled sense when she first entered the center of Los Angeles with Brandon and Keenan, when the mob confronted the councilman in Huntington Park, and when the woman of *los tres* strikes plotted her escape and then surrendered and wept. She wanted to take all the exhausted American people she'd seen and give them freshly starched clothes to wear, and she wanted to take all the misplaced ob-jects and polish them and put them back where they belonged.

"These laws you have. In some ways they are pretty," Araceli said. "But in other ways they are ugly."

The American police would politely release you if they knew the truth of your innocence; they would not accept bribes, apparently, and they placed the property they took from the people they arrested in transparent bags for later return. And yet their courts would blackmail an innocent woman into a devil's bargain, just so they could keep the flow of the accused moving swiftly through their concrete buildings.

"*Entonces, a pelear*," Araceli said.

Ruthy Bacalan beamed. "Yes, we fight." She explained what would happen next: the court would schedule a "mini-trial" called a preliminary hearing. "I'll push for that quickly. If we lose that, and we likely will, we go for a full trial."

The two women shook hands and gave each other a half embrace before leaving the room via separate doors. Araceli took a slip of paper from the guard and followed a yellow line on the concrete floor that led away from the room and twisted and turned down a labyrinth of corridors. On those few occasions when she ventured out of her cell, the expanse and openness of the county jail surprised Araceli: the prisoners shuffled back and forth without escorts, up and down the hallways and escalators, women walking with leisurely strides in groups to the cafeteria, carrying trays of food and boxes and envelopes, guided by a greasy rainbow of painted floor lines. The jail had the structured bustle of a huge office building, a weird corporation where the secretaries wore their hair in dirty strings, or shaved at the sides, and every employee dressed in a blue or a yellow jumpsuit.

She walked back to her cell block, ten minutes through a corridor maze, and remembered what she had told the deputy public defender: "I am not a fighter." But perhaps she was. She could be a Mexican superhero wrestler, the Masked Inmate, springing into the air in her yellow jail overalls, with ankle-high pink leather boots and a purple cape trailing behind her. She gave another solitary chuckle and thought that it was nice to be able to get out of her cell and talk to Ruthy for an hour, and then to jostle through the rushing crowds of secretaries in the yellow jumpsuits who crowded the passageways.

Halfway back, just past the point where the orange line turned off toward the cafeteria, Araceli felt a jolt to the head and stumbled, tumbling through an instant of blindness. She landed facedown on the floor and regained her sight, touching yellow and blue and green lines on the cement, trying to remember which one she was supposed to follow.

"Baby stealer!" someone shouted above her. "*Kidnapper!*" Someone kicked her in the spine as she tried to rise to her knees, sending her back to the hard coolness of the floor. *Someone is trying to kill me.* The inmates formed a circle around her, she could see their feet sticking out through the rubber sandals everyone had to wear, toenails freshly painted ruby and tangerine. *Where do they get nail polish in here? How did I miss the dispensing of the nail polish?* A whistle sounded and all the painted toenails ran away, replaced by the heavy black shoes of a guard. Araceli looked up and saw a tall uniformed and muscular Scandinavian giant with a ponytail. The guard pulled her up, but Araceli's head wanted to stay on the ground. "Gotta get you outta here, girl," the guard said. "Get up. Or the crowd will re-form." Araceli's legs wanted to give up, but the guard wouldn't let her fall, and they started to walk back toward the cell, Araceli taking three good steps for every bad one that couldn't support her weight, being held up by this woman with the torso of a weight lifter. "You gonna make it?" the guard asked.

"*Creo que sí,*" Araceli said.

They started to move forward again, the guard's arm around Araceli's waist. Suddenly the guard lifted her into the air with a grunt, and all of Araceli's thoughts were erased by the unexpected sensation of being embraced by the stout construction of the guard's arms as she carried Araceli over the lines on the floor. Araceli wanted to coo, it felt so good, all the tension in her spine and face and the pain of the blows suddenly slipping away.

Maureen opened the front door at 4:50 in the afternoon, thinking that it was Scott, but found instead an older, heavier, and slightly darker version of her husband. John Torres carried a suitcase and wore the expression of a man forced to rescue a drowning woman too stupid to know she couldn't swim. "It has come to my attention that you guys are kind of falling apart here," he announced. "That's why I'm back. And that's why I'm gonna move in. I'm going to take that little house in the back your maid had, since I'm assuming she ain't coming back. I'll stay four nights a week, which is probably as much as I can take."

Maureen opened her mouth to speak, but could not find words to resist the affront.

"I can cook. I can clean as well as anyone," he said, with a kind of

wounded determination. "And I sure as hell know how to make a bed, which is more than my son knows. I won't do the dishes, but I can cook a pretty mean pot of beans and just about anything these kids will eat for breakfast. You can leave your boys with me here and I can babysit, and you can take a break with my granddaughter, which I take it was what led to this mess anyway. And I'd say you probably need a break too, because, to be frank, you're looking kinda worn down, daughter-in-law." He took in her frazzled appearance with a quick up-and-down. "I know you're not supposed to say something like that to a woman, but let's get down to brass tacks here. You need the help. You're wearing out like some of the guys I used to pick lettuce with. I'll work for free. Just let me eat my own arroz con pollo is all I ask."

El abuelo Torres disappeared into the kitchen and then into the back-yard and the guesthouse. Scott found him thirty minutes later, with his head in the refrigerator.

"Dad? What's going on?"

"I'm looking for a decent cheese to make these kids a quesadilla. That's something I know they'll eat for dinner."

Scott walked away, feeling he had entered a nightmare in which he sleepwalked through scenes from his childhood, the past returning with an eerie and familiar sense of doomed domesticity.

"My father is cooking dinner?" Scott asked Maureen in the living room.

"And living with us."

"In this house?"

"In the guesthouse, yes."

"Why?"

"Not my idea."

"Can we make him leave?"

"I suppose we could," Maureen said. She took in the smell of melt-ing cheese wafting in from the kitchen. "But can we afford to?"

After serving his grandsons and granddaughter a dinner of quesa-dillas and sliced apples, with the boys grinning at him and calling out, "Can we have another one, Grandpa?" the elder Torres returned to the silver range. He prepared baked potatoes and chicken thighs spiced with tarragon, the kind of simple but hearty meal you might get at a diner, and slid it across the kitchen table to his son and daughter-in-law.

"Enjoy," he said flatly.

"Thank you," Maureen answered weakly.

When they were finished he left the dishes in the sink for Maureen and went out in the backyard and grabbed one of the footballs and yelled out to Brandon, "Go long." After a few tosses Keenan joined them and they played catch for thirty minutes, until the elder Torres began to cough and he plopped down on the grass and said, "Let's sit down and take a rest and look at this pretty desert we've got growing here."

Grandfather and grandsons admired the stiff petals of the prickly pear cactus, the spiny yuccas, and held very still when they saw a crow perch itself on top of the ocotillo. It turned its head side to side to examine the humans below with each of its eyes.

"Damn, that's pretty," the elder Torres said. "It's been a long time since I seen the desert like this. Grew up in the desert, you know."

Brandon sensed his grandfather was drawn to the cactus in some profoundly adult and emotional way, and he half heard and half imagined a cowboy twang in his speech. Perhaps he was a south-of-the-border cowboy like the venal gunslinger with a Mexican accent in that spaghetti western Brandon watched with his father once, until the cowboys started cussing and his father told him he had to leave.

"Is this what Mexico looks like?" Brandon asked.

"Wouldn't know. I'm from Yuma, in Arizona." The elder Torres looked at his grandchildren, saw their expression of innocent confusion, and allowed his natural defensiveness to slip away. "My father was from Chihuahua. I was born there, but it's been a long time. I suppose it probably still looks like this."

"Are we Mexican?"

"Just a quarter. By me, I guess."

"Only a quarter?" Keenan said. He thought about the math lessons at the end of second grade, and did not understand how a human being could be divided into fractions. One-quarter, two-thirds, three-eighths. Were his bones and muscles split into Mexican parts and American parts? Could his greenish-brown pupils have a quarter Mexican pie slice, two American pie slices, and an Irish pie slice, and if he looked in the mirror with a magnifying glass, could he see the slices and tell them apart?

"Yeah," their grandfather said. "Just a quarter."

"Is less Mexican better than more?"

"Don't know. Some people think it is. These days, though, I ain't so sure."

At 8:45 p.m. the elder Torres retired to the guesthouse, and by 9:15, when Maureen entered the kitchen to make herself some tea, she could hear him snoring, a faint animal rumbling of stubborn helplessness squeezing through the two walls that separated them.

The next morning he awoke at 6:00 a.m., entered the kitchen, and made his son a ham, tomato, and cheese omelet for breakfast. When Scott had finished eating, his father gave him an order.

"Do me a favor and scrub out a couple of toilets before you leave for the day."

"What?"

"Listen. Your wife is allergic to the toilet bowls, and I'm gonna have a lot on my plate today."

"But I'm going to work. I'll be late."

"I thought you were the boss there."

Twenty minutes later the elder Torres found his son on his hands and knees in one of the home's four bathrooms, attacking the porcelain with a scrubber.

"Man, this is gross," Scott said.

"You've got two boys. What did you expect?"

Scott rose to his feet, lowered the toilet cover to sit, and took a break, studying the sink and the tub, both of which were awaiting his attentions.

"Did Araceli really do all of this? By herself?" Scott asked. He looked at his hands, which smelled of bleach. "You made breakfast, and dinner last night. Maureen's doing the baby's laundry. I'm cleaning the fucking toilets. I can't believe that one woman did all of these things."

"Yeah," the elder Torres said. "And she did them well." He examined his son's work on the toilet, and added, "Don't forget to scrub down on the sides. You need to get back down on your hands and knees to do it right."

For the next few days Scott and Maureen remembered Araceli in their muscles, and in their wrinkled and bleached hands, until the tasks became familiar and routine and her prominent place in their memories began to fade, very slightly.

23

"Somebody paid your bail." The guard named Nansen, who had carried Araceli to safety just yesterday, looked a little disappointed. "Ten grand, paid in full." Araceli walked through the jail corridors for what she hoped was the last time, trying to imagine who her benefactor might be—a man, a tall man, a gringo? Would his act of kindness present additional complications? After her clothes were returned to her at the Inmate Reception Center, she walked through one last set of doors into a room where the guards didn't care about her anymore, a waiting area with plastic chairs and the feel of a seedy bus station. Standing in the middle of the room, with the lost look of a passenger who had missed his connection, was a thin, white-haired, and pale man of about fifty with ruddy, cratered skin, in a brown tweed jacket and a white cotton dress shirt that dangled over the top of his jeans.

The attorney opened his arms in greeting. "Araceli! I've been here for over an hour. I'm Mitchell Glass. From the South Coast Immigrant Coalition," he said. "We paid your bail."

"Why?" Araceli realized, of course, that she should say thank you, but her need to understand what was happening outweighed any pretense. There was a moment of awkward silence while Glass considered the question.

He explained, in slow and condescending English that sped up and was less condescending after Araceli frowned at him, that the coalition had received the funds to free Araceli from a group called the Immigrant Daylight Project, a large circle of benevolent and open-minded people from Manhattan, Austin, Santa Monica, Cambridge, and many other places. "Usually they pay bail for people who are in immigration detention. So they can get out and live among free people while they appeal the verdict. Out of the shadows and into the daylight. Get it? The directors thought that, given the attention to your case, they would pay your bail too. Plus, it wasn't a huge amount."

"*¿Y qué tengo que hacer?*" she asked.

"Nothing," Glass said. "These people just want you to be free while you fight your case."

Araceli did not know it, but not long after her second arrest the Daylight Project had sent off a flurry of emails and posted letters calling on its members to "help throw a wrench in the prison-industrial complex" by "emancipating Araceli N. Ramirez, the latest member of the fastest growing sector of the incarcerated population"—undocumented immigrants. The group's fund-raising literature was a bit heavy-handed with its use of slavery metaphors, and included broken chains on its logo and references to the Underground Railroad in its brochures. But they dealt almost exclusively with those in federal detention and their decision to pay Araceli's bail caught Ian Goller and his office completely by surprise. It had been ages since the Orange County District Attorney's Office had a defendant whose fate worried faraway liberal crusaders. Generally speaking, alien inmates without family members on the outside stayed inside the big house, there was no habeas corpus for them, no writs, no appeals, no purchased freedom.

For the moment, however, Araceli was a happy and unlikely beneficiary of the Bill of Rights, as free of overbearing authorities as the New Englanders who stood up to King George, a startling fact which she confirmed by scanning the street and the parked cars as she walked toward the jail's parking lot. *No one is following me.* Qué milagro. *The sun is shining on my face. Daylight.* She wanted to ask about her public defender, but instead Glass told her something about a "rally."

"What?"

"We're going to a little meeting," he said as they entered his car. "Your case inspired us to organize this."

They arrived at the campus of a Catholic church and its affiliated school and parked on its basketball court, then marched briskly around the chapel, Glass leading the way to a collection of nearby bungalows and square buildings painted industrial-tan. *Is this a political meeting?* she wanted to ask. *I am not a fan of politics.* Araceli began to feel annoyed with this Glass, even though he had liberated her from jail. He was a step ahead of her, but she reached out to grab him by the dusty sleeve of his jacket.

"Wait," she said. "*Necesito saber.*"

"What?" He stopped his forward march and gave her a mildly flustered look.

"What do I have to do for the money?" Araceli demanded. "For the bail? What do they want?"

"Nothing. All you have to do is go to court on the day they tell you."

"*¿De veras?*"

"Yes. Let's go now," Glass said. "Please. People are waiting for us." They resumed their frantic scurry across the school's black asphalt playground, with Araceli wondering why the playgrounds and classrooms were empty of children, until she remembered it was the middle of summer and school was out.

They entered a long room with high ceilings that was filled with people sitting in rows of folding chairs. A speaker was addressing the audience in Spanish from a small stage, a very short, light-skinned woman who spoke in an amplified, high-pitched whisper. "*Es que son unos abusivos,*" she said in a Central American accent. "*A mí no me gusta que me hablen así.*" Most of the audience turned toward Araceli and Glass as the door opened, and several people smiled at Araceli when they saw her, though none beamed broader than a wool-pelted, bureaucratic-looking, and unmistakably Mexican man and his equally well-dressed acolytes sitting in the front row. These men now rose from their chairs as one, rudely ignoring the speech that was still in progress onstage, and moved toward Araceli with outstretched hands.

"No, Consul, not now," Glass said brusquely as he moved his body forcefully between Araceli and the Mexican diplomat.

"That's the consul of Mexico in Santa Ana," Glass whispered into Araceli's ear as they climbed up the little steps to the stage. "A real publicity hound. Don't talk to him. He's useless."

Now Araceli stood on a platform, above an audience of about one

hundred people, nearly all of whom were gazing at her with the delight of unexpected recognition. They knew her face from the television reports. She was a celebrity, a realization that brought a sardonic grin to Araceli's lips which, in turn, only seemed to make everyone around her happier. *The liberated inmate is grateful because our movement has set her free.* Araceli had a moment to marvel at the power of television and newspapers to make her face known to strangers. There were younger people, most of them Latino college students, it seemed, and older people of European stock in distressed cotton. One of the college students, a young woman with hair worked up into a kind of half beehive, raised a phone to take Araceli's picture.

Glass stepped up to the microphone. "Just a few minutes ago, we posted bail for our friend here, Araceli Ramirez," he began. At this the audience broke into a hearty applause. Was that big guy in the back Felipe? *Could it be? No.* Now everyone was beaming, except for three severe-looking young men with identical close-cropped haircuts and earrings that opened weird, hollow spaces in their lobes. They were members of a club with rules Araceli did not recognize, and their jaws were locked in grim defiance, as if they had been the ones put in jail, not her, and they seemed to be making a point of cupping their hands and clapping harder than anyone else.

"We're going to ask Araceli here to say a few words, but first . . ."

Say a few words? She looked at Glass and wanted to tap his shoulder to ask if she had heard him correctly, but he was still addressing the audience. "You and I, we all know what this case is about," he said, his bass voice finding a Brooklyn rasp or two as it rose in volume. "This is about racism; it's about the powerful imposing their law on the weak." Several people in the audience nodded in assent because Glass had spoken a truth that Araceli could see too, even through her stage fright. "Well, we're here, all of us are here to say that we're tired of the police raids, we're tired of our young Latino men and women being harassed, we're tired of the *migra*." His voice rose even more to match the ascending volume of the audience, the people calling out, "Yes!" as if this were some sort of evangelical service.

"And this case, this case our friend Araceli has against her, this is the worst. She has done absolutely nothing wrong. Nothing!" He was spitting into the microphone now. "And if they can lock up Araceli

Ramirez and take away her freedom for nothing, then they can do it to any of us. Now we're saying we're not going to tolerate this. We're not going to allow our Latino men and women to be railroaded!" Nearly everyone rose to their feet, a few were shouting words Araceli couldn't make out, they wanted to hear more, but Glass seemed to have run out of steam. He turned to Araceli, who was standing at his shoulder, and looked at her: it was her turn.

She whispered into his ear, "*No sé qué decir.*" Out in the audience, a hundred people were standing before their folding chairs, their eyes locked on her.

"Just tell them you hope there is justice," he said.

Glass put his hand at her back and nudged her toward the microphone. She brought her lips close to it and spoke softly. "*Quiero justicia.*" The sound of her voice, turned to metal, bounced off the walls. "*No hice nada.*" She stopped, wondering what to say next, suddenly at a loss for words, as if she'd picked up a text of her speech and found all the pages blank. *Is that all I have to say?* "*No hice nada,*" she repeated, feeling parrotlike. "*Soy inocente.*" They expected a waterfall of words, and suddenly she didn't want to disappoint them, but her sense of urgency only muzzled her more. "*No sé qué más decir,*" she said, and the words came out with a nervous near-giggle that she would remember as the sound of her failure. One of the shaved heads in the back started clapping, all alone. And then it was as if he'd opened a faucet, because everyone joined in and the applause became a wave of sound, growing denser as it approached the stage and crashed at her feet. Now she thought of what more she could say: she would thank the people who paid her bail, and Glass for coming to get her out of jail, she would say that she agreed with everything Glass had said. But now that she had the words, she couldn't speak them, because the applause kept on going, it had a momentum of its own, people were making a point of keeping it going, to show it would not die. All the clappers looked at her with what seemed to her an overwrought pride, as if she'd just had a medal pinned to her chest. There was a young, thin man in the first row, wearing a loose-fitting leather belt of chrome pyramid studs, and jeans fashionably ripped at the knees, and she had time to think that she liked his style. When she studied him closer, she saw he was crying. *He would fit in in Mexico City, except for the fact that he's clapping and crying at the*

same time—in my city, we are either happy or morose but rarely both at the same time. Maybe if she started clapping too, they would stop. Glass put his hand on her back again and she understood: she stepped away from the microphone and followed him down from the stage, where everyone reached out to shake her hand.

If Giovanni Lozano hadn't been crying and laughing when Araceli spotted him, she would have taken more time to admire his outfit, and the familiar, punk-inspiring stylings whose fashionability endured in Mexico City as much as Los Angeles. On his black denim blazer he wore a NO HUMAN IS ILLEGAL button next to another of Joey Ramone, and he walked to his car in his ripped jeans with a studded leather belt and the leaning, I-don't-give-a-shit gait of an oversexed musician. He tossed his raven bangs back before stepping in and listening to the engine of his old Dodge turn over with a clank and shuffle that sounded like the prologue to a folk song. As the engine revved and warmed up, he resisted the temptation to fire off some text messages to his friends, because the event he had just witnessed was too big, too monumental, he decided, to be reduced to the usual texting acronyms and abbreviations. Giovanni Lozano, a twenty-six-year-old Chicano Studies maven and perpetual Cal State Fullerton undergrad, had been following Araceli's case on television for days. He was the most active and most read poster on the La Bloga Latina page dedicated to Araceli's case, where he had a large following among the small but growing segment of Spanish-surnamed population that Giovanni called "the Latino intelligentsia, such as it is." His readers were a largely college-educated and over-qualified bunch, their ranks including underpaid municipal employees, unpublished novelists, untenured professors, underappreciated midlevel executives, unheralded poets, and the directors of underfunded nonprofits seeking to house, feed, and teach a tragically undereducated people. These readers appreciated his Spanglish wit, his Orange County Chicano, *Y-Qué* attitude—thanks to them, he was winning the war on Google, outpacing the One California nativist website on "Araceli Ramirez" searches by nearly two to one. As he drove he began to craft, in his head, a succinct summary of the events that had just unfolded: *Araceli Noemi Ramirez is free on bail! La Bloga's campaign—successful! We just saw her at a church in San Clemente. ¡Qué mujer! Her speech: short and to the*

point. Her attitude: arty and defiant, como siempre. *A tall, big* mexicana, *she waltzed past our local, do-nothing consul as if he wasn't there! Ha!* From his very first glimpse of her running in that footage shot under the electric transmission lines in Huntington Park, Giovanni saw in Araceli a symbol of *mexicana* hipsterhood victimized. This vision of her was only strengthened by the details he found buried in the news accounts of her two arrests and double jailing, including the revelation, reported near the end of a story by Cynthia Villarreal in the *Times,* that police had found "disturbing art" in Araceli's room. Giovanni had understood, instinctively, that Araceli was being victimized not only for being a *mexicana,* but also for being an individualist and a rebel. He had studied the photo essay on the web that accompanied the *Times* story on the rearrest, and drew his readers' attention to the tiny silver studs Araceli wore on her earlobes, the too-tight leggings, and the wide blouse with the wide-open neck and small embroidered fringe that was tastefully Oaxacan without being too folksy.

Araceli's presence was an antidote, somehow, to all those sad stories of workplace raids and deportations; she stood for the sophisticated place he and his mostly American-born readers imagined deeper, urban Mexico to be. She was an event of history that had been dropped into Giovanni Lozano's provincial corner of the planet, a force with the potential to separate the Spanish-surnamed masses from their complacency and denial. People like his immigrant mother, who tended to her roses in their home in Garden Grove, telling Giovanni that she felt the Holy Spirit in the faint breeze that blew between the flowers. His mother pretended not to care when he told her how she and her people were being belittled on the radio and on television, in the courts and in the supermarkets, by the racists who attached that slur "illegal" to anyone and everyone with Mesoamerican blood in their veins. *Don't you see, Mother?* he wanted to say. *They want to destroy us! Deport us all! It's a war against our culture!*

No, my people don't understand shouting. They understand victims and heroes, he thought. So he would give them an icon. He would take one of those photographs of Araceli from the newspaper website, and he would make a work of art, a portrait-poster. He would take Araceli's face and multiply it, so that many Aracelis floated above the marching crowd at the next rally, in a Warholian statement about the power of her ordinariness and her celebrity. He would paste her to the walls,

and put some text underneath her. Perhaps Araceli's own statement from the newspaper. "¡*No les tengo miedo!*" And why not in English too? A Mexican woman with her mouth open to the words: "I am not afraid!"

"I don't know what I know anymore," Maureen said fifteen minutes into the interview with Deputy District Attorney Arnold Chang. Maureen and Scott were confused and evasive about time and their own actions during the disappearance of the children, and they were unwilling or unable to say anything about the defendant that would bolster a felony child endangerment conviction. They were freshly showered and scented, appropriately polite, but also distant to the man who was there to be their champion in court against the woman charged with endangering their children.

"She never did anything you found strange?" Chang asked.

"Strange? Oh, yes, lots of things," Maureen said. "We called her Madame Weirdness."

"You'd say hello and she wouldn't answer," Scott said.

"I got kind of used to that after a while. Who needs to hear 'hello' all the time in their own house?" Maureen said. "But she did seem unhappy a lot of the time."

"Almost all the time," Scott said. "But that's not a crime, I guess. Unhappiness is not against the law."

"What was she unhappy about?"

Maureen and Scott thought about this question for a few moments, reviewing their memories of the four years they had lived with Araceli for some insight into their employee's inner life. They looked at each other blankly, then separately gave the prosecutor a startled and embarrassed shrug.

"We have no idea," Scott said.

"I'm guessing that she was lonely," Maureen said. "That she expected more from life—because, you know, she's obviously very smart. But she worked hard. We have to give her that."

"She did everything," Scott said. "Everything. And never complained."

"She grumbled," Maureen corrected. "She was rude. But did we ever hear a real complaint? No."

The "victims" wanted the case to go away, the deputy district attorney concluded, and that was a common enough reaction. They wanted to return to their normal, untroubled lives. But then the husband took it a step further.

"I'm not sure Araceli needs to be prosecuted," Scott said suddenly, bluntly. "I really don't think she did anything wrong."

Maureen lowered her eyes, feeling suddenly exposed and naked, but not entirely surprised. She allowed Scott's statement to fill the space above their dining room table unchallenged, knowing that her silence was a loud proclamation of assent. *If Araceli didn't do anything wrong, then what about me?* She had contributed to Araceli's jailing with that small lie to the 911 operator, and then she had all but denounced her former maid in a television interview, with insinuations that caused the Mexican woman to be jailed again. A simple statement by her husband had forced her to confront these truths. And it was all happening here in the living room, before yet another stranger.

"But she took them, or placed them, rather, in a situation of peril," the deputy district attorney said.

"Because of us," Scott said. "It was our fault."

"Stop," the deputy district attorney snapped, raising his palm like a traffic policeman, and both Maureen and Scott understood why.

"Can't you just let this go?" Scott said, with frustrated insistence. "Because the longer it goes on, the deeper you're digging us into a big mess. I mean, the media, everything. It's going to swallow up our family."

"There's something you need to understand," Deputy District Attorney Chang said after a few moments. "It's not your decision to make. This case doesn't belong to you. It belongs to the People now."

"**W**ell, that went smoothly," Scott said once the deputy district attorney had left.

"We spent the last twenty minutes talking about the desert garden and about his kids," Maureen observed, and with that she turned away from Scott and walked over to the portable playpen in the middle of the living room and took out Samantha.

"She's spending a lot of time in there," Scott observed, but his wife

ignored him and gave him the baby, and in a few moments she had disappeared into the kitchen and then emerged again with an apron.

"There's some things we need to talk about," Scott said. Before the arrival of the representative of the district attorney's office, Scott had spent the morning on the phone, speaking to a representative of Child Protective Services. He had to sit down with his wife and sort through how they were going to work their way out of this mess, but now she walked away from him again, tying the apron around her back and disappearing into the kitchen. *How is it that women are so good with their fingers behind their backs and we men are not?* The image of motherly dexterity and purpose stuck with him as he took the baby and headed for the backyard. He took Samantha outside and rolled a ball around the grass with her, and enjoyed the crazy, baby-tooth giggle she gave when it slipped away from her. "Ball," his daughter said, her voice mostly a big, squeaky vowel. When they had finished playing he looked for his wife, thinking that he might grab and hold her attention with the momentous news that their daughter had just uttered her first word. He found her in the boys' room, on her knees, examining the contents of the boys' bookcase.

"Hey, Samantha is talking now."

"I know. She said 'milk' a few days ago. Didn't I tell you?"

"No." He studied his wife, who was taking books and dropping them into a box with harried relish. "What are you doing?"

"I had an epiphany," Maureen said, giving a scan of the room Araceli called El Cuarto de las Mil Maravillas. "We have too much stuff."

"What?"

"The kids have toys they haven't played with in two or three years. And books like these that they'll never read again." She held up two slim volumes from a series of detective mysteries written for young readers, one for each letter of the alphabet. Their precocious younger son had finished whipping through all twenty-six more than a year earlier. "Why have we kept these? It's all this stuff gathering dust that's just making it that much harder to keep this place clean."

"Okay," Scott said in the tone with which one addressed children and madmen.

"Of course, the real solution is to move to a smaller house," Mau-

reen continued. "That's what we should have done a while ago." It pained her to think she'd soon have to leave this home built with so much time and care. But there was no other way out. Not any she could see. "We can't have your dad staying with us forever. And if we're not going to have any live-in help, then we can't be in a place that's this big. If we can get rid of about half the stuff we own, we can fit into a smaller place. Maybe a place with a public school district that's half-way decent."

Scott could see his wife would now approach the task of divesting herself and her home of these superfluous objects with the same vigor she had applied to their accumulation. The household was her domain, and he and all the children would live according to whatever principles she embraced: baroque beauty and excess, or simplicity and moderation. *What do they call it when women run everything? Matriarchy? Feminocracy?* He imagined a leaner household, smaller credit-card bills, and a less imposing flat-screen television. Or perhaps no television at all. Hadn't it been that way once, in some other time, in the prehistory of his American family, a time his Mainer great-grandfather would remember? He allowed himself to imagine living in that emptier household with children, perhaps with a vegetable garden in the back instead of cacti or semitropical plants—and then he remembered the nagging matters of the present.

"We need to talk about some things."

Maureen heard him but chose not to respond, because if she did she would lose the momentum that was carrying her through the domestic juggling act of her day. If she stopped she would curl up like a ball on the bed with a bowl of ice cream and the television turned on to faux courtrooms and talk-show hosts who filled the day with common sense and scolding rants delivered to knucklehead moms. Better to sort through this bookcase, separating out the old Dr. Seuss and other very early reader books Samantha might still enjoy. If she could leave the boys' room looking less cluttered, the sense of minor accomplishment would stay with her and lift her through the preparation of lunch. Afterward, she would strap up Samantha for a walk through the neighborhood to see if she might fall asleep, because the baby was starting to skip her naps, which transformed her into a moody afternoon screamer. The visit of the representative of the district attorney's office had

thrown Maureen off, set her back, but now the sight of these books had her back on track again. Each book had a little of their past and their hope attached to it, and it would be hard to part with the brightly colored pages of trucks, trains, and spaceships, many with dates of purchase and a name written inside: *Brandon's favorite, Age 3.* There was a poetic order, she could now see, in the seemingly haphazard collection of topics and images in these books. *Here a slice of ancient Egypt brought to life with meticulous drawings, there a child's primer on human evolution. Australopithecus, Homo habilis.* They had purchased these books to transform their children into little cosmopolitan princes. But all this was too much. She considered a collection of art-history primers, which her sons never cracked open. Michelangelo and his Sistine Chapel were gathering dust, because her sons were unmoved by the hand of God touching Man.

"The child services people called this morning," Scott said behind her.

"Uh-huh."

Scott lowered Samantha to the floor and allowed her to begin walking through the room, thinking perhaps that would get his wife's attention away from the books she was sorting. There was something remarkable, and also very predictable, Scott thought, about this moment: he and his wife had been thrust into a public crisis, suffered embarrassment on television, in the newspapers, and on the Internet, and yet the essential dynamic in their marriage remained unchanged. *I'm trying to help us avoid disaster and she is still not listening.*

"Maureen, we need to focus," he insisted. "Child Protective Services got set off by the stuff about the spa. About you being at the spa alone. Apparently there's another, quote, unquote, 'wave of anger' building against us. The media found out about MindWare, and me being a software millionaire, supposedly, and how much our house is worth. Peter Goldman said they're calling us 'symbols of excess.'"

"Peter told you that?" Maureen asked, finally turning to face him. "You talked to him?"

"Yes. This morning. I called him after I talked to the child services people and that nut Ian Goller. Goller called just before his guy came out here. He said we should go to the courthouse when Araceli's hearing starts. And this time we should take the boys."

"But he said last week we didn't have to."

"Not to the trial. To a rally outside. On the same day."

"A rally? A rally against the immigrants? What for?"

"Because of the kids. Goller says it'll keep pressure on child services to leave us alone. That's why I told that guy I wanted to drop the case. Because this whole thing is getting too crazy and weird. But now I don't know. What happens if I tell the child services people the same thing I told the DA guy? That it was our fault. What do we say?"

Instead of responding, Maureen took a deep breath to gather herself, then walked over to the room's large closet and opened it. She allowed the quiet to linger, and then focused her eyes and attention on the next challenge before her: a half dozen plastic containers filled with toys. The only solution here was to order the boys to go through everything and decide what they wanted to keep and send the rest to Goodwill. *Responsibility: they are just the right age to learn a lesson about managing their living space.*

"Maureen," Scott insisted. "Please! We have to talk about this."

She turned to face him and spoke in a calm but determined voice. "Don't you understand? I'm trying to take control of our lives too." She stretched out her arms and held her palms upward and gestured around the room filled with the artifacts of their frenetic overcollecting, the stuffed shelves of make-believe objects, and the overflowing plastic, paper, and fabric inside the closet. "What we need to focus on to keep our family in one piece is in here. In these rooms. Not out there."

"I saw this woman and those two boys crossing the street on Broadway. And it was two days before they show up on the TV 'kidnapped.' I'm certain of it," Judge Adalian told the cable host from the network's Burbank studios. "I told this to the district attorney's office in very clear terms. First on the phone, and then in writing. So what do they do? They ignore me. There is no follow-up. So I insist. I'm a judge and I'm used to getting my way, I guess. They still haven't called back. I find this a bit irritating. So I called up the public defender's office and told the very nice young deputy they have working on this case. And she was very happy to hear that a municipal judge is making a statement that corroborates the defendant's version of events."

Ian Goller listened to the news in his quiet office on a Sunday afternoon and rubbed his temples and tried not to think about the Angels'
pitching rotation instead, or the endangered state park at San Onofre,
or any other of his usual topics of procrastination. He kept his focus on
the news host as she went on to point out other tidbits of information
that appeared to "tilt the scales of believability" in favor of the Mexican
defendant: "the sighting of Mrs. Thompson, without her husband, at a
desert spa during the alleged kidnapping," and "numerous statements by
a city council member of Huntington Park, who we choose to believe,"
the host said sardonically, "even though he has a Mexican last name." The
case against Araceli was falling apart very publicly and very quickly—or
so it seemed on one cable network. Against this latest and predictably
skeptical report, there was the steady flow of letters, emails, and television commentary for his office to continue its aggressive prosecution of
Araceli N. Ramirez, especially now that she had been unexpectedly set
free on bail. Ian Goller had countered the flow of opinion favorable to
the defense with a series of incriminating leaks, including selected passages from the transcript of Brandon's description of his days in the
mystery-land of Los Angeles. Ian Goller had fed these bits of info to three
different reporters at a Santa Ana Denny's, and had felt oddly spent and
empty afterward. Media warfare was tedious and base, but he was forced
to wage it: the alternative was to allow the district attorney's office to
look ridiculous, and to permit the idea that the DA was pursuing a "ra-
cially motivated prosecution" to taint the institution. The subsequent news
accounts of Brandon's tales of "war," "slavery," and "bombs" had done the
trick, fostering the expected reactions of suspicion and revulsion—one
talk radio host asked, "Where did that animal take those boys?" The
clamor would not yet die, in some venues it was growing stronger, and
for this reason Goller was optimistic. His own view of the case was that
a misdemeanor child-endangerment conviction was entirely fair, because of the mental suffering, albeit of a passing nature, that Araceli's
actions had inflicted on the two children. He would almost certainly
get a misdemeanor plea if he won at the preliminary hearing and the
judge ordered her to stand trial on the felony charge—and there were
several recent reforms to criminal procedures in California that aided
him in that goal. Most important was an initiative recently approved by
crime-weary voters that allowed police officers to give hearsay evidence

at preliminary hearings, sparing the alleged victims the trauma of doing so. This new law would keep Scott Torres and Maureen Thompson and their sons out of the courtroom, which was especially fortuitous because it was clear that, despite her strong performance in her television interview, Maureen would likely fold on the stand. His lead deputy on the case, Arnold Chang, had returned from his one and only session at the couple's home shaking his head.

"Our witnesses are a bit mixed up."

"They often are," Goller said. "Such is the nature of human memory."

"No, this is worse."

"I figured it might be."

"It's bad."

"They're traumatized parents."

"No, this is worse. They don't want to go forward. They don't want us to charge this woman with anything."

"Did you tell them that the case belongs to the People now?"

"Yes."

Goller nodded that he understood. "Well, it doesn't matter really."

"Boss," his deputy said, "I'm not sure this will fly."

Assistant District Attorney Goller considered this assessment for a few moments and said, "Lucky for us, our case involves a deportable alien. So it only has to fly a little."

"How little?"

"If you toss a chicken in the air and it flaps its wings for two seconds or so, you can call that flying. Right?"

"At least, Señor Octavio, allow me the pleasure of making a salad." Araceli was cutting lettuce, slicing tomatoes in the living room, while in the kitchen Octavio Covarrubias toiled at another meal in her honor, this one to celebrate her rerelease from jail. In a bid to top his previous efforts on her behalf, and to communicate his ever-elevated respect for her immigrant martyrdom, Octavio had decided to prepare the most difficult dish he and his wife could make, the jewel of Mexican cuisine, a sauce so elaborate that he had called in his elderly aunt from the San Fernando Valley to help him prepare it. *Mole*, the chocolate nectar the Aztecs served their emperor and his court, spread over

tender chicken breasts. "We spent four hours tracking down the Oaxaqueño with the best *mole* in Orange County," Octavio said. "These people are harder to find than drug dealers."

They sat for the meal, with Octavio looking expectantly at Araceli as she ate the first bite very slowly. Finally, she pronounced, "*Espectacular.* Like honey." Octavio smiled broadly, as did his wife, though the aunt did not—she seemed confused as to why her nephew and his wife were infatuated with a tall *indocumentada* who lorded over the table and spoke as if everyone were obliged to listen.

"They are probably going to deport me, one way or the other," Araceli said casually in Spanish, between bites. "That's how my lawyer explained it to me, *más o menos.* They will probably offer me a deal, where they forget about the more serious and ridiculous accusation against me and just give me a traffic ticket—like when you go through a red light. A traffic ticket for taking the boys to a dangerous place. But if I sign the paper accepting this ticket, then they will take me away. *Para el otro lado.* If I don't take the deal, I might go to *el bote* here in California for a couple of years before they send me to Mexico—that's if we lose the case. And if I win, they might still come and get me. Probably here at this house, or wherever they find me." She looked around the table to judge their reactions—Octavio lowered his thick eyebrows and gave a defiant squint, while his wife opened her eyes theatrically wide with worry.

"Can't you just run away? Just leave right now?"

"No. Because I made a promise to the people who paid my bail. That I would go to court."

"So what are you going to do?" Octavio asked.

"It seems that getting the ticket is the best deal," his wife said.

"Well, a lot of people want to see me fight it," Araceli said.

"Just to show them that our people won't be intimidated," Octavio said.

"*A fin de cuentas, se trata de la dignidad de uno,*" she said, and had time to think that it been a very long time since she had used that abstract word—*dignidad*—in reference to her person. "But sometimes you have to be practical. Why suffer in those cells, where any *loca* can hit you on the head, just to prove a point? There isn't much *dignidad* in those American jails."

After the meal, Araceli was sitting alone on the porch steps, thinking about the choices she had made and how quiet the block seemed. Perhaps the neighbors had gone into hiding at the news of her return. She took in the summer stillness, the heat that was dissolving into the fiery twilight sky, the sparrows that were flittering about the jacaranda and maple trees. Just a few days earlier she had stood on the narrow cement walkway that cut through this lawn, facing the police sergeant who had come to arrest her. She was free again, at this same spot, but there was no one to photograph and memorialize her moment of liberated boredom. An ice cream vendor pushed past on the sidewalk, glancing up at Araceli and waving. A moment later, a big red pickup truck turned and pulled onto the street and parked in front of the Covarrubias home. The driver inside looked vaguely familiar.

"¡*Gordito!*" she called out, but quickly realized she didn't know him well enough to address him that way. "Felipe!"

Felipe looked both taller and wider than she remembered, and his black curls longer. He waddled up the path in white pants splattered with yellow and peach paint stains, and gave her the expectant and nervous look of an autograph seeker. *He thinks I'm a celebrity too. How funny!* He reached the porch and stood before her with his hands tucked deep into his pockets. "They told me you stayed here, on this block, but I didn't know which house. So I was going to park my truck and knock on the doors and ask around. But then I saw you sitting here."

"¿*Qué pasó?* I was waiting for you to call me. And then everything happened with the boys."

"I was going to call you, and then my uncle got us a job up in San Francisco for a week. When I got back, you were all over the television. *No lo podía creer.* I called that number you gave me three times, but they hung up."

He sat on the porch steps next to her, putting a pair of large hands on his knees and releasing a big man's exhale. An hour passed by as they talked about her arrest, and all the different television and radio shows in which her case had been covered and discussed, and what Mexico was like and how it would be for Araceli to go back there if she were forced to do so. Not having lived in Mexico since he was eight years old, Felipe had a benign vision of the place as a land where uncles and grandparents lived on *ranchos* amid cows, horses, and poultry,

though he knew Mexico City was another world. "I've never been to El De Efe, but I remember Sonora as a beautiful place in the desert." Felipe had gone to school in the United States for the most part, Araceli now learned, and he spoke both English and Spanish impeccably. She prodded him to say something in English, and when he did she gave a mock shiver and said, "¡*Ay!* *Qué* sexy *eres* when you speak English." He was one of those people who moved easily back and forth between English- and Spanish-speaking orbits without being fully appreciated in either. With each minute they talked, Araceli heard more she liked. The sky began to surrender its glow, the lights turned on in the houses around them, and still they talked, stopping only when Luz Covarrubias stepped outside and gave them two glasses of *agua de tamarindo* and said, "*Qué bonito* to see a young man and a young woman talking so much on my porch."

Out of the awkward quiet that followed, the noise of an engine emerged, and soon Araceli and Felipe were watching as a blue van with a satellite dish turned the corner and parked behind Felipe's pickup.

"Oooh. *La prensa,*" Araceli said. "*Vámonos.*"

They rose to their feet, turned, and headed for the safety of the front door, but before they could escape Araceli heard a strangely familiar voice call out with the brio and accent of Mexico City's upper classes: "*¡Araceli! ¡No te me vas a escapar! ¡No te lo permito!*"

They turned simultaneously to face a man in a midnight-blue suit and yellow tie who was sitting in the van's passenger seat, with one leg hanging outside the open door. "Where have I seen that guy before?" Felipe said, though he was instantly recognizable to Araceli. He had a Mediterranean complexion and black-brown hair that was lightly moussed, and presented a sartorial package of male refinement so striking that Araceli could already imagine the cloud of sweet musk enveloping him, even though he was still on the other side of the lawn. Then his name came to her, and she spoke it out loud, the last of the nine Spanish and French syllables coming with the rising inflection of a question.

"*¿Carlos Francisco Batres Goulet?*"

"*¡El mismo!*" he said.

He was the second-most-famous man on Mexican television, the host of a morning news-talk show produced by a network with a near-monopoly on the Mexican airwaves. He walked up the path with an

outstretched hand, and Araceli straightened her spine as if to greet royalty, remembering the television set her mother had had going in the kitchen every workday, this man on the screen sitting on a studio couch engaging in casual repartee with rock stars, rebel leaders, and cabinet ministers, or in the field with the weeping families outside a mine disaster in Sonora, or wearing a yellow parka while awaiting a hurricane before the turquoise waters of the Yucatán. Carlos Francisco Batres Goulet was only a few years past thirty, but he was already a kind of walking history book, and as he reached over to shake Araceli's hand in greeting it was with the bearing of a benevolent, outgoing prince of the people.

"*Qué gusto conocerte,*" he said.

"*El gusto es mío,*" she mumbled back.

Carlos Francisco Batres Goulet had been in Malibu in the morning, having flown out from Mexico City to interview a Mexican actress who was a big crossover success in the United States. He had traveled to her recently purchased home, which cantilevered over a rocky stretch of the beach and the Pacific, and afterward he had phoned the network's headquarters in the San Ángel district of Mexico City to suggest an interview with the famous *paisana* who had been falsely accused of kidnapping. Now he entered the Covarrubias home with a greeting of "*¡Hola!*" and raised a palm in greeting to Octavio, who had stepped out of the bathroom with wet hands, and who now stood dumbstruck in his own living room.

"Carlos Francisco Batres Goulet?"

In a few moments, the newsman's crew began to fill the Covarrubias living room with lights and cables. Batres Goulet and his field producer had quickly decided Araceli would sit on the couch with the newsman facing her from a director's chair. With its faded purple cushions, and with the velvet painting behind it, the couch was an evocative symbol of Mexican working-class humility and bad taste, and both Batres Goulet and his producer knew the setting would resonate with their demographically diverse audience in many different ways. "You will sit here," he told Araceli in Spanish, making it sound more like an artistic inspiration than a command.

After the application of a few daubs of powder and makeup to both their faces, and a sound check, Batres Goulet began the interview. He smiled at her and addressed her with a gentle nod: "*Araceli Noemí*

Ramírez Hinojosa," he said, pronouncing her two given names and paternal and maternal surnames slowly and with the formality appropriate to the reading of an encyclopedia entry, as if recognizing her admission into Mexican celebritydom. Araceli heard the four names and thought about all the places in Mexico they would be broadcast: from her mother's kitchen, to the television next to the stacks of cigarettes in the *abarrote* sundry store on the corner in Nezahualcóyotl, to her father's village in Hidalgo and the little stands with small black-and-white televisions where children and men with machetes stopped to drink *atole* and watch the news, to the breakfast restaurants of Polanco in Mexico City, where businessmen would see her as they ate their *chilaquiles*.

". . . *es usted una criminal, tal como nos dicen las autoridades del estado de California?*"

"No," she answered, her face brightening with amusement, she was not a criminal, no matter what the California authorities said. "I am just a woman who came to this country to work and to do my job," she said in Spanish. "And I ended up getting in trouble for trying to do it."

Guided by Batres Goulet's gentle but skillful questioning, she explained the circumstances that had led her to leave the house with Brandon and Keenan, including the fight between her *patrones* and the broken coffee table, details that now became public for the first time.

"It sounds like chaos, this house you worked in."

"It was only that night and that weekend. For a long time they were good people to work for. *Exigente*, yes. Everything had to be a certain way, but I didn't mind that. You can imagine what it's like to work for a *norteamericano* family with as much money as these people have, and with good taste. The food was excellent. This woman I worked for, *la señora* Maureen, she has a great eye for a tomato. And in this country, it's harder to get a good tomato than back home. That I don't understand."

The newsman laughed out loud and brought a winning smile to Araceli's face, and for a moment she had the jolly look of a Mexican everywoman. He let her go on a bit more and then brought her back to the subject at hand.

"So the moment came when you decided to leave with these boys."

Araceli now explained, because she assumed most people in Mexico would not know, how it was that the American authorities took children from parents and put them in an institution called Foster Care.

"I had to decide. Between taking care of them or calling the police. Obviously, looking back, I should have called the police. Then the parents would be in trouble instead of me. I wish I had called the police!" She said this with a volume and vehemence that was unbecoming, and that bespoke her anger at being chased by the police, tackled on film, and tossed into jail—twice—and finally beaten, all for an act of selflessness. She mentioned all these indignities to Batres Goulet, though much of her harangue was never seen by the Mexican viewing public, because Batres Goulet and his field producer would later edit the three-minute segment to make Araceli look as sympathetic as possible. Her desire to protect Brandon and Keenan had only brought her trouble, she continued, and Araceli could see now that you survived in this country with a certain kind of coldness and distance from others. This was what people said back home about the United States, and it was a cruel thing to have seen that pearl of wisdom confirmed. "I don't even really like taking care of children," Araceli said. "But what was I going to do? *Los niños no tienen la culpa.* I couldn't let them go to the place where the *norteamericanos* take lost children. No."

"Is there a message you would like to send to your family back in Ciudad Neza?" Batres Goulet asked.

"I'm sorry I haven't called," she said with a casualness that suggested she was not sorry at all. That remark too would be cut from the broadcast.

Batres Goulet left the Covarrubias home, navigating through a crowd of about one hundred people that had gathered on the lawn, spilling over onto the sidewalk and around the van. News of his presence had spread quickly through the neighborhood, causing a sort of reverse effect of the appearance of the police on the day Araceli was rearrested. As long as Carlos Francisco Batres Goulet was among them, they sensed, his perfect skin and aura of Mexican television power would protect them, and they repeated the newsman's name with the reverent tones in which one spoke of holy places and holy people. "Carlos Francisco Batres Goulet . . . Carlos Francisco Batres Goulet." When he opened the front door and stood on the porch, there was a girl scream or two, and he waved at the crowd and shook some hands, and in two minutes he was gone and in his wake people still repeated his name.

"Carlos Francisco was here! Carlos Francisco Batres Goulet!"

Thirty minutes after the crowd and their chants had dispersed, Araceli was back on the porch with Felipe. They talked and joked in the restored evening quiet about the newsman and his visit, until the moment when a sport-utility vehicle rolled up and a semi-familiar face emerged at the head of a squad of suited men. The oldest of the men pulled at his lapels as he approached the steps, then gave a distracted "*Buenas noches*" as he peeked inside the Covarrubias home. "*¿Qué se hizo Batres Goulet?*" he asked.

"*Se fue,*" Araceli answered curtly. "*¿Y quién es usted?*"

"*Soy Emilio Ordaz Rivera,*" the man said with the odd, faraway grin of someone accustomed to having his greetings rejected. "*Soy el cónsul de México en Santa Ana.*"

Behind him stood three men who mimicked his general appearance, with dark sunglasses in their shirt pockets and cuff links and thin chains on their wrists, filling their tailored gray and black suits with the self-important bearing of men groomed from an early age for glory in Mexico's federal bureaucracy. They were pelted animals that had been baking all day in the California sun at a pointless community function, and judging from the ennui painted thickly on their faces, they thought these surroundings too were somehow beneath them.

"I was hoping he was still here. So I could contribute a little to the story."

"You wanted to be on television? With me?"

"Yes."

"Why?"

The consul lowered his voice and spoke in her ear, with a deliberate frankness that he thought of as a kind of intimacy. "Why does anyone want to be on Televisa? Because it's Televisa, of course."

The consul was in midcareer mire, looking for something more glamorous than Santa Ana, because he was thirty-eight years old and was losing the battle with time and the byzantine hierarchies of the Foreign Relations Ministry. A year earlier, they had offered him the number two position in the embassy in Tegucigalpa, Honduras, and like an idiot he had turned it down, because it seemed that being inside the Southern California media market would be better, but he could see now that the consul in Los Angeles got all the press, all the photo ops with the starlets and the meetings with the visiting ministers. He'd

even take the number two spot in Lagos now, if they offered him that, anywhere but Santa Ana, with its long lines of desperate and poor people, where the most important thing he did was ship home the bodies of *paisanos* killed in car accidents, roofing mishaps.

Araceli did not know about the longings and insecurities of the overeducated, frustrated, poetically inclined career diplomats of the Secretaría de Relaciones Exteriores, but she could feel this man's desperation to please his superiors and to be noticed, even as she and Felipe retreated to the living room, closing the door as the consul squeezed in one last plea.

"Call me if Batres Goulet comes back!"

24

Araceli had told herself she wouldn't look at the crowds, and as she ascended the courthouse stairs with Ruthy Bacalan, she kept her gaze fixed downward, using a hand to shield her eyes from the sun. When she raised her head for an instant, a flash of black-and-white caught her eye, a poster of an enlarged X-ray of a skull with a rod running through the middle. There was a caption that meant to explain the image, but did not: KILLED BY ILLEGALS. She looked at the protesters grouped behind and around the X-ray and saw a tired-looking woman in a nurse's uniform holding it up, and alongside her stood a group of men and women clutching at various pieces of red-white-and-blue fabric, shouting at Araceli and shaking their fists, raising the volume because she had deigned to look at them. They carried other signs that were just words: MEXICO = DISEASE + DEATH + DESTRUCTION. They screamed "Go home!" to Araceli and also to the group of counterprotesters standing to her left, and now Araceli followed their shouts to study this other group too. Araceli recognized a few people from the gathering at the church where she had failed to give a speech, and they were all holding posters composed of a ridiculous photograph taken when she was about to be arrested for the second time. There were ten two-dimensional

Aracelis bouncing on the staircase, and she thought that she should turn and raise her finger and open her mouth in silent imitation of her pose in that impromptu portrait—that would be a good joke—but she stopped herself when she remembered she was standing on the steps of a courthouse and should respect its solemn function even though the competing bands of protesters were not. A policeman took a step toward the flag people, walking down and across the wide staircase, his arms outstretched, saying, "Keep back!" She had a moment to think how unusual that was, to have a policeman protecting her, and looked to her left when she heard someone yelling her name: a young woman was swinging a Mexican flag back and forth, and Araceli caught the eagle in the coat of arms and thought her *bandera* seemed awfully medieval next to the Stars and Stripes on the other side. As for the United States flag, she didn't understand why so many stripes and stars were crowded into such a small space. *That flag is written in English.* Both sides seemed to be held back by some invisible boundary, allowing Araceli and her attorney to advance in the wide path between them, and Araceli wondered if there was a line drawn on the steps to keep them back, like the Chinese chalk she scratched on the floor underneath the cabinets and inside the closets to keep away the ants on Paseo Linda Bonita. There were a few more students in the group of people who had come to support her, people in their twenties it seemed, their lithe frames inside bright and seductive cottons. Their expressions were wounded and aggrieved, like children who've been betrayed by alcoholic parents. Araceli thought they looked handsome and dignified next to the older and less lithe red-white-and-blue crowd, who all seemed to share the outrage and embittered superiority of good people who've been victimized by slum-born criminals.

Suddenly, the woman in the light green nurse's uniform crossed the invisible line and rushed toward her, causing Ruthy Bacalan to scream, "Hey!"

"Tell the truth!" Janet Bryson screamed a few inches from Araceli's face, and then she uttered the first complete sentence she had ever spoken in Spanish, a four-word phrase she had manufactured herself with the aid of an Internet translation program: "¡Diga la verdad, usted! ¡Diga la verdad, usted!"

Standing on the other side of the steps, Giovanni Lozano watched

in outrage as the woman in green verbally assaulted his martyr-hero, and now he too crossed the invisible line and rushed toward Araceli, reaching out to push Janet Bryson away. A man of about forty in a bus driver's uniform shirt rushed forward to grab Giovanni, and in seconds the two groups had merged into a single mass of vocal cords and flexing muscles on the staircase behind Araceli and her lawyer. Ruthy Bacalan grabbed Araceli by the elbow and said, "Almost there," as they reached the top of the stairs and stepped between a grunting squad of sheriff's deputies heading down into the crowd with batons drawn, and a moment later Araceli and Ruthy entered the still quiet of the new Laguna Niguel satellite courthouse and its concrete plaza.

Surrounded by palms and a crowd of briefcases and the men and women who carried them, the building's faux-Mission architecture and terra-cotta tile roof suggested a resort where lawyers came to unwind. Araceli and Ruthy joined the line of barristers and passed through the center of three tall arches and headed toward a glass door, where a group of men and women with cameras formed a phalanx. *They've come to photograph me again*, Araceli thought, and she raised her head and gave them a good look at her *mestiza* face. But only one of the photographers stepped forward to snap her picture, with all the others looking behind her, causing her to turn to see what had caught their attention, but there was only the empty concrete plaza she had just walked through. She was vaguely disappointed and felt a brief and absurd sense of rejection. *What? There's another celebrity* mexicana *bigger than me? Who is she? A serial killer? She must have done something very, very bad.*

Araceli swung open the last set of glass doors, and she and Ruthy Bacalan stepped into the courthouse and its icy air.

When Olivia Garza was twelve, a Kern County social worker visited her home. Young Olivia was impressed by the ability of a woman armed with mere plastic credentials to put the fear of God and the law in her father, who never again got quite as drunk or angry. In the years that followed, her mother was never again forced to visit an emergency room on a Saturday night with her children in tow, leading Olivia the young woman to conclude that she wanted to become that person—a stranger who could wield the power of reason and the law over a family

in their own living room. After she went to college and joined Orange County Child Protective Services, she came to realize that there were certain mothers who had seen her in their dreams long before they had met her, because they too had been girls who watched a stranger with a clipboard step into their living room. As Olivia Garza entered Paseo Linda Bonita alone for the first time, she sensed that Maureen was one of these people—it was the peculiar air of recognition and fear about her, the sense that she was being forced to repeat a very old and demeaning family ritual.

"Is it just you?" Maureen asked as she guided Olivia toward a large, long dining room table with a platter in the center. "We made you some cupcakes. The kids decorated them."

Maureen had been preparing for the scheduled arrival of the representative of Child Protective Services for two days, drafting everyone in the family but Samantha into the cleaning of the home, and then including Samantha in the final spreading of cupcake frosting and sprinkles, which allowed Maureen to announce to the social worker that "even our little girl helped with these." *El abuelo* Torres had cut the front lawn—again—Brandon swept the path, Keenan helped clean his sister's room, Scott finished the bathrooms, and Maureen had wandered into the succulent garden to pick the tiny explosions of milkweed and sow thistles. It was like the preparation for another birthday party, except that Araceli wasn't around to help this time, which left Maureen more frazzled than she would have been otherwise, and the boys sulking, because they didn't like the idea of "working," since that was something grown-ups did. "Are we slaves now?" Brandon asked his mother, who did not hear him. *If the social worker knew my mom had me sweeping,* Brandon wondered, *and that my hands will soon have blisters from holding that broom and that rake, would it get us all in trouble?*

When Olivia Garza arrived, Brandon and Keenan greeted her in the living room with freshly combed and moist hair, and their hands in their pockets, in a loose approximation of soldiers standing at attention, until their mother told them they could go to their room to read while the adults talked in the dining room. Maureen brought coffee and sat at the table next to her husband, and Olivia felt compelled to reach over and take a cupcake. "Thank you," she said. Looking at the couple and at the baby who was sitting on her mother's lap with frosting on her worm-sized fingers, Olivia Garza asked, "So, how have you been doing?"

Maureen kneaded her lips and looked down at the oak table and the Guatemalan embroidered place mats that covered the freshly polished surface, and said nothing because she was trying very hard to convey her mastery over the situation, and saying just one word about how she was "feeling" would unleash her emotions and set them off to entertain this stranger. As she blinked against the tears welling in her eyes, she did not know, or intuit, that Olivia Garza had arrived at the conclusion that this family's essential normality posed no threat to its children, and that she would soon make the final entry in the case file before formally closing it. It was a decision she'd arrived at moments earlier, in a burst of insight triggered by seeing this living room without police detectives or district attorneys for the first time. She could now *feel* this home and see it properly. And what she saw was a mother whose only crime was trying too hard.

"We're okay," Scott said finally. "Just trying to get back to normal."

There was just one topic to cover, the most recent entry in the file, and Olivia Garza jumped straight to it. It was an allegation of domestic violence related to an open case, and she had to ask.

"So, tell me a little about what happened that night with the table. With the argument you had. The argument that set all this off."

"How did you know about that?" Scott asked quickly.

"The woman who used to work here mentioned it last night on Spanish-language television." Maureen's forehead and cheeks suddenly matched the color of her daughter's blouse. "No one told you? It was on Channel 34, but I'm pretty sure it was mentioned later on cable in English."

"We've been screening calls," Maureen said.

"I imagine it's the table that used to occupy that spot right there," Olivia Garza said, pointing to an empty rectangle of tiles framed by two couches.

"I fell backwards," Maureen said.

"Because I pushed her." Scott sensed he could not lie to this woman who carried a clipboard but wrote nothing down, and who seemed to study everything with a neutral expression. If he lied, she would know, and this would send them into new and ever more tortuous predicaments.

"We were arguing," Maureen said. "It got out of hand."

"Yes."

"It's never happened before," Maureen continued. "We never had a fight like that before. He's not a violent person. It's not the way he handles things."

"I'm a programmer."

"He's a gentle person. I said things. We were just stressed out over money."

"It's not a good situation, the money."

In the course of fifteen minutes all the truth fell into the room. Scott began by laying out the details of their finances: how much they had purchased their home for, the cost of their two sons' private school, how they had spent more because of certain complications in Maureen's pregnancy, and the loss of expected income from investments that "didn't pan out." Maureen was struck by the blunt math of it all; Scott had told her these things in parts, but she had never understood it altogether, how complex and rooted their financial follies were. Together, she saw now, they suffered from a disease of outlook in a chronic and advanced stage, a bloated and myopic way of life.

Scott arrived, finally, at the argument over the garden and the moment he laid hands on his wife. "I just lost it. It was an instant. She was on the floor. The next morning we both left. Separately. I guess Araceli cleaned everything up."

"I went to the desert," Maureen said. "Alone. With my daughter." The sound of her own contrition surprised her. *No, I am conceding too much.* "But Araceli shouldn't have taken them into the city. If she had just waited a day longer."

The social worker nodded, and for the first time scribbled something on her notepad: a sentence, a phrase, a conclusion, an "assessment."

"You mind if I go talk to your boys, alone, for just a minute or two?"

Scott led Olivia Garza to the space Araceli had called the Room of a Thousand Wonders, where Keenan was on his bed reading a graphic novel modeled after a fictitious boy's diary, while Brandon read a little paperback, his stomach on the floor, though he sat up straight at the sight of the social worker.

"I'll leave you, then," Scott said.

"Thank you."

Olivia Garza greeted the boys and pointed at their bookcase. "So many books. You guys read all these?"

"Most of 'em," Brandon said.

"We had more, but Mom threw them away," Keenan said.

"No," Brandon said, giving his brother a hard look. "She gave them to the poor kids' library."

"We read a lot," Keenan said.

"Me too," Olivia Garza said. "When I went to college, I took some classes in reading, though they don't call it that there. They call it literature." The social worker mentioned some of her favorite books, including a thirteen-volume series about the fantastic misadventures of three siblings who retain their innocent spirits and optimistic outlook even as they are orphaned and wander through a cruel adult world.

"I read all those twice," Brandon said. "They're really funny."

Talking to children was the hardest thing in the world to do, and the aim in these "interviews," Olivia Garza had learned long ago, was not the soliciting of information, but rather a sounding of the waters of the subjects' moods and fears, a passive probing of their dispositions. To her practiced eye these boys communicated both intellectual curiosity and a touch of the loneliness that was entirely common in well-off families. And perhaps a little preadolescent ennui from the older one. If they had been traumatized by the flight of their parents, and their journey into Los Angeles, it was not immediately apparent.

"What are you reading now?" she asked Brandon. He showed her the cover of the paperback and then handed it to her in the same way a teenager surrenders a pack of cigarettes to a school principal. "Wow, a classic. This is an advanced book for your age."

"I'm a pretty good reader."

"But do you understand everything that's in it?"

"About eighty percent. No, ninety. When I get to a part I don't get, I just pretend the words don't exist."

"Interesting."

"That way I keep going."

"I should learn to do that."

"It's like the best book I've ever read. It's really real. Next to that, everything else I've read sounds kind of phony."

Olivia was holding the book and leafing through it when Maureen appeared at the doorway, holding Samantha and trying too hard to project an air of motherly nonchalance.

"Is everything okay?" she said with a smile.

"Yes, yes. We were just talking about the book Brandon was reading. What page did you say you were on, Brandon?"

"Ninety-three."

"Do you mind if I borrow this for a second? I'll give it right back, I promise."

Olivia Garza said goodbye to the boys and left the Room of a Thousand Wonders with Maureen.

"Is everything okay?" Maureen repeated when they reached the living room, because she sensed they were not.

The social worker held open the book to page ninety-three and gave it to her. "I'm not sure he's quite old enough for this. And especially passages like this one."

Maureen took the copy of *The Catcher in the Rye*, a book she had never read, though she knew the name of its protagonist. The social worker's thick index finger had been resting on a page where Holden Caulfield was using the cool slang of the middle of the last century, smoking cigarettes and preparing to talk to a prostitute: "She was sort of a blonde, but you could tell she dyed her hair. She wasn't any old bag, though." Just a few pages later the protagonist was talking to her pimp, arguing with the man, the narrator's voice suggesting the casualness and loose morality of an ancient American era.

"Oh, my God. Why is he even reading this? Where did he get this?"

Maureen held the book and looked at the representative of Child Protective Services, and felt the weight of a judgment that was at once holy and official. Her shame deepened when she realized that the social worker had discovered this transgression after just fifteen minutes of conversation with her son. COUNTY OF ORANGE, said the official seal on the social worker's plastic badge: three pieces of the eponymous fruit rested in a green field that itself was nestled inside the center of a sun ablaze with a corona of dancing yellow arms, and for an instant that seal was as disturbing as those dusty old icons of Saint Patrick in her Missouri home, the ones with the snakes at his feet and flames around his head. Her eleven-year-old was consorting with pimps and prostitutes, having been transported to a seamy corner of Manhattan via the art of fiction, and he was doing so in Maureen's very house, in her very presence. *Because I am not really looking at him. I am not here in the*

room with him. Now the saints that looked after the Irish and the County of Orange both knew this secret.

"I'm so sorry. I'm so sorry," Maureen said, directing her words not just to the social worker but to everyone she knew. "I thought I was in control of everything. I thought I had it all under control."

Underneath all the order and beauty around me, things are not as they should be. I've glossed it all over so it doesn't look like Pike County, but underneath everything is just as frayed as that old couch in our living room, as those unpolished and splintering floors. She felt foolish for expending so much effort uselessly, and when she thought of herself puttering around this living room amid its leather, oak, and wool, she felt an empty sorrow, as if she were standing at the beginning of a dirt path that led back to the places she had run away from. "I'm so sorry." She plopped herself down on the sofa, still carrying Samantha on her hip. She wanted to cry, but could not. Instead she sat there, defeated, and thought about how Brandon had betrayed her, and that she shouldn't be surprised, because he was a man, after all: and then she stopped herself from thinking that, because he was eleven years old and that was absurd. *This is why women go crazy. We live with men who act like boys and boys who want to be men, and we're trapped between what we know is right and what little we can do, between what we can see and what's invisible to us. It's all impossible.* She shook her head and mumbled the word out loud. "Impossible."

"It's not really that big of a deal," Olivia Garza said, reaching into her purse and handing Maureen a tissue from the large supply she carried.

Maureen realized now that there were tears in her eyes. She wiped her face and began to speak, in a voice that was eerily steady. "We are going to change."

"Excuse me?" Olivia Garza said.

"We're moving. To a smaller house."

"Maureen," Scott said. He wanted to stop his wife before she went too far, because she always took things too far.

"We're going to put our kids in public school. In another city." It was a necessary sacrifice, Maureen thought. A surrender. A defeat. They would leave their Eden, and that would be a fair punishment. "If they go to public school, if we live in a smaller house, how much will we save? Twenty, thirty thousand a year? No, more. Right?"

"Yes," Scott said. He felt defeated seeing his wife like this—fighting off tears one moment, and then telling a stranger about a new beginning the next. *I am responsible for this.* In a few weeks or months, when they were living at another house, she would come to the same conclusion, regret all the things she had said, and find a way to blame him for it.

"Well, that sounds all very positive to me," Olivia Garza said. "But don't worry. We don't take away kids because their parents let them read Salinger." She allowed herself a hearty, big woman's laugh. "I really just thought you should know what he's reading. I think it's just the tone—that's what he likes about it. He told me he just skips over the parts he doesn't understand. The rebellious tone. Get ready. Puberty hits earlier these days."

Scott led her to the door, and after what he hoped was a final hand-shake, the social worker pulled him close and spoke in a low, furtive voice.

"You have nothing to worry about," she said.

"What?"

"I'm not supposed to say this, but I will: my office won't bother you anymore. And no one else can or will. Not the sheriff or the DA. No one."

"Really?"

She took a moment to size up Scott with her large eyes, wondering if he could be trusted with the information. "Go about your lives. But I never said it. You didn't hear it from me."

"We're free and clear? Why are you are telling me?"

"You're a smart guy, Torres," she said, rolling the *r* in his surname suggestively. "I'm sure you'll figure it out."

It was another mystery, like how to cut a lawn cleanly, or the rules of the stock market, and Scott wondered if he'd ever understand. For the moment, he decided he'd keep it a secret, even from Maureen.

The following morning Child Protective Services issued a two-sentence press release concerning "the events surrounding two children at a home on Paseo Linda Bonita in the Laguna Rancho Estates." "CPS has investigated this matter," the release said, "and has closed the case without further action." The memo was transmitted to news agencies via the press office at the Board of Supervisors, falling into the report-ers' mail slots along with releases from other agencies announcing the

unemployment figures, the number of county residents receiving public assistance, and the upcoming celebration of Orange County Weights
and Measures Day. By then only a few dedicated scribes noticed or cared,
and just one penned a news brief that appeared alongside the summa-
ries of traffic accidents and robberies in the Orange County daily newspaper. The minds and eyes of the reporters on the county beat had been
spirited away by another drama, playing out on four channels of the
county press room's cable television hookup. This new story involved a
single missing child and had begun to unfold the previous afternoon in
Stanton at about the same time Olivia Garza was leaving the Torres-
Thompson home and Araceli Noemí Ramírez Hinojosa was sitting before
a judge inside the Laguna Niguel satellite courthouse. The protagonists
were a missing eight-year-old girl in a Hello Kitty blouse and her stepmother, an elementary school teacher, and the supporting cast included
crews of divers searching the bottom of a lake. It was a case whose
cruelty and gruesomeness would invite no ambiguity, uniting a city in a
sense of tragedy and revulsion once the child's body was found.

The dead girl had four siblings whose custody would soon become
Olivia Garza's concern, along with the fate of the level one caseworker
who had visited the trailer park where the girl lived twice the year before to investigate several anonymous complaints. Olivia Garza fired the
caseworker herself, and visited the siblings in their Foster Care homes
several times. Many weeks later, after her role in that horrific case had
ended, Olivia Garza remembered her pleasant visit with the Torres-
Thompson boys on Paseo Linda Bonita and how she had reencountered
The Catcher in the Rye again, after twenty years. She read the book on
her first Saturday afternoon off and decided, belatedly, that it was probably okay for a bright eleven-year-old to read.

25

The ants marched in from their hidden nests in the soil outside and every day they conquered new territories of tile, particleboard, and porcelain. They gathered in pulsating masses around pieces of chicken underneath the dining room table, over the toilet paper in the bathroom trash cans, and inside the kitchen sink, carrying away whatever it was that settled at the bottom of the garbage disposal. As the number of days without Araceli in their home grew, Maureen came upon more fresh swarms each morning, when Scott was still snoring in the last few minutes of post-dawn coolness, with Samantha awake and in her mother's arms, drinking her first bottle of the day. At first Maureen assaulted the insects with water and soap, simply smothering them with wet sponges and paper towels, reclaiming the kitchen and other spaces a square foot at a time, washing both their corpses and their still-slithering bodies down the drain. Within a day the effectiveness of this fight back diminished and the swarms returned in their original ferocity. The ants appeared next in the bedrooms and garage, and in the kitchen there were always two or three ant scouts on the counter where she prepared meals, probing in every direction in an odd shuffle, until she killed them with a squeeze of her fingers. *How did Araceli keep the ants away?*

The ants triggered memories of the time before Araceli worked for

them, in that first year in the Paseo Linda Bonita home, when the trails
the insects forged into the kitchen during a summer-long siege led
Maureen to briefly consider moving out. It was her helplessness before the ants that had finally convinced Maureen she should hire a
housekeeper, and she had gone through various women who struggled
with the insects as much as Maureen did, until she found Araceli. Now
Maureen suspected that Araceli had secretly applied some potent and
probably illegal Third World insecticide to defeat the ants, deciding on
her own to disobey Maureen's admonition not to use chemical poisons.
For a day or two Maureen searched cabinets and shelves in the kitchen,
laundry room, and garage for the bottle or can that contained this magic
potion, but she could not find it. Araceli had defeated the ants, Maureen finally concluded, merely by being extremely vigilant, by never flag-
ging in the disciplined daily upkeep of all the ant-prone surfaces of
the home, by never allowing garbage to accumulate, or spills to linger.
Maureen did not have the energy to imitate this behavior, nor did her
new domestic helper, her father-in-law. The old man cooked, he looked
after the children—sort of—and made the beds, but he would not clean
the floors, no matter how many hints Maureen dropped. *Probably he
thinks mopping a floor is women's work.*

Maureen finally mopped the kitchen, bathroom, and living room
floors herself one night, with Samantha asleep and Scott reading stories
to the boys in their bedroom, and for a moment she felt renewed by the
fake-lemon scent of disinfectant and the wet gleam of clean tile. As she
leaned into the mop Maureen noted the presence of fading chalk lines
along the base of several walls and wondered if Araceli had placed them
there for some reason, and what those lines could mean. They were like
crop circles, an apparition with mysterious and alien meanings, and another example of Araceli's many minor imprints on the household landscape, like her decision to save instant-coffee powder in the refrigerator,
or to leave basil leaves in a bowl of water by the kitchen window. *Basil?
Is that some sort of cure? But for what?* Maureen wiped out the chalk lines
with the same desperate insistence that a student uses in erasing an
incorrect math equation on a chalkboard.

When Maureen awoke the morning after her first assault with the
mop, it was with the anticipation of ant-free surfaces. Instead she found
a new trail entering the kitchen through one of the light fixtures and
splitting into two branches, one crossing the room to the pantry, where

the ants were devouring a loaf of stale French bread. Yet another trail entered from the backyard underneath one of the sliding glass doors, across the former path of one of Araceli's chalk lines, and Maureen followed it to the remains of a dead grasshopper that had somehow been trapped behind one of the bookcases. *This is more than I can take.* She could not look at the sickening nodes of their dirt-colored bodies a moment longer. Several times a day, she felt one or two crawling on her legs and arms, racing for her neck and breasts, and she fantasized about finding their colony's nest, and bringing some cataclysmic destruction upon it that would end ant culture and ant history on this hillside. Finally, that afternoon, she stood in a supermarket aisle she always tried to avoid, and purchased two different cans of poison. When she got home she was so desperate to see the chemicals work that she didn't bother to get the children out of the house before she began spraying.

In the evening Maureen had rearmed herself with the spray can, determined to find any ant scouts or trails that had escaped her initial offensive, and was wandering the various rooms of the house when the phone rang.

Scott answered in the kitchen. "Hello, Mr. Goller," he said, and Maureen listened, watching as he spoke in profile, either unaware or unconcerned that she was eavesdropping.

"No. We're not going to do that . . . We really don't want to be there. No. We've made our statements . . . You go ahead and do that, and we'll be there if you force us to. And you know what: we're pretty clear on exactly what happened . . . Meaning that we left separately and didn't . . . If you'd just let me finish . . . Well, I guess you could say that, but I'm past being embarrassed now . . . No, neither will my wife . . . Right . . . Child Protective Services was already here . . . It was a very nice visit . . . Well, I got the distinct impression we don't have anything to worry about . . . I'm sorry, Mr. Goller . . . I think that would be an injustice, Mr. Goller. Supremely unfair, for reasons that should be clear without me having to say why . . . I understand what the laws are, yes . . . I have to go, Mr. Goller . . . Kids, you know, and dinner . . . Good-bye, Mr. Goller . . . Goodbye."

For the first time since that night he'd pushed her, Maureen allowed her eyes to settle and linger upon her husband. He was as exhausted as she was, but also completely in the present, his eyes pale brown embers giving off the same serene and low-burning glow of a

woman in the days after childbirth. *Men don't often look like that.*
Scott had somehow understood, from one moment to the next, that
they were no longer at the mercy of the melodramatic machinery of the
media and the criminal justice system. It had hit him, Maureen sensed,
with a eureka suddenness and intensity, like the solution to a programming conundrum. *These prosecutors and bureaucrats have no power over
us. None. Because we haven't done anything wrong. We're just as innocent
as Araceli. Aren't we?* Every so often her husband did something brilliant like this, shifting his thinking as easily as he might shift his posture or his feet, finding a solution suddenly falling into his arms, simply
because he'd stepped out of the box of a problem and examined it in an
entirely different light. *That's something he can do that I cannot.*

Looking at him, she began to see the possibility that the original,
simple, and indefinable feelings that drew her to him might return.

"Is it over now?" she asked.

"I think it is."

"Really?"

"I don't think he'll be calling us again."

"Thank God."

She was still holding the yellow can whose steel skin was emblazoned with drawings of bugs and a thousand words of warning in mi-
nuscule fonts.

After several visits to courtrooms, police stations, and jail-
houses, Araceli now understood that Americans associated justice with
two dominant architectural styles: the austere cement cubes where
walls, floors, ceilings, and passageways blended into a single smooth
surface; or the woody hominess of dark paneling that suggested shad-
owy forests of mystery. This new Laguna Niguel satellite courthouse
had a bit of both, and the mood was as somber as those other places,
despite the presence of large Latino families with children sitting on
some of the benches in the hallways and playing with toy cars and dolls.
The look on the faces of the mothers and wives said, *This is where I
come to say goodbye to my* viejo. Adiós, pendejo, *and yeah, I'll look after
the kids, because what the fuck else can I do?* This was a place, Araceli
understood, where the damned were released temporarily from their
dungeons to intermingle with the undamned. The presence of the in-

mate fathers and brothers in their shackles and jumpsuits sent everyone around them into a funk. The gloom was there to see in the faces of the mothers and the daughters, the judges and the lawyers, including Deputy District Attorney Arnold Chang and Ruthy Bacalan, who had lost the sheen of pregnancy on her cheeks and looked older somehow as she took a seat with Araceli at a table before the judge. There was sadness too in the look of pained exertion on the face of the first witness of Araceli's preliminary hearing, a police officer she had never met before.

Deputy Ernie Suarez was not dressed in police clothing as he sat in the witness box, but rather in jeans and a collared short-sleeve cotton shirt that revealed his rather excessive musculature. He wore a small loop earring that was meant to convey masculinity, but whose effect, Araceli decided, was completely the opposite. Only the badge on his belt identified him as a member of the tribe of law enforcement.

"You are, at the moment, working?" the prosecutor asked by way of explanation.

"Yes."

"Are you working as what they call an 'undercover' officer at the moment?"

"Yes, sir."

"What is this, 'undercover'?" Araceli whispered to Ruthy. It didn't sound good.

"I'll tell you later."

"At the time of the incident involving the Torres-Thompson children, you were a patrol officer assigned to the Laguna Rancho area, correct?"

"Yes."

Guided by the prosecutor's questions, Deputy Suarez proceeded to tell the story of his arrival at Paseo Linda Bonita, of the "distraught" state in which he found Maureen and Scott, and his search of their home for clues of the boys' whereabouts, and how Maureen paced and held the baby.

"Had the defendant left any communication of any kind with the parents?"

"We didn't find any note or message of any kind, sir, no."

"So the parents had no idea where their children were?"

"That's correct, sir. And they were pretty shaken up about it."

Listening to the deputy, Araceli saw the events inside the home on Paseo Linda Bonita that day through the eyes of Maureen and Scott for

the first time. Her employers were adrift and afraid in that orderly house Araceli had left behind for them. *I cleaned the sinks before I left, but I didn't think of the most obvious thing: to leave behind a note. I made a mess of things as much as they did.*

As the court session moved on, Araceli could see the prosecutor was building a tale of foreboding around her acts of naïveté and stupidity. The deputy district attorney was a short man in boxy, scuffed black shoes, and a tie that was knotted too loosely. Now he began to fiddle with a computer and a projector, and raised a screen inside the empty jury box. An image appeared on the screen, a video from a Union Station surveillance camera that showed Araceli, Brandon, and Keenan, seen from an eye high above the waiting area, the shiny floors reflecting the atrium daylight into an odd glare, so that Araceli and the boys stood in a menacing glow. The prosecutor had a sheriff's detective state the video's provenance and act as narrator. "The defendant enters the frame at one forty-five p.m. . . . You can see the victims walked in after her . . ."

"Were you able to determine if the two boys have any relatives in the vicinity of that station?"

"To the best of our knowledge, they have no relative within thirty miles of the station."

The video representation of Araceli turned her head in several directions, mulling which direction to take as the boys studied the high ceilings above them. Video Araceli walked away and out of the range of the camera without saying anything to them and they followed after her. Araceli looked at that footage and saw what everyone else did: an impatient woman who never wanted to take care of children, who rushed out of the home without leaving a note because she was too anxious to be rid of them. The video doomed her. *Am I really that selfish and mean?* But how had she allowed herself to be placed in such a predicament in the first place? *You are going the wrong way, woman! Go back to the house and wait!* Why was she always at the mercy of other people? Seeing this stupid woman projected on the screen, Araceli felt an impotent rage that made her want to stand up and shout in Spanglish, *I am a pendeja! Looking for the grandfather?* ¡Pendeja! But she said nothing, and slumped back in her chair suddenly and folded her arms, and shook her head with silent violence. "What's wrong?" Ruthy Bacalan asked. *They are going to put that woman in the video back in jail and then send*

her home with plastic ties around her wrists because she is a callous sim-pleton. Araceli fought to hold back the water welling behind her eyes; she couldn't let these people see her cry. *Now I understand why there are all these boxes of tissues in the courtroom.* There was one box on the table before her, another perched on the railing where the witnesses stood, two more in the empty seats of the jury box. *People come to cry here. To see their follies projected on a screen, and then to weep.*

The prosecutor turned off the video, the deputy left the courtroom, and the next witness entered the courtroom.

Detective Blake marched down the gallery aisle like a middle-aged man in a hurry, rose to the stand, said "Yeah, I do" in response to the oath, and plopped down into the witness chair. He was soon asked to relate Brandon's tale of his journey with Araceli.

"The neighborhood this boy described to you," the prosecutor began. "Would you say it bore a general resemblance to the neighborhood near the intersection of Thirty-ninth and South Broadway?"

"Very general. Yes."

"What did Brandon tell you about that place?"

"That it was dirty and grimy. That a lot of people came and went there. That he heard a man screaming. That he slept on the floor, next to a child who was a slave, or an orphan, or something like that."

"On the floor, next to an orphan?"

"Yes."

"Did he say anything about seeing people with scars on their faces?"

"Yes."

When the prosecutor had finished, Ruthy Bacalan rose to begin her cross-examination. She was dressed in her own idiosyncratic version of summer courtroom dress: a white jacket with gold-braided epaulets on the shoulders, and wide white pants and white sandals, an outfit that suggested she had come to represent a defendant being brought on trial before the captain of a luxury cruise liner.

"Generally speaking, during the hour or so you spent with Brandon, did he seem frightened to you?" she asked the detective.

"No."

"Did he appear intimidated by his experience with the defendant?"

"No. Probably the opposite."

"The opposite?"

"Yeah, he seemed like he was having fun telling his story. It was all sort of, uh, fantastical to him. 'Magical' is the word, I guess."

"And how much of that story were you able to verify?"

"Excuse me?"

"Did you make any effort to find out how much of Brandon's story was true? For example, did you find anyone who looked like they had been through a war, like the, quote, 'refugees' Brandon mentioned?"

"You mean, did we find the war refugees Brandon told us about?"

"Yes."

"No." For the first time, the detective dropped his guard and grinned. "Didn't know where to start looking for them."

"Brandon also mentioned something about time travel. In a train."

"Yes."

"Able to verify that?"

"We punted on the time travel, ma'am."

From her chair, Araceli felt the mood in the courtroom turning light, inconsequential. The judge rolled his eyes—twice! *My Ruthy is winning!* The prosecutor was starting to look ill, he was grabbing the table before him with two hands, as if the building were shifting, very slowly, and the floor of the courtroom were suddenly afloat and tossed about by rough seas. "Brandon said his brother had been, quote, 'holding fire,' unquote. Did you find any burns on Keenan Torres-Thompson's hands?"

"No, ma'am."

"Did you find any fires burning underneath the surface of the earth?"

"Excuse me."

"It's in the statement. Brandon says he saw a fire burning in the ground."

"There was a pig cooked, apparently. At the home in Huntington Park."

"And what about the, quote, superhero? Mr. Ray Forma?"

"We were able to ascertain, to a high degree of certainty, that there have been no sightings of any such man."

On the bench, the judge gave a bemused smirk that matched the one on the face of the detective.

"No further questions, Your Honor."

Ray Forma sounded like a stage name to Araceli. There was a student she knew in art school who worked as a clown for children's parties and called himself Re-Gacho. "Really Uncool" was a typical Mexico

City clown who amused and annoyed in equal measures, harassing the moms with double entendres that their kids didn't understand. Yes, Re-Gacho would fit perfectly in this courtroom, where even the bailiff looked grateful for the brief levity of superheroes and time machines at the end of a day of slogging through the calendar. Cover the oak with red and yellow streamers, bring out the balloons, and put a big top hat on the judge. *Qué divertido.*

"The People rest, Your Honor," the prosecutor said, causing the judge's face to come alive again with a sparkle of astonishment. The judge was a balding man with a sallow complexion and a fringe of white hair: up until that moment, he had maintained a temperament of studied even-ness and congeniality. The judge considered the seated prosecutor for an instant, and then his face collapsed into a mask of disapproval, as if the exit doors had been thrown open inside a darkened theater, inter-rupting a bad movie and revealing the sticky, trash-strewn aisles.

"That's it?"

"Yes, Your Honor."

"Ms. Bacalan. I see you have one witness," the judge said after a pause. "Is he here, by any chance?"

"No, Your Honor. I didn't anticipate the prosecutor cutting short his witness list."

"Right. So, tomorrow at nine a.m.?"

"Yes, Your Honor," Ruthy and the prosecutor said in unison.

Sitting in the last row of the gallery with his legs crossed, Assistant District Attorney Ian Goller fixed a dagger stare at Madame Weirdness, the Mexican woman who could make his life easier by making the ra-tional choice and taking the plea bargain. In his desire to avoid defeat he had assembled a squad of attorneys and investigators dedicated to keeping alive the machinery of case AB5387516, in the hope that he would eventually pressure this stubborn woman to accept the inevita-ble. But as he watched the defendant leaving the courtroom behind her attorney, Ian Goller realized she would not give up. Araceli Ramirez was a Mexican national with nothing going for her but a strong work ethic, apparently, and lived unaware of her powerlessness relative to your average American-born resident of Orange County. She owned no prop-erty and had no social security number or credit rating, but walked past him like an exiled empress in denim and sneakers because she inhab-ited another, Spanish-speaking reality where those things didn't matter,

a world of people happy with the plebeian pleasures of hurdy-gurdy music and pickup trucks. The assistant district attorney knew, in fact, that there was a pickup with a driver waiting for the defendant in the parking lot. Goller had that information thanks to the investigator he'd assigned to track her movements—an egregious misuse of scarce resources—but the assistant district attorney only now realized how unhealthy his obsession with this case had become. Could it ever be a bad thing to want to win, Goller wondered, when the side you were on was called *the People*? He wanted this woman to make the rational calculation of a defeated American criminal, but of course she would not. His experience with the Mexicans that crossed his path was that they expected the worst and were immovable once they latched on to the idea that the DA's plea offers were the ploy of English-speaking grifters. Thinking of all of this, Ian Goller slipped into a depression, because Araceli's surrender was the only path to victory in the case.

Maybe he should just go hit the waves and cuddle with the moving water and its shifting shapes, with its power to lift a man and make him fly.

Assistant District Attorney Goller was in the parking lot, opening the trunk of his car and confirming the presence of his wet suit and mini board in the back when his phone beeped with another text message: his investigator was following the defendant from the parking lot and was wondering whether to continue surveillance.

No, the assistant district attorney wrote back.

He saw *The People v. Araceli N. Ramirez* more clearly now. It was unusual to be burdened at this relatively late stage with so many bad facts: the parents caught in contradictions, the paper trail of their lies, and the older boy and his elaborate fantasies. In the name of efficiency they usually tossed unwinnables like this one out the door. And yet there was still the march of institutional logic, the overwhelming likelihood the judge would order the defendant to stand trial, adding the passage of time to the equation. It would be four months, at least, until the trial: that kind of time often worked wonders, since it brought into play the predilection of defendants to muck up their lives. The defendant might run afoul of the law while free on bail, allowing her to be arrested on another, unrelated charge. Or they might get their deal. If none of those things happened, there would always be another illegal immigrant to arrest and try in another high-profile case, eventually, inevita-

bly. The math suggested it would happen again soon, though it was hard to imagine a case as perfect and full of possibility as two handsome boys spirited away by their humorless Mexican nanny.

Ian Goller had closed the trunk of his car and was contemplating the best route to the sea when his phone chattered again with the announcement of another text message.

Araceli did not notice the assistant district attorney as she left the courtroom and entered a hallway filled with people in sagging, end-of-the-summer day clothes. She walked a step behind Ruthy Bacalan, who was talking into a cell phone, and then into a long corridor where a man and a woman were walking toward them, backs and heels first—after a moment, Araceli saw they were two photographers aiming lenses at a subject, walking backward as the subject walked toward them, as if walking backward were the most natural thing in the world.

The smart-stepping photographers tangoed in reverse past Araceli and Ruthy and suddenly the two women were alone with the subject, a sapphire-eyed man with a light, sun-kissed complexion and a wheat-field of hair that looked as if it had been born on van Gogh's palette on one of the painter's sunnier mornings. He was an A-list movie star, internationally recognized and swooned over, and he was in the courthouse to testify at and savor the trial of an annoying paparazzo. The sight of the A-list star caused both Ruthy Bacalan and Araceli to stop in the center of the hallway to admire him. Suddenly he spotted Araceli and stopped his advance down the hallway.

"Hey, I know you," he said to Araceli. He reached out, shook her hand, and said, "I've been following your case."

"*¿De veras?*"

"I have." He smiled, spectacularly, and then added, "And I just want to say, good luck to you, señorita," in a voice that seemed a conscious imitation of Jimmy Stewart or Cary Grant or some other star of a bygone age, and in a moment he was bygone too, headed down the hallway to Department 186B to witness the sentencing of a man who would hound the beautiful people of Laguna Beach, Brentwood, and Bel Air no longer.

"Wow," Ruthy said, with a hand at her chest.

"*Sí*, wow," Araceli agreed.

He left them in a trance as they followed the hallway to the door

and the concrete plaza outside and its long-shadowed brightness. None of the distracted newspeople standing in the center of the plaza had noticed that Araceli was walking among them. Five of them were gathered in a semicircle, talking to one another and contemplating the black slabs they held in their raised palms, as Hamlet had the skull of his poor friend Yorick, summoning news of a tragedy with their thumbs. A girl's body was being pulled out of a suitcase in the lake, her stepmother had been arrested, and Ian Goller was speeding toward the scene. The newspeople were all wondering where they would be deployed next, because it was an all-hands-on-deck moment, but Araceli did not know this and assumed that they had simply grown bored with her, and she gave herself a moment to think about how fickle they were, how short their attention spans. None of them had been present to see Ruthy in her white nautical outfit destroy the prosecution in Department 181.

Araceli parted company with Ruthy and made her way to the parking lot, where Felipe was waiting for her. He'd been there for four hours, waiting, sitting in the cab of his truck with a pad of paper and a pencil, drawing, and he tossed the pad into the back of the cab as soon as she approached. They drove back to Santa Ana, and she told him about how Ruthy had taken apart the prosecution, and when they reached the Covarrubias home he walked her to the front door and said goodbye in a very chaste way, as if he were holding back other, deeper things he wanted to express but was too afraid to say. There was something that was supposed to happen next between them, and Araceli wondered if he would allow that thing to be.

"¿*Mañana*? At the same hour?" he asked.

"Yes. But only if you want to."

"I do. I really do. I don't have any work now—things are slowing down. But even if I did have to work, I would be here, *porque es importante.*"

"*Hasta mañana entonces.*"

"*Hasta mañana.*"

This is a formal, too-polite parting, filled with unspoken yearnings, like in the villages back home, Araceli thought, and she reached out for his hand. Their fingers lingered together long enough for her to inhale and exhale once, very slowly, and in that moment Araceli felt infinitely more electricity pass through her skin than when the A-list movie star had touched the same hand.

26

On the morning of Araceli's second day in court the large crowds of protesters had disappeared from the front steps of the court-house. In their place there was Janet Bryson, alone, scanning the street and the parking lot for the friends she had made yesterday, at first per-plexed by their absence and then, finally, disappointed by their lack of resolve. "They said they would be here," she said to herself aloud, and when the defendant in *The People v. Araceli N. Ramirez* appeared at the bottom of the steps with another Mexican, Janet Bryson barely noticed, because she was so upset with the unpunctuality and flakiness of her fellow Californians. *What are they doing that's so important that they can't be here? What's on their televisions that's so captivating; what excuses about traffic will they concoct?* Araceli walked up the steps with Felipe and didn't see Janet Bryson. The shouting woman of the day before had dis-solved into the background for Araceli, because at the bottom of the stairs Felipe had reached over to take her hand.

Felipe had wrapped his fingers around Araceli's suddenly, in-stinctively, because he was swept up by the emotion of leading his new friend into a courthouse, which he thought of as a place where people went to disappear and never come back. They could take Araceli away and send her to one of those prisons in the desert, in faraway valleys

where people trekked to visit incarcerated fathers and brothers on pathetic road trips where an ice cream for the kids at Burger King on the way back was supposed to make it all better. Felipe had suffered such trips to see his older brother—who was still in that prison, thirteen years later—and when he reached over to take Araceli's hand, it was to comfort himself as much as her. He knew she was someone special and brilliant whose freedom and future were under threat. They walked up the stairs with palms joined for twenty-four steps and thirty-eight paces to the door with the metal detector, until he let go and allowed her to enter the court building alone, and said, "*Te espero en el* parking lot, just like yesterday."

Inside the paneled courthouse, the proceedings resumed with Ruthy Bacalan rising to her feet and announcing, "We call Salomón Luján, Your Honor." The Huntington Park city councilman entered the courtroom, in black denim jeans and a thick leather belt whose bronze buckle bore the initials SL. His nod to the formality of the courtroom was a freshly ironed plaid shirt with mother-of-pearl buttons, and boots polished so that they resembled the skin of the oak table on Paseo Linda Bonita. Once on the stand he recounted the phone call that brought Araceli Ramirez to his home, and the arrival of the defendant and her two charges at her front door. "She told me she was looking for their grandfather," he said in moderately accented English, "because the mother and father had abandoned her in the house, alone, with two *gringuitos*," he said.

"With two what?" the judge interrupted.

"Sorry. I mean with two little American children."

"And did these children you saw," Ruthy asked quickly, "did they seem to be well taken care of?"

"Yes. They look a little tired. But this lady, Araceli, she was in charge. Their hair was long, but she made them comb it. She was taking care of them, yes." After asking Luján to recount how Brandon, Keenan, and Araceli had all slept in his daughter's room—"She's the one going to Princeton, correct?"—and having Luján confirm that he was a member of the Huntington Park City Council, Ruthy moved to the moment at which Araceli fled his home, alone.

"Did she tell you why she was leaving?"

"Yes. Because of the immigration."

"She was afraid because she felt she might be detained for her immigration status?"

"Yes."

"And when she left, did she leave the children in your care?"

"Yes. She could see, on the television, that their mother and father were back home. So she didn't need to take care of them anymore."

"And you had them until the police arrived?"

"Yes."

"Nothing further, Your Honor."

Arnold Chang said he didn't have any questions for the councilman—the prosecutor seemed as eager as Araceli to be out of the courtroom.

"The defense rests, Your Honor," Ruthy said.

"Any affirmative defense or motions?" the judge asked.

"Motion to dismiss based on insufficiency of the evidence," Ruthy said. "I would like to be heard, Your Honor."

"Go ahead."

Araceli watched and listened as Ruthy rose to her feet again and launched into a spirited monologue directed at the judge and, with the occasional sidelong glance, at the prosecutor. "It strikes us as a misuse of prosecutorial power to file charges against the only adult in the household who acted responsibly," Ruthy said. She sometimes held her belly in her palm as she spoke, and she leaned on the lectern once or twice as she described Araceli's attempts to find a safe place for the children first with their grandfather, and then in a "traditional home with a respectable family" in Huntington Park. "Clearly," she concluded, "these are the actions of an adult who's taken the responsibility of caring for two children seriously." When she finished she plopped back down into her chair, and all the men in the courtroom seemed relieved that she did, because it seemed she might go into labor if she kept on talking.

"And the People?" the judge asked.

Now Arnold Chang stood up and began using the same legalisms Ruthy had pronounced, but with a dismissive tone, as if firing tennis balls back across the net. "The facts in evidence establish the vulnerability that is at the essence of the endangerment statute," he said, and

Araceli wrinkled her brow at him because despite his at times abstract and difficult English, the meaning of what he was saying was clear in his flustered, strained brow, and the way he stretched out his arm in Araceli's direction to make a point. "The vulnerability need not be an actual physical threat, but may also include a looming emotional threat over the psyche of the victims. The People argue that the disturbing nature of the journey undertaken by the defendant with the two minor children, into an area of persistent physical dangers, all thanks to the poor decisions of the defendant, falls within the definitions of the statute."

After the prosecutor had stopped and returned to his seat, the judge leaned back into the cushions of his swivel chair and said, "Well, then." Araceli understood that it was now his turn to decide the next stop on her journey through these buildings and their rooms of concrete and wood paneling. He rubbed his bald head vigorously with both hands, in what felt like some odd judicial ritual, then looked at a clock on the wall. He allowed the second hand to advance in its circular motion and kept on looking as it reached the six at the bottom and swung back and began climbing again toward the twelve, leading Araceli to wonder if he was peering into the clock's face and studying it for a message only he could discern. Finally, he turned to the lawyers.

"I'm going to grant your motion, Ms. Bacalan."

This short statement was followed by a long silence whose contours Araceli did not fully appreciate, because she did not know what "motion" meant, precisely, in this context. *Motion.* Moción. *Something is moving. The judge will allow something to move. Me? Do I move? But to where?* The prosecutor sat up straight, as if preparing to launch into new arguments, while Ruthy leaned back in her chair and gave her pen a jaunty twirl between her fingers.

Addressing the prosecutor, the judge said, "You're not even anywhere near a preponderance of evidence."

"I respectfully disagree, Your Honor."

"Well, you can make a trip to the Court of Appeals if you like, counselor. If you feel it's worth it. This court has rendered its decision."

"Your Honor, before you adjourn," Arnold Chang interjected, "there's also the matter of the defendant's immigration status."

"Excuse me?" the judge snapped. He leaned forward and glared at the prosecutor.

"Objection," Ruthy said, almost spitting the word out as she rose quickly to her feet.

The judge motioned for her to sit down, then leaned back in his tall padded chair and brought his hands together before his face as if in prayer. "Counselor, there's a couple of things," he began. "First, I've got a pretty full docket here. Unfortunately, I don't have the luxury of an hour, or even fifteen minutes discussing facts not related to the charges before this court. And second, and most germane, is that big bronze seal that's floating over and behind my head. See that?"

"Yes, Your Honor."

"It's got the San Francisco Bay and a lady with a spear, and it says 'State of California.' Is there an immigration law in the California code that you'd like me to enforce, counselor?"

"No, Your Honor."

"Case dismissed," the judge said. "Ms. Ramirez, you're free to go." He pounded the gavel, which sounded with an odd clack-clack, and rose to his feet and retired to his chambers, carrying an empty coffee cup he intended to fill before returning to the bench for the next case.

They walked up a wide staircase of weathered granite into the open house, a family of five, Maureen holding Samantha's hand as the little girl raised her legs high to navigate each step, Brandon and Keenan and their father following after. Maureen stopped in her climb to look longingly at the Prairie style, Frank Lloyd Wright–inspired windows, each an eye-pleasing geometry of nine glass rectangles separated by thin strips of wood. The windows were authentically old and American, as were the pillars of river stones that held up the rafters of the front porch, and the polished floors in the living room whose brown mirror greeted the Torres-Thompson family as they walked through the front door.

"This is nice," Scott said.

Of all the Craftsman homes they had seen in South Pasadena, this was the purest gem. It wasn't as big as some of the others, but it was the best preserved, and it seduced Maureen with the triangles of its eaves, the sturdiness of its exposed rafters, the long beams that loomed over the living room and jutted out over the porch outside. It was a squat

story and a half, perched halfway up a gentle rise above the concrete wash of the Arroyo Seco.

The boys ran through the living room to the stairs and climbed up to the two rooms of a second story that was tucked underneath the sloping ceilings of a pitched roof. The floors creaked and moaned with each of their steps. "It's like an eagle's nest up here," Brandon said, and he lay on his stomach and looked out a window frame that was only six inches off the floor. He scanned the neighborhood, the billowing canopies of the sycamores and oaks, the spotted green fruit of a black walnut tree, and the shadows and shafts of light that cut through leaves and branches to dapple the sidewalk below, and he remembered the tiny talking forest creatures of a novel he'd read a long time ago.

Down in the living room, Maureen paced the echoing floors and thought about how she liked the simplicity and directness of the Craftsman design, with its embrace of early twentieth century American values of openness and restraint. Sunlight and breezes raced through its spaces, which seemed familiar and somehow midwestern. This house embodied the new person she wanted to become, and she felt it was a good sign that at this property, unlike all the others, the Realtor had not done a double-take when he saw the notorious Orange County family from the television news walk up to the door.

"It's from 1919," Scott said, reading the brochure as he climbed the stairs behind them. "The plumbing is probably not great."

"Who cares about the plumbing?" Maureen said. *We're looking for a new beginning,* she thought, *and some old pipes aren't going to stop us.*

She returned to the porch and admired the street, with its wide oaks and denuded jacarandas, each standing in a pool of purple flowers. It was a version of an America that was, a Main Street USA, a *Music Man.* She thought, *Only the streetcars are missing. This is the kind of street where the boys can ride their bikes.* There were no walls separating this neighborhood from the rest of the city, and yet there were no bars on the windows either, no suggestion that the residents lived in fear. *This is as it should be.* Yes, the air was still and dirty here; she would miss the sea breezes living inland. She was losing the California home of her dreams—she had been chased away from it, really, but perhaps it was for the best. *I paid for my ocean view with that horrendous isolation, up on that hill, in that gated and insular place.*

"It's just nineteen hundred square feet," Scott said. "Can we squeeze in?"

"That's the point," Maureen said. "To make do with less."

Scott examined the asking price, a nose more than seven figures, and more than he had paid for the house on Paseo Linda Bonita five years earlier. *Now I might be paying more for less house and no ocean view.* It made sense only for the supposedly excellent local public schools, and for having a home small enough to take care of without a Mexican living with them.

"What if we offer a little less than that?" Scott said to the Realtor, a man with slippery hair and ruddy skin who was just reaching the top of the stairs.

"They may take it. You're lucky; it's a good time to buy. The prices have sort of stabilized the last month or so."

"Do you think the prices will start to drop?"

"No. Not a chance."

Up on the second floor Brandon was still on his stomach, still looking out the window, a bit disappointed by the failure of this new landscape to trigger any vision or hint of adventure. And then a girl of twelve or thirteen appeared below. From his perch he watched her pass before the house, hands folded over her chest holding a book, a long black braid bouncing on the back of her neck, advancing with a slow, feminine glide over the sidewalk squares. The sight of her brought forth an unfamiliar sensation deep in his stomach. *That's a pretty girl.* He quickly forgot about forest creatures and everything else on the street until the girl disappeared from his field of vision, and for the next hour he didn't think about any of the books he was reading, about Holden Caulfield or the dragon in Eragon, and instead he secretly wished they would move to this house so that he might see that girl again and maybe even talk to her.

Maureen walked out the back door and climbed down the stairs with Samantha, and allowed her little girl to roam the fescue lawn in the backyard. There was neither a pool nor room for one. Good. Better that way. The yard was separated from the neighbors not by the high walls of the Laguna Rancho Estates, but by a picket fence not much taller than Samantha herself. Standing at the door that led from the kitchen to the backyard, Maureen could look directly into the property

of another Craftsman next door. She saw a woman there in a large straw hat leaning over a row of plants with a hoe. A garden occupied much of the woman's yard, and it was filled with emerald globes and sunflowers reaching skyward, and corn plants that would soon be man-high, each looking as stiff and sturdy as a tree.

"Hi, there," the woman said.

"Hi," Maureen said.

"That's a great house."

"Yes, it's lovely."

"Gonna buy it?"

"We're thinking about it."

The woman smiled and rose to her feet and grabbed a box. She walked to the picket fence and lifted the box to show off the contents, a collection of a dozen red spheres, each the size of a tangerine. Maureen walked across the lawn to take a look and the woman used her gloved hand to shake off some bits of loam and handed a tomato to Maureen.

"They're beautiful."

"I've got too many, believe it or not. I'm taking these to a friend of mine."

"You grew all these?"

"My summer crop. Black cherry tomatoes, planted in April. They're heirlooms, organically grown."

"Organic," Maureen repeated, and thought that the word carried lovely sounds to match its meaning—proximity to nature, purity, simplicity.

"Do you garden?" the woman asked.

Maureen opened her mouth to say no, then yes, but sputtered and said neither.

Finally she asked, "Is it hard to learn?"

"That hardly ever happens, you know that," Ruthy said. "Every once in a while, we get these tiny miracles. I guess that's why I haven't quit yet."

"*¿Se acabó todo?*" Araceli asked. They were standing alone, outside the courtroom, and she was still confused. At one moment, she was a woman with the ligatures of United States jurisprudence affixed to her skin, at another she was free to leave the courtroom and travel about

the continent again. The judge had decided the government was wrong, but was a judge allowed to do that?

"Yes, it's over," Ruthy said. "The case was dismissed. There are no longer any charges against you. Like the judge said, you are free to go. *Se puede ir*. In fact, you should go now, and not hang around here at all. Because the DA's office has gone totally nuts. The deputy DA wanted the judge to hold you for the immigration people, which is totally inappropriate. It's sort of amazing to hear a county prosecutor say such a thing in open court. Did you see how angry the judge got? So don't even go back to that address in Santa Ana. That'll be the first place they'll look for you—because he's probably calling the ICE people right now."

"Thank you, thank you so much for everything," Araceli said, placing her hands on Ruthy's shoulders, as if to hold her steady. She gave her a Mexico City kiss on the cheek goodbye, and as Araceli made her way down the hallway alone, she took one last glance at Ruthy's turning, round silhouette and the hand that rested atop the cotton hillside of her belly. She walked briskly toward the parking lot, to give Felipe the good news and to think about what she should do next. Just outside the courthouse's glass entryway, behind the nylon cordons that blocked a patch of concrete now empty of photographers, Araceli passed Janet Bryson, who was standing alone with a rolled-up sign she had only briefly displayed on the courthouse steps.

"They're letting her go?" Janet Bryson said, having heard the news seconds earlier from the departing deputy district attorney. "Where is the media? Where is the outrage?"

Next Araceli walked past Giovanni Lozano, who had his poster-portrait of her dangling upside down in his grip. "They're letting you go?"

"*Sí*," Araceli said breathlessly. "*¡Me voy!*" She hustled as fast as she could without breaking into a jog, the memory of her failed sprint from the Huntington Park police alive in her thighs and the panicked tom-tom beat inside her chest. *Don't run, because that will get you in trouble, but move quickly,* mujer, *because they might grab you at any moment.* The ICE agents wore either stiff forest-green uniforms or navy-blue wind-breakers, and she scanned the path to the parking lot for them. There was a man following them back from the courthouse yesterday, in a car, driving slowly—perhaps he was with the ICE. Now she turned and saw a swarthy, middle-aged man in a suit, running after her with long strides of his tailored wool pants—could it be? Yes, it was the Mexican

consul. "*¡Araceli!*" he called out. "*¡Ramírez!*" She was about to break into a run when she felt a hand land decisively on her shoulder and heard his Mexico City accent call out her name: "*¡Araceli Noemí Ramírez Hinojosa!*"

With his full arm over her shoulder, the consul now guided a still-surprised Araceli back down to the courthouse plaza and a waiting cluster of suited men.

"We're here to help you," the diplomat said, and Araceli detected that sly sprinkling of irony with which Mexican officials flavored their pronouncements. "And, more important, we have something to give you."

One of his suited assistants produced an envelope and gave it to the consul, while another stepped back and aimed a camera.

"We received a request from some people in Santa Ana," the consul said. "We took the account number they provided us. And with the very kind cooperation and signature of your former *patrón, el señor* Torres, we secured the money from your account. As you requested."

"I never requested that. From you."

"Well, someone contacted me. And you should thank them. And thank me. Pedro here works in the consulate and is also a freelance writer and photographer for *Reforma*. He'll do a little article for us. Right, Pedro?"

"*Por supuesto, licenciado.*"

Araceli peered into the envelope. "This is a check."

"A cashier's check. Safer than cash. And, if I may be permitted to say, for an amount that is surprisingly large. It's so good to see one of our *paisanas* doing so well for herself. It's made out to the name on your voting card. And if you lost that one, here's another I had made for you and sent from the Distrito Federal. And also a passport, which I think you never obtained."

She examined the new documents, with their seals and hologram squares, and remembered how people suffered a *via crucis* of lines, forms, waiting rooms, and belligerent officials to get these in Mexico City. Now they gave them to Araceli without her even asking: it was a bureaucrat's idea of a Christmas present.

"If you don't mind, we'd like to take a photograph or two to illustrate the story."

"You want to take a picture of yourself giving me my own money?"

"It will just be a second. And it will help us here at the consulate tremendously."

Araceli could not say whether the consul was a good man or a bad man. Clearly, he was at the mercy of that clubby Mexico City culture that took bureaucrats, professors, and even painters and poets and transformed them into obsequious babblers. Araceli had escaped from all that, and she thought she should tell the consul to go to hell and leave her alone, because, after all, what had her government done for her? *They said they would give me classes in drawing and professors who could teach me to master oils, but it was all a trick, because they don't give you brushes or a canvas, or a studio, or the time to become what you dream. Instead our government gives us the roads we take in our northward escapes, and the policemen picking at their teeth and sizing us up to see if we can pay a bribe. It gives us the cartoon pictures of Juarez in our textbooks, and the lessons about the agrarian reform and the Constitution of 1917.*

Araceli wanted to be angry, but in the end she felt pity, and she turned and posed, foot forward and leg extended, like a beauty contestant, because in the end it was all a joke, and because if the police or the ICE caught her again, she might actually need this bureaucrat's assistance. Click. Click-click. Click.

"*¡Gracias, paisana!*"

He offered his business card and she took it, mumbling "*Gracias*" and slipping away, and thinking that a paper rectangle printed in Mexico City was a poor defense against the ICE. *They can grab me at any minute and send me back into tiny, locked cubes, because the eyebrows on the television and the screaming woman on the staircase demand it.*

Araceli found Felipe asleep in the cab of his truck, a baseball cap pulled down tight over his eyes, his largeness barely contained by the weather-scarred red skin of his pickup. His mouth gave little wet puffs, but even in this unflattering state, she found him attractive: above all, because she sensed an innocent, incipient devotion in him. He would wait for her an entire day, without eating, if he had to. Finally she woke him up.

"You're back," he said, startled.

"*Ganamos*," she said.

"You won?"

"I am free. *Se acabó todo.*"

"*¿Estás libre?*"

"Yes, except that now I have to run away."

"Right."

"How much gas do you have in this truck? Because I need to get far away."

Felipe maneuvered his pickup through the streets of Laguna Niguel with an aggression she had not seen before, squealing through a couple of turns, accelerating with controlled desperation, and after a few minutes they were on the freeway, headed north, his truck settled into a fast cruise. "We need to get out of the city," Araceli said. Towers covered with razorlike antennas loomed over the highway, and danger seemed to lurk in every off-ramp, in every Denny's and every Taco Bell, in every parking lot: a reporter, police officer, or immigration agent might ambush her from any of these urban hollows at any moment.

"So we go to the desert, to the east," Felipe said. "That's the fastest way out."

"And after the desert?"

"The desert is big. If we keep going, we get to Arizona. To Phoenix."

"Will you go with me, that far?" Araceli asked.

"Anywhere you want to go. For as long as you want. After Phoenix is New Mexico. After that, Texas, I think. And then, *no sé*. Tennessee, maybe? It's a big country. All the way on the other side is Carolina. *Carolina del Norte y Carolina del Sur.*"

Felipe looked out over the asphalt, the white lines, the traffic drifting toward him and away, and turned and gave Araceli a gentle, mischievous smile. They were beginning a journey without a destination, without limits, on the spur of the moment, with only the clothes on their backs. Araceli guessed he was not normally a rule-breaker or risk-taker. Probably he owed money on this truck. He took no chances with his wardrobe either; he was a man of steady and unchanging habits. And yet, he kept driving. Soon they were on another freeway, headed east toward a place called Indio, according to the green signs that floated over their heads. Felipe said the hard part of the drive started after Indio, when you passed into the Mojave Desert, which you had to cross to get to Arizona. But before they got to the desert there was more city to contend with, the serpentine flow of trucks and campers and convertibles and station wagons all moving very slowly, as if each bumper were attached to the next, a conga line of blinking red lights following the

curves of the freeway around office complexes, up into hills of dry grass and their crowns of nectarine-colored condominiums. Felipe's air-conditioning didn't work, so he lowered the windows, the roar of the traffic and the wind joining the grind of the engine, and when they spoke they had to shout. "I think we should buy some water!" she said. "So that we can drink when we cross the desert!" They pulled off the freeway and stopped at a gas station and jumped back on again. Araceli expected to see cactus at any minute, but the traffic was slow and the metropolis went on, exit after exit announcing a new district of the city unknown to her—Covina, Claremont, Redlands—more malls and parking lots extending from the freeway's edge like crops growing along a riverbank. Los Angeles did not want to let her go; it kept its hold on her with its sprawl.

"It's a long drive!" she shouted. "When do we get to Indio?"

"*Una hora más.* I do this drive once or twice a year. To see my family in Imuris and Cananea. Sometimes I go with my father. We go to Phoenix, then Tucson, and from there we drive south, into Mexico. I was born in Cananea, did I ever tell you that? You know, we could go there. I wouldn't mind that. It would be a good place to get a new start. Mexico isn't that bad. You're poor there, but it's *más calmado.*"

She thought about Mexico and the check in her pocket. The amount was a small fortune on the other side of the border. She could start a small business, or buy a house and build a barbecue in the back and cover the patio with bricks. Or she could rent a studio with big windows to let in the light and a concrete floor that she could spill paint on.

On the other hand, there was still the United States, and the promise of even greater riches, and the smooth satisfaction of being a woman who stood her ground. She could find an apartment in this Phoenix place if she wanted to. It was a city in a desert valley where people couldn't survive without air-conditioning, and Araceli wondered if she could live in such a place, without rain, clouds, and seasons, especially now that the traffic had sped up and they had finally reached the outskirts of Indio, the landscape turning dry and chalky. They drove past trailer parks rising from dirt lots, the wind spraying brown dust devils along the ground. A tumbleweed bounced along the strip of dirt in the middle of the freeway, and she sat up and pointed it out to Felipe. "*Mira, Felipe, es una de esas malas hierbas. ¿Cómo se les llama?* Tumbleweed!" She felt

proud of herself for remembering the name, wondering how and why she would have learned such an obscure Americanism. Tumbleweed, the plant that rolls like a wheel, which is what the specimen she had just seen was doing, headed toward Arizona like Araceli and Felipe.

A hot wind blew in through the window, the heat of the desert and the black highway rising into the pickup truck, making Felipe sweat, the perspiration dripping down his neck and covering his T-shirt. She reached down between her feet and pulled up another bottle of water and opened it, handing it to him, and you would have thought she'd given him a bouquet of roses. *Even the smallest kindness from me makes him happy—he must be in love. But when will he kiss me?*

"How far is Carolina?" she asked.

"Very far. Maybe four or five days."

"Would you drive five days with me?"

"Yes. Of course."

"Aren't you worried?"

"About what?"

"Getting caught. By the immigration."

"No. I'm a citizen."

"Of the United States?"

"Yes. I got my papers last year. Through my uncle. It took ten years."

"But I don't have papers, and you could get in trouble for helping me. You're breaking the law."

"So?"

"And you still want to drive with me. And help me escape?"

"Yeah."

It took a moment for this small miracle to sink in and feel true. Yes, it was there to see in his serene and satisfied study of the road ahead of them. It was the look of a housepainter after a day of flawless work. He was a big man with big sexy hair, and he was hers. He would even break the law for her.

"*¡Qué romántico!*" she shouted, and laughed, and he laughed too, in a muted and nervous way.

"After we get to Phoenix, we have to decide," he said. "There's two ways we can go. We can keep going east, and go to Texas or Carolina. Or we can go south, to Sonora and to Nogales and Imuris—to my *tierra*. If we go south, we can't come back north, because there are check-

points with *la migra*." He turned to look at her and asked, "Where do you want to go?"

"*A mí me da igual*," she said, because she could see herself following either path.

Soon the last human settlement was behind them and they sped across a vast, open plain of sand the color and texture of flour, covered with skeletal shrubs, maroon mountains rising in the distance, rocky and lifeless. "We reached the desert," Araceli shouted. The road had become a straight line, dipping over the horizon in a watery mirage.

"It's the Mojave," Felipe shouted back.

They were in an eastward flow with sports cars in bright primary colors that zipped past their truck like low-slung missiles, and big sedans with people inside reading books and looking at tiny screens, passengers and drivers cool and comfortable behind shields of tinted glass. They were people of all the American colors, and carried an air of affluent confidence and anticipation: *The road belongs to them and they know it*, Araceli thought, *and they even appreciate it*. There were great big vehicles the size of small homes too, with license plates of many different colors that announced their owners resided in the LAND OF ENCHANTMENT and VACATIONLAND, or that they were headed to a SPORTSMAN'S PARADISE.

The plain of shrubs and sand undulated as if it were a vast pool of liquid, or an ocean, with mountain ranges standing like islands in the distance. An hour went by wordlessly as they crossed this sea, and Araceli would think later the time swam by, it slid along so smooth and quiet and lovely. She imagined gliding across this desert ocean, with Felipe at her side, until they reached Carolina del Norte, or maybe even Veracruz, and the real sea at the end of their journey, to begin life anew.

Now several tall plants were growing alongside the highway, the long succulent fingers of the ocotillo, their barbed, candy-cane digits reaching for the white sun. Suddenly there were dozens of them, and now hundreds, covering a mountain slope. Araceli was going to comment on the beauty of the ocotillos when another pickup truck identical to theirs began to roll alongside them, the two vehicles cruising together long enough for Araceli to stare through the open windows and examine the face of the driver. He was a *mexicano*, like her, though perhaps ten years older, with a freeway of worry lines carved into his forehead, and a muddy

complexion that suggested Michoacán or Guerrero, or some other corner of her country where the people raised corn. He was looking at the
straight highway with faraway eyes, as if remembering other journeys on
other highways like this one, and suddenly she realized this man was the
person she might become if she stayed in the United States. She imagined a biography for him, a story of crossings, arrivals, money, and disappointments. *There are so many of us on these roads. So many of us from
adobe villages and cinder-block colonias. We are scattered on this highway
between the motor homes and the sports cars, we scrubbers and builders,
we planters and cooks, searching for the next place, the next hope.*

"A lot of people are going to Arizona," Felipe said. "I have a cousin
who lives there. He says no matter where you go, you can find a job in a
day. We'll be there in an hour. The border is the Colorado River. When
we go over the river, we're in Arizona."

Araceli had never been in another state besides California. *It's
called the United States because there are many, fifty altogether.* She wondered if there would be authorities at the border, an official checkpoint
where they would demand to see her documents. If so, they would discover she lacked the necessary stamps of U.S. eagles—she had a passport now, but a passport without a visa was just another reminder of her
Mexicanness. The anxiety about crossing the river and the coming
frontier distracted her until they reached a place called Blythe and the
signs said Arizona was just five miles away.

"What happens when we cross the border?" she finally blurted out.

"What?"

"In Arizona. Do they ask for my papers?"

"No. You just cross."

"They don't check anything?"

"No. Just the trucks carrying fruits and vegetables."

They rattled down the highway, toward an oasis of tree canopies
and green bushes. Soon they were on a wide bridge, rolling across to the
other side. LEAVING CALIFORNIA said the sign as they passed over a muddy
river.

"*¡Adiós, California!*" she yelled with her arms raised in the air, as if
on the last drop of a roller coaster.

"'Bye!" Felipe shouted in English, and they laughed and shouted
together.

On the other side they were greeted by a sign that said WELCOME TO ARIZONA, decorated with what she assumed was the flag of that state, red and yellow rays rising from a patch of blue, a copper star in the middle. Araceli admired its simple abstract expressiveness and thought, *That's what a flag should look like.*

They drove past the checkpoint for trucks Felipe had mentioned, and started to climb away from the river and into a rocky landscape. *This is Arizona, these red stones, already the landscape looks different. I have seen these fire-colored rocks in the movies and thought it was in California, but I was wrong.* She had arrived in a new place, and suddenly days and weeks of worry and fear lifted, and she lay her head against the door, feeling she would fall asleep any minute in this peaceful, rust-colored place, where a dozen tall saguaros had raised their arms to greet her.

Araceli fell into a soothing darkness and dreamed, for the first time, of Brandon and Keenan, that she was guiding them by the hand along the red Arizona rocks, away from a pool of water. Then the sun caught her full in the face and her dreams turned yellow and while these golden dreams lived they wiped out the memories of many years, of all her highway travels, her border crossings, her goodbyes and hellos.

She awoke to the taste of humid air and looked around to see that they were still in the desert. The forest of saguaros had grown thicker and a bank of percolating thunderclouds with bright white roofs and dark gray bellies was looming over the horizon with cathedral-like majesty. For a moment, Araceli wondered if the clouds were an apparition, or an extension of her dream, because the sky had been empty and blue when they crossed the river.

"Look at those clouds," she said.

"*Es un* monsoon," Felipe said. "You see them in the desert in the summer. Looks like we're driving right into it."

The air cooled and thickened and soon the sun disappeared behind the storm, shooting out rays in the patches of blue between the clouds, lines that spread out like a fan, the image in the Arizona flag she'd seen when they crossed the border, yellow streaks radiating from the star. She tasted the humid air again and understood that this storm came from the south, from somewhere deep in the tropical heart of the earth, from Mexico or some other wet and needy land.

Soon they were underneath the cloud bank and it began to rain.

First a few drops, each one large and heavy on the windshield, then thick sheets that covered the road with swirling streams, so that Felipe had to pull over to the shoulder and wait for the storm to pass. Araceli opened the window and let the warm water fall on her face, a rain stronger than any she could remember, a downpour that washed away all the dust of the desert and turned it to mud.

She turned and saw Felipe's face was wet too, and at that moment she leaned across the cab to kiss him. Their lips met in a moist caress. And then another one. And one more, until they stopped and looked at each other and Araceli suddenly felt lighter and younger, and she kissed him again and their arms and hands reached for one another too, until she gently pushed him back and said, "Slow."

The rain stopped and the sound of cars splashing by on the wet road brought them back to where they were—on the shoulder of a highway in Arizona, in flight.

"We have to keep going," she said.

They rejoined the road and in a few minutes they were entering a metropolis, Phoenix, with its low-slung warehouses, and neighborhoods with homes of rocky front yards and cactus landscaping. The sun returned, the clouds retreated, and the highway grew wider, spreading out from two eastbound lanes to three, until they reached the city center and the glass towers pulsated in the returning heat. The highway sank below the level of the street and spread out into four and then five lanes. Several green and white rectangles loomed on the overpasses above them, with odd-numbered highways and new destinations. 17. FLAGSTAFF. 225. TUCSON.

"So we have to decide," Felipe said. "Which way are we going? To Flagstaff if we stay in the United States. To Tucson if we go to Mexico."

Araceli looked up at the signs and thought, *Yes, it's my choice.*

She raised her hand, stretched it out until it almost touched the windshield, and pointed with her index finger.

"*Para allá,*" she shouted above the roar of wind and engines, and then she said it in English too, just because she could.

"That way."

Discussion Questions

1. What were your initial impressions of the Torres-Thompson family and Araceli? How did your understanding of them change throughout the novel?
2. Maureen and Scott, along with their friends, consider themselves to be progressive. How would they need to change if they were to bring about true progress in their community? Are the newly rich of this century very different from wealthy entrepreneurs from other generations?
3. Do Araceli and the other servants in the neighborhood have any leverage, or are they entirely powerless with their employers?
4. Discuss Los Angeles as if it were a character in the novel. What personalities and history are captured in the neighborhoods Araceli travels to, with and without Brandon and Keenan? How do the extremes of rich and poor affect the city as a whole? Do Brandon and Keenan see the world the same way as other characters in the novel, even though neither one of them has traveled far before (except through fiction)?
5. In Maureen's and Scott's minds, what does good parenting look like? How is this different from Araceli's parenting standards? How does Brandon and Keenan's childhood compare to their parents' childhood?

6. Does Maureen treat her baby daughter, Samantha, differently from her sons? What does it mean for her to have a little girl in a household of males? When Maureen and Scott have power struggles, does gender come into play?

7. In the scenes depicting Araceli's time off, what is most striking to you about her true self and her lost dreams of being an artist with a college education?

8. What would America look like—economically, socially, and otherwise—if Janet Bryson had her way? Were you surprised when the author revealed how much Araceli earns per week ($250 cash, on top of room and board), as well as Pepe's annual salary range (in the four figures)?

9. At every turn, Tobar finds a place for humor while keeping the story line tremendously realistic. What makes satire the best way to understand the issues of class and immigration raised in the novel? How did it affect your reading to know that the author is a Los Angeles native whose parents emigrated from Guatemala?

10. Discuss the translation and language issues that arise in *The Barbarian Nurseries,* including the moments when non-native speakers try to use Spanish. Is Araceli in some ways protected by the fact that her English is limited?

11. Ultimately, whose fault is it that the Torres-Thompson children were briefly without parents? Could something similar have happened in your household? If so, would you have been grateful to Araceli or suspicious of her?

12. Why is Scott so different from his father? How has Grandfather Torres evolved since the time the photograph was taken?

13. The title is referenced in chapter eight, when Maureen looks at the landscapers and thinks to herself, "*What am I doing, allowing these sweaty barbarians into my home?*" In chapter ten, Araceli uses the expression *qué barbaridad* when she thinks about Maureen's not telling her where she's gone. Who are the barbarians in this novel? What is being nurtured in the "nurseries"?

14. In the closing scenes, many of the characters experience newfound freedom. What did they have to sacrifice in order to gain that freedom? How did their definition of freedom change?

15. How would you have answered Felipe's question—"Which way are we going?"—in the novel's final lines?

"There are a lot of books and courses about succeeding with women, but this book is the best out there. I highly recommend it as the first thing any man read."
—Marshall Sylver,
creator of *The Secrets of Persuasion & Influence*

"I am a great admirer of [their] work—this is the best book on the subject."
—Leil Lowndes,
author of *How to Make Anyone Fall in Love with You* and many others

"Sexperts Ron Louis and David Copeland have great advice for men on the prowl."
—Jennifer D'Angelo, editor, Fox News

"You're holding in your hands the undisputed heavyweight champion of seduction guides. Whether you're a seasoned player or a rookie in the dating game, *How to Succeed with Women* remains the essential book on this subject."
—Rob Wiser,
coauthor of *M.A.C.K. Tactics: The Science of Seduction Meets the Art of Hostage Negotiation*

"Ron Louis and David Copeland have come up with the best dating information available, and I recommend every man read their book and use their material."
—Jerilyn Walter, *Playboy* Playmate

"Know that when you enter a room full of women, you're not leaving alone. *How to Succeed with Women* totally works! Get the girl you want, anywhere you go. Read it, learn it, live it."
—*Swank* magazine

"*How to Succeed with Women* by Ron Louis and David Copeland is one of the best books available on understanding dating from a male perspective."
—Shari Mindlen, dating columnist

D0017113

How to Succeed with Women

Revised and Updated

RON LOUIS and
DAVID COPELAND

PRENTICE HALL PRESS

PRENTICE HALL PRESS
Published by the Penguin Group
Penguin Group (USA) Inc.
375 Hudson Street, New York, New York 10014, USA
Penguin Group (Canada), 90 Eglinton Avenue East, Suite 700, Toronto, Ontario M4P 2Y3, Canada
(a division of Pearson Penguin Canada Inc.)
Penguin Books Ltd., 80 Strand, London WC2R 0RL, England
Penguin Group Ireland, 25 St. Stephen's Green, Dublin 2, Ireland (a division of Penguin Books Ltd.)
Penguin Group (Australia), 250 Camberwell Road, Camberwell, Victoria 3124, Australia
(a division of Pearson Australia Group Pty. Ltd.)
Penguin Books India Pvt. Ltd., 11 Community Centre, Panchsheel Park, New Delhi—110 017, India
Penguin Group (NZ), 67 Apollo Drive, Rosedale, North Shore 0632, New Zealand
(a division of Pearson New Zealand Ltd.)
Penguin Books (South Africa) (Pty.) Ltd., 24 Sturdee Avenue, Rosebank, Johannesburg 2196,
South Africa

Penguin Books Ltd., Registered Offices: 80 Strand, London WC2R 0RL, England

While the author has made every effort to provide accurate telephone numbers and Internet addresses
at the time of publication, neither the publisher nor the author assumes any responsibility for errors,
or for changes that occur after publication. Further, the publisher does not have any control over and
does not assume any responsibility for author or third-party websites or their content.

PRINTING HISTORY
Reward Books trade paperback edition / October 1998
Prentice Hall Press trade paperback revised edition / January 2009

Prentice Hall Press ISBN: 978-0-7352-0435-5

The Library of Congress has cataloged the Reward Books edition as follows:

Copeland, David.
     How to succeed with women / by David Copeland & Ron Louis.
        p. cm.
     ISBN 978-0-7352-0030-2
        1. Dating (Social customs)—United States.   2. Women—United States—Psychology.
3.   Man-woman relationships—United States.
I. Louis, Ron.   II. Title.
HQ801.C716   1998
646.7'7—dc21   98-27038 CIP

PRINTED IN THE UNITED STATES OF AMERICA

10   9   8   7   6   5

Most Prentice Hall Press books are available at special quantity discounts for bulk purchases for
sales promotions, premiums, fund-raising, or educational use. Special books, or book excerpts, can
also be created to fit specific needs. For details, write: Special Markets, Penguin Group (USA) Inc.,
375 Hudson Street, New York, New York 10014.

CONTENTS

8. The Seduction Date 245

The Eight Components of a Successful Seduction Date *246* ▪ Before the Seduction Date *257* ▪ The Seven Steps to a Knockout Seduction Date *260* ▪ Mastering the Seduction Date *265* ▪ From Raging Bull to Purring Kitten in Nine Easy Steps *273* ▪ After the Date "Did" Checklist *276* ▪ After the Date "Didn't" Checklist *277* ▪ How to End the Seduction Date *277*

9. Closing the Deal: The First Kiss and More 278

The Secret to Getting the First Kiss *279* ▪ Review of the Pre-Work *280* ▪ Testing Her Readiness *281* ▪ Test Checklist *285* ▪ Going for the First Kiss *285* ▪ How to Go for the First Kiss *287* ▪ If She Says No *288* ▪ The Ten Crucial Mistakes That Blow the First Kiss *290* ▪ Taking the Kiss Further *294* ▪ Passionate Kisses! *295*

10. Being the Man of Her Dreams in Bed 297

The Triangle Offense: The Three Keys to Improving Any Man's Sex Life *299* ▪ Creating the Physical Setting for Romance to Turn to Sex *302* ▪ Setting the Mood with Sensual Talk *304* ▪ Topics to Avoid in Bed *305* ▪ The Art of Foreplay *305* ▪ The Main Event *306* ▪ Enjoying Afterplay *307* ▪ Possible Problems and How to Solve Them *307* ▪ Staying Alive: Safer Sex *312* ▪ Condoms: Every Man's Necessary Weapon *313*

11. When Babes Attack: Handling Problems Women Cause 314

Bad Dates from Hell *314* ▪ So How Do You Handle Problems? *318* ▪ Gauging the Maintenance Spectrum *319* ▪ Low-Maintenance Women *319* ▪ Medium-Maintenance Women *320* ▪ Too Hot to Handle (High-Maintenance) *321* ▪ The Eight Secrets of Handling the Problems Women Cause *323* ▪ The Three Ways Women Fight and How to Handle Them *332* ▪ The Four Classic Women to Avoid *337* ▪ The Twenty-Three Problem Women *340* ▪ The Sixteen Problems Caused by Your Tendencies *341* ▪ How to Handle the Top Problems Women Cause *348*

INTRODUCTION

We were no different than you might be. Our relationships with women were dependent upon two things: luck and the whim of women who happened to be attracted to us. When either of us had sex, it was because we quite literally "got lucky" and a woman decided to have us. We had little choice or power over when we had sex and relationships, and what women we had those interactions with. Sex and relationships, it seemed, were a crapshoot. Perhaps we'd meet someone, perhaps we wouldn't. Needless to say, we got tired of it.

Finally, we decided that we would do whatever it took to find out what worked with women. We wanted to know how to seduce women and more—we wanted to know how to develop relationships with women that would be fulfilling for both us and them.

We set out dating as much as we could and comparing notes after each and every interaction with women. Looking back, many of our interactions with women seem unskilled or even laughable to us now, but we stuck with it through the failures, frustrations, and successes. We found that as we kept at it and kept working together, we began to see the underlying structures of successful dating interactions. We found that we could start to predict how interactions would go and how certain women would respond to us. We began to take our interactions with women less seriously and to have more fun. We started to see how most of our problems with women had been generated by our own behavior. We began to develop the set of principles that has evolved into this book.

Now we know that we can have as many women as we desire simply by using the technology outlined. For instance, we understand the messages we send to women through our personal styles (Chapter 3) and how to make those messages as seductive as possible. We know how to get women to naturally think of us as possible romantic material when they first meet us, rather than relegating us to the role of "friend" (Chapter 2). We know how to flirt successfully and how to use that flirting to get the first date (Chapter 5). We know how to take a coffee date (Chapter 7) and make it into a full-blown seduction (Chapter 8). We know how to go for the first kiss—and more (Chapter 9). We know how to handle problems when they arise (Chapter 11), and how to end things with women when the time comes (Chapter 12). Our lives with women are much easier and more successful than they ever were before, simply from using these techniques.

Over the course of writing this book, we often found ourselves saying to each other, "If only I'd had this book ten years ago, I'd have made so many fewer mistakes!" This book contains a program that can change your life with women, forever. To get the most out of it, you may want to take on the following practices:

Be coachable. It won't do you a bit of good to read this book if you go through the entire thing rejecting everything we say before you have even tried it out. Of course, you will inevitably disagree with some of the things that we tell you to do, or when we explain what has worked for us or our students. But don't worry about it.

Think of us as your personal dating coaches. Part of a coach's job is to push you into trying something new. Imagine a professional basketball player who argues with his coach every time the coach tries to teach him a new move or critiques his performance. The player would fight a lot and get nowhere. As a man being coached, you have to be willing to set aside what you "know" to be true and to try out something different once in a while. So if you want to get the most out of this book, don't run mental arguments with us as you read it. Pretend what we are saying is true and try it out, at least for a while, and see how something new works for you. After all, if you already know everything about success with women and have exactly the sex life you want, why are you reading this book?

Have a study partner or better yet a "wingman." Do you know why, on the average, Asian students get better grades than non-Asian students? According to the experts who study this kind of thing, it is not because they are inherently smarter. It is because they are much more likely to study together than alone. Students who study with other students master the material faster, have more fun, and get better grades than students who study alone. You would do well to take advantage of this principle.

If you know another man you can study seduction with, then by all means study with him. You can discuss the chapters and the ideas together and egg each other on to try out the techniques that we will teach you. A study partner can be someone to get pumped up with before an interaction with a woman and someone to debrief with after. He will be able to give you feedback and coaching on email you send to women, love letters you write, and how to handle the variety of experiences you will have with women once you start using the program. He will be able to celebrate your successes with you and help you quickly get over your disappointments.

It worked for us. We developed the material in this book by working together. We were able to master the various distinctions faster through our conversations, and we were able to learn from each other's experiences.

The only trick of this is to find the right guy to work with. He needs to be someone you can kick back and have a good time with, who won't be offended by the idea of studying ways to romance women. He should not be a blabbermouth. If he tells everyone that you are studying seduction, he is likely to put off women you might want to seduce. You do not need to be overly secretive, but no useful purpose is served by telling everyone. You will find that having someone to work with you while studying this material, although not essential, will help you quite a bit.

Write in this book! We know that you were probably taught to never write in a book. Well, that's ridiculous. Feel free to customize this book to make it work best for you. Underline things you think are important and take notes in the margins of ideas or questions you might have. This will help your retention of the material substantially and make it easier to find parts that you may want to refer back to later.

We have learned that good intentions and being a good guy are not enough. These qualities are important, but, by themselves, they will almost never generate romance with a woman. If you are going to have success with women, you must be able to create romantic structures. You must be able to intentionally create interactions, conversations, events, dates, and moments that, by their very nature, make women feel romantic feelings and think romantic thoughts about you. Sometimes these structures just happen, but with a little know-how, you can insure that they happen consistently and with the women you desire. You must know how to construct them. Teaching you to do just that is what this book is about.

Remember, dating is a game. It is an important game, but it is a game. All games are frustrating when you are first learning the rules, and dating is no different. But, like other games, dating becomes fun as you master it. Stick with it through the first few tries and the possible confusion. Keep at it, and it will become fun.

Before we get started, though, there's one more thing you need to know.

Before you take seduction advice from us (or anyone else), we want to give you an important warning that can save you from a lot of trouble: When it comes to seducing women, you must get good advice. You must get advice from someone who has an established track record helping normal men get the women they desire.

You've got to take advice from someone who has more credentials than "I'm a young pretty boy and I get laid a lot, so think I can make a quick buck putting up a website about it."

If you try to do what works for the "pretty boys"—the guys who are young, attractive, and "naturals" with women—you'll just end up failing with women and blaming yourself, even though it's not your fault that their "pretty boy" techniques didn't work for you.

If you want to succeed with women, you must take advice from someone who has extensive, real-world credentials in helping normal men.

Does that make sense?

So before we get into the "nitty gritty" of how to succeed with women, we want to "come clean" and be up-front with you about who we are, and why you probably want to listen to us. Take a second to read the following,

and then decide if it makes sense to believe that we can help you get the women you desire:

- We have been dating coaches since 1996—even before we had a website.
- The first edition of the book you are holding in your hands was published in 1998 and has more than 250,000 copies in print in eight languages worldwide (English, Spanish, Portuguese, Hebrew, Japanese, Korean, Chinese, and Lithuanian). Our techniques work for regular guys, all over the world.
- Our seduction methods are so "spot on" that major magazines— from *Playboy* to *Men's Health* to *Maxim*—have interviewed us about them. Numerous major TV networks, from ABC to CNN, have reported on the success of our methods.
- MTV even did a dating documentary (called *Sex2k*) about our seduction seminars. That's real-world recognition!
- For the past ten years, we have been helping all sorts of men—young men, middle-aged men, older men, shy men—to get the success they want with the women they desire. We've had thousands of men come through our seminars and coaching program.

We're not telling you this to brag, or boast, but to make a point: When we say these "How to Succeed with Women" techniques can totally change your life, we know what we're talking about.

And with this new second edition, we've updated old material, removed stuff that doesn't work anymore, and created new sections that will help you seduce women in today's world.

As an owner of this new edition, you are entitled to special extra chapters, a free mini-course on "How to Make Women Pursue You," and a lot more at www.howtosucceedwithwomen.com/owners.

Since writing the first edition of this book we've created a lot of other great material that might be of interest to you if there are specific areas of seduction that you want to get ongoing education in. We've created a sixteen-CD, thirty-two-day Mastery Program, which will walk you through a total overhaul of your dating system. We've created a program specifically

about How to Talk to Women that might interest you if you want to focus on speaking romantically to women. We have a special CD program that helps extra shy men overcome the "Nice Guy" syndrome, and a monster fifteen-DVD course on The Advanced Bad Boy Training Program that you can use with the material in this book to get women to pursue you. Our seminars and coaching program also have helped men all over the world. You can find out about all of these programs and more at www.howtosucceedwith women.com, or contact us at ronl@howtosucceedwithwomen.com.

Enjoy the book, and have fun learning how to succeed with women!

Ron Louis and David Copeland

1

So You Want
Success with Women

Greg came to us with a problem. See if you can relate to it. He said, "I can't seem to get women to like me. I mean, they like me as a friend, but when I try to make things more romantic, it never works out. I haven't had sex in over a year. What should I do?"

We hear stories like Greg's all the time. All sorts of men come to us with their dating problems. Some are young, some are middle-aged, some are older. Some are salesmen, some are computer programmers, some are executives. We've worked with college professors, as well as men who are their students. We've worked with men who've never been married, and men who've been married and divorced multiple times. We've worked with rich men and poor men, attractive men and ugly men. We've worked with men from as many different walks of life and socioeconomic strata as you can imagine.

All of them have come to us with the same problem: They can't seem to get women to have sex and relationships with them. They desperately wish they could be successful with women, but they aren't, and it seems like the harder they try, the worse things get. Greg says, "I've all but given up dating because I'm so tired of the pain and humiliation." His feelings are common among these men.

To make matters worse, there's a whole world of newly minted "dating gurus" who, for a fee, promise to solve all your dating difficulties. We know, because practically every day we clean up after the problems these so-called gurus have made in some poor guy's life. As you'll discover in this book, you don't have to dress like a clown, learn complicated and crazy "patterns," or insult women to get what you want. The men we work with are often recovering from the humiliation of trying techniques that work only if you are young, attractive, or an accomplished performer for women or for groups. The guys we work with aren't like that.

These are good men. They are sincere and honest and would make good lovers, boyfriends, and husbands. But they can't seem to get women even to give them the time of day. They all find themselves living in hope—hoping that someday they will meet a woman who likes them, hoping that someday they will magically figure out how to attract women, hoping that someday they will, through some mysterious process, turn into superstuds.

Obviously, living in hope doesn't work, especially about something important like relationships with women. It's like hoping that your apartment will get clean, but not cleaning it. It's like hoping that you will have enough money for your retirement, but not saving for it. You have to take the proper actions consistent with your commitments, not just live in hope.

Very occasionally you may meet a woman with whom everything goes right, no matter what you do. But such occasions are rare. Romance rarely "just happens." Hope alone will not give you the relationships you want with women. Leaving it to chance will very likely cause you to end up alone. You've got to take continuous action.

But what to do? What can a man do that will make him so attractive to the women he's interested in that they'll not only like him, but they'll want to take their clothes off and rub their bodies against him? Answering that question is the subject of this book.

We won't lie to you, or hold out some ridiculous claim that simply reading this book will instantly make you into a superstud who can go from meeting a woman to getting her into bed in ten minutes or less. That's snake-oil salesmanship, and not part of our program. Effectively

seducing women is work. The reason this book will change your life is that it will show you, for the first time in your life, *exactly* what the work is. It's up to you to follow through and to implement the "science" we'll teach you (though we'll show you exactly how to do that, too). If you are willing to do the work, the tools we'll teach you in this book *will* work for you, just as they have worked for us and the many men we've taught. The principles are simple and extremely useful. The steps are easy to learn and easy to remember. With practice, you will master them, and will be more success-ful with women than you ever imagined.

WHAT THIS BOOK WILL TEACH YOU

This book will teach you, step by step, how to find women, meet them, se-duce them, and build relationships with them. We'll cover every aspect of seduction, so at each step you'll know where you are, where you've been, and what there is for you to do next.

This book will give you the ability to pursue and date as many women as you want, and to pick and choose from among them the one that works for you long-term.

We'll teach you:

The seven habits of Highly Effective Seducers

There are a number of habits that all master seducers follow. We'll show you what successful seducers do every single day that makes them consistently successful with women. We'll also show you how to stop mak-ing the most common seduction mistakes, which you probably are mak-ing continuously. When you take on the habits of successful seducers and stop making these few common errors, you'll be more effective with women instantly.

The elements of style

Your deepest communication to women is carried out by your personal style and your level of confidence. What you "say" to a woman through these two key areas can easily make the difference between a successful and a failed seduction. We'll show you how to develop a personal style,

both through how you dress and how you behave, that is a genuine expression of who you are and that women will find absolutely compelling.

Flirting without disaster

You use flirting to go from seeing a hot woman to making her your date. You build the basic structure of your relationship through the quality of your flirting. Will you be a woman's lover, or will you be her friend? Much of that will be decided by how you flirt. If you don't know how to flirt well, you will screw up your future with a woman and not even know you did it. We'll show you how to flirt your way to the date, effectively overcoming her natural fear of you and building a bond of fun and excitement between you. We'll then show you how to effortlessly turn that connection into an accepted invitation for a date.

A crash course in romance

Many practical-minded men don't know how to be romantic in a way that will really make a woman feel special. Furthermore, romance seems passé; in this age of equality, a man shouldn't have to romance a woman, should he? Well, yes, he does. You have to be romantic because it can be a fun way to make a woman see you as special and exceptionally attractive. We'll show you how to do it.

The priming and seduction dates

We'll teach you about the two kinds of dates, priming and seduction. We'll show you how each is a different, yet critical, part of effectively seducing a woman. You'll learn how to find what she desires in a man, and how to fulfill those desires by bringing those parts of you alive. You'll learn how to reliably make romantic conversation, and how to construct romantic experiences that will turn her on, connect her to you, and that she'll remember for the rest of her life.

Closing the deal: the first kiss and more

Done properly, the first kiss is easy. Done improperly—which is the way most men do it—the first kiss seems more like pulling teeth. We'll show you exactly how to create an experience in which the woman is thinking

about the kiss and desires it. We'll teach you the specifics of how to go for that first kiss, and how to take it much, much further immediately.

Being the man of her dreams in bed

The master seducer understands that he must always be improving his ability to enjoy sex and to please a woman. We'll show you how to improve three key areas—your communication, your attitude, and your technique. We'll show you how to create that moment when the date turns sexual, how to excel at foreplay and afterplay, and what to say and not to say during sex.

When babes attack: handling problems women cause

Sadly, not all of your interactions with women will be easy. In our experience, and in the experience of our students, the same basic problems tend to show up again and again. We'll teach you the nine secrets of handling the problems women cause, and walk you through, step by step, handling the most common dating difficulties. Because women are only half the problem (if that), we'll also show you how to handle the problems *you* cause in dating situations.

Breaking up is easy to do

All short-term relationships come to an end, sooner or later. We'll show you how to figure out when it's time to end it, and how to break up in the most merciful way possible so you end up friends. We'll also show you how to determine if she might be a good candidate for a long-term relationship.

Along with all this, we will ask you to be responsible for your life. We will constantly show you how many of the problems you blame on women or on "life" are actually caused by your behavior. Not to worry, though, we'll also show you how to change your behavior to make you more responsible for your life, and to get more of what you really want. As you learn and use this material, you will naturally become less whiny. You will become more of a man who is able to go for what he wants, both with women and in other aspects of his life.

At its core, this book is about generativity—your ability to be creative, inventive, results-producing, and fun. As you take on the practices we will teach you in this book, you will naturally become more of all those things in your life. This is important because it is this characteristic—your ability to create a life that turns you on—that will ultimately attract women to you. All the exercises, steps, and processes we'll show you are simply means to the end of turning you into an exciting, generative man. You'll find enhancing this trait will make your entire life better, not just your relationships with women.

THE SEVEN DATING MYTHS (PLUS ONE BONUS, THE "BIGGEST MYTH" OF ALL)

You are ready to do the work to get women into your bed; now all you need is for us to tell you what that work is. But before we tell you the secrets to creating an abundant sex life, we must explore and dispel the seven dating myths (plus the bonus "Biggest Myth" you can't afford to believe). You've probably bought into most or all of these myths; the first thing to do now is to clear them away.

Myth 1. If you are nice enough and interesting enough, you will get a woman

It's great to be nice and interesting, but it is not enough; it's not the same as being seductive. Most men don't understand this. Your average man thinks that if he likes a woman, and she says that he is "sweet," "interesting," or a "wonderful friend," that he's moving the relationship toward eventual romance. He isn't, because, as we've said, being nice and interesting is not the same as being seductive.

If you don't believe us, then just look around at all the jerky men who have plenty of women to have sex with. Women certainly aren't panting around these men because they are so nice and so interesting. They are panting around them because they are exciting, romantic, challenging, and fun. When you learn how to be exciting, romantic, challenging, and fun, you too will be surrounded by willing, interested women. You won't

have to give up being nice and interesting in order to do this; just remember that being nice and interesting isn't what turns women on.

Myth 2. You are a nice guy, who only has nice thoughts and desires

Men who believe that they are really nice guys, who only have nice thoughts and nice desires, are often the men who break women's hearts the most cruelly. The men who know that they aren't always sweet, and who know that they don't always have kind thoughts and desires, are often much more humane.

How can this be? After all, men who are committed to always being nice in every way should actually be nicer, shouldn't they? Sadly, it doesn't work out that way.

Look at it this way: Over the course of any relationship, you have the opportunity to feel a wide variety of feelings and behave in a wide variety of ways. Statistically speaking, you can't always be at your best. Sometimes you'll be at your best, most of the time you'll be at your average, and some of the time you'll be at your worst.

When you are at your worst, sometimes you'll have feelings and desires that aren't very nice. Actually they will probably be downright unkind. You'll want to retaliate against something some other person said, or you'll feel angry about how some other person is behaving. If you believe that you are a nice person who only has nice thoughts and desires, you'll be less able to be responsible for your behavior. You'll do things that most definitely are *not* nice, but you won't even notice you did them. After all, you'll tell yourself, no way could you be mean: You're a "nice man." You will ruthlessly refuse to admit that you are ever unkind. Women tell us repeatedly that it's the "nice men" that they have to watch out for. They tell us that "nice" guys are more likely to express their anger indirectly, and to hurt them emotionally, all the while acting innocent and claiming to be victims themselves.

Men who know they are not always "nice guys," and who know that they don't always have nice thoughts and desires, are much more able to be responsible for themselves. They can acknowledge when they are angry, or

when they want to retaliate, and can handle it appropriately. They are much more straightforward and forthright than "nice" men are. Women trust them more and like them more (and want to have sex with them more, too). In the long run, they are much less hurtful to everyone around them.

Some "nice" men pride themselves on being especially sensitive to women's feelings and women's needs. Women often tell them they are "special" or "not like other men." They often consider themselves ardent feminists and are ever-vigilant for anything that might hurt a woman in any way. They are naturally suspicious of other men and determined to not be like them. We call this kind of man a "SNAG," or "Sensitive New Age guy." Don't get us wrong—if you are one of these men, we aren't against you personally. In fact, we relate to you quite well—many years ago, both of the authors used to have some SNAG characteristics, as well.

Here's what we've learned about it, though: You don't have to give up being a good, honest, sensitive man who loves women in order to get sex. If you read this book and use the techniques we present in it, you will be able to do that without having to endure the humiliation of being a Sensitive New Age Guy.

Myth 3. Just "be yourself" and women will desire you

People who don't understand our method sometimes think that we are teaching men how to be manipulative. "It's wrong to study seduction," they whine to us. "Why can't you just be yourself?"

It's a mistake to think that using the techniques in this book is a substitute for being yourself. It isn't. We are not suggesting that at all. It's actually harder to get women into bed if you are trying to be someone else. That's one of the reasons that so many manipulative "seduction techniques" sound good on paper but don't work when you try them. Women notice, of course, that you are acting strangely. And even if you do succeed in getting a woman into bed by hiding your true self, you won't enjoy it as much as you thought you would. You'll know that you, yourself, weren't good enough for her and that you had to pretend to be someone else. The whole experience will hurt your self-esteem and your self-respect.

We are, however, suggesting that some parts of you are more appropriate in some situations than in others. This isn't such a strange idea. After all, you probably don't swear or burp loudly in church, even if you feel like doing so. You don't put your feet up on the tablecloth at a fancy dinner party, even if you want to. And you don't come on to a woman giving you a job interview, even if it would be an expression of who you truly are at that moment. None of these actions would be appropriate to getting the outcome you desire.

But isn't that being manipulative? After all, if you find the woman at the job interview attractive but you want the job, aren't you manipulating her by not "being yourself" and asking her out? Aren't you just "putting on airs" to try to get a job? And at church, shouldn't people like you without you having to go through all the contortions of dressing a certain way and repressing certain kinds of behavior? Aren't you just manipulating the people there into accepting you? Shouldn't you just be able to "be yourself"?

Isn't your self-expression being limited at the dinner party by not putting your feet up on the tablecloth if you want to? Shouldn't you be able to "be yourself" and be liked for that? Why should you have to manipulate everybody into liking you with all these special behaviors that might not come naturally to you? Shouldn't you be able to just "be yourself"?

Of course this makes no sense. "Being yourself" doesn't mean that you are utterly impulsive and driven by whatever behavior is most convenient for you in the moment. In different situations, you naturally bring out different parts of yourself. In church you follow a certain "code of conduct," but that shouldn't repress you. It's simply an opportunity to bring out the more formal, religious part of yourself. At the dinner party, you bring out the more cultured, sophisticated part of yourself. At the job interview, you bring out the professional part of yourself. You're not "repressed" because you don't ask her out. You are simply expressing a different part of yourself at that moment.

Our belief is this: It's critical that you bring out different parts of yourself in seduction situations than at other times in your life. Furthermore, we believe that you probably don't know much about those parts of yourself,

and that you will need guidance to bring romantic, seductive behaviors to the forefront.

That's what this book is about. Just as you were probably taught how to behave at a formal dinner, before you act without external guidance, you must learn how to behave when dating. When you do, you'll be able to bring out and explore romantic, seductive, powerful, and interesting parts of yourself that you may not have spent much time with before. After all, women do this, too. When they put on makeup and their push-up bras, you could say they are being manipulative. Or you could say that they are bringing out the seductive, sensual side of themselves. That's what we believe, and you must learn how to do it, too. You'll grow and have fun, and women will be captivated by you, all because you were willing to go beyond your normal knee-jerk behavior and to try something new.

Myth 4. Women know what they want, and they will tell you

Have you ever noticed that women will talk about the kind of man that they want, and end up with someone completely different? It happens all of the time. What women say they want and what they actually respond to are often totally different.

This is actually a very human trait: There are probably things you say you want in your life that you only *think* you want. Women are no different.

The bottom line is that women love men who are generative and creative. If they have to tell you how to get them, what to be like, and how to behave every step of the way, they aren't going to be turned on by you. It's your independent nature that gets them going, not your dependency on being told how to act.

Ironically, some of the traits in men that women complain about the most have in them the seeds of the traits women find most attractive. In the film *The Full Monty*, a bunch of out-of-work male steelworkers decide that they will make their money by putting on a strip show for the local women. The plan has "trouble" written all over it—none of these guys is particularly great-looking. It also speaks to a basically male trait that women find both aggravating and attractive: Men are troublemakers.

They take on silly projects, push them to their limits, and even sometimes make them work. This troublemaking quality is the flip side of the generative creativity that women desire so much in men. If you count on women to tell you what they want, and how to behave in order to get them, you short-circuit this creative, troublemaking nature that women love so much.

Women can't tell you what they want in a man—they can only tell you what they *think* they want in a man. There's a big difference. They also aren't attracted to men who approach as supplicants, begging for the easy keys to melt a woman's heart. Don't fall into the trap.

Myth 5. Be a woman's therapist, and you'll get sex

We'll talk about this more in the next chapter when we discuss the Seven Habits of Highly Effective Seducers. For now we will simply point out that being a woman's therapist is one of the worst ways imaginable to get sex. Many men think it will work, but it almost never does.

Myth 6. Being "honest" means telling her the worst things about yourself

Many men seem to think that the best way to be honest with women is to tell them the worst things about themselves, the sooner the better. "Full disclosure!" seems to be these men's motto. We think this is foolishness.

It's good to be honest. There's only one time that we ever suggest that you not tell a woman the truth. (You'll learn about that in Chapter 7.) The rest of the time, we believe that dealing with the consequences of the truth will almost always be easier than dealing with the eventual consequences of lying.

However, this doesn't mean that you should tell a woman every thought or desire you ever have. That simply isn't useful. A man who believes this myth will often tell a woman his problems right away, or will talk to her about his abusive childhood. He believes that by sharing the worst parts of himself he is being emotionally vulnerable, and that vulnerability will make the woman he is interested in desire him.

Nothing could be further from the truth. A man who "spills the beans" about his problems and his defects right away may bond emotionally with a

woman, but she won't desire him. She'll think of him as a friend, but she may also think of him as a nutcase. As you'll learn in this book, many men think that if they get any positive emotional reaction at all from a woman, they must be on the way to a romantic encounter. This simply isn't true. While you shouldn't lie about your flaws, you shouldn't share everything right away, either.

Myth 7. Dating should be fair

This one myth gets men in more trouble than almost any of the others. If you are a man who whines about how dating isn't fair, and how you have to do all the pursuing of women, you must stop that right now.

We hear it all the time: "Why can't a woman ask me out for once?" "If women really believed in equality, they'd kiss me first!" "I'm tired of doing all the pursuing with women. It's their turn now." Blah blah blah. If it makes you feel better, you are right: It is unfair that you have to do all the pursuing, and that you have to take all the emotional risks by making all the "first moves."

We've known men who confront women about their not pursuing men. One man named Cameron made it a habit of confronting women who didn't do "their fair share" of the pursuing. He'd tell them in no uncertain terms that if they wanted to date him, they'd have to do at least half of the initiating, the pursuit, and the emotional risk-taking. "It's the age of equality," he'd explain to them. "You get equal rights, so now take equal responsibilities!" Cameron didn't have many second dates.

Other men we know just complain about it. They whine to their friends about how women just aren't willing to do the work to make a relationship happen. They complain about how every time a real risk has to be taken, it's "the man's move." They say they are waiting for a woman to pursue them.

Our advice is to get over it. If you don't have the sex life you want, it's *your* responsibility to get it. It is not women's responsibility to take care of you and to make sure you have what you want in relationships. Expecting them to do so is just immature.

You can also look at it this way: If dating is naturally unfair, and if you have to do all of the initiating, that just means that you get to make it work

the way you want it! You can pursue women when you want to, and not pursue them when you don't. You can set up dates for times that work for you, and go for that first kiss when you feel like it. Having to do all the initiating puts you in the driver's seat. Use it as an opportunity to make your relationships the way you want them to be and stop complaining about it.

Bonus Myth. The "Biggest Myth" of all

There's a "dirty little secret" that most so-called dating gurus have in common. That secret is the "Biggest Myth" that is at the core of almost all of the programs most dating gurus teach. This Biggest Myth is making you fail with women—and is causing you pain and making you feel bad about yourself.

When you believe the Biggest Myth, you make a mistake so fundamental that it causes more failure with women, more problems, and more out-and-out *pain* than any other mistake men make. But it's the most popular, favorite mistake for men to make. And a lot of scam-oriented dating teachers make a lot of money teaching it to men like you.

But before we get to what the Biggest Myth is, we have to talk about its effects.

Have you tried manipulative approaches with women—perhaps trying

- "being cocky and funny,"
- hypnosis,
- or "patterns"?

And have you been left feeling like you were doing something wrong? You probably have. Did it feel "unnatural" to try these things? It probably did. And worst of all—did you feel bad about yourself, as if it was *your* fault that those approaches felt wrong and didn't work? Well, it's not your fault. It's the fault of the scam artists who sold you on the Biggest Myth.

So what is the Biggest Myth—and how can your get what you want with women by understanding and avoiding it?

We want to explain the Biggest Myth in an unusual way—by talking about the movie *Groundhog Day*. (Don't worry—we're going to let you in

on the secret that will let your interactions with hot women be easy, automatic, and overwhelmingly successful. This is just the fastest way to do it.)

Groundhog Day stars Bill Murray as a man who gets caught living the same day (it happens to be February 2, Groundhog Day) over and over. He can learn and change his behavior each day, but no matter what he does, the next morning everything around him resets itself, and it's the previous day all over again.

Have you ever felt that way with women? Have you ever felt like, no matter what you do, the same thing happens again and again? If so, this will make sense to you.

When Bill Murray's character discovers that he's living the same day over and over, he realizes it's a chance to try to "get" a woman he's attracted to. He decides to become the best manipulator he can. He starts collecting information about her and to try to figure out the "perfect thing" to say to her.

And he falls into believing the Biggest Myth: It's the belief that if you can only become manipulative enough and controlling enough, you can get what you want with women—and thus be happy.

So Murray tries to become the expert manipulator with the woman he desires. He finds all her weak spots and hot buttons, and slowly develops a routine he can go through with her. He tries to find the mechanical path that will get him into bed with her.

Because each morning she's forgotten the day before, he can test, over and over, different "scripts" with her, until he finds the script that works best. But no matter how good his manipulation gets, she feels it. She feels manipulated. She pushes him away. And it hurts him, too. The more he treats her like an enemy he has to outsmart, outmaneuver, and defeat, the less happy and successful he is. (Does that sound familiar to you?)

He bought the Biggest Myth—the belief that some manipulative act is the "answer" with women.

Most so-called dating gurus make their living by selling a bogus bill of goods to unsuspecting men. They sell this crap to men who just want to have relationships that they enjoy with women they are attracted to. But these men get sold on the Biggest Myth.

If you've tried to be "cocky and funny" and ended up just feeling like a jerk, then someone sold you on the Biggest Myth, too. If you've tried hypnosis, NLP, or "patterns," and ended up just feeling like there was something wrong with you, then you also got sold the Biggest Myth.

We didn't become the original, bestselling, and best-respected dating gurus by "selling the myth." We teach the simple principles that will never go away. We teach the principles that will always work, naturally, because our approach *is* natural. And that's why our work has been so successful, all over the world. And that's why it will work for you, too.

We won't give away the end of the movie, but will simply tell you this: Finally, for him to get what he wanted, Murray had to stop focusing on manipulation and strategizing and learn to discover who he was and to express his natural romantic self.

That's what you must do, too.

While it is true that there are some tools and techniques that can help you bring out your romantic self so you can easily get what you want with women—there's a world of difference between that and simply focusing on becoming a better manipulator of women. In fact, as you read these words, men who are no better than you are getting the women you desire. They are doing it by bringing out their natural, romantic selves. You can do it, too. And this book will help you.

If you've believed any of these myths in the past, we suggest you stop believing them now. To recap: First, being nice and interesting is great, but it won't get you sex. It will get you women who think you are nice and interesting, which is not at all the same as getting women who think you are arousing. Second, you aren't a nice guy who only has nice thoughts and desires. You'll be much better able to be responsible for your behavior if you admit that sometimes you are nice, and sometimes you are not. Women will also find you more attractive, because you'll be more trustworthy. Third, just "being yourself"—meaning impulsively doing whatever you feel like in the moment—won't get you women. You need help bringing out the more seductive parts of yourself, and the first few times you bring those parts out, they won't feel natural at all. Fourth, even if women did know what they wanted, they wouldn't be attracted to a guy they had to spell it out for. Women are attracted to men who are generative

and creative, not men who come groveling to them, asking how they should behave. Fifth, being a woman's therapist won't get you sex. It simply doesn't work. Sixth, being "honest" does not mean telling her the worst things about yourself right away. "Full disclosure" of everything that might make her dislike you is not necessary. Seventh, dating isn't fair. Men who complain about that fact need to grow up. Men who accept that fact can have as many women as they like. And finally, becoming a better manipulator is *not* the best way to become a better seducer. And if you commit yourself to becoming a better manipulator, you are likely to seem like a real weirdo and to scare women more than you arouse them.

It's as if dating is a dance. In the past, everybody knew their steps and could dance together. A man knew that if he was interested in a woman, he could do certain things to show that interest, and a woman knew the proper responses to show interest or lack of it. In the modern world, those dance steps have been largely lost, and we have been left on our own to figure the new ones out. Oftentimes, rather than dancing together, it feels more like we are crashing into each other, and stepping constantly onto each other's toes.

This book is about changing all of that. By helping you understand the dance women are doing, and showing you how to dance with them, this book will teach you how to put music, rhythm, and grace into your interactions. They will be attracted to you, because you seem to "just know" how to be romantic with them. With this skill in hand, you will be able to have as much success with women as you desire.

2

The Seven Habits of a Highly Effective Seducer

UNDERSTANDING WOMEN'S BIGGEST FEAR

We've been lucky enough to date and befriend many extremely hot and sexy women. Since learning the "tricks of the trade," we've been with women we would have only dreamed of earlier in our lives. We've been with hot blondes, brunettes, pierced and tattooed girls, exotic dancers . . . women of every description, all from using the material in this book.

One of the authors has a good friend and former lover named Dawn. She is twenty-four years old, long blond hair, big blue eyes, tall, great legs, a huge chest, and loves to wear seductive clothes. She also loves sex, and gets off on doing whatever makes her lover happy. In short, Dawn embodies many men's fantasies.

Before dating one of the authors, she used to go out and flirt with guys at bars. She told us about entering a bar and seeing how the men would stop talking and stare at her, drooling like dogs. She said she enjoyed the attention, but she rarely gave out her phone number to or dated any of the men who came on to her in bars. Why? Because she was afraid. She would be attracted to a man and then get afraid of being physically abused or

raped by him. After all, she didn't know him; she just met him at the bar. So she'd stay distant, unattainable by the many men who desired her.

Fear of being abused, hurt, or raped by men is *the* biggest concern women have in dating. Dawn and most other women smartly scope out men to make sure they won't be physically hurt by the ones they date. They want to be sure they can trust the men they are attracted to before getting physically vulnerable with them.

If you want to have success with women, you must be aware of this most basic female concern. You must deal with the fact that women you meet will be testing you to see if you are "safe," or potentially violent.

We think this concern makes total sense. If we were women, we would have the same concerns, and so would you. Put yourself in a woman's position: If you became aware of stories of rape, spousal abuse, torture, and murder of women every day in newspapers and on TV, you'd be paranoid, too. Women need to be a bit paranoid because so many men are psycho. It simply isn't worth the risk for a woman to go home with a man who could hurt her. What this means for you is that you must do the things to create trust with a woman, while still being exciting, interesting, and challenging. It's a tall order, but you can do it when you follow our steps.

YOU CAN BE A NERD AND STILL SCORE

In writing, speaking about, and researching dating dynamics, we've talked to men from every age group and occupation. We've counseled middle-aged lawyers from farm towns in Wisconsin and young up-and-coming musicians in New York. We've counseled computer geeks in Washington and writers in San Francisco. In the process, we've observed many of the hidden sexual dynamics between men and women.

The men we talk to often have a laundry list of problems, concerns, and complaints about their relationships with women, both past and current. Men often come to us in desperation, at the end of their ropes. They've read other books, bought programs on the Internet, tried subliminal CDs and pheromone-scented colognes, and nothing has worked. They usually come to us looking for confidence with women. They want to be able to meet women and make them into lovers. We give men the same advice

and information you will get in this book: a systematic approach to transforming your relationships with women.

One of our first clients was an attractive man in New York City. We will call him Todd. Todd was, and still is, a very popular musician who travels all over the country, puts out CDs on major record labels, and is respected by many people in the music industry. He's beautiful, too—the guy even models and has been in commercials. He's a solo guitar-playing singer/songwriter who performs in front of thousands of people each year. Many women find him sexy as he stands on stage, playing his guitar and singing with his amazing, satiny voice. You know as well as we do that women love rock stars. With Todd it is no different.

During our first meeting with Todd, we couldn't believe that this man was having trouble getting women. We looked at each other and laughed out loud. At first glance, we were hoping Todd might give *us* some advice. We hoped he might let us be roadies at one of his gigs so we could meet the women who were attracted to him, and maybe go home with them. But here he was, with a problem!

After just a few minutes of listening to him, we discovered the problem that kept Todd from being successful with women. Todd suffered from a severe lack of confidence. While he was in a situation that many men would kill to be in, constantly surrounded by hundreds of available women, he didn't have the confidence to follow through and seduce any of them. He told us he never knew what to say to women. He would look out in the audience and see lots of attractive women ("a sea of amazing breasts" is how he put it), but even though he was the big star, he didn't have the slightest idea how to start a conversation with any of them. He even admitted that women would wait to talk to him after a gig, but he rarely would go out with them. It was hard for us to restrain from smacking him, that he would dare to have a problem with women in this situation. We put him on a three-month program of coaching, goal-setting, and dating. He made commitments about how many dates he would go on and how many women he would talk to. It took a lot of effort, but Todd now has sex with as many women as he wants.

Todd is a useful example because he shows that even men who are surrounded by available women can have a profound lack of confidence. At the same time, other men are very confident with women, but are not in

situations where they have much contact with them. Some other men are not even all that attractive at first glance, yet embody the Habits of a Highly Effective Seducer so well that they have as much success with women as they want.

Blake, for example, is a computer programmer for a large firm in Chicago. He is thirty-eight, has epilepsy, and has scars on his arms from an accident as a child. At first glance Blake looks like a computer geek and is not particularly attractive. His glasses look a bit out-of-date, and he even has pens in his pocket (though, thankfully, no plastic pocket protector). He wears goofy ties and white tennis shoes. He is balding and has a bit of a gut. He looks like the type of guy who is much more comfortable with computers than with people.

However, as you get to know him, it is easy to see why he dates as many women as he wants, and even knows some who just like him for sex. It is pretty funny that a computer geek like Blake can have so many women, and a guy who is a successful rock star could hardly get a date to save his life! But it is true.

One of Blake's strong points is that, unlike Todd, he is very easy to talk to. Unlike many computer geeks, he is very personable. He has studied how to be romantic and is able to be sweet to women and be compelling to them at the same time. Women find Blake attractive because he's fun to be around and it's easy for them to trust him. Blake has learned that he must pursue many women, and he doesn't seem upset when he's rejected. He knows it is all part of getting the sex life he wants.

The bottom line is that if Blake can get sex and Todd can't, then you most definitely can. Yes, we are speaking to you, the one who is reading this right now. Even if you're not a model-quality beauty or are older and balding, you can still have wonderful relationships with as many women as you want. You can cultivate the skills to be a dating machine.

IT'S NOT ROCKET SCIENCE

People tend to make things they don't understand more complicated than they really are. It's only natural. Older people often think that using a computer will be so difficult that they are too intimidated to even turn the

thing on. Other people are so intimidated by the simple task of balancing their checkbook that they never learn how to do it. We all tend to complicate topics we do not yet understand.

One of the authors gives this example from his childhood: "When I was six years old, football seemed so complicated. I could understand the basic ideas of the game: The quarterback throws passes and someone catches the ball. Guys try to score touchdowns, block the other team, and make goals. That, I could understand. The rest of the strategies involved, however, didn't make any sense. Even after my father explained it to me dozens of times, the strategy of the game still seemed like a foreign language that I'd never understand. I decided to keep watching games and have my father continue his explanations. By the time I turned eight, things had started to make sense and I began to understand some of the more complicated aspects of the game."

Meeting and dating women is just like any other skill. At first it seems overly complicated and difficult. Most men simply give up because the task seems too large. It's not. In fact, many men are less successful than they could be because they overcomplicate matters by being overly involved with their own thoughts about how difficult dating is.

Let's introduce you to a man named Bob. He spends hours a day preoccupied with scenarios about women. He carefully constructs imaginary conversations with beautiful women at the pizza place he frequents. He creates comeback lines for all of her reasons why she won't go out with him. He daydreams about seductive conversations with young women he imagines he could meet on the bus. He studies manipulation and seduction on the Internet and argues about seduction techniques on discussion boards. In short, Bob is so "in his head" about talking to women that when he talks to a real, alive, breathing woman, he flips out and becomes tongue-tied. He's made it overly complicated by thinking about seduction too much, and taking action too little. He's made it into rocket science, and left himself unable to deal with it.

We have purposefully written this book in a very straightforward manner. We want you to understand that this material is not rocket science; the first steps to becoming a successful seducer are simple, and you can start today. We want to dissolve once and forever the idea that other men know

something that you don't, and that these skills are out of your grasp. That just isn't true. Once you get over the idea that it's complicated and beyond your reach, you'll find you can easily learn and apply our system and get women, no matter what your age or level of physical attractiveness. So let yourself relax, and enjoy learning this material.

YOU'VE GOT WHAT IT TAKES

If you've ever learned any skill, then you can learn how to get women into bed. You've simply never been taught how. Like any skill, once you learn the basics, the rest seems easy.

Most guys try to talk to women and fail. Bob tries and tries, but still can't manage to get a woman in bed. "I'm sincere," he moans. "I'm a good guy. I'm nice. I listen to women and try to give them what they want. Why haven't I had sex in two years?"

So Bob becomes more and more upset. He tries to psych himself up, to "get out there" more, and to be more confident with women. He resolves that he'll change with women, that *this* time he'll be the confident man he knows he is inside. This time he'll actually go up to that woman he's attracted to and ask her out. But when he does, he gets the same results he always gets: failure, or another female "friend"—the same thing as failing as far as his sex life is concerned. His self-esteem and self-respect plummet, especially as he tries to be more of a nice guy or a better friend, in the hope that this will inspire women to feel romantic about him.

Exasperated, he has even confronted women about their lack of interest in him. Several years ago he had a woman friend named Susan who told him that she wasn't ready for a relationship. He accepted this, even though he was attracted to her. Susan was young, cute, with long legs, almond eyes, and jet black hair. Hoping to be the first man on the scene when she was finally ready for a relationship, Bob spent lots of time with her just hanging out. He knew she liked him, because she spent time with him. He knew they shared the same interests in music and movies and were intellectually compatible. He knew he wasn't particularly bad-looking. In fact, lots of men who had girlfriends looked much worse than him. He

knew he had what it would take, and he hung in there, spending time with Susan whenever she wanted.

One day she told him in an offhand manner, "Remember what I said about not being ready for a relationship right now? Well, I met a guy who it's really working with, so I guess I was wrong!"

"Wait a minute!" Bob came back. "Why didn't you choose to date me? I'm a good friend! I'm always there for you! Why won't you date me?"

"I don't know," Susan responded. "I just don't feel that way about you. To tell you the truth, there's something weird about you, you seem kind of desperate. I like you and everything, but Joel makes me feel different." Once again Bob has been passed over for another guy who, predictably, he later learned, was not nearly as sensitive as he is.

If you are like Bob, you've had this happen to you. You've resolved to try harder, to be more confident. Secretly, like Bob, you've wondered if there's something basically wrong with you. You've thought that there is something you can't see about yourself, that everyone else sees and that repels women from you, just as Susan was repelled from Bob.

The good news is that nothing could be further from the truth. Sure, you've got problems. Everybody does. But, as you've no doubt seen, plenty of guys with more problems than you are dating women and having sex and relationships. We know a wheelchair-bound paraplegic who has an ample sex life with attractive women. We know a man who was horribly disfigured by fire who has a constant stream of women in his life, who would never dream of thinking of himself as sexually inadequate. There's nothing wrong with you that keeps you from having sex with as many attractive women as you like. If you can communicate at all, even if it's typing out messages with a pencil between your teeth, you can get women to desire you.

What's missing is the simple technical skills required to get women experiencing romantic feelings and thinking romantic thoughts about you. As we said, if you can communicate at all, you can have success with women. But you need to know *what* to communicate, and how to communicate it. Just as important, you need to know what *not* to communicate, and how not to communicate that.

Some men intuitively know this material already. They are the "naturals," who seem to have women all around them no matter what they do. Sadly, they usually can't teach you the technical skills of success with women because they don't know how they are doing it. They just do it. Even if they did understand what they were doing, they wouldn't particularly want to share those secrets with you.

In the *Dilbert* comic strip, someone once comes to Dogbert and asks him the secret of his success. He says, "Sleep with a vat of Jell-O by your bed. Set an alarm to wake you every two hours. When it goes off, stick your head in the Jell-O and scream, 'Boy, I'm tired!'" He ends the strip saying, "Beware of the advice of successful people, for they do not want company." If you've ever gotten useless or even destructive guidance from sexually successful men, you've experienced this personally, and perhaps even let it discourage you. Perhaps you used it as another example of how you don't have what it takes to seduce women. This is completely wrong. You don't need to be a "natural." You just need the technology in this book.

"IT'S AN ATTITUDE"

What would you say if you'd never driven a car before and we told you that driving was all a matter of your attitude? We seat you behind the wheel for the first time in your life, give you the keys, and say "Okay, drive!" First, you look at us like we are nuts. You fumble around and possibly manage to get the thing to turn over a few times before it dies. "Hey," we say, "don't get down. The secret of confidence with driving is having a good attitude, everybody knows that. Look at you, you are getting stressed-out. Now, try again, but have the right attitude!" You take a deep breath, take on a "good attitude," and try again. Perhaps this time you get the car moving, just enough to drive directly onto someone's front yard. "It's no use," you say. "I can't do it." "Well of course you can't," we come back, "with an attitude like that! We certainly can't help you till you get that attitude fixed!"

It's obvious what's missing here: We never told you anything about the technical skills of actually driving a car. We never taught you how to start the car, how to stop it, to steer and to shift. We never taught you the rules

of the road and all the skills you'd need to be a confident driver. Of course you didn't have the right "attitude." Of course you failed.

Now imagine that we've taught you everything you need to know before seating you behind the wheel for the first time. You've studied the textbooks, learned about how other drivers tend to behave, and the best ways to interact with them to get what you want. You've spent time in an automotive simulator where you could make mistakes with no real-world consequences, and when you first get behind the wheel, you know exactly what to do. What might your attitude be like then?

We think that saying, "The secret of success is to have a better attitude," is about as useful as saying, "The secret of success is to have success." In our opinion, the word "attitude" is horribly overused and tells you nothing useful. Attitude and success are both outcomes of doing certain things on a consistent basis. When you understand driving inside and out, know what to do when and how to do it, you automatically have the right attitude and have success. When you understand sex and dating inside and out, know what to do when and how to do it, you again automatically have the right attitude and have success.

Just as it does with driving, the attitude that creates success with women comes from understanding and using tools and technology. When you understand and start to use the tools in this book, you will have the "right attitude," which will lead to success. Furthermore, you don't have to somehow come up with it. We'll show you exactly how to create it.

WE LEARNED THE HARD WAY

There's no reason to give up because you haven't known how to get women in bed, or because you don't have some elusive thing called "attitude." As a matter of fact, we used to have the same problems you do. For both the authors, sex was sometimes plentiful and sometimes elusive. It seemed to be at the whim of luck, or at the whim of whatever women we happened to be around. Then we decided to put an end to the uncertainty and to discover the fundamentals that separate the master seducers from the men who spend Saturday nights alone.

There was work involved for us, the same as there will be for you. But

the difference is, using the material in this book, *you will finally know what the work is.* No more guesswork, no more accidentally destroying budding sexual relationships with rookie mistakes, no more spending Saturday night alone. But it *is* work, and it will take practice.

We committed ourselves to experimenting and going about seducing women in new ways, ways we would have never previously dreamed of. We realized that we were getting very few results using our then-current strategies, and so we decided to try new approaches. We once heard that the definition of insanity is doing the same thing over and over and expecting different results. We took this advice and set out on a completely new course for seducing women. We are sure that you can do the same thing, probably in much less time than it took us. We'll show you how to master these skills step by step, but you must be persistent.

MODELING EFFECTIVE SEDUCERS

In our quest to become reliably successful with women, we made use of the concept of *modeling*. Modeling, in this case, does not mean runway models or centerfold models. It means that we modeled our behavior after men we met who seemed successful with women.

Modeling means to imitate someone else. Knowing how to model someone who is successful is an essential skill for anyone who wants to achieve that same success. Modeling is based on the belief that anything someone else can do, you can do, too. You simply need to be able to think the way that person thinks, believe what that person believes, and take the same actions that person takes. Do this, and you'll get the same results. Along the way, you will learn what works for you and what doesn't.

For instance, a friend of ours returned to college at age thirty-two. He did this after being out of school for ten years. He decided that, this time, he was going to figure out how to be the most effective student he could be. He wanted to study the least he could but also get the best grades he could. So he set about finding and modeling the most successful and least stressed students. He observed the best students in his classes. He observed how they took notes, and he took notes in the same way. He sat in the same parts of the classroom they sat in. He studied with them to learn their

study habits and interviewed them about how they thought about going to school. By modeling his behaviors on theirs, he was able to take the same actions they took, and to get the same excellent results.

You can also use modeling in learning about success with women. Say you know a man who always seems to be in romantic relationships with hot women. He never seems to have any problems getting as many women as he wants, and seems to have exactly the sex life he wants. If you were to make this man your model, you wouldn't simply ask him how he does it, because he probably wouldn't know. (You certainly don't need more blah advice like "Have a good attitude!") What you would do is observe him. You'd look at how he dresses and moves, and dress and move the same way. You'd watch how he behaves with women, and try to behave the same way. You'd ask him what he's thinking at different times in a date, and think the same way. You'd ask him about his beliefs about women, and believe the same things. You'd listen to how he talks to women, and use the same words and sentences. In time, you'd have the same success he does. And you would be able to adapt what you've learned from him to best suit you.

As we modeled successful seducers for this book (and became successful seducers ourselves), we noticed trends. We were able to determine the basic habits that are common to all Highly Effective Seducers. If the only thing you get out of this book is that you incorporate these habits into your behavior with women, you will get your money's worth—and a *lot* more sex with women.

But be warned: As important as "modeling" is, there are some successful seducers who it really doesn't make sense to try to model, because the things that they do to succeed with women are *not* things you can replicate.

For instance, a really gorgeous guy will literally have beautiful women offering themselves to him, for no other reason than because of his beauty. This may not be something you can model (at least, not without costly plastic surgery!), so forget it. This is also the case with expert seducers who have many many years of experience as actors or performers. Sometimes the approaches they use are so subtle, developed over so many years of training and practice, that it's just too much to think you can model them.

Put another way: You don't want to model a young, gorgeous performer who's never failed with women, unless you are young and gorgeous, too. When we wrote this book, we modeled successful seducers who were like us: not too gorgeous, not too successful, not too young, but amazing with women. Those are the men we have modeled for you, and those are the types of men we suggest you model in your own behavior.

THE HABITS OF A HIGHLY EFFECTIVE SEDUCER

A Highly Effective Seducer never grovels for sex

Little kids whine. If you look at any group of kids, you'll see them whining, trying to get what they want. We aren't sure if it is a genetic or cultural trait, but it certainly is true about them. Can't you just hear the irritating sound of a kid whining, "Mommy, I don't want to go to sleep!" Or imagine that same statement screamed at you by a kid who's crying and pounding his fists into the wall next to you. How pleasant!

We were recently at lunch with one of our students, Paul. He had brought his six-year-old son, Benjamin. Paul is a divorced single father and is looking for a woman for a casual relationship. During lunch Benjamin drew quietly while we discussed dating strategies. Just as we paid the check, Benjamin threw a tantrum because Paul wouldn't buy him a second dessert. Benjamin screamed, pounded on the table, and spit on us. Incredibly, he even punched his father in the stomach. People at nearby tables stared. Paul apologized to us and seemed embarrassed. Finally, in desperation, after five minutes of Benjamin's bad behavior, Paul gave in and ordered him a second dish of ice cream.

Benjamin's throwing a tantrum to get what he wanted was similar to the way many men go about trying to get women to have sex with them. Some men approach seduction like they are needy little boys. If a woman says no, they try to manipulate and cajole her. Or they become obviously upset and pout. Another common strategy is to wear the woman down by begging her for sex. All of these behaviors convey a sense of neediness. From our perspective, they are forms of whining.

Clearly, people don't respect whiners. They are seen as childish, not worthy of respect, people who can't take care of themselves, and as wimps

who could be taken advantage of. While people often give children what they want just to shut them up, adult whiners get judged very harshly. The biggest cost to people who whine is a total loss of respect from others. Though you don't realize it, you've probably groveled for sex in much the same way as kids whine for ice cream.

When you grovel to a woman for sex, she thinks you are a worm. If the woman has kids, she will automatically think of you as one of their peers. She will lose any respect she had for you. Some women will move you from the category called "man" to the category called "boy." They probably won't have sex with you, and will disqualify you from any possible relationship. They may, moreover, think of you as a chump and take advantage of you.

You know what? Some things are more important than sex. And, to a man's man (which is what you will become if you follow the system in this book), self-respect is far, far more important than a momentary sexual experience. On the one hand, the more self-respect you have, the easier it is to be successful with women. On the other hand, you can sometimes get sex by throwing away your self-respect and groveling and begging to a woman for it, which a Highly Effective Seducer would never do.

Let's look at the typical groveling situation. Guy goes out with girl. Guy knows nothing or very little about seduction. Girl has nothing better to do, and allows some kissing and petting to happen. Girl gets turned off at some point and decides she doesn't want sex after all. Guy begs with "Aw, come on," "Why not?" and "You don't know how it hurts a guy," until she finally gives in and lets him have six minutes of unsatisfying—for her—sex. Afterward she looks disgusted and tells him to get the hell out of her bedroom. She thinks he's a jerk, and she's right.

Groveling may get you sex, but let's look at the cost: First, even though groveling may have gotten you sex this time, it won't work in the future. Groveling erodes your self-respect, and a man without self-respect is not sexually attractive to women. So this leads to more groveling and begging for sex, which erodes your self-respect even *more*. Eventually you have no self-respect, no self-esteem, and must live as a worm groveling through every interaction with women. Is that what you really want?

Second, how you are in pursuing sex is how you are in pursuing your

life. If you are able to have fun, be playful, and pursue a goal consistently but not be attached to the outcome, you will be successful both in life and with women. However, if you get into the habit of groveling and begging with women, you will be a groveling beggar in the bigger realms of your life. To some degree you'll grovel to your boss, to sales clerks, parents, everybody. You will be a true loser with no self-respect, no self-esteem.

Third (as if that's not enough!), women may become sadistic with and take advantage of a groveling, no-self-respect man. They'll take your money, time, and will toy with you sexually, finally ditching you without putting out. In the process they will purposefully make you miserable. One woman told us about a man she dated who would always grovel for sex. Whenever he wanted her, the man would snivel and whine in a way that she found disgusting. As a result, she made him buy her all sorts of expensive gifts. She even made him give her his credit card so she could use it to buy expensive clothes. The problem with this guy was threefold. One, he didn't realize that he was being exploited and punished for his whining. He lost his self-respect and was too naive to realize it. Two, he didn't notice that he was being overcharged for sex with this woman (we will go into this later). Three, he inevitably lost her. He never really got the sex he wanted, and she got rid of him when she became bored.

While we could focus on the woman in this situation, and examine how exploitative she was, we won't. We want you to take the focus off external circumstances and always bring it back to yourself. Rather than blaming women, we want you to always look for what you could change in yourself, what you could bring to the party, and what you could alter to create the situations you want. Men like to blame women for their problems, but blaming, after all, is just another form of whining. Whining, begging, and groveling for sex are behaviors you must stop if you want to become a Highly Effective Seducer.

A Highly Effective Seducer knows it's his job to pursue sex; and that she has the final say

Men and women play a very elaborate game of cat-and-mouse. Men pursue and women either accept, reject, or play hard to get. As men, we often love the process, even though it seems tedious at times. A woman

likes to know that you are persistent, appropriately challenging, and worthy of her affections. As men, we love the conquest. We love the accomplishment of taking this woman who at first seemed like an impossibility and of knowing that we now "have her."

As research for this book, we interviewed hundreds of women on their attitudes and experiences with dating. One woman explained why she loves being chased by men. "I like knowing I can turn him down. I like knowing he wants me and would do anything to have me sexually. I love the moment before we kiss, knowing it is the beginning of a long series of interactions. The whole process drives me crazy. I must admit, it leaves me feeling all hot and bothered."

Pursuing is paradoxical. On one hand, it is your job to pursue sex and go after what you want. On the other hand, she always has the final say. You must go at her speed and yet push at the same time. Even if it doesn't seem "fair" to you, you must stop when she says, no matter what. Warren Farrell, researcher of men's issues, figured out that men have to initiate over a hundred interactions with women to get them into bed. Men risk rejection each step along the way. These initiations include eye contact, kissing, petting, getting the phone number, and more. You must listen when she says no and behave accordingly.

When men don't listen to women's no, they are risking many severe problems. The biggest one is being accused of rape. This is a real threat.

A Highly Effective Seducer doesn't get upset at her no's

One of the myths in dating and seduction is that as a man you should be able to just go out and meet a beautiful woman on the street and have her back in your bed in minutes. We can recall times in high school thinking that a "real man" could just go out and pick up a woman effortlessly, which we later realized is a near impossibility. If you are especially gorgeous, a rock star, or already very famous for some other reason it could happen, but for most of us there is almost no chance. Ninety-eight percent of the online dating industry is built on the false idea that seduction can be instant and effortless. While it can be fun, it's usually not instant, and it does take some effort, even if it ends up feeling like a game.

We once heard a story about a man who was willing to go to extreme

measures for sex. No, he didn't have sex with a prostitute—he had his own ploy. He would stand at a bus stop in Los Angeles during rush hour and approach every woman getting on the bus, off the bus, or waiting, and he'd say, "I want to sleep with you." The story goes that he would do this sometimes hundreds of times. Women would laugh at him, spit at him, slap him, and run away in fear. Occasionally, however, there would be a woman who would say yes. He'd say, "Let's go to my place," and the sex would happen right away.

This guy had no problem accepting a woman telling him no. While we are not telling you to go and live out this crazy ploy, the man did act with a kind of bold courage and balls that you could probably use more of. Of course the guy was a bit off-kilter for risking so much trouble, like getting VD, sleeping with women he didn't know, having enraged women attack him, having boyfriends of the women kick his ass, getting arrested immediately, and not acting with self-respect. The part that is worth modeling is not being upset when women turn you down.

To meet women and have sex with them is often a lengthy process. Along the way you will have to face all sorts of trouble, problems, rejection, etc. The number one thing that stops most men from being successful is that they give up when women ambiguously or uncertainly say no. We view the dating scene as a game, and part of it is that women will, predictably, say no at some point. You have to improvise a way to stay motivated and focused on your goal without pushing them in a way they resent. Just like the one fellow who was nuts about asking every woman for sex, you need to develop a tougher skin regarding rejection.

Most men faced with no stop because they feel as though they've done something wrong. Have you ever been with a woman and thought things were going great, only to find out later that they weren't? You were holding hands, having great discussions, staring into her eyes, and just counting down the moments before you went in for the kiss. As your heart raced, you slowly brought your lips close to hers for a long, hot French kiss. Just as your lips touched hers, she pushed you away and said, "No. I'm not ready for that yet. I can't believe you just did that."

First of all, you are not alone. We all have miscommunications with women and let our hormones dictate our experience. The problem in the

above situation is that most men stop at that point and never go back, because they fear another rejection. The type of attitude we are teaching would have the man stop when the woman says so, all the while knowing that this was a step along the way, that he has other women he is working on, and that the door is still open for kissing or even having sex with this woman later.

A Highly Effective Seducer knows that rejection is the key to sexual prosperity

You're on the second date. You know it's time to make your move. She seems to like you. But who can tell? Maybe she's still wondering why she decided to go out on a date with you in the first place. But you have to make your move now. After all, *you* are ready. But what if she says no?

Or perhaps you aren't even out on a date yet. Maybe you are looking across the room at her, that unmet angel, that wonderful woman you wish you could bring yourself to talk to. You could go up to her. This could be your only chance. But what if she rejects you? What if she's mean to you? What if she says no?

Fundamentally, you are scared of women for one reason only: You are afraid of the pain and humiliation you'll feel if she rejects you. If she says no, you'll interpret it to mean all sorts of things: that you'll never get a woman, that you're not good enough, and that there's something fundamentally wrong with you. You'll feel humiliation and pain for days, perhaps even longer. Each rejection makes you even less likely to initiate anything with a woman again, which makes the next time you actually do initiate something seem even more important and significant to you. It will be extra-important to you that you not get rejected again, which will make you seem weird to the woman, who will then reject you. Then back to more pain and lonely nights ahead. This chain of events is enough to make your head spin. Many men that we've seen have experienced a similar cycle when they were rejected. The strange part is that most of us are not even consciously aware of these crippling thoughts.

For Bob, doing something as simple as asking a woman out is a very significant task. "If she says no," he muses, "I'll look like a fool. I can just see that horrified look on her face already. I wonder how she'll say no?

Then she'll tell all our mutual friends that I, of all people, tried to ask her out. They'll all laugh at me and make fun of me behind my back. My reputation will be ruined."

Bob puts himself in so much pain by picturing the worst possible outcomes that he paralyzes himself with fear. He's picturing all these terrible outcomes when he approaches a woman, and his sheer level of fear alone, if nothing else, makes women say no to him. He acts so strangely and so hesitantly that he's at his worst, rather than at his best. Few women would choose to go out with him. Women are not stupid; they can sense hesitation in a man. They don't want to be the source of you becoming depressed if they are not interested in dating you.

Like many people, Bob feels it's his duty to imagine the worst of what could happen in a risky situation, so he can "steel himself against it." He thinks that looking realistically at the "downside" of being rejected is the best way. He is wrong. Drawing lots of unpleasant pictures of being rejected, and getting completely absorbed in fear of how you'll feel if you are rejected, makes rejection almost inevitable.

The Highly Effective Seducer sees things completely differently. Rather than seeing rejection as a reflection of his value as a man, the Highly Effective Seducer has one rule about rejection: "Rejection is the key to sexual prosperity." An Effective Seducer thinks about rejection differently than does an ineffective seducer. He makes better decisions about what a woman's rejection means to him.

For instance, imagine you are at a grocery store, and you flirt and joke with the attractive young woman behind the counter (as we'll teach you to do). Perhaps she says, "Would you like a bag?" You smile and jokingly respond, "Oh no . . . bags are dangerous! Haven't you read the suffocation warnings on them?" She responds with a dark glare. You continue to joke with her, and her only words for you are a cold-sounding "Thank-you-come-again" when she hands you your change. In every way that she can, short of outright insolence, she rejects you.

Let's look into the mind of an ineffective seducer after this interaction. He might be thinking, "Wow, I really blew it with her. I can't believe I said that stuff. I must have been really out of line. Once again, I scared a woman I was attracted to. What's wrong with me? Won't I ever be able to talk to

women without something weird happening? She's probably talking about me right now, telling everybody what a jerk I am." The ineffective seducer explains the interaction to himself in a way that causes him humiliation and shame.

To the Highly Effective Seducer, rejection is a stepping stone to massive sexual success because he sees it as one more no he doesn't have to hear on the way to an inevitable yes with some other woman, or even the same woman. After that same interaction, an Effective Seducer might say to himself, "Wow, she sure didn't have much of a sense of humor. I wonder if she's not feeling well. Perhaps she had a friend die from suffocation in a plastic bag. Who knows?" If he does think that she didn't like him, his only thought is "Well, it's a good thing I found out now, before wasting more time and energy on her. Now I can concentrate on all the women who will want to be with me!" The Highly Effective Seducer explains the interaction to himself in such a way that he feels good about himself. He's gotten one more no out of the way, and can move on to the yes he knows is in his future somewhere.

When asking a woman out, the ineffective seducer thinks differently as well. Imagine you are at a restaurant and about to ask your waitress out. You say, "Hey, you seem pretty fascinating. What would it be like if we went out for coffee sometime? Could I have your phone number?" She responds, "Gee, uh, no. Would you like some dessert?"

Here's how an ineffective seducer might think about this: "Man, how humiliating. I can't believe I did that. What a slap in the face! That's what I get for thinking any attractive woman would want to go out with me. She didn't want me. I mustn't be good enough. I feel like crap. I will never do that again."

Meanwhile, here's how the Effective Seducer thinks about it: "Wow, how 'bout that. She must have a boyfriend or something, or really got hurt somewhere along the line. That kind of thing happens, I know. Perhaps she's just caught up in her own little world. Well, that's one more no I don't have to hear on the way to getting a yes from a woman. Too bad, she was cute. What's on the dessert menu?" The Effective Seducer explains her rejection in a way that's not personal; it doesn't mean anything about him, except that it's one more no he won't have to hear again.

Effective and ineffective seducers differ if they are rejected when going for a kiss, as well. Say you've been on a date that went okay, but not great. You were bored and found an excuse to take her home early. In the car in front of her house you look into her eyes, run your fingers lightly through her hair, and as you begin to move toward her, she says, "Please don't try to kiss me."

By now you can probably see the difference already. While the ineffective seducer is plunging into depression at her rejection, the Highly Effective Seducer is already planning how he's going to spend the rest of the evening, thinking something like "Huh! I guess she was as bored as I was. That's one more no on the way to yes. What's on TV later?" While the ineffective seducer is letting it wreck his evening, the Effective Seducer is planning how to get her out of his car as quickly as possible, so he can get on with his life.

Here are the basic principles the Highly Effective Seducer follows in the face of rejection, which you must also follow. First, he leaves his self-image out of it. He comes up with an explanation for her rejection that has to do with her or with circumstances, rather than with him. He thinks to himself that "She must have a boyfriend," rather than "I must not be attractive."

Second, he redirects his attention. Rather than giving his brain an opportunity to dwell on the rejection, he thinks about something else instead. He asks, "What's on the dessert menu?" or "What's on TV tonight?" If his brain does go back to the rejection, he reminds himself it's one more no he won't have to hear on his way to an inevitable yes. The Effective Seducer does not allow rejections to mean that he is unworthy or bad in any way. Though we dislike the overly New Age/positive-thinking movement, we saw a poster recently that poignantly summed up our point. It said, "You miss 100 percent of the shots you don't take."

A Highly Effective Seducer sees dating as a numbers game

Highly Effective Seducers constantly remember that dating, like so many areas of life, is a numbers game. Crass as it may seem, dating women is like selling a product. Instead of selling a vacuum cleaner, however, you

are selling *you*. Salesmen know that they rarely make a sale on the first call they make. They know that if they do, it was luck, and they can't count on it again.

Let's watch a top salesman at work. Martin sells insurance, and has for four years. He's twenty-nine, and he has stunned his company by again and again meeting and beating his sales goals. He's made himself their best salesman by following a simple philosophy. He's learned, through keeping records, that for every seventy-five people he calls, he makes four appointments, and out of those four appointments he makes one sale.

Unlike his associates, who don't sell as much as he does, Martin has accepted these facts of life. He understands that it's not personal when people hang up or aren't home or yell at him. It's all part of the numbers game he's playing, a game in which he knows he will eventually, inevitably, make the sale. All he has to do is keep dialing the phone, and sooner or later he *will* sell some insurance. So he keeps dialing, with that end in mind.

His associates that fail don't see it as a numbers game. They take the rejections and difficulties personally. Instead of knowing that they are working their way through inevitable rejection to get to inevitable success, they get caught up in the momentary bad feelings and lose sight of their goal. They eventually give up, while Martin goes on to succeed. Martin is like the infamous Energizer Bunny. He keeps going and going, unwilling to be stopped by pitfalls along the way. Sure, Martin sometimes gets flustered, upset, and angry when things don't go his way. But he is able always to bring it back to the numbers game he is playing.

Highly Effective Seducers see seduction as a numbers game as well. Even the most successful seducers we know don't bed every woman they approach—far from it. They know that most of their "cold calling"—that is, flirting with women—will not lead to anything more than that one interaction.

An Effective Seducer expects that one in ten of the women he flirts with he'll go out with, and that one in four of the women he goes out with he'll have sex with. He's accepted these facts of life. He thinks it's like baseball: those who hit the most home runs also have the most strikeouts. He understands that it's not personal when women say no to him, don't show

up, or reject his advances. It's all part of the game he's playing, which he knows will eventually get him in bed with women he desires. All he has to do is keep initiating, flirting, asking women out, and following the principles in this book, and sooner or later he *will* be having sex. So he keeps initiating, with that end in mind.

Even better, the Effective Seducer knows that each of those interactions—even the "failed" ones—can be fun and energizing for him, even though they don't lead to sex. In that way each interaction charges him up for the next one, creating a snowball of flirting that inevitably leads to sex.

Ineffective seducers don't see seduction as a numbers game. They take the rejections and difficulties personally. Instead of knowing that they are working their way through inevitable rejection to inevitable success, they get caught up in their momentary bad feelings. As a result, they lose sight of the inevitability of their goal. They eventually give up, while the Effective Seducer goes on to succeed.

At the beginning, when you are first developing your seduction skills, your numbers may be more daunting. Unlike the practiced seducer, you may have to flirt with twenty-five or thirty women before you ask out three, and of those three only two may decide to go out with you. You may have to date six or seven women before you get one in bed, rather than the two or three needed by a more experienced seducer. You must understand that it doesn't matter when they say no. As long as you realize that your persistence makes success inevitable, you'll be able to stick with it and keep pursuing women until you finally have the success you want. That success will bolster your confidence, and you will have an easier time getting the next woman. As long as you remember it's a numbers game, you will have success with women.

Geoffrey is a student of ours who took this habit to heart. Forty-two years old, divorced, and slightly overweight, he hadn't had sex with a woman since his divorce three years previous. He was a sensitive fellow who'd make a devoted lover, boyfriend, or husband. His chances of that were slim, however, as he had been taking any negative sign from women extremely personally. If he made a joke and a woman didn't laugh, he was crushed. Since the last woman who said no to him two years ago, he hadn't

asked any woman out at all. He was living in hope, wishing that somehow he would find the love and relationship he wanted. Geoffrey was depressed when we met him, desperate for female companionship.

We shared the Habits of a Highly Effective Seducer with him, and he changed his approach with women. Instead of seeing their rejections as reflections of him, he kept his mind focused on the numbers game. He told us, "I figure I'll have to ask out ten women to get one yes, and date four woman before I'll have sex. Fine, I'll do it!" He even showed us a chart he'd made to keep track of how many women he'd asked out and how many women he dated.

It turned out that Geoffrey's predictions were overly conservative. Three of the first six women he asked out said yes, and one of those ended up having sex with him within three weeks. "Thinking of dating as a numbers game gave me the ability to move on to the next gal when one said no," he told us later. He now has a girlfriend he loves, and whom he's planning to marry.

Seeing dating as a numbers game will give you the confidence to go on in the face of anything that happens. From the man who approaches women on the street and asks, "Will you have sex with me?" to Geoffrey's search for a girlfriend, the numbers game will make you a Highly Effective Seducer.

Some men object to the idea that women's rejections should just roll off their backs. They want to be sensitive men; they think that seeing women's rejections as the key to sexual prosperity somehow gives license to men to be even more insensitive than they are already. After all, don't women complain that men aren't sensitive enough?

We think you should be sensitive to what women say and do, but *not* in the early stages of dating. When you are first getting to know each other, too much sensitivity to what she says or does is sexual suicide. The objection is that if you don't feel bad, you won't do what it takes to keep yourself "in line." You'll just be an example of the huge male ego we've all heard so much about. If you aren't hurt by her rejections, this line of reasoning goes, you must think you're God's gift to women. At least if you are hurt, you know you're not overly egotistical.

Bob takes this route. When a woman rejects him, he's devastated. If

you suggest to him that he might explain the rejection in some other way, he'll worry that then he'll be inaccurate: After all, maybe there really is something offensive about him that he needs to fix! If he keeps feeling good about himself after being rejected, he might be one of those egotistical guys who women sneer at behind their backs! He might become a macho pig, and we wouldn't want that.

Bob doesn't realize two things. First, that women may sneer at those guys, but they also have sex with them (for reasons we'll get to later) more than they do with apologetic men. Second, while he should always be refining his style and approach with women, feeling bad about himself will not help him do that. In the atmosphere of early dating, you simply have no choice but to be insensitive in the face of rejection. If you want any kind of relationship with women, you must be thick-skinned. Simply follow the steps the Highly Effective Seducer follows, realize it's one more no you won't have to hear on your way to success, and move on.

A Highly Effective Seducer always pursues more than one woman

In interviewing and modeling the behavior of Effective Seducers, we learned a terrible truth: If you are trying to become an expert seducer, pursuing only one woman is worse for your sex life than pursuing none at all!

Why is this so? Because when you are pursuing only one woman, you have no backup plan. You have all your eggs in one basket. You can't be playful and pursue her unconcerned with outcomes, because if she's your only prospect, she's your only chance for sex. You'll get overly concerned that if things don't work out you won't have anyone else to pursue. It most likely will make you dependent on her in some way. You will likely push her away with this dependency attitude. Further, if after a few dates she doesn't like you, then you will feel that there is something wrong with you. Your inability to relax with her will drive her away and leave you feeling bad about yourself.

Many of our students have fallen into this trap. You can follow all the other habits of the Highly Effective Seducer, but if you pursue only one woman, you will never experience an abundant sex life.

Leo, the manager of a dry cleaner, didn't believe us. When we started coaching him, he hadn't had a date in six months. "It's been so long since I've had sex," he joked with us, "that I think I've forgotten how to do it!" We trained him in the Habits. He followed them all except one. He pursued only one woman at a time. He flirted with one woman, returning to the store she worked at to see her again and again. He fantasized about how wonderful it would be to go out with her, to have her as a lover. Leo ignored other women, not exploring them as we recommended he do. But he had a problem: Every time he saw the woman he desired, he felt more tense. It became harder for him to joke with her, and he became more afraid of saying or doing something that would offend her. By the time Leo decided to ask her out, he was so nervous he was actually sweating. If she said no, all his work would have been for nothing, and all his dreams with her would be dashed! When he tried to ask her out, he stumbled on his words and blushed. She said, "Gee, thanks, I like you and everything, but I don't think it would work out." Because she was the only woman he was after, her response became so meaningful to him that he lost all ability to relax and be himself. Seeing his tension, she naturally didn't want to go out with him.

Leo returned to us and asked our advice. We told him again how it was important to go after more than one woman at a time. After all, we asked him, would he seek out only one client for his dry-cleaning business? Of course not. He began following our advice, using the system we outline in this book, and soon had success.

If you do this, too, adding in more women all the time and dropping ones that don't work out for you, no single woman's response to you will take on much significance. You will be able to relax, be playful, and unconcerned about her responses to your seduction. You'll be able to say to yourself, "Hey, if she doesn't want me, there are plenty of women waiting in the wings to take her place," and know it's true.

Pursuing more than one woman also makes you more patient with the women you are seducing, because you have a variety of women at different points in your seduction. Now it doesn't matter to Leo if one of the women is being uncommunicative, is mean to him one day, or is moody. He knows he doesn't have to rush her in any way, because he has his needs met other

places. This makes him an easier man to be around, and much more attractive to women.

Following our advice is also important when you finally are having sex. If you stop going after other women once you have a lover, she *will* become your girlfriend, whether you like it or not. Studies have shown that men's body chemistry actually becomes physically addicted to a woman he sleeps with on a regular basis. That's fine if you want a girlfriend, but if you want casual short-term relationships with women you *must* continue to pursue other women, even after you've got the first one in bed.

Women are attracted to men who are relaxed, creative, and exciting. Pursuing more than one woman brings out these qualities because it keeps you engaged with life in a creative, exciting way. When you know the woman you are after is one of many, her response matters less than it would if she were your only hope for sex. You can be more relaxed, because you aren't risking offending your only possible sexual partner. If you do lose her for some reason, you can just move on to the next woman.

A Highly Effective Seducer initiates everything with women

Men frequently fail to initiate with women. They either forget that it is essential, or they resent doing it. Perhaps they've been frequently rejected a lot by women. Perhaps they think they are so special that women will approach them and ask them out. Whatever the reason, here is what Highly Effective Seducers know: The man must *always* make it his responsibility to initiate every step of a romantic encounter. Effective Seducers never forget it! If you slack off, another man will be having sex with the woman of your dreams while you are home alone masturbating.

Men commonly think women give signals of interest the same way they do. This is a big mistake. Most men don't realize that women do *not* do things the way men do. You must understand the crucial differences in how men and women respond to initiation.

For instance, if one of your buddies doesn't call you back when you've initiated getting together, it is fair to assume he doesn't want to accept your invitation. This is not the case with women. Women are trained to play hard to get, and are programmed to give mixed messages. It isn't per-

sonal. In fact, you will be a much happier man if you just keep initiating; don't take anything a woman does personally.

A case in point: A hot woman will never ask you out and will rarely call you back. If you really want her, you will have to prove you are persistent, patient, challenging, and that there is something that sets you apart from the others. When a friend of ours met a beautiful twenty-year-old woman at a bar, he initiated and got her phone number. He called her several times and she didn't call back. He kept initiating phone calls and finally talked to her. They set a date for coffee and she didn't show. He initiated another call and set up a date with her. On that next date he slept with her. His success was built on his persistence and willingness to initiate. What he didn't do was take it personally, resent the woman, whine to her, or give up.

We know many men who are angry that they have to initiate. They complain that it isn't fair, and that if women really believed in equality, they would approach men. Or they complain that it's scary to approach a woman they don't know and risk rejection. Our advice to these men is to grow up and deal with it. If you are resentful, no woman will want you. Just get over it. This may be more easily said than done, but initiating without resentment is essential if you want success with women. This is the law of the jungle, and you must learn it to survive. You have no chance of changing the terrain, only of adapting to the harsh conditions. A master seducer will have the inner discipline to overcome his fear and resentment to get to his eventual goal of abundant sex.

Try looking at it this way: Initiating gives you power. Rather than feeling resentful for having to do all the work to get a woman into bed, an Effective Seducer knows that initiating gives him the opportunity to make dating work for him. If you are the initiator, you get to talk to her when you want to, set up dates for times that are convenient for you, approach any woman you want, and eventually sleep with any woman you are attracted to. You're not powerless; in fact, you have total societal approval to make it work for you! From this standpoint having to initiate is pretty great for men.

Just in case you are totally brain-dead, here is a list of initiations you must make: the first eye contact, the first smile, talking to her for the first time, keeping the conversation going, asking for her phone number, calling

her up, calling her again when she doesn't call you back, asking her out, asking her out again when she "forgets" to show up, all eye contact and touching on the date, the first kiss, every single sexual initiation, and any subsequent dates. In a short-term erotic relationship you will also have to initiate the breakup.

A Highly Effective Seducer is always prospecting

A Highly Effective Seducer turns every situation with women into a prospecting situation. If you want an abundant sex life, you must learn to do this as well. One of Bob's fatal flaws is that he has tunnel vision in his pursuit. Though he is consistently unsuccessful, he thinks he "knows" that there are very few places he can meet women. He is wrong. The fact is, women are everywhere. There is no shortage of places to meet them. Some of the best places are ones you are in every day that you don't even yet realize. Because Bob doesn't realize this, he only flirts with women when he feels like it, not as practice. He doesn't turn every situation into a prospecting situation.

Before taking our seminars, reading our books, or getting our CD or DVD courses, many of our students stumbled through their days. They were unaware of the multitude of women around them at almost every moment. They constantly thought they were flawed in some way, never aware of the constant flow of sex available to every man as his birthright. If you read this book carefully and follow our advice, you will be able to notice who the women are that you have contact with every day and turn many of them into lovers, just as Highly Effective Seducers do.

Effective Seducers are like successful salesmen. Let's examine how a successful salesman views his life. To him, every situation poses the potential for a sale. A hungry insurance salesman, for example, will do many cold calls, ask his friends for leads, call up long lost relatives for leads, put ads in newspapers, leave his business card at restaurants, and do other outrageous things to make sales. He will do whatever it takes to get the sale. The Effective Seducer has a similar type of rigor and intensity about his quest for women.

The Effective Seducer is also like a hunter. A good hunter is constantly outside of his comfort zone. This means that he doesn't hunt only

in places that are easiest to get to. He goes to areas where he thinks the deer are, whether or not those places are always convenient. He makes it a higher priority to get his prey than to be in a comfortable situation. He gets up before dawn, hikes in the dark, sits in the cold, and waits patiently for a deer that may or may not come, because he knows that if he is consistent, he will eventually be successful. This is a model for us all.

A hunter scans the landscape looking for any signs, smells, or sounds that might lead him to his prey, just as an Effective Seducer does. He observes the whole landscape and investigates anything that moves. Most lonely men could also use this trait. An unsuccessful seducer is so caught up with how a woman isn't quite pretty enough that he turns down the opportunity to practice on her, or to use that situation to meet other women. He also fails to scan the landscape and to stay aware of all the women who are potentials. The hunter analogy, though crude, is useful for you to use on your path to becoming a Highly Effective Seducer.

Look at every situation you are in as a potential for meeting women. You can even look at every interaction with a woman, be it at a restaurant, in an elevator, while pumping gas, or at the doctor, as an opportunity to initiate the steps to getting a date and practicing your skills as a seducer.

A Highly Effective Seducer always acts with an outcome in mind

If you were cold-calling for your business, would you call up a potential customer and not have any idea of what you were going to say? If you wanted a raise, would you go into your boss's office and have hours of meandering, meaningless conversation in the hopes that a raise would "just happen"? Would you take a potential client to seemingly random events and social occasions, hoping that for some reason he would decide to make a purchase?

Of course you wouldn't. You'd always act with an outcome in mind. If socializing or conversing were part of getting to your outcome, of course you would socialize and talk. But you'd always have in the back (or even near the front) of your mind the outcome you wanted to produce. You'd do the things that brought you closer to that outcome, and not do the things that had no impact or that might even take you away from your goal.

That's what Highly Effective Seducers do. Successful seductions are built on planning, and having outcomes in mind for every step of the way. Where there is no planning, there is room for problems and breakdowns.

Having an outcome before the date means that when a man is talking to a woman for the first time, he is focused on giving her romantic feelings or getting her phone number. On the date, the outcome may be to have sex. After the date, the outcome may be to see her again, to keep her feeling special and interested, or to move on. You must always be asking yourself, "What is my goal?" and "How do I want her to be feeling?" If you want her to feel safe, you must appear safe and not be too outrageous or scary. If you want her to feel romantic, you must ask her romantic questions and do romantic things. If you want her to think of you as intriguing, you must challenge her in some way. If you don't want her to feel disgusted, you must not burp, make crude jokes, or do other disgusting things.

If your goal is the first kiss, and you have that goal in mind, you will automatically tend to choose activities and behaviors in line with that goal. And step by step, your goal will be fulfilled.

Men who don't have an outcome in mind are at the whim of circumstance and are bound to fail, and most men fall into this category. They go with the flow and want to "just see where things go." As a man following the Habits of a Highly Effective Seducer, you know your outcome, and pursue it.

A Highly Effective Seducer always makes life work for him

You met her last week. Attractive, fit, blond, and in her mid-twenties. You had fun talking together, she readily gave you her phone number and agreed to meet for coffee. You arrive ten minutes early and are all ready for her to show up. You are waiting at the time she said she'd be there, waiting ten minutes past that time, and still waiting thirty minutes later. She still hasn't shown up. The question is, did you make it work for you, or didn't you?

A man who makes life work for him has no difficulty in this situation. He's brought some work to do, or some reading that is important for him to complete. He set up the date at a place and time convenient for

him, so that if she didn't show up it wouldn't wreck his day. He works, and flirts with the other women at the coffee shop, and ends up having a good time anyway. After waiting thirty minutes, he leaves. When he calls the woman who didn't show—and we'll show you the best way to do this in a later chapter—he's not filled with unproductive resentment that she didn't keep her word. He made life work for him and had a good time anyway.

A man who doesn't make life work for him is so astounded that the woman said yes in the first place, that he bends over backward to meet her for the coffee date. He may have canceled something important, rearranged his schedule, and come to an inconvenient place to meet her. He'll have arrived ready to socialize and have no backup plan in place for when she doesn't arrive. Even if she does arrive, forty minutes late, he's so angry and upset and humiliated that he can't have a good time with her. He's made himself a victim by not making life work for him.

This is a huge mistake that many of our students make. They expect others, or their circumstances, to make life work for them. The man who is victimized by his date not showing up was expecting *her* to make the date work for him. As a result, he was a victim, just as you will be if you leave making your life work in the hands of other people.

Steve is a tall, balding man in his late thirties. He has an important presentation to make at 8:00 a.m. the next morning. It could make or break his getting that big promotion. After wrapping up the final details for his presentation, he decides to go out with the guys for a couple of drinks. It is now 9:00 p.m., and the bar seems really hopping. Brenda, an attractive woman in a slinky tight silk dress, is giving him a lot of attention. He dances with her and buys her drinks. Brenda touches him, smiles, and even leans over off her bar stool to kiss him lightly, pressing her breasts into him. "Finally," Steve thinks to himself, "I'm finally gonna get lucky."

Unfortunately for Steve, Brenda has no intention of leaving before closing time: 2:30 a.m., still three hours away. Steve is tantalized with the prospect of sex dangling before him. He drinks and dances with her until 2:30 a.m. Then she begs him to take her to an after-hours party until 3:30 a.m. Finally, he gets her back to his apartment, where they have sex until 6:00 a.m. Still drunk and exhausted, on one hour of sleep, Steve gives a terrible

presentation the next morning. He doesn't get the promotion, and his boss's boss wonders aloud what is wrong with him.

The answer is simple: Steve didn't make life work for him, at least not in this situation. Once a woman comes on the scene, he becomes a victim. He hopes her whims get him sex and that his life will still work. He becomes a victim of his own unwillingness to take control of his life. He is also blindsided by his own urges and has no ability to prioritize the things in his life. He acts out of desperation, not like a man with a plan.

When Robert, who's worked with us, finds himself in the same situation, his choices are easy. He knows that for life to work for him he must leave the bar by 11:00 p.m., whether or not there's a woman on his arm. He tells Brenda he has to leave, and she's disappointed. He tells her he'd love to see her again, and gets her phone number. He leaves, gets to bed early, and aces his presentation the next morning. He gets the raise, and is so pumped up by his success that he goes out that night and picks up another woman and has sex with her all night. Plus, he still has Brenda's number to call later!

The difference between Steve and Robert is that Robert is committed to making his life work for him, while Steve isn't. Steve might say he is, but the possibility of sex makes him throw away his control over his life. If we observe both of them, we can see that Steve is more committed to being a victim of his circumstances and to instant satisfaction than he is to long-term gain. Robert sets his intention and moves toward it. He's leaving the bar by 11:00 p.m., because he knows that's what it'll take to make his presentation work. His presentation is his top priority. He knows a night of drunken sex isn't worth risking the raise he's been working on for three months. Robert is an Effective Seducer. Steve is not.

Do you make life work for you in every situation, or are you willing to throw away control of your life when there's a possibility for sex? Highly Effective Seducers set up their lives so that they get the kind of life they want, whether women are in the picture or not. They count on themselves to make their lives work, rather than counting on women. As a result they are happier, more in control of their lives, more successful, and more attractive to women.

It is said that sex is the world's most expensive commodity. It often seems that way for men. Men's need for sex topples empires, loses them

jobs, gets them landed in jail. If you've ever done something that hurt your long-term best interests in order to pursue the possibility of sex, then you are not making your life work for you. If you've ever felt like a victim in your interactions with women you've dated or tried to date, then you, too, haven't been making life work for you. In both situations you haven't been a Highly Effective Seducer.

This habit of Effective Seducers branches beyond dating. Men who are committed to always making life work for them are always asking themselves how they can improve their experience of *any* situation. If an Effective Seducer is on a business trip and gets caught in an airport for a four-hour layover, he doesn't whine about it—or if he does, he gets it over with quickly. He asks himself, "How can I make this work for me?" and he keeps on asking until he comes up with an answer that works for him. He may make calls that need to be made. He may set up his laptop and get some work done. He may find the airport bookshop and find a book he's been meaning to read. He may even call phone sex on his cell phone from an empty bathroom stall.

A man who always makes life work for him is willing to be outrageous to have that happen. He wants a life that he lives fully. When caught in the airport, he may set himself the goal of flirting with ten women and getting one to have sex with him. He may call an ex-lover who lives in the town he's stuck in, and try to seduce her. He decides the quality of experience he's going to have, and creates his life to achieve it.

If you are going to be a man who has a life that works, you must do this, too. Here are some of the questions a Highly Effective Seducer constantly asks himself:

- How can I make this experience work for me?
- What quality of experience am I committed to having, no matter what happens?
- What is a physical action I can take, right now, to create that experience for myself?
- What's most important to me in this situation?
- How can I get that?
- What would make this situation most fun?

By asking yourself these questions, and committing to making life work for you rather than counting on women to do it for you, you will become the kind of man women are most attracted to.

A Highly Effective Seducer is never a prospect's therapist or friend

Pop quiz: The best way to get a woman to desire you sexually is to help solve her problems, listen to her difficulties, and to prove yourself to be an excellent friend. True or false?

Every Highly Effective Seducer we studied knew that this statement is false. Being a woman's therapist, confidant, or pal is one of the *worst* ways of getting a woman in bed. In fact, if you are a woman's therapist, confidant, or pal, you almost certainly destroy your chances with her sexually. While you may want to have women as pals on your own time, if the woman is a prospective sex partner, this could be the death blow.

The Therapist Ploy. The man who tries to get sex by being a woman's therapist thinks that if he solves her emotional problems then she'll naturally want to have sex with him. He bases this faulty reasoning on the fact that if an attractive woman solved *his* problems, he'd want to have sex with her. Given the fact that he'd probably want to have sex with an attractive woman even if she added to his problems, his logic doesn't make sense.

Gary is a man who tries to seduce women by being their free therapist. He was very attracted to Diane, as any man would be; she was blond and bouncy and smart and large-breasted and everything he was looking for in a woman.

But Diane had problems. She'd had a difficult childhood, and it seemed like she always dated men who ended up being jerks to her. Sometimes she was happy and sometimes she was miserable. Her problems gave Gary something to talk with her about, and he secretly decided that he could get her in bed if he solved her problems. She'd see how wonderful he was and reward him with sex. He took on being her personal therapist.

So Gary listened to Diane's problems and gave her wonderful advice. Then he listened to more to her problems and gave her more advice. He thought about her problems all the time, figuring out innovative solutions.

He talked to his friends about how difficult she was, how she didn't seem to want to change. Gary encouraged her to call him in the middle of the night if she had nightmares—and she did. Gary was certain that he was getting closer to her and that she would soon be his. After all, they were so intimate. She called him all the time!

Gary's plan fell apart when he took Diane to a party where he noticed she was very flirty with lots of other men. One of his male friends told him later that she had said to him, "You know, it's odd. I want to have sex with every man in this room, except for Gary!" She ended up going home with Gary's best friend. He was devastated that she didn't desire him. He couldn't figure it out. After all, hadn't he helped her solve her problems?

This is a common story of ineffective seducers. When a man discusses a woman's problems with her, she associates him with her problems. Even if he manages to come up with solutions, he's still the last person who saw her with the problems. Either way, she'll want to get away from him. Effective Seducers know that women are attracted to men who take them into a different, romantic world, in which they seem to have no problems and feel wonderful. If a prospective lover shares her problems with an Effective Seducer, he may listen, but he will never offer solutions. He'll distract her from her problems by being charming and exciting, get her feeling the way he wants her to feel, and continue the seduction.

When Jake, a Highly Effective Seducer, meets a woman like Diane, he handles her completely differently. He doesn't take the bait of talking about her problems. Instead, he sets up romantic experiences that blow her mind and make her associate being with him with feelings of pleasure and attraction. (We'll show you how to do this when we talk about the "priming" and "seduction" dates.) She wants to be with him because he's exciting, not because he's a good therapist. He may even cause problems for her, and she'll put up with it, and keep wanting to see him. She'll complain about him to someone like Gary, but she won't be able to wait to see him again. All because Jake knows not to become her therapist.

The Friend Ploy. The man who tries to get into a woman's pants by being her friend fails with women just as much as the man who tries to be her therapist. As we will discuss later, women we've interviewed have told us

that they often decide if a man will be a lover or a friend in the first two minutes after meeting him. Once you are in the friend category, it's very difficult to get out. Donnie was friends with Kathy, whom he met at a personal growth seminar. She thought of him as a friend, and often told him so. He wanted to be her lover, but every time he pursued it, she'd say things like "I like you, but I don't want to spoil our wonderful friendship," or "I just don't feel that way about you. You're more like a brother to me." (Once she even said he was like a *sister* to her!) Effective Seducers understand that if a woman is a prospective lover, a man must avoid being her friend, and let her know about his romantic interest right away. When Jerome, a Highly Effective Seducer, meets a woman like Cathy, he shows his interest right away, as we'll show you how to do in this book. By doing this, he puts himself in the lover, or at least potential lover, category, avoiding the trap of friendship altogether. While Donnie is stuck in the friend category, Jerome has a foundation he can build his seduction upon, without her being able to object that romance might spoil their friendship. After all, they never had a friendship in the first place.

Women can be great friends if you have absolutely no sexual interest in them. If you are interested in a woman as a lover, take a cue from the Highly Effective Seducers: Don't be her friend or her therapist!

A Highly Effective Seducer is always willing to walk away from the seduction or from the woman

Have you ever seen a man totally at the beck and call of a woman, and miserable about it? Have you ever been that guy who is so dependent on a woman that you've forgotten what you are about and what your boundaries are? Have you ever felt "taken" by a woman?

Once the relationship starts, many men tend to give a woman everything she wants and sacrifice their self-respect in hopes of getting a steady supply of sex. Men often stay in unsatisfying relationships because they don't see any way out. Or they think no other woman will put up with or love them. As a result, they stay in relationships, sometimes for years, miserable and knowing that they should break it off, but somehow never mustering the courage to do so.

Ed, a thirty-year-old social worker, dated Pam, a modern dancer, for six years. She came from a wealthy family and paid the rent on their apart-

ment. Ed became semidependent on Pam during the four years they lived together. They were even engaged during the last year.

At first, he explained, "things seemed so exciting, and the sex was great. She would often prance around the house in her sexy leotards and we would cherish the nights we had at home." Later, she withheld sex and demanded that he do all the housework because she was paying the rent. He felt trapped in the relationship. He worried that no other woman would love him, and besides, he was dependent on her. He didn't like doing all the work, and didn't pursue his interests in the meantime, but somehow he couldn't turn down her demands.

Highly Effective Seducers are willing to cut off relationships with women if they don't work for them. If you are not willing to leave the relationship, you no longer have any power or say in what happens. If you aren't willing to walk away, she will assume that she can walk all over you. A woman, like anyone else, will try to take as much as she can from you if you don't show her the bottom line.

The same principle can be applied in business situations. A man who isn't willing to quit when things become intolerable is at the whim of everyone's opinions and desires. He probably doesn't advance at his job or ask for what he wants because he is so busy being subservient to others that he ignores going for what he wants. The willingness to walk gives a man confidence in himself in any situation, especially with women.

This book will show you how to stay in the driver's seat and get sex whether you are in a committed relationship or not. If you don't want a girlfriend or a committed relationship, you must learn the power of being willing to walk away. If you want a committed relationship, you must be willing to walk away from women who do not seem like the type you want to spend the rest of your life with.

Being willing to walk integrates a hard-bottom-line attitude while not being cruel. It is not a personal attack on her. In fact you are really saying, "I want 'x.' You can either produce that or I'll replace you." An Effective Seducer knows what he wants and cuts to the chase, saving himself and the woman time and energy. A man who is willing to walk away, even from sex, is respected and cannot be taken off the course he has set for his life.

If Ed had known about our ideas, he could have ended the relationship

with Pam much earlier and would have been able to create relationships he wanted with other women.

A Highly Effective Seducer makes it look like he's not working on the romance

What is one key difference between seducing a woman and having a job? At work you need to look as if you are working—in fact, the harder you look as if you are working, the better it is. The Highly Effective Seducer knows that when seducing a woman, the opposite is true: When you are with a woman, you absolutely must make everything look easy, even if you worked hard to set up the perfect romantic evening, or even if you hunted for hours to find the perfect little romantic gift.

One of our students, for example, spent his spare moments over a two-week period searching online for a T-shirt for Rachel, the woman he was pursuing. He knew she would love the shirt and it would lead to a "reward" of some sort. When he gave it to her at an unexpected moment, she threw her arms around him and gave him a huge passionate kiss. The response was better than he could have imagined. Had he told her that he only bought the shirt to charm her, to make her feel romantic, and that he methodically looked for it for weeks, she wouldn't have been so happy.

A common bonehead mistake an ineffective seducer makes is that he expects a woman to acknowledge and thank him for all the work he's done in seducing her. This is suicide. A woman will rarely, if ever, acknowledge that you have pursued her, called her, created good feelings for her, risked rejection in asking her out, risked rejection in touching her for the first time, kissing her, and every other initiation that you've made. After all, the seduction is happening effortlessly for her, isn't it? It must be effortless! You will be happier if you don't even expect a woman to understand what you have gone through to make the romance seem effortless. She won't appreciate it anyway. It is best to boast to your friends about your seduction schemes, rather than to your date.

Bringing up the fact that you are putting in effort that she isn't appreciating will offend her. Look at it this way: She expects romance to just happen, and the last thing she wants is a guy plotting how to get her. If you tell her about the work you are doing to seduce her, you break the magic spell,

and she *will* accuse you of treating her like an object, not really caring about her as a person, and manipulating her to get sex, and she will be angrier than you can possibly imagine.

On a recent date with Jennifer, Bob idiotically admitted to her that he believed dating is a matter of "constructing a meticulous plan to charm and romance a woman." They got into an argument about the merits of planning out dates versus "just going with the flow." Bob went on to admit that he believed that romance was "just a matter of working hard enough to get a woman into a sexual mood." To make things even worse, he admitted that he had put lots of thought into his last date with Jennifer—the date on which they ended up kissing in front of his fireplace while her favorite band played on the stereo. Jennifer was shocked and offended that he had worked to set that up. She thought it had "just happened." She became so angry and upset with Bob that she made him leave her apartment and told him that she never wanted to see him again.

When Bob opened up his big mouth and wanted Jennifer to acknowledge the work he had done to seduce her, he made a number of terrible mistakes. First, as you will see later, fighting with a woman will usually not lead to sex. It most often leads to more trouble. Second, Bob didn't realize that women will not understand that sex and dating are work. While he was correct in realizing it was work, she would never understand this. In fact, she responded appropriately. No one wants to feel manipulated. To admit planning out a date *will* be misconstrued by a woman as manipulation. Last, Bob expected to be acknowledged for all the work and energy he put into the seduction dates he created with Jennifer. When he talked about it, he bit off more conflict than he could possibly chew, and it wrecked his chances with Jennifer.

Do what the Effective Seducers do. Make it look like you're not working, and the women you desire will be yours!

A Highly Effective Seducer is appropriately challenging to women

Have you ever felt like the more you did to connect with a woman, the more it felt like she was slipping away from you? You probably gave her everything she wanted, did whatever she said, never disagreed with her,

and racked your brain to figure out how to please her. You were interesting, agreeable, curious, and complimentary. You looked for things you had in common and brought those to her attention.

But the more you tried to connect with her, the more disconnected, distant, and uninterested she seemed to become. And so you felt that horrible feeling of a beautiful woman losing interest in you, and slipping away. But because you didn't know what else to do, you just kept trying and trying, being nicer, being more agreeable, until she wouldn't return your calls and all your interactions with her became totally awkward. Have you had that experience? You probably have. You gave her everything she could want . . . Yet she still slipped away. Well, we're about to tell you why that happened. And better yet, we're about to tell you how stop it from ever happening again. But first, let us explain why that woman slipped away from you.

You see, when you gave that woman everything she could ever want, you removed any challenge to her from the interaction . . . and that made you worthless to her. You need to carve this incredibly important fact into your mind, because it's at the core of seducing beautiful women: If you never challenge a woman, she will have no place to go but away.

So think about the last time a woman seemed to slip away from you. If you tried to connect with her and fulfill all her desires, never disagreeing with her and never challenging her, you ended up pushing her away.

It's true that it is very important to be able to create a sense of Connection with the women you pursue. But it's also critical that you be able to create some challenge, and be able to face challenge if it comes up in your interaction.

We call that creating seductive "Disconnections." When you can both Connect and Disconnect with a woman, you create chemistry far better than you would through Connection alone. Disconnections—disagreements, differences of opinions, or even, sometimes, saying harsh-seeming things to a woman—show a woman that you are challenging, interesting, and not like other groveling men.

When you create Disconnections with a woman, you are appropriately challenging her and give her desires for you that are unfulfilled, and which therefore draw her in your direction. When you create Disconnec-

tions, you show her that there's a difference between you and her, and that challenges her to work for your approval. When you create Disconnections with a woman, you directly show her that you have a higher "value" than she does, which intrigues her and makes her want to associate herself with you.

When you appropriately challenge women using Disconnections, the women you desire pursue you, rather than the other way around.

Doesn't that sound a lot better than what you've been doing?

We've written an entire book and created a fifteen-DVD course about how to create seductive Disconnections with women. The book is called *How to Be the Bad Boy Women Love*, and we've made a six-lesson mini-course for you that you can download from the Owners Page on our website. This course covers specific ways to create seductive Disconnections with the hottest women, how to use "Truth Disconnects" and "Canned Disconnects" to make women explain themselves to you, how to use silence to make women seek your approval, and a lot more. We suggest you download that course right away.

For here and now, though, it's important that you start to develop your Disconnection muscle by learning how to disagree with a woman.

Using Disconnections with Women. One great way to start using Disconnections is to begin challenging women by disagreeing with them. Once you start doing this, you'll see that being challenging to a woman by expressing yourself—even expressing your disagreements and incompatibilities with her—can be very attractive.

That's because sometimes a woman needs to know that you are different from her, and that your inner world is something that you value. She needs to see that your "inner world" is different from hers, valuable—and that if she's lucky, she just might be able to enter it.

Having said that, here's an important point: Being willing to Disconnect through disagreeing and being challenging does not mean just being disagreeable. It does not mean just arguing for the sake of arguing, or showing random hostility, aggressiveness, or defensiveness. That's just going to seem crazy.

Disconnecting by disagreeing with a woman means being willing to

have there be moments in the interaction where the woman really sees that you are different from her. She sees that you are not a jerk about your disagreements. But she also sees that you have an inner world that you are not going to abandon just for her.

This is important: Being willing to disagree, and take a stand for what's important to you, actually makes you more valuable in a woman's eyes. When you value something more than you value having sex with her, it's like saying, "Hey, there's something in my life more valuable than you are."

And the coolest part is this: She'll want to achieve that same level of value, so she'll start working to be with you, and to get into your world, rather than you always having to work to get into hers.

This works especially well on hot women, who are used to having men do anything to get closer to them. Suddenly she's "competing" with something that's more important to you than being close to her. So she tries to get closer to you.

Disagreeing can give you magnetic power with women, if you do it properly.

How to Compellingly Disagree with a Woman. You compellingly disagree with a woman by showing her that you are willing to take a stand for what you believe in.

But—and this is important—you do it without having to be combative, obnoxious, or making her "wrong." There are two steps to making that happen:

1. Challenge her by stating your disagreement.
2. Change the subject, without trying to change her point of view.

Let's give you an example:

She may have said something you really disagree with, like "I think war is always, always wrong." This might really go against what you believe. So you wouldn't run away, or smooth things over, or lie. You'd be willing to disagree. You'd say something like "I believe that there are times when you have to take action on what you think is right, and be willing to pay the price for that. I don't agree with every war, but to me, there are

times when a country has to take drastic action to protect its citizens, just like a man might have to take action to protect his family. I support that."

She may respond with her point of view. Let her, but don't get sucked into a discussion about it. The secret is to allow her to have her points of view, while you have yours. You can say something like "I certainly don't want to argue about it, and you make some good points. I'm just a man who believes what he believes."

This shows her that you are not one of those many men she runs into every day who would step over their grandmother's bodies for a chance of having sex with her. You are showing her that you are interesting. You are showing her that you have a world that is more important than sex with her, and that's a world she will probably want to be a part of.

Then be willing to change the subject. Provide a new subject for conversation, by saying something like "Hey, you said before that you were really into [something she told you she was into]. Can you tell me more about that?"

The thing is, a lot of men are frustrated with women. They are angry because they have felt helpless with women they desire. They've felt like they have either had to abandon their own beliefs in order to try to get a woman, or had to fight with women about what they believe in. Both approaches lead to failure.

As you develop the skill of challenging women through Disconnections, you'll find that women respect you more, and are more attracted to you.

3

The Elements of Style: Dress and Confidence

What kind of woman do you want? What's most important to you in a woman? Is it that she be tall, or short? That she have wonderful breasts? That she be blond, or brunette? That she be smart, or rich? That she be twenty-five, thirty-five, or forty-five? What exactly do you want?

These may seem like confrontational questions. For men who are living in a sexual desert, the answer may well be "any woman at all"! Strange as it may seem, you'll have better chances of getting a woman if you are looking for one with specific qualities than you will if you are looking for any woman at all. So we ask again, what kind of woman do you want?

Most men to whom we ask this question go a little nuts at first. They get like the proverbial kid in a candy shop. "Nineteen years old with perfect skin and a model's body," one man says. "She's aggressively bisexual and loves sex." "A Victoria's Secret model," says another. "She's so rich, I quit my job and she supports me. We have sex twenty hours a day, every day she's not working! And she sets me up with other supermodels, too!"

When they are allowed to ponder the question, however, most guys calm their desires down. They don't *really* want to date nineteen-year-olds, but they *do* want to date women who are young and very attractive. They don't *really* want to date Victoria's Secret models and quit their jobs. What

they *do* want is women who are more beautiful, more sexual, and more intelligent than they've ever been with before. The supermodel fantasy is just the expression of that desire. The bottom line is that most men don't really desire the extremes, but they *do* desire women who are "out of their league."

So think about it. What kind of woman do you really want? Most men dream about women they wouldn't really want, and end up getting women they would never dream about and don't particularly desire. We want you to get women you would dream about, and want in real life. So let yourself dream, let yourself imagine the kind of women you want. Think "out of your league." What do you get?

Most men we asked desire women who are extremely attractive, young, intelligent, mature, and who love sex. They want women who have a great sense of style, who are confident and outgoing, who take care of their bodies, and who are not snobby or overly obsessed with their own comfort. They want women who fulfill their particular physical desires: great legs, or large breasts, or long hair, or perfect butts. Men usually find they desire women who are well above the level of the women they have been dating, but not actually superstars or supermodels.

There's an old saying: "If you don't have any destination in mind, any road will take you there." You really have to decide what you want in a woman to make use of the information in this chapter to find out what you need to do—what roads to take—to get her. And the more specific you can be with what you want, the better this process will go.

Once you have an idea of what you want, here's the next step: Think about the kind of woman you desire. Think about her style, her grace, and her beauty. Now ask yourself: "If I were to have a woman like this, what kind of a man would I have to be?"

This question is crucial because it will guide you in your quest. What kind of a man would you have to be to have the kind of women you desire? The first mistake men make in answering this question is that they think they would have to be more than they could ever possibly be. They doom themselves with answers like "To have the women I really desire, I'd have to be a millionaire," or "To have the women I really desire, I'd have to be a professional basketball player." Or they come up with criteria that doom them

from a physical standpoint: "To have the woman I desire, I'd have to be taller," or "To have the woman I desire, I'd have to be more handsome," or "To have the women I desire, I'd have to be younger," or "To have the woman I desire, I'd have to not have [whatever you think is wrong with you]."

That's all nonsense. You don't have to be fundamentally different from what you are to get the women you desire. You don't have to be richer, or taller, or better looking. Look: The truth about women is very simple. You can have the woman you desire if you can make her feel the romantic feelings she most wants to feel when she is around you and see you as interesting, sexy, passionate, and authentic. When we ask, "What would you have to be like to have the women you desire?" we are simply asking you to think about the parts of yourself you'll have to accentuate if you are to make the women you desire feel romantically about you.

The second mistake men make in answering this question is that they decide that they have to become somebody they are not—fake men, or supermen. They imagine they'll have to become basically different from what they honestly are. They think they'll have to become James Bond, or some sort of a "tough guy" action hero who they really aren't. They imagine that they will need to dress in crazy outrageous clothing, wear pimped out jewelry, and look and act like a clownish version of themselves. Some men believe they need to memorize hypnotic patterns, canned stories, and essentially lie to women to get a date or a sex partner. In essence, most men believe that to get women, they'll have to betray themselves. They are afraid of trying to be who they aren't, and for good reason. Most men who approach women trying to be completely different from who they basically are come across appearing insincere and immature, and put forth a distrustworthy vibe. As you'll see in this chapter, you'll need to stretch yourself, but not betray yourself.

When you think about the kind of man you'll have to be to get the kind of woman you desire, what kind of answers do you get? Most men we work with say things like Ken did: "Well, I'd have to be more confident, and talkative with women, I think. And I'd have to look sharper, too, I think . . . If I'm going to be with a woman who looks and dresses as hot as I'd like her to, I'd probably have to be fit and wear clothes that look good on me, too. I might have to clean my car, and what about my house? I'd probably

have to put those pictures up, and water the plants more often, if I'm going to be the kind of guy who gets the woman I desire."

Most men discover that while they don't need to be different from who they really are, they do need to more thoroughly develop who they are. They find that they need to develop their personal style, which has two parts: *style*, that is, how you dress, and *confidence*, how you behave. While you don't have to change who you are as a person, you will probably find you have to change how you express who you are—your personal style—if you want to get the woman of your dreams.

WHY HAVE PERSONAL STYLE?

Bob doesn't want to change anything about himself to get women. He's sure that if he changes his looks or his behavior in any way, he'll be "being fake." "I want a woman to like me the way I am!" he asserts. Many men tell us things like "If only women could know me, I'm sure they'd want to be with me." But, for some reason, the women they'd like to know never seem to want to know them. When we examine how these men dress and their level of confidence, we find again and again that they dress and behave in ways that put women off.

Sidney was one of these men. Very proud of the fact that he always did things his own way, he called himself a "maverick" and a "rebel." He liked to wear torn-up clothes that looked terrible: His favorite sweatshirt was so shredded that he had replaced one of the sleeves with an old pant leg from a pair of jeans. His clothes were not only torn up, they were *wrinkled* and torn up. He prided himself on not owning a clothes dryer, and proudly said, "I will *never* iron a shirt!" Sidney had a great body as well, but would never wear clothing to show off his physique. He didn't care at all about how he looked and was surprised that women who *did* care about how he looked were never interested in him. In fact, it seemed that most women went out of their way to avoid him. Day after day he looked terrible, and day after day he wasn't attractive to the women he desired. Strangely, day after day he was surprised by this fact.

He fared little better in his confidence—that is, his behaviors with women. As we worked with him, we discovered that he worried his way

through every interaction with attractive women. He was always asking himself, "What am I doing wrong? Am I offending her? What if she doesn't like me? Am I scaring her?" He never had any idea about what to say to women and often ended up sputtering and apologizing for "bothering" them. His confidence was terrible, and he never varied his approach. Day after day he approached women in the same ineffective, apologetic way, and day after day he wasn't attractive to the women he desired. Again, day after day he was surprised by this fact.

The funny thing was, Sidney was obviously a great guy. He was well read, well educated, and a great cook. He was a marathon runner, in great shape, and had a lot of interesting ideas. He obviously would have made a wonderful companion, and any woman who was with him would have been lucky. But Sidney had a fatal flaw that left him helpless with women: He was unwilling to change anything about his dress or approach. As we said before, a person is insane when he does the same things over and over and expects different results than he got before. This is exactly what Sidney was doing, and it is what many men, quite possibly you included, do as well.

Think about it. When you have not had the success you've wanted with women, have you tried changing your looks and behavior? We are willing to bet that you probably haven't. Like Sidney, you've probably done what you've always done, and not known any different approaches to try. As a result you've behaved insanely, doing the same things over and over with women, expecting each time that perhaps, through sheer luck, something better will happen. To truly succeed with women you are going to need to try out new behaviors, approaches, and be willing to step outside of your comfort zone to become a new and improved version of yourself.

As we taught Sidney the material in this chapter, he began to change. He began to see that, rather than needing to be someone other than who he was, he needed to develop his personal style and confidence to better express who he really was. Sidney learned, as you will learn, that his attire and confidence were ways of expressing himself more fully and attractively, not a way to hide or be fake. And as he started developing his personal style and confidence, he began to be the man he'd have to be to get the women he wanted.

DEFINING YOUR STYLE

As we said before, women are attracted to men who make them feel the romantic feelings they so desire. Don't be fooled by the simplicity of this statement; teaching you how to make women feel romantically inclined is the fundamental goal of this book and should be your primary goal as well in all your interactions with them. Everything you can do toward this end, you must do.

Your style—how you dress and your level of confidence—is the first thing a woman sees about you. You must make it work for long-term outcome. You must make your style automatically generate romantic feelings in the women you encounter. Your clothing can have you come across to women as just another sloppy boring guy, or as someone who is interesting and attractive.

Your personal style is your unique expression. It's your first "advertisement" to the world about who you are and what you are about. Through your style, you tell people what is important to you. Your style is a reflection of your passion.

THE COMMITMENT OF STYLE

Would you go to a job interview in your workout gear? Would you show up at your job wearing torn, dirty, or even smelly clothes? Would you wear a suit and tie to play in your local softball league? Or wear swim trunks to a business meeting? Of course not.

The simple fact is that different activities have different uniforms. If you want to be successful at a job interview, you invest the time and money in getting the right outfit for it. If you want to look professional at your job, you invest the time and money in getting the right clothes for it. And if you are playing softball on the local team, you don't wear a suit and tie; you wear the clothes that are proper for the activity.

Your life pursuit is now "getting women." If you are serious about this, you will invest time and money in getting the right clothes for the job. Because every day, every interaction you have with women will be a

"job interview" of sorts, you need to wear clothes that are attractive for the job.

What, exactly, those clothes will be will vary from man to man. A man who is a mechanic, for instance, will express his style through clothes that are different from those of an executive. But both men, if they wish to be successful, will make the commitment to thinking about how they look to women every single day.

Our level of success with women skyrocketed when we first understood the importance of proper dress when meeting them. We each developed "dating uniforms" which we knew would make us into the kind of men we'd have to be to get the kind of women we desired into bed. We became willing to spend the time and money on getting the right clothes and keeping them clean, pressed, and mended. This simple commitment has made all the difference in our level of success with women.

WHAT YOU SAY WITH HOW YOU DRESS

A wise person once said, "I've never met a person who wasn't carefully costumed." We agree. No matter how you are dressed right now, on some level you have chosen your outfit because it makes a statement you want to make. Sidney, in our example above, wore torn clothes as a way of saying that he was a rebel and a maverick. On a subconscious level, it was more important to Sidney to show what a rebel he was than for him to get women.

When women look at how you dress, it makes a statement to them. To women, Sidney's way of dressing said, "I want you to look good, but I'm not willing to look good in return." Not surprisingly, women were not very attracted to this. Other men make other statements. One of our clients, Ray, was an older man who had been having trouble getting dates for many years. He wore garish, brightly colored clothes that clashed and from a stylistic perspective looked terrible. His ex-wife told him he "made a mockery of style." On top of this, he rarely bothered to bathe or shave, so he often smelled bad. On a subconscious level, by wearing clothes women wouldn't like, Ray was constantly saying, "Go to hell!" to women. He was saying this to his mother, to women in his life now, and to every woman he'd ever felt controlled by. He would complain about how women didn't

like how he dressed, and wouldn't date him, but as we got to know him, we saw that it was more important to him to insult women's sensibilities than it was for him to get sex. Because of his style, his mere presence offended women. And he wondered why he couldn't get them into bed!

Men like Sidney may make less bold, but still destructive statements to women through the way they dress. At best, they send the message "I don't care about how I look," and at worst, "I'm immature and you don't want to go out with me." When it's more important to Sidney to show what a rebel he is than to get the women he desires, women end up thinking, "He's immature, and not a real man."

Other men make more constructive statements to women through the way they dress. Think about some men you know, or have seen, whose style of dress is attractive to women. You might think of John Travolta, playing the character Chili Palmer in the film *Get Shorty*. He always looked good, wore clothes that fit, and had a style that fit him. His style said, "I'm an attractive man who knows what he's about. I'm not stuck in making some immature statement. You want me in your life." This is what you want to say, too.

As we worked with Sidney, he changed his style and thereby changed what he was saying to women. He realized that saying he was a rebel was not as important as being attractive to women. He decided that, in order to be the kind of man that got the kind of women he wanted, he'd have to have a style of dress that said, "I'm an attractive, mature man," rather than making a teenage statement of rebellion. He made the changes, as you'll learn to do in this chapter, and immediately noticed improvements in his relationships with the opposite sex.

What does your way of dressing say to women? Does it say that you are mature, attractive, in love with your life, confident, and of interest to her? Or does your way of dressing send out a more immature message? Let's find out.

WOMEN DO IT!

Focusing on your style may be new to men, but there's one group of people it's not new to: women. Almost all women spend time thinking about how they look to men, and spend a lot of time trying to improve their

attractiveness. Heck, they even put paint on their faces to make themselves look better! We're not suggesting you go that far, but since women spend time thinking about how they look to the other sex, perhaps spending a little time on it yourself is not so unreasonable.

Women actually set an encouraging example. How many women do you know who look noticeably more attractive "done up right" than they do when they don't think about how they look? Probably most. One of our female dating coaches, Cindy, is on the low end of average-looking when she's wearing torn-up, poorly fitted house clothes and her hair is a mess. However, when she makes herself up, does her hair, and puts on attractive clothes, she looks great. If you are going to get the women you most desire in bed, you must learn to accomplish the same kind of transformation.

THE THREE HELPERS THAT MAKE YOU LOOK BETTER

If you are like most men (and you probably are, right?), you aren't going to be able to transform your style of dressing without help. We will go over the basics in this chapter, but to really create a transformation in how you look, you'll also need help from other people.

1. Stylish men

We suggest you look around for the resources you already have to help you develop your style. Who do you know who has a great sense of style? Approach stylish men you know, and ask them for advice. Ask them where they shop for clothes, and where they get their hair cut. Then go to those places and ask the salesclerks to help you with a "new look." They'll often suggest clothing you wouldn't normally get for yourself, but that your style could "grow into." If you know any gay men, they often have a much better fashion sense than the average straight guy you know. They can be extremely beneficial in helping you create a new look and a sharper fashion sense. Another great resource are men's magazines such as *GQ*, *FHM*, *Maxim*, and so forth. These magazines give you a sense of what fashionable men are wearing and give examples of male models with a variety of ages and "looks."

2. Women

Another intelligent way to shop is to find a stylish woman who you are not interested in sexually, and ask her to go shopping with you. One of our dating clients, Jim, had a tremendous experience the first time he did this. He went to Cindy, our dating coach mentioned above, and she took him shopping and gave him an entire makeover. It turned out she gave him great advice, and for less than $1,000 had him looking like a rock star. Cindy had him buy a great leather jacket, jeans that fit him perfectly, and a few more items that created a great look for him. For months he got compliments from women on how great he looked, all because he was willing to commit himself to looking good. "It was hard at first," he said later. "A lot of the clothes she told me to buy, I didn't really like at first. But it turned out to be great, and did a lot to help me create my personal style."

3. Male friends

It's good to go clothes shopping with other men who are also developing their personal style. The right men friends can encourage you to take fashion risks. The right male friends can push you to take risks and to step outside of your comfort zone and challenge you to try something new.

In time you will develop relationships with stores you like, where you know you can trust the clerks to suggest new style ideas that will both express your true self and make you even more attractive to women. One of our students who often wears a cowboy hat that looks great on him got the hat that way. "I'd never considered a hat like that before," he says. "But when the clerk brought it over and set it on my head, it looked great. I knew right away it was right for me, and I never would have found it by myself." As you buy more clothes, you will discover what you really like, and what kinds of clothes really make the kind of statement you want to make to women.

WHAT IS THE LOOK YOU WANT
TO PRESENT TO THE WORLD?

Think for a moment about the sort of look you would like to present to the world. If you want to be a rebel, that's fine, but how could you be a rebel with style? While women love bad boys, they want the guy to look clean, strong, and to be wearing clothing that fits his body well. We are not suggesting you need to always wear a suit or always wear business clothing—that would be stupid. But you can have a variety of looks that convey your personality in an attractive way.

Think about the UFC fighter Chuck Liddell—he is extremely attractive to women, but is always seen in a T-shirt and jeans. The question is, does he look fashionable and good in what he is wearing? You bet. The rock star Tommy Lee dresses in sloppy rock star wear—but he looks good in what he is wearing. Look at how many actors and musicians dress—hip, modern, current, comfortable, and of course cool.

Other men want to wear a suit, or casual business wear, or go after a more refined look. Whatever the look you are going after—make sure it fits you. And make sure you look "interesting." By interesting, we mean you add an interesting detail to your attire like a cool watch, fashionable shoes, a ring that is odd, or some other accessory that can be a discussion piece.

Sidney, as mentioned earlier, dressed like a slob, and he failed to show off one of his best assets—his muscular body. We've had many guys attend our seminars in the past who have worked for years to have hulky bodies, but been afraid to show them off. If you have a great body— experiment with tighter shirts that show off your arms and body. Take the risk to attract more attention from women.

Whatever look you are going after, it has to be congruent. This means your look has to fit your personality. If you are a fifty-five-year-old man who lives in Maine and are normally a business-suit-wearing guy, you are probably going to look like a moron wearing a cowboy hat and trying to come across as an urban cowboy. The same is likely true for the thirty-eight-year-old trying to dress in hip-hop wear with big baggy jeans

and chains. It looks stupid and is not congruent. Find ways to come up with a "look" that fits you in a realistic manner.

THE FOUR RULES OF CLOTHING

Most men are "clothes blind." They don't see dirt in the same way women do, and they don't think about style as much. Here are the basic rules about clothes that men need to learn.

First and foremost, *clothes must fit well!* It doesn't matter how great a shirt is if it looks ill-fitting. It doesn't matter how much a pair of pants has been marked down if it pulls into a pronounced "starfish" shape where the legs meet the crotch. Simple clothing that fits well is far better than fancier clothing that just "doesn't look right."

If you are interested in pursuing a casual, ragged, torn-up clothing look, proper fitting is the difference between looking sexy and looking like a slob. Next time you see a man or a woman who looks great in the torn-up style, notice how well the clothes fit them. You'll notice they fit perfectly, which is why the style works.

Some clothing stores are better for the average man than are others. If you are a bit overweight, some of the more hip and upscale stores may not have clothes that fit you well. Very often one store will have an entire line of pants, for instance, that don't fit you well. It's just the way the clothes are cut. Another store, on the other hand, might have a wide variety of pants that fit you. It's a good idea to keep shopping around until you find a store where the clothes fit, they look good, and the salespeople help you expand your style.

How do you know when clothes don't fit well? Often, the salespeople will tell you, though you can't count on that. The men you are shopping with can tell you. The bottom line is simply this: If you don't feel that the clothes fit, they don't. If you honestly do not feel you will wear an article of clothing because it seems too flashy or too outrageous, don't waste your money, and move on to the next piece.

The second rule of clothing is that *clothes must be clean!* Because most men are "clothes blind" and can't seem to tell when clothes need laundering, let's briefly go over how you know when it's time to wash something:

- If it's underwear, and you've worn it more than once, wash it.
- For shirts and pants, you can be more discriminating. To tell if shirts and pants are dirty, look at them under bright light. Are there any spots or stains? If there are, rub the spot with stain remover (buy it where you buy detergent) and wash. Pants need laundering when they start to get baggy and wrinkled. Blue jeans are especially susceptible to stretching and getting baggy. When this happens, it's time to wash them.

The third rule of clothing is that *clothes shouldn't be wrinkled!* Yes, you might have to iron your shirts and pants, or have them ironed. Think about it: You are more attracted to women who are wearing clothes that aren't wrinkled and sloppy. Women are no different. Of course, not all clothes need ironing, but if you want to send a message to attractive women that you are the kind of man they want, ironing may be required. Having your shirts and pants laundered professionally is a possibility for men who can afford it and don't want to iron.

The fourth rule of clothing is that you must *keep clothing in good repair!* Look under "seamstress" in the local yellow pages, and get buttons sewed back on, holes patched, and rips mended right away. If your clothes are totally ripped up and irreparable, throw them away and go shopping.

Wearing clean, well-fitting, ironed clothes that are in good repair has multiple benefits. Not only do you look good, you also *feel* good. Your style of dressing will naturally send out the message to a woman that you are attractive, together, and of interest to her.

THE THIRTEEN-POINT BODY MAKEOVER
FOR BEING ATTRACTIVE TO WOMEN

By working with men like Sidney, we've developed a thirteen-point "body makeover" that focuses men's attention on the particulars of their look. We'll start at the top of your body and work down, giving you time-tested style pointers along the way to guarantee that you will look attractive to women.

Bobby came to us because the women he was attracted to were not attracted to him. He was twenty-eight years old and thin and wiry. He was

a gifted computer system administrator, and had a style that could best be described as "lazy hippie." His hair was long and unkempt, and his beard was unruly. He had thick-framed glasses that looked old, and he seemed to have to squint a lot to see through them. He wore T-shirts under messy and out-of-date, unbuttoned button-down shirts, and a variety of old jeans and beat-up sneakers. As we worked with Bobby, it became clear that through his dress, he was telling women, "I'm still a boy. I'm not good enough for you." We took Bobby through our thirteen-point makeover and changed his message to women to "I'm together and interesting, and you'd like to talk to me." Here's how we did it:

1. Hair

Bobby looked like a "wild man" when we first met him. His hair was long and shaggy, and it looked like he hadn't had a haircut, or even combed his hair, in months.

Hair has to be taken care of to look good: The movie stars who seem to have rumpled, disorderly hair actually spend a fortune in time and money to get it to look "just so." While short hair doesn't always look better than long, many men who have long hair used to look good with it but now that they are getting older, don't anymore. We determined that Bobby had looked good with long hair as a teenager, but should try a shorter, more orderly style now. He got a new, shorter haircut, which immediately made him look more professional and, we thought, more in charge of his life.

He learned to style his hair, something he had resisted for years. He discovered that he needed to use styling gel to get his hair to look more orderly and properly fashioned. He noticed an immediate change in his life; women seemed more interested in him. He decided that, in view of the newfound feminine attention, having to use hair gel was not such a big problem.

It's important that your hair looks good. It should not be greasy or out of control, and you should not have dandruff. Go see a real hair stylist, and get a look that is good for you. Go to a real salon; avoid the cheapo haircut chains. It is worth spending the extra money to get a great cut and style.

Men who are balding have several options. Even if you are balding, your hair can still look good and be styled well. Just watch out for the trap balding men fall into of combing just a few hairs across the bald top of their

heads. It doesn't work, and women, especially, find it unattractive. Just re-member *Star Trek's* bald Captain Picard, and let your bald head shine.

We've also known balding men who have created a powerful, attractive look by keeping their heads shaved. Admittedly, it takes some guts to do this, but if you have an attractive skull, it can really look good. There are dozens of popular and hunky bald men, such as Michael Jordan, Michael Stipe (from the band R.E.M.), Moby, Samuel L. Jackson, and Jesse Ventura.

2. Eyebrows/ear hair/nose hair

Most men don't have a problem with their eyebrows, but it makes sense to check yours and be sure. Some men's eyebrows grow very long and need to be trimmed. Several of our students have gray hairs in their eyebrows that grow, if unhindered, to an inch long or longer. These men must pluck or trim these hairs on a regular basis.

Ear hair and nose hair must be trimmed regularly. You might not notice if this hair grows long, and your male friends might not notice, but women you find attractive *will*. You can use little scissors or special trimmers to trim these hairs at least once every two weeks. Hair should not protrude from the nose or ears. Stray hairs growing on your ears must be trimmed.

3. Glasses

Like many men, Bobby wore glasses. His looked old, scratched, and he seemed to need to squint to see through them. We sent him to his optom-etrist to get his prescription updated, and then accompanied him to find the right pair of frames.

If you wear glasses, choosing the right frames is very important. The bad news is, really stylish frames cost some money. The good news is that having to wear glasses is a great opportunity to choose frames that will enhance your attractiveness noticeably. It's worth shopping around for the frames that look the best on your face. Go to high-end stores as well as the cheaper ones. Every woman who sees you will see your glasses, so it's worth getting ones that really look great.

Some guys look significantly better with contacts, rather than glasses. It is definitely worth experimenting with contact lenses. Wearing contacts can often make you look younger and more approachable. We highly rec-

ommend men over the age of thirty check out contact lenses to change their look around. LASIK surgery is another option, but obviously more risky.

4. Snorting and phlegm

Brian had a problem. He was attractive and dressed well, but always seemed to need to clear his throat and spit. He became so used to this that he hardly even knew he did it anymore, but every time he'd take a big snorting inhale, women noticed, and didn't want to be around him.

Women find snorting and spitting of phlegm *very* revolting. We know you find it disgusting, too, but take it from us, what you feel is nothing compared to how women feel about it. While it may seem obvious to avoid clearing your throat and making that terrible snorting noise, many men make this mistake and end up ruining an otherwise good date or interaction with a woman.

If you find that you have problems with phlegm, you must find out why and solve them. Many people who have excess phlegm have allergies to dairy foods and find it clears up if they avoid milk products or take enzymes to help them digest lactose. If you have these problems, seek professional help and get the phlegm cleared up, or the message you'll send to women will be "I'm disgusting. Stay away from me."

5. Facial hair

Bobby had a beard, and, at first, we suggested that he try shaving it off. Unless a beard is well kempt and trimmed regularly, it won't be attractive on most men. We thought Bobby's beard made him look like a slob, so we suggested he shave it off.

While many men look better without beards, Bobby wasn't one of them. "My God," he said after he shaved it off. "I look terrible, like a fat guy with a weird-shaped face!" We agreed that it wasn't the right look for him, and he grew in a short, well-trimmed beard that went with his hair and looked great on him.

The biggest problem men have with beards is that they let them get too wild. Pick a style and keep the beard neat. The biggest problem women tell us that they have with men's beards is that the beards tend to get scratchy. If you do have a beard, be sure to use conditioner on it to keep it soft.

6. Lips

And speaking of soft, if you plan to be kissing women, you need to keep your lips soft. If they are rough, women will notice, and not want to kiss you. We know it seems petty, but it's true. Remember, when you are first dating a woman, she has you on probation. Sure, you're exciting, but dating you puts her at risk of emotional entanglements and getting hurt. While you are thinking of how great it's going to be to have sex with her, she's looking for a reason to send you back into the slammer with all those other guys, so she can get back to her nice, orderly life. For this reason you *must* have your details in order. And for this reason, your lips must be soft. Use lip balm.

7. Teeth

We also sent Bobby to the dentist to get his teeth cleaned, and if you haven't had yours cleaned in the last six months, you should make an appointment, too. Bobby didn't want to go, so we had him create a reward that would motivate him. He decided that as a reward for getting his teeth cleaned, he'd take himself out to the local strip club and have a good time. With the prospect of naked women dangling before him, he was able to get in and have more than five years of crud scraped off his teeth. They looked whiter, and felt smoother and cleaner to him. After all, if you expect a woman to stick her tongue in there, you want your mouth to be as clean as possible. You may want to invest in high-quality teeth whitener, or have a dentist perform a teeth-whitening process on you. Men who are smokers and/or heavy coffee drinkers often have stained teeth and need to get them whitened more frequently than those who are not.

It is critical to mention that if you have crooked teeth, are missing teeth, have a misaligned bite, or in any shape or form have anything preventing you from smiling around women, you should seriously consider coughing up the money to get your teeth corrected. For one of our seminars, Mike flew into Chicago from London, where he currently lives. He ended up meeting many women and learning the basic skills of seduction, but he had crooked teeth and was in desperate need of teeth whitening. After getting his teeth fixed and cleaned, his success with women skyrocketed—as did his confidence.

8. Skin

Smooth soft skin is important to women, especially on your face. If the skin is rough on your face, shave more frequently and make sure to use a moisturizer. If you have rough hands, start using moisturizer to soften them up. Most women aren't interested in men who have rough, sandpaper-like hands.

9. Smells

It's hard to underestimate the negative consequences of smelling bad to a woman. A surprising number of the women we interviewed said that they had been on dates where they would have had sex with the man, if only he hadn't smelled bad. It is important that you bathe regularly, own deodorant, and use it. Remember, if you think you might smell bad to women, then you probably do.

You should know that, as one woman we interviewed said, "nothing is more of a turnoff than the smell of feces." If you tend to have gas, then you *must* do something about it. Products like Beano can help you pass less gas. You may even need to see a doctor if you have a serious gas problem.

This is no small concern. Studies show that women have a more developed sense of smell than men do. Smells that don't seem too bad to men can be quite repellent to women. If you want to have sex with attractive women, then you must manage your smells. Men who refuse to handle this problem send the message to women that they are more interested in passing gas than they are in having sex with women. Women conclude that such men are immature, and they are right.

It's also critical that you have good breath. Again and again, the women we interviewed told us that men who have bad breath turn them off. Reena was typical of these women when she said, "Sure, I can think of a number of guys I was ready to have sex with, but then noticed they had bad breath. I figured I didn't want them after all." You must brush your teeth regularly, and if you think your breath might be bad, it is. Carry mints with you, but don't use them in front of her. For some reason, women seem to think that men who take steps to have good breath are vain, even while they say that

men who smell bad are slobs. Excuse yourself to the bathroom and put the breath mint in your mouth there.

If you use aftershave lotion, be sure to not use too much. As the saying goes, a dab'll do. Women aren't attracted to guys who wear so much lotion that smell rays seem almost to be radiating from their bodies. The man you'd have to be to get the kind of woman you want probably doesn't smell too bad, or too good.

10. Pockets

Just as you can have a wonderful, expensive desk, and overload the drawers to the point where they can't be closed, you can have wonderful, stylish clothes, and overload the pockets to the point where your nice slick clothes make you look like an old lumpy mattress.

While women carry purses that they overfill, men overfill their pockets. If you want to be attractive to women, you must carry as little as possible in your pockets, so you don't look lumpy and your clothes don't get stretched.

Bobby overfilled his pockets. He routinely had so many pens and papers in his shirt pockets that the weight pulled the shirt down, and he overfilled his pants pockets as well. Like many men, he had lots of keys, which made a big lump on his leg when he put them in his pocket. We had him remove the keys he didn't need, and carry as few as he could get away with. Other men who absolutely must carry lots of keys have benefited from carrying them on their belts rather than in their pockets.

Bobby's wallet was thick, disorganized, and bulging with papers and old receipts. We explained to him that women do check out men's bodies, just as men check out women's, and how a thick wallet made his butt less attractive to women. A huge wallet also made Bobby look like a slob whenever he would pull it out. He got rid of the excess papers and bought a thinner wallet. Problem solved.

11. Belt

Your belt is one of the small particulars of your dress that you must have under control if you want women to be attracted to you. If you are wearing a cheap cardboard belt, or if your belt is falling apart, you won't be sending an attractive message to women. Likewise, if you are using the

biggest or the smallest hole in your belt, you might look silly, and should consider getting a belt that fits you better. If you are at all overweight, it's better to not have too fancy a belt buckle, as it will draw attention to your waist, which is not where you want women to look. Get a simpler belt buckle until you've slimmed down.

12. Socks and shoes

If you'll look closely at your socks, you'll find that there is an inside and an outside, and that it's possible to wear them inside out. Though few men would ever notice this, women tell us that they do. Wear your socks the right side out. But that's not all women judge you on—they judge you on having clean socks, and whether or not your socks match your outfit.

Women also evaluate men by the quality of their shoes. It's hard for most men to comprehend the amount of time women spend thinking about shoes. They have conversations with each other about shoes; they spend discrete blocks of time shoe shopping; they sit around thinking about what shoes to wear with what outfits. The more attractive a woman you are interested in is, the more time she probably spends thinking about shoes. Ron once went on a trip with an ex-girlfriend, who was a psychopathic fashion model. For a one-week trip the woman brought two huge suitcases—one for clothes and the other just for shoes. Ron learned that women love shoes and spend tons of time thinking about and shopping for shoes.

With this in mind, you shouldn't be too surprised to find out that a woman also judges and thinks about your shoes. So you should be ready. The sad fact is that you surely need more and better shoes. Bobby had his dirty sneakers, his messed-up dress shoes, and a very uncomfortable pair of loafers that he wore two times a year. Through his work with us, he realized that to be the kind of man who attracted the kind of women he wanted, he'd need some new shoes. He visited a number of stylish shoe boutiques and got several pairs of sexy new shoes. To keep current with men's shoe fashions, check out a *GQ* magazine and get several different styles so you can put together different looks for different situations you will be in. Get some cool boots, some fun but clean-looking tennis shoes, some fashionable dark shoes, and other items that can enhance your look.

13. Posture

Bobby had what we call "adolescent posture." He slumped like a teenager and shuffled when he walked. His shoulders were rounded and his head was forward. He looked unobtrusive and timid, but realized that he needed to look powerful and decisive to get the women he desired.

There are a lot of kinds of bodywork you can get if you, like Bobby, suffer from poor posture. You may want to explore chiropractic, which is often at least partially covered by insurance, to improve your posture. Other men get regular massages or go through a process called Rolfing or neuromuscular therapy to improve posture. Some men have reported that going to yoga class has helped them stand up straighter and have more powerful posture, as well as correct back pain.

Bobby started getting chiropractic care and regular massage treatments. He soon was standing straighter and taller, his shoulders seemed broader and less tense, and he walked straighter and more upright. As a plus, his lower back pain cleared up. "I feel more solid now," he told us, "and more able to meet attractive women on their own ground." Better posture made him more into the kind of man who would be attractive to the kind of women he desired.

Bobby followed our thirteen-point makeover plan and developed an entirely new look for himself that brought out the parts of him that he wanted to express to women. He looked and felt more confident, mature, adult, and attractive. With his good posture, clean look, and neat, interesting, well-maintained clothes and shoes, he said, "I'm a together adult man, ready to take on the world. You are interested in being with me." Women noticed this and began responding at once.

DETAILS: THE KEY TO WOMEN'S HEARTS (AND PANTS)

One important key to seducing women, which we will return to again and again throughout this book, is *details*. Women feel romantic when the little details are taken care of, whether those details are perfect candlelight,

clean sheets, or the small particulars of how you dress. You may have noticed how many parts of the makeover focused on the details; that's because properly managed details make women feel romantic.

You've probably heard women talk about how important the "little things" are to them. While women usually don't give useful advice about how to seduce them, in this case they are telling the truth. A man who can manage the details will always get women in bed. In upcoming chapters we'll show you how to manage the details in every aspect of a seduction. Here's how you can make the details of your appearance work for you.

The "little things" in how you dress tell a woman a lot about you, and have a big effect on how she treats you. Evan has the "sloppy attractive" look mastered. He seems to wear torn, ratty clothes, but they look mysteriously good on him. Attractive women constantly surround him. What is his secret?

Evan understands the importance of details. He knows that it's not important that his clothes are torn; what's important is that the details of his look all work together to make him look good. Torn clothes are part of his style. What makes him different from other, unattractive men who wear torn-up clothes is how he manages the details of his appearance.

First, even though his clothing may be torn, he still follows the four Rules of Clothing closely. His clothes are clean and orderly; we've seen him iron ripped blue jeans, and throw away clothes whose rips don't look "right' to him.

Second, his details are all wonderful. His style has a Native American air about it, even though he's not Native American himself. His belt is from a Pacific Indian clothing store, and his watch, rings, earrings, and necklaces reflect the same style. This attention to detail makes him look like he's thought about his look, which he has, and sends an attractive message to women no matter what else he is wearing. He never carries much in his pockets, and his glasses fit his face perfectly. He looks like he's just thrown on whatever is around, and looks great. The reason he looks great is that he's thought about and managed the details of his appearance. Women notice, and find him fascinating.

You can use the details of your appearance to stand out from other men. Extra-nice or interestingly coordinated shoes, belts, wallets, backpacks,

briefcases, watches, or hats are all ways to show women that you pay attention to details and care about looking nice.

Slightly unusual details in your dress can even get women to begin conversations with you. One man we know wears a striking copper bracelet he got in India. Women often ask him about it, and he gets to tell them about the time he spent traveling there. Another man wears an artistic pin on the lapel of his suit, which women comment on. Another man has a cowboy hat that fits his style perfectly, which women often comment on.

Tattoos, if you have them, are another kind of detail of style that can start conversations with women. One man we know has several beautiful tattoos and uses them to start conversations with women who have tattoos and piercings. "I like your tattoo. Where did you get it done?" will often lead to interesting conversations and eventually dates with women he's attracted to.

Details to avoid

Once upon a time, tobacco was cool. You could light up a cigarette, hold it casually, breathe smoke, and look suave and intellectual.

Those days are past. Cigarettes are no longer attractive to women and, in our current cultural climate, are actually repellent to many beautiful, health-conscious females. While it is true that many young women smoke because they think it will keep them thin, you won't be any less attractive to them if you don't smoke. And you will be more attractive to nonsmoking women, who outnumber the smokers. To be attractive to women, you must go smoke-free, too.

Even though cigars have come into vogue in recent years, most women still think they smell like burning commodes and find men who light them up very offensive. Jake learned this the hard way. He was on a business trip to a distant city, and there he met Anne. Anne was thirty-three, tall, with fiery red hair and remarkably upright, beautiful breasts. He seemed certain to score with her; she knew he was in town for only a few days but still wanted to be with him. She must want to have sex with him, he reasoned. What could possibly go wrong?

They went out to a sushi dinner together, ate and drank, and were en-

joying each other's company, when Jake made his mistake. With studied casualness, he took a cigar out of his pocket and lit it up. "I've never seen a woman's mood change so quickly," he told us later. "She wrote me off immediately, became cold, and couldn't get away from me fast enough. Even after I put it out, she still wouldn't warm up to me. Needless to say, I slept alone that night." Don't make the mistake Jake made. If you smoke cigars, do it around other guys. Don't do it around women you are trying to seduce.

WHAT IF YOU ARE FAT
AND OUT OF SHAPE, OR UGLY?

Your style needs to send a message to women that says, "I am mature and interesting and you want to be with me." Accomplishing this is more about what you do with what nature gave you than about how subjectively beautiful you are. We all have seen men who, at first look, are no "feast for the peepers" but who are dating very beautiful women. They are able to do this because they make the best of what they have and have developed their personal style into something they can be proud of.

Carey is one such man. Weighing in at well over three-hundred pounds, Carey seems, at first look, to be a guy who would only get sex if he were willing to pay cash for it. Nothing could be further from the truth; Carey has a constant stream of women in his life.

How does he do it? Carey has style. He never smells bad and always looks great. Everyone who knows him agrees that his clothes look great on him and that he "wears his weight well." He follows the guidelines of the rest of this chapter, and his home and car look wonderful and are extremely inviting. He also has confidence, which we will cover later in this chapter. Carey's style shows that he is in love with his life, is a mature man, and that he pays attention to details. Subsequently he is attractive to a variety of women.

Carey is careful to never be apologetic about his weight. "I know I'd be healthier if I was thinner, and I'm working on it," he says. "But I know if I start acting like there's something wrong with me, I'll never get another

date again. I just think of myself as a big, attractive guy. The ladies seem to agree." If you express your own true style, it doesn't matter if you aren't naturally beautiful to look at. You'll send the right message to women, they will feel romantic feelings about you, and you'll do well with them.

Tips for overweight men

Here are some tips for overweight men: Some "genius" self-help people out there will tell you to go lose weight, plain and simple. We know from personal experience that losing weight takes a lot of work and isn't something you can do overnight. It takes discipline and work—especially if you are over thirty-five. It is worth noting, however, that if you are overweight, going to the gym and putting on some additional muscle will make you look more attractive. If you regularly include weight lifting in your life, within a few months you can put on enough muscle in your shoulders, back and arms to greatly increase your level of attractiveness.

Furthermore, people tend to associate fat people with being sloppy, unattractive, and ugly. So your first task is to *always* wear clean clothing that is not wrinkled. Let's face facts: People judge fat people much more severely than they do thin people. So you must do everything in your power to present a clean image. A skinny, in-shape dude can get away with being a little dirty, but you can't. Deal with it.

Next, make sure your clothing fits you properly. Properly fitting clothes will make you appear less chunky. However, super-baggy clothing will make you look even bigger, and tight-fitting clothing will highlight your weight. It's fine to wear untucked shirts, just make sure they are clean and pressed.

Darker colors tend to hide the bulge better than lighter colors. Lighter colors are great for body builders, but if you have a gut wear darker colors to give you a slimmer look. Shirts with vertical lines are great for chubby guys. Vertical lines will give you a "longer" look. V-necks are another great item for overweight men. V-necks help hide the double chin and focus attention away from your neck toward your chest area.

Speaking of your double chin, sometimes growing a goatee can help hide your fat face. The important pointers about growing a goatee are to

keep it short and well kempt. A goatee can greatly hide the flab and change the look of your face to be more attractive to women.

THREE WAYS TO MAKE YOUR CAR
INTO A ROLLING SEDUCTION CHAMBER

By now you've learned what you need to know to give women the right message with how you look. You've learned the importance of developing your personal style, looking good, and taking care of the details. You're looking hot and feeling good. You have a good chance of getting a date, so now it's time to start thinking about the other expressions of your personal style that women will see: your car and your home.

One of the most common lies women tell is that they don't care about men's cars. In a sense, we suppose, they are telling the truth: Intellectually, they don't care, and don't think such silly things could sway them emotionally. Women often like to make fun of men's cars as "extensions of their penises" (as if that's a bad thing!). On an emotional level, however, women do respond to the kind of car you drive, and to how clean or dirty you keep it. They'll just rarely tell you the truth about it.

This was brought home to us vividly when Esther, a female friend, started dating a new man. Esther is a powerful, can-do kind of woman. She's very successful in her business and is known for her hard-edged, no-nonsense attitude. She would often list her requirements in a man to her friends, and was very clear that there was no way she'd have sex with a man right away. Or, anyway, that's what she thought until she met Keith.

Esther put it this way. "We had dinner, and everything was going well. We had met at the restaurant and he was about to give me a ride home. It turns out he has a Cadillac Coupe de Ville! When he set me into that plush leather seat, and closed the door with that satisfying 'click,' I said to myself 'I'm having sex with this man!'" Keith's car was so cool that it impressed Esther greatly. She ended up having sex with him that very night.

We were shocked by her revelation, but it taught us something important: The experience a woman has in your car can make or break your seduction. Most of us don't have cars as nice as Keith's, but there are still

things you can do to make your car a more seductive space for the women you date.

Like your way of dressing, your car sends a message to women. Your car can be an important part of your seduction strategy. Teenagers aren't the only ones who have sex in cars, and many successful sexual experiences start in men's cars and move to the bedroom later. Here are the three ways to make your car into a rolling seduction chamber.

1. Make your car clean

It'll be hard to create the right romantic mood in your car if it is messy. In this society, where people are increasingly living out of their cars, it's easy to fill it with work projects, books, fast-food garbage, and things you've been meaning to remove but have been too much of a slacker to actually take out of your car. If you are going to give a woman a ride somewhere, it's important that your car not seem like a Dumpster with wheels. Remember, you are sending a message to women with every expression of your style that you make. She is judging your style to see if she wants to have sex with you or not. If your car is clean and comfortable, you've made it past another hurdle. If it isn't, she'll get the message that you are a slob and not in control of your life and be less attracted to you.

If you do need to carry a lot of stuff, get some organizer baskets to keep in your car, or better yet, store all your crap in your trunk. Dwight had to make a lot of overnight trips for his work, and had to keep files, product samples, and personal belongings in his car all the time. He was not a naturally organized person, and his car was always a mess of papers, trash, and dirty laundry. Though his guy friends didn't mind the mess, women were repelled, and he wondered why he had so few second dates.

We had Dwight buy a number of plastic baskets, tubs, and organizers, and simply organize and store unnecessary items in his car. Once everything had its proper place, the car looked neat, even though there was a lot in it. Instead of making him look like a slob, his car made him look like an organized man who was serious about doing his job well.

If a woman sees your car messy, we suggest that you don't bother apologizing. Women are sick of guys who apologize for being slobs rather than

having their lives together. Simply take the time to clear room for her, act like nothing is out of the ordinary, and hope you can see her again with a neat car.

2. Make your car romantic

If you are going to use your car as part of your seduction strategy—and you should—you should have the right equipment to make your car romantic. We suggest you have blankets and pillows in the trunk, in case a romantic walk in the woods becomes something more. You should have good romantic music on the stereo, and condoms hidden in the glove compartment.

You should not have anything in the car that will turn a woman off. *Penthouse* air fresheners, complete with naked centerfold pictures, should not be hanging off your rearview mirror. Ditto for fuzzy dice. Your car shouldn't smell, either. The scent of old burritos or stale cigarette smoke is not a turn-on for women.

You should remove any signs of other women in the car, as we'll show you how to do in a later chapter. One of our students ran into trouble when he was dating several women. One had folded a pretty paper swan for him and written "Christy and Mike" on the wings. She had given it to him in his car, and he put it on his dashboard and kissed her so passionately that they went back to his house to have sex. Unfortunately, after he drove her home later in the evening, he forgot about the paper bird on the dashboard. The next day, when he picked up Jane for their date, she saw it immediately, read the message on it, and took great offense.

Your car should be comfortable, romantic, smell good, and not remind your date of other women.

3. Make your car work

Doors and windows should work on your car; women don't like to have to slide across the driver's seat to get to the passenger's. Your muffler must work. A loud car tells a woman that you are an immature teenager and that your life is most likely out of control. If you can't take care of your car, how will you take care of her? A loud car sends the message that you are obnoxious and unsafe and not to be trusted.

THE FIVE SECRETS OF A SEDUCTIVE HOME

Think about your home. Think about the kitchen, the living room, and your bedroom. Picture it in your mind. Now ask yourself the following questions:

First ask yourself, "Is this a home that will make the women I most desire want to have sex with me?" Most of the men we work with have to answer no. When they look at their homes from the perspective of the women they desire, they find they can understand why these women wouldn't want them.

Second, ask yourself, "What's the message my home sends to the women I'm attracted to?" Most men find that their home doesn't send the message they want to send. It sends messages like "I'm still a boy," or "I'm not really going anywhere in my life." Most of the men we've coached seem to have homes that look like disastrous bachelor pads where a woman would definitely not want to go to have sex. If your home doesn't seem like a comfortable place to spend romantic time in, then you are sending a message that "romance isn't important to me."

Now think about homes you've seen that seem to send romantic messages to women. While many of these homes may seem expensive, and expensively furnished, their style follows basic principles you can follow, too, to make your home more inviting and romantic. While this entire list needs to be followed only right before a date, it will be easier for you if the basics are in place all of the time.

1. A seductive home looks like an adult lives there

A seductive home is not a dorm room, a closet, a warehouse, a garbage dump, or a science experiment. It's not a place for random friends to hang out, or a pornographic poster supply house. Any of these things will leave women thinking that you are still stuck in your adolescence, and they won't desire you.

2. A seductive home is clean

Specifically, the details should be clean. It's best if the mini-blinds are clean, and there are no dust bunnies in the corners. The areas that are most important to your date should be cleanest, and the areas that are least im-

portant, or that you think you can keep your date out of, can be ignored. If she wouldn't see your kitchen unless she spent the night, for instance, you can get away without cleaning it. Because she will already have had sex with you by the time she sees it the next morning, the fact that it is a mess won't wreck your chances with her.

The bathroom, on the other hand, must be absolutely clean. There is no middle ground on this one. One man we coached tried to get around this by taking the lightbulb out of the bathroom so his date couldn't see how dirty it was. This only annoyed her. You must clean the bathroom thoroughly before a date comes to your house. This means cleaning the damn toilet, cleaning the piss stains off the floor, having hand towels, and making sure you're stocked with toilet paper.

3. A seductive home is properly lit

The lighting should be subdued and controlled. Bright overhead lights will make your date feel tense, like she's being interrogated. Try soft, reflected light. This can be a lamp with a 40-watt bulb rather than a 100-watt bulb, or candles, or light coming in from the next room. There should be shadows and patterns of light and mystery. It should be welcoming, not antiseptic. This idea is hard for many men to grasp, because they are used to lighting spaces in order to get things done in them. Did you know that some women try to stay out of fluorescent lighting because of how it makes them look? Your seductive rooms aren't workshops. Be sensitive to having romantic lighting.

4. A seductive home is unpacked and set up

It's amazing how many people still live out of boxes years after moving into their homes. One man who's lived in his house for four years still hasn't put up his pictures. When we told him it could make his house more romantic, he replied, "What's the point of putting pictures up if the house isn't clean?" While we agree that it's important to have a clean home, it's important to have a set-up home. Unpack those boxes, and hang those pictures! Make the home look like an adult lives there.

5. A seductive home has romantic potential

A seductive home makes a woman feel like she's in a place she can relax. Think about the places in your home where you are most likely to be "making a move" with a woman and concentrate on those areas first. This means getting a comfortable couch that is clean and can fit two people lying on it. A couch can begin a seduction when you invite a woman over to "watch movies" or just hang out.

The pictures on the walls don't have to be originals, but they should be framed and hung properly. The furniture is clean, and if it's old or funky, it has a throw cover on it. The carpet has been vacuumed recently and there are no piles of paper or random belongings around. The music is soft and sexy. Everything seems to have a proper place, and is in it.

One of the most important rooms, if not *the* most important room, in a seductive home is of course the bedroom. The bed should be made and large, at least a double bed in size. There should be plenty of pillows, pictures on the wall, and, of course, the sheets should be clean. Set up a music system near your bed, a dim light, and stash condoms in out-of-the-way places for easy access. You should clean out the sports memorabilia, stinky socks, and paramilitary tactical guides from your nightstand.

If you are going to have romantic dates in your home, coordinate your seductions with your roommates beforehand. (And if you're over twenty-five, you better not have roommates, period.) If you want the living room for the evening, for instance, talk to housemates and see if they'll stay out of the house till at least a certain hour. You don't want to be interrupted by people coming in just when you are going for that first kiss.

And speaking of interruptions, turn your cell phone off once a woman comes over. More than one of our students has been ready to make that first move when the phone rings and their date, of course, becomes annoyed and suspicious. Avoid this problem by turning off your phone whenever you have a woman over.

Your style in how you dress, how you keep your car, and how your home looks tells women a lot about you, and helps them decide whether to make you into a hot lover or a lowly "friend." You must take control of these areas, and make sure that the messages you send with them are at-

tractive, intriguing, mature, and adult. Everything else you learn in this book can be undone by poor personal style. Make sure that you have it handled.

HOW TO BECOME CONFIDENT WITH WOMEN: OVERCOMING THE THREE STUMBLING BLOCKS ON THE ROAD TO CONFIDENCE

Confidence Stumbling Block 1. Fear of rejection

As we covered in Chapter 2, you are afraid of rejection because of what you make rejection mean to you. While the successful seducer knows that every no is only another step on the way to the inevitable yes, a man who fears rejection fears it because he makes it mean that there is something wrong with him. Take it from us, after working with thousands of men in our seminars and coaching programs over the past decade, we have seen that the fear of rejection is the one issue that will block your success more than anything else. Here are some solutions:

The Thirty-Day Program for Getting Over Fear of Rejection. You must get yourself so used to rejection from women that it no longer has any negative meaning to you. A simple way to do this is to start small, with our easy-to-follow, thirty-day rejection-stomping confidence-building program.

If you are scared to talk to women and scared of rejection from women, this simple program will get you talking to them daily, and laughing in the face of rejection. It's straightforward, painless, and easy to do. It's based on a simple two-letter word that, when you use it with women, will build your confidence, start you talking, and be the first step in getting women into your life.

Are you ready for the word?

The word is "hi!" To build your confidence with women and to overcome your fear of rejection, for the next thirty days, say hi to women in public at least six times a day. That's all there is to it. You are walking down the street, you see an attractive woman, you say hi to her, and walk on. You see the next attractive woman, and you say hi to her, too. And so on.

Don't be deceived by the simplicity of this program. If you are willing

to actually do it, and to actually say hi to a number of women out in public every day, your confidence will rise, your fear of rejection will diminish, and your success with women will improve. Here's why:

First, your confidence will improve because you actually will be talking to women. Saying hi is wonderful because the interaction ends quickly. Like some other techniques we'll show you for building confidence, the hi interaction doesn't put your ego on the line, and doesn't give her much chance to reject you. What's the worst thing she'll do, glare at you as you walk by? Who cares? It's not like you've risked your whole ego by asking her out or trying to kiss her. You'll get into the habit of seeing women who attract you and talking to them. And that's good.

Second, women's responses to you will become less important to you. You'll find that you are being the kind of man you want to be, the kind of man who says hello to whatever kind of woman appeals to him, no matter what her response might be. You'll become less scared of rejection as you notice that some women smile and say hi back, that some women are in their own world and don't even seem to notice you spoke, and that some women glare at you darkly and reach for their police whistle. You'll start to see that it doesn't matter; all that matters is that you are making life work for you by starting to approach the women who attract you.

Third, you actually will get into more conversations with women if you set a precedent of talking to them right away. Have you ever been in a situation in which you would have spoken to a woman, but the fact that you've initially ignored her makes it hard to start? This happened to our friend Bob just the other day. "I was in a line waiting to buy tickets to a movie. There was a gorgeous girl in line in front of me, but when I first saw her, I went back into my old fear mode and didn't look at her or say hi. After about five minutes of waiting, I really wanted to start talking to her, but it seemed a lot more awkward because I hadn't said hi at first." After you've practiced saying hi for a few weeks, it'll be second nature for you to see that woman in line, look her in the face, smile, and say hi. You'll be relaxed and not concerned with her response. And it will then be natural for the two of you to talk more, and for you to be able to use the tools from the rest of this book to seduce her.

Do you think saying hi is too simple and too easy? Not complicated

enough for you? Here are some other simple approaches you can use to massively increase your confidence with women and begin to master approaching any woman anytime, anywhere:

- Ask for directions—ask where a nearby coffee shop is, or a bookstore.
- Ask a woman for her opinion about where a great nearby restaurant is.
- Ask a woman what time it is.

Other Ways to Overcome the Fear of Rejection

- *Have a "piece on the side."* As you are just beginning to develop your harem of available sex kittens, you are at a disadvantage. As usual, success breeds success. The more sex you are getting, the more confident about sex you will become and the more new women you will attract. But at the beginning, you don't have the confidence of lots of past success, and that slows down your ability to get that first woman on a date and into bed.

  Though it is not available to every man, having a "piece on the side" can generate the erotic confidence that allows you to get even more women. A "piece on the side" is a woman you have occasional sex with—say, once a month—though you might not really want her very much. She is a woman you *know* you can have, but who isn't attractive enough for you to try to start a relationship with. An occasional sex partner like this can build your sexual self-esteem and enable you to take the risks that get you into bed with the women you really want.

  So who could be a potential "piece on the side"? They may be ex-girlfriends, women who are not extremely attractive, much older women, close female friends, women who understand you don't want a relationship, or married women. When you have a "piece on the side," you know you aren't a total loser. If you look hard enough at your life, you will usually find at least one woman who would sleep with you. Try her out and see what happens.

We've had students say, "Yeah, the date didn't go so well, so afterwards I went to the house of my 'piece on the side.'" They were able to get sex when they wanted it. As a result, they were empowered to pursue the sex they really wanted.

• *Get your validation from your life, not from women.* Too many men rely on women for their sense of validation, self-respect, and self-esteem. They live as if women's opinions of them are what matters. If they have a good interaction with an attractive woman, they feel good about themselves. When an interaction goes bad, they feel badly about themselves. This need to be validated by women in order to feel good about themselves robs these men of their confidence with women.

Bob has this problem big-time. His whole picture of himself is based on his latest interaction with a woman. When he asks a woman out on a date and she says no—as they sometimes do, even to the best seducers—Bob is crushed. He thinks, "What a jerk I am. Why do I even bother asking women out in the first place? There must be something wrong with me. I'm a failure. Let's see, how long has it been since I've had a date? What a bummer." He stops being able to concentrate on work, doesn't work out, and generally lets his life go to hell. On the other hand, if an interaction with a woman goes well, Bob is on top of the world, at least for a while. When he has a date that goes well, or meets a hot woman who seems interested in him, he dances through his life. He thinks, "See? I'm not such a bad guy after all! I'm okay! Things are going to be great!" He sets himself up for a letdown by making his self-esteem and validation dependent on his success with women.

We tell men to listen to what former UCLA basketball coach John Wooden used to tell his players. He said, "I always told them that I didn't want excess dejection at a loss, or excessive jubilation after a victory, and that I hoped that, after a game, no one could tell whether you won or lost by your behavior." Coach Wooden knew that the best path to success is to get your sense of validation from your life as a whole, not from momentary wins or losses. Wooden's teams' record-setting levels of victory make this approach seem pretty smart.

If you want to have an easy sense of confidence with women, how do you make this work? Practically, this means finding ways to be in love with your own life, and to have the things you are up to in your life be validating for you. Success with women and success with life are similar. Just as women won't go out of their way to bring you sexual success, life doesn't go out of its way to bring you life success. Just as your sex life is your responsibility to make the way you want it, your life as a whole is your responsibility to make the way you want it. If you want success with women, it makes sense to have long-term goals for your life that inspire you and that you are moving toward, no matter how slowly. If you do this, you'll get your validation from your life, rather than from women.

Don is a good example. As a computer programmer for a large insurance company, it was easy for him to allow his life to get into a rut. Day after day he'd go to work, program, come home, watch TV, and go to bed. He had no goals and no direction. He became passive with his life and, not surprisingly, with women. He blamed his company for his lack of enjoyment of his job, and blamed women for his lack of an abundant sex life. His future looked like it would be just like his past. He looked to women for validation in his life, because he couldn't find it anywhere else, and when they didn't validate him, he became depressed. Thus the cycle worsened: The more depressed he became, the more he wanted women to make him feel validated and, predictably, the less attractive he became. The less attractive he became, the fewer women validated him, and the more depressed he got.

This was the state he was in when he came to us, complaining about his relationships with women. We taught him the tools in this book and had him begin to set goals for his life. We had him go to his local bookstore and get a book on goal-setting, and got him to really look at what he wanted his life to be like in ten years, five years, one year. We got him to write down goals that inspired him, and to put them into his date book where he'd see them often. As he began to get excited about what was possible for him in his life, the cycle began to break apart. He started getting his validation from his life,

rather than from women. This made him more attractive to women. Rather than wanting to be with women so he could have a life, he began having a life that validated him, whether women were in it or not. Naturally, women were intrigued by his passion for his life, and wanted to be a part of it.

We advised Don to make more male friends. Don tended to have many female friends and few male ones. We aren't against having female friends, but there are two kinds: the ones you don't want to have sex with and the ones you do want to have sex with but who don't want you. When a man has many women in his life that he wants sexually but who only want to be friends with him, it's hard on his confidence. Don was always around women who didn't want him, and this made him feel undesirable. It convinced him that women only wanted him as a friend, which really meant that women didn't want him as a man. Being around these women got him into the habit of being nonsexual friends with desirable women, rather than being their lovers. He began treating all women like friends, and they treated him the same way.

At our advice, Don stopped spending so much time with women he desired but who didn't desire him, and started spending more time with other men. These male friendships were able to validate him without putting down his sexuality or showing him that he was undesirable. He found he could get a kind of support from men that he could never get from women he desired who insisted on being "friends." This validated him and made women's reactions to his approach less disturbing.

Women are attracted to men who have passion and fire for their lives. They aren't any more interested in providing the validation for your life than you are in providing the validation for theirs. When you have goals, male friends, and a life that inspires you, you'll be validated by what you are up to, and women will want to be a part of your life. It won't matter to you if they say yes or no when you ask them out, seduce them, and go for that first kiss. You'll be validated by your life and easily able to move on to the next woman.

Confidence Stumbling Block 2.
Fear of hurting women

Some men are driven by the idea that their sexuality hurts women. For instance, Walt always felt like there was something bad about his sexual desire. A tall, thin man in his early thirties, he grew up with three sisters, his mom, and no father. "I was privy to lots of girl talk about how bad guys were, how much they only wanted women for sex," he told us. "With no men to tell me that sex was great, I only got the picture they gave me—that men were insensitive bastards who only cared about using women for their own gratification. I remember being around when my sisters would come home from dates and put down the men they had been with. I so much wanted to be a good guy, to not hurt women with my sexuality."

When Walt first started dating girls as a teenager, he strove to always be polite. "I wouldn't even think about them sexually, 'cause I knew that would be rude," he says. "I masturbated looking at women in magazines, and I even felt guilty about that! Finally I was lying on top of my girlfriend in her bedroom while her parents were away. We were making out, but I was avoiding touching her breasts, because I didn't want to 'use' her, like those guys did with my sisters. Finally she said to me, 'Do you realize you are avoiding touching my breasts? Don't you desire me?' and she took my hand and put it on her breast. I'll tell you, that turned my world upside down."

While most men don't have this fear of hurting women as much as Walt did, many men still have it, and usually don't even know it. They've bought into the myth that men are insensitive bastards who only want women for sex. They've bought into the idea that when a man has sex with a woman he is somehow taking something from her for his own selfish gratification. After all, we say that women "put out" sexually; that must mean that men take what women put out. Many overly nice guys like Walt believe that women are delicate flowers who can get hurt if men are sexual with them. Instead of challenging this belief, these men try to be harmless and are overly sensitive to women's needs. And guess what? They don't end up having much sex.

Men like Walt are committed to being sensitive to women's needs—not being macho, unfeeling jerks who hurt women. Unfortunately, this fear

makes them tepid companions for women, and drains them of their confidence by making them hesitant and self-doubting in all their interactions. In fact, they come across as boring wimps who, at best, women keep around as lowly friends.

"Sensitive" men wonder too much about what women think of them. They spend their brainpower, which should be spent being charming, assertive, funny, and romantic, on self-absorbing concerns about what women think of them.

One of the main fears a man might have is that the woman he is talking to will think he's going to hurt or assault her. As a matter of fact, women you talk to *do* worry that you are going to hurt or assault them. Rightfully so—dating is dangerous for a woman. What these "sensitive," unconfident men don't know is that *indulging her fear of you makes her fear you more.*

Let's look at how this works. When a woman is afraid of you, as most will be when they first meet you, they are looking for signs that their fears either are, or are not, well founded. If you are afraid that you will hurt her, it gives her the evidence she needs to justify avoiding you. You'll be hesitant, unconfident, and self-doubting. You'll treat yourself as if you are dangerous. Of course she'll notice this, and want to get away from you.

If, on the other hand, you *aren't* afraid, you'll be confident and relaxed. She may be afraid that you'll hurt her, but she'll notice that you aren't afraid that you will. Your confidence, your certainty, will help her relax, and make you more attractive. This is one of the reasons that jerks get women; they aren't worried about hurting them. They simply don't care. The jerk's lack of fear allows women to relax their fear. It's ironic that jerks—the men who hurt women the most—can get sex by not worrying about it, while men who would never hurt women, who worry about it all the time, can't get sex at all. This happens because men who are afraid don't have the sense of freedom or the confidence they need to be successful with women.

We advise men to get over the fear that, by their mere presence, or by having simple conversations with women, they are going to be hurtful. It almost certainly will be stressful for women when you first approach them, but the best way to relieve their stress is to model being fearless, not to indulge their fears. Women are tough—if your saying hi to her disturbs her, she'll get over it. Relax. We advise men to realize that if you are afraid you'll

hurt a woman, and that fear drives women away, they don't ever get the benefit of being with you romantically. They never get to experience the pleasure you'd bring them, the romantic feelings, the thrills.

Some men lose their confidence because of false ideas about what women want. Men tell us that they are afraid that they'll end up hurting women emotionally, because with most women they meet, they only want short-term, sexual relationships. They are certain that no woman could possibly want this, and so they avoid the entire seduction, so they don't accidentally cause a woman emotional harm.

This is simply not right, for several reasons. First, there are plenty of women who just want to have sex with you and get rid of you, just as much as you might want to have sex with them and get rid of them. We are reminded of a situation comedy in which a guy decided that he needed to have his first one-night stand. True to the make-believe world of television, he easily accomplished this with a beautiful woman. The next day he was hanging out with his friends, bragging about his conquest. He mooned over how wonderful this woman was and decided to call her and see her again. He called the number she'd given him and—lo and behold!—she had given him a fake number! He was beside himself. "She used me!" he said. "She used me for sex!" A friend asked him, "How does it feel?" After a pause, he responded, "Pretty good, actually." She only wanted him for sex, then she wanted to get rid of him.

Television is rarely an accurate reflection of life, but if you get good at seducing women, you will find yourself in this exact situation. It comes as a shock to many men that women might want sex without a relationship, because it seems like they never meet those women. Bob moans, "Where are these women who just want sex? I never meet them. Where are they?" Well, they are all around him, all the time. The difference between men who just want sex and women who just want sex is that men who just want sex act like it, while women who just want sex act like they want long-term relationships. As far as we can tell, there's not a reliable way to tell if a woman is up for short-term sex without seducing her. After you've had sex with her, you'll start finding out if she wants to keep seeing you, or to get rid of you right away.

We advise men to not worry about dashing women's hopes for

long-term relationships, because, at least at the beginning, she may well only be checking you out for sex, too.

But what if she really does want a long-term relationship? Well, she has the same opportunity you do: If she desires you badly enough, then she can try to be wonderful enough to convince you to have a relationship with her. You'll only get to know that as you spend time with her. You are depriving her of a possible relationship with you if you stay away from her because you feel guilty about only being interested in sex.

Some men lose their confidence with women because they are ashamed about being male. They've known women who've been very hurt in relationships, and they have decided that there must be something basically wrong with men. These men are often feminists, acutely aware of the violence men do to women and committed to not being like other men. Other men are ashamed of their sexuality because of their religious upbringing. All this shame makes men unconfident with and unattractive to women.

Overcoming Fear of Hurting Women. We admire men for not wanting to hurt women. Not being a hurtful person either emotionally, physically, or sexually is rightfully important to many men and is commendable. At the same time, we do take issue with how many men try to keep themselves from hurting women by being constantly worried about it. As we've seen, men who are overly concerned about never hurting women often don't get to have relationships with women at all because they are so hesitant and scared of what they might accidentally do. What can you do if you are one of these overly cautious men?

First, being aware that you are paralyzed by your fear of hurting women can help you start to change. Realize that you are hurting women anyway, in a sense, because they don't get to have relationships with you and have to have relationships with jerks instead. When you start to see that you really aren't helping women, and are hurting your chances with them, it's easier to let go of fear, and be more seductive.

Second, you can decide to change your belief system about women. You can make the decision that you are no longer going to tolerate thinking of women as helpless, delicate flowers, and of yourself as somehow dangerous to them. You can commit yourself to taking on the ideas in this

book and making them part of your daily behavior, rather than simply passively reading about them. This will immediately increase your confidence with women.

The first stumbling block on the road to confidence—the fear of rejection—is basically the fear that you will get hurt in your interactions with women. We've shown you how to get over this fear, by saying hi, talking to women all the time, having a "piece on the side," and getting your validation from your life, not from women. If you follow these steps, you will become almost immune to rejection, and be free and confident to initiate with women anytime you want.

What If You Are Shy or a "Nice Guy"? We have a lot of experience helping self-proclaimed "nice guys" become more seductive without becoming jerks in the process.

We have created an entire course just for shy and nice guys on how to overcome this syndrome: This four-CD set along with a workbook covers everything you need know to reform your inner shy or nice guy into a seductive machine without losing your humanity or the essence of your authentic personality. The purpose of the course is to help you be a good guy and still get women—be respectful of women and still get sex. You can read more about the course at www.howtosucceedwithwomen.com/owners.

Shy men have a unique and special set of problems. Very often shy men know exactly what they "should" do with women. They "should" say hi. They "should" ask women out. But for some reason, they can't get themselves to do it. We now understand these reasons and know how to overcome them—and so can you, with this new audio course.

If you are a shy guy, all the "techniques," "pickup lines," or "motivational visualizations" in the world won't help you. The problem is deeper than that, and has to be addressed or you will stay shy. This course addresses those deeper issues and gives you concrete, tested ways to become less shy with women.

Imagine going from feeling guilty, afraid, or ashamed with women to feeling good about showing romantic interest, and having it work for both you and the woman! That's what Overcoming the Nice Guy Syndrome is about.

Shy men are usually very respectful of women. The problem is they define "respecting women" in such a restrictive way that showing any romantic or sexual interest in a woman seems disrespectful to them. So they end up friends with women, and sexually and romantically frustrated. In this audio course you will learn how to both respect women and show romantic *and* sexual interest in them.

Shy men don't realize it, but they are very tense and controlling with women. Because they are so scared of being hurt by women, or of upsetting women, shy men always have to control every outcome in their interactions with them. This kills any spontaneity in the interaction, and leaves the woman feeling repressed. When a woman feels like she can't express her true self with you (because you are so controlling), she decides that you will be "just friends" and your chances with her are over.

The result is that these women have to date jerks, as the jerks are actually less controlling, less difficult, and more exciting! "Bad boys" are so successful with women because they bring risk into their interactions with women. It's risky for women to be around them, and women find that exciting.

Shy men are hung up on providing a sense of safety for women, believing that being "safe" (i.e., "controlling") is more respectful of women than being risky. The result is that women don't like shy men; they don't feel free around them or excited by them.

Paradoxically, you actually provide more safety for a woman when you provide risks and let her have her own responses to you. You'll learn exactly how to do this—with precise instructions and examples—on this audio course. Knowing how to take appropriate risks with women gives you the "bad boy" quality with them, without having to actually be bad.

In many ways, the ultimate expression of respect for women is being willing to express yourself honestly and appropriately, and to not try to control reactions to you.

Of course, this sounds dangerously like the often-given and utterly useless advice "Just be yourself." It turns out, however, that there are specific ways shy men can learn to express themselves more with women, ways that are seductive to them.

Shy guys are so worried about staying in control that they can't be curi-

ous, because curiosity takes them into the unknown. If you are curious with a woman, you don't know where the interaction might go. You have to be willing to risk things getting out of your control in order to be curious with a woman.

However, curiosity is a critical part of seducing a woman. When you follow your curiosity with a woman, you take risks and provide opportunities for her to risk with you. The result is that you become closer with her and exciting to her. And the cool thing is, being curious is not the least bit manipulative or scam-oriented.

Imagine . . . being able to both respect women and let them know about your sexual interest in them . . . knowing that your intentions with women are good, even if you are only interested in short-term sex . . . being able to provide both safety and risks for women . . . not having to control outcomes with women . . . not being stopped by fear or rejection . . . being curious about women and life, and letting that guide you.

Imagine being a nice guy who is interesting and exciting to women, and who is able to get sex and relationships with them.

Confidence Stumbling Block 3.
Fear, anxiety, and panic around women

Many of our students have had to overcome massive obstacles to succeed with women. Some men are so stopped by fear and anxiety that they literally feel as if they are going to die if they approach a woman. And no matter how hard we push, cajole, or force them to do so, nothing will help. So we had to research and understand how anxiety and panic operate.

Kirk was a very hip, well-dressed guy who was interesting and well spoken. He came to us after reading book after book about seduction and dating and not being able to even approach a woman to say hi. Kirk had massive fear of approaching women. We taught Kirk several tricks to handling panic and anxiety, and after a few weeks he was well on his way to approaching women with confidence.

First of all, as with any phobia, the more you avoid the thing you fear, the more intense the fear becomes. In other words, the more you do not approach women, the larger an issue it becomes in your life. So to start

attacking the fear, you need to put yourself in harm's way and start out doing small things like saying hi or going out with friends in social situations.

Next, this is a biological response. This is your own fight-or-flight syndrome going off and creating unpleasant physical symptoms in your body. So you need to do things to calm down your physiology. The most effective treatment is to learn to breathe from your abdomen and slow your breathing rate. When you are scared, your breathing rate increases and becomes shallow; when you train yourself to slow down, you can also slow down your breathing and this will reduce the symptoms of anxiety. Kirk was able to train himself to slow down, and it greatly helped him keep his cool.

The next technique you can employ is to pace or walk around to help calm down your body. Many people feel calmer if they walk around the block, pace for a while, or even do push-ups or jumping jacks to release excess energy. You can even go into your car and scream really loud to help calm down (if that works for you). Kirk found that doing as many push-ups as possible worked for him. It helped tire him out, and the aftereffect was relaxation. He also found that doing a few yoga poses and stretching his body helped keep him feeling relaxed.

Some people find that using hypnotic relaxation techniques can be very beneficial. You don't have to go to India and learn to meditate on a mountaintop to train yourself to calm down and feel more confident. You can, for example, imagine a calm scene in your mind. This calm and peaceful scene, such as a beach or waterfall, can hopefully help you focus on something other than your anxiety feelings long enough to change your inner state. Another technique is to imagine someone you trust, like Ron Louis and David Copeland, there with you offering encouragement and support, and cheering you on.

In the end, Kirk was able to greatly relieve his anxiety by using a variety of the techniques we listed above. After we worked with him for a weekend, he emailed us and said, "Thanks, guys, for the great coaching. It was amazing to finally feel free of the panic I used to feel. I can even laugh about it now. It seems actually funny that I've avoided women this long, and now approaching them seems fun—almost like a game."

OTHER CONFIDENCE BUILDERS: EASY WAYS
TO RAISE YOUR CONFIDENCE LEVEL

Be in "the zone"

Peak performers talk about being in "the zone" or in "the flow." You are in the zone when you are at your best, when all your inner resources are available to you, and when you seem to automatically handle everything well.

We've all had these moments. Sometimes they take place during sports, when a rock climber, for instance, is so engaged in the climb that he forgets about everything else in the world but what he is doing. Surgeons report that when they are doing surgery, they are so involved that it's like they are in perfect harmony with the world around them. If you can remember a time when you effortlessly and peacefully performed beyond what you usually were able to do, you have been in the zone.

People who are falling in love are in the zone. You probably have felt it. When you were with her, it was like time stood still. You could do no wrong, and life, when you were with her, seemed effortless. When you were together, you were creative and happy, and not worried about yourself or about your life. This is the zone as well.

Nick had this experience when he first met Kay. "I'd seen her at a couple of parties and been very attracted to her, but from the start I didn't feel tense or nervous around her, like I usually do when I meet women I'm hot for. It was like I knew in my heart that we'd get along fine, and I wasn't worried about it. I felt like, if it were meant to be, then it would happen. I really didn't worry about it.

"I remember running into her at a park, and we talked a bit and sat together on the grass. I didn't feel like I had to say anything, and there were these long periods when neither of us said anything, but I knew it was just fine. I felt present and happy and didn't need to fill the silences.

"After one of those silences, she said to me 'I just want to tell you everything about me.' It was the start of our relationship. I was in the zone that day, that's for sure."

How did Nick do this? What made him so irresistible to Kay that she couldn't help but open up to him, even though he said very little? Nick

accidentally did what all peak performers do, and what you can do with women, too. He pursued his outcome (being romantic with Kay) and, *simultaneously*, let go of having to make that outcome happen (having faith that if it was meant to be, it would happen). He stopped worrying about whether she would like him or not, and simply pursued her. Any outcome would have been fine with him. If she had not wanted to be with him, he might have been disappointed, but he wouldn't have been upset. Similarly, he wasn't overly excited about her interest, even though he was pursuing it.

Let's look at the opposite example. Randy was very interested in Donna. He thought she was cute and mysterious, and he very much wanted to have a romantic relationship with her. It was terribly important to him that all of his interactions with her be great for her, so that she'd like him and want to go out with him. He was so focused on this goal, and on how bad it would be if she didn't like him, that he was weird and distracted when he was with her. "I was such a jerk," he says now. "I so wanted to impress her that I talked a mile a minute, made jokes that weren't funny, and was all-around a tense, jumpy guy." Because he couldn't stop thinking about his outcome—having her like him—he could never be relaxed and unconcerned with her. "I scared her off," he says. "I was so wrapped up in what I wanted to happen with her, I never was present with her when we were together." His inability to pursue his goal with her, and give up worrying about the goal at the same time, made him out of the zone, forced, and not attractive.

Women you have chemistry with are women you are pursuing but you are not worried about the outcome. For some reason, with certain women, it's easy for you to not worry, and to get into the zone. You can, however, train yourself to worry less and less in your interactions with all women by simply making that your intention. When you go into interactions with women, you can remind yourself that the outcome isn't important. When you do this, you'll find that you are getting into the zone, that you are more relaxed, and that you have better chemistry. When Randy learns to not be worried about how it goes with Donna, and has some faith that everything will be okay, he will relax, and it will make it easier for Donna to get to know him and to find him attractive. All the rest of the tools you learn in this book—seduction strategies, meeting women, going for that first kiss, and more—will be much easier to practice and have success with if you train yourself to follow this credo.

Make decisions

Decision-making is a muscle that gives you control over and confidence in your life. But you must practice. You don't want to be a control freak with women, but you don't want to be a useless wad of indecisiveness, either. Being decisive means you never, ever say, "Oh, I don't know, what do you want to do?" It means that when those little meaningless choices come up during the date—such as what table to sit at—you decide quickly and easily. If she'd rather sit somewhere else, then you can say, "Sure," but always make decisions quickly when you are with her. This means you make decisions when you are on the phone with her or when you are making plans with her. Being decisive can go a long way to having you appear as a confident and powerful man. This shows her that you are a guy who is in charge of his life and not wishy-washy, and will put you miles ahead of most of the other guys she meets. This seems obvious and simple, but it builds your confidence and sets the stage for seduction.

FOUR THINGS YOU CAN DO *TODAY* TO BE CONFIDENT WITH WOMEN

1. Groom yourself like a man who is confident with women

Think about your grooming. Today might be a good day to try a new aftershave, or to get a better quality shampoo or conditioner. You may want to make an appointment with a good hairstylist to get your hair cut in a new way. Or you may want to get your teeth cleaned. Wash and style your hair, and trim any unwanted hair in your nose and ears. Take a second to think about a few ways you can improve your grooming and what actions you can take this week to do so. Notice how much more confident you feel when you are well groomed and looking good!

2. Dress like a man who is confident with women

Go to your closet and look at your clothes. What are the best outfits you have for seducing women, and what are the worst? Notice the shirts and pants that you should wear more often, and those that you should wear less,

around women. Look at your details: What are the most attractive shoes you own? What is your most attractive belt? What bracelets, rings, or other jewelry do you have that might be attractive to women? What clothes fit your body best and are in best repair? What clothes make you feel most attractive when you wear them? What is your most attractive outfit?

Be aware that your most attractive outfit may not be the most elegant, or the most expensive. You may not look best in a suit, for instance; you may look best in a well-fitting sports shirt and a pair of clean, ironed jeans, with nice boots and a black belt. Whatever it is, put it on and wear it today. If you need to iron it first, do so. Notice the confidence wearing this outfit gives you with women, and commit yourself to developing a wardrobe of clothes that make you feel the same way. If you haven't been shopping recently, go shopping within the next few weeks and add a few new items to your wardrobe. Maybe you buy a new, cool-looking shirt, hip jeans, boots, or something else that looks great on you.

3. Move like a man who is confident with women

At any time, you can change the way you hold and move your body, and change your level of confidence and how you feel. If you don't believe us, try slumping and slouching, letting your shoulders come forward as if you were terribly depressed. Breathe shallowly. If you really take on this posture, you will feel less confident, and will eventually actually *become* depressed!

Fortunately, this works both ways. The same body you can use to make you feel unconfident and depressed, you can use to make you feel just the opposite. Try it now. Take on the posture of a man who is confident with women. As weird as it may seem, imagine that you are inside his body. How does he sit? How does he stand? Are his shoulders forward or back? Put your shoulders there. Is his head up or down? Put your head that way, too. Does this confident man breathe deeply? Do it! What's this confident man's facial expression? Try it out! It may seem crazy, but if you try it, you *will* notice a difference; you may even want to stand up and practice walking around with the posture of a confident man.

Imagine how useful this could be when you are approaching a woman. Before talking to her, you take on the posture that makes you feel more confident and, breathing deeply, tall and relaxed, you approach her. If you

practice this posture every day, you'll find it brings out your innate confidence and becomes natural for you.

4. Pursue like a man who is confident with women

Now groomed, dressed, and moving well, commit yourself to having an interaction with a woman today in which you pursue her romantically, while at the same time not worrying about whether your outcome happens or not. Put yourself into the zone and give yourself the freedom of not worrying about the outcome. You may want to commit yourself to asking a woman for her phone number. You may want to approach ten women this week or simply practice saying hi to as many women as you can. You may want to ask a woman out—or ask out several women. You may simply want to make it clear to a woman you meet that you are attracted to her. Whatever it is that you do, make it a little more risky than you are comfortable with—and, most important, give up worrying about whether she says yes or no.

Think again about the first questions we asked you at the beginning of this chapter. What kind of woman do you want? What's most important to you in a woman? Is it that she be tall or short? That she have wonderful breasts? That she be blond or brunette? That she is smart or rich? What exactly do you want?

And then think again about the next questions we asked you: What kind of a man will you have to be to get that woman into your life and into your bed? Are you that kind of man already? What changes do you need to start putting into place in your life to become that powerful man who is successful with those women? Write down what you feel you need to change in your life and get to work on changing yourself and your life. You really can do it. We've seen our lives dramatically change with women as our confidence skyrocketed, and we've seen the lives of thousands of men change by using this book as a guide to succeeding with women.

If you are like most men, you've realized that you aren't yet the kind of man you'll need to be to get the kind of women you desire. What you need is to develop your personal style—your way of dressing and your confidence.

You've seen how the way you dress sends a message to women, and have learned how to take control of that message so that it says, "I'm interesting, mature, and attractive. You want to be with me." You've learned that it doesn't matter what nature gave you; what matters is what you do with it in how you dress, move, and act. You've learned how to make your car and home romantic, and how to overcome the two stumbling blocks to confidence with women: fear of rejection and fear of hurting women. You've seen the importance of not relying on women to validate you, but rather getting your validation from your life. You've learned how to be in the zone with women by giving up worrying about the outcomes of your seduction and simply pursuing what you desire, no matter what happens. And you've found out the four things you can do today to be more confident with women than ever before.

As you develop your personal style, you will discover many benefits it brings beyond simply being attractive to women. And as that happens, you'll find women are more attracted to you than they've been before.

4

Where the Girls Are:
Meeting Women
for Sex
and Relationships

Imagine this scenario: After reading this book, Jim decided to call us because he was filled with questions and wanted to attend our world famous "How to Be Successful with Women" seminar. He explained that he was our "number one" fan. He told us he had even recorded a homemade CD of our book so that he could listen to it while in his car, on the train, and while working out in the gym.

After a few minutes of discussion, we invited him to a course, but we refused to tell him where or when it was being held. We simply told him to get on a plane and meet us, still not telling him the location or the date. Jim got annoyed with us because we didn't give him any useful information. We just kept telling him to come to the course without telling him how or where. He finally screamed into the phone, "If you are not going to tell me any of the specifics, I'm not coming to your damn course!" We replied in a calm and methodical manner: "We're sorry you feel that way. We'd love for you to attend the course," yet still refused to tell him when

and where it was. We told him what to do, but not how to do it. Of course he eventually went nuts. Anybody would.

This is a good example of how most seduction "authorities" will teach you to meet and date women. They'll do what we did with poor Jim; they'll tell you what to do, but not how to do it. They will tell you the impractical theory without the telling you how to practice. Or they will show off for you and not explain to you in real terms exactly what they are doing. Some experts will use such complicated seduction "tricks" that if you follow their advice, you end up feeling like an idiot or insincere, and decide, instead, to just give up. Only learning principles leaves most people feeling frustrated, empty, and worse off than when they started.

The majority of men we've trained haven't had very good experiences using empty theories like "Be more hard to get" or "Be more outgoing" to get women, or just "Be more confident" or even just "Act cocky and funny." Dating advice usually takes the form of unhelpful locker-room talk and equally useless bombast. Plus, the guys who talk about getting women usually aren't the ones actually getting them. You probably know men who are all talk and no action, always bragging, yet always sleeping alone. You probably know guys who spend endless hours online researching and reading about seduction, but cannot take any action to save their lives, while the most successful men seem to be surrounded by women with no apparent effort or planning. These are the guys who go out to have fun and effortlessly approach women without fear. Remember the guys who got girls in high school? They were not always the brightest of the bunch, but they didn't have to force themselves to go out and approach women. Often, they were the bad boys who would skip class and get in fights, or they were football players who made a routine out of punching your lights out if you didn't do their homework for them. They didn't have theory or any ideas at all, but they had the proper action and managed to get the girls. Some guys you meet are "naturals" who without any effort on their part easily get women. Most of our readers are not, however, "naturals," and they know that they will have to actually put in the work to transform their dating lives. Most of our readers have found it difficult to navigate the maze of dating and have come up empty-handed when it comes to understanding the very complicated dance of male-female relationships. Thank God you have this book in your hands.

Theory alone will not get you sleeping with the women you desire. You need to learn to take action with women—massive action. This means getting out of your house and approaching and meeting a ton of women. You know how hard it is sometimes to take a new idea and actually use it those first few times. This chapter will show you how to integrate seduction into your daily life. We'll also explore where to meet women in a variety of settings and places.

One common myth among single men is that there is a scarcity of single and available women. Single men usually fail miserably to notice all the women they have contact with in a typical day. Most men are surrounded with women throughout their daily routines, but are too blinded by the myth of female scarcity to notice. The solution is simple in theory, but much more difficult in practice: You must notice the women around you, ask them out, and create seductions. You need to open your eyes and see women around you and know that you, yes you, have a shot with them.

The myth of female scarcity is not grounded in reality. Our research shows that there are, at this moment, millions of single women waiting for you. They are not hiding in the mountains or in caves; they are at bookstores, shopping centers, bars, on the street, at work, behind the checkout counter, in restaurants—everywhere. You simply need to contact them. This chapter will show you how to turn every aspect of your life into situations that could lead to seduction.

We will start with a blow-by-blow description of our desperately lonely guy, Bob, and of all of his boneheaded mistakes. We will compare him to our master seducer, Bruce, and show you all the things he does throughout a typical day that attract women.

The fundamental difference between Bob and Bruce is that Bruce has many practices in place that have his success insured. He doesn't only know the theory; he knows how to put the theory into practice. Let's start by looking at the typical, non-woman-meeting day of Bob.

7:30 a.m., Bob wakes up to the loud ringing of his alarm clock. Bob sits up thinking, "Oh no, another day. Can't I just go back to bed and pretend I'm dead? This is going to be even worse than yesterday. God, I wish I were

sick today. Maybe I should call in to work and tell them that I have the flu. I haven't met any women in over two years."

Bob doesn't take time to shower. He looks around his dirty bedroom floor for a pair of semi-clean underwear. He finds a pair under his bed along with a wrinkled shirt that he puts on. His hair is messy and he tries to make it look nicer by running his fingers through it. He stares into the bathroom mirror and grunts to himself, "I hate this." He finds an old pair of slacks in his closet hamper, puts on his shoes, and off he goes to work.

7:45 a.m., on the way to work. Bob swears at the other drivers on the road. At a stop sign he stares at a beautiful woman in the car next to him and wishes he could be with her. She catches him looking and glares at him as he quickly looks away. "I should just become a card-carrying fairy," he says to himself.

7:55 a.m., the drive-through at McDonald's. Bob grumbles to the female employees and orders his normal breakfast. He pays the cute young female cashier. She smiles at him and he rolls his eyes. He drives off. He snarfs down his coffee and quickly takes bites of his Egg McMuffin. Flakes of the muffin drop onto his shirt and pants. He ignores the greasy flakes and mumbles, "I hate being late! Why am I always late?" as he drives the rest of the way to work.

8:15 a.m., at work. He enters through the door to the office and the receptionist, Patty, smiles and says, "Good morning, Bob." He grunts, "Hi. Traffic sucked this morning. I hate that, all that god-damned traffic!" Having vented his frustration at this attractive young woman, he goes to his desk.

As he gets comfortable in his cubicle, his former girlfriend Laurie calls to invite him to a party she's having later that month. Bob gets angry and says, "Look, Laurie, I don't want anything to do with you or your stupid parties! I hate parties!" She hangs up on him and he gets to his work.

A few male employees stop by to say good morning to him and he tries his best to get rid of them by typing and concentrating on his computer

while they talk. On a short break from work he gets on the Internet and looks at the personals ads on dating sites. He thinks they are stupid. "I could never meet women that way. I bet they are all psychopaths, or guys pretending to be women." He pops over to his favorite Internet porn sites, drools over the hot women on them, and then gets back to work.

12:30 p.m., lunchtime. Bob does his best to avoid people during his lunch break. He either gets food from the company cafeteria and brings it to his cubicle, or brings a book and reads in a corner. While other people joke and laugh, Bob looks at them with disgust. "What the hell are they so happy about?" he thinks to himself. He stares at Marcia, the most attractive woman at the company. She is sitting with a guy named Bruce and having a great time. "What does that guy have that I don't?" he asks himself. "He's not even that attractive."

Today Bob waits in line to pay for his chicken casserole. He doesn't talk to any of the other employees in line or the friendly forty-year-old cashier. He looks at women he wishes he could talk to, but knows in his heart that they would just be unfriendly to him. "Besides," he tells himself, "there's a big difference between a conversation and actually finally getting some sex. I can't see why I would even bother." He slumps back to his desk.

1:20 p.m., back to work. Martin, Bob's high school pal, forwards him sexy emails from women he has met online. Martin wants to know if Bob would be interested in going on a blind double date with the women Martin has met. Bob thinks that Martin is crazy and emails back that he has standards and would never go on a blind date. "Blind dates are for losers," he explains. "It's like admitting that you can't get a woman any other way." Martin gives up and finds somebody else.

6:00 p.m., time to leave work. Bob goes home to watch TV alone for the rest of the night. He orders a pizza and drinks two beers. He watches a porn video, masturbates, and goes to bed.

From the start to the finish of his day, Bob lives in a vacuum. Even when there are women around, he avoids them and rationalizes his lack of contact

by telling himself that the available women either aren't good enough or would never want him anyway. He stays horny, lonely, and depressed.

Now let's look at a day in the life of our hero Bruce, who leads fundamentally the same life Bob does. The only difference is in the approach.

6:00 a.m. Bruce is suddenly awakened by his very loud and obnoxious radio alarm blasting the Jimi Hendrix song "Foxy Lady." As the radio blares, our gallant hero tries to smile. He rubs his eyes, stretches his arms in the air, and thinks to himself that today will be a day full of flirting, fantasy, and fun. He sings along with "Foxy Lady" and improvises his own lyrics: "You know you're a sweet little heartbreaker. Oh, yeah, you are my hot and sexy foxy lady. You turn me on so bad. Oooooooh yeah!" He laughs out loud and smiles.

He's unfamiliar with the next song, and it fades into the background as the female DJ's sexy voice says, "The tenth caller will win tickets to the coolest new movie and five new CDs." Bruce, halfway through shaving, grabs his phone and dials with a passion. Though the line is busy, he calls and recalls until he gets through. Though he doesn't win the contest, he boldly flirts with the DJ and lets her know that he is a fan. While talking to her, Bruce decides that he will make her his newest "project," and he vows to call her a few times per week. Could he get a date from this?

He brushes his teeth, puts on his clean, well-fitting, stylish clothes, and packs up his gym gear and briefcase for the next adventure.

6:38 a.m., on the way to the gym, in his car. Bruce is feeling good and sings along with songs on the radio. As women pass in their cars, he smiles, winks, and waves at them. Some glare, some smile, some ignore him. He doesn't care.

He calls back the lovely DJ on his cell phone and asks her out. She says no, and Bruce, undaunted, tells her a silly joke. He asks for her email address at the station so he can send her a silly note. The DJ laughs and gives him her email address and Bruce celebrates his small success.

As he nears the gym, a beautiful brunette in a sporty car passes. She has

pouty lips and looks like an erotic receptionist who would pose in a "Sexy Secretary" *Playboy* pictorial. Even at this early hour, Bruce is mesmerized by her. They seem to be going in the same direction, and Bruce smiles, waves, and winks at her as they work their way through the busy traffic. She smiles and waves back, and Bruce thinks he sees her blushing. He mouths "I love you" to her, and at the next stoplight he pulls up next to her, writes "I'd love to meet for coffee—please call!" on his business card, and tosses it through her open car window. He takes the next turn and is almost at the gym.

7:00 a.m., at the gym. Bruce goes to the gym at the same time four days a week. Consistently working out at the same time pays off because it lets Bruce know the "regulars" who work out at that time. He can build on his successes with the women he meets there, and slowly chip away at his seductions.

As he walks up to the door, he flirts and talks with Janet, who is on her way in. Bruce has seen her in the gym lots of times. She is with her six-year-old son. Bruce says hi to the son, opens the door for Janet, and checks her out. "So what if she has a kid," he says to himself. She works out all the time, has a great body, and besides, it's all practice anyway. As he walks into the club, he smiles and flirts with the girl checking IDs. Her name is Pauline, she's twenty-three, and from a small town. He always jokes with her about going to a bar to watch the local college sports team. She always kids him back, and he knows that they will indeed go out sometime soon. He patiently flirts with her, knowing that if he keeps at it, his success with her is inevitable.

While working out. Bruce changes into workout clothes. Even though he's no perfect physical specimen, he's chosen workout clothes that make him look good. They are clean, look neat, and smell good. While working out on cardio machines, he smartly positions himself near a large-breasted, sexy-looking, mid-thirties woman. Bruce hasn't seen her in the club before. "Are you new here?" he asks, creating an opening for conversation. After he introduces himself, she tells him her name is Fiona. They discuss her regular workout schedule. As she gets up to leave, he asks for her phone number. She turns him down, but tells him to meet her back at the club

some afternoon next week. He accepts her request and enjoys watching her walk away. Bruce feels even more confident because he had the balls to ask Fiona out.

On the way to the weight room, Bruce smiles and says hi to other cute female regulars. He uses every opportunity to talk to women. Even if the women are not all that hot, he flirts anyway because he is as smart as Bob is dumb. He initiates and maintains conversations with women of all ages and all levels of beauty. Bruce asks women open-ended questions at the gym, questions about the news, great places to go on vacation, and even about health- and workout-related topics. Because of his persistence, Bruce has dated and had sex with several women from the gym.

He showers, dresses well, and prepares for his next adventure.

8:30 a.m., he goes to his regular coffee shop. Bruce enters the Coffee Hut, his favorite place for flirtation, coffee, and breakfast. He has selected a coffee shop to frequent that is convenient for him and that has a large clientele of women. It doesn't have the best food in town, but Bruce knows that the real focus here is finding women to date, not getting the best food or coffee.

Bruce is already pumped up from his workout and is ready to smile and talk to the lovely twenty-two-year-olds behind the counter. The woman making the coffee drinks is named Vicki. He has nicknamed her "Cappuccino Mamma." She and several of the other women working there are very beautiful. Bruce talks to them about some silly item in the news. They laugh and smile. He even thinks they look forward to him coming in; at least they seem happy to see him.

While in line he talks to another woman. She is tall, dark, and conservative-looking. He talks about coffee and she seems distant and scared. He introduces himself and talks to her until she gets her coffee. She sits far away from him. Once again, he doesn't care. He knows that the important thing is not how women will respond to him, but that he's being the kind of man he wants to be.

Bruce sits down with a muffin, coffee, and a newspaper, his regular routine. He strikes up a conversation with yet another woman, who is sitting near him. Having a newspaper helps him, because he can comment

on something funny or weird in the news. He makes plans to go to happy hour with her and readies himself for work.

9:15 a.m., our boy wonder arrives at work. The first thing Bruce does upon entering work is flirt with the receptionist, Patty. He leans on her desk and smiles, saying, "How's the Goddess of Reception doing this morning?" He knows his company policy on dating and is sure to never appear to be sexually harassing while he flirts with the women at his workplace. At the same time he figures that Patty could be a good person to bring him to parties with her friends, and to possibly introduce him to new social circles he is not yet a part of. Bruce knows that having several female friends is just as important as having many female lovers.

Bruce gets to his cubicle and checks his email. He has been seducing several women he met online, and several lusty responses are waiting for him. He composes a hot, letters-to-*Penthouse*-type reply, and with only minor changes sends it to two of the women who wrote him, as well as to a woman he had been seducing but with whom he's lost contact. Bruce also text messages several women he has been in contact with. He is at work filling up his social calendar for the rest of the week and into the next one. He aims to go out at least four times per week and is constantly looking for new dates and social opportunities to check out.

A little while later, a cute woman from the local print shop enters the office to drop off brochures. He locks eyes with her and they have a conversation. He finds out the type of movies and music she likes and decides to call her sometime at the copy store to set up a movie date.

Lunchtime, 12:30 p.m. All this running around and working so hard has made our hero hungry. He goes to one of his favorite lunch spots. While the food is below average, it is near his office and many businesswomen eat there. Bruce selects his lunch spots just like he selects his coffee spots: He goes where the beautiful women are.

While in line, he smiles at two very sophisticated women waiting to be seated. "Isn't it fun to be waiting?" he asks in a sarcastic tone. The two women smile and he introduces himself. As one reaches out to shake hands, he kisses her hand and tells her that it is an honor to make her acquaintance.

Bruce talks more to the women and they invite him to sit with them during lunch. He ends up exchanging phone numbers with one of the women and using his cell phone to take a few silly photos with both of them.

After the experience at the restaurant, Bruce sits in his car for a while and jots down in his notebook a list of women as possibilities for dating. He can't even remember the names of all the women he is in the process of pursuing. Bruce always uses his lunch hour as a time to flirt and practice his seduction skills. Even if he is busy at his job and under deadlines, he always uses some of his lunchtime hour to hone his seduction skills. He practices on women who are eating lunch near him, waitresses, servers, and will even go to places like Starbucks on the way back to work to squeeze in a few more approaches.

1:20 p.m., back to work. Bruce arrives back to work and checks his email again for more responses. A few more bored women, also at work, have responded. He flirts through email and sends them more seductive Internet messages. He continues to text-message women, work on his MySpace page, and keep in contact with his male buddies and wingmen to see if they have any leads on interesting parties, outings, or any other ways to meet women. (Secretly, the authors of this book wonder how Bruce keeps his job with how little time he actually puts into it.)

6:00 p.m., time to leave work. Bruce stops at a coffee shop and flirts with a few women on his way home from work. He also goes into a Target store and flirts with several women shopping. He keeps practicing his approach skills with women and his ability to close the deal. When Bruce gets home, he focuses on what fun events he will pursue that night. Every week he looks in the "Happenings About Town" section of his Sunday paper and figures out what options most appeal to him. Maybe he will go to a lecture about dogs tonight, or attend a burlesque convention.

He calls several women on his list and makes a date for 11:00 p.m. at Suzi's house. Suzi has been an off-and-on lover of his for several months. She's always happy to hear from him, and says that tonight she wants to cuddle in bed and watch DVDs with him. Bruce plans to go see Suzi after hitting a few bars on the way to her house.

Bruce goes to bar number one, a cool lounge. He approaches a few women and has lukewarm conversations. Some blow him off—and he doesn't care. He then approaches a group of four women sitting drinking wine and laughing. He chimes in to their conversation, sits down, and continues to talk to them for a while. He ends up flirting with Becky, who is a slightly shy twenty-eight-year-old. He whispers in her ear several times and she blushes with Bruce's comments. He ends up telling her to put her cell number into his phone. Before he leaves the bar, he texts her, "You are a silly girl. I look forward to seeing if you're still a brat when your friends are not around." Becky quickly texts him back calling him a "bad boy" and asking when they can go out. He plans to take Becky out a few nights later for drinks.

After meeting Becky and getting her number at the bar, our hero finally ends up at Suzi's house. They watch movies, have a few drinks, and have sex for hours. Bruce falls asleep and wakes up to a new day.

THE FOUR EXCUSES THAT KEEP YOU FROM MEETING WOMEN

The reason Bob is so unsuccessful is that he lets negative beliefs run his life. He is probably a lot like you, and certainly a lot like us before we learned the secrets of seduction. His negative beliefs and concerns dictate how he acts, which in turn dictates how successful (or unsuccessful) he is with women. The concerns and beliefs become excuses that Bob uses to keep himself from pursuing women. The following four excuses are often occupying Bob's mind, and they destroy his success with women. If you don't deal with them, they will destroy your success with women, too.

Excuse 1. "It takes too much time."

Bob looks at his daily schedule and whines that he simply doesn't have enough time. He can't meet women, he claims, because he is always busy. He claims he's not scared of women, just too rushed, overloaded with too many responsibilities. We know this is not true. In fact, meeting women is not as time-consuming as you may think, and much of the "dead time" in your life—waiting in lines, for instance—is prime women-meeting time.

As Bruce demonstrated, however, flirting and dating women does take *some* time; there's no way around it. But it is worth it. While dating women may take time up front, after the women are in place, the time required to maintain the relationships is very minimal.

Bruce doesn't view flirting with and dating women as time-consuming because he enjoys it so much. To him, it is his fun time. It is one of the things that bring joy to his day. Bruce feels that meeting women is an outlet for his self-expression and a way for him not only to connect with women, but to be the man he wants to be. Bruce views meeting women as his social time, and he includes hanging out with his buddies and having new experiences as part of his self-expression as well. Occasionally it seems like work, but usually he finds himself naturally interacting with women and talking without any effort on his part.

Mastering any new skill does take an initial time and energy investment. If you want to become a great basketball player, you have to buy the right equipment and put in the time to learn the basic moves and strategies. As your playing gets better, it isn't as hard anymore. You can get away with simply maintaining your skills and condition, which takes a lot less time.

The same thing is true of dating. Once you have skills and structures in place, you won't have to spend nearly as much time working on them. On a daily basis Bruce does several things and takes many actions that all help him succeed in dating. He talks to women, smiles and says hi, and flirts—these things don't take much time on their own, but their cumulative effect is tremendous.

Excuse 2. "It'll hurt my reputation."

Many men, Bob included, worry too much about their reputation. They fear being "found out." They worry that their friends will think they are desperate and won't respect them. They worry that people will think of them as a "player" or as someone who is a jerk. Some men are even concerned that if they ask a woman out in a bar, those around her will think of him as a jerk.

Bob uses concerns about his reputation as an excuse to not get out there and talk to women. He says, "What if I do ask out that woman I'm so

interested in? I can just see how disgusted she'll be by the idea, and I just know she'll tell all our mutual friends. I can see them now, laughing at me." He also moans that he doesn't like to go to pick-up bars because he fears he will see someone he knows. These fears are totally stupid because if you see someone you know, each of you has the same knowledge of the other. If you keep your mouth shut, so will he.

The bottom line is this: You no longer need to apologize to anyone for your interest in dating women. You no longer have to apologize or hide the fact that you are a seducer. You no longer have to worry that others will judge you negatively. Dating is natural and guys of all ages date. If we could lift a magic wand and take your concerns away, we would do so right now. We can, however, impress upon you that it is now time to let go of this excuse and no longer use it to keep you from meeting and seducing women.

Excuse 3. "I just can't do it."

All of our students, at some point, have felt as though they were fundamentally inadequate when it came to meeting women and dating. Perhaps they were just beginning to learn how to date women and it all seemed too overwhelming. Or perhaps they had asked out ten women in a row, and all said no. Maybe the last three women they seduced had gotten almost to the point of having sex with them, then decided to just be friends. Whatever the reason, it is only natural to sometimes feel as though you just can't do it. And it's natural to feel frustrated, aggravated, and want to quit at times.

In a way, feeling like a failure is good because your dissatisfaction can get you in action, ready to fight back and prove that you *can* do it. Seen this way, feeling like a failure is actually an opportunity to prove that you aren't one. You've probably experienced feeling bad about something until suddenly you felt so pissed off that you couldn't stand feeling bad about it anymore. People who are depressed often report that this happens; they can't stand being so down anymore, so they begin changing and improving their lives. It's sometimes said that it's best to kick a man when he's down; that way, he'll get up faster. When thinking you can't approach women gets painful enough, you'll naturally start to approach them just to get rid of the pain of feeling like such a wimp.

The main thing you must do if you feel like you "just can't do it" is to get support from other men. Mark found himself in this situation. He was just learning how to seduce women, and it seemed like everything he tried made him fall flat on his face. His attempts at witty banter with women came across like drunken street-person ranting, and every interaction with women seemed awkward. He was ready to give up entirely, and came to us dejected.

"I just can't do it," he said. "It's hard and I'm not good at it and I just can't go on with it anymore." He needed support, so we gave it to him, just as you must be able to get support when your seduction failures get you down. "Look," we reminded him, "of course it's going to be difficult at first. If you hang in there, it will get better." We went over his interactions with him, and gave him coaching about how they could be improved in the future. By reminding him that his dating problems were temporary, and by going over his recent dates with him looking for problems, we were able to give him the support he needed to get out there and keep trying.

When you want to quit, you can also use the time off to refine your game. You can study more of our materials, reread this book, or simply take a break to regain your strength and confidence. Sometimes we all have to take a break from seducing women.

You must make sure you get support when you think you can't do it. If you have men friends who are also reading this book, go to them to be reminded that things will get better, and to be reminded of the long-term goal you are working for. Go to men who will remind you of your successes with women so far, no matter how small they may be. If you do not have friends like this in your life, contact us directly and correspond with us— share your questions, concerns, and successes with us directly at ronl@ howtosucceedwithwomen.com.

When you have support, you'll be able to keep trying.

Excuse 4. "I don't know how to seduce women."

No one taught you, or any of us, how to meet and seduce women. Some men are just "naturals" at it, while the rest of us have been relying on hope and luck. In a way, "I don't know how to seduce women" is a reasonable concern. After all, it's true, isn't it?

You are holding in your hands the answer to this final excuse. Once you finish this book, and you know what there is to study and practice, all you have to do is keep trying, and you will succeed. You can continue to work with us in a variety of ways—from reading more of our materials and working through our audio courses, to working with us directly at our seminars and coaching programs. As the owner of this book, you are entitled to tons of new information about succeeding with women. Go to www.howtosucceedwithwomen.com/owners for more information.

These four excuses keep men from taking action to get the women they want. You must give them up and stop whining if you are going to become a seduction machine. As he goes through his day, Bob indulges in these excuses constantly. Bruce does not.

LESSONS FROM THE MASTER

As you can see, Bruce acts in a masterful manner throughout his day and produces results with women. While Bob acts like a putz, Bruce is unstoppable. He focuses his attention, and his activity, on getting women and having a steady supply of dates.

Bruce flirts with every woman

Many men complain that their one or two attempts to meet women and get dates didn't produce results. These men give up if they don't get instant gratification from women. They think that all the time they spend thinking about sex and admiring women's bodies is the same as being out there flirting and asking for dates. Bruce is not like this. He knows that each woman he comes into contact with is another possibility. He flirts and flirts and flirts. He doesn't count on any one woman to be his source of sex; he is unrelenting in meeting new women. Bruce learned a long time ago that "he who hesitates, masturbates," so he flirts with women at every opportunity.

Bruce knows that every seduction is built on a thousand interactions. Whether you want a one-night stand, a long-term relationship, or anything

in between, you'll do much better remembering that every seduction is made up of a thousand interactions.

Most men we work with get sloppy in their approach with women and try to complete an entire seduction in a few small interactions. They think that once they've met a woman, or asked her out, the work is done. They fail to realize that successfully keeping a woman happy and romantically/sexually interested is an ongoing task. Bruce realizes this and knows that there is always work to do. He never gets complacent with women. He is always doing follow-up calls, emailing women, visiting familiar waitresses, and making dozens of other bold moves.

The small, consistent steps Bruce makes add up to big seduction success. Always remember that it takes dozens if not hundreds of initiations to get a woman in bed. You must do the work, just as Bruce does.

Bruce turns every situation into a prospecting situation

As mentioned in Chapter 2, a successful seducer is always prospecting. What makes Bruce so successful is that he never gives up; he is constantly making every situation into an opening to meet women and flirt.

All women are potential prospects for you. This means that they are potential dates, girlfriends, one-night stands, marriage partners, casual sex partners, or anything else you desire. When you prospect, you are looking for women to interact with and interacting with them. You are like a salesman. When a salesman goes out looking for prospects, he is looking for prospective clients or customers. And a salesman is constantly networking with other people, because the broader his social contacts the more likely that he will find new customers and sources for leads. A successful salesman will use any situation he is in to ask for a sale, and ask everyone he knows if they know someone who could be a lead or a potential sale. In this way, he turns every situation into a prospecting situation. You have to do this, too.

One of our students, Derek, was a very successful real estate agent. Over coffee he told us about a famed salesman who makes millions of dollars every year in real estate. "So what?" we asked him. "Lots of people make a killing in real estate. What's the point?" Derek told us that the

point was how this man had made his money. This agent, he told us, walked house to house, knocked on every door, and spoke to every single resident of his city. He asked them if they wanted to sell their home, if they were looking for a broker, if they had friends looking for a real estate agent, or if they were looking for a new house. He was relentless in his pursuit, talked to everybody he could about real estate, followed up every lead, and it paid off for him.

You must be like this with women. Bruce is. If Bruce thought that he could get the women he desired into bed by going door to door, he'd do it. He's willing to do whatever it takes to meet women he desires. You must do what Bruce does and flirt and interact with all women. We know you only want to talk to the really hot ones, but that probably won't be useful in the beginning; you'll be too scared of them to flirt effectively, anyway. We say, talk to all women. At this point in your quest for women, the only quality they need for you to flirt with them is that they must be breathing. It is that simple.

Bruce makes it a game

When we say "game," what do you think of? Many men associate games with competition—often fierce competition characterized by battle, conflict, hard feelings, losing, and being upset. Or you may be the type who associates games with intellectual, manipulative ploys. Another type associates games with fun, creative expression, freedom, and wonder.

For the sake of this book, "game" means something that is fun and has no negative consequences if you make mistakes while playing it. For most men, dating is serious, and any screwups have negative consequences to their self-esteem. Dating seems difficult, like a test of manhood. We want to change that idea. Dating will be radically easier for you if you take it less seriously and make it fun.

Bruce thinks of dating as a game, and you must, too. Then you create lightness and a freedom in your life. Bruce's attractiveness with women comes as much from his game attitude as from anything else. He's fun, playful, not too serious, and has a life women want to be a part of.

Here are the rules of the dating game:

Rule 1. Nothing is personal. Have you ever been playing a game with other people when it suddenly stopped being a game and started being personal? One man tells us about a soccer league he was in. The game was going great, when suddenly one of the players attacked a guy on the other team. "Suddenly it wasn't a game anymore," he tells us. "He took personally a move the other guy made, and just lost it." This is one of the quickest ways to destroy a game; then it starts being real.

No matter what a woman does, don't take it personally. Does this mean you can kiss a woman and grab her body and ignore her saying no? Absolutely not. But when you say hi to a woman and she glares at you, or when you ask a woman out and she says no, you should simply not take it personally. You do not even take it personally if you are in the bedroom with a woman, about to have sex, and she wants to stop. You stop and do not take it personally. If you do, you will suffer and not get the sex you desire.

For example, you may want to tell yourself that a woman's rude response to your smile is because she must have just found out about a death in her family. Or when a woman ignores your hello, you might tell yourself that she has a hearing problem and didn't hear you. You may also blame a woman's coldness on the fact that she has a stomachache from eating too much chocolate. The point is, you don't really know the reasons why she rejects your advances or blows you off. If you take her behaviors personally, it won't be a game anymore, and it won't be fun.

Bruce isn't pulled off course by women's negative responses. He takes it in stride. When you do the same thing, you will be light-years ahead of most other guys.

On the other hand, if a woman responds favorably to your flirtations, then you should take it personally. You should remember that she is attracted to you, and that you are the one who made it happen. So feel acknowledged when things go well, and don't take it personally when things don't work out.

Rule 2. Be playful. Recently we observed a below-average-looking, overweight fifty-five-year-old insurance salesman pick up a beautiful young woman at a restaurant. He asked the cashier about some of the paintings on the wall and joked with her about how ugly and out-of-date

they were. She laughed and smiled at him. She asked him if he wanted to be seated, and he said that he was going to the nearby grocery store to do his shopping. He reached out his hand to say good-bye to her. She extended her hand and he kissed it slowly and said, "It has been a pleasure meeting such a lovely and beautiful woman." She blushed and fanned herself with a menu pretending that he had made her hot and bothered. She gave him a drink in a to-go cup and asked him to stay and talk to her. Because he was able to be playful, he created an opening to charm her. This guy, even though he is below-average-looking, has learned to seduce women and get them to date and have sex with him.

Rule 3. Don't give up. Just as in any game, persistence makes a difference. Even if you don't think you'll win the game, you'll enjoy it much more if you don't give up and you play to win, anyway.

This is Bruce's attitude. It doesn't matter to him if he wins or loses, just how he plays the game, and he plays to win even when the odds are against him. Most of the women he flirts with he never sleeps with, but he doesn't care. He simply pushes each interaction as far as it can go, then moves on to the next one. He knows that if you give up in a game, the game is over. Because he enjoys the game, he wants to stay with it.

Being persistent and playing to win makes you into a man who doesn't give up easily, and being a man who doesn't give up will bring you more success than you ever thought possible. There's a story about a boy in a math class. He had dozed off, and awoke to find the teacher writing a problem on the board. Thinking that the problem was a homework assignment, he scribbled it into his notebook and took it home with him.

For the next two days, he spent every free waking moment working on the problem. Finally, he got the answer and took it to his teacher. She was shocked—it turned out the problem was supposed to be insoluble, and she had only written it on the board as an example. He was able to solve it because he played to win, and didn't know that he "couldn't." He didn't give up when the going got rough, just as Bruce doesn't.

Rule 4. Use probabilities. One of the great things about sports announcers is that they always throw probabilities into their commentaries.

They talk about how well a batter has batted against the pitcher in the past, and compare this to his other averages. Announcers then go off into the minutiae, talking about how this batter does against right-handed pitchers and compares this to left-handed pitchers. They talk and talk until no one cares anymore. By that time a new batter is up.

In the dating game, probabilities are fun, too. They make the game more fun and make interactions with women more about numbers than about some huge ego risk. On a particular night you may see a beautiful woman across from you in a bar and use probabilities to create the percent chance that you could go home with her. You might give yourself a 5 percent chance that she will talk to you. There might be a 1 percent chance that you could buy her a drink and a .05 percent chance that you could sleep with her tonight. If she's less beautiful or she's drunk, your probabilities may go up. It sounds silly, but using this technique creates a framework of fun.

Rule 5. Have fun. You must find ways to make the dating game fun; otherwise you will never have the stamina to succeed. Have you ever noticed that fun is contagious? We sure have. People who are in a good mood, laughing, and enjoying themselves tend to seem more open and attractive than people who are overly serious and closed.

One of the reasons Bruce is so successful is that he finds ways to enjoy himself when he goes out to find women. He enjoys meeting new people, learning new things, and pushing himself in new ways. Bruce frequently asks himself how he can increase the "fun factor" in his life, and it helps him be even more successful with women. At the same time, the more fun and playful Bruce is, the more interest he seems to get from women.

Rule 6. Play on your terms. Sometimes you need to walk away from an interaction from a woman. Sometimes, as you know, women can be nasty, mean, and downright rude. In these situations you need to get away from them as quickly as possible. Taking a lot of crap from women is not the same as being a loving guy. We are not saying to be mean to women, but you have to treat yourself with respect. And you can start rebuilding that self-respect now. A lot of guys are confused on this point, so let's repeat it: Being good to a woman and giving up your self-respect are not the same thing.

So many men are afraid that no woman will ever want them that they give up their self-respect and become unwilling to take care of their own feelings, or even to walk away from abuse. Well, get this through your head: Letting a woman walk all over you doesn't get you the girl. Not only is it painful, it doesn't work. So stop doing it!

In any situation with a woman where you think your self-respect may be being compromised, ask yourself this: "What would the man I'm committed to being do in this situation?"

You can also ask: "What would I do in this situation if there was an abundance of sex in my life?" Then take the risk of losing the girl, and act with self-respect.

The important component of this rule is that when you feel a woman is mistreating you or being rude, you need to remove yourself from this situation and/or bust her on her bad behavior.

When you follow the rules, dating becomes more like a game, less threatening and scary, and more fun for everybody. You know games have ups and downs, wins and losses. You don't go into games putting your ego on the line, or feel like there's something wrong with you if you don't win every time.

We've written an entire book and created a fifteen-DVD course about how to create seductive Disconnections with women. The book is called *How to Be the Bad Boy Women Love*, and we've made a six-lesson mini-course for you that you can download from the Owners Page on our website. This course covers specific ways to create seductive Disconnections with the hottest women, how to use "Truth Disconnects" and "Canned Disconnects" to make women explain themselves to you, how to use silence to make women seek your approval, and a lot more. We suggest you go and grab that course right away.

Have your friends egg you on

As men, whether we admit it or not, we love competition. It is useful to use our innate competitiveness to motivate ourselves and our friends to date more women, and to do outrageous things to meet and succeed with women.

The authors of this book used this principle frequently to push each

other to get out and date more. We would tease each other and dare each other to approach a beautiful woman. We placed bets on each other's success and failure rates.

Once again, it's important to have male friends who are supportive. If the competition becomes something that has you feeling like a failure, stop doing it immediately. We are encouraging you to have friends to both console you when things go bad and encourage you when you get scared and are not able to be in action. No one understands all the potential pitfalls, problems, and pleasures of dating better than another man. If you are a guy with few men friends, who mostly hangs out with women, this must change. Having male friends egg you on will produce results that far exceed any advice that women will give you.

Bruce relentlessly follows up leads

Bruce is relentless in his quest for women. He is hitting on so many women in one day that he couldn't care less if one or many don't work out. He is focusing on the long-term goal of having dozens of women he can call in an instant and sleep with that night.

He is constantly following up leads at bars, restaurants, on the phone, by email, and in the stores and other places he frequents. Like the hungry salesman, he does what it takes to get as many women as he can.

Bruce knows it's a numbers game

Bruce lives his life from the "numbers game" analogy we discussed in Chapter 2. He knows that, like sales, dating is all about numbers. He knows that if he flirts with ten women, one will give him her number. If he sets up ten dates, four women will actually show up. He knows that of those four, he will sleep with at least one. Bruce uses this philosophy to boost himself up when he is rejected. To him it is just one more interaction with a woman that will eventually lead to a yes.

Bruce flirts with and prospects lots of women

We've explained that master seducers not only play it like a numbers game, but they also don't put all their eggs in one basket. They pursue lots and lots of women.

Even if women are not receptive, the practice is well worth the effort. Bruce views flirting and prospecting women as part of the reason for his success. When you practice something long enough, you will develop mastery. By flirting often, you master your speaking skills with women. All of us can point to skills in our lives that we studied for a long, long time, until we could do them effortlessly. Riding a bike, tying your shoes, and memorizing multiplication tables are all examples.

Flirting with lots of women also generates a high level of vitality and confidence in yourself that is infectious to women. When you are talking to many women, your successes build on one another and that helps you to get more dates and be more vital in other areas of your life. One definition of vitality is that it is a reflection of how bold you are in life. It can be measured by how much of a public personality you are, how willing you are to be outrageous. Women want you to be powerful and confident in public and private. Flirting with lots of women will help develop these qualities in you.

Another reason to flirt with lots of women is that it will eventually lead to big results. We believe that small, consistent actions eventually lead to success. We all know the story of how successful the turtle was because he was slow but steady, unlike the hare that was quick but got sloppy and lazy. The same is true with pursuing women. When you constantly flirt with women it will have a multiplier effect, and aid in current and future successes with women.

Bruce is constantly studying seduction

Bruce is constantly working on his seduction game. He is constantly working on his skills in approaching women, sustaining conversations with them, and closing the deal. Bruce frequently attends our seduction seminars and frequently reads new books on dating theories. Bruce never allows himself to get stagnant in his seduction skills.

Bruce pretends he is a world-class stud

We mentioned in Chapter 2 about the importance of modeling other men. It is useful to model your dress, approach, lines, and general demeanor after a highly successful seducer.

One of the things that Bruce does constantly is act like he is *the* man. He acts in a confident manner. Secretly, Bruce models himself after a character John Travolta played in the movie *Get Shorty*. He also uses his friend Sam as a role model. Sam is always surrounded by women, and dates frequently. Bruce has learned that if he acts the way Sam does around women, he tends to be much more successful than when he doesn't model his behavior after Sam's.

Bruce leaves the house ready to party

Looking good at all times, no matter what, is an important part of success with women. Many men make the mistake of leaving the house not ready to meet women. We are not suggesting that you always have to be wearing a suit. However, we are suggesting that you seriously consider what you are wearing and consider whether or not it is appropriate for meeting a woman. You read about this in depth in the previous chapter. Even if you are wearing sweat pants and a T-shirt, you can present yourself in a manner that will be attractive to women. Keep it in mind.

Bruce is always ready to flirt, no matter what. It's part of being a world-class stud. Behind all of the flirtation are many hours of preparation. He has memorized seductive questions and opening lines. He has decided ahead of time how many women he will talk to in a day. In later chapters you will learn pickup lines and approaches to meeting women. Bruce can easily use many different approaches and ways to meet women, so he is ready to flirt in any situation.

Bruce has studied seduction in great detail, like a martial artist who studies and anticipates every situation. Like the martial artist, Bruce prepares for all the different options and is ready to create new alternatives that are easily applicable to any situation that may come his way.

THE FIVE BEST PLACES TO MEET WOMEN

Bruce is in the habit of visiting the same places regularly. This practice opens up many opportunities to ask out women and creates a basis for rapport. Social scientists have shown that the more you see someone and have contact with that person, the more attracted you are. This is called attraction by

familiarity. This fact alone should inspire you to find ways to interact with the same people on a regular basis. Here's a list of places you can go on a regular basis to meet women and create an attraction by familiarity:

1. Coffee shops

Coffee shops are rapidly becoming the hottest new place to meet women. Singles all over the country are using them as potential pickup spots. Women there are often reading and open to chatting with strangers. In most of our seminars we take men to coffee shops to meet women, and many of our students have had massive success in coffee shops all over the United States. The best part about coffee shops is that there are tons of them all over the place. You can check one out and then drive a few miles away and find another one. The important thing to remember is that depending on what time of day you visit them, they can either be packed or empty. You need to figure out the optimal time to go that best fits your schedule and has the maximum number of women.

Bruce demonstrated how useful it is to become a regular at a coffee shop. They tend to be like small communities. The same cast of characters shows up at approximately the same time every day. It is good for you to get into a routine with a place. This way you can get to know the regulars. A woman may be sipping hot java and hanging out with her friends, or she may be reading a book or writing in her journal. Knowing many of the employees and regulars will also make it easier to meet other customers.

2. Malls

Malls are one of the single best places to meet women, period. We're not talking about your grungy crappy mall on the bad side of town, but the huge thriving mall that on weekends is packed with thousands of hot women. The best malls are the ones full of high-end women's clothing stores and other hip fashion stores. The reason why we think they are so great is that you have the opportunity to interact there with a huge amount of women in one spot. You can practice approaching women and utilize the hi program, or you can approach groups of women and look for quick sex hookups. You can find sexy twenty-one-year-old women at malls, and you can find attractive women in their forties and fifties. On a good day at

the mall you can find just about any kind of woman you can imagine. Malls are perfect environments for you to go and work on your skills for a few hours.

Sam attended one of our seminars in Chicago. We spent two days going to malls (and at night would go to bars). Sam was able to approach more than one hundred women in one day. He ended up having lunch with a different woman every day and got several phone numbers from women he met at the mall. Sam was happy because he could meet so many women there so rapidly.

To master your seduction skills, we highly recommend you spend time at malls on a weekly basis. Malls are perfect places to meet a huge variety of women quickly.

3. Bookstores

Are you looking for a sexy, smart, and untamed woman? By frequenting bookstores, you can meet lonely intellectuals. Women you meet in bookstores will often be receptive to you because there you will find women who are smart and who can't find a guy. Why do you think women read so many romance novels and weird fiction anyway? Many bookstores are packed with women on Friday nights. They are looking for something, and it isn't just another Martha Stewart book.

One of our students met an attractive woman looking at books in the Sex section of a large chain bookstore. Though he thought it was corny, he made a joke about the book she was reading. She was receptive to him and they joked about penis enlargement toys. Later, he got her email address and they wrote back and forth for a few weeks, and later dated.

We recommend meeting women in bookstores for all of our intellectual students. The other added bonus about bookstores is that many of them have attached coffee shops, so you can meet a woman and then take her out for coffee right away to continue the seduction.

4. Bars

If you are looking for short-term sex, bars are a must for you. Women go out to bars to meet people and to socialize—and let's face it, drunken women are easier to get into bed than sober ones. As a result, we highly

recommend bars as one place to practice and master your seduction skills. The trick is to find the right type of bar that matches your interests, age group, and personality. There are many types of bars and it's important for you understand some of the basic differences. Some bars are mellow and quiet and full of people in their thirties and forties just hanging out. Other bars are full of drunken college girls who are so cliquish they won't talk to anyone they don't know. Some bars are loud dance clubs where you must be young, hip, and attractive to succeed, while others are full of country music fans line dancing.

Bruce loves going to bars, because they are fun, full of energy, and he is able to practice his seduction skills on a variety of super-hot women. Much like the variety of women who are attracted to shopping at the mall, Bruce knows that sexy women are nearly always at bars (Thursday, Friday, and Saturday nights especially). Bruce appreciates being able to approach women in different ways, depending on the environment he is in. He likes being able to carry on a more serious conversation in a mellow bar, and he enjoy being obnoxious, silly, and playful in loud bars late at night.

Your first task is to start looking around your area for the type of bar you would feel most comfortable in. Find the quiet bar if you like that, or find the large sports bar on a packed Friday night to meet women. Find the bar that plays classic rock, or the bar that has swing dancing on weekends. Find the place that fits your personality the best and practice your skills. Better yet, try to spend time weekly or monthly at a variety of bar settings.

Happy Hour. Many of our students have had success at happy hour. Happy hour starts early, usually around 5:00 p.m. during the workweek, and attracts women who want to go out for a drink after work and be home before 10:00 p.m. Bars that feature a happy hour tend to attract professional women in their thirties and forties, many of whom are single and have a difficult time finding men to date and have sex with. Another useful feature to happy hour is that it tends to be more mellow, and women are easier to approach, and because it is fairly early in the evening, they are more receptive to you approaching and talking to them.

5. The Internet

While almost all of the information in this book is timeless, there is one area that has changed dramatically since we wrote the first edition. That area is the Internet.

When we were writing the first edition of *How to Succeed with Women* in 1996, the Web was in its infancy. Very few women were online, and the truth was that most of the women online at that time were overweight. We advised men that "You have to leave the Web alone and log on to Usenet to find discussion groups to meet women." And it was true. Back then the Internet was a place to practice your seduction skills and to meet women for phone sex, but in-person hookups were usually disappointing, unless you liked women with more than a few extra pounds.

How times have changed. Today the Web is basically synonymous with the Internet, Usenet is practically dead (you've probably never even heard of it), and for all intents and purposes every woman you could possibly desire is online. You must make use of this fact.

Changes happen too quickly in the Internet world for us to give you a technical step-by-step in using any particular service or site; by the time you read this, such instructions would be obsolete. What we can do, however, is give you an overview of using the Internet, and give you the basic steps you must take to use it for seduction, no matter what website or service is the next "big thing" at the time you are reading this.

Using Dating Sites. Most experts agree that the Internet has had two stages so far, and is poised to move into a third stage. The first stage—often called "Web 1.0"—was the text-based Internet. There were a few pictures, but mostly it was made up of static, written webpages you had to read. There was very little room for interaction on the Web itself, and mostly, if you wanted to communicate, you used email.

This is the model that most dating sites use. You post a profile (or more than one profile), then send messages to women who interest you. Most guys post a simple, generic-sounding profile, then hope women contact them. Unless you are particularly attractive or rich, this is unlikely to work.

As usual, you must do "something extra" to get things to work for you. Here's what you should do to make dating sites really perform for you:

- *Test a variety of sites.* You can find our up-to-date list of suggested dating sites, and info about the kind of women you are likely to meet on them, on our website. You'll want to check out a variety of sites, and here's why:

  First, different sites succeed in different geographic areas. Once a critical mass of people goes to one of the major sites in an area, that site will continue to "win" and get most of the women. You need to check around to see which major site has "won" in your area.

  Second, different types of women gravitate to different types of dating sites. Some sites will attract more women who are interested in long-term relationships. Some more "edgy" sites will attract more women who are looking for "off-budget" no-strings sex. You need to do some investigation and find out which women show up at which sites in the area you live in.

  Third, there are specialty sites you should check out. There are sites that specialize in dating for people with specific sexual fetishes and sites that specialize in people of specific religions, and many other options in between. There are online dating sites for pet lovers and online dating sites for video gamers. Make a list of your interests and do some Internet searches using that interest with the word "dating." You'll be surprised how many options you find.

- *Use more than one profile, which showcase different "personas."* Why only take one shot at the women you desire? By posting multiple profiles, you can highlight different aspects of yourself and have a much better chance at getting the women you want to notice you.

  Most guys try a scattershot approach to their profile. They list everything they can about themselves in the hope that one or more of those qualities will attract a woman they desire.

  That approach does not work. Listing everything about yourself, with no central focus, is more likely to make you appear bland than to make you appear fascinating. What you really want to do is hit a hot women's desires in one category, and hit those desires accurately

and without distraction. The way you do this is by creating separate profiles, each of which highlights a certain aspect of your personality.

This is similar to the approach successful marketers take when marketing a new product. Successful marketers don't list every conceivable feature and benefit right away. If they did, their ads would be confusing and unreadable.

Instead they come up with the "big idea," the one thing they are going to focus on for the ad, and make that one thing as compelling as they possibly can.

When you develop "personas" for your personal ads, you do the same thing. You paint a big, bright singular picture, rather than a diluted mess of thoughts and ideas that have no central focus or point.

So ask yourself this: What are your passions? What are you good at? What are you into? And how can that passion or interest be turned into a persona?

For instance, if you love camping, you might want to have one of your personas be the "rugged outdoorsman." Your profile would put 80 percent of its emphasis on this aspect of your personality, and everything else would be left out or given very little mention.

Or if you are a computer programmer who has a motorcycle, you might develop a "Biker" persona, and 80 percent of your profile would be about how great it feels to be biking, how the wind feels in your hair, the wildest adventure you've had on your bike, and what it would feel like for the woman who eventually ends up with you. Such a profile will be a lot more successful than one that talks about your ten main interests, with each interest getting 10 percent of your profile.

Remember, there is a lot of competition online, not just from other men, but from every other website on the Internet, each of which is just a click or two away. When you focus on a persona, you give a woman an easy-to-relate-to picture of you that will intrigue her and draw her in. You may need to sign up with several sites to test your different personas at the same time, or you can do them one at a time on a single dating site. Either approach is good.

- *Get a good picture.* It's amazing to us how often men use unflattering pictures of themselves in their personal ads. Either the pictures are just plain bad, or have other people in them, or have some other distraction that makes them useless.

    Most women will judge you immediately on your persona and on your picture. You have got to get a good picture of yourself for your profile, even if it means paying a professional photographer. This is important—do it right.

- *Describe feelings, feelings, feelings.* You'll have a lot of space to write about yourself and what you are looking for in a woman. You want use that space to describe yourself and what you want in a way that paints romantic pictures for the women reading the ad.

    To do this, you use romantic, poetic images in your writing. You could say something like "Are you looking for a guy to date?" But you are better off saying something like "Are you looking for your heart of the ocean, the one you will 'never let go' of?" You could say something like "If you respond to my ad, I'll be happy to meet you," but you'd be better off saying something like "If what you've read here intrigues you, then why don't we meet? I'll be waiting for you at the top of the grand staircase, by the clock."

    Think about the things women find romantic. What are books that are currently romantic hits, or movies? What images from those things sum up the romantic feelings in them? "The top of the grand staircase, by the clock" is the perfect image to sum up the romantic feelings from the movie *Titanic*. What are some other such images you could use? After you have written your ad, go through it again, asking the question "What romantic images can I add to this ad?"

    Most Internet personals services give you specific categories to fill out, like "favorite music." You should feel free to make use of this space in any way that you want. If the service asks, "What was your favorite rock concert ever?" don't just describe the concert; describe the way it made you feel. "Seeing [band] was an incredible experience. Have you ever felt completely swept away by music? Like you just disappeared, the music entered your body, and you felt total joy and as one with the music? That's what it was like—that kind of

experience would only be better if I could share it with the right woman."

If you have only one thought when filling out your profile, it should be to describe romantic feelings. Do this and you'll be way ahead of your competition.

- *Use video (and audio) if you can do it well.* Dating sites are increasingly allowing the use of video. You should use video, if you can do it well. Here are a few things to remember as you set up your dating video:
  - It doesn't need to be professional. In fact, if it's too polished, it will be creepy, so keep it informal. It's okay to do some editing and to add some pictures, but don't do too much. Don't start with titles, just start with you talking.
  - Remember that women watching your video want to get a sense of your vibe, a feeling for how you move and the sound of your voice. You don't need some big production to do that; it's more important for you to be relaxed.
  - Talk about the passion of your persona, and how that passion makes you feel. Tell a brief story about it, and paint a picture with your words of where a woman might fit in with that passion.
  - Take general notes of what you want to say, but don't use a script! Have a few bullet points you want to cover, and do a few takes. Don't take it too seriously.
  - Smile.
  - Keep the video short. A couple of minutes is plenty long to get your point across.

  These points also are good if you create a short audio about yourself, which you should do.

- *Respond to a lot of women's ads.* One of the biggest mistakes we see men make is that they do not respond to enough ads. They answer one or two profiles of women they like, then leave it at that.

  If you want to succeed, you need to respond to a lot of profiles. If you can respond to a hundred of them, do it. You want to get energy moving. You do not want to be a guy who sends out three responses

to women's profiles then checks his inbox every thirty seconds in hopes of a response. Answer a lot of profiles.

- *Make your responses quickly.* Never spend more than five minutes on a response to a woman's profile. Ideally, you won't spend more than a minute. Create a simple email that says you read her profile and liked what you saw. Mention one or two details from her profile so she knows you actually read it. (This is a big deal to women, and an important part of your response.) Ask her a question or two about things she mentioned in her profile, then invite her to check out yours and say hi if she likes.

If you are a guy who would naturally tend to spend a lot of time answering women's profiles, then set a timer for three minutes and discipline yourself to be fast. You must move quickly and not overly invest in any one woman.

Using Social Networks. As we write this, "Web 2.0" is gaining a lot of traction. Web 2.0 is the social, interactive Web. It's sites like MySpace and Facebook, where people create pages, have virtual friends, join groups, and interact a lot.

You need to join the most popular social networking sites and spend some time creating your profile page. The tips from above are still important. Have a central focus, a "persona" that you use, and create an easy-to-understand personality on the page.

Aside from that, the big rule of social networks is "interact, interact, interact." A lot of the interactions on social network sites might seem dumb. As of this writing, Facebook allows you to "poke" people, and to send them a virtual fish. As moronic as it might seem, such little interactions keep people connected and thinking warmly about each other, so you must do them too.

Join groups that interest you, and participate until you find out either (1) it has women who interest you, or (2) it does not have women who interest you. If it has women, focus on communicating with those women, using your words to paint pictures of feelings as much as possible. If it does not, move on right away and throw yourself into something more promising.

The Future of Internet Dating. The Internet is moving toward "Web 3.0," which is likely to involve virtual worlds where you have a 3-D-rendered "avatar" who walks or flies around and interacts with other people. Such environments already exist, with a service called Second Life currently leading the pack.

While sex is a primary activity in virtual worlds, you should be aware that, at this point, most of the "virtual women" you interact with will be other men pretending to be women. In a lot of ways, dating in virtual worlds is in the same place that Internet dating was when we wrote the first edition of this book. It's primitive, mostly populated by guys, and kind of hard to use. But it's also worth keeping an eye on as it probably will be the next big Internet dating phenomenon.

If you want to learn more about dating online, check out our resources at www.howtosucceedwithwomen.com/owners.

THE SEVEN SECRET PLACES TO MEET WOMEN

What follows is a list of places that you probably don't associate with prime woman-meeting spots. However, these are wonderfully secret hidden sources of lonely women waiting for you. We recommend that if you show up at one of the following events or places and there are no women you are interested in, move on immediately. If you quickly move on, and keep going on to the next opportunity, you are destined for success.

1. Yoga classes

Your local yoga class is a great place to meet New Age women. Yoga, in case you don't know, is a form of exercise similar to stretching. Yoga comes from India and was used as a form of transcending the body and mind together. We won't go into any more detail, to avoid scaring you. Over the past few years yoga has become a popular form of exercise among health-conscious women. Most cities have many classes, and women are usually the main ones teaching and attending those classes. A woman who has been active in yoga for years usually has a wonderfully toned body. That's another added advantage!

Fred attended a local yoga class and found himself in a room full of

twenty women and no other men. Since he was a beginner, he failed miserably at the yoga "poses." Fred kept asking women nearby for help. By the end of the hour-long class, he had four women offering to help him outside of class. Other women were friendly and receptive to him coming back. "It was great," Fred said. "I am all over yoga class, like a hobo on a ham sandwich. I love talking to these calm, airy-fairy chicks. They are fun to talk to and even more fun to look at. I'm even finding some physical benefits from the classes."

2. Dance classes

Dancing close to a woman is still one of the most romantic things you can do. The old-time male sex symbols are still popular among women because they possess a flair for charm and romance. Fred Astaire, Bing Crosby, and others are still the fantasies of many women. Part of their charm was their ability to sweep a woman off her feet with dancing and romantic talk. They could be subtle and forward at the same time.

Dance classes are great places to meet women and start a seduction. First, women respect men who learn old-time romantic activities like dancing. They will hopefully cut you some slack if you are a crappy dancer—after all, you are attending the class to learn, aren't you? Second, they will likely want to dance with you because so few men take dance classes that you are a rare commodity. And third, you will be able to flirt with them over multiple weeks and seduce them slowly.

Ballroom dancing is a great way to hold women close to you and perform the same moves they've seen master seducers do on TV and in movies. Many people report that they feel "high" because of the aerobic effects of dancing and that it adds to the feeling of romance. Learning ballroom dancing will also be helpful for weddings, formal events, and even out in a dance club.

Brian, a thirty-one-year-old computer programmer, used ballroom dancing to meet several women. He was having a problem meeting interesting and sexy women to date. His job forced him to be inside most of the day, and he wasn't into the bar scene. Brian saw an ad for the ballroom dance club on a local college campus. He decided to start attending classes. To him it was good exercise and a great way to meet attractive students.

After a few months he became quite good at dancing, and many of the women in the club asked him to dance during their events. Brian had been used to having a primarily solitary life, and the new attention was fun and thrilling for him. He became a regular member of the club and attended two dances per week. Brian not only created a new social circle, but also eventually began to seriously date one of the women.

3. Church

A few years ago we had a student who claimed that church was the ultimate place to meet women. His name was Bart and he was the poster boy for geeks everywhere. He wore fifties-style glasses and outdated pants. However, Bart was always active in his church and a devout follower. He decided to use his faith to get women.

Bart began attending singles events on weekends. He confessed to several members of his congregation that he was looking for a woman of faith. A number of churches like to promote dating and relationships from within their communities, and many members of Bart's congregation began setting him up.

The thing that amazed us was that these women had sex with him. "Like bunnies," he told us. "Most of them couldn't wait to get into bed." You may want to go to church this coming week and check out the chicks while you pray.

4. Outdoor music events

What could be more romantic than a concert under the stars? Women eat up this type of event. Depending on the kind of musician who is performing, a concert can prove to be well worth the time and money.

Such a music event is a great place to meet women. Single women attending in small groups are open to meeting men; indeed, many of them go with that as their goal. If the music is jazz, classical, or pop rock (not punk or hard rock), it will be easier to make a connection. The hard-rock outdoor shows will have lots of drunken underage women. Obviously, you have to watch out for women who look attractive and seem mature, but who in fact are seventeen. The other problem with hard-rock concerts is that they tend to be so loud you can't talk or hear someone else talking.

The authors of this book once attended a jazz festival in Concord, California, called the Concord Jazz Festival. Miles Davis played as the headliner. It was a long day under the sun, and when night came it was cold. We used the cold as an opportunity to invite three women sitting near us to cuddle under our blanket; they had worn shorts and weren't prepared for the cold. Because we had talked to them off and on all day long, they felt comfortable with us. We cuddled with them and later invited them to join us in our hotel room for after-hours action. They accepted.

Because there is no magical solution, you won't always be so lucky. However, you can be persistent in going to places and attending events where women will be open to dating, and you will eventually have success.

5. Personal growth seminars

Do you want to meet an emotionally open woman who is willing to see you as a magical solution to her problems? Could this solution include a hot night with you? A personal growth seminar may be your ticket.

One of the key elements of most seminars is the deep level of bonding that quickly happens between participants. At a personal growth seminar, you will be in a group of people who are there to break out of their normal day-to-day routines and try something new. This can be a good environment for you to experiment with new behaviors with women who will be much more receptive than those on the street or in a cafe.

Another element of most seminars is that they stress honesty. Usually this means emotional honesty. People who reveal their innermost secrets are often rewarded by the group leaders and gain the respect of fellow seminar attendees. This environment is perfect because you can come across as Mr. Sincere and Mr. Emotionally Honest and Available when you are actually just hitting on women.

On a break you could walk up to the most beautiful woman in the room and say something like "I've never told anyone this before, but I am finally realizing that I am a fully sexual being. A sexual man who has both emotional and sexual needs. Does that make sense to you? Have you ever thought you were not honest with yourself or people in your surroundings about what you really want in relationships?" In an environment that stresses honesty and sharing, you can approach many women and honestly

express your attraction, ask them out, get to know them better, and practice your new skills.

Another advantage is that most women attending will be open to meeting you, and may even approach you first. Some will actually be attending with the sole purpose of meeting a man. Some will even be there just to find sex partners! There will also be women attending because they want to explore some inner turmoil, and they may suffer from both the "innocent victim syndrome" and the "unbelievably gullible disease." This is both good news and bad news. It is good because they will be open to dating and sharing with you. It is bad news because they may have psycho tendencies and may end up being more of a pain than they're worth. Later we'll teach you about psycho chicks and provide you with the necessary diagnostic tools to spot these women. In the meantime, some may be fun to date.

You may find the information presented at the seminar useful, too. We've observed that the clearer a man is in his purpose in life and the more clarity he has about his relationships, the easier time he has with women. A seminar may help you in this task.

The only major downfall of seminars is that they may cost too much money. For the untrained man, the personal-growth-seminar world is a mess. You have all the New Age crystal healing courses, meditation classes, self-esteem seminars, anger management courses, erection problem support groups (avoid these for meeting women), divorced dads groups, and then companies, like Career Track, that run seminars, too. The prices range widely, from $50 for a day to $3,000 for a weeklong course in how to become a spiritual master. We are suggesting spending, at the most, around $350 for a weekend course.

6. Volunteer for causes

Do you remember what the biggest obstacle is when you meet a woman? The correct answer is that she will be concerned about whether or not you are violent and will harm her. When she meets you at a volunteer event, this concern can disappear quickly. What kind of men volunteer to help worthy causes? To a woman, a man who volunteers for a cause must be trustworthy, honest, and responsible.

Many opportunities to volunteer for causes will lead to meeting women. You will usually be working side by side with a woman, or will have a woman leading a team of volunteers (this is an added bonus for all the submissive guys out there). Women volunteer for causes much more than men, so in the crowd of women volunteers you will be a novelty. Women will think that you are sensitive, moral, and safe, and your net worth to them will increase.

If you follow the Seven Habits of a Highly Effective Seducer, you will be a man with direction in his life, and one who consistently focuses on his values and expresses them in the world. This type of inner discipline, determination, and focus will make you stand out to women. Being a volunteer can not only help increase your confidence in yourself, but can lead to having a life which you love. As a result, you will be that much more marketable to women. When a man does things to help his community, stands up for a cause he believes in, participates in a political campaign, or raises awareness for an issue he feels strongly about, he is seen as a leader and commands the respect due one.

Imagine that you are helping with registration at a 10K Run for Nature. You show up early on a Saturday morning and meet all the hot women there to compete in the race. You flirt openly with them. In the process, you get to check out hundreds of women dressed in tights, short shorts, and various degrees of undress. Additionally, you probably work with many women who are there to volunteer and have fun. You meet a woman at a nearby table and talk to her after the race begins and make dinner plans for that night.

José, a forty-year-old divorced father, volunteered to be part of a fund-raising banquet for children. As a father, he wanted to help raise Christmas funds as well as awareness in his town about child poverty. Besides, he thought, it would help get his mind off women. He was lonely during the winter season and wanted to think about "larger issues." He spent two months attending weekly meetings and calling local restaurants to donate food. At the first meeting he noticed Caroline. She was bubbly, forty-two years old, and above-average-looking with a good body. José decided to work with her on a committee. They were in frequent contact

on the phone and José suggested they get together at a bar for meetings. Over the two months José not only solicited several restaurants to donate food, but he also began dating Caroline.

Volunteering is a good way not only to meet women, but to increase your net worth around them. You develop confidence and begin to focus on someone else for a change. This is a skill you will need if you ever want to have a long-term relationship.

7. Get your friends and family to set you up on dates

Most of the men we have coached never ask friends and family to help them find dates. We realize it may sound a bit crazy at first, but think about it, your friends and family actually do care about you and want to see you happy. Some of them may have leads and know single women who you may be interested in dating. Your friends and family may have no idea you are looking to date, and if they did know, they might just help you out. We recommend you ask friends, relatives, coworkers, and even acquaintances to help you find dates.

USING NICHES TO MEET WOMEN

At its best, a niche is an entry point into a community that contains women. It is like a fishing spot—and a good fisherman has at least several fishing spots he can explore. A niche helps you interrupt women—it gives you some mutual ground to stand on, something shared to interact about. When you are in environments or communities that contain women, you can practice the hi program, start conversations, and meet women in a more mellow environment in which women will be more open to meeting you.

What a niche does
A niche does two things:

- *Puts women in front of you.* If the yoga class, for instance, doesn't have any women in it, or any women you're attracted to, it's not a niche for you. You want the yoga class only if there is one that has at least a few hot women in leotards.

- *Gives you an excuse to interact with these women.* A dance concert is probably not a very good niche, because it doesn't practically force interaction between the people there—you can go to the concert and not interact with any women, and they probably aren't expecting to be approached and spoken to. A dance class, however, could be a niche— the other students will have to interact with you during various exercises, and it wouldn't be unexpected if you were to talk with them.

A niche is an entry point into a community that includes women. The ideal niche is not just a "one-off"—it's a way to get involved with a group of people over time.

Examples of niches

- Classes
- Art openings
- Fund-raising parties and events
- Art fairs
- Museums
- Film festivals
- Singles events
- Political campaigns and debates

To find your niches, you'll need to make a habit of getting whatever weekly paper in your area has a social calendar, and looking it over for events you could go to that meet at least two of the three criteria for a niche. Then put them into your date book.

Remember, the hardest moment of niche work is getting off the couch and actually going to check out the niche. This is the only moment you need to think about after you've decided what niches to explore.

How to find a niche

- Look in your local weekly and/or daily paper for events that might lead to niches. Look for both one-offs—events that probably

wouldn't connect you with a group over time—and events that might be an entrée into repeated interactions with a community of people.

- Make a preliminary list of possible places that might be niches for you. List communities you could explore, people who might help you, events you might go to, and anything else you can think of.

Questions to answer for finding niches

- What are niches from the newspaper that you might want to check out?
- Start by looking in your life at your interests and hobbies and think about places and groups you could get involved in. What are you interested in?
- What business, sports, wine tasting, theater, or political activities could you get involved in?
- What are your social networks?
- What groups are you are involved with, even in a peripheral way?
- What possible social contacts are you not exploring fully?
- What niches are in your life already that you are not exploring fully?
- In your life, what are some health-oriented places that might be possible niches?
- In your life, what are some volunteer opportunities that might be niches?
- In your life, what are some spiritual, New Age, or religious opportunities that might be niches?
- In your life, what are some personal growth or self-improvement opportunities that might be niches?
- What are some opportunities or places you routinely go in your life that might be niches?
- What support could you ask of family and friends for finding niches? What could they introduce you to?
- What might be some clubs, bars, classes, or "dance nights" that could conceivably become niches?

Condense the above list to a list of niches you might want to start pursuing, and create a plan for how you could start pursuing them.

Make a list of all potential social groups, organizations, and social networks you are part of. Come up with a plan for how you can get involved in these groups. Start making weekly and monthly commitments in your calendar. Actually write into your calendar what you are planning on doing—schedule it in like a real appointment.

In closing, you no longer can make the excuse that there are no women out there, or that you are too scared, or that meeting them is too hard or takes too much time. You no longer have to wait until you "get lucky" and meet a woman, and you no longer have to live a life of helplessly hoping for better times.

Women are everywhere. You encounter them constantly, and regularly pass up opportunities to surround yourself with them. This is not just "positive thinking" or some other New Age noise. If you give up your excuses, flirt with every woman you see, allow your seductions to build over time as a thousand little interactions, turn every situation into a prospecting situation, make meeting women a game, have friends egg you on and support you, follow up on every lead, and leave your home looking good and ready to party, you'll be ready to meet women. If you frequent a coffee shop, the Internet, malls, bars, and bookstores, you'll also find women to meet.

If you take the trouble to go to a yoga class, a niche event, a personal growth seminar, or a church, you'll also find plenty of women you could meet.

You now know *where* to meet women. The next thing you need to know is how to meet them. That is the topic of the following chapter.

5

Flirting Without Disaster: So You've Found the Women to Talk To, Now How Do You Do It?

Many men are very analytical in their approach to life. They think about life practically, and they think about women practically. They get caught in the paralysis of analysis. This is a huge error. Romance is not practical, logical, or even sensible.

Bob thinks women and romance should be logical. When he's been attracted to women and had the nerve to actually approach them, he's figured that it's best to be direct. "After all," he says, "women like men who are direct and honest. What could be more honest than telling them about my attraction to them?" He's tried to seduce women friends by explaining to them how logical it would be for them to have a relationship. "You say you like me, and I like you. It doesn't make any sense for us to not get involved!" He's never understood why they've said no to him. His practical, logical approach drives women away.

WHAT IS FLIRTING?

To date women successfully, you must master flirting. Flirting is not practical, obvious, or direct. But it does follow basic principles, and once you understand them, you'll be miles ahead of other men in talking to and being successful with women.

Think about kids playing together. They don't try to accomplish anything; all they are interested in is games. They take on roles with each other effortlessly. They play cowboys, and one kid is the cowboy, another is the Indian. Or they play house, and one kid is the father and the other is the mother. Or they play doctor, and one kid is the doctor while the other is the patient. (That's the kind of playing you want to do with adult women!) They dress up to get into the roles better. They let their imaginations run free. It's all ultimately meaningless, but they don't care; they just want to have fun.

Kids love games, both premade and ones they make up. And most of the time, they aren't overly concerned about winning. Just being together playing is enough to make them happy. Kids relate by playing, and if they can play, they can relate to each other, though they don't think about it that way. Playing is a way of being in the zone together.

Adults play differently. First, let's look at how men play with men. We usually don't think of it as play, but watching sports together, or talking about sports, is a way men play with one another. After all, sports are ultimately meaningless: Which team wins the NBA title this year really isn't going to make that big a difference in the grand scheme of things. It really isn't. Sorry. But the point is, by caring about it together, by watching the games, yelling and screaming at the players together, and keeping track of the players' statistics, men play together. Because of all this, they feel the togetherness and unself-conscious love for one another that kids feel.

The other way men play together is through joking with one another and playing jokes on one another. The little jokes that men make about one another, the loving insults traded back and forth, are bonding for men.

Men and women, on the other hand, play together differently. As most men have discovered, playing with women the way they do with men doesn't work. Women aren't interested in sports statistics. And the jokes you make with

your buddies only offend the women you know. Having learned this stuff the hard way, men decide to not play with women at all. They approach women the way Bob does, logically and practically. And they get no results at all.

Flirting is the way men and women play. If you can't flirt, you can't play with women, and if you can't play with women, they won't be romantically or sexually interested in you. Flirting is one of the ways women find out what you'll be like as a lover, and what you'd be like in a relationship. If you aren't playful, imaginative, and fun to be with when she first meets you, what will you be like to date? And what will you be like in bed? Bob impresses the ladies as a cold fish. He seems stiff, analytical, and calculating. Even if he can logically show them they should be interested in him, his lack of playfulness doesn't touch them inside. His outcome-oriented approach is anything but playful.

Let's look at how Bruce, an accomplished flirter, handles women he is attracted to. At the bank, for instance, he flirts with the cute female teller as he makes his deposits. "So," he asks with a smile, "do you get to keep a percentage of all the money you take in each day? It only seems fair, don't you think?" She laughs and says, "Oh, that would be nice, especially on payday." He jokes, "But then you might get docked a percentage of the money that goes out! We can't be having that happen to you!" She laughs again, and notices her connection with him. As he leaves, he says, "Thank you, O Banking Goddess!" "It's not a bank—it's a credit union!" she laughs after him. He leaves, and thinks about how happy she'll be to see him next time.

Bruce knows that flirting with a woman creates opportunities. It's a chance to have fun interacting with a woman, to build up to asking her for a date, and to prequalify women to see if they are interested in sex and relationships. When Bruce flirts, he has fun and makes women like him. He finds out how responsive they are to him, and prepares them for going out with him. Teaching you how to do this is the focus of this chapter.

YOUR GOAL IN FLIRTING

When Bruce leaves the bank, he's left the teller delighted, and looking forward to seeing him again. Indeed, this is Bruce's goal. In any flirting situation with a woman, your goal is for her mind to connect the idea of seeing

you with pleasure. Any effective seducer knows that women respond to their emotions, not to their logical minds. An effective seducer uses flirting to get women to have happy emotions every time they see him.

Flirting makes women happy to see you through a process called "anchoring." Anchoring simply means that a certain stimulus—be it a sight, a sound, a smell, or a person—is always connected to a certain feeling. Most people, for example, see a police car in their rearview mirror, siren blaring and lights flashing, and connect it with the feeling of fear. Their feelings automatically respond to the police stimulus; their hearts pump, and they feel afraid. The two are anchored together.

Similarly, Bruce knows that he is the stimulus, and the feeling he wants to create is happiness in the woman. Just as a person automatically responds with fear to seeing a flashing police light, Bruce wants women to automatically respond to his presence with pleasure. He knows that flirting is the structure in which he makes this happen.

WHAT FLIRTING DOES

Flirting is the key to a successful seduction. If you master flirting, you will master the art of seduction and vice versa. All masters of seduction are masters of flirting.

You build rapport
"Rapport" simply means that she likes to talk to you, and feels good doing it. When you are flirting, you usually aren't talking about anything heavy or deep. You are probably talking about something fun or silly. She feels pleasure, and you feel pleasure. This creates rapport. Rapport can also be built by having a woman feel related to you at a deep level. This creates trust, connection, and a common bond.

You make her feel safe by returning to the same topics again and again
As you'll see in this chapter, in flirting you'll often have a "running joke" with a woman. For example, Frank, a forty-four-year-old college instructor, has been flirting with a woman at his local health food store for

several weeks. She's pretty, red-haired, tattooed, and in her mid-twenties. Frank thinks she's quite beautiful, and that she'd probably be a lot of fun in bed. The first time he met her, she was wearing an old military shirt and jeans, and he joked with her about her being a marine. "Hello, Major," he said to her. "I see you are wearing your fatigues. Doing some covert operations here at the health food store?" "Oh yes," she responded, immediately drawn into his silly idea. "I'm here watching everyone, to make sure there are no foreign spies." They joked along this line for a while, and as he left, Frank said, "I'd better leave—I don't want to blow your cover!" and she laughed. Since then, every time he's come in they've built on this comic scene. She's always happy to see him, and loves the special little world they create together. Plus, he always has something to talk with her about.

Flirting lets you get to know her to see if you want her

Contrary to what you might think, you really don't want to get involved with every attractive woman you meet. Simply understand that flirting is a chance to find out if a woman is dangerously unstable, or a cold fish who is not interested in sex.

Ted found this out the hard way. Carolyn was attractive, drunk, and interested in him. He met her in a bar, and they went to bed within fifteen minutes of meeting. "We met, she said, 'I want you,' and we went to my house immediately," Ted relates. "It was cool to get sex so fast, but immediately after we had sex, she said, 'Wow, it's so great to have a boyfriend at last.'"

Ted's personal hell had begun. From then until he finally got rid of her, Carolyn was a constant, unwanted fixture in his life. She broke into his house and was in his bed when he got home; she called and filled his answering machine with crazy messages again and again. She harassed his friends and wouldn't ever leave him alone. He finally had to call the police to get her out of his life. "I wish now I hadn't been so 'successful' with her that first night," he says. "If I'd taken the time to flirt with her more, I might have found out how crazy she was."

So how do you use flirting to evaluate a woman's stability? First, flirting helps you gauge her fear of you. If she has an enduring fear of you, she might not be worth pursuing. It's important to understand, however, that

there is a difference between this enduring fear and the temporary fear that almost all women will experience when they first meet any man.

At first, you'll be flirting through her fear, overcoming it with your certainty that everything will be okay. After your second or third interaction with her, however, she should be lightening up and joking back with you. If she isn't, you can certainly keep flirting with her to stay in practice, but you should probably give up on her as someone you'd want as a sexual partner. A woman who can't play with you will not be fun to be in any kind of relationship with.

Similarly, you may discover that she is extremely sensitive and easily offended. If your flirting with her makes her angry, or if she delivers a lecture about how "there are some things you just don't joke about," you know that you want to avoid her. Likewise, if she starts to cry, or interacting with her scares *you* or makes *you* want to cry, you should avoid her as well. If Ted had taken the time to flirt with Carolyn, he would have seen her fundamental instability, and steered clear.

Flirting helps her feel safe with you

Remember women's number one fear when they first meet you? They are rightfully worried about whether you are dangerous or not. If you are able to be playful with a woman, she relaxes. Subconsciously she reasons, "He's making me feel good. Therefore, he's not dangerous." Men who can't flirt often scare women because they are so tense and cold that the woman's natural fear of men is amplified, rather than dampened. When you can flirt playfully, you show a woman you aren't overly concerned about hurting her, which, as we discussed in Chapter 3, will make her less concerned about getting hurt.

Flirting helps her associate fun and playfulness with you

When you are first getting to know a woman, there often seems to be an endless trail of hoops to jump through. While it is critical that a woman feel safe around you, it is also important that she have fun while she is with you and that you come across as a guy who doesn't always take life too seriously. One of the reasons why Bob has no game with women is that he has no

ability to laugh at himself and to joke around. He seems overly serious, and women do not tend to feel comfortable around men who act overly serious and significant about life. At the same time, if you are always joking around and never serious, a woman won't feel comfortable either—because she will be concerned that you never take anything seriously, including her feelings. It's a tricky game to play, but you must do your best to have a woman associate a spirit of fun and playfulness with you.

Flirting gets her used to the idea of being romantic with you

When you flirt with a woman, you create a different, imaginary world for the two of you. It's a small step from this world of flirting to the world of romance.

Flirting gives you opportunities to practice your seduction skills

We suggest that all our students flirt with women constantly. Flirting gives you a chance to nibble away at learning it, like a mouse eating cheese, until you have mastered it. When you are first learning to flirt, it is important that you do it with all women, not just the ones you are attracted to.

Flirting gives you the opportunity to gauge her interest in you

If you said hi to that woman at the coffee shop when you first saw her, and she didn't say hi back, you'd have a good idea that she's not very receptive to your approaching her.

With some women, you really might get the sense that there is a wall around them, that they are really in their own world. In that situation, the average guy will make this mistake—he'll assume that if he was better with women, he'd be able to break down that wall, talk to that woman, and get her into bed in twenty minutes or less.

Then the average guy will feel bad about himself. Has that ever happened to you?

The truth is, some women are highly unreceptive, and it doesn't have anything to do with you, and there's nothing you are going to be able to do

about it. Stop idealizing her as the "perfect woman, who got away" and stop beating yourself up about it.

If you are around anyone, you are likely to make accidental eye contact—unless that person is making an effort to make sure that eye contact does not occur. If you can't catch her eye, it doesn't mean that the game is over, but it might mean that she's less open to you than you might like.

Flirting makes you generative

When you flirt, you are always creatively making up new ways to delight the women who interest you. You can't do this if you are into being depressed, needy, resentful, moody, or shut down. To flirt well, you have to be energetic and creative. Ultimately, women like to be with men who are generative. Fortunately, practicing flirting as we describe in this chapter will actually take you out of your moodiness and make you into the alive, vital kind of man who gets women.

Flirting gets you the date!

There's not much more to say. The more you flirt successfully with a woman, the more natural it will be for her to want to go out with you.

HOW TO CREATE FLIRTING CONVERSATIONS

A flirting conversation is made up of two elements:

1. Asking questions
2. Making statements (and telling stories, sharing opinions, and experiences)

Statements can be either canned (usually in the form of stories) or improvised, which means you come up with them on the spot.

You need to work on both asking questions and making statements. And you need to sit down and craft out stories to share with women when you are seducing them.

Improvised material is much more difficult, but also critically important. So many things happen when you talk to a woman that you couldn't possibly plan for, and many of those things are great to talk about. She might

glare at you, and you can include that in the seduction. Or she might share the same birthday as you or have some other very unexpected thing in common with you. These all become part of the improvised dialogue.

It is so important to practice your improvisational skills so you can feel comfortable talking to new women and also thinking on your feet.

When you work on all of these key skills, your success rate will rise dramatically.

Wide and deep rapport

You need to connect deeply on several topics when seducing a woman. By *wide* we are talking about connecting on a variety of topics. When you connect on a variety of topics, she feels deeply connected to you and feels that you two share many similarities.

Wide rapport also gives her the sense that you two know each other, which builds her feeling of comfort, safety, and attraction.

By *deep* we mean you connect in a deeply emotional way. She feels special, that she knows secrets about you, so that the two of you are no longer strangers, but deeply bonded. She feels that there is intimacy in the relationship and therefore trust.

How do you create wide and deep rapport? You need to specifically ask questions that elicit stories of intimate experiences in her life, and also share your own intimate experiences.

The five key topics women love to talk about

A great starting point to developing wide and deep rapport is to use the Five Topics Women Love. This is not an exhaustive list, but very basic and bottom-line, so you can easily memorize it.

Here are the top five topics you can use in any conversation with a woman to create a decent connection:

1. Travel/vacations
2. Food/restaurants
3. Fashion/clothing
4. Movies, books, forms of drama
5. Celebrities, people in the news, current events

Talking to women is an essential component of seduction. If you master your conversation skills with women, you can succeed in any environment, but if you can't talk to women it will be hard to succeed. Our book *How to Talk to Women* is a powerful resource in succeeding with women. In the book we teach you, step by step, how to talk to women, and even include a CD along with the book so you can actually hear us talking to real live women. This resource has helped many men greatly improve their game, and it can help you, too. Read more about this useful program, along with more information on talking to women, at www.howtosucceedwithwomen.com/owners.

Do's of flirting conversations

- *Do smile and say hi.* Your expression is an important part of your behavior. When you approach a woman to flirt, it's best to be relaxed and to smile, make eye contact, and say hi. Many men approach flirting with women in an overly serious manner. They are resentful about having to do it, or are indulging a bad mood. They don't look relaxed and they don't sound relaxed.

  As we said in Chapter 3, you must overcome adolescent posture. It may be necessary for you to get some bodywork or to take some yoga classes if you habitually radiate tension. If you are relaxed when you approach a woman, she sees it on your face and in your eyes.

- *Do ask them about things they know.* Unusual questions are good, as are questions about personal appearance. As we'll discuss later, one good line is "What's the story behind that . . . ?" If, for instance, she is wearing an unusual necklace, you might say, "What a beautiful necklace you are wearing. What's the story behind it?"

- *Do ask questions.* Along the same lines, it's a good idea to ask questions. After all, you want to find out about her, and asking the right questions can give you important information. It's not an interrogation, so don't badger her with questions, but do make inquiries about what she cares about. For example, if she's holding a flower, ask her about it: "That rose you are holding is beautiful. Why did you pick a rose? How does a rose make you feel?" Or you could ask, "Why do

you think women love flowers?" Either way, you are engaging her, through your questions, in a conversation that is about her likes, her dislikes, and her feelings. That's the kind of conversation that could become more romantic later on.

- *Do describe feelings for her.* Your goal in flirting is to get her to think romantic thoughts about you, and to want to act on those thoughts. To do this, you must describe romantic feelings.

Have you ever been with someone who was describing something disgusting? Perhaps a friend had been sick and later described to you, in intimate, loving detail, every step and every nuance of how it felt to be about to throw up. Can you remember how you felt as he described his sickness? Did you start to get sick, too?

Or have you ever wished someone would stop describing some horrible event or accident, because you are starting to feel how it must have felt? You probably have. These people have used a simple principle on you, that to *describe a feeling to someone makes them experience that feeling.* That's why you feel sick when your friend describes getting ill, or you feel queasy when someone talks about a disgusting accident.

To flirt successfully, you absolutely must take advantage of this principle, only in reverse. You must describe the feelings you want her to have—romance, attraction, arousal—in lush and lavish detail. As you describe these feelings, she'll start to have them.

The principle is simple: When someone describes something to you, you must imagine it to be able to understand what that person is talking about. If I'm describing my new car to you, and tell you that it's a minivan, and it's blue, you can't help but imagine it. Even if I tell you *not* to imagine something, you have to imagine it to know what not to think about. If I tell you *not* to imagine a minivan, you must think of one, so you know what thought to avoid.

The same thing happens when you describe a feeling to a woman. Whether she wants to feel the feeling you are describing or not, she must feel it to even know what you are talking about. The extent to which she feels it is dependent on how well you describe it. For instance, Sven is talking to the attractive young woman behind the

pastry counter. "I can imagine you must feel so great and special behind the counter, goddess of the whole store, and people come to worship you," he says to her. "Those great feelings of people coming to see you must really make you feel wonderful." He's playfully described feelings of specialness to her, and if she is to evaluate what he's talking about at all, she must go inside and feel those feelings. While looking at Sven, she starts to connect his visits to her store with feeling those special feelings. In time, this will lead her to "naturally" feeling attracted to him.

Poets are the get-laid kings of all time. Poetry is a wonderful tool in teaching you how to make beautiful, and detailed, descriptions of romantic things. After all, 99 percent of poetry is about love. If you look at most romantic poetry, you'll find it's made up of descriptions of romantic, loving feelings. Romance novels, in much the same way, are unending streams of descriptions of romantic feelings. Learn to speak romantically by describing romantic feelings, and you will be much more successful with women.

FLIRTING WITH HUMOR

Remember this: You want to make women laugh. If you can make a woman laugh (so long as she isn't laughing at your expense), then you are delighting her, and she'll want to see you again. However, as most men know, women often find different things funny than men do. It's easy to misuse humor with women, and to frighten and offend them instead. With that in mind, here's a list of do's and don'ts for flirting with humor.

Don'ts

- *Don't joke with a woman as roughly as you would with a guy, and don't make jokes about her appearance.* This is very important. When a guy drops something, for instance, it's a funny, bonding joke to say, "Way to drop that, bozo!" Among men this is great humor, occasions for high-fives all around. Such jokes are how we men play together. When a woman drops something, you must be much more gentle on

her. It's best to not make fun of her mistakes at all, or she will be offended.

It's also better to not make jokes about her appearance, unless you are sure that the joke can be taken only in a positive way. Women are taught to be paranoid about their looks; if a woman can misinterpret a remark about her appearance, she will. When Robert told Greta, "Wow, you've got such a nice, big butt. I like big women," he really sincerely meant it. Greta took offense, and so will every other woman in Western civilization.

- *Don't joke about violence unless you are absolutely sure she'll like it. And she probably won't.* Once again, play among men and play among women is different. Among men, jokes about violence are funny: You might ask a man for some information only to have him reply, "I'd tell you, but then I'd have to kill you." To guys, this is funny. To women, it's scary. There's a big difference. Kenny met Rachel at a daylong personal growth seminar. Afterward they took his car to a nearby bar. Along the way, Kenny made his error. Thinking he was joking, he said, "Oh, what the heck. I think I'll just take you out to the woods and kill ya." Rachel became upset, and only the fact that they were just then pulling into the bar kept her from freaking out entirely. "The thing is," he told us later, "I had used that line on a girl I met at a punk-rock concert a few weeks before and she thought it was hilarious!" Most of the time, women hear jokes about violence as threats of violence. They aren't flirty, and you shouldn't make them.

- *Don't use physical humor with women.* Guys play with one another using physical humor. They play-punch each other, give each other noogies, and generally get rowdy together. They make physical jokes about pissing, farting, and feces. Men find this great fun, but it doesn't work on women. Just don't do it. These jokes *will* offend her. You have to decide which is more important: joking or seducing.

- *Don't make yourself the butt of any jokes.* This is very important. Remember what we've said: When a woman is first meeting you, she's deciding what position you will have in her life. Will you be a lover? A friend? Someone she avoids? She's trying to figure out what level of respect to give you, and one way she figures that out is by

watching how you treat yourself. If you make jokes at your own expense, she knows that you aren't worth wasting time on.

Some men are so used to making themselves the butt of a joke to entertain women that it's hard for them to stop. Jerry was always the class clown, was a little overweight, and was used to making fun of his heaviness as a way of entertaining women. "I learned that if I made fun of myself, they'd laugh," he said. "But I noticed I never got any sex. It was hard to give up being the butt of my jokes, but I did it, and now I've got a girlfriend."

Do's

- *Do make "creative misinterpretations."* When you approach a woman, you've got to be alert and have your eyes open. Look for the details in her appearance or in what she is doing that you can safely make jokes about. You do this by putting a new spin on something normal. When Bruce asks the bank teller, "Do you get to keep a percentage of all the money you take in each day?" he's creatively misinterpreting something in her environment and using it to flirt. When he asks if she gets to keep a percentage, he's being silly in a way she can relate to. It gives them a joke to talk about and creates a little separate world for them together.

  Similarly, when Frank jokes to the girl at the health food store about being a major in the marines, he's taking something at hand and creatively misinterpreting it, recasting it as something they can joke and flirt about. Every time he sees her, they return to this joke, and she feels more comfortable with him each time.

  You should try to make your misinterpretations complimentary to her. For example, misinterpreting the woman collecting the money as you leave a parking garage as the "parking goddess" would be more effective than misinterpreting her as, say, a trash collector who got lucky and got her current job. The first is a joke; the second is an insult. Keep track of the difference.
- *Do be confident that your joking is okay.* One of the top flirting mistakes men make is that they wait for the woman to be comfort-

able with the flirting before *they* become comfortable with it. We can't emphasize this enough: When a woman first meets you, she is trying to decide if you are dangerous or not. If you are uncertain and hesitant, you come across as though you, too, are afraid that you are dangerous. You act as though you are scared of yourself, and she will become scared, too. You must decide to have certainty that you are not hurting her, are not a threat to her, and that your flirting is fun and relaxed for you both.

Bob has this problem. He tries to flirt, but to him it is such a big deal, and he's so afraid that he's going to scare his prospect away, that he's a big ball of tension. When he talked to Natalie, the dental receptionist where he goes to get his teeth cleaned, he was as frightened as a cornered mouse. He has to work himself up to talking to her, and his heart pounds. He keeps asking himself, "What if she doesn't like me?" and worries about potential rejection. "So, I guess a lot of people get hurt here," he "jokes" with her, his jaw muscles throbbing with tension. She just stares at him, wondering what kind of a psycho he is. He notices her fear, and becomes more upset himself. "Uh, I mean, that's a joke," he says weakly. "Oh, heck. When's my appointment?" His fear, and his need for her to not be afraid of him, makes him fail with the receptionist, as he does with all women.

Now let's look at how Bruce handles the same situation. When he sees Natalie, he knows he desires her, and knows that she may or may not be induced to desire him. He knows that she may not respond to him, and doesn't care. Bruce has decided that his joking is fine, and is certain that he is charming, even if she doesn't think so. When he walks up to talk to her, he is smiling and relaxed, radiating confidence rather than tension. "So, you are the guardian of this ba-a-ad, evil place, eh?" he says to her in a laughing way. She looks at him to decide if he's a threat, but he's so relaxed and seems so certain that everything is fine that she decides to laugh in response. "Oh yes, I'm the guardian, all right," she says. He continues in his confident, joking manner, "How could I persuade you to put a spell on me to keep me from harm here? In fact, I think I can feel you putting a spell on me already. You are bewitching me, Natalie," he

says, reading her name off her name tag. She laughs at his joking. "Now I feel like I can go in there, protected by the spell you have me under. I'll just say to the dentist, 'The beautiful and charming Natalie put me under a protective spell.' How do you think that will work?" "You can try it," she responds, laughing. "But I'd still take the Novocain." He comes back with "Oh, I don't need painkiller after seeing you. Have you ever had the feeling of meeting someone, and it's like your heart can only feel good feelings, can feel no pain? After meeting you, I'm sure I won't need anything else." She blushes. "Well, thank you!"

Bruce makes this interaction work because he is certain that it will work. If he appeared uncertain, like Bob did, and waited for Natalie to give him approval before he allowed himself to relax, he'd have the same failure Bob had. Because he's not waiting for her to feel good for him to feel good, he's able to create the good feelings for them both.

- *Do be romantic and sensual with your humor.* Just being a clown makes you come across like a chump. You must make it clear that you find her attractive. In the above example, Bruce doesn't only make Natalie laugh; he uses their flirting to let her know that he finds her beautiful and charming. He does this by slipping in the occasional compliment, sideways. When he says, "I'll just say to the dentist, 'The beautiful and charming Natalie put me under a protective spell,'" he's telling her that she is beautiful and charming, and that he's thinking of her as more than just a friend. By doing this, he makes her choose what category to put him in, friend or potential lover. If she keeps flirting with him after he says these romantic things about her, then she's accepting the fact that he's a potential lover.

Only if she rejects his compliments will she be able to think of him as just another lowly male friend. But because she's having so much fun flirting with him, she's unlikely to do that. By being romantic with his humor, he puts himself on the inside track for being her lover. When you look at how Bruce flirts with Natalie, you can see how she would have a hard time thinking of him as "just a friend," because of the romantic quality of his flirting. You, too, can do this, if you show your romantic interest as you flirt.

Conclusion of do's and don'ts of humor

Men make two main errors when they flirt with women: Either they play (that is the essence of flirting, after all) with women the way they would with men, or they don't play with women at all, and seem stiff and nervous. If you follow the guidelines we've taught you, you'll never make either of those mistakes again. You've learned how flirting relies on humor and play, how men and women play and joke differently, and how to play and joke so women think of you romantically. You've learned to avoid joking with women as roughly as you would with guys, to not joke about violence, to not use physical humor with women, and to not make yourself the butt of any jokes.

You've learned how to "creatively misinterpret" with women, to engage in romantic "pretend" with them, and to ask them questions. Can you see how these skills can be useful in your interactions with women, starting today? Of course, learning to flirt with women will take time, and your first interactions may not be as wonderful as you would like. No matter. All that matters is that you start talking with women, joking with women, and playing with women. As you practice, you'll get better at it. Now that you understand these basics of flirting and humor, you are ready to learn how to flirt your way to the date.

FLIRTING YOUR WAY TO THE DATE

With these basics in mind, we'll now take you, step by step, from meeting a woman all the way through asking her out. We'll look at the specific problems of each step, and show you how to overcome them.

The main problem you face is that women, like everybody else, resist change, even change they would like. It is entirely possible that dating you would be the best thing that has ever happened to the women you desire. It's even possible that having sex with you would be the best thing that ever happened to the women you desire (especially after you've read Chapter 10, "Being the Man of Her Dreams in Bed").

If you do what we teach you in this book, you may well provide a woman with more romantic feelings, passion, and happiness than any

man ever has before. Even if you are only interested in a short-term sexual relationship, you still might easily provide her with a fling she'll be grateful she had for the rest of her life.

In spite of the truth that you could well bring her nothing but pleasure, she'll resist you because she resists change. You represent the *potential* for pain, discomfort, or, at the very least, unfamiliarity. You are a monkey wrench of disorder in her otherwise orderly life. While you are dreaming of wonderful nights of hot sex with her, she's imagining you leaving your dirty socks around and messing up her life the way other men have. So even in the best of times, when you meet a woman, you may encounter resistance.

It's really no different than any other sales situation (which seducing a woman fundamentally is). If you've ever been a salesman, you know that people resist most products and services on principle, even if the products and services you offer would improve their lives. While you are thinking about selling them this great product, they are wondering how badly you are going to rip them off. It's exactly the same with women. Each of the steps below takes you through the process of getting through her fear, and helping her see the desire she has for you.

GETTING HER TRUST

Before you can flirt your way to the date, you must handle her natural fear that you will hurt her. You must show her you are trustworthy.

From time to time, Bob has noticed that women seemed afraid of him when he first talked to them. He's tried to handle this directly, with horrible results. "I'm not dangerous, you know," he said once to an attractive receptionist at an auto parts store. "I'm just a regular guy. You really don't have to be afraid." She got pale and her eyes got wide with terror. No doubt she was asking herself, "Why is this guy telling me he's not dangerous? Why would he think to say that? What's he gonna do to me?"

As we've said so many times, a woman's first concern is that you are going to assault, rape, or kill her. Saying that you are not dangerous only makes her more frightened and suspicious. You alleviate her fear over time—either over the course of the flirting interaction, or over the course of a number of flirting interactions. As you are persistent in your flirting,

and as you consistently cause her to laugh and feel good, she'll naturally start to trust you, and to know that you are safe. To overcome her fear that you are dangerous, you must demonstrate certain qualities. If you don't, you will never get past her fear. It's been sad for us to see so many wonderful men striking out with women because they don't know how to show that they aren't dangerous in a way women can understand.

THE ESSENTIAL QUALITIES YOU MUST DEMONSTRATE FOR A WOMAN TO TRUST YOU AND FEEL SAFE

• *Build trust by respecting her.* Bob thinks he's being respectful when he tells a woman that he's not dangerous. Actually, he's just being scary. Bob's mistake is that he doesn't understand that actions, as the old saying goes, speak louder than words. Have you ever known someone who said they were one way, but actually were another? Of course you have. Perhaps it's been someone who has talked about the importance of being on time, yet who chronically showed up late. His words didn't match his actions, and you probably found yourself suspicious of all his talk about being on time. It's exactly the same with not being dangerous. Talking about it only makes it worse; you must demonstrate it. And the first way to demonstrate it is by being respectful.

Respecting her is not the same as groveling before her, or treating her as if she's better than you, or superior to you. That's not respecting, that's fawning and toadying, and no woman wants to be around it.

Most important, you must respect her when she says no. A woman likes to move at a certain pace during a seduction. She feels safe knowing that she is in control of the speed. You'll get to know this pace by her use of the word no. You must back off when she says no. When you do this, she will feel respected.

When you are first flirting with a woman, you may say something that offends her. She'll look unhappy, or a little irritated, and you'll notice the flow of the flirting interaction slow down or even stop. You must respect this, notice it, and work with it.

• *Build trust by not being desperate.* Nothing makes a woman feel used faster than a man who seems needy for female companionship, lonely, or desperate for sex. Women immediately and correctly decide that the guy isn't really interested in *them*; they decide that he's only interested in *sex*. While you might think it would be great if a woman was only interested in you for sex, take it from us when we tell you that even women who *are* only interested in you for sex will be put off if you are desperate and obvious.

Desperation shows up most often in three situations:

1. *When you are only pursuing one woman.* As we discussed in Chapter 2, when you are only pursuing one woman, have all your bets on one horse, you are likely to get desperate. You have no backup plan, so things *must work* with the woman you are with. This "it must work" pressure destroys your ability to act freely. You won't be able to say, "It doesn't matter how it goes with this woman; there are lots of others to choose from." You'll get tense, and she'll feel it and get tense, too. Then you'll get tenser, because, after all, this woman is your only chance. Once you have that thought, it's all over. Unless you can remind yourself forcefully that there are lots of women available to you, you are likely to continue looking desperate.

   The solution, of course, is to always be "working on" a number of women, as we discussed in Chapter 2. Having a number of potential lovers "in progress" will keep desperation far away.

2. *When you are overly terrified of rejection.* When you feel this way, you often become desperate. By this time, we hope we've impressed upon you the importance of overcoming rejection and fear, and that you are committing yourself to taking on the anti-fear practices we described in Chapter 2.

3. *When your life is otherwise lonely and meaningless.* If you are lonely, and your life seems meaningless, you also appear desperate to women. You must have something you are into, that gives your life meaning, above and beyond a relationship and sex with some woman. If you are trying to get meaning for your life out of your interactions with women, they will always

notice it, and not want to be with you. Men, too, won't respect you.

You may have noticed that women like successful men. It is true that they are attracted to the money, but that's not the whole story. They are attracted to men who are passionate about their lives and have fire and drive. Some of these men have money, but some don't. Money is less important than being a dynamic man, tackling his life head-on.

We've all seen garage-band rock guitarists who get sex easily, even though they never play anywhere but in local bars. Their passion for something in their lives makes both these kinds of men, the men with money and the guitarists, more attractive to women.

Along with passion, women are attracted to men who have deep social connections. In essence, women are attracted to men who have social status—which means a man has plenty of friends (both male and female), is frequently participating in social activities, and is involved in several different social circles.

We're not going to walk you through an entire life-overhaul here, but you'll find that the principles of being successful with women are the same as the principles for life success. You'll notice that the Seven Habits of a Highly Successful Seducer are also habits that will serve you in your life outside of your relationships.

It makes sense to act with an outcome in mind, not just with women, but also in every area of your life. It makes sense to see life as a numbers game, to not take the events of life personally, and to pursue more than one project at a time. It makes sense to be willing to walk away from work or business situations that aren't paying off, just as it makes sense to be willing to walk from women. And it makes sense to make life work for you, just as it makes sense to make dating work for you.

Keeping these dating principles in mind as you design your life will help you live with passion and success. You'll be able to use the principles of planning and follow-through, which we

will discuss in upcoming chapters, in creating a life you are passionate about. When you are passionate about your life, and care about something other than sex, you won't be desperate.

Men become desperate when they are lonely. This especially happens to men who have many female friends and few male friends. If you don't have buddies you can kick back and really relax with, you should get some. Having male friends makes interactions with women less important sources of love and validation. It will be much easier for a woman to trust you and be relaxed once she knows that you are not desperate for her attention.

If you have any of these problems, you are in danger of becoming desperate with women.

- *Build trust by being patient with her.* Being patient with a woman is an important way of showing her that you are not dangerous and are worthy of her trust. It's easy, however, to confuse "patient" with "stupid." We don't mean to say that you should let a woman walk all over you, or jerk you around. We are saying that a flirting interaction that can lead to dating and sex requires patience. Furthermore, if a woman feels you are pressuring her for a phone number, for a date, or for sex, you will turn her off and she will likely not want to see you or interact with you anymore.

You must be patient in the flirting interaction over time. You must be willing to go see her again and again, and have multiple flirting interactions, before you go out with her. Jim used to think that in one interaction, he could build her trust, interest, and attraction, and ask her out on a date that would end in sex. Although this is certainly not impossible, most women won't be seduced that fast. You must be willing to be patient, and to take the time to have multiple flirting interactions, before you finally go out with her.

Knowing people in common also helps build trust, as long as the people you know in common are not other women you've "loved and left." If she knows a friend of yours, or if a mutual friend introduced you, you have an implicit recommendation from that friend; this, too, helps her trust you.

You can also build her trust in you by giving her your card or cell number. She won't call you, so don't count on that. It can be used as a simple way of showing her that you are willing to not keep your address and identity a secret. It's part of the patient process of getting her trust.

- *Build trust by avoiding unnecessary conflicts.* It's important that you moderate what you talk about, if you want a woman to trust you. Remember your outcome: You want this woman to desire you. To this end, it's important that you avoid unnecessary conflicts while you are flirting with her. Who cares if she spouts some opinion that pisses you off?

Remember what you are after: romance and sex. When Kurt first went out with Sally, he was doing everything properly . . . until she started talking about feminism. "Women always get the short end of the stick in this society," she said. "Men have everything, and don't even know it." Kurt, who was involved in the men's movement, got angry with her when she said this. He quoted the statistics about how men really are abused by their wives, how more men die in wars than women do, how men get raped in jail, and about the damage done to men by infant circumcision. Arguably, he was right about everything he said, but it didn't matter.

Sally finally interrupted him: "Hey, you're talking really loud now, and it's really scaring me. I don't like this about you." Kurt wrecked a perfectly good seduction by getting drawn into a fight about men and women's issues, when he should have been romantic. He never did get into her pants.

You have to decide what's most important to you: arguing with a woman or having sex. If men's behavior is any indication, the average man is more interested in fighting. He gets into fights about why sports are important to men, or gets drawn into fights about men's and women's issues. You must be different. The correct way to handle a woman's invitation to fight is to let her know that you heard her, and to introduce a different topic of conversation. When Sally spouted her opinion about men and women, Kurt should have taken it in stride. He should have said, "Really? That's interesting. Do you remember

how it felt the first time you thought you were in love?" By not arguing with her, and changing the subject, he would have avoided losing
Sally's trust, and the seduction would have continued.

• *Build trust by showing her you're not weird.* Have you ever known
a man who was odd, or out of the ordinary, who was successful
with women? You probably have. It may be someone you know
who is tattooed all over, with green hair, and multiple piercings. It
may be someone you know who is very tough-looking, decked out
with black hair and a leather jacket. It may be someone with some
other eccentricity. You notice that these men seem to have made their
eccentricities work for them. They are comfortable with themselves—
tattoos, piercings, green hair, odd tastes, and all—and they have no
difficulty getting women.

You may have known a man who was odd, or out of the ordinary,
who felt self-conscious and ashamed about it. He may have had unusual tastes in music or dress, but no different from the men who are
"odd" and still have success with women. You notice that this second
group of men seem to be uncomfortable with their eccentricities,
and they have trouble getting women.

A man who is "weird" in some way, but is comfortable with it, is
an inspiration to women. She sees that he is unashamed of his passions, and sees him as a man who is willing to express himself fully.
These are arousing qualities to women, who find such men "cute" or
"artistic." They trust such men, because such men trust themselves.

A man who isn't comfortable with his eccentricities, on the other
hand, is frightening to women. Because he seems to think there is
something wrong with him, women will think so, too. His shame
about his passions make women see him as "weird" and untrustworthy. They don't trust him, because he doesn't trust himself.

The solution is to look at any "odd" behavior or mode of dress,
decide if you want to keep it, and, if you do, to integrate it proudly
into your style. You make this decision by asking yourself, "What
message does this send about me?" When Luther wanted to decide if
he should keep his ponytail and goatee, he asked that question. He
not only asked himself, but also his friends and family. Luther

learned that many folks found that his ponytail looked immature. It sent the message that he was a boy in a man's body, someone unwilling to grow up. After thinking about this feedback, Luther agreed. He cut off his ponytail, shaved his goatee, and found he was happier and that people began to interact with him differently. Women suddenly seemed to feel more comfortable around him.

Clarence had a different experience. Even though he lived in a large eastern city, he was always more comfortable in cowboy gear. He constantly wore a cowboy hat, shirt, and cowboy boots—eccentric in the area in which he lived. When he asked his friends what message they thought his hat and boots sent to people, they were all positive. "It just seems like 'Clarence' to me," one said. "It really seems like you've found your style." Clarence agreed, and kept his cowboy gear. He even accentuated it with a new, flamboyant hat that he wore proudly. Women were comfortable because, through his style, he was expressing who he really was. They trusted him. Luther, on the other hand, was expressing his fear of aging with his style. When women saw that, it made him seem weird and untrustworthy.

Often a man appears this way to a woman because he is looking for validation from her. We've been over this again and again: Get your validation someplace other than from women. Needing women's validation creates problems in every area of seduction. If a woman needs to take care of your feelings, and you are using her to make you feel good, she's not going to be interested in you as a lover.

Many men accidentally come across to women as "weird" by worrying about their eccentricities. They look to women to validate their oddness, and end up seeming weird and scaring women off.

- *Build trust by leaving her happy.* All these practices will make you more trustworthy to a woman. If you respect her, are not desperate, are patient with her, don't fight with her, and show her you are not weird, she'll have every reason to feel trust in you. If you leave her happy, she'll not only trust you; she won't be able to wait for you to return.

THE THREE STEPS OF A FLIRTING INTERACTION

Step 1. First meeting her

When Bob first met Brenda at a party, he was terrified. Brenda, a twenty-six-year-old copywriter for an advertising firm, had straight blond hair, a toned, supple body, a beautiful face, and intelligent eyes—though the first thing he noticed was her ample bustline, truth be told. "I knew I had to make a good impression," he later told his friend, Scott, "so I made sure that I didn't do anything that would scare her off." Bob was so scared that she wouldn't like him, or that she would be offended by him, that he was unable to interact with her normally.

He adopted his usual, unsuccessful approach to attractive women: trying to appear harmless. "What do you do?" he asked Brenda. When she told him, Bob initiated a conversation about work, overtime, and different kinds of computer systems that businesses use. She found him harmless, and mildly interesting, but when he finally got the nerve up to shakily ask her for her phone number, Brenda said, "I like you and everything, but I have to tell you you're not really my type." He was aware that she was initially afraid that he was dangerous, and he had handled that danger. She certainly wasn't afraid of him now. So what went wrong?

It is true, as we've said, that a woman's first concern upon meeting you is that you will hurt her in some way, and that you must handle. This doesn't mean, however, that you should allow her fear to sanitize you and make you tepid, as Bob does. You must allay her fears and, if you ever want to have sex with her, show your romantic interest right away.

As we've mentioned before, women decide about men immediately. She determines whether you are a potential lover or a lowly friend in the first few minutes of knowing you. It is important that you take advantage of this fact by presenting yourself as a romantic interest immediately. If you don't do this, making her feel safe only leaves her wanting you to be a friend, while she seeks romantic excitement with other men.

Lines to Use When Approaching Her for the First Time. Students often ask us for lines to use when approaching women, or when asking for the

date. They seem to think that there is some magic formula that works with every woman, and if only they can figure out what it is, they'll be successful in asking out women.

The truth is, there is no "right" way to ask a woman out, and no "perfect" opening line. This should make you happy, because that means that whatever you feel like saying—something simple and honest, perhaps—may well be the perfect thing.

Some men favor joke lines. They'll go up to an attractive woman and say, "Wow, did heaven lose an angel? 'Cause I'm seeing one right here!" Our interviews with more than three hundred women indicate that they don't like these lines. You might as well say "Wow, did heaven lose a couple of angels? 'Cause I can see them bouncing around inside your blouse," which we highly do not recommend. We also don't recommend "If I told you you had a beautiful body, would you hold it against me?" All these hokey, adolescent lines tell a woman is that you aren't really a grown-up man. Give them up.

Opening Approaches. Earlier we told you about the "hi" program. We told you to practice simple approaches with women to increase your confidence with them as well as to help you become more outgoing. We are now going to offer some great approaches you can use when talking to a woman for the first time.

Asking a woman for directions is always a good way to get her to start talking to you. Ask her where a nearby Starbucks is located, or a Borders bookstore. Or you could ask her if there is an amazing restaurant nearby. These may sound corny, but they are the type of questions that get a woman talking to you—and that is exactly what you want.

We have already told you about creative misinterpretation and using humor with women. These both work very well.

Another way to start a conversation is to comment about something in the news, or a current event. Ask her for her opinion about this event and keep asking questions and responding to her.

You can also ask open-ended questions in the form of opinion approaches. These types of questions are designed to get a woman talking and then stretch into a much longer conversation. You can ask questions like "What do all women wish men knew?" or "What are the coolest places

around the world to go on a vacation?" Or "If someone gave you a million dollars, what would you do?"

Step 2. She starts to think of you as romantic material

If you've done everything properly in Step 1, the woman you are interested in will trust you. She will then start thinking of you as romantic material. You've made your interest known, gotten her feeling safe with you, and left her happy every time you've interacted with her. You've flirted with her using humor, as we outlined earlier in this chapter. You haven't gotten into a stupid fight with her, or scared her in any other way. She's enjoying your company, and knows you are interested romantically. You are thinking you're home free. She's starting to think, "This guy is cool. Why shouldn't I go out with him? Why not?" What could possibly go wrong?

Now that you've overcome her early fears, it's time for her to give you the next problem in your seduction. As she becomes attracted, she starts to answer that question "Why not?" Remember, women are like everyone else—they try to avoid change, even change they would like. As we said before, while you are fantasizing about nights of great sex, she is dreading having to sleep on the wet spot. In order to preserve her orderly life, she starts coming up with reasons to disqualify you. Your next challenge is to overcome these reasons, to continue to give her good feelings, and to move the seduction forward.

So what kind of answers will she have to the question "Why not"? She'll tell herself—and you—that you are not her type, that she doesn't want to spoil the friendship (more on this later), or that she's still getting over some other guy. Like anyone contemplating trying something new and potentially risky, she thinks up any and every reason to not go out with you. You just have to handle it.

"Why not" problems are usually general, rather than specific in nature. She's not saying no because she doesn't like you, or doesn't like something you did; "why not" problems seem to be free-flowing, general problems with whole classes of relationships. "I don't date men shorter than me" is a "why not" problem. So is "You're not my type" and "I'm not looking for a relationship right now." Other "why not" problems are "I don't have the time," "I don't have a car," and anything along the lines of "I have to wash my hair."

"Why not" problems are different from the problems you have when she simply doesn't like you. If she says to you, "Hey, I don't ever want to talk to you again. I'll never go out with you, and I want you to leave me alone," she doesn't like you. Leave her alone, and move on to women who like you. But if she says something more vague, thrown out as an almost offhand problem, a problem more with the idea of relationships themselves than with you specifically, then you must gently persist with her.

Many of our students are older men who want to date younger women. Predictably, at some point early on, the young woman tells the man that he's disqualified because of his age. This happened to Marvin. At thirty-eight years old, he returned to the university part-time to finish up his undergraduate degree. Suddenly he found himself surrounded by unbelievably hot, stripper-quality nineteen- and twenty-year-olds. He went to work on them immediately, but found them to be very frightened and untrusting. "That first step just takes forever with these girls," he told us, "but I found that if I hung in there, eventually they started to trust me."

The first woman he dated from school, a twenty-two-year-old senior named Jennifer, only went out with him after seeing him in class and talking to him over and over and over. "We were a third of the way into the semester, when I finally decided that she trusted me enough to go out for coffee. I asked her, and she said, 'Well, okay, but there's something I have to tell you. I've thought about it, and I can justify dating a man up to twenty-eight years old, but not a man as old as you are.'" A man who hadn't been taught by us might have given up at that moment, or stupidly begun a fight with her about what she meant by "justify." Marvin knew she was probably just answering the question "Why not?" and set up the time and location for the coffee date.

"I knew she might really mean it," he told us, "but that's the breaks of the game. If I tried to kiss her later, and she said no, then I'd know she meant it, and didn't like me. But I figured it was a 'why not' situation, told her I understood, and went on with the date." Three dates later, using the techniques from this book, he had sex with her, which she later told him was "the best experience of my life." Marvin knew that by being persistent, being willing to accept her no, and staying with it, he could get past her "why not's."

Your persistence in making her feel good is the key to getting past her "why not's." Eventually she'll see how wonderful you are and want to continue with you. Or she'll decide you are basically an obnoxious jerk and tell you to get lost. Either way, you are on your way to sex, either with her or with a woman who does want you.

Tips for Older Men Wanting to Date Younger Women. We've been running seminars and coaching men on dating and seduction since 1997, so we've worked with tons of older men wanting to date younger women. Here are some basic tips on how older men can succeed with younger babes:

First, you must realize that many younger women are more attracted to older men than they are to those drones their own age. They want someone who is sensitive, mature, and experienced. In case you didn't notice, that's you, bucko!

So you want to find those twenty-year-olds who want an older man. Don't blow it by trying to be "hip" like the guys her age. You'll just look like an idiot if you try to dress like a teenager. At the same time, don't draw attention to her comparative youth. The worst is to lecture her about how you were when you were her age and what you have learned. If women your age don't care, why should she?

To get sex with younger women, you must convince yourself (and thus, her) that your age is a benefit. Some girls will reject you because of your age, but others will sleep with you because of it, too. So muster up the courage to ask out that beautiful twenty-year-old. She may well be the girl for you.

Step 3. You ask her out, she says yes

There are three different kinds of situations in which you meet women. How quickly you ask them out has to do with which of the situations you are in.

First, there is the emergency situation. You see a woman you are attracted to, and you must ask her out right now, because she's about to leave, and you'll probably never see her again. Have you ever seen those personals ads in the "one-to-one" column where some sad guy is describing some woman he saw, pathetically begging her to call him? "I saw you from across the room, but was too scared to approach you," he might

write. "You were tall, blond, built, and talking to a buff weight lifter. I was the guy cowering over in the corner, pretending to make conversation with the potted plant. Please call me!" Not very likely.

If you don't want to be that sniveling guy, you've got to talk to the woman you may never see again. This can be as simple as approaching a woman at a gas station, for instance, and saying, "Hi, I saw you here, and I just couldn't let you walk out of my life without saying hi. I don't usually do this, but I wonder if I could give you a call sometime?" She may well say no, but she might say yes. If you are especially scared, you can give her your card, though the likelihood of her calling you is vanishingly small. You certainly have a better chance of dating her if you ask than if you don't ask. After all, if you don't ask, your chance is exactly zero. If you go up and talk to a woman in line at a coffee shop or walking around a mall, you might just end up having a longer conversation over coffee or have an instant date right then and there. Many of our students have turned cold approaches into instant dates. You gotta get up your courage, however, to do so.

The second situation gives you a bit more time. You perhaps have a few hours, or a full day, to work on her. This might be at a party, or at a full-day class, for instance. You can have numerous interactions with her, then, before you both leave, say, "You know, you seem cool. What would it be like if we went out sometime?" and set it up from there.

In the third situation, you work the flirting over a period of time. This is the woman you see reliably: the woman who works out the same time you do, the clerk at the coffee shop you frequent, the waitress at your favorite restaurant. This is the lowest-stress situation, because you can work on the woman over a long period of time. You can give her all the time she needs to get used to you, to feel safe, and to imagine you romantically as part of her life. Then, at your leisure, when the time is right, you can ask her out.

It's important that you figure out which situation you are in with any woman you are attracted to. It does you no good to be full of flirting and seduction skills if the woman of your dreams walks out of your life while you do nothing to stop her. When you figure out which class a woman is in, you can plan the urgency and velocity of your flirting accordingly.

USING THE PHONE TO ASK HER OUT

One of the most common mistakes men make is to think that a woman is not interested when she fails to return phone calls. As a result, guys will stop calling, whine about women's lack of responsiveness, and—worst of all—give up. We know this is not intuitively obvious, but the fact of the matter is that women call when they feel like it. They don't act rationally. Remember, a woman is not here to make your life easy. You will be happier if you stop expecting them to simplify things and call you back, ever.

The secrets of using the phone to ask women out:

- It is always preferable to ask a woman out directly on the phone. Leaving a message is a much weaker approach. If you do leave a couple of messages and she doesn't call you back, quit calling her for a week or so. Otherwise you start to sound desperate and become, in her mind, "that guy who's always calling me."
- Leave messages about specific places and dates where and when you might want to meet her. Ask her to meet you at Joe's bar on Thursday at 11:00 p.m., for example. Or invite her to a comedy club on Friday evening. Do not call her up without a plan in mind and say something like, "Uh, wanna go out?"
- Don't ramble when you are on the phone or when leaving messages: Be decisive.
- Don't call just to "talk." You'll only create opportunities to do something stupid and screw up your chances. Don't call unless you have something seductive to say or a date to ask her out on.
- Keep all phone calls short.
- Sound friendly when you leave messages. Smiling makes your voice sound friendlier.
- Never call when you are upset with her.

If she doesn't call back, never ask why she didn't call back—it'll call attention to the fact that you are a wimp she stood up on the phone who has come back for more. Simply act like the first message never happened.

While you do need to be patient and not expect her to call you back, you don't want to be a doormat, either. You could try the three-call rule: If after three calls she hasn't called back, move on. We sometimes advise men to call her back after she has failed to return the second call and warn her. Say something like "I'd love to see you again, but you've failed to call me back twice. I hate to do it, but if you don't call me back, I can't call you again for a long time." This gives her a message that you like her, but that you aren't willing to sacrifice your self-respect to be with her.

Flirting via text messaging

Text messaging is a great way to flirt with women and to ask them out. Most young women are used to text messaging, and it is a fun way to chat with them. You can send short flirty messages throughout the day. You can send something like "Hey troublemaker, what sort of trouble are you causing today?" or "Just wanted to say hi to you. Looking forward to seeing you soon." Or you can simply use text messaging to set up your next date with her.

Whatever level of flirting and conversation you do via text, it only adds to your seduction—because the more frequently she communicates with you, the more connected she will feel.

Flirting via email

In Chapter 4 we discussed how to use the Internet and email as ways to seduce women. We just want to reiterate how important email can be in your overall seduction strategy. Email is great because, like texting, it helps create a bond between the two of you. Email is a great forum for you to practice writing seductive messages, and a way to communicate with a woman on a frequent basis. The other cool thing is that you can save time on the priming date (which you'll read about in Chapter 7) by laying the sensual groundwork via email.

WHAT IF YOU SCREW IT UP?

Your problems aren't over when you finally ask her out and she finally says yes. You are as capable of screwing it up as she is, if not more so.

The time comes when she is primed. You have a strong connection

with her, either in one interaction or through a series of interactions. You've made your romantic interest clear by showing your attraction to her. She's become used to the idea of thinking of you as a potential romantic partner. You've flirted with her consistently and successfully. She's happy every time she sees you, and you leave her feeling good. It's time to ask her out.

This is where you'll foul it up if you aren't careful. Let's go over the bonehead mistakes you are likely to make, and show you how to avoid them:

You wait too long to ask her out

If you do this, you risk losing your "window of opportunity." If your flirting is building a sense of attraction and connection in the woman you are working on, you must take advantage of it before her mood changes. It's hard to know exactly where this point is; practice will teach it to you. If you wait too long, the woman will decide that you must not be interested in her, and will start to think of you as a friend. So you must make your move when the time is right.

As you become more skilled at seducing women, you'll start to find that there are, in fact, women whom you've started to seduce, but in whom you aren't interested. It may not seem possible to you now, but once you start pursuing women using the tools in this book, you really can have more women to date than you have time for. That's not a pipe dream; both of the authors, and many of our students, have made this happen. When it happens to you, you'll find that one way you show your lack of interest is by not asking women out in the "window of opportunity." Until you get to this point of disinterest, make sure you ask a woman out once you've got her interest.

You don't have a plan for the date

When you ask a woman out, always have a specific idea of where you want to go with her on the date. (We'll talk more about this in the upcoming chapters.) *Never* ask a woman out without a date plan in mind. This means that, in advance, you think about the kind of dating experience you want to have, and think about where you could go together and what you

can do. As you'll see later, there are two kinds of dates: priming dates and seduction dates. When you ask a woman out, you must know which kind you are asking for, and what you will do on it.

If a woman accepts a date with you, and you don't have a plan in mind, you are probably doomed. You'll end up saying, "I dunno, what do you want to do?" which is the worst thing you could possibly say. It makes you look like a sloppy jerk who isn't creative and relies on her for everything. Believe us, she won't find it attractive.

When you ask a woman out, you can say something like "Hey, you seem cool. How about we go out for coffee sometime?" When she says yes, you then supply the details, and gently direct the conversation toward getting everything worked out. "How about we go to Joe's coffee shop sometime next week? I'm free on Tuesday, after work, around five-thirty. Would that work for you?" You don't make her supply any of the details, and you make sure the plans are clear.

You are indecisive

One easy way to make yourself into a more powerful, attractive man is to practice making decisions quickly and with a minimum of fuss. The more easily you make decisions, the more successful you'll be in every area of your life, including with women.

You don't want to be bossy, but you should present a clear invitation. If she wants to change it, be flexible, but decide quickly and easily on the details. Setting up the date is an important interaction, in which she learns a lot about how you approach your life. She'll be looking at you to see if you are weak and indecisive, or strong and decisive. Do you expect me to make all the decisions and create the plans, or do you come up with ideas? Remember, women are attracted to men who are generative. This means you must come up with the ideas and get the details ironed out. If you are indecisive, you'll blow all the work you've already done.

You seem too available

Like everybody else, women like things that are rare and hard to get ahold of. If you ask a woman out and say, "Oh, anytime is good for me," it makes you sound like an unemployed bum who has no social life. Even if

you are an unemployed bum with no social life, it's important that you not sound like one. Have a couple of times available, and be reluctant to reschedule other things to be with her. Make sure the date is at a place and time that works for you, too, since it's more than likely that she won't show up anyway. When offering times, you may want to say something like "I can do it at four o'clock Wednesday, but I only have about an hour." If you sound busy, though not inaccessible, you'll be more interesting to her.

If you manage to get through asking her out and setting up the date without screwing it up, congratulations! You have a date!

If you follow the flirting steps, you will be able to easily overcome the problems that will arise during flirting, and you will get the date. You won't be stopped by her fear of you, her "why not" problems, her specific problems with you, or by yourself. You'll move the seduction forward and do much of the romantic groundwork that will make sex with you seem natural to her later. You'll use flirting, humor, and creative role-playing to make her feel connected to you and happy to see you. You'll play with women in ways that make them desire you, while still being strong, decisive, and generative. Do all this properly, and a successful date is almost assured.

Will there be more problems during and after the date? Of course. But don't worry; we'll show you how to handle each and every one of them.

THINGS YOU CAN DO TODAY TO IMPROVE YOUR FLIRTING, NO MATTER HOW TIMID YOU ARE

Now let's give you some specific, useful information about precisely how to flirt with women. What follows is a daily routine of exercises and activities that will build your "flirting muscles" and make you ever more attractive to women:

Saying hi

Remember this exercise from Chapter 3? By simply saying hi to six women a day, you'll be interacting with women and improving your flirting skills. Use the other approaches we've taught you so far in this book so you can master the art of approaching and interacting with women.

Smile

You must smile at women. You probably think you smile now, but you don't really. You should practice your smile in the mirror—to be big enough to be noticed, your smile will probably have to be bigger than you are used to. Smiling sends the message that you are open, friendly, and fun to talk to. Start smiling immediately!

Winking and waving

Much of flirting is in how you move your face and body, rather than what you say. One of our students tells us about being on a subway in New York City. A gorgeous black woman got on the train and sat across from him, a few seats up. "I wished I had the nerve to go sit next to her and talk to her," he told us, "but I didn't, so I used the 'wink and wave.' I winked at her, smiled, and waved when I caught her eye. She smiled back, and to my amazement, she came over and sat down next to me!" They ended up kissing on that same train ride, and later having sex at her apartment, simply because he was willing to do some simple flirting, the "wink and wave."

Stopping while it's still fun

Men who are shy and learning how to flirt frequently stay at parties or flirt with women for too long. When you are learning to flirt, it's wise to stop while it's still fun.

One of our students, Michael, had this problem. He was shy, but was committed to getting over it. So when he flirted with a woman, he'd make himself stay around her until she basically asked him to leave. "I'd start out pumped up, but as the interaction dragged on and on, I'd feel more and more uncomfortable and humiliated. I didn't know it was okay to leave while I was still having fun with her. I guess I thought that as long as it was going well, I should stay." After learning this, he was able to flirt with more women more successfully, and to have a lot more fun doing it.

Look into her eyes "too long"

This is simply holding eye contact a little bit longer than you normally would. While you are conversing with her, you want to be sure to have eye contact at least some of the time. At least once it's a good idea to hold the eye contact a little "too long," just a fraction too long, so there's a brief, more intimate moment between you.

The "good-bye" compliment

The "good-bye" compliment works well when leaving while it's still fun. If you are at a party, bar, or other social engagement, the "good-bye" compliment allows you to do some more aggressive flirting, even if you are very timid.

The "good-bye" compliment makes use of the fact that most any man can generate enough confidence to say one flirty thing to a woman. The problem, for some men, comes right after he says something flirty. What should he do then? What if she doesn't like it? What if she gets mad, or looks at him like he's something she scraped off her shoe? How to handle the tension? What to do next?

When you use the "good-bye" compliment, all those problems are solved. When you are ready to leave the bar, party, or whatever social engagement you are at (while you are still having fun, preferably), you simply approach the woman you've been too scared to approach, compliment her, and leave immediately.

These compliments can be simple, such as "I've gotta go, but before I do I just wanted to tell you that you look great and have a wonderful sense of style." They can also be more aggressive, such as "Wow, you look great. I just wanted you to know that if I didn't have to leave, I'd stay here and try to seduce you." After the "good-bye" compliment, you leave. It gets you flirting confidently, but with much less stress.

Ask, "What's the story behind that?"

Bruce was served at his favorite coffee shop. Sandy, the girl who was getting him his coffee, was a cute redhead in her early twenties, probably a coed at the local college. He noticed that she was wearing an

unusual necklace; it looked old and like it might have been from India. "Wow, that's a wonderful necklace," he told her. "What's the story behind that?"

This opened the conversational floodgates. She launched into a three-minute account of how she'd gone to India and got the necklace there in one of the most meaningful experiences of her life. She was open and sharing, and he learned a lot about what made her feel good.

For those few minutes she was back in India, having that peak experience again as she told him about it. By the end of her account, and their conversation about it, she was feeling very close to Bruce. He ended by saying to her, "Wow, you seem like a fascinating woman. I'd love to hear more about this sometime, and get to know you better. Can I call you?" She said yes; after all, if he was good enough to tell one of her most intimate experiences to, then he must be good enough to go out with, right?

"What's the story behind that?" is an immensely powerful flirting question. It gets most women to open up immediately and tell you intimate details about themselves. After they've told you these details, it's harder for them to think of you as a jerk—after all, if you were a jerk, why would they open up so much to you?

When you are talking to a woman, be it a salesgirl behind a counter or a woman at a party, notice if she is wearing anything that looks unusual or personal. It might be a pin, a necklace, a piece of clothing, or a bracelet. Notice it and ask her, "What's the story behind that?" It's a powerful conversation starter.

You've read a lot in this chapter about the specifics of flirting with women. You've read examples, general principles, and do's and don'ts. You've learned things you can do to start flirting more, today, and hopefully have become inspired about what's possible for your sex life if you start using these tools. We want you to use them, and be successful with women, but our experience shows that one question holds men back from actually using this flirting material: "What do I do if I 'blow it' with a woman?"

Men mean different things by "blowing it," but their fears have some general qualities in common. They are often afraid that they'll become flustered and not know what to say. They are afraid that the woman will just stare at them, terrified, like a deer in oncoming headlights. They are afraid that instead of seeming funny, they'll seem offensive.

Well, first the bad news. If you really are practicing, all of this will almost certainly happen to you. Women will respond to your witty openings with stunned silence. Sometimes you'll get flustered. Sometimes women will seem scared of you. It's all part of learning to flirt, and it even happens to master seducers. There's just no way around it.

Look, you have a choice, both with women and in life. You can choose to not try anything until you are absolutely sure things will go exactly the way you want them to, or you can throw yourself into life and trust that it'll come out okay. If you wait to flirt with women until you think you can do it "good enough," you will never flirt, and never be a success with women. And, incidentally, if you take this approach to life, and never try anything you aren't sure is going to work, then you'll never be a success in life. You'll be trapped in only doing what you've done before, again and again. That kind of behavior will never take you where you want to go, in any area of your life.

And now the good news: If you practice, you will succeed. Sure, there will be the occasional problem. But if you hang in there, you will get women.

It makes sense to think about your personal definition of success. We suggest that you define a successful interaction with a woman as an interaction in which you learn something about seduction. If you learned something, the interaction was successful. If you failed to learn something, then you failed, and you can make the interaction a success by figuring out what you learned. If you make this your personal definition of success, no matter what you do, you won't have really "blown it," and you can feel good about yourself.

6

A Crash Course
in Romance:
How to Sweep Her
Off Her Feet
and Into Your Bed

On a beautiful spring afternoon, Simon picked up his girlfriend Molly from her job. Earlier that day he had called her and suggested they go on a secret outing. "Expect the unexpected," he said. "Only pack a light jacket, and bring boots that can get muddied. Leave the rest up to me." Throughout the day Molly looked forward to seeing him, excited about the adventure ahead. She even told a few of her friends, "I don't know what to expect. Simon is so unpredictable. He always keeps things so exciting."

As she walked toward his car, Simon got out, hugged her, kissed her lips lightly, and whispered, "You look more beautiful than ever. I've been looking forward to seeing you all day." He then opened the car door. Fresh flowers, a card, and a few Hershey's kisses were waiting for her. As they began driving toward country highways near the outskirts of town, Simon popped in a tape of *her* favorite music.

After driving for nearly an hour down gorgeous country roads, they arrived at a remote nature preserve famous for its view of a river from a high rock ridge. It was a perfect spot on a perfect day that would inspire anyone to feel joyous and excited.

Simon knew that Molly loved nature and wasn't allergic to grasses or pollens. These details are essential when planning the perfect romantic date. (If she was allergic to something in nature, Simon would have planned the date totally differently.) This outing was custom-designed to melt Molly's heart (*not* her sinuses).

Simon had meticulously planned this event. He thought out every detail ahead of time. That made it easier for him to relax and have fun with Molly. It was in his self-interest to plan ahead.

As they walked along the ridge, holding hands, Simon was very happy with himself, basking in his success at sweeping Molly off her feet. After fifteen minutes of hiking, they relaxed at a beautiful spot. Simon pulled the blanket around them and they began kissing. She thanked him for being such a wonderful boyfriend and for going through all the work to have the date go well.

The view from the ridge was breathtaking. Molly wrapped her arms around Simon's neck and they kissed passionately, like hungry lovers. They ended up on top of a huge flat rock with the blanket under them.

After they lay together on the rock for a while, the temperature started dropping and they got dressed and headed back to their car. They laughed together, imagining how crazy their friends would think they were to be out in the woods, partially undressed, and totally turned on. Simon pulled out a gift for Molly. It was a necklace that fit her sense of style perfectly. She was thrilled at the gift.

In the near dark Simon took Molly down an alternative path, one that was much quicker than the one they'd used to get up the hill. Once again, Simon's planning paid off. They arrived at their car quickly. Molly even commented that she was impressed with how familiar he was with this park.

They soon left the park for the next adventure. Simon pulled out a map and navigated them to an out-of-the-way, elegant, cozy restaurant. Simon had made reservations ahead of time. They sat together, held hands, ate,

and drank wine while sitting beside a huge window overlooking pine trees and woods.

During dinner Simon pulled out more small gifts. One was a stuffed bear. It was something cute and cheap that he knew she'd like. They had seen stuffed animals in a store window a few weeks before, and she had mentioned how much she liked this particular one. The other gift was a book of poetry they'd looked at and read from at a bookstore months ago. Simon had kept the title in the back of his mind, waiting for a perfect opportunity to buy it for Molly. Covertly, he thought it would be great to read the poems to her while they were in bed together.

After a slow-paced meal they left to go back home. Simon drove straight to Molly's place and she invited him in. Simon let her get a head start toward her apartment so he could enter with more secret gifts. A few minutes later, he entered with a few items in wrapping paper. She tore the paper open like a kid on Christmas and discovered sexy lingerie, a bottle of wine, and massage oil, all the fixings for a romantic night alone. Molly pulled Simon into her bedroom. They made love all night long.

LIGHTING THE FIRES OF ROMANCE

Romance is the focus of this chapter. If you want success with women, you must be skilled in romance. You must understand how to create romantic situations and feelings in women. All women love romance and the attention it focuses on them. While all women are not looking for the exact same thing, and desires vary greatly, all women do want the feelings that come from being romanced, and commonalties do exist. And there are ways to think about specific situations and interactions that will produce romantic interactions and feelings in a woman. You will learn these in this chapter.

If you want a short-term relationship, romance is a large part of it. You have to sweep a woman off her feet if you want to get her into your bed. She must be taken by the experiences you provide for her if you expect her to want to have sex with you. Romance is the key to melting her heart and having her want to have you. In a long-term relationship, romance is what

holds it all together over time. Romance is what will have the intimacy and sex last over years and years together. Romance is what will make the relationship stay "fresh" and fun.

It's a man's job is to bring the romance to relationships with women. If you want a steady supply of sex with a woman, romance is your meal ticket. It is worth making the effort to study this topic and become a romantic master.

We make a distinction between sex symbols and romance masters. Guys like James Dean were sex symbols because of their looks and attitudes on screen, but they had little skill in being romantic. John F. Kennedy was able to sleep with many women because of his power and status, not because of his skill in seduction. Someone like Casanova, however, was able to "be" romantic and embody classic romantic moves. Romance masters like Casanova and Don Juan got the way they were by being generative. They were generous with women and were able to give them exactly what they most want.

In the example that started this chapter, Simon acted the part of the romance master with Molly. He not only swept her off her feet, but created a lasting bond between them that would work to his advantage for a long time to come. He created a memorable experience, tailored precisely to her. Molly would later look back on their magical afternoon together the same way she would a vacation or a cruise. And romance isn't only applicable in long-term relationships, like Simon and Molly's. A relationship at any stage will be accelerated and sexualized by romance.

For women, romance is an individual, highly personal, intimate, and loving experience. Women experience a certain "otherworldly" quality about romance. Because girls often learn to value romance at an early age, they are well prepared to respond to your romantic moves. Books and even cartoons aimed at kids all show situations in which women are swept off their feet, saved by daring and brave men, or rescued from castle towers. Women are socialized to expect and want men to romance them. Men, on the other hand, often try to fight this fact. The authors, however, have accepted it and used it to improve our relationships with women and to increase our successes. You can fight all you want, but if you want success, you will learn to be consistently romantic.

When Simon took Molly to the bluff and brought out a surprise necklace, Molly felt romanced. When she first entered his car, she could see from the card, candy, and flowers that she was being romanced. The combination of having all the details handled, of having Simon taking care of her, of his generosity and planning, and of the excitement of it all, created a feeling inside Molly that was magical and mysterious.

Women love to know you are thinking about them. When they realize that you are, they feel romanced. They want to imagine you are hanging around thinking about them, like they often are of you. Even if you aren't, you need to take actions that make them think you are. They want to know that you appreciate it when they give their bodies to you. They want to be certain that, if they are going to be in a relationship, you respect them. One of the main reasons Molly was so thrilled was that she realized Simon had put so much thought into the experience and he was thinking of her while shopping and creating the date. She felt special. In some situations it isn't even the gift itself; it is the fact that you thought of the woman when you weren't with her that makes her happy.

Be aware: Romance is not a "one-size-fits-all" proposition. It is defined by the woman you are romancing. If you buy her flowers, for instance, and she hates them, that's not romantic. Some women may think it's romantic if you purchase fake blood, bite her neck, and pretend you are a vampire. It is completely subjective. You need to look to her reaction to determine if you were successful in your romance or not.

For example, Bill had been dating Karen for a few weeks. They liked each other, but didn't connect as well as he thought they could, and the sex certainly wasn't happening. They had kissed and fooled around a few times, but it never seemed to "click." After attending a seminar with one of our trainers, Bill realized that he had failed to provide her with any romance. He was trying to push the sex too quickly and never put any attention on "charming her." He realized that he wasn't giving her what she really wanted: romance.

The next week, Bill set up an evening experience for Karen. He purchased a few inexpensive but nicely wrapped gifts and took her out to dinner. He did the things he thought *she* would like and kept his attention on her. He restrained himself from talking about work and how much he

looked forward to deer hunting season a few weeks away. Immediately, they seemed to get along much better, and had "deep" conversations. After dinner, they went to his house and talked and kissed in front of his fireplace. That night, they had sex for the first time.

Ironically, when Bill stopped focusing on his own needs, sex just happened naturally without any pressure on his part. We propose that sex will just seem to happen as soon as you refocus onto the woman. Romance is the way you shift this focus.

A form of psychology called Neuro-Linguistic Programming (NLP) contends that people experience love and appreciation in different ways. Some women feel loved when you touch or hug them. They connect through physical contact. Other women experience love when you say certain things to them. Certain words and phrases are what give them the feeling of love. Still others feel loved only when you buy them things, when they can see what you have purchased.

The same is true with romance. Some women feel romantic only when you say certain things to them. They may need romantic poetry or sweet comments in order to feel romanced. Others need physical contact like kisses, hugs, massages, and other touch-related experiences. Still others need presents and unusual experiences like trips to new places.

Let's get into the specifics. A romantic situation is one that takes a woman out of her day-to-day routine and into a special world. Simon achieves this by taking Molly into a new environment. He drives her out on country roads, into areas they rarely visit. He also creates a mood by giving her gifts and planning experiences for her ahead of time. Simon successfully creates this date as an "event," not just another night out.

You don't need to create as elaborate an outing as Simon to have a memorable date. You could just as easily take her to a cultural event, exotic restaurant, or even spend an evening of pampering at home. The one requirement is that it is special and out of the ordinary.

Along the same lines, you could also look at romance as a celebration of being together. This celebration is that you can fully be with her, enjoying her company, and having fun in the process. If you are not enjoying yourself and having fun, what is the point of going out with a woman anyway? So much of our lives is spent working at jobs. Most of us don't even like the

jobs we're at. So why not fully have fun and celebrate being with her when you are together? Even if it is a one-night stand, why not play full-out?

Romantic masters live life fully, knowing that magic happens only in the present moment. They don't waste time imagining the future or bitching about the past. Imagine how different it would be if you interacted with women as if each interaction was a celebration. We are not getting all mushy or New Age-y on you; we are simply proposing a way to act and interact with women that will provide the most fun, ease, and sexually prosperous experience possible.

SECRETS OF COURTING

If you are looking for a girlfriend or a long-term relationship, you will have to court the woman to some degree. We define courting as a process in which your actions "prove" to a woman over time that you want to be with her. The term itself has links to medieval times of kings and queens, knights in shining armor defending the court. In these times courting was a long process during which the man, boy, or prince had to prove his worth not only to the girl or princess, but also to her parents, the community, and whomever else happened to be around.

Fortunately, you don't have to jump through nearly as many hoops, but these same ideas are still very much alive. Women want you to prove to them that you are worthy of having them. Sure, this is not the most feminist idea in the world, but after interviewing hundreds of women for this book about what they look for in dating partners and how they select a man, we have determined that the medieval notion of courting remains important today.

The key to courting is to prove that you are patient. You are demonstrating that you are dependable, honest, good, moral, and that you have other noble qualities. In short, you are proving that you really want her as an individual, not just a one-night stand. This means that you consistently pursue her over time. Most women, especially those worthy of having a long-term relationship with you, want to know that you like them for more than just their bodies and sex. While in a short-term relationship, sex is probably your primary objective, in a longer-term relationship, it isn't.

When you court a woman, you are getting to know her and creating an opening for her to "give herself to you" over time.

The flip side to courting is that you also get to "test her out." Is she a bitch to you, or someone you can spend hours and hours with without fighting? Is she complimentary toward you, or is she demanding? If she is nasty, mean, or doesn't fit with your picture, you can stop dating her as well.

As you read this, you might think it isn't right to "prove yourself" to a woman. You may think she should just take you for who you are. Or maybe you think this idea is ridiculous and outdated. Nothing could be further from the truth. If you are naive enough to think that women don't still want you to court them and sweep them off their feet, you are dead wrong. While you *might* get a one-night-stand without courting, it is unlikely you will get much else. We will go much more in-depth about how to maintain a long-term relationship in a later chapter. For now, we just want you to understand courting's basic importance.

Here are a few question she will be asking herself about you. You must get over these hurdles during the courting period:

- Do I trust him?
- How much do I trust him?
- Does he have a violent temper?
- Does he want a long-term relationship?
- Is he just a player?
- How far will he go to prove himself for me?
- How demanding can I be?
- Can he stand it if I withhold sex?
- Would he be a good father?
- Is his career going well?
- Does he have drive to succeed in the world?
- Do my friends like him?
- Would my parents like him?
- Is he attractive?

Overcoming these hurdles takes time. Strangely, our experience shows that even women who say they aren't looking for a long-term relationship

usually ask themselves questions like these. It's a fact of life that you will have to prove yourself to women you have sex with. Romance, it turns out, is the fastest way to do this.

ROMANCE IS NOT WEAKNESS

Having said all that, here's an important caveat: Being romantic is *not* the same as being weak, a pushover, supplicating, or groveling for sex. It is *not* the same as selling yourself out, pretending to agree when you actually disagree, giving things you don't want to give, or doing things you don't want to do. This is an important point, so let's focus on it for a minute so you get it right your first time out of the gate.

There are two ways that you can be romantic: You can be romantic in a way that hides your true self, is supplicating and weak (*not* the way we recommend), or you can be romantic in a way that shows who you really are, is forthright, generative, and strong (which *is* the way that we suggest).

Remember this: While most successful seducers succeed with women because they create romantic connections with them, it is critically important that you also provide the woman some sense of challenge to show her that you are a strong, independent man rather than a slimy weasel who will do or say anything to get into her pants. (You may actually *be* such a slimy weasel, but even then you'll have better seduction success if you show the woman you are strong and independent.)

Remember back in Chapter 2, when we talked about challenging a woman appropriately? We said that it's good for a woman to know that sometimes you may disagree with her, and that your approval is something that she sometimes has to work for.

So when you are being romantic, you also need to be true to yourself. You do this by asking yourself these questions:

1. *Do I want to be doing what I'm doing?* If you don't want to be doing the romantic activities you have planned, you planned poorly. Remember how a successful seducer makes life (and the seduction) work for him? It can be a real joy to do romantic activities with a woman you are seducing.

When you are planning your romantic activities, remember that *you* need to enjoy them, too.

2. *Do I want to be giving what I'm giving?* Sometimes men fall into the trap of thinking that if they simply give enough—enough time, enough money, enough listening to her problems with an empathetic ear—the women they desire will feel so overwhelmed with love that she'll spread her legs for sure.

Well, listen up: Giving too much does not make a seduction work. It will simply end with her using you, her possibly thanking you, and her definitely going off with another man. You make sure you don't give too much by asking yourself, "Do I want to be giving as much as I'm giving?" If you feel like you are giving too much, you probably are. Don't confront her about it—that would be moronic—simply back off, focus on what brings fun to *you,* and balance will come back into the seduction.

3. *Do I actually agree with what I'm agreeing with?* Sometimes when you are seducing a woman, you'll be tempted to simply agree with every word out of her mouth because it's easier, and because it seems like the fastest route to getting her in bed. But that's not true: Agreeing with everything a woman says is not particularly romantic, and it's actually the fastest way to seeming utterly boring to her, and even to pushing her away.

If she says something you disagree with, you don't have to hold your tongue. Review what we said in Chapter 2 about the best way to disagree with a woman—state your opinion and be willing to move on. Remember, disagreeing is almost never a big deal unless *you* make it a big deal. If you disagree and move on, you show that you are a strong, independent man . . . and you also show that you are a man she may have to do some work to get.

Keep these points in mind as you romance a woman, and you'll enjoy it a lot more *and* have a lot more sexual success.

HOW TO WRITE A LOVE NOTE
THAT MAKES HER MELT

The historic romancer was skilled in writing love letters. Because he rarely saw the woman before they were married, he often had to communicate through letters. Letters were how he created hot romance, and you must learn to write them, too.

Most women love letters. We have both had wonderful success using love letters as tools for seduction and to aid the courting process. For us, these letters have taken the form of emails, cards, notes, and letters. Women love the thought and effort it takes you to write a note and send it off to them. It can be a few stanzas of Shakespearean poetry, or something simple like "I miss your lips touching mine" or "I can't wait until our next secret outing this weekend" or "When we left each other Friday night I forgot to tell you how beautiful your eyes are." Some women can also handle the hard stuff, like "I can't wait to get you in bed," but that's risky and to be done only after you've been having sex with her. It's up to you.

Let's look at this from a purely economic standpoint for a second. For $3.50 you can buy a great-looking card from a specialty shop. Then, for the price of a stamp, you can send the card. These simple actions can easily cause the woman to melt in her seat. Is it worth it or not? Even e-cards—those free, online cute cards that are delivered to the woman by a link in an email—are great for romance. Perhaps it's one of the differences between men and women that men find e-cards to be barely any better than spam, while women find them loving and romantic. Whatever the reasons, cards and e-cards work.

Here are some tips for writing love notes. First, shorter is better. A few great lines that pack a punch are much better than some long, cheesy monologue that offers more opportunities for the woman to dislike the note. It is better to leave her wanting more than to overdo it and have her confused or thinking you are lying or manipulating her.

Here are the three elements of every successful love note:

1. Acknowledging how wonderful she is

The more specifically you can compliment her the better. For example, commenting on how her "beautiful brown eyes reflect in a candlelit room" is much better than commenting on how nice her eyes are. Here are a few of the top things to comment on:

- Her hair
- Her eyes
- How sweet she is
- How you just love to look into her eyes
- Her lips
- The beautiful way she moves

Avoid saying overtly sexual things about her body. Here's a few to avoid commenting on:

- How great her breasts would look in a wet T-shirt
- How awesome her lips would be for oral sex
- How great her ass looks in tight jeans
- How you wonder what she'll look like in the morning

2. How great she makes you feel

Next talk about how wonderful she makes you feel. Once again, say something specific. Here are a few comments to make:

- When we are together, I lose myself.
- I get that warm feeling all over when we are together.
- I've never felt so comfortable with a woman before.

3. You are thinking of her

Lastly, mention that you are thinking about her and can't wait to see her again. Here are a few possibilities:

- I can't stop thinking about you.
- I am holding my breath until I see you next.
- The image of you won't fade from my mind—and I never want it to.
- You are special in my life beyond words.

If you must enhance the letter, go through Steps 1 and 2 a few more times. When you begin, however, we recommend you keep the notes short and sweet. And don't forget to sign it!

THE SIX KEYS TO ROMANCE

Now that you are beginning to get a feel for sensuality—no pun intended—you are ready to start learning about romance. There are six keys to romantic behavior with women. Here they are:

1. Romance is generous, it's never needy

In Chapter 3 we showed you how to get over being needy by getting the validation for your life from somewhere other than from women. But how do you become generous? When you are being romantic, the focus is on her, not you. You have to put out for her, not vice versa. This is how you express your generosity in a dating situation.

At first it will probably be hard to put the focus on her. You may resent having to do the up-front work for the date; you may feel like she should be acknowledging you for taking all the risks you've taken to flirt with her and ask her out. Either get over it or plan some other romantic outing that you can feel good about. After you've practiced being generous for a while, you'll find that it's much more fun than being angry. If you get resentful, remember that you are doing all this for a reason. By being sensitive, sweet, and generous, you melt her heart and open the road to sex. But again—you are not just a giving machine, without needs. We would never send you into a situation to be a doormat, or to be a man who gives and gives, receiving nothing in return. In later chapters we will discuss how to cut off relationships with women who give you nothing back, and when to do so. For now, however, you must do the up-front work. She won't do it, and if you don't, you won't succeed.

Generosity is really a basic principle of being a powerful man. Men who command respect are not needy, groveling worms. They are men who are mature, know when to give and when to take, and who are not looking for people, especially women they desire, to take care of them.

If, for example, you seem needy, and try to get a woman to "reward" you for being good to her, she will likely and reasonably think you are a jerk who's only trying to manipulate her. If you are generous, but not a doormat, it will make all the difference.

2. Romance is patient

When you are creating the perfect romantic situation, don't push her too hard. We all hate to be patient, but during a seduction, it's necessary. Nothing turns women off more quickly than a guy obviously trying to score and only hitting on her for sex. It doesn't seem romantic at all. Impatience is especially devastating after an evening of seduction. If you push too hard at the end of the date, she will probably think the whole night was just a scam, a ploy to get her to have sex with you. It will blow all the work you've put in up to that point. The solution is to be patient and learn to go with the flow.

Jason, for example, always blows dates by being too forward and intense with women. Instead of being patient, he always goes for sex right away when a little bit of patience would serve him much better.

On a recent date he took Catherine out to dinner and a dance club. He immediately started "dirty dancing" with her, shoving his pelvis into her hip. He failed to notice that she didn't like it and kept pulling away from him. In fact, he was hurting her by shoving himself into her too hard. Later, when she seemed noticeably upset, he learned the truth from her. "Why didn't you just tell me I was hurting you? I didn't know any better," he said truthfully.

Jason is what we like to call a "helpless idiot." He has no idea how to charm a woman or be seductive. He is still caught up in being an adolescent with women. He still wants and even expects instant gratification without being sensitive or patient. We all do stupid things, like Jason, and until we realize they don't work, we continue to do them and continue to fail. Remember, be patient, and initiate sex while also going at her speed.

3. Romance is truly appreciative of her

As we said before, the focus of romance is on *her*. It is your job to romance her and give her the romantic feelings she wants. Start by appreciating her beauty, her eyes, her intelligence, her hair, or her apartment. You've got to understand that a woman cares deeply about her appearance. She'll spend hours teasing her hair to look just "right." She will put on an extra-special dress, wear perfume she thinks will attract you, and wear the perfect bracelet because it matches her shoes. If you can notice any of these easy-to-miss details and tell her so, it will certainly impress her.

You can also show your appreciation of her by focusing on the details in your own appearance. Even though you don't care if your socks match, or if your gold football medallion matches your tie, women do. Look over Chapter 3 again, and make sure you are paying attention to the romantic details of your own look.

Master romancers like Casanova understood how to really appreciate the beauty of a woman and make her feel like she was the most special person in the world. You must do this as well. By appreciating the details of her appearance, you convey to her that she is the only one in the world you would want to be with tonight, even if that isn't necessarily true. When she believes that you are totally focused on her, she will be much more likely to "reward" you with sex.

4. Romance has an air of the unexpected and unreal

Alert! Alert! This is very important, and will serve you in every step of your seduction. When we show you how to create a "seduction strategy," we will rely again and again on your understanding that romance has an air of the unexpected and unreal. Master giving women unexpected and unreal experiences, and you can have almost any woman you desire. Do this by creating surprises and doing things you normally wouldn't do:

- *Surprises.* Unexpected and unreal romantic situations often contain wonderful suprises. We started off this chapter with the example of Simon taking Molly out for a romantic afternoon. One of the reasons why the afternoon went so well was because Molly had no idea what

was going to happen next. By filling the afternoon with surprises, Simon was able to take her into another world, a world outside of their normal, day-to-day routine.

- *Doing things you normally wouldn't do.* One woman we interviewed told us that "if a man can capture my imagination and mind, he can have the rest." When you create activities that you normally wouldn't do, you show the woman you are with that you are fun, adventuresome, and, most important, that you are willing to go out of your way to make her feel good. To plan a romantic night, add the spice of the unreal and unexpected—go to a new part of town after a movie, or to an out-of-the-way bar after a romantic walk. You want her to feel like a queen, like a princess, like a character in a movie. Creating an out-of-the-way, romantic event is a wonderful way to do this.

5. Romance is confident

If you want to ruin a romantic moment, date, or conversation, be a guy who has no confidence and who isn't able to be bold. The man who has mastered romance is able to be confident in every moment with a woman. This is not being dominating or controlling. Rather, a man with confidence makes decisions, isn't wishy-washy, is able to be straight with a woman about his expectations and not be apologetic about his sexual or other desires.

Ken, for instance, is your typical sensitive man. He rarely makes the first move and is embarrassed when women touch him in public. Though he is thirty-five, his face looks like a twenty-year-old's. He has a successful job and makes a decent income, but few people respect him. Men usually think he is a wimp, with no real opinions, who is more concerned with catering to everyone's whims than to his own desires. When we told him about using romantic talk on a date, he didn't think he could tell a woman anything romantic. He was concerned that she would be offended. Needless to say, Ken had gone for the past three years without sex. To make it worse, his last girlfriend made him buy her presents ("Just look at my Amazon wish list" she would sigh), loan her his credit card, and even stole money from his house. Ken is a classic sensitive New Age guy whose inability to be confident about going for what he wants makes him a victim of his circumstances.

Isaac, on the other hand, is confident. Though it hasn't come naturally to him, he has learned to charm women and create romantic evenings that are very successful. Even better, he has sex whenever he wants.

Isaac has studied our material and learned to be confident on dates with women. "I often feel nervous before dates and sometimes even when I'm out with my date. I just don't let it get to me. I know the Seven Habits of a Highly Effective Seducer, and I've memorized them. I just keep going when I mess up, and women continue to be interested in me."

Specifically, Isaac is confident when giving a woman a card, paying for the date, opening the door for her, making the first move, kissing her, being decisive, and asking for follow-up dates.

You may be saying, "Wait a minute! You just told me to be patient! Now you're telling me to be confident and bold! What's going on here?" The truth is, you must be both patient and confident. While you are waiting for her to be ready to be your lover, you must be confident and certain that everything is okay, and that you are fine, no matter what happens during the seduction. This confidence will give you the ability to be as patient as you need to be.

6. Details

We know it is totally redundant to even mention the importance of details at this point of the game, but because men are so resistant to integrating essentials into dates, we are mentioning it once again. Details will make or break the date. Use "take care of the details" as your mantra when setting up all dates.

TALK THE TALK

You can probably remember what it felt like the first time you really "got it" that someone loved you, can't you? And perhaps you can remember what it felt like the best time you experienced "love at first sight." And when you think about one of the best times you've ever had with a woman, what do you feel?

Sometimes you just feel connected to someone. Have you ever felt an overwhelming trust, even though you may not know why you felt it? Like

when you met someone, and it just seemed that you were connected, as if you had known each other forever. Do you know what we mean?

Most people will have emotional reactions to the preceding two paragraphs. That's what makes those paragraphs examples of romantic talk. Questions and descriptions of romantic feelings will usually create those feelings in the person you are talking to. This is why you must talk the talk of romance.

As we've said before, when you describe a feeling, the person listening will automatically remember times when he or she felt the same way. So, for example, if you ask a woman what was the first time that she felt totally swept off her feet and completely enthralled with a man, she will automatically remember that experience. She will begin to reexperience that feeling in the moment.

This is a very useful tool in creating romance. By spending a little time before the date, you can memorize many romantic questions that will help to create a state of mind in the woman. You can also discuss romantic topics with her and get the same results.

Here are a few examples of romantic questions you can ask a woman:

- What is it like when you feel totally happy and carefree?
- Imagine that you have a week of vacation with the man of your dreams. What would you do next?
- What was the most romantic evening of your life?
- What was the most romantic movie you've ever seen?
- Which actor do you find most attractive and why?
- What does it feel like when you are in love?
- How do you know you are in love?
- What is your favorite thing about kissing?
- Who was your best boyfriend and why?
- Describe your favorite princess story.
- What did you think romance was like when you were a little girl?

Asking these questions will put her in a more romantic mood. We'll go into more detail about this in the next chapter.

Be warned, however: Not only positive feelings can be created this

way. We could get you in the mood to be scared and edgy if we asked you to recall a time when you felt threatened by another man. "What was it like?" we might ask. "Tell us all the details. What were you thinking and feeling? Did you have adrenaline pumping through your veins? How did that feel? Was the guy big or small? What did he look like? Did he have a weapon? Did you feel victimized?" Can you notice as you read this how we could psych you up to feel scared? This is the mistake you make with women when you get into conversations about violence against women, war, and rape. When you do this, she starts imagining all that violence happening to her. Don't allow the discussion to get into descriptions of violence and horror, or you will destroy the romantic mood entirely.

This may seem like complicated stuff, but let's look at your competition. The average guy is nowhere near understanding these ideas. He treats women as he would treat really sexy men, doesn't create special occasions for them, doesn't treat them as if they are special, rarely compliments them, and is either needy or a bully to them. He's completely non-sensual and is resentful that he has to put the focus on the woman if he wants to get sex. He is as likely to describe something violent, and make women feel scared, as he is to accidentally say something romantic. Heck, women tell us that most men don't know enough to bathe before dates, much less write romantic love notes. If you avoid the common mistakes, and do even half of the romantic things we recommend in this chapter, you'll leave women desiring you and panting for more.

7

The Priming Date

Wendy worked at Bruce's health club. While she wasn't glamorous, she was fit, with a small, tight body. After flirting with her a few times, Bruce realized that she was an intellectual. She was reading a book almost every time he saw her, and she told him she was working on her PhD in zoology. She seemed cute and sweet. He found her attractive and asked her out for coffee. She said yes, and they arranged to meet at a coffee shop near the health club at four o'clock the following Tuesday. "I'll only have about an hour," Bruce told her, "but that should be enough time for us to explore each other a little bit."

Bruce asked Wendy on what we call a *priming date* (though, of course, he would never call it that to her). The purpose of a priming date is to meet with a woman for just long enough to create a romantic connection with her, to get her thinking about you in a romantic way, and to find out the best way to sweep her off her feet on the *seduction date*. The priming date also gives you an opportunity to decide if this really is a woman you want to pursue. It's cheap, and being only a coffee or meeting for a quick drink, it allows most women to feel more comfortable than a big multi-hour extravaganza.

It's usually wrong to ask a woman out for an extravaganza, such as to a movie and dinner, for your first date, because you won't be ready. You won't know enough about her to arrange an efficient seduction, and thus you will

be more likely to make devastating mistakes with her. If you ask her out for an evening event first, she's more likely to be put off by the intensity and intimacy of such a first date. You appear calmer and less desperate when you ask a woman out for coffee or a drink, rather than for an entire evening. You are telling her you want to see her, but aren't needy and trying to rush things. This lets a woman know that you have a life outside of seeing her, which is very important, especially with very attractive women.

On a priming date, you are priming her for your seduction. It's like preparing a camp stove before lighting it; done properly, you only need a few simple moves to create quite a hot little fire. Without proper preparation, you are always working too hard to get what you want to happen. With priming, you leave the first interaction ready to go.

THE THREE ELEMENTS OF A PRIMING DATE

1. The priming date is short

When you are seducing a woman, you want to spend as little time with her as possible before having sex, because the less time you spend with her, the less time you have to make a mistake fatal to the seduction. You want to take as much time as necessary, but not an instant more. Every unnecessary interaction is just another opportunity to bungle it up.

Before the date, a woman is looking for reasons to get rid of you. Earlier we talked about how, when a woman dates someone, her orderly existence becomes shaken up. All of us resist change, even change that would make us happy. In some corner of her mind, the woman you are interested in is looking for some justification to get you out of her life. The more time you give her to find one, the more likely she is to do just that.

Once a woman has had sex with you, the rules change. Now instead of trying to justify getting rid of you, she's trying to justify why you were worth having sex with in the first place. Instead of being on the hunt for your bad points, she's more likely to be on the lookout for the good. If you spend lots and lots of time with her before sex, you spend too much time on the wrong side of the equation. Priming dates, while important, should be short.

When Bob went out with Marcella for the first time, he disobeyed this

rule. He had told her that the date would last no longer than an hour. He met her for coffee. Things went so well he figured he would stretch the date out even longer. Eventually Marcella had her fill of him and suggested that it was time for her to leave. "Oh, do you have to? Gee, when can we go out again?" Bob found himself whining. He had put himself into a powerless, one-down position and, as a result, looked like a jerk.

When Bruce met Wendy for a beer at a bar, he knew that if things went well, that was an even *better* reason to keep the date short. "Well, I really have to go," he said after thirty minutes. Wendy looked sad that he was leaving, because she was having such a good time. He left her wanting more rather than satisfying, or even overdoing, her interest in him. As a result, she was very receptive to his idea that they go out again.

We suggest a priming date be thirty minutes to seventy-five minutes long, and no longer. If you are having such a great time together, that's wonderful. Leave before you blow it, and invest her enjoyment of you into your seduction date.

2. The priming date takes place in coffee shops, mellow bars, or other quiet public places

Having the priming date in a public place, like a mellow bar, helps her feel safe and non-pressured. After all, she reasons, what can you do to her in a coffee shop or a bar? Contrast this to a first date where you invite the woman over for dinner at your house. That is a scary first date for most women. Many will find a reason to back out at the last moment. A coffee date, on the other hand, is in full view of everybody, so she knows she will be physically safe.

You want to choose a place that isn't too noisy, and where you won't run into your friends or hers. If you know that a certain coffee shop is a hangout for her and her friends, suggest a different one. You don't want her distracted, or showing off for her friends.

You shouldn't choose a restaurant. You want her to be focused on you, not her food. If you invite her out for a meal, she is more likely to see you as just a dinner companion or, worse, a ticket to a free meal. You don't want her to be distracted by the waiter or by the taste of her food. You want the focus to be on you and the romantic possibilities

between the two of you. Besides, a restaurant date will take longer, start to finish, and is more of an emotional commitment for her than a coffee date is.

When you ask her out, you must have a place in mind. Be sure the location of that place is clear. One student, Larry, asked a woman to meet him at "the Cafe Espresso on Main Street," not realizing that there were actually *two* franchises of that cafe on opposite ends of the street. His date went to one, and he went to the other, and they never did meet up. Be clear where the date is, and be able to give her simple directions if she needs them.

3. The priming date is not a time to socialize

By "socialize" we mean "hang out and talk without a purpose." That is the *last* thing you want to be doing before you've had sex with her. Hanging out and talking without a purpose is something you do with your male friends. With a woman, you must remember that dating and friendship are completely different, and cancel each other out. You can't serve both masters. You can only do one or the other. It's like drinking and driving; you either get to drink, or you get to drive. You can't do both. You must decide whether a woman is going to be a friend or a potential lover, and stick with it. Just hanging out and talking without an outcome in mind will default you into "friend" mode every time.

Your purpose for the priming date is to charm her, find out if you are attracted to her and interested in seeing her again, and to get her ready for the next level of your seduction. This chapter discusses exactly how you go about accomplishing these noble goals.

BEFORE THE PRIMING DATE

As you are well aware by now, you must do much of the work of the date before the date actually begins. In this way, dating a woman is like painting a house. When you think about painting, you probably imagine using a brush or roller or sprayer, slowly and methodically covering the surface of the building with paint.

If you've done much painting, you know that the actual painting is

only the most glamorous part of the project. In advance you have to prepare the surface, which can take a lot longer than the painting itself does. You have to get off the old paint, layer by layer. You spend days scraping, or slopping on paint-removing chemicals. You have to make sure the wood itself is sound, and if it isn't, you have to repair or replace it. Only once you have everything set up properly does the painting go easily and smoothly. Even then, you have to put on a priming coat before you put on the color you really want. If you refuse or forget to do the pre-work, your painting experience will be a disaster.

Likewise, when you think about dating a woman, your mind probably tends to jump right to the actual date itself. After you've practiced our techniques, however, you'll understand that the date itself is only the most glamorous part of the project. Just as you must prepare the surface before you paint, you must prepare for the date before you go on it. The downside is this takes some time and energy. The upside is if you do it properly, it will make the date a thousand times more successful.

Here's what you must do to prepare yourself for a priming date:

Think about what kind of woman she might be

You probably know her well enough to make some guesses about the kind of woman she is. Is she an intellectual, a party girl, an artist, a plain Jane, a shy fawn, an overworked mom, a rebel, or another type we've left out? Making these judgments beforehand will help you in your preparations. If the woman is an intellectual, you know you'll want to prepare to be smart and funny. It might make sense to bring along some intelligent book you are reading, so she can see and comment on it. If she is more of a rebel, it might be appropriate to bring forth the more troublemaking part of yourself. This would be a time to wear your leather jacket and dark glasses. If she's an artist type, you might want to be reading a magazine on performance art when she comes in. This isn't to say that you should invent parts of yourself that don't really exist. That would be too much work, and wouldn't work well, anyway. What you should do is take dating these different types of women as opportunities to bring out and explore the different sides of yourself. This will make the date more fun for you, and make you more successful with your prospect.

Set up the date at a time and place that truly work for you

Remember, she may well not show up (more on handling this later). If you inconvenience yourself terribly to get there, and she blows you off, you're going to feel pretty stupid.

This is actually pretty simple to do. Simply make sure that the date works for you, and don't agree to anything that doesn't. This doesn't mean that you become unwilling or intractable; any coffee date with a woman is going to be less convenient than sitting at home. But canceling an important meeting or driving two hours for a date with a woman who may not show up is simply unacceptable.

Know what you will do if she doesn't show up

Bring some work to do, or a great book to read. Be ready to flirt with the other women at the coffee shop. If you're in a bar, find other people to talk to before she arrives. Never *ever* let yourself get into a situation where you are sitting waiting for a woman to show up with nothing to do. It's humiliating and it makes you resentful. Your attitude should be that you are just as happy being there alone as you are with her showing up. Bringing things to do that will satisfy you is the best way to do this.

Remember your outcome

Before you go on the priming date, it's critical that you get clear about what you want your outcome to be. Do you want her to feel attracted to you, interested, aroused? Make sure you know how you want her to feel at the end of the date, so you'll have a target to shoot for, and a standard against which to measure possible topics of conversation.

Create a list of romantic and sensual questions you can ask her

We talked about the importance of romantic questions while flirting with a woman. Those questions are also important on the priming date. Remember, asking the proper romantic questions is one of the fastest ways to achieve your goal of getting her thinking romantically about you.

This isn't just "making conversation." This is where the rubber hits the road.

Most romantic questions have three parts:

1. The excuse
2. The description
3. The question

While this isn't always true, and the three parts aren't always in this order, if you follow this pattern, you'll be easily able to create romantic questions, which will get women talking about romance.

The *excuse* is the part where you briefly explain why you are about to ask the question. The excuse is something like "A friend of mine and I were talking about this, and I wonder about your opinion on it . . ." or "I saw a TV show last night that got me thinking about the idea of attraction . . ." or "I've been having a lot of fun lately asking people this question about romance . . ."

The second part is the *description*. Before asking the romantic question, briefly describe the feeling you want her to experience. This might be "It was so romantic, the way they felt drawn together, the chemistry slowly building until they had that romantic, passionate first kiss." It might be "Your heart just opened up, and you could feel your defenses dropping for that incredible man."

The third part is the *question* itself. It is "What was your first kiss like?" or "What's the most romantic thing you ever experienced?" Put it all together, and it looks like this:

- "You know, I saw a TV show last night where these two teenagers fell in love and were having their first kiss. It was so romantic, the way they felt drawn together, the chemistry slowly building until they had that romantic, passionate first kiss. It got me thinking . . . I'd be curious, what was your first kiss like?"
- "Do you remember the first time you fell in love? Everything seemed so fresh and new and amazing, remember? It was like that first time

when you really understand that someone really likes you, just the way you are. If you don't mind me asking, what was that like for you?"

- "My friend Mary was just telling me about the most romantic date she was ever on. It was amazing. Imagine this: You are out with a man you really like and find really attractive. You are sitting in this gorgeous outdoor restaurant, overlooking a lake. The autumn colors are just perfect. The air is fresh and smells so great, you feel like you don't even need to eat, just sit there and breathe that sweet air. Anyway, that's how she put it. And you have this incredible date as the sun goes down over the water, the stars come out, and then the moon rises, and the two of you feel so connected, so in love, you know what I mean? What would you say is your most romantic moment ever?"

- "I was having this discussion with my friend, and I wonder what you think. Do you believe in love at first sight? Where you see someone and you just feel that 'click,' and it's like, even though you are meeting for the first time, you feel like you've known him forever? Or does that feeling of attraction just build inside of you, slowly? Have either of these ever happened to you?"

- "Do you believe in destiny, like certain things or relationships are predestined to happen? I am sure you know the feeling when you see someone and you just feel that 'click,' and even though you are meeting for the first time, you feel like you've known him forever? Has that ever happened to you?"

- "My friend Suzy is falling in love. It's so fun to watch. She was telling me about meeting this man and feeling like she'd known him all her life. Like she felt like 'Oh, it's you,' even though they had just met. Have you ever met someone and just felt like you'd known him forever?"

- "I've been thinking how great it would be to take a vacation, and asking people what they've done that they really loved. It's been fascinating to hear about people's ideal vacation experiences. What's your absolute fantasy vacation?"

- "You know, it's interesting how different people feel special in different ways; it's like each person has his or her own code for feeling special, connected, and really loved. I'm curious: How do you know when a man really appreciates you?"

If these questions seem too personal, you can always ask questions about *women*, rather than about her. She'll tell you the same kind of answer, either way. For instance, instead of asking, "How do you know when a man really appreciates you?" you can ask, "How does a woman know when a man really appreciates her?" The answer will be the same.

Men tend to think the mood has to be right to ask questions like these. It's a tricky issue, because the mood that is right for these questions is created by questions precisely like these. By asking these and similar questions, you help build the romantic mood that makes this kind of talk appropriate. You've just got to jump in and start asking them.

Also, don't be afraid to memorize these questions word for word, exactly the way we've said them here. There's a huge difference between asking about a first kiss the way we put it here and saying, "Hey, what was your first kiss like?" with no excuse or description.

You also won't want to fire these questions off in a row. It'll sound odd. You're not interrogating her. If you do ask a romantic question, and then want to ask another one later, you can simply say, "I don't know why my mind seems so fixated on romance. Has that ever happened to you? Anyway, for some reason I'm wondering . . ." Be subtle and stay on task with these questions and it will greatly speed up the seduction process.

Learn from what she tells you

What she reveals about herself in these romantic conversations will be the base for the seduction date you will design for her later. If she tells you that her most romantic experience was when a man cooked for her, you'll want to make dinner for her next time. If she tells you she loves romantic walks, you'll want to set one up, complete with blankets and wine and cheese. Remember, you aren't just making random conversation. You have a job to do. The beauty of romantic questions is that they not only put her into a romantic mood, but also give you the data you need to get her clothes off as efficiently as possible. Pay attention to what she says. Excuse yourself to the bathroom to take notes if it'll help you remember. Definitely take notes right after the date, while it's still fresh in your mind.

Have answers to those romantic questions prepared

As you ask your romantic questions, you'll find that, aside from answering them, your date will often also ask them back to you. Very young, attractive women will often go an entire date without asking you *anything* about yourself. This is just as well. The less she learns about you, the less she can learn that will make her decide that she shouldn't date you. Much of the time, though, most women *will* ask romantic questions back to you and want your opinion as well. They'll give you an answer, and then say, "I don't know. What was your most romantic moment?"

The common mistake in this situation is to tell a woman about your most romantic moment as you experienced it. This is all well and good, but it doesn't necessarily forward the seduction. If you want to move forward, you must answer this question by describing your romantic experience, or a generic romantic experience, from her point of view. This gives you another opportunity to describe romantic feelings of attraction to her, and gets her even more into thinking about romance with you.

Here's how you do it. Suppose you asked your date, "What's it like when you feel really special and appreciated?" She answers, and finishes up with "Well, I guess that was it. What's it like when you feel special and appreciated?" Follow these guidelines, and you'll be golden:

- *Answer the question from her point of view.* The way you do this is to say, "You know what it's like when you . . . ?" You'd answer, "It's great when I feel special and appreciated. You know what it's like when you feel like someone is seeing you as you really are. That person cares deeply about you and just thinks you are really great?" It's also useful to describe those feelings in the present tense. This makes it easier for her to have those feelings *now*, rather than simply imagine having had them, once upon a time. Say, "It's like you can let go and be romantic," rather than "It's like you felt you could let go and be romantic." Both will work, but using the present tense works better.

- *Describe the feeling you want her to have.* Now describe the feelings

you want her to have, from her point of view. You might say, "It's like you feel as though you are melting, it's so great. You feel so connected, so much immediate trust, it's like you've known each other for years. Those are the most romantic moments for me."

- *Be general in what you reveal.* If you describe a specific experience, do not describe the woman you were with, or how crazy you were about her. This will only put off your current date. Say, "It was an incredible evening. You can imagine what it was like: walking under the open starry sky, the air, the perfect temperature, and the smell of flowers. Then later, great wine in a candlelit room. Just perfect, you know?" Don't say, "I was with Jessica. What a woman! She was so awesome and had an amazing body! The best time was when she'd go down on me for hours!" This will annihilate your current seduction. Keep your descriptions general so that your date can feel included.

Turn romantic questions into romantic conversations

The seduction date focuses on creating experiences to make a woman feel sexual and romantic toward you. The priming date focuses on creating conversations that give her those feelings. If you want her to feel romantically attracted and strangely fascinated, you'll have to design conversations about those topics. You turn your romantic questions into romantic conversations by asking conversation-extending questions. For instance, if you ask a woman, "What was the most romantic experience you ever had?" she may tell you, "It was at a restaurant in Italy. It was a perfect night, that's for sure." Don't let her stop there! Even though she's answered your question, you want her to elaborate, for two reasons. First, you want her to talk about her romantic experience so she'll remember how it felt, and start feeling that feeling now, with you. By explaining the memory, part of her will go back to that experience and begin to relive it. Second, you want to get data to use on the seduction date. If she's willing to tell you what worked on her before, you bet you want to listen! Here's a list of conversation-extending questions you can ask to keep romantic conversations going:

- "Wow. What was it about that that made you feel best?"
- "I am very impressed. Will you tell me more of the details?"
- "Fascinating. Tell me more about [some part of the experience]."
- "How did that make you feel?"
- "That's amazing. Have you felt that way since?"

The three steps to practicing talking on the date

When faced off with a real live woman, you might be nervous. So it makes sense to practice whatever you can beforehand, so that it's easier to do. For this reason, we suggest you practice your romantic questions and answers *out loud* before the date. We know it sounds silly, but it can really make a difference in how well you lead the conversation when it really counts. By practicing, you will get used to saying romantic things and begin to relax and speak with an easier flow. Use the following three steps of practice, and the romantic questions will melt any woman in sight:

First, practice the questions, as they are written above, out loud until you think you can say at least a few of them by heart. Second, imagine her responses, and practice saying the conversation-extending questions out loud as well. Third, practice answering all your romantic questions, in case she asks them back to you.

Create a list of interesting questions to ask her

Not all questions and conversations are going to lead to romantic conversations, but you need to prepare for both types of conversations. Your goal is to seduce her, and a big part of that is having her think you are interesting, intelligent, and deep. Asking interesting questions and having interesting answers are important components of that process.

When choosing questions, try to find open-ended questions that can lead to deeper and more intimate conversations. Avoid asking yes or no questions, because those types of questions tend to end a conversation rather than expand it. You might ask a woman what was the most fun event she has had in the past three months. Or you could ask her to describe an embarrassing moment in her life.

Here are some additional interesting questions you can use on a priming date:

- If you could script the basic plot for the dream you will have tonight, what would the story be?
- What's the most ridiculous pickup line a man has ever used on you?
- Is it better to be rich, famous, or free?
- What was your most disastrous trip or vacation?
- Has any book had a major impact on you?
- What was the craziest thing you ever did when you were a kid?
- If you could live anywhere, where would you live?
- If you could date any celebrity, who would it be and why?
- What cartoon character best represents your personal philosophy?
- What is the weirdest gift you have ever received?
- What's the best dinner you ever had?
- What was your worst summer or part-time job?
- If you wrote a book about yourself . . . what would it be about?
- What is your very favorite part of your day?
- What is one thing about you people would be surprised to learn?
- What one modern convenience could you not live without?
- What is one secret that you haven't told anyone?
- If you had a "theme song" that played whenever you walked into a room full of people, what would it be?

Get yourself psyched up

Use the techniques we described in Chapter 3 to get yourself ready for the date.

Prepare for success

Our students are often caught by surprise when these techniques work. At the end of his priming date with Jeanette, Morris went for the first kiss (as we'll show you how to do), and succeeded. "I was shocked, as I was kissing her," he told us. "I couldn't believe how enthusiastic her response was. I found myself walking away after the kiss, dumbfounded. I didn't realize till later that I could have kissed her more, and perhaps even gone somewhere and had sex with her right then!"

You prepare for success by being ready to have the outcome you ultimately want happen much faster than you anticipate. Have a condom

along, and have an idea of where you could go to have sex if it turns out she is ready. If she really responds to your first kiss, go for more. You don't want to be kicking yourself later, like Morris was, for walking away from a primed and ready woman.

BEFORE THE PRIMING DATE CHECKLIST

- Bathe
- Smell good
- Shave
- Brush your teeth
- Look in the mirror at your general appearance
- Style your hair
- Check your clothes: they should look good on your body, be ironed if needed, and not be stained or dirty
- Have things to do while you wait for her
- Have a watch with you
- Have prepared at least three romantic questions/conversations
- Be psyched up
- Clean your car
- Plan to stay only 30–75 minutes
- Have money
- Have your outcomes clearly in mind
- Have a place to go if she wants sex
- Have condoms
- Have practiced romantic questions/conversations out loud
- Leave home on time to arrive early
- Have a plan for what you would like to do on a next date

USE YOUR BODY TO CONVEY THAT YOU HAVE VITALITY AND GENERATIVITY

Before you go to meet her, it's worth looking once again at that slippery beast called *attitude*. All the tools, skills, practices, and checklists in this book are designed to give you a sense that you know what you are doing,

which will help you have that confident attitude women respond to so well. But remember, what skill and "attitude" really convey is vitality and generativity. If you are a vital, fully alive, creative beast of a man, women will desire you and want to have sex with you. As you are carrying out the technology in this book, it's critical that you do it with a vital and energetic flair.

When you are feeling vital, powerful, and alive, you move your body differently than you do when you are feeling depressed, unhappy, and hopeless. By changing the way you use your body, you can alter how you feel, and thus how other people relate to you. Remember, the woman is looking to you for certainty that the date is going well. If you look to her for that, you are doomed. By using your body, you can create that certain, powerful feeling that will help her feel safe.

Try this now: As you are reading this, move your body so you are sitting as though you are reading the most fascinating, exciting thing you've ever read. You may find you lean forward, and that your expression changes. Now sit as though you are an incredibly together, attractive, powerful masculine man who is on fire about his life. Breathe that way. Actually do it! This is the kind of posture you want to have when you are on the priming date. You don't have to start out feeling powerful and certain to do this. You can create the feeling anytime you want by using your body.

If you do this, and don't rely on her for validation that the date is going well, you will have presence and charisma that she will notice. You will have that mysterious thing called "attitude." And attitude combined with romantic questions and conversations, equals a woman who will surely desire you before the date is over.

ON THE DATE

Okay. You've done all the pre-work. You asked her out, set the time and place that was convenient for you, and committed yourself to not more than about an hour of your time. You've prepared and practiced your romantic questions and conversations. You are absolutely crystal clear about what your outcomes are. You've psyched yourself up and are using your body to convey your vitality and generativity. To return to our painting metaphor, you've prepared the surface and you are ready to paint!

Men often ask us if they should be late for the priming date. After all, they reason, if you make her wait, you'll have power over her, and won't be in one-down position. There are several flaws in this way of thinking. First, she will almost certainly be later than you. If you get into a little competition to see who can be latest, she will probably win. Second, if you arrive late and apologize, you don't appear especially powerful; you just look as if you have no control over your life. If you arrive late and don't apologize, it's even worse. In that case, you just look like a jerk.

We recommend that you arrive early, with something to do. When she arrives you are so involved in what you are doing, you may not even notice her until she arrives at your table. This shows that you are just as happy being there alone as you are being with her. As women routinely miss priming dates, it makes sense to be enjoying yourself anyway.

YOUR PRIMING DATE TO-DO LIST

As the priming date proceeds, you'll want to do things that convey your romantic interest and which pique hers. Every moment of the priming date won't be taken up with romantic talk. For most women, that would appear strange. It's perfectly acceptable to ask her about her job, family, and so forth. And to touch her.

There actually is an art and science to moving a woman from a platonic friend to a lover, and the natural sequence you will go through includes various stages of kinesthetic touch. These include friendly touching, personal touching, silly and fun touch, flirty and sexy touching, and then sexual and beyond. On the priming date you want to touch a woman in a friendly way, personal way, and in the realm of silly and fun ways, too. Here are a few ways you can include physical touch and flirting moves on the priming date.

Touch her at least five times

Touching a woman casually and non-intrusively establishes a precedent that will help you touch her more intimately later. It gets her used to accepting your touch, and even shows her that it can feel good.

These touches are quick, gentle, and over with before she has a chance

to get uncomfortable. You may touch her arm for a moment when talking, to emphasize a particular point, or touch her back while directing her to your table.

Sometimes men get flustered and find they have forgotten how to do this simple thing. It's easy: As you gesture, there are times when your hands are far from your body. Those are the moments to push one hand a bit farther and to touch her.

Touch her hand at least once

This touch is a bit more intimate, a bit more intrusive. You simply put your hand on hers for a moment to emphasize some point you are making, look into her eyes, then take it away.

Touch her in a playful manner at least once

This type of touching conveys that you are a playful guy and includes thumb wrestling, giving her a high-five, or playing footsie with her.

Look into her eyes "too long"

This creates a moment of intimacy that shows her your romantic interest. You should look into her eyes when you are talking to her, at least from time to time. It's not a staring contest, and hard, long stares are commonly considered aggressive. But even if you are in the habit of never looking into a woman's eyes when you interact with her, you should at least do it occasionally. It shows her you aren't scared and, if you do it in a relaxed manner, shows her you are willing to be open and honest with her.

Once during the date, you should establish eye contact and hold it for a fraction of a second longer than is comfortable, then look away to some other part of her face. This is especially intimate and romantic. It's a subtle way of getting her to open her "personal space" to you, which prepares her for opening up even more, later.

Check out her body one time

Wait, wait, wait! Before you ogle her like a stripper at a bar, let us explain to you how to check out a woman's body without offending her. It's a weird dichotomy. On the one hand, women are offended if you ogle their bodies. On the other hand, they go out of their way to make their bodies attractive to look at. If you look the wrong way, she may be offended. If you don't, however, you run the risk of giving the impression that you aren't interested in her sexually. You handle this problem by looking at her body quickly. Start by looking in her eyes, then quickly, in less than a second, let your eyes sweep over her body. Then return to her eyes. By returning to her eyes, you show her that you are not ashamed of having looked at her body, and that you still want to connect with her. Do this once or twice (but not more) during your conversation with her, and it will help reinforce the romantic mood.

Make decisions easily

We've talked about this before, and will only touch on it now to remind you of its importance. Being decisive is attractive. Being indecisive is unattractive. Choose.

Wink at her one time

Winking creates a little moment of intimacy between you and someone else. Have you ever had a woman wink at you? You shared a special connection, a momentary little world just for the two of you. When you wink at a woman, you do this for her. Make the wink fast; it's not like lowering a garage door. And smile; it's not some big, significant event.

Ask your romantic questions

The first step to having romantic conversations is asking your romantic questions. If you never do this, she is *much* less likely to think of you as potential romantic material, and you may find yourself in the friend category once again. Just open your mouth and say the lines you've memorized, even if you are uncomfortable. You can only start at the beginning and go from there.

Manage romantic conversations

Draw out her responses by asking the conversation-extending questions, which you, of course, memorized before the date. You'll probably find this part easier than you think. When a person starts telling you about her peak experiences, it's easy to become genuinely interested. When she returns the questions, and asks you about *your* romantic peaks, be ready to tell her about them by describing lush romantic feelings.

Keep your body powerful

Keep sitting like you are fascinated and fascinating.

Work on your vocal technique

Your voice is the delivery vehicle for your words, the physical connection between your mind and hers. A strong, melodious voice can greatly attract a woman, just as an unattractive, screechy voice can swiftly turn a woman off.

It is very important for you to take time to work on your voice and delivery when approaching women and throughout the seduction process. A powerful voice will grab a woman's curiosity and interest, and compel her to listen to what you have to say.

Make sure she can hear what you're saying

Many men mumble and wonder why women do not pay attention when they talk. To start, you better talk loud enough, especially in a loud environment, so that women can hear every word you are saying. You may need to practice speaking loudly.

You probably need to slow down your speaking pace around women, as well. If you speak too fast, a woman will assume you are scared and likely disregard what you are saying. Do not allow your words to slur into each other like a drunken slob's; slow down and articulate when you speak.

Get variety by changing pace

Pull out the key words and phrases and practice slowing them down. You'll be amazed at how slow you can actually go—and how much more interesting you sound. And for added effect, introduce pauses, especially just before key words. This will draw a woman's attention in.

Work on using emphasis when you talk. Yes, practice talking out loud and try saying a phrase several different ways.

Try saying this sentence in a variety of ways: "I am always surprised at how amazing a full moon can look when there is not a cloud in the sky." Practice saying this phrase out loud in the following ways:

- Full of sensuality
- Commanding and bold
- Energetic and enthusiastic
- Romantic and softly

Having flexibility with your vocal delivery will help you greatly when you communicate with women. Make sure to slow down your pace and avoid mumbling when talking to women.

Use "seduction" words

Some words are more romantic than others. Words like "urine" or "foreclosure" are less romantic than words like "seduced," "attracted," "romance," or "love." You want to use romantic words in your conversation as much as you can, without looking like you are crazy. This means using the words more than you are comfortable with, but allowing other conversation to happen as well.

Here's a list of romantic words and phrases. You may find others to add to this partial list:

- Seduced
- Attracted
- Falling in love
- Romance

- Warm and safe
- Elegant
- Sensual
- Dreamy
- Passionate
- Feeling in your body
- Exquisite
- Exotic
- Erotic
- Magical
- Special

Whisper or change vocal tone at least once during the date

While this isn't appropriate on all priming dates, if things are going well, it can help push the romantic interaction to the next level.

Whispering to her is powerful for a number of reasons. First, when you whisper, you command her attention more fully. If she doesn't pay attention, she'll miss what you are saying. Second, when you whisper, you create a little world that is for the two of you only. Third, you have to get closer to her to whisper. If you lean across the table to whisper, your mouth can get perilously close to her ear. It's intimate, yet easy for her to accept. This makes it easier for her to accept your romantic approaches later.

Compliment her three times

Obviously, your compliments won't be too sexual in nature. "Your breasts look so great in that outfit, I can hardly keep my hands off them" is only one step above professing a fascination with serial killers in terms of destroying any possible romance. Try complimenting her shoes, if they are at all nice. Tell her she has a wonderful sense of style or a beautiful smile. Find *something* and praise it.

The only exception to this rule: If a woman is extremely beautiful, and knows it, a man complimenting her is nothing unusual. In fact, some such women may hold it against you if you do. One woman told us, "A guy compliments my body. Great. Another guy who wants me. How

original. Who cares?" If you must compliment them, find something un-usual to focus on. Oscar met Sheila at a global warming lecture. She was staggeringly beautiful. He didn't want to just be another guy groveling before her good looks. On their priming date he told her, "You know, you're real pretty and everything, but I knew I had to meet you when you asked that question at the lecture. I said to myself, 'I've got to know this woman.'" He managed to compliment her on something unusual—her intelligence—while still acknowledging her good looks. She was im-pressed, rather than simply throwing his compliment on the pile with all the others.

Have fun

Like "Have a good attitude," "Have fun" is one of those commands that people give you without ever telling you how to do it. We suggest that, on the priming date, you remember that one of the purposes of going is to have fun, and that if the opportunity arises to actually enjoy yourself, you should take it. Study all these guidelines before the date, but on the date, let yourself relax and forget them from time to time. If you've studied first, your brain will be able to keep you on track. While this is work, it shouldn't be laborious. Remembering to have fun can help.

NINE POSSIBLE PROBLEMS ON THE PRIMING DATE

Not all priming dates go hitch-free. Lots of things can, and do, go wrong. However, everything doesn't have to go right for the date to be a success. The moment a problem happens on a date, most men panic and think the whole thing is ruined; this simply is not true. But you do have to be able to handle problems as they arise. Fortunately, you have our watchful guid-ance to help you solve whatever they might be.

1. She doesn't show up

The most common problem is that she doesn't even bother to show up. Astonishingly, women "forget" coffee dates very, very often. Attractive women in their early twenties are especially susceptible to this. As you be-gin dating a variety of women, it is inevitable that some will stand you up.

Actually, having a woman stand you up is a good experience. It teaches you not to take dating so personally. It teaches you not to rely on women to make you feel good, or to solve your problems. When a woman stands you up, you remain responsible for your feelings, your beliefs about yourself in the face of rejection, and your life. Here's how to make a "stand-up" work for you:

- *Don't take it personally.* Of course your date is late. Of course she's standing you up. This doesn't mean she doesn't like you, or won't eventually end up sleeping with you. She just got scared, or involved in something else that seemed more important, or just didn't feel like coming to the date. She may even have forgotten. Don't worry about it. We'll show you in a bit how to turn the entire scenario around on her and actually use her standing you up to forward your seduction.

- *Don't jump to conclusions.* Amazingly, she still might be very interested in you. She just didn't feel like showing up. We know this is astounding, but you must get used to it. Some extremely attractive women would literally never think to lift a finger to pursue, or even keep their word with, men they want to be with. Denise was one of these women. When she met Steve, she was very interested in him. She told her friends, "He seems so cute, and smart, and fun." But she never did anything to pursue him. In fact, she did quite the reverse. She didn't return his two phone calls, and when he finally did set up a priming date, she didn't show up. But she was still interested. You must understand that this kind of thing really does happen.

  And, of course, there may be a legitimate reason for her absence besides she "forgot" or didn't feel like coming. People do get lost or have emergencies. When Sunshine didn't show up for her priming date with Alvin, it turned out that two of her friends had died in a car accident. His anger disappeared pretty quickly when he found this out, and he offered his shoulder for her to cry on instead.

- *How to handle a no-show.* First, you wait only fifteen minutes for her to arrive. If you are still there when she arrives twenty, thirty, or forty minutes later, all you are doing is showing her that you are a

worm who will still be there for her, no matter how she treats you. If she shows up thirty minutes late and you are gone, it shows her that she has to treat your time as respectfully as she'd like her own treated. If a woman isn't there by fifteen minutes after you've scheduled the date, there is only a small chance she will show up anyhow.

- *Use your cell phone and call her directly and ask her why she's late.* Sometimes when a woman is running late, or can't make it, she'll call your cell phone or text-message you to let you know she's running behind schedule. After waiting fifteen minutes, check your phone. Try calling her and asking her where she is. If she doesn't answer, wait another fifteen minutes and then split.

If she's running late and tells you, it is permissible to wait, but you should still cut the date off quickly.

2. She doesn't show up repeatedly

We suggest you adopt a "two strikes and you're out" rule in your dating. If a woman doesn't show up to the *second* priming date, it's probably best to move on and quit pursuing her. You may want to contact her a month or so later and try again, but if a woman doesn't show up for two priming dates, she probably is not interested in spending time with you.

3. She brings a friend or girlfriend

If she brings a female friend, she's probably bringing a chaperone to check you out. Be charming, but less pushy with the romantic questions. You can still show your interest, of course. You may even ask the other woman how she met your prospect, and talk about how you felt when you first saw her. You can say to her, "Isn't Sheila beautiful?" as a way of complimenting your date. When you call your date later (if you decide to), joke with her about hoping that you passed the test with the chaperone. She'll deny she brought the friend to help her check you out. Accept this by saying, "Of course. I was just kidding," and set up your next date.

If she brings a guy friend, your problem is more serious. Why has she brought competition? Is she so popular that she has to date in groups? It could just be that she is extremely thoughtless. Or it could be that she is psycho. Use your psycho-spotting skills, and scale back the seduction

significantly. Leave after twenty or so minutes; you won't get much done with that guy there, anyway. If you decide to call her later, again joke about hoping you passed the chaperone test. When you ask her out again, humorously request that this time she come alone.

4. She is boring or weird, but you still want to have sex with her

You will meet the occasional woman who seems strange and is completely uninteresting to you intellectually, while you're still hot for her body. In these situations you must move faster, take more risks, and either push the romance to its conclusion or offend her and get her out of your life. The most common mistake men make in this situation is that they decide that making the romance move faster means not doing all the little things that will make her desire you in the first place.

When Bob decided to push his seduction of Maria forward because he found her boring, he stopped touching casually, looking into her eyes, winking at her, or doing anything to make her feel special. It's as if he decided that because she wasn't special to him, he could seduce her by treating her that same way. Needless to say, when Bob lunged at Maria to plant an awkward, unprepared-for kiss, she recoiled.

A top seducer understands that in these situations, you don't stop the romance. You stop everything else. From there it can go either way. She may well reject you, saying that though she is attracted to you, she "wants to know you better first," or she may have sex with you. You can decide from there if you want to keep seeing her.

5. Your romantic questions and talk seem to make her uncomfortable

Sometimes women squirm or get quiet when you are romancing them, because they are attracted, but scared. Sometimes they do exactly the same things because they are repelled, and scared. It's hard to know the difference.

You'll learn the nuances of handling this as you practice your dating skills. As we've said before, every woman will resist dating you at first, because they are resisting change. You have to push forward and keep being romantic, and wait for her to get over it. If she is profoundly uncomfortable

with your romantic talk and not attracted, you'll naturally slow down. She may even tell you she's not comfortable. One option is to talk about less romantic topics and rely instead on the interesting questions listed earlier in this chapter. Some women require extra time to be open to romance and sex. If you feel as if the date is going well and you are both having fun, that's still a good sign and a reason to see her again. If she never lightens up and keeps acting uncomfortable and critical of you, then don't date her again.

6. You push too hard and too fast

When you first use these tools, you are basically practicing. Because you are awkward and inexperienced, your new set of behaviors, discussion, and dress styles may seem unnatural and strange to you. However, that doesn't mean that it will seem strange to her. After all, she doesn't know how you normally behave. She doesn't know that you don't usually wink, or check women out, or make romantic talk. Only you know that. Most of the time, you will be the only one feeling weird about it. That huge risk you take when you ask her about her most romantic moment doesn't seem risky to her; it is only in your head. Don't mistake your own tension for hers.

Especially at first, she may feel that you are coming on too hard and fast. She'll seem offended or pull back when you touch her. She may even ask something like "Are you doing some weird thing to seduce me?" Tell her that you like her and are interested in her, and apologize (briefly) if you are coming on too strong. Have neutral conversation about her job for a while, then start bringing the seduction back in.

You should also know that priming dates can sometimes lead to one-night stands and sex. You never know how attracted a woman is to you unless you push things, and while you must always stop pushing the sex if a woman tells you to do so, you never know if she likes you unless you test out the waters. So be open when pushing the sexuality—be open to stopping, to going all the way, and to changing direction and slowing things down.

7. Her beauty intimidates you

When you first go out with a very attractive woman, it's easy to get overwhelmed with your concerns about things going wrong. After all, she's so beautiful, you'd better get it right. More than likely your fear will

drive you to do things your old, unsuccessful way. This will only leave you with another beautiful female friend. Don't default into your old ways; they won't serve you.

The best solution is to go into dates with beautiful women as if they were an experiment. When Russ first set up a date with Tina, an actress, her beauty overwhelmed him. And she was a real looker. She had been on the beauty pageant circuit before becoming an actress. He came to us for help preparing for the date. "I can hardly talk to her, she's so damn hot," he told us. "What can I do?"

First and foremost, we counseled Russ to look at this date as an experiment. Because this was his first truly beautiful date in his entire life, he was likely to screw up since he'd never had any practice before. We advised him not to worry about it. "The idea isn't to bed her in this case," we said. "The idea is to see how far you can get without screwing up, and to learn as much as you can from any screwup that you make. The more you learn from this beautiful woman, the farther you'll get with the next one you find." We also told him to make sure to use his body powerfully, and to do all the confidence-building things we teach in Chapter 3.

He took our advice and approached dating her as an experiment, rather than as a task at which he had to "succeed." As a result he learned a lot from his interactions with her and actually got to the point of kissing her before she rejected him. Russ was thrilled he got that far, rather than depressed, and the next very hot woman he pursued, he had sex with.

8. She offends you, or you disagree strongly

Sometimes a woman is so unpleasant to be with that you change your goal. You quickly decide that it would be more enjoyable to give her a piece of your mind than it would be to sleep with her. If that is the decision you make, then by all means fight with her. Have a ball. But don't kid yourself and think that you'll ever have sex with her or change her mind. You won't. But fighting with her is your right, if you want to do it.

If you disagree with her strongly, or she offends you, but not enough to put you off entirely, you can argue, but tone yourself down. There is a huge difference between having a passionate and heated discussion and an all-out rageful argument. It's okay to disagree with women, but if she sees

you get angry, she will likely label you as an "angry man" and not feel safe around you.

9. She wants to cry on your shoulder, but doesn't want to have sex

This is the worst case scenario, and sometimes it does happen. Reggie liked Wanda, but when they went out she confessed that she was very confused about her sexual identity. "I really wish I wanted men, but I only desire women," she told him. "But I want to get married and be a normal person!" She went on in this vein for their entire priming date, continually rerouting all romantic conversations back into laments about her problems. At first Reggie thought she might be worth the effort. He instantly fantasized about sleeping with Wanda and one of her sexy friends, every man's fantasy. Sadly, when he asked her, "Have you tried being with a man and a woman at the same time?" she was deeply offended, saying, "Why do men always say that?" If you desire a woman who won't stop using you as a therapist, you should accelerate your seduction and either get her into bed or get rid of her. When Reggie tried to kiss Wanda at the end of the date, she refused, and he never called her again.

Remember your purpose. Most of the time, a woman who wants to cry on your shoulder but doesn't want sex will continue to not want sex with you. You don't have time for this.

ENDING THE DATE AND DANGLING THE BAIT

You are leaving the priming date. How do you know if you should make a pass at her or wait until the next time?

In terms of the seduction, you are better off kissing her quickly if you can. If you kiss her, she's left having to give herself reasons why she did the right thing by allowing it. If you don't kiss her, it leaves her more easily able to think of you as a friend. The downside of kissing her at the end of the priming date is that if she's not ready, you risk blowing what you've worked for.

There are logistical considerations as well. If she decides to stay behind at the coffee shop, it's harder to kiss her. If you are walking her to her car,

however, the relative privacy of a parking garage might be more conducive to the first kiss. We'll discuss how you go for the first kiss (and more) in Chapter 9.

Even if she refuses your kiss, she may simply be telling you she's not ready yet, but will be. Ken tried to kiss Mindy standing next to her car after their priming date. Realizing he was rushing things, and not sure how it would be received, he warned her first. "Oh my," he said. "I don't know if I can resist kissing you." "Please don't," she said, smiling. "It's just too soon. But you call me, how about that?" "Oh, so you want to be pursued more," Ken laughed. "I can do that. I have a feeling you are worth every minute." She laughed, and got into her car, and he walked away. A success, even though he didn't get what he was after. Mindy made it clear that all he had to do was more work, and he could have her. Ken didn't object to doing the work, so he left feeling happy and confident about the seduction.

If you have a clear idea in mind for the seduction date, it's perfectly fine to ask her out and make the plans at the end of the priming date. Simply say, "This has been great, and I'd like to see you again." It's better to nail things down when you are with her. In this age of phone tag and people who can't make plans without their BlackBerry, it can be a lot easier to just set up the next date right then. It is also good to ask her out while she is right in front of you, feeling the joy that you created on the date, rather than later when she's had lots of time to think about why you are a jerk. Be general, unless you have a seduction date strategy already in mind. Set a date, and ask her when the best time is to call her to set up the details. Your next stop is to design your seduction date strategy.

AFTER THE DATE "DID" CHECKLIST

- Asked the romantic questions you memorized
- Conducted the romantic conversations you prepared
- Touched her hand
- Looked into her eyes a little too long
- Cut the date short (75 minutes tops)
- Touched her non-intrusively and casually

- Made decisions quickly and easily
- Made her smile and/or laugh at least one time
- Pursued your goals
- Made your romantic interest known
- Were early and absorbed in something else when she arrived
- Gathered information about her romantic needs
- Complimented her three times
- Had fun for at least 40 seconds
- Checked out her body in the way specified
- Used seductive language (seduce, attraction, falling in love, romance, etc.) seven times
- Used interested body language
- Whispered at least once
- Took notes afterwards about what makes her feel romantic

AFTER THE DATE "DIDN'T" CHECKLIST

The nine date-killers:

- Didn't treat her like a friend
- Didn't insult her
- Didn't complain
- Didn't complain about other women
- Didn't check out other women
- Didn't grab her ass
- Didn't rely on her for certainty that the date was going well
- Didn't allow yourself to get upset when you forgot your lines, etc.
- Didn't take anything she said or did personally

AFTER THE DATE STUDY QUESTIONS

We recommend that you sit yourself down and ask yourself a few questions after the priming date. Whether or not it went the way you wanted, you can learn from the experience and be a more skillful seducer in the future.

- Is she worth the work she will probably be? How much do you want her? How much work are you willing to put in?
- What did you learn about what is important to her in relationships and dating?
- What worked and made her feel especially connected to you?
- What didn't work and seemed to make her feel more separate from you?
- What did she like about you?
- How responsive was she to romantic and sexual talk?
- How was the date a success?
- What did you learn about seduction?
- What does your intuition tell you about seducing this woman?
- How psycho is she?
- Does she live with her parents or in some other arrangement where it might be hard to have sex with her?
- Does she seem to prefer you acting dominant or submissive?
- What topics should you avoid and/or pursue?
- What seductive conversation worked best?
- What is the cost/benefit ratio?
- Is she one of the four kinds of women to avoid? (See page 337.)

PASSING THE PRIMING DATE WITH FLYING COLORS

When Bruce went out with Wendy, he passed the priming date with flying colors. When she arrived, he was absorbed in his book, an intellectual work called *Sex and the Brain*. Her "hello" popped him back to reality, and he greeted her. "Wow, hi. I was so absorbed in this book, I didn't see you come in." Wendy, an intellectual type, was immediately impressed and interested in his book. This led to conversation about sex and how men and women become attracted to each other. Bruce took the opportunity to use seduction words like "romance," "attracted," "chemistry," and so on.

He also used the conversation as an opening to ask Wendy about her romantic experiences, and how those experiences felt to her. After telling him about her most romantic date ever, Wendy laughed and said, "I feel

like I'm telling you everything about me! Now you'll know everything about romancing me!" "Well, that's just great," Bruce responded. He leaned forward, whispering more intimately, "But trust me, I have a few romantic surprises for a beautiful woman like you that you haven't seen before." He smiled conspiratorially. "You'll see," Bruce said, as he leaned back, and winked. For the duration of the date he made decisions easily and used his body to convey his vitality and interest in her. He touched Wendy's arm several times, and then placed his hand on hers.

At one point, while Bruce was describing a romantic experience of his in response to her "What about you?" question, he said, "It felt so beautiful to connect, you know what I mean?" and reached out to lightly touch her cheek for a moment. She blushed, and they went on with their conversation. Later he held her eye contact a fraction too long, and, as he was getting up to leave, he checked out her body one time.

Wendy was awed by and attracted to Bruce's confidence. She was surprised by how naturally she found herself thinking romantically about him. She didn't realize that he'd left her little alternative. He was obviously not going to be a friend; all of his behaviors told her that. Bruce showed his interest in her romantically and skillfully. She had to think of him either as possible romantic material or as a pushy jerk. Either way was fine with Bruce, because either option moved him closer to his goal. If she thought of him romantically, she was more likely to go to bed with him. If she thought of him as a pushy jerk, she'd get out of his life and he'd have more time to pursue other women.

After forty minutes Bruce got up to leave. "Well, it's been great seeing you," he told her. "How about we get together again?" "That'd be great," she said. "Please call me!" At that moment, he could have set up the date, gone for an early kiss, or left and called her later. He had choices, power, and the date was cheap and didn't take too long. By following our directions, Bruce put himself on the road to romance. If you follow them, so will you.

8

The Seduction Date

After a successful priming date, Bruce knew Wendy was interested in him. She seemed sad that the date had ended, and had kept staring and smiling at him throughout the time they were together. When he winked and checked out her body, she still smiled. Bruce knew that if he had made the first move, they definitely would have been making out near the coffee shop, but he didn't want to push things too hard, too early. Bruce looked forward to turning up the romance on a seduction date. He found her attractive, intelligent, and sweet. His next step was to create an afternoon adventure, a date that would provide fond memories. A magical afternoon.

Bruce waited until Thursday to call Wendy. She sounded happy on the phone. After a few minutes of chitchat, he asked her out for Saturday. "I can hardly wait to see you," she said. "We will be going on a secret adventure," Bruce warned. "I love secret adventures," she responded. Bruce hung up the phone excited about the date. He couldn't wait.

The purpose of a seduction date is to create romantic experiences that lead to sex. Priming dates create rapport through *conversations*; seduction dates do this through *experiences*. A seduction date assumes that she knows you are interested in her romantically and she is still interested in dating you. On priming dates you research the qualities she looks for in a man and the experiences she considers romantic. All this information comes together on a seduction date.

After four priming dates with Kathy, Bob decided to take her on a seduction date. Even though she didn't seem that interested in him, and they never came close to kissing, Bob wanted to move things to the next level. He failed to notice that Kathy had ended all the dates first. On one date, she asked to borrow money, and she kept asking him to buy her dinner at expensive restaurants. At no point did she show any interest in him at all. Not only was Bob a sucker, but he was nowhere near ready to be on a seduction date with this woman. He didn't generate any romantic feelings with Kathy on the priming dates, nor did he create much of a connection. He rarely asked her romantic questions, and he gave off a weird vibe. Bob did not come across as boyfriend material. He would have been better off going out with any other woman, rather than trying to force Kathy to be on a date with him.

On his thirty-minute priming date, Bruce left Wendy wanting more. They constantly talked about romantic topics. He found out her favorite type of movie (science fiction), food (Chinese), that she loved nature and animals. Her ideal Sunday morning was to wake up with her lover, have him go out and get the *New York Times* and bagels, and have them cuddle in bed, drinking coffee, reading for hours. He frequently touched her and even kissed her hand. By the end of the date, they were laughing, having a great time.

THE EIGHT COMPONENTS OF
A SUCCESSFUL SEDUCTION DATE

1. The seduction date takes longer than a priming date

On the priming date, you focus on *not* spending too much time with the woman, because there was a good chance you would blow it by saying something stupid. The purpose of priming dates is to leave the woman wanting more. On a seduction date, it is useful to spend more time together. Romance and feelings of sexiness usually take several hours to build. They are a series of progressive successes stacked on top of one another. Another reason why the seduction date takes longer is that women usually love the courting process. For them it is like a cat-and-mouse game. It's a fun game to play, and playing it brings them enjoyment.

Another reason why seduction dates take longer is that they give the woman a justification to sleep with you. Most women feel bad about themselves when and if they meet a guy at a bar and go home with him. They often regret the experience and avoid the guy. When you spend hours with them, it is much easier for them to justify to themselves being sexual with you.

Be aware, however, that just as Abe Lincoln said a man's legs should be "long enough to reach the ground," a seduction date should last long enough to get her in bed and not a whole lot longer. Sometimes you will go on a seduction date where things go quickly. It'll be obvious that she's ready for sex, and, in those cases, you shouldn't take longer than you need to.

This happened to Luther on a seduction date with a girl named Penny. He went to her house to pick her up for the date, and when he came inside he noticed that she had slow dance music playing on her stereo. He said to her, "Would you like to dance before we go out?" She said yes, and he took her in his arms and they danced . . . then kissed . . . then had sex right there on her living room floor.

If you practice your seduction enough, and use our techniques, this kind of thing will happen to you, too, and you should be ready for it. If Luther had insisted on going out for the entire seduction date before making his move, it might or might not have worked. But since he saw the opportunity and took it, he got to his goal much faster.

Jim took Sandy on a more regular seduction date. It was winter in Colorado and snowy. On a priming date he found out that they both loved winter sports, especially skiing. He had been an avid skier for the past fifteen years, and she, too, loved to be on the slopes.

As a result of their shared interests, Jim set up an afternoon ski trip for the two of them. He found a remote resort few people visited. It was out of the way, and only the most devoted ski bums knew of it. Though it wasn't as high quality as the more popular sights, it would be a better place, he figured, to create a romantic outing. They arrived around one in the afternoon on a warm Sunday. It was a perfect day to be out, and there was hardly anyone else skiing. Jim flirted with Sandy all afternoon. On a break, they held hands, talked, and laughed. The seduction date took them away from her normal circumstances, and it gave Jim hours to flirt and connect with her. Later that evening, after a delicious meal, they went to her

apartment and kissed for hours. They did everything short of making love. The date ended perfectly.

2. Seduction dates make the woman feel special

Seduction dates focus on deepening the connection between the two of you. How you relate to each other changes, from acquaintances to possible dating partners. The date invokes romantic feelings between the two of you by making her feel special and appreciated. Priming dates address her concern about whether or not you are safe to date. Seduction dates address her questions about whether she wants to have sex with you.

If you are like most men, you would sleep with a woman regardless of whether or not she seems like a potential girlfriend. Women, on the other hand, often search for a potential mate. Single women over thirty tend to focus on men who are "marriage material." Your job is to come across as the type of man who can fit her desires, no matter what they are. When you spend hours together, it helps you seem like the boyfriend she has always wanted. You are not only spending quality time with her, but courting her in the ways she wants.

A woman—any woman—wants to feel special. It is your job to make her feel that way. For most women, the man of their dreams appreciates how they dress, the topics they discuss, their interests, and much more. Given that you are striving to be viewed as a potential boyfriend, you should take an interest in these subjects. Her ideal boyfriend would most likely give her long back rubs, hold her close, pay for dates, and enjoy kissing softly in the moonlight. If that is what she desires, do those things. You'll probably find you even enjoy them. Seduction dates work best if you go into them looking to have a fun time giving her what she wants, rather than expecting her to give you what you want.

As a rule of thumb, stay focused on her and her desires throughout the date, making her feel special, but find a way for you to have a good time, too. Do this when you plan the date, are on the date, and afterward when you evaluate the date. Later in the chapter we will cover the specific techniques you can use to acknowledge her and make her melt.

If a woman feels as though you are just using her for sex, she probably

won't sleep with you. Even if she is the type to have one-night stands, she will want to know that you appreciate something about her personality. She wants to know you think of her as more than just a woman to have sex with. The most efficient way to accomplish this is to imagine you are her, and imagine what you would like to do, and how you would want to be treated. Chances are that you won't be able to fully understand where she is coming from, but it will be a good way to guide your behavior nonetheless.

. . . .

From Trash to Treasure:
THE ROMANTIC POWER OF LITTLE GIFTS PROPERLY GIVEN

Another way to show your appreciation is through little gifts. Women love gifts; who doesn't? The great part of "little gifts" is that you can give her a very inexpensive gift and it will melt her heart almost as much as an expensive one. We highly recommend that you do this on seduction dates to increase the feelings of romance and affiliation.

Little gifts serve many purposes. First, their "surprise factor" can be used to get her attention. By giving her something she doesn't expect, you show you are interested and thoughtful. Second, it shows you are generous. Third, she will feel appreciated and cared for because you went through the trouble of purchasing something for her. Fourth, little gifts give something tangible from the date to remind her of you after she goes home. If it is a gift she enjoys, she will probably stare at it or use it long after the date is over. Even something silly like a Wonder Woman key chain can help remind her of how fun and crazy the date was. She will probably look at the chain and laugh, thinking about a joke you told, or how surprised she was to see a plastic statue of her childhood cartoon superhero. The gift will actually anchor more romantic and good feelings to you, even when you are not around.

As important as the gift itself is how well it is wrapped. This is critical. The act of unwrapping a present is an exciting ritual for her, and you will enjoy watching her do it. If the gift is inexpensive, as it should be, wrapping it well makes it ten times more special than it would be unwrapped. Remember, you want to give her a good experience. Unwrapping a gift is an experience she'll remember for a long time to come.

The five rules for gift giving

1. It must be wrapped nicely.
2. It must be in good taste (nothing like a huge vibrating hand or a deck of cards from Hooters).
3. It must be inexpensive.
4. It must be either fun, funny (to her), or romantic.
5. It must be given at a random time. You don't want a woman to start expecting and demanding gifts on every date.

Examples of cheap gifts women love:

- Stuffed animals
- Chocolate
- Cute cards
- Funny pens
- A memento you buy while on the date
- Flowers
- A CD of good romantic music
- A funny toy
- Food
- Massage oil
- A goofy hat
- A shell from the ocean
- A book

. . . .

3. The seduction date takes place in an out-of-the-ordinary place

You must take a woman out of her ordinary surroundings on a seduction date. Remember, you want to create a memorable experience. One way to create such an experience is to break out of the normal routine and go places you've never been—different scenery, smells, sights, vibes, everything. By doing so, the experience will seem exciting, bold, and adventurous.

The date can take place at a museum, a shop across town, a sporting event (only if she has mentioned her love of sports), a concert, a special restaurant, or any other place she is likely to enjoy. The only condition is that you don't go to places she tends go to in her normal routine. So if she

goes to the museum every week to check out the Egyptian artifacts, don't go there. If, however, there is a helium balloon show nearby, or an art show she wants to attend, it's perfect. These experiences are new for her, and more likely to be an "event."

Jason racked his brain for hours thinking of where to take Shannah. At age forty, he thought of himself as successful and attractive, but very shy. He wanted to date Shannah, a woman he met at a neighborhood coffee shop they both frequented. Jason flirted with her over a few weeks, and slowly found out details of her life. After nearly a month, he finally mustered up the courage to ask her out for coffee. Since he had been to one of our seminars, he knew enough to take her to a *different* coffee shop than the one they both enjoyed.

After the priming date, he felt he was ready to seduce her. Though he had lived in New York for the past ten years, every place that came to mind seemed clichéd and silly. He racked his brain thinking of places she would like. Finally, Jason decided to take her to the Statue of Liberty. He reasoned that it would be romantic to be on a boat, and he knew she had always wanted to go. Shannah had said so a month ago when he first started flirting with her and finding out about her life.

The date turned out wonderfully. The boat ride was fun, and the tour of the statue was more interesting than Jason had imagined it would be. Afterward, they walked around neighborhoods Shannah had wanted to visit. They looked at architecture, churches, and other points of interest. They walked, holding hands, occasionally stopping for coffee, donuts, or just to rest. At the end of the date, they went back to her house and kissed passionately. It was the first of many dates for them.

One reason the date worked so well was that Jason took Shannah to a place she wanted to go. Second, the date took them both out of their normal routines and into "foreign" territory. Third, by being together over time, they began to bond with each other. In the coffee shop they could talk to other people and retreat into their books or newspapers. On the boat ride and while walking, they had to be together. They could either enjoy each other or suffer. Being out of their normal routine forced them to bond, which moved the seduction forward.

4. The seduction date includes the element of surprise

When we interviewed women about their most romantic dates, most said that the place was less important than how the date was structured. What made it romantic was that the man had taken care of all the details and that she felt like she was in another world. One woman commented that on the best dates, she felt "transported into a romantic world." Surprises are a wonderful way to create such feelings.

Since childhood, most of us have loved surprises. We've been conditioned to appreciate them. Why, for example, do kids love scary movies? Why do kids love roller coasters or even hide-and-seek? The element of surprise turns a mundane activity into an event. It transforms the ordinary into the extraordinary. The element of surprise creates a quickened bonding process and invokes fun, ecstasy, and romance.

Creating a wonderful surprise for a woman also brings out the playful parts in you, which is always a good idea while getting to know a woman. Most women want a man who is sensitive and fierce, fun and playful, and at least somewhat unpredictable, all at the same time. When the date is full of surprise, you are unpredictable, exciting, and it is difficult *not* to have fun. We highly recommend experimenting with surprise on seduction dates and keeping it going while in a committed relationship. It adds spice and freshness.

During our interviews we also asked women what made the best dates go well. Part of the magic, women told us, was doing things they didn't normally do. "I want to be taken out of my environment," one woman said. "I want a guy to bring me somewhere I'd probably not go alone or with my girlfriends. Even if it is just a funky coffee shop on the other side of town, or to a ballet, what impresses me is when a guy treats me like I'm worth putting in effort for." Secrets, surprises, and mystery all drive women crazy.

5. You pay for the date

Some men aren't so skillful. Along with being a bumbling idiot, Bob is a cheapskate. He doesn't like to spend money on himself, on a woman, or on anybody. "I don't want to blow any money if sex isn't going to happen," he says. "Why should I spend my hard-earned money on a woman?" One

reason Bob is such a failure with women is because he is unwilling to put out for them. He expects them to just throw themselves at him and beg him for sex, even though he isn't willing to do much of anything for them. We're not talking about spending lots of money on a woman. That would be stupid and naive. But we are talking about providing for her on some level. A seduction date is about supplying the woman with fun and excitement, romance and appreciation. Part of how you create these is by taking financial responsibility for the date.

By refusing to spend even $20 on a movie date, Bob shoots himself in the foot and ruins his chances of success. By being overly paranoid and stingy, he turns women off. But Bob is not alone in this—many men fall into this trap. When you pay for a woman on a date, you are demonstrating your ability to be generative. You are showing her that you are willing to do your part. Most women expect you to pay for them and will think less of you if you don't. You are welcome to argue about the fairness of this all day long if you want. You can be right about it until the cows come home. We don't care. The bottom line is, you need to set up the date so that it works for you financially, and so that you can pay for it for the woman.

If you have little money, don't worry. Spending lots of cash isn't necessary. Creating a memorable experience for her and taking charge of managing the date are more important than spending money. It would be a fine, memorable, and *free* date if you took her to a free museum and then on a walk around a lake. If you know her better, you can rent movies and make her a special, romantic dinner. Another option is to make it a road trip, visit a nearby town, and window shop down the main street. These are all cheap options, and the world is full of many more. The important part is that *you* are creating experiences for *her* and taking responsibility for the date rather than expecting her to do so.

Murray was quite knowledgeable about plants, having majored in horticulture in college. He had researched forest ecology and could identify nearly every tree, shrub, and plant in the botanical gardens nearby. He decided to take Beth on a visit to the gardens. In an earlier conversation she had mentioned her love of exotic birds, plants, and trees. Murray saw the botanical gardens as a perfect place to walk and bond. From there he planned to take her to a lunch spot, and then to a chocolate store. The

whole date, he figured, would cost around $15. It would give them an opportunity to be together in a romantic spot and have the date be memorable.

Howard is a dating master. He always has a steady stream of women to date. He meets them everywhere he goes. Over the years, Howard has developed a list of dating laws that he strictly follows. One is the $40 rule: He never spends more than $40 on a seduction date. He simply decides ahead of time his spending maximum, and never spends more. This rule has served him well, and never leaves him broke or resentful.

We recommend you take Howard's lead and do the same thing. Set aside a fixed amount and design a date that won't go over it. Gamblers who decide how much money they are willing to lose ahead of time, and never exceed that amount, leave casinos happy. They live within their means and don't mess up their lives by chasing something that is improbable, like beating the odds at the blackjack table.

The same thing holds true on seduction dates. If you are not winning, and a connection is not being made, don't force the issue. If a date begins going badly, don't fall into the trap of spending more money in an attempt to fix it. That's desperation, not confidence, and it doesn't work. Spending more money won't help things. You will probably leave feeling even worse, and no closer to your goal.

Even though we recommend paying for the seduction date, you shouldn't believe that paying for dates negates the importance of creating and maintaining the romantic mood. Money is not a substitute for the other work required. If you take a woman to a very expensive restaurant, she may be impressed, but if you fail to create any romance, she will only view you as a sucker whom she can manipulate into buying things for her. You must create a balance: The work on the date must be done in tandem with paying.

6. The seduction date is not a time to socialize

Just as the priming date wasn't a time to socialize, neither is the seduction date. Sure, having fun is part of the date, but you are still "at work." You are still focused on your goal of creating sexual tension between the two of you that you can have fun resolving later. The other task you are working on is creating romantic feelings. As a rule of thumb, be clear about

your goal every time you interact with your date. When you stray from this focus, get back on track. If you forget your goals, you will likely fail.

7. Seduction dates are on a flexible schedule

Priming dates have a definite format. They are short, usually forty to seventy-five minutes. You focus on discovering the woman's likes and dislikes. Seduction dates follow a completely different format. While they are goal-driven, the pace is slower and less intense. The goal of the seduction date is sex, and there are many paths to it. The easiest one is to let go of having to make your plans work perfectly, while at the same time pursuing your goal. Does this seem confusing? It should. We are telling you two completely opposite things at the same time. But it's still true.

Most guys have a hard time just "going with the flow." They prefer to know ahead of time how every moment is going to be spent. Then they fret when things don't go as planned. The likelihood of your success will be greatly improved if you can let the ambiguity and uncertainty be there, while still following the other principles. Otherwise, you'll turn into a control freak. After a few seduction dates, this formula will make much more sense.

When Danny took Amy to an art opening, he never expected that they would be invited to the artist's hotel room for a private show. While he was a bit worried that the artist would hit on Amy, he went anyway. They ended up talking to the artist for the next few hours, drinking wine, and getting to know him and the few other people who had been invited as well. Afterward, Danny took Amy home and they ended up having sex. Because he was open to changing his plans, while still remaining focused on the outcome, he gave her a very special experience, and was successful.

Most people go through life busy and hurried, without allowing themselves much time to be relaxed and to enjoy what is going on in front of them. When you allow for the date to unfold in its own time, you create a relaxed environment for her, and this will greatly aid you. This in no way means you don't plan out the date meticulously and have an abundance of options at your fingertips. You do plan. But you must allow for both a tightly structured outing and one that is flexible.

Remember also: Few women want to be with a man who is constantly trying to rush into sex. If you try to hurry things, a woman won't respect you and won't desire you. Men who are unsuccessful with women lack the ability to be tactful. When you relax and let the date unfold and go at her pace, and still follow your plan, she will respect you and eventually give you sex.

8. Seduction dates plan for success

While planning a date, you must assume that sex will happen and do the steps necessary to get ready. This means that you prepare mentally, physically, practically, and emotionally. You also prepare your environment to lend itself to a sexual experience. To put it bluntly: You must end up someplace you can "do it."

Calvin, a successful student, reported that one of his first seduction dates failed because he didn't plan properly. The date had been going well and he and a delightful young woman wound up at her home. So far, so good, he thought. They began by kissing passionately on her couch, and after a while they moved things to the bedroom. Calvin took off her top and played with her breasts. They kissed more, and she pulled off his pants and underwear. They continued and she took off her bra. Calvin was in heaven. After another half hour of foreplay, she begged him to enter her for the wild ride of his life.

At that exact moment, Calvin realized that he didn't have any condoms. "I felt like a total idiot," he recalls. "I had no idea things would go so far on the date. If I had, I would have planned. I still kick myself when I think of my blunder." Calvin's lack of planning cost him a great night of sex, and he looked like a bumbling idiot in front of a woman who desired him.

Most men are so used to failing with women that they expect the worst. After many rejections, they expect to strike out. They don't plan for success and are surprised when it happens. Like Calvin, they don't bring condoms on a date because they don't even think they could possibly score. They don't bother cleaning their bedroom because they don't think the date will lead to the woman coming home with them. They don't dress well because the woman probably won't like them anyway. We could go on and on, but we suspect you get the idea. You must plan for success.

In our experience, holding on to negative beliefs and pessimistic atti-

tudes will give you what you've always gotten: poor results and lukewarm-to-cold responses from women. We recommend that from now on you plan for success. It is crucial that you be ready for things to go your way. If you aren't, you will end up a chump, and the only one you will be able to blame is yourself.

BEFORE THE SEDUCTION DATE

We always stress the importance of preparation for a date; you should know this by now. Planning, after all, is 90 percent of the work. Imagine all the work set designers do before a movie shoot. They are on-site weeks before the actors even show up. They spend weeks constructing buildings from scratch, parking lots from cornfields, saloons from barns—anything needed to match the movie script. After all the preparation is done, the actors stroll onto the set and shoot the scenes. Filming usually takes place for less than a month. The designers are there before, during, and after, making sure everything works as planned.

Successful dating works in much the same way. It requires hours of pre-work to set the scene. The work is constant. The demands are great. But the hard work pays off when the actors (you and her) seem to create magic from thin air. Here are guidelines of things you must cover before the date:

Assess the attraction level between the two of you

Here is a short quiz for you to take. Your answers will help you measure her level of interest in you. If you answer yes to three or more of these questions, she is likely to be quite interested. If you answer no to three or more, there is a minimal connection and more bonding is necessary.

1. Did she seem interested when you asked her romantic questions?
2. Did she seem excited about the idea of another date, or was she just being polite?
3. Does she seem willing to alter her schedule to see you?
4. Does she seem happy when you touch her non-intrusively, or does she squirm to get away from you?
5. Has she complimented you on your looks or behavior?

6. Has she welcomed discussions of anything sexual?
7. Has she mentioned that she talked about you with her friends?

By realistically assessing her current level of attraction, you allow yourself to prepare intelligently for the date. You are likely, however, to fall into one of two traps. First, you might think that if you are really attracted to her, she must be really attracted to you. Remember, you want to assess the amount of attraction *between* you, which will probably be mediated by her, not by you. Second, you may let your fear do the assessing for you and decide that there's no way she could be attracted to you. That's not realistic, either. Look at the situation as if you were an outsider watching a budding relationship, and make your assessment from there.

Create a sexual goal for the date

Now that you have measured the degree of attraction between the two of you, it will be easier to create a sexual goal for the date. Remember that, by definition, all seduction dates aim to create an opening for sex.

You want to pick goals that are attainable. It is okay to push yourself to a new plateau, to stretch and reach beyond where you've been in the past. But the goal must be doable and realistic. Many men choose goals that are out of reach, beyond their skill level. They would rather live in a dreamworld than face up to gritty reality. By choosing something beyond your skill level, you will hurt your self-confidence. By not being honest with yourself, you perpetuate boyish, delusional ways of thinking that will prevent you from the life you want. If Bob, for instance, really thinks his date will sleep with him, he is nuts. It would be miraculous for him to even kiss her, given the way things are going.

While Bob has zero chance with his date, Bruce is likely to bed Wendy on their seduction date. She has already shown signs of sexual interest in him, and the chemistry is right. They already have a strong attraction to each other and they seem to like each other. If he creates and executes a date that she enjoys, sex will probably happen. Whether you are in a situation similar to Bruce or Bob, you must decide how far you think things can go, and plan from there. Each seduction must be custom designed to match the individual woman and circumstances.

Make sure the time and place work for you

Do you really have enough free time to devote to a date? If not, either create the time or don't have the date. When you plan, you must make sure you have the free time required to make the date a success. If you have a demanding job, like most of us do, it is likely that you occasionally are expected to work on weekends, or extra hours during crunch times. We strongly recommend that you never mess up your work schedule for a date.

At all times, you must remember that your work is more important than a woman—especially during the beginning stages of a relationship. It is lunacy to put your job in jeopardy to date a woman, no matter how attractive she is. Out of desperation, men often harm themselves to get women. In the end, acting from desperation will cause more problems down the road. If you skip work to be with a woman, you will probably be preoccupied anyhow, and the date won't work. The solution is to set up a seduction at a time and place that truly works for you.

Decide how much money you are going to spend on the date

As we discussed earlier, you must decide ahead of time how much you are willing to spend on the date. Budgeting is important because it acts as a safety measure to insure that you don't feel taken advantage of by a woman. Some men tell us that they tend to feel used by women; they report that women often only seem interested in dating them for gifts or for free meals and entertainment. In these situations, the men end up paying more for the date than expected. At the same time, they don't get any sex. If you are to avoid falling into this trap, you must decide ahead of time how much you are willing to spend, and stick to it.

Use the information from the priming date to guide how you plan the seduction date

Priming dates function as fact-finding missions. By asking a woman romantic questions, you find out what she looks for in a man, what turns her on, and what turns her off. You also learn about her likes and dislikes, interests, and topics to avoid. All of this information, including your intuitive

sense about her, helps you plan the seduction date. Begin by looking over your notes about the priming date. Go over everything you know about her. Recall her likes and dislikes, everything that seemed interesting about her, anything that seemed wacko, and any other details that stand out. This data will help you decide where to take her and what the most effective strategy with her will be.

THE SEVEN STEPS TO A KNOCKOUT SEDUCTION DATE

Your success depends upon how you construct the entire date. Merely taking her to a beautiful park or getting great tickets to an opera is not enough. You must create the romantic and sexual mood. Remember, you want to create sexual tension. If you take her to an amazing place, but don't create the mood of attraction and sexual attention, everything you do will be pointless. Just as spending money doesn't ensure success, having one great place to go, in a vacuum, doesn't ensure success either. The seduction date must work from start to finish. Here's how you create a knockout seduction date:

1. Recall insights you have had about the woman and things she seems interested in.
2. Make a list of potential places she might enjoy.
3. Pretend that you are her and pick the two that seem the most romantic and fun.
4. Write down a basic timeline for the date.
5. Find creative ways to string the two activities together.
6. While on the date and while planning, constantly ask yourself what could make the experience more romantic and sensual. When you come up with an answer, figure out how to include it.
7. Ask yourself what you could do to turn up the fun to the next level, and add that into your dating structure.

Part of the planning process is to call ahead of time and make sure the place where the date will happen is actually open. Find out the hours they

are open and if there are places nearby that might interest you and your date. Also, find out if reservations are needed and what the cost will be. If you accomplish all seven steps, but don't call ahead and make sure the place is even available, you may be creating another failed date.

Here are two lists; one offers possible places to go on the date, and one places to avoid. If you read these lists and still feel stuck, call her and get her opinion. Most women will be honest with you about where they'd like to go, and it will help ensure that the date goes well.

Potential places to take her

- A movie in an out-of-the-way or art-house theater
- Nature (only if she is a nature lover)
- A road trip to a nearby quaint little town or exciting city
- A part of town that is safe and that neither of you frequents
- Museums
- Concerts
- Offbeat or unusual restaurants
- Parks where you can feed bread to birds
- Out for ice cream
- Amusement parks
- Botanical gardens
- A drive in the country
- A planetarium
- A dance club
- A drive-in movie
- Plays
- Zoo
- Aquariums
- Cooking together
- Wine-tasting parties
- Tourists' spots
- Bike rides
- Comedy clubs

Places to avoid taking her

- Anywhere dangerous
- Martial arts demonstrations and professional wrestling matches
- A sporting event, unless she specifically mentioned she *loves* sports
- Anyplace where there will be lots of guys who will hit on her
- Gory movies
- Strip clubs
- An enrollment event for your multilevel marketing company
- A baseball card convention or *Star Trek* convention
- Anyplace your buddies hang out
- Anyplace *her* buddies hang out
- A concert where you aren't sure if she'll like the music
- An overnight trip
- Any lecture that could lead to a political argument between the two of you
- A sports bar
- A nudist colony
- Anyplace too private if you think she still might be afraid of you

These lists are only partial and are here to get your imagination going. You will best be able to come up with something that suits her perfectly by listening to her and using your imagination. Remember, each woman is different, and the ultimate seduction date for one might be a total turnoff for another. These lists, however, should get you started.

The importance of a backup plan

Seth had created the ultimate date for Stephanie. He set up a picnic in a nature preserve. After that, he planned that they would attend a performance of *Romeo and Juliet* at a nearby outdoor Shakespeare festival. He knew Stephanie would enjoy everything. It all looked perfect.

On the day before the date, he grinned to himself, thinking he was so cool for planning such an awesome date. He daydreamed about having sex with Stephanie outside. He imagined pulling into a country motel

because they would both be so full of lust that they couldn't wait to make it home.

On Saturday Seth woke up to shocking and upsetting news. It was raining outside. In fact, the sky was dark and thunderstorms loomed overhead. He panicked, not knowing where else to take Stephanie. In the end, he canceled the date because he had no other options. By being overly cocky, and not having a backup plan, Seth created a losing situation. The same thing can happen to you if you don't have a backup plan in place, because any plan can be ruined at the last moment. We recommend that you pick three or four places to take a woman for a date and have them planned out, just in case any problems occur.

Purchase at least one surprise gift for her

When Bruce went out with Wendy, he surprised her with several small gifts. He got a small box of chocolates for her. He also purchased a bookmark, with quotes from her favorite author. All told, he spent about $10 on the gifts. In her mind it seemed as though he went to great lengths to create a perfect date for her. These gifts earned him a lot of points with her. It was also fun for Bruce. He got a kick out of being generous and seeing Wendy happy. Creating fun for both of you is a great way to ignite the magic of romance.

Be prepared

Like any Boy Scout, you must be prepared for every circumstance. If you have been paying even the slightest amount of attention, the following list of things will be old hat. By the time you are done reading this book, they will hopefully be second nature. If you haven't been paying attention, let's go through it again. Remember to:

- Clean your car
- Bring condoms
- Clean your bedroom
- Put clean sheets on your bed
- Have candles in the bedroom ready to use
- Make sure your housemates (if you have any) won't barge in on you
- Dress for success

Generate romantic questions to ask her

The priming date chapter covered how to create romantic questions. We recommend that you memorize them and practice them often. On the priming date, you peppered them into the conversation throughout the date, creating romantic feelings and gathering information about her. You may have had some full-blown romantic conversations, but because the date was short, those conversations were also short. The seduction date is different. We suggest you get into longer and deeper conversations about romantic topics. Your romantic and exciting settings will make this easier.

During the first hour of his seduction date with Jodi, Shane began asking her questions about her most passionate kiss. At first he jokingly asked her these questions, but he was surprised at her detailed answers. Jodi described how good the man's tongue felt in her mouth and how much she enjoyed being close to a man. She went on and on, leaving Shane shocked. Finally, after discussing various kissing techniques, he went for the kiss. That began a long and hot make-out session.

The success that Shane experienced stemmed from his ability and willingness to use romantic questions on seduction dates. It is important that they be used to open up longer conversations. Many of the questions can be used as foreplay throughout the date.

Memorize her phone number

During our interviews, several women noted that they were impressed when a man memorized their phone number. Though it may sound trivial to you, they found it to be a sign that the guy was thinking of them often, and it made them feel special. It is an easy feat to accomplish and will help shed a better light on you in the future.

Get psyched up

Use the techniques we described in Chapter 3 to get yourself ready for the date.

MASTERING THE SEDUCTION DATE

It is a major accomplishment to get this far. You should congratulate yourself and be proud. By getting this far, you are way ahead of 90 percent of other single men and you are certainly on the right course.

Look at some of the hoops you've already jumped through: You asked her out; survived at least one priming date; prepared your clothing, car, and home; created a great seduction date plan; prepared for sexual success; practiced romantic questions; created a timeline and a budget; created a backup plan; and much more. She will never know all the things you did to make the date go smoothly, but we do, and we salute you. You are very close to being a true Seducer.

If you have laid the foundation properly, the date should go well. If you haven't, problems are inevitable. Whether you have done the pre-work or not, it is important that you put it all behind you once the date starts. On the date, focus your attention on her. Things will go much more smoothly if you tune all the expectations, thoughts, opinions, and regrets out of your head. We know this is very difficult, and something few people can do perfectly. But if you can do it, every seduction will go better.

Be punctual

Though a seduction date goes at a different pace than a priming date, it is still important for you to be on time. Based on our research and personal experiences, dates flow best when they start on time. Women tend to respect men who are punctual compared to men who tend to be late. Which man would you count on in a pinch? Who would you want as a husband? One who is on time, or one who is late? Punctuality is a wonderful habit to have. It gives you breathing time and helps you concentrate on the date, rather than on how you are going to explain to her why you are tardy.

Now, some "seduction gurus" will tell you that you should be late to make her wait, and to show her that you are more important than she is. If you want to get into that sort of a squabble with women, that's your business,

but we suggest against it. If you feel the need to "show a woman who's boss," use the techniques in the bonus mini-course that comes with this book, which you can get at www.howtosucceedwithwomen.com/owners.

Be polite

A great number of men have a hard time understanding modern-day dating norms. In a time of extreme political correctness and dramatic change, they repeatedly comment on being confused about how to treat women. "I've been on dates over the past year where the women got mad when I opened the door for them," one guy said. We know it can be puzzling to know how to act around women. We recommend you conduct yourself as a man of exceptional manners. For example, open doors for her, take her coat when you go out, help her with her coat when she puts it back on, make sure she sits at a table before you do, and don't start eating a meal before she does. If she mentions it, just shrug and say, "Yeah, I guess I'm an old-fashioned guy." While women may outwardly rebel against it, the majority will be secretly turned on by it. Use that to your advantage.

Treat a woman differently from the way you treat your buddies

It is important that you watch how often you use "vulgar" language, and that you generally act "civilized." The hackneyed cliché "There is a time and place for everything" is useful in this situation. When you are with your buddies, it's great to swear, burp, fart loudly and laugh about it, drink beer from a can, and slap the guy next to you on the back. These behaviors don't cut it on a date. Most of us know this intuitively, but we often fail to manage ourselves properly on the date itself.

In our research for this book, numerous women told us that men show up for dates smelly and dressed like slobs. They also told us that many men do stupid things to "ruin" the date. The man might burp loudly and then laugh to himself, or maybe he talks about how all his coworkers are stupid, and he may even indulge in "colorful" language. When you do these things, the woman will disqualify you as "lover material" and start planning how to cut the date short. By being clear about which behaviors are appropriate around women and which aren't, you will avoid these dating pitfalls.

Focus on your date, not other women

You probably don't even realize it, but if you are like most men, you constantly look at women on the street, in bars, in restaurants—everywhere. For a single man, the world is his shopping mall. Why not ogle an attractive woman? Most men stare and wonder what women are like in bed, if their breasts are real, and what the chances are of dating them. These are perfectly natural reactions.

While it is all right to look at women on the street, when you are on a date it is totally unacceptable. Do you want to anger the woman you are with and blow the date? Of course not. When you stare incessantly at other women, she will probably feel angry, jealous, and sad. When she feels upset, it is more work for you, and it delays creating the sexual mood.

The first step is to realize that you habitually check out women. The next step is to decrease the frequency with which you do it. Third, when you find yourself doing it on a date, stop instantly. After a while you will have a handle on this habit.

Darrell was on a seduction date with Betsy. They were having a fun time at the zoo. It was summer, and they sat on a park bench in the shade eating snow cones. Sitting on a nearby bench were two amazing-looking twenty-year-old women who, frankly, were much more attractive than Betsy. They both wore very short skirts and tight-fitting shirts. Their breasts were nearly popping out, and their nipples were clearly visible. Darrell couldn't stop staring at them.

After a few minutes, it became obvious to both Betsy and the young women that he was checking them out. Betsy became upset and threatened to leave if he didn't stop. "Why did you even ask me out if all you are going to do is look at other women?" she asked. "I thought we were having a romantic time and I was starting to like you, but now I am not so sure." It took hours for Darrell to regain the mood he had lost in the park. He learned the hard way that while it is natural to look, you must restrain yourself from checking out other women when you are on a date.

Be affectionate

Most men have a difficult time being affectionate. They reserve affectionate words and touching for the bedroom. In day-to-day life, men are apt to worry about being viewed as "soft" or wimpy. Women, however, love it. You can speed up your seduction and begin to "sweep a woman off her feet" by being affectionate.

Affection can take the form of compliments. Here are a few examples:

"Joyce, I really enjoy spending time with you. I am amazed at how close I feel to you after such a short time."

"I must tell you that you look even more beautiful on this date than I've ever seen you look before. It is a delight to be able to look at you."

"I am having such a fun time being with you. I want to thank you for being such a great date and being so easygoing about the plans today."

"Joyce, you are the type of woman I've been waiting to meet for a long, long time. You are a very special woman and I really appreciate being with you."

What links all the above examples together is that the woman is thanked, complimented, and acknowledged. You must do this in your own way, in your own unique style. If you use our words, and they are contrary to your own, your affectionate words will sound awkward and insincere.

More frequently, affection is expressed through actions. These can be soft and gentle touching, notes, a quick phone call, or a surprise gift. The same rules apply, as we discussed earlier. The action must acknowledge, compliment, and thank her in some way.

Ben took Erin to the movies. They saw the latest "chick flick." Toward the end of the movie one of the main characters was on her deathbed in the hospital. The character was explaining to her granddaughter all the hardships of growing up on a farm in the 1930s. Erin began crying during the scene. Ben thought the scene was silly and unrealistic. However, he reached for Erin's hand when she began to cry, and held it while she sobbed. In that moment, he displayed affection and caring for her. She was impressed at his level of sensitivity.

Touch her at least six times

During the priming date you began touching the woman non-intrusively. You did this to set the stage for more affectionate touching. On the seduction date more deliberate touch is required. You want her to be frequently reminded that you are interested in her. By setting a precedent of touching her, you build a mood of sensuality for later.

You may wish to hold her hand, touch her face lightly, touch her hair, run your fingers on her neck, or touch her back and waist. We highly discourage you from touching her breasts, butt, lips, or thighs. It is important that you kiss her before touching any of these "private" areas. You must start small and build from there.

Warning: Some women will be uncomfortable with you touching them so often. While they may even like you, and want to sleep with you, they may feel freaked out. Always pay attention to a woman's response. It is crucial that you be respectful and don't upset her. Realize that religion, culture, and family norms all play a part in how she responds to you. A highly religious woman may feel uncomfortable no matter how you touch her, while another might enjoy holding hands and passionate kissing in public. It all depends on the woman. It is your job to note her reactions and act accordingly. If she is not ready for your touching and recoils from your hand, then *back off* and build more of a seductive connection. Remember, we live in a world where a simple touch can be grounds for a lawsuit. It's your responsibility to make sure you don't go too far.

Compliment her often

One of the best ways to make a woman feel special is through compliments. It is important, however, that you be truthful when you compliment her. Women are highly skilled in their ability to spot insincerity and can usually spot a lie a mile away. If they think you are lying, they will undoubtedly hold it against you.

Women are likely to be flattered if you compliment them on something most guys wouldn't notice. We've explained how important it is for you to set yourself apart from other men. When you compliment a woman in a sincere manner about something most people don't notice, she is likely to

be impressed. For example, noticing an interesting barrette in her hair or a necklace will show her that you are aware of more than her breasts and her butt.

Here are a few examples of things to compliment her on: the clothes she is wearing, her eyes, an article of jewelry, her smile, her hands, an intelligent remark she makes, her presence, or her sense of humor.

While on a canoe ride, Zach and Chrissy had a deep conversation about Eastern religions. He was surprised at how much she knew about the subject and immediately complimented her. Later on, he told her how cute she looked with a canoe paddle in hand and a life preserver around her neck. He also commented on how good her hair looked in the sun. By paying attention to Chrissy, Zach had an easy time coming up with several ways to compliment her.

Some men fear that complimenting women puts them (the men) in a "one-down" position. And it's true that it can become that way if your behavior consists of nothing but a groveling stream of fawning compliments.

But think of it this way: When Zach tells Chrissy, "I'm impressed you know so much about Eastern religions—I don't get to meet many women I can have this sort of conversation with," he's telling her that *he* is a man who is capable of making judgments about people, and that she has had the good fortune to pass his test of her. He is not being weak. In fact, he's showing her that he believes he has the right to decide what is worthy of complimenting. This makes him appear strong and moves the seduction forward.

Talk about upbeat topics

It is important to discuss upbeat topics. We don't mean that you come across as some Pollyanna type of guy, who is always smiling and happy-go-lucky. We do say that being negative and criticizing everyone and everything will not work, however. If you frequently discuss harsh topics, complain, talk about things you hate, insult your date, and seem preoccupied with sex, the date won't go well. Remember, the purpose of the date is for her to have fun and enjoy being with you. If you create a negative mood through your conversations, she will likely find you creepy and look for ways to avoid you. After all, most of us avoid being around people who scare us or who seem nuts. Your date is not any different.

Some men also tend in general to be overly serious. This works just as badly as discussing death or war or how much you hate your job. You create fun by talking about upbeat topics, and this helps the woman relax.

Bob was a strong believer in recycling. He shared his views with Carla on a seduction date. He told her in no uncertain terms that he hated the mayor of their city for being so lax in his recycling campaign. "The mayor is such a jerk," he said. "I think politicians are mostly morons. Many of them would be better shot in the head than serving our communities. Don't you agree?" Carla became nervous with Bob's violent comments. Though she, too, believed in recycling, his intensity scared her. If he had said the same thing in a milder manner, Carla could have discussed the topic with him, and even agreed. Instead, he looked like a freak.

On his date with Wendy, Bruce told her about many of the international trips he had taken in his life. He shared his experiences visiting the rain forest in Brazil and climbing in the Swiss Alps. While he was forthright about a few political issues that came up on the date, he made sure Wendy always felt like she was part of the conversation. Bruce frequently asked Wendy about her opinions. He made sure not to say things that would be construed as too intense or harsh, and often brought the conversation back to upbeat topics when it threatened to get glum.

Topics to avoid discussing

- Controversial topics that could offend her
- Anything too overtly sexual
- Violence
- Death
- Children being harmed or abducted
- How much you hate your boss or job
- How much you hate marriage
- How much you hate, well, *anything*
- The IRS
- Your fascination with serial killers
- How you collect cigars
- Past girlfriends

- How often you like to have sex
- Cruelty to animals, especially cats and dogs
- Topics she is not interested in, like cars, math, gaming consoles, *Star Trek*, *Doctor Who*, sports, etc.
- Your bad habits that you really need to overcome

Make decisions

On a seduction date it is important that you come across as confident. Women want to know that you are comfortable with yourself and not apologetic for who you are. We've said it before and we'll say it again: One easy way to demonstrate confidence is to be decisive—in planning the date, when talking to her about where to go next, what restaurant you desire, what table to sit at in the restaurant, what music to listen to in the car, and what section of the museum to check out first.

At the same time, you don't want to come across as a control freak, or a condescending jerk. Just remember this: A man kills a date when he constantly responds with "I don't care what we do next. What do you want to do?" or "I don't know" in the face of a decision. Being wishy-washy shows that you lack confidence and lack direction. Make decisions on the date and you will increase her level of respect for you. If you haven't learned this yet, learn it now.

Listen to her opinions

As we mentioned before, it is important that you take her opinions seriously and always include her in the decision-making process. Many women complain that men don't listen to them and don't care about what they think or feel. When women express their opinions, men tend to view them as nagging or demanding. It is natural to sometimes feel this way. However, it is still important, whether you think she is being a nag or not, to listen to her opinion and to let her talk.

When a woman begins opening up to you, it means that she has begun to view you as a potential mate. She trusts you enough to tell you her thoughts, opinions, and ideas. One of the hidden costs of dating is that you will have to put up with things you don't want to. Our advice is to notice

when you are upset or annoyed that the woman talks too much or is overly demanding, and simply keep listening anyway.

Cheryl loved to talk. Talk, talk, talk. She spouted off her badly informed opinions to anyone who would listen. Dean was attracted to her physically, but occasionally could not stand to listen to her nonstop talking and unfounded opinions.

Dean's tendency was to argue with women. He would meet a woman, they would date for a few weeks, and he would finally tell her what he really thought about her and her opinions. She would, of course, promptly dump him. After a few years of repeating this pattern over and over again, he realized that the way he interacted with women fundamentally didn't work. Soon after, he became one our students and his problems vanished. He realized that women mostly want someone to just listen and take their opinions, so he stopped getting upset. He found out that he could be bored when Cheryl talked, while still listening to her. He also noticed that after a few minutes Cheryl would usually be done giving her opinions and the date could continue. Because he listened to her, Cheryl felt very close to him and wanted to be sexual.

FROM RAGING BULL TO PURRING KITTEN IN NINE EASY STEPS

As you've seen, seduction dates are dramatically different from priming dates. But problems do occur on seduction dates. Given how much time you are spending together and the fact that romantic feelings will likely be in the air, you both may be more tense than usual. She will be off in her own world, thinking of reasons why you could or could not be a couple. You will probably be off in your world, thinking of the stupid things you've said, worrying about whether she is having fun, and wondering when you'll get to see her naked. All this can create trouble.

Another thing that makes seduction dates even more volatile than priming dates is that by this time you both have more of an investment in each other than you did before. This creates expectation and tension, which can create problems.

You'll know you have a problem if she gets upset about anything. You may say or do something that offends her or that goes against her values. The two of you together might have an upsetting experience, and she may need to talk about it. No matter what happens to upset her, the solution is the same. This model is effective on any date, with any woman, at any step along the way. If you modify some of the steps, you can use them in long-term-relationship conflicts as well.

1. Listen to her

When they are upset, most women just want someone (you) to listen to them. If your date can express her problem, concern, or misunderstanding early enough, it will likely go away easily. We recommend that you just listen without interrupting her or trying to fix it. When you listen to her, she is likely to calm down quickly.

2. Repeat back what you heard

A woman not only wants to know you listened to her, but she also wants to make sure you completely understand everything she said. When you repeat back what you heard her say, it gives you an opportunity to clarify anything you may have misunderstood, and an opportunity to demonstrate that you really are listening, which will also help calm her down.

3. Thank her

Even if you feel angry that she is telling you all her thoughts and opinions, and you really couldn't possibly care less, thank her for taking the time and the risk to talk to you. In her world, she is taking a risk by telling you her problems or concerns. By getting it off her chest, so to speak, she is likely to feel more relaxed and more connected to you.

She may also be testing to see how you respond. When you thank her, she can see that you are caring and sensitive. It also foreshadows, for her, how you might respond during a future conflict. When you behave like a gentleman and respond like a caring guy, she will trust you more and want to be sexual with you.

4. Continue to listen to her

It is likely that after she has one problem, another will surface in conjunction with the first. Once again, let her tell you any other problem she feels is necessary. Your job is to listen, repeat it back to her, and to thank her.

5. Make promises and apologies if it makes sense to do so

If you follow the previous four steps, she will calm down, and there won't be a lot more for you to do. If you can see how your behavior might be something to change, then you can promise to change it. If you can see that you have something to apologize for, why not apologize?

There's a real power with women (and with people in general) to keeping your promises about changing your behavior. If you are constantly doing something that upsets her—like making jokes at her expense, for instance—and she finally gets upset about it, you can really increase her level of trust in you a lot by apologizing, promising to stop doing it . . . and actually not doing it again. When she sees she can trust you to keep your word and make the changes you say you'll make, she'll feel safe sharing much more of herself—like her physical self—with you.

6. If you really, truly don't care

If she has a huge problem with something you think is insignificant, determine if you want to end the date or not. Determine if you think sex will happen. If you are attracted to her and foresee future dates with her, and if you can honestly do so, apologize. If she doesn't seem worth the hassle, end the date then and there. Quit wasting your time and hers. If she does seem worth it, let all your frustrations go and move on to the next step.

7. Let it all go

Given that she was upset, you are likely to be also. We strongly recommend that you don't fan the fire by telling her your opinions or showing her your anger. You have to keep yourself focused on your long-term goals. If you tell her how wrong she is, and logically prove how stupid she is to be upset with you, the date will likely fail. If you want success, you must let it go.

8. Compliment her

When things have calmed down, we also recommend that you compliment her again to end the whole thing. Most guys who make it through these steps fail to leave the conversation on a good note. Complimenting her leaves the whole conflict clean and complete. Then you can move on to something easier and more fun. She will likely be impressed if you compliment her on her ability to be straight with you and on her communication skills.

9. Repeat this process as many times as it takes

Then get on with the date.

AFTER THE DATE "DID" CHECKLIST

- Made her feel special
- Gave her at least one small gift
- Took her outside her normal environment
- Had surprises on the date
- Paid for the date
- Were flexible with time
- Made her smile and/or laugh at least one time
- Planned for success
- Assessed the attraction level
- Created a sexual goal for the date
- Scheduled the date at times that work for you
- Decided ahead of time how much money you were willing to spend and stuck to that amount
- Used information from the priming date to guide the date
- Took her to a romantic spot during the date
- Used seductive language (seduce, attraction, falling in love, romance, etc.) seven times
- Used interested body language
- Whispered at least once
- Constructed the date using the method we recommend
- Created a backup plan

- Prepared yourself and your surroundings
- Got psyched up before the date
- Were punctual for the date
- Acted with exceptional manners
- Treated the woman differently from your buddies
- Focused on your date, not other women
- Were affectionate
- Touched her at least six times
- Kissed her at least two times
- Complimented her often
- Were easy and fun to be around
- Talked about upbeat topics
- Made decisions
- Listened to her opinions

AFTER THE DATE "DIDN'T" CHECKLIST

- Didn't treat her like a friend
- Didn't insult her
- Didn't complain
- Didn't complain about other women
- Didn't check out other women
- Didn't grab her ass
- Didn't rely on her for certainty that the date was going well
- Didn't allow yourself to get upset when you forgot your lines, etc.
- Didn't take anything she said or did personally

HOW TO END THE SEDUCTION DATE

If you've done all the steps we recommend, the date should end with you both feeling romantic and sexy. Since you have planned for success, you will end the date near someplace where you can explore each other's body. If there is sexual chemistry and the mood is right when you get to the end of the seduction date, go for it. In the next two chapters, we will show you how to get the first kiss, get her into bed, and be the lover of her dreams.

9

Closing the Deal:
The First Kiss
and More

On the rare occasions that Bob has actually attempted to kiss a woman, everything has gone wrong. Having decided that he was sick of being alone and that it was time he "made his move" on his friend Sherry, he invited her to see an arty, NC-17-rated documentary about the sex industry at the local art film theater.

During the movie, which showed many people having sex, Bob noticed that Sherry was sitting as far from him as possible without actually moving to a different seat. In view of that, he decided not to put his arm around her. After all, he reasoned, why make her uncomfortable? They were both watching people have sex: Of course she would just naturally want him the way he wanted her after seeing that.

After the film, Bob was almost shaking with nervousness, but figured that they had just seen a (sort of) romantic movie, so it was now or never. While still in the lobby, he took Sherry by the shoulders and tried to kiss her. She recoiled, pulling away from him and turning her face aside. "Please!" she said. "Bob, I like you as a friend! As a friend!" He was crushed, and when Sherry said, "I must leave now," he didn't even

walk her back to her car. His first kiss had failed, and he was alone again.

Men often ask us why getting the first kiss is hard for them. They find themselves ready for it, but the right time never seems to come. Or they wait for the woman to make the first move, which she almost never does. They find themselves waiting for that one woman who is so obviously attracted to them, with whom the chemistry is so overwhelmingly great, that the first kiss seems to "just happen." While such chemistry does exist in the world, and most men have experienced at least one time when getting sexually involved with a woman seemed easy and effortless, if you wait for "magic" to happen, you will have a long, long wait.

If you learn nothing else from this book, learn this: Waiting for magic, and hoping that something good happens, will never get you the life you want. It won't give you the sex life you want with women, and it won't give you the results you want in the rest of your life either. Besides, being a man who waits and hopes for magic will actually make you less attractive to women, who tend to go for men who actively create the lives they want. You must commit yourself to learning what it takes to create the life you want, and follow through until you achieve that result. When it comes to the first kiss (and more), you can't wait for magic. You have to learn and apply the necessary knowledge. Waiting for magic will leave you lonely once again.

THE SECRET TO GETTING THE FIRST KISS

The secret of getting the first kiss is so simple that once you understand it, getting the kiss will be a trivial risk rather than a huge event. The secret is the pre-work. By the time you go for that kiss, you must have her so ready, so prepared, and so desiring that kiss that she is more than good to go. Once again, it's like lighting a camp stove. If you just lunge at the stove with a lit match, of course it won't light. If the stove doesn't light, the problem isn't with the match you are using, how you are holding it, or the way you struck it on the box. It's not a defective camp stove and it doesn't hate you. You just haven't primed it properly. If you focus on thinking that you are doing something wrong during the "lighting" stage of anything, when

the problem is that you haven't "primed the stove" properly, nothing you do will work.

The first kiss—and the first time having sex—is the same. If you prime the woman properly, the kiss is easy and seems natural. Men believe that getting the first kiss is difficult, or that there must be some complicated move or line that they are missing. They tend to focus on the wrong side of the problem. Understand this: The end of the date is *too late* to start preparing her for your kiss. Rather than focusing on the moment of the first kiss, you need to focus on taking the proper steps leading up to it.

When Bob went in for his first kiss with Sherry, he'd done none of the necessary pre-work. First, Sherry saw him as a friend, and he'd never given her any reason not to. He hadn't shown any credible romantic interest before his attempted kiss. If he had, he would have found out that she wasn't interested. Knowing this ahead of time would have disqualified her from the running before he wasted time dating her, or he could have worked on the very early steps of building her interest through flirting, rather than jumping right to the date. By taking her to an erotic film, without any romantic prelude, Bob created a situation that made her scared of him. Then he had the nerve to wonder why the first kiss seemed hard to get!

Bob needs to be more like Bruce. Bruce realizes that the first kiss is simply a result of properly making romantic moves earlier in the date. When he first kissed Wendy, she was ready for it. He had prequalified her as an interested woman immediately and showed his romantic interest consistently. He asked romantic questions and engaged her in romantic conversations. He did everything we teach, "by the book." By the time he went for the first kiss, she was ready and willing, and responded passionately. Bruce knows that the first kiss is not difficult. It's the work that leads up to it that he must pay attention to.

REVIEW OF THE PRE-WORK

By this time, you already know most of what you must do to get a woman thinking romantically about you. If you need more information about these things, reread this book! The preceding chapters have covered everything you need to know to prime a woman for physical involvement with you.

Before going for the first kiss, you must have:

- Asked romantic questions
- Conducted romantic conversations
- Touched her hand
- Looked into her eyes a little too long
- Touched her non-intrusively and casually
- Made decisions quickly and easily
- Made her smile and/or laugh
- Been clear about your goals
- Made your romantic interest known
- Gathered information about her romantic needs
- Fulfilled her romantic needs on the seduction date
- Complimented her three times
- Checked out her body in the way specified
- Used seductive language (seduce, attraction, falling in love, romance, etc.) seven times
- Used interested body language
- Whispered to her

These are the bare-bones basics. If you haven't done most of these things, don't even consider the first kiss. Go back and do more of them. Create more romantic conversations. Put her into more romantic situations. Get the basics handled, then move on.

After you've done the pre-work, there are only two steps left for you: testing her readiness and going for the kiss.

TESTING HER READINESS

When you are going for the first kiss, certain conditions must be met or your attempted kiss will fail. Until all of these conditions are met, you might as well not go for it; she's only going to say no. If, on the other hand, you have fulfilled these conditions, feel free to try! She's ready. You should know, however, that these conditions may be met faster than they are in the examples in this book. If the chemistry is there and if it "feels right," no

matter when it comes, go for the kiss. This may be at the end of, or even during, the priming date. It may even be *before* the priming date, if you notice that her stove is primed and ready to be lit. It can even be when you first meet a woman, if she's attracted to you and the energy is right.

The conditions you must meet before going for the first kiss are:

- She is not surprised by the kiss.
- She is thinking of the kiss, and more.
- She knows that you want her, and likes the idea.

But how can you know if these conditions are met? We've developed a series of tests for our students to use before they go for the first kiss. These tests will tell you if your date is ready, and help continue to prepare her at the same time. We suggest you perform these tests and check out her responses before you try for it.

The touching test

You can test her readiness by gauging her responses to casual and romantic touching. Casual touching is simple and fast. It's when your fingers touch her when you give her a cup of coffee, or when you touch her arm or back to guide her to the table you've selected. Casual touching is ambiguous; you might be touching her as a friend, or you might be touching her as a potential lover. Romantic touching is more intrusive. If you are touching and holding her hand, or rubbing her arm, or keeping your hand on any part of her body for more than a few seconds, you are touching her romantically.

You want her to welcome longer and longer periods of touch from you. First, touch her casually, and see how she responds. More than likely, she will have no visible response at all. If she pulls away, keep your touching extremely brief, and keep up your romantic conversations. If she continuously shrugs away from your touch, consider getting rid of her and moving on. There's no reason to stay with a woman who is cold, unresponsive, and doesn't want to be romantic with you.

If she does respond positively, touch her for longer periods of time. If

she gets more relaxed and animated, if her skin flushes, or if her eyes get shiny and reflective, these are all signs of positive response. In this scenario, move to putting your hand on hers for longer periods. Don't make a big deal of this, just let it seem to happen.

The hug test

One way to find out how a woman feels about you is to see how she responds to being hugged. Like casual touching, hugging is something you can usually get a woman to accept just by doing it. When you hug a woman and don't make a big deal out of it, much of the time she'll just assume that you are a guy who hugs, and not make a big deal out of it either.

We usually recommend that you avoid hugging a woman much before you are having sex with her. Hugging is a friendly thing to do, rather than a lover-ly thing to do. If she gets use to being in your arms without kissing you, it's easy for her to resolve the apparent incongruity by telling herself that you are simply a friend. Also, hugging is a time when men who are starved for touch accidentally show some desperation. They grab hold, get caught up in how good it feels to them (rather than to her), squeeze too hard, and don't let go. One woman told us about a guy she met at a party who hugged her when she was leaving, after knowing her for less than an hour. "He hugged me, then put his hands on my hips, and held me close while he said good-bye to me. It seemed really weird to be held there. I felt like I couldn't get away." The hug is a chance to screw up, so if you do it, you want to be sure to do it properly.

The first rule of hugging a woman that you are dating is that you keep it short. Short, short, short. Use it as a test of her readiness, not as a chance to get your sexual or touch needs met. You'll get enough of that later on. When saying hello or good-bye to her, you can often simply take her in your arms and hug her. If you keep it short, it won't scare her, and you'll be able to gauge her response. Does she press into you? Does she seem to want to really hang on? That's a good sign, and you might want to move to kissing her right then. If she seems to want to get away, then you know you have more work to do in making her feel romantic feelings.

The face kiss test

Along with hugging, you can try face-kissing. This is when you kiss her cheek to see how she responds. If she leans into the kiss, and smiles, she's into it, and will be receptive to your lip-kiss later. If she pulls back, or winces, then it's back to the drawing board again. She most certainly won't be receptive to a lip-kiss if she won't take one on the cheek willingly.

The enthusiasm test

You can also gauge a woman's level of interest by her level of enthusiasm. This will be shown in her overall demeanor, but it's best shown in the time between one activity and the next. It's *between* the activities that you do together, rather than *during* them, that she has the best opportunity to claim she is tired and needs to go home. Watch her level of interest. After the movie, is she eager to go out for coffee or a drink, or does she seem reluctant? Does she seem to be looking for a juncture at which she can end the date, or is she up for partying with you all night long? It's these "between spaces" that will tell you her level of interest.

When Mike went out with Kary, he was careful to notice how she behaved between events. He took her to the local botanical gardens for their seduction date, and afterward invited her to get some ice cream with him. "Great!" she said. He knew that she was enthusiastic, and would probably be interested and responsive when he tried to kiss her later.

A few weeks earlier, when he had taken Kelly to that same botanical gardens, she had said, "Well, I really have to get going. I've got a lot of work to do, so . . . well . . ." At this point he knew she wasn't interested, and that she probably wouldn't be responsive to a kiss. He let her leave at once, and didn't ask her to stay, whine, or, most important, try to kiss her.

The pretend kiss test

This test also primes the woman for your kiss. You begin by moving toward her, as if to kiss her, at some point "change your mind," and back off again. If, as you move toward her, she backs away, she probably doesn't want to kiss you. If she stays still, or moves slightly forward, she's probably interested. The pretend kiss can "seal the deal" for the real kiss later. If she

hasn't moved away, then you both have acknowledged that a kiss in inevitable, and it's only a matter of time.

When Bruce seduces Wendy, he does all the pre-work. As the date progresses, he also tests her readiness by touching her, hugging her, and kissing her face, noticing her level of enthusiasm moving from one activity to another, her responsiveness to compliments, and her response to his "pretend kiss." All these actions also improve her readiness for the kiss. Anytime he gets a response he doesn't like, he returns to building their sense of connection by doing more of the pre-work. By the time he goes for the kiss, her response is passionate and displays obvious interest.

TEST CHECKLIST

For your convenience, here is a list of the tests.

- The touching test
- The hug test
- The face kiss test
- The enthusiasm test
- The pretend kiss test

GOING FOR THE FIRST KISS

If you've done the pre-work, and she's responded well to the tests, you are ready to move ahead and kiss her for the first time. She's well primed, ready, and all will almost certainly go smoothly. We have to cover only a few elements of technique to finish your preparation.

Timing

In every sexual and romantic interaction, timing is everything. When you go to kiss a woman, you have to be in a romantic moment *right now*. Not yesterday, not a few minutes ago, not last week on the phone. In time and with practice, you'll learn to feel romantic moments as you create them. When the romantic moment is present, make your move. Don't wait to kiss her outside her door, like men do on TV and in the movies. When

the mood is there, go for it. You never know how long the mood will last, and it may not come back for hours.

Timing is one of the most difficult skills to teach. Learning this art requires practice, and a willingness to mess up. We believe that good timing is natural to all men—we just do things that destroy it. With that in mind, we can tell you the basic blocks that destroy it in romantic interactions with women:

1. *Lack of confidence kills timing.* By now, this should sound like a broken record to you, but we keep repeating it so it will become ingrained in your brain. Managing your confidence level with women is one of the most important things you can do. The biggest way men destroy their confidence is to look to the woman for assurance that the date is going well. Don't do it. Go with your gut, and move when you feel certain the time is right.

2. *Being attached to the outcome kills timing.* When you are acting with complete confidence, you are fully present in the moment, paying attention to what is going on around you. If you are worrying that your desired outcome won't happen, you won't be paying attention to the woman in front of you. Because you won't be paying attention, you'll mess up. Let go of your outcome—she's either going to respond, or she isn't. When you are relaxed and are goal-focused, while knowing that anything that happens is fine, you will have much better timing.

3. *The wrong attitude kills timing.* Just as on the rest of the date, your attitude should be one of confidence, caring yet a bit distant, knowing that if this woman won't kiss you, another will. You must show her that she is special and you enjoy her company, but have many other potential lovers as well.

The biggest way to destroy your attitude is to think that having success with this woman, today, will be the thing that validates your life. How many times must we say it? Nice as it is to be successful with women, you shouldn't base your self-image on whether or not the woman you are dating wants to have sex with you. Keeping that in mind will help create

the proper attitude for that first kiss, and make you more attractive to her.

HOW TO GO FOR THE FIRST KISS

So you've done your pre-work, run some tests, and think she is ready for the kiss. You feel confident, have given up your outcome, and you are both feeling the romantic mood. How do you go for that first kiss?

There are four ways. They are: the "just do it" method, the "ask" method, the "announce" method, and the "she kisses you" method. Let's go over these methods one at a time.

The "just do it" method

When the feeling is right, you simply kiss her. This can happen in many different ways, depending on the circumstances. It may work best to take her in your arms; it may work best to simply lean over and kiss her lightly. The details will change depending on the situation, but the foundation of this method is consistent. You kiss her, you just do it, and don't worry.

The "ask" method

In this politically correct world of ours, this is the most legally unambiguous way to get the first kiss. After all, kissing a woman without her permission can be considered assault. Of course, if you've used the techniques in this book, you are very unlikely to be trying to kiss a woman who would be so offended by it that she presses charges.

The problem with the "ask" method is that it works worst of all, and some women, even those who are interested, are turned off by this approach. A surprising number of women have told us that they are offended by men who ask if they can kiss them. Natalie, one of our interviewees, commented, "I hate it when a man asks if he can kiss me. One guy did that a few months ago, and I told him to bug off! If a guy wants to kiss me, the least he can do is be man enough to do it without asking!" It's a hard quandary for men. On the one hand, some women are telling us that we must get absolute, crystal-clear consent from them every time we touch them.

On the other hand, women tell us that they are turned off by men who ask before the first kiss! We suggest that, most of the time, you not ask before kissing a woman, but that you definitely do the pre-work and the testing first. Asking first simply creates more problems than it solves.

The "announce" method

This method can work quite well, and gives the woman an out if she doesn't want you to kiss her. By making some sort of announcement about what you are going to do, you aren't actually asking permission—which, as we have said, puts some women off—but you are still giving her a chance to tell you to bug off if she doesn't want a kiss. You might say, "Oh, my. You are so beautiful . . . Try not to panic, I'm about to kiss you," and then go for it. The "announce" method works well, and keeps you on "the right side of the law."

The "she kisses you" method

This method is just what it sounds like: She gets so aroused and romantically inclined that she kisses you. You're probably saying to yourself, "Boy, that would be so great if it ever happened," but as you begin to master the material in this book, you'll start to understand that the first kiss is no big deal, however you get it. It doesn't make a huge difference if she kisses you or if you kiss her. It's just another step in her inevitable seduction.

IF SHE SAYS NO

Congratulations! A woman rejected your kiss! While this probably won't happen often, it may well happen. Welcome! Join the club! Here's what you should and shouldn't do when a woman spurns your attempted kiss:

Decide what you are going to make it mean

Your first action, when this happens, is to decide what you are going to make it mean to you. Left to your own devices, you would probably make it mean that you are a loser and a jerk, a guy who's destined to always be alone. Don't leave yourself to your own devices. *Decide*, in advance if possible, what you are going to make a rejection mean.

We suggest that you interpret her rejection to mean that she isn't ready yet to kiss you. It is as though she were saying, "Not now, but some other time." You may also want to take it as a sign that you have more pre-work to do. We strongly advise you to avoid making it mean that you are a loser. If you want success with women, you must make a more empowering decision about what rejection means. From our experience, no man ever has constant success without first having to face many rejections.

Never ask "Why not?"

Asking "Why not?" is a typical rookie mistake men make. First, it will make you sound like a wimp. It calls to mind a little kid, whining "Why not?" to his mother. Asking "Why not?" also seems like a form of begging. This will make her want to kiss you even less. Second, when you ask her "Why not?" she'll tell you, and that's the last thing you want. It forces her to come up with justifications for not kissing you. The more she comes up with, the less likely it is she will *ever* kiss you. Asking this question is seduction suicide.

Never argue with her about it

Arguing is the other rookie mistake men make in the face of women's sexual rejection. It does the same thing as asking "Why not?" because it makes her dig into her position more completely. We know of no instance in which a woman has changed her mind and wholeheartedly kissed a man because he argued with her rejection. All it does is ensure that she will never kiss you, ever. She will think of negative thoughts when she thinks of you, and avoid you in the future. By arguing with a woman's decision, you are saying that you don't respect her opinion and her boundaries, which will likely turn her off more.

Never beg her

Don't beg, don't cajole, don't "Aw, c'mon, you don't know how it hurts a guy." Begging a woman shows her that you are a wimpy, powerless man, who can't handle waiting for what he wants. It shows her you have no resolution to make your life what you want, and demonstrates to her that you

go groveling through life. Don't do it. You will definitely lose your self-respect by lowering yourself at her whims.

Try again later

She's only rejecting you *now*, not later. While you don't want to badger her, it's a good idea to remember that some women will just want to see how you handle them saying no. Others just aren't in the mood for it today, but they would be another time. Still others will be willing to kiss you, but only after you've done more work to show you really like them, not just their bodies. Some women simply don't want you, and never will. Remember that each no is a stepping stone to an eventual yes, if not with this woman, then with some other.

THE TEN CRUCIAL MISTAKES
THAT BLOW THE FIRST KISS

By now you realize that most of your dating problems have come from the dumb things you've done to wreck seduction situations. You've been a friend, or have treated a woman as you would a guy, or you've been indecisive. Let's look at the top mistakes men make going for the first kiss, and show you how to avoid them.

Mistake 1. You announce your intention to seduce her

Here's a very dumb thing that you may be tempted to do: Tell your date that you have a seduction book, are studying it, and intend to use the techniques on her! You may think no one would be this dumb, but we've known plenty of men who've done it. Needless to say, she won't want to kiss you after that.

Mistake 2. You offend her by saying or doing something stupid

There's no shortage of ways to offend a woman you are dating. A women's magazine article gives a few examples of stupid things men have said or done on first dates:

- The man who asked his date, "Why is it that all the good women are taken?"
- The man who said, "I'm so intrigued by the mind of a serial killer. The rage and passion he must feel while actually killing someone is fascinating to me."
- The man who offended (and mystified) his date by saying, "I shower four times a day. I have to."
- The man who felt compelled to admit that "When I have sex with a woman, I always have to imagine I'm with someone else."
- The man who said about marriage, "I'm not a big fan of the institution myself."
- The man who said about his ex-girlfriend, "Some people just *need* hitting."
- The man who invited a woman for dinner at his house and, at the end of the date, said, "To keep this relationship devoid of any sense of anyone owing anyone anything, why don't you pay your half?" He then presented her with an itemized bill of what he'd spent.

You can also alienate a woman by discussing your love of pornography, commenting on other women's bodies, or taking a position on a political or gender issue that she profoundly disagrees with.

You can further offend her by lighting a cigar (unless she lights one first) or engaging in a prolonged scratching session. If you do something that insults her deeply, back off at once, apologize briefly if you think it will help, and go on with the date as if nothing happened. Sadly, you often won't know what she feels. She won't tell you; she'll simply write you off, and get away from you as quickly as she can. She certainly won't kiss you.

Mistake 3. You approach the kiss as though it was a business transaction

This is a common problem for men who want to get to the bottom line and "get down to business." You may have this problem if you are used to the business world, or are just very practical.

Men who fall into this trap have a harder time than others accepting

that they must go out of their way to make a woman feel special. They see all the work involved as false, manipulative, and dishonest. They don't like it one bit, and seem set on proving us wrong. Sadly for them, we aren't wrong, and when the practical-minded man approaches a woman for a kiss, she inevitably ends up rejecting him. She tells him that he seems too "cold and calculating," which he is. You want to be warm and kind, and this is achieved by being romantic, doing the little things, and following the guidelines laid out in this book.

Mistake 4. You are indecisive

When you decide to go for the kiss, go for it! Whatever method you use, this is the time when "he who hesitates is lost." Women want a strong, decisive man, and that is never more evident than on the first kiss. This does *not* mean that you become overly forceful, or that you ignore her if she protests. If she doesn't want to be kissed, of course don't kiss her. But you shouldn't weasel around about it. If you've done the pre-work, and she's passed the tests, go for it!

Mistake 5. You act like she is doing you a favor by kissing you

When Bob eventually gets that first kiss, he thanks his date! This is a mistake. You can say, "That was very nice," but don't act like she's doing you a favor that is any bigger than the one you are doing her.

Mistake 6. You get flustered by minor problems on the date and give up

Giving up is almost always worse for the seduction than any mistake you made. Men often get flustered if a conversation doesn't go well, if she becomes offended, or if she seems suspicious of their romantic questions. Remember, she's either going to respond to you or she isn't. It doesn't mean much about you. If you get flustered, you can often pretend nothing happened and move on. She may be looking to you for verification that the date is still okay, even if there was an awkward moment or odd exchange. If you don't give up, she'll see that things are fine, and probably relax.

Mistake 7. You push too hard, too quickly

Every seduction has its own pace. You can destroy the effectiveness of any of the techniques in this book by doing them too hard, too fast, and inexpertly. We know this may be hard to hear, coming as it does after hundreds of pages telling you how important it is that you take action in the seduction, but it's still true. You must take action, and you must also move at her pace.

Practically speaking, this means you must learn to pay attention to her responses. If she is consistently resistant and unresponsive, you may be scaring her or making her angry by pushing too hard, too quickly. Slow down and back off a bit.

If she says that you are coming on too strong, don't worry. It's great that she gave you the feedback. Remember that she's not necessarily telling you to stop seducing her, she's probably just telling you to slow down. Just say something like "Am I coming on too strong? Sorry," and compliment her. "It's just that you seem like a great woman. I'll slow things down." By saying this type of thing, you've shown her that you were only moving so fast because she's so great. By reassuring her that you will slow down, you also acknowledge that you are seducing her, and will continue. If she accepts this, the entire interaction will move the seduction forward.

Mistake 8. You surprise her by trying to kiss her "out of the blue"

Women like subtlety. They don't like aggressive surprises that seem to come out of nowhere. Your first kiss should be the culmination of a long sequence of actions and activities between you. If your kiss surprises her and seems "out of the blue," she'll conclude that you are insensitive and she will not desire you.

The solution is to distinguish between your desire and your romantic-feeling moments, which will come and go. Make sure you kiss her in a romantic moment, not just because you are horny. Using the "announce" method will give her at least a few moments to prepare herself for kissing you.

Mistake 9. You ram your tongue into her mouth

Many women have told us about men who wrecked kisses they would have succeeded with by tongue-kissing too hard, too soon. The first kiss is a gentle touch, not a long French kiss. The gentle kiss acts as a prelude to a longer, more intense one. After Bruce first kissed Wendy, she said, "That was the most gentle kiss I've ever had." That's the kind of response you also want.

Mistake 10. You taste like garlic, have bad breath, or otherwise taste bad

It's no use doing all the pre-work, passing all the tests, and really establishing a connection with a woman if you are just going to ruin it by having bad breath or tasting bad. A number of women have told us that men who have tried to kiss them have disgusted them with bad breath. You must not let this happen to you, and you shouldn't trust your automatic thought that your breath always smells good, and that it's a problem that only happens to other men. It can happen to you, too, so you should think about it.

The solution is to make good breath a priority on a date. But—this is important—*never* squirt a breath spray into your mouth in front of a woman. For reasons we don't understand, women find this a total turnoff. It actually *angers* them. If you have to secretly bring a toothbrush and toothpaste to the date, and excuse yourself to use them after dinner, do so (though don't tell her you brought them). Most of the time, using some kind of breath freshener, gum, or breath mint will suffice.

TAKING THE KISS FURTHER

If she allows the first kiss, you should consider going for more right then. Ideally, you will push your kissing to the point *right before* she stops you for "going too fast." Gauging when a woman is about to stop your kiss is about as easy as cooking a soufflé until just before it burns. You can do it, but it's likely that you will end up burning it, no matter how careful you are, until you have a lot of practice with it.

Allowing the kiss is not the same as enthusiastically responding to it.

If she presses her breasts into you and kisses you hard, stay with it. If you are in a place conducive to more intense kissing, do it. When Josh first kissed Lynn, she responded enthusiastically. He had walked her to her car after their priming date. They both had to go to appointments. At Lynn's car, Josh kissed her. She responded well, pressing her body into his and wrapping her arms around him. He kissed her more, and they started French kissing. "Why don't we get into the car?" he asked. They got into the front seat together, kissing more and more passionately. Josh started touching her body as she panted enthusiastically. Finally he said, "The heck with my meeting. Let's go to my house." She agreed and drove him there, where they had sex.

While this will rarely happen, on occasion it will. You've got to be ready to take a first kiss as far as it can go. You must be gauging her response and continually taking your interaction to the next level if you can. If she seems uncomfortable, slow down or back up. If she seems to be into kissing, take it further. If you aren't paying attention, you will either take things too far or not far enough.

Keep in mind, this is not a race. If you've done all the pre-work, she will actually desire you. As a result, you can go back for more later. In many ways you are better off leaving her wanting more. Women aren't used to men who can walk away from an offer of sex, and it impresses them. After all, you may really have something else to do. You must make it work for your schedule, as we've said so many times. You want to tell her something like "This is great, but I really do have to go. You are really something special. Can I come over later tonight, say around ten p.m. after my evening commitment is over?" Get directions, set it up, and finish making love to her, at your leisure, later that night.

PASSIONATE KISSES!

You now have no excuse for wondering what you are doing wrong at the moment of the first kiss. You now understand that that moment is comparatively trivial when compared to all the important steps that come before it. You understand that there is little work that needs to be done to improve the moment of the first kiss; the real work is during every single moment leading up to it.

You start preparing a woman for the first kiss when you first meet her, when you start setting yourself apart from men who end up being friends. You also prepare for the kiss when you show your romantic interest and flirt like a man who is interested in her. After you have her feeling good, after one or more interactions, you either ask her for her phone number or you ask her out. If she says yes, you proceed to the priming date. If she says no, you move on to the next woman, or keep working on her and ask her out again later.

On the priming date, you prepare for the first kiss by being decisive, looking into her eyes, touching her, continuing to make your romantic interest known, making her smile and laugh, using interested body language, checking out her body, whispering something romantic to her, asking romantic questions, and conducting romantic conversations.

If you don't kiss her on the priming date, you continue to prepare her for the first kiss on the seduction date. This is done by repeating much of the priming date, plus setting up experiences that create romantic feelings in her. These experiences leave her feeling special, attracted, and cared for. You test her readiness, which also prepares her further. Finally, when you kiss her, she is not surprised, is totally ready, and has been thinking about it, too. You are finally ready to proceed easily on to the next step—being the man of her dreams in bed.

10

Being the Man of Her Dreams in Bed

After months of work, Bob finally brought home a woman. Barb was in her late thirties, fairly attractive, with a cute face, and tall, but overweight. Earlier in the evening they had watched football at a sports bar. Bob kissed and held her as they stood in the crowd. As soon as the game ended, he suggested that they move the date to his home. She agreed.

Minutes later, they entered his dark and gloomy house. Dirty clothes were strewn around the room, as were empty pizza boxes and dishes with moldy food stuck to them. Stacks and stacks of paper were all over the floor.

Bob shoved the garbage away to create a path to the couch. The hot and sensual feeling had been lost among the mess. Barb sat on the couch and Bob immediately began stroking her hair and kissing her. He tried to touch her breasts. She pushed his hands away. Once again they kissed, and he attempted to grab her breasts. When she pushed him away a second time, he felt embarrassed and angry.

Bob stopped touching her, crossed his arms, and sat looking angry. Luckily, Barb said, "This isn't working. Let's start over again." She made the move and kissed him gently. He kissed her roughly. She pushed him away again. "Bob, that hurts. Be gentle with me, or I'm leaving," she said. Bob told her that "Pam, my ex-girlfriend, always liked it when I kissed her

hard." She responded, "Look, either be gentle with my body or I'm leaving."

He made a greater effort and touched her more gently. Barb calmed down and the mood intensified. She then took off her shirt, slowly undid her bra, and placed Bob's left hand on her right breast. "Touch it gently, like this," she explained. He enjoyed himself, rubbing circles around her nipples with his fingertips. She moaned, and asked him if they could cuddle in his bed.

"Now I am going to get some," Bob thought to himself. "All the years of waiting are about to pay off." They walked hand in hand into his bedroom. "Let's get naked," he exclaimed, as he began throwing off his clothes. "No, please hold me. I just want to snuggle next to you and feel how much we like each other," Barb replied. Once again, he felt upset, but he complied. They held each other in his bed. He softly stroked her hair and kissed her all over. Barb laughed when he kissed her neck. He immediately responded in a defensive manner, "What are you laughing at? What did I do this time?" She told him, "I like how you are touching me. My neck is just ticklish, that's all." He seemed so inexperienced, and luckily Barb found it kind of cute. As they were kissing passionately, the phone rang and Bob stopped to answer it. Barb stared at him in disbelief. She couldn't believe that he would stop a romantic moment to talk on the phone.

Once he got off the phone, she kissed him and pushed him onto his back. She pretended to ride him like a horse, much to his enjoyment. Bob began unbuttoning her jeans and running his fingers over her panties. He pinched her thigh very roughly and it hurt her. Once again, she asked him to be more gentle. As she was telling him this, he looked at his watch. "Do you have an appointment sometime soon?" she asked him.

Bob continued to make every mistake in the book. Even so, Barb was ready for intercourse. She asked him where he kept the condoms. "Gosh, I didn't think we would get this far tonight. I don't have any. If you want to wait, I can drive down to a nearby all-night grocery store." Barb stared at him in disbelief and shrugged her shoulders. "I have one in my purse." She ran into the living room and returned with one in hand.

"Why do you have condoms in your purse? Is this something you do often?" he asked her. "Shut up, Bob!" she said. "If you offend me one more

time, I'm leaving. What I do in my life is none of your business. You're lucky I am letting you touch me at all. Besides, *you* didn't have any condoms. I would say that beggars can't be choosers." Bob felt humiliated, but wanted to have sex so badly he didn't dare respond.

He ripped open the package and quickly put the condom on. He immediately tried to enter her. "Not so fast. Slow down, cowboy. Kiss me first," Barb said. He kissed her insensitively, jamming his tongue into her mouth, and then attempted to enter her again.

By this time Barb could not believe how strangely and uncomfortably Bob was acting. Being an unnaturally forgiving woman, she continued to have sex with him. Throughout the experience, he refused to look at her. She kept trying to look into his eyes, but the more she did that, the more uncomfortable he felt. He even interrupted the process to turn off the lights to avoid seeing her face. Never did he attempt to see if she was enjoying herself, or if he could do anything to improve her experience. Bob went on, only concerned with his own pleasure.

After he was satisfied, Bob turned over, without saying a word, and instantly fell asleep. Moments later, Barb got dressed and stormed out of the house. She felt angry and used, and vowed never to see Bob again.

We know you're not Bob, but you think you're Casanova, and you're not. You think you satisfy a woman every time and are the opposite of Bob, but it's not true. You assume your sexual communication skills are wonderful, but they aren't. You know that you are easy to get along with, but it's a lie. No matter how great you are in bed, there is always more to learn.

This chapter will teach you the basics of how to be a great lover. We will cover the common problems and concerns men go through when having sex with a woman for the first time, and during a relationship. We'll also discuss strategies to use before, during, and after sex.

THE TRIANGLE OFFENSE: THE THREE KEYS TO IMPROVING ANY MAN'S SEX LIFE

Bob is a terrible lover because he hasn't mastered the three critical areas in the bedroom: communication, technique, and attitude. This chapter will give you hands-on (no pun intended) skills in these three areas. As you

increase your degree of mastery, your sex life will also inevitably improve. Better yet, each of these three areas supports the others. So, for example, if you better your technique, your attitude will improve. When your attitude improves, so does your technique. As your communication improves, you'll get more information and your technique will improve. Besides, spending time perfecting these areas can be a lot of fun.

We know you have a busy life and you don't need yet another set of things to do. There are hundreds of other books that describe sexual etiquette and women's hottest fantasies, including the fascinating *Sexpectations* by Ron Louis. But if you spend even a little time increasing your knowledge and skill level in each of the following three areas, you will become a master in the bedroom.

Communication

Any problem can be resolved through communication. Any concern, fear, mood, or thought can be transformed by opening your mouth and talking. We are always communicating. Body language, listening skills, vocal tone, word choice, and volume all play a part in communication. In the bedroom, communication skills are particularly essential if you want to be a hot and memorable lover. They can make or break the mood. If a woman feels afraid during sex, a good communicator can quickly calm her down and comfort her. Someone like Bob, however, will make the problem worse.

A chronic complaint among women is that men just don't communicate and talk enough. For our purposes, let's bring communication into the bedroom. Given that all women's bodies are different from one another and respond erotically to different types of stimulation, you will have to ask questions during sex.

Sexual masters asks questions; amateurs do not. The master knows that talking will intensify things, not interrupt them. Rod, for example, was in bed with Patricia. He began licking her left breast and she moaned. He continued, and began touching her other breast with his hand. She moaned even more. This continued on for several minutes. Rod took a short break, and asked her how hard she liked her breasts to be touched. "Because my breasts are so large, they also need a lot of stimulation," she said. "You can squeeze them hard and pinch the nipples a lot." This is not

obvious information, and is exactly the *opposite* of what a lot of other women need to get turned on. (In fact, a lot of women would be turned *off* by that kind of treatment.) When Rod touched Patricia again, he used more force. She moaned even louder. By asking a simple question, he turned her on even more.

Technique

Your technique is made up of your knowledge of female anatomy and your familiarity with different types of sexual interactions, such as different positions, fantasy-fulfillment and role-playing, lubrication products, foreplay, afterplay, kissing, sex toys, and anything else that you or a woman can think of during sex. All these forms of sexual interaction make up a body of distinctions called "technique."

Bob treats Barb so roughly, he fails to keep the mood. He has no idea how to be gentle when touching her vagina. He has no idea what or where a clitoris is, or why she would want it touched. His technique is nonexistent. To learn more, he should start studying and understanding what women want in a lover. This information is readily available on the Internet. Simply search for "sex education" and browse whatever pages don't look like porn sites.

Attitude

We recommend that you adopt a fun, outrageous, confident, playful, and easygoing attitude in the bedroom. If you want to be a memorable lover, you will have to leave her feeling special, full of passion and fun. Besides feeling totally unsatisfied, Barb left Bob's house vowing to never see him again. In fact, the sex was so bad that she kept hoping it would end so she could finally go home. If Bob had talked to her, and had been open to having fun, then they both would have had a better time. She might have instructed him on how to please her, which is a perfectly acceptable (and even desirable) thing for a woman to do. Instead, Bob was so caught up in trying to look like he knew what he was doing, and pleasing himself, that he missed the opportunity.

To improve your attitude, study men who interact with women in ways you respect. Sean Connery, Clint Eastwood, John Travolta, and Jack

Nicholson all tend to play strong male figures who have no problem meeting women and going to bed with them. They do this on screen and off. They display a playful yet very strong male presence that drives women wild. Study their attitudes, and they will rub off on you. Before you go to bed with a woman, decide what attitude you want to convey. Use the exercises to psych yourself up, and then create the ultimate experience for the woman you are with.

CREATING THE PHYSICAL SETTING FOR ROMANCE TO TURN TO SEX

You don't have to be a genius to realize that a romantic mood can be created. We've told you this in every way we know how. What follows is a list of basic qualities to make a physical space more romantic. Just as you've been preparing yourself mentally for dates, by psyching yourself up and practicing romantic questions, we also recommend you prepare the physical space and get it ready for hot and heavy fun. These tips may seem basic, but it's worth a few moments to go over them and to make sure your physical space is handled correctly.

Soft lighting

No one in their right mind feels sensual in a brightly lit room. In fact, studies have shown that people tend to relax in a dimly lit room and become tense in a brightly lit one. This phenomenon can be used to your advantage. When kissing a woman, it works best to dim the lights. Do it discreetly. A woman won't be impressed if she thinks you are a playboy trying to be smooth and are trying to seduce her. Be subtle. Lower the lights and let the mood shift slowly. You may decide to install a dimmer switch, or to get some three-way bulbs to help you easily create the right mood lighting.

Music

The same geniuses who spent time finding out that dim lighting mellows people out also realized that music alters the mood. We bet you aren't too surprised to find out that blaring Led Zeppelin at full volume has a dif-

ferent effect than playing gentle classical music at background levels. Good music can become your sex friend. It not only blocks out background noise, but creates an atmosphere conducive for sex. It is important, however, to play music she enjoys. If you get the chance, find out which artists she likes before the date. Better yet, let her browse your CD collection or iPod and pick the music she likes. Make sure the music fits the purpose of creating the magical mood, and you will be that much closer to a memorable night for everyone.

Incense

Women are much more sensitive to smell than are men. As a result, we recommend *not* burning incense unless you are sure she enjoys it. Since smells are very personal, there is a high likelihood of burning something she will dislike, which may then actually turn her *off.* The same is true for air fresheners, aromatherapy, aftershaves, and potpourri. You can create the association between sex and a scent early on if you go to a perfume store, or health food shop, and have her pick a vial of aromatherapy essence, incense, or aftershave. Or simply ask her. "I'd like to light this incense. What do you think of its smell?"

Candles

Candles are part of the traditional romantic scene. They create a soft, flickering, natural light. Candles truly set the mood, and leave everyone happy.

Try not to set your house on fire.

Fireplace

Fireplaces are awesome and romantic. If you have one, use it. You can get wood in bundles at most grocery stores, and can also buy cheap "firestarter bricks" if you don't know how to get a fire going on your own. Gas logs are great, too. Again, don't burn down your house.

SETTING THE MOOD WITH SENSUAL TALK

In our interviews, most women mentioned feeling nervous the first time having sex with a man. Each woman feared that her sex partner wouldn't like her body. From this information we saw the importance of complimenting a woman's body during sex. Compliments create and maintain an atmosphere in which she feels safe; they alleviate her fears. Compliments are a great way to turn her on and make her want you even more.

What to compliment her on

1. *Her body.* Compliment specific body parts. Compliment her on the sparkle in her eyes, or the way her skin glows in the candlelight. Be careful, however, not to be crude. Saying something like "You have great tits" won't seem like a compliment. "Your breasts are beautiful" will. Go through her body and compliment specific areas.

2. *Beauty.* An important aspect of being a memorable lover is to have the woman leave the experience feeling like you had an outstanding experience with her. She wants to be noticed as an individual, not just as any woman. Compliment her beauty. Let her know that you are attracted to her. Let her know that she is special and that you are thrilled she is with you.

3. *Technique.* Most guys don't realize that women want to be complimented for their sexual performance. Once again, women want to know that they please you. They know that sex is one of the most important things to guys; if they can be hot-looking and be good in bed, a man will more interested in them than if they aren't. By complimenting a woman on her sexual technique, you will make her feel closer to you, and the chances of a repeat performance increase.

TOPICS TO AVOID IN BED

Compliments will aid the mood, but there are numerous topics that can kill it. Read these over carefully to ensure you don't screw up a hot moment. We also recommend that you prescreen her for offensive talk by asking questions during the foreplay time such as "Do you think women like guys who talk dirty during sex?" You will then get the lowdown on if she likes that sort of thing.

Avoid:

- Talking about other women
- Your love of pornography
- Admitting that you don't understand her body, or any other woman's
- How long it has been since you've had sex
- Using vulgar words, unless she starts
- Telling her when you are about to have an orgasm
- Insulting her body
- The future status of your relationship with her
- Talking about topics not related to sex, like sports scores or work

THE ART OF FOREPLAY

If you had to pick one sexual position or act that the majority of women report as essential to satisfying them, what would it be? Is it having an orgasm? No. Is it being bitten on the nape of the neck? No. Is it penetration? No. Is it having their breasts touched? No. If you responded yes to any of the above questions, you are wrong!

Women consistently report that foreplay is, to them, the most satisfying part of sex. They also reported that men consistently don't spend enough time on it. Most men avoid it. Instead, we go right for intercourse. Your new job is to satisfy her, and blow her away with your skills in the bedroom (while, of course, still having a great time yourself). We strongly advise you to alter your routine from focusing on yourself and your needs, to focusing on her and what makes her hot. You'll be surprised how hot that makes the entire event.

To be clear: Foreplay is all the kissing, touching, and talking that comes before intercourse. Remember all the steps and preparation that went into the first kiss (flirting, casual touching, romantic talk, tests for readiness, etc.)? Foreplay is the pre-work for having sex. It is the necessary activity that ensures a memorable experience. All master seducers spend time on foreplay. Even if they just want to cut to intercourse, they spend time doing the pre-work because they want to please the woman and increase the chances of a repeat sexual experience.

We recommend that you change your sexual habits and stretch out the amount of time you spend on foreplay. We also recommend that you go from five minutes of foreplay and three minutes of sex to at least fifteen minutes of foreplay and twenty minutes of sex. It may seem weird to "go by the clock" in your sexual interactions, but trying it a few times might really help you. How long to do you really spend on foreplay? How long do you really spend on intercourse? Try intentionally stretching it out a few times. You may find a new world of pleasure opens up for both her and you.

THE MAIN EVENT

Now that the foreplay is finally over, let's move on to the main event. In case you didn't know, most women can't orgasm solely from intercourse. (We know that might seem like a design flaw to you, but it's the truth, just the same.) Usually, spending time touching, rubbing, or licking her clitoris is required. If you aren't sure where the clitoris is, and how to touch it, get on the Internet and find some basic anatomy info. This knowledge isn't secret, and you should avail yourself of it before you get into bed with a woman again.

During sex, you might want to try bringing her to orgasm first. Most guys have no problem achieving orgasm quickly. In fact, there are millions of men who suffer from premature ejaculation. If you get her off first, you can justify coming quickly. Your job is nearly done.

A good lover is also generous in the bedroom, and most men are more satisfied knowing that the woman had a good time. Men often report feeling a sense of confidence knowing that they brought her to orgasm. We recommend you spend whatever time is necessary learning how to bring a woman over the edge.

ENJOYING AFTERPLAY

Most men fail to realize that afterplay is an important part of sex. Now that the action is over, you probably just want to turn over and go to sleep, or get her the heck out of your home so you can go about your business. If you are trying to build a relationship, then holding her after sex is the perfect way to deepen the bonding between the two of you. Afterplay doesn't require hours and hours of time; even five to ten minutes should suffice. Spoon with her, give her a few kisses and compliments, and you can be on your way out the door or to a night of relaxing sleep.

Another key reason to spend time cuddling is that the first time you make love with a woman, she usually decides if it will happen again. If you hold her, compliment her, and follow the other steps mentioned, sex will probably be repeated. If not, she probably won't want to see you again.

POSSIBLE PROBLEMS AND HOW TO SOLVE THEM

Whether they come at convenient times or not, problems in the bedroom are inevitable. Sex will frequently trigger emotional responses for you, and especially for a woman. Here are a list of potential problems, so you won't be caught off guard when they inevitably happen. Refer to the conflict resolution techniques explained in Chapter 8 to guide you through most conflicts.

"I am not comfortable with the speed we are going at."

In sexual situations women usually think that the man is going too far, too fast. The solution is simple: Slow down! Perhaps it was so simple that you missed it, so we'll say it again: Slow down! A successful seducer never pushes a woman. He respects her wishes and immediately slows down. Bruce realizes that if a woman feels that things are going too far, respecting her wishes is crucial. He wants the date to go well, for her to be happy, and able to stop the sexual process at any time she wishes. In these sensitive times, he knows that if you don't stop, or slow down, when a woman asks, she may consider it harassment or worse, and put him at legal risk. He never wants to be in this position.

Think about it this way: If you and a woman are kissing and heavy petting, she obviously likes you. It is also likely that she is interested in spending more time with you. Even if you end up spending a half hour touching and kissing and she wants to stop, do it. It will make the next time that much better. Most men find it useful to take the long-term view toward sex. By stopping, you ensure that you will probably see her again. If you feel that she has required you to stop prematurely, go on to someone else and come back to this one later.

"I'm sort of seeing someone."

The classic moral dilemma: Do you or do you not date a woman who has a boyfriend? The first question to answer is whether or not you feel comfortable having sex with someone in a relationship. We've had students who care and those who don't. We refuse to make this moral decision for you. The most important factor is always to act consistent with your beliefs. If you care, don't date her again. If you have no moral dilemma, go for it.

Having said that, you should be aware that almost every attractive woman has a guy in her orbit somewhere who she is "sort of seeing," and it may really mean next to nothing. She may also be telling you that she is "sort of seeing" someone because she wants you to be aware that this is "off budget," noncommittal sex for her. In other words, she may want you to be her sex buddy. This arrangement may work perfectly. The larger strategy is to *not* make her comments a big deal. Stay calm, cool, and collected, and then move forward.

"I really care about you and I want more than a one-night thing."

Many women date in hopes of meeting a special man for a committed relationship. Men often date in hopes of pure sex.

At this point, you have a decision to make. Some women are very simple and naïve, and would never dream that you might want to have sex only one time and then move on. Such a woman might be devastated by you taking her to bed if you clearly have no intention of seeing her afterward. It really might hurt her a lot. What do you do?

Tina is a woman we know who, though in her mid-thirties now, still feels bad about how she lost her virginity. She was eighteen, wide-eyed and naive, and traveling abroad alone for the first time. In Germany, she met a man in his mid-twenties who "seduced" her. She told him, "I want more than a one-night thing," and he assured her that he did, too. After having sex with her, he promptly disappeared, never to be seen again. There's still a part of her that's hurt about his betrayal, even all these years later.

If you find yourself faced by a woman who is naive like that, you might want to decide you are better off *not* being the guy she feels manipulated by and whom she regrets meeting for the rest of her life. You can decide to get your sex somewhere else. Sometimes that's the best thing to do.

But much of the time the situation is not that severe. Often a woman will say, "I'm looking for something more" because she is, even though she's also perfectly happy to have sex with you once and see what happens.

Here is something you could say in this situation:

"I am unsure about my long-term goals. Eventually I want a serious girlfriend, but now I'm not so sure. If the right woman came along, why would I wait? And I like you a lot and hope we can continue getting to know each other."

The fact is, a *lot* of relationships start with casual flings, and a lot of men and women find themselves in long-term relationships when they weren't looking for them. That might happen to you, too, so why rule it out?

"I have an STD."

Hopefully the woman will mention a sexually transmitted disease (STD) *before* you sleep with her. If she admits this to you *after* sex, leave and break things off with her immediately. A woman who lies to you and puts your health in jeopardy is trouble and has already put you at great risk.

If she tells you about a disease *before* sex, stay calm and don't get upset. Don't jump to conclusions. First, find out what she has and if it will *definitely* interfere with your sexual relationship. Getting the information will help you make an informed decision about things. Talk to a doctor or pharmacist about it. Be smart.

If you see a future with the woman, purchase the necessary protective gear for sex. A dental dam, for example, allows you to explore her vagina

without getting the secretions in your mouth. For other pointers, look at a guide to safe sex.

If she has a chlamydia or gonorrhea, stop being sexual with her until she is cured. Both can be knocked out with medical treatment.

HIV is a much more serious problem. Definitely don't have sex with her, even with condoms. The risks are too great. You might want to touch and fondle each other, and stop there. But for most men this won't be satisfying for long. If you fall in love and foresee a long-term relationship, however, you'll want to investigate how HIV-positive people make it work.

Unfortunately, if she has a disease, or diseases, you shouldn't see her until you understand it, or them, better. We are not doctors and cannot give you the advice you need. As ministers of sex, however, we know that many STDs are treatable and can be gotten rid of. We recommend that you spend time on the Internet, in a bookstore, or talking to a pharmacist or doctor, finding out the facts. Always talk to a medical professional if you have any concerns. In this day of such dangerous diseases, you must take care of yourself.

"If I were to get pregnant, I'd keep the baby."

No matter on what side of the abortion issue you stand, when a woman tells you she would keep a baby, it is reason to worry. Why is she telling you this? She has already decided what to do if, and when, someone impregnates her. You should be fully aware, too, of the risks here for you. If you have unprotected sex with a woman who is committed to keeping a baby, you can easily get stuck with child support payments for the next eighteen years. This does happen. Don't let it happen to you. We recommend that you proceed with such a woman with great caution. Don't depend on her to provide the contraception. Even if she uses an IUD, is on the pill, uses a diaphragm, or anything else, always use condoms religiously and use caution. Stop often to make sure that the condom is still on and hasn't broken.

"I hate condoms; we don't need to use them."

When a woman tells you that condoms aren't necessary, an alarm should go off in your head instantly. You can be sure that the woman is incredibly stupid, dangerously so. If you follow her moronic advice, you

are risking not only your future health but also your future finances if she gets pregnant. Also, you are probably *not* the first man she has said this to, and who knows how many of them took her up on the offer? Who knows what diseases they have given her? You need to watch out.

Even though she may be dumb, you can still sleep with her if you have a condom. She may just really like you and feel swept up with the heat of the moment. Once again, proceed with caution and make sure to wear a condom. Although generally, in cases like this, we would advise you to avoid this woman. She will probably cause trouble down the road.

"I am still healing from old relationships and I can't risk getting hurt again. My heart just can't take it."

All of us are vulnerable after ending a relationship. Women going through the healing process are particularly sensitive because they are acutely aware of the potential pain that comes from breaking up. Women in this position are usually looking for an informal relationship, not another serious one. They are on the mend and are looking for a transitional fling to get their feet back into the dating world. They probably want a man who is fun, easy to be around, and not demanding.

When a woman tells you she is still healing from a breakup, she wants to make sure you are not going to fall in love with her or become dependent on her. She wants to avoid the hassle of taking care of you and worrying about yet another man's feelings. We recommend you tell her that while you are open to a relationship, you are more focused on having something fun that's *not* serious. A woman on the mend probably wants to avoid a serious relationship. If she thinks you are looking only for something serious, it will be another strike against you.

She cries during sex

Some women cry during sex. They cry for many reasons, such as the emotion of it all, the intimacy, because they care so deeply for you, as a release after an orgasm, because they remember a traumatic sexual experience, or for no reason at all. Most of the time, just staying calm will make everything fine.

When the woman reacts to sex with all-out sobbing, stop having sex immediately. Hold her and find out what is going on. If you continue with sex, it will be trouble later. After being held and talked with for a few moments, the majority of women will calm down. You can then move back in for more action. If not, be patient and weigh whether or not sex will happen again that night.

STAYING ALIVE: SAFER SEX

There are two things to worry about: sexual diseases and pregnancy. Whether you care to admit it or not, both problems affect you. While each can cause massive problems, they can also both be easily avoided.

Most men blame the heat of the moment for not using condoms. Or they pass off responsibility to women for such things. The immature man fails to use condoms because he doesn't stay aware of the dangers. He will ultimately be full of regret for not taking a long-term view of things and only going for momentary pleasure with a woman. Using condoms until both you and your monogamous lover have been tested for STDs is the only sensible solution. We know it isn't easy. But you do have to do it.

The most common STDs and parasites are chlamydia, crabs, genital warts, gonorrhea, and herpes. Consult with your local Planned Parenthood organization, credible websites, or a local bookstore to find out a lot more about these topics. We will cover the most simple basics, and we strongly recommend you do more reading to fully understand the dangers.

If you have an STD or crabs, we advise you to tell all the women you might have infected. While it may be embarrassing, it simply is the right thing to do. Many of the diseases can be a serious problem if not treated soon after infection.

We always advise you to see a doctor the moment there are any problems. There are free clinics all over the United States that can help if you don't have money. STDs are nothing to mess around with. They are very serious, and can cause you and your partner an array of health risks, including death. We are in no position to advise you on any medication or cure; only doctors can help with this. Get help if you need it.

CONDOMS: EVERY MAN'S NECESSARY WEAPON

Birth control and prevention against STDs is *your* responsibility. The days of unprotected sex are long gone. So are the days of depending on women to provide the protection during sex. Here are the facts: If you don't use condoms, and you aren't in a monogamous relationship, you have a huge chance of contracting VD.

No form of birth control is 100 percent effective, even when used in conjunction with condoms. This includes Norplant, a diaphragm, an IUD, a cervical cap, and the rhythm method. They are all risky. No forms of birth control, except condoms, prevents the spread of STDs. This is why condoms are required for every man.

The only kind of condom that is effective at blocking the spread of disease is latex; lambskin condoms feel better, but they don't prevent the spread of diseases. We recommend that you purchase a box of condoms tonight, and keep them handy. They are your required weapon against diseases and pregnancy. Every successful seducer has made peace with the fact that condoms must be worn during every sexual experience.

There are many ways to botch up a sexual experience. If you are like Bob, you forget to treat a lady like a lady, don't spend time on foreplay, fail to prepare a room romantically, are overly rough with a woman, fail to understand her body, don't talk during sex, try to rush things, don't hold her or cuddle after sex, answer the phone or look at your watch during sex, don't have condoms on hand, insult the woman, and do many other stupid things.

All of these mistakes boil down to the three main areas of sex in which you must become proficient if you are to be a master man in the bedroom: communication, technique, and attitude. This chapter has covered how to learn, study, and master all three techniques. We recommend that you be rigorous in your studies and you will soon see progress. It may take months or years to become familiar with them, but it will be well worth it.

If you follow our advice in this chapter and master communication, technique, and attitude, you will soon become a sexual master and have many nights of mind-blowing sex.

11

When Babes Attack: Handling Problems Women Cause

BAD DATES FROM HELL

Date 1

When Jacob went to meet Zoe for their first date, he was expecting her to be a little nervous. She was a girl who worked at the health food store where he shopped. She was tiny, punky, and cute, and responded well to his flirting and romantic overtures. After a few weeks of romantic banter, she'd come running out of the storeroom to see him if she heard his voice. He set up a coffee date with her at a nearby coffee shop. The shop was convenient. The plan seemed foolproof.

He arrived at the coffee shop, armed with an interesting book in case she didn't show up. But she did show up, shortly after the agreed-upon time . . . with a guy.

"This is my roommate, Tony," she told him. "I figured you wouldn't mind if I brought him along."

"Of course not," Jacob responded, realizing instantly that his seduc-

tion of Zoe wasn't going to move very far that day. The three of them sat down. Jacob immediately noticed that Tony was not a stable person. His eyes and face looked wild and very unattractive. He seemed preoccupied by conspiracy theories. After making polite conversation for about twenty minutes, Jacob concluded that if he pursued Zoe further, this psycho guy would probably cause him plenty of trouble. Two days later, when he called Zoe, she told him, "Tony and I are moving out of town tomorrow. He thinks you're stalking me." To his relief, Jacob never saw Zoe again.

Date 2

Dennis was new to dating. In his early twenties, he'd always been too scared to ask women out. The few women he'd dated had pursued him, and he had always let them have all the power in the relationships. They decided everything. He passively hoped the relationship would go the way he wanted, though it never did.

The one woman he did ask out was Daria. She was nineteen and elegant-looking, and for reasons he couldn't explain, she seemed to really like him. On their first date they sat on a park bench and talked, and she kept leaning forward, "accidentally" making it easy for him to look down her shirt. He asked her out again, she said yes, and he figured he had it made. Not having read this book, he took Daria to dinner and a movie for their first date.

Trouble first started when he met her for dinner. "We had our whole meal, and I guess I made kind of a slip," he told us. "I said, 'You are paying for yourself, aren't you?' and she said, 'I don't have any money.' From there it went downhill."

It turned out Daria was completely unable to take care of herself in any way. She had no money, and then when they got to the movie—an R-rated one—she didn't have any ID, and they had to go to a children's movie instead. "She just got madder and madder with me," he says now. "Each time I paid for something, I tried not to make it a big deal, even though it was to her." After the movie, he dumped her off at her house, and left behind the most uncomfortable date of his life.

Date 3

"We went to see the movie *Schindler's List*," Fritz told us. "I had no idea she'd be so upset by it. She started crying about ten minutes into the movie, and was still crying in the car all the way back to her apartment. She couldn't stop, she was really freaked out by it. Needless to say, my seduction plans were destroyed for that night."

Date 4

Anna had the punk look down cold. Amazingly beautiful to start with, she had bright orange hair, leather clothing, torn-up T-shirts, chains, and combat boots. She was extremely sexually attractive, going through life looking like some sort of dressed-up fetish dolly. Brett was thrilled to be going out with such a hot woman, but there was one problem.

"Of course people stared at her, because she was so aggressively hot," Brett says. "And she hated it. If guys looked at her, she'd glare at them, and say things like 'What are you looking at, jerk face? Wanna make something of it?' Then *I* had to deal with these huge, angry guys. After I got punched trying to defend her, I finally broke up with her."

Date 5

Thirty-six, tall, and tan, Rebecca had taken care of her body and was often mistaken for a woman in her twenties. The first time Sal had sex with her, they were at his house, and she was incredibly aroused. "Oh God, I'm so turned on," she told him. "Do me without a condom! I hate those things! Don't worry, I won't get pregnant! Even if I do, I don't care, I don't mind having your baby! Just do me without a condom!" Needless to say, Sal used a condom anyway, but found himself worrying about Rebecca's attitude even as he was having sex with her. "How psycho is this?" he asked us later. "To want me, a virtual stranger, to possibly get her pregnant or give her a disease? What is going on here?"

Date 6

Rich and Roger were housemates. Roger had been dating Jill, an unstable, neurotic, highly sexual woman. "I love crazy women," Roger told Rich when he started dating her. But soon her crazy behavior was driving

them both mad. One day Rich was sitting home when the front door opened and in stalked Jill. "Where is he?!" she screeched. "Where are you, Roger, you jerk! I've let you have my body ten times, and now you are going to give me what I want! Where are you?" Roger had to call the police to have Jill removed, screaming, from their house.

Date 7

Bob and Yolanda were on their third date when she flipped out. They were talking about gender issues, and how women and men are different, and she, as he put it later, "just went nuts on me." She started ranting about all the bad things men do to women, about females being used as sex slaves, and female circumcision. "I started realizing that she was nuts, and I asked her to change the subject. That's when she hit me!"

Date 8

Dwayne and Emmie were friends. She often came to him with her emotional problems, of which she had plenty. She seemed almost like the "trauma of the week." One week it was "My dad abused me," the next "I think my mother killed my twin brother." Dwayne had no way of knowing if these traumas really happened to her or not. He assumed they must have, or she wouldn't have been so unstable.

One night she came over late, talked to him for a while, then slept on his couch. Four days later, she called him. "You sexually abused me while I was asleep the other night." She told him, "I'm calling the police." Fortunately, he had saved many of her crazy, ranting, self-contradictory phone messages, which gave him a good chance in court, so she decided not to press charges. If she had, he might be in jail today for a crime he did not commit.

Date 9

Henry picked up Jean in a bar. He couldn't believe his luck. She was sexy, slutty, had large, full breasts that seemed to defy gravity, and a completely flat stomach. It was his dream come true. They went to his house, had drunken sex, and when he woke up in the morning, she was gone.

And so was his wallet, his checkbook, and some of the more valuable knickknacks around his apartment. He never saw her, or his money, again.

Date 10

Albert went out with Wendy, a chiropractor who lived in his town. They had several dates and were checking out the possibility of being romantic with each other. They'd had some long phone conversations and generally felt pretty connected. One day when he called her, she said, "I'm gonna stay in alone tonight and watch a movie. What do you recommend?" He told her about a film he'd rented recently, *The Addams Family*. She rented it, watched part of it, and called him up the next day. "I just had to tell you," she said, "that I can't date anyone who would like that movie. I can't see you anymore."

SO HOW DO YOU HANDLE PROBLEMS?

Has anything like this ever happened to you, or to a man you know? If it hasn't, it probably will. We don't say this to curse you, but simply to warn you. Not every woman you get to know will be stable, mentally healthy, and sincere when she interacts with you. Some will be difficult, strange, unpleasant, scary, or even possibly dangerous. This chapter is about how to handle difficult women.

The best time to handle a problem is before it becomes a problem. If Henry had seen the warning signs in Jean, he might not have been so quick to fall asleep before getting her out of his apartment, and could have saved his wallet and his valuables. If Roger had known how dangerous Jill could be, he would have thought twice before dating her often, or letting her know where he lived. If Dwayne had seen the warning signs in Emmie, he would never have let himself get into situations where she could accuse him of sexual impropriety. By taking simple precautions in advance, these men could have easily made their lives much simpler and safer.

Men tend to be extremely naive when it comes to women. They think that nothing bad could possibly happen to them in a dating situation. Nowhere is this naiveté more more common than in sex. Many men idiotically—and incorrectly—think that they are exempt from needing to wear a condom, for instance. They won't get a woman pregnant. They won't catch HIV or some other STD. This sort of "everything will be fine"

thinking permeates men's relationships with women and makes them unable to see, in advance, the problems women are setting up for them. This chapter will help you give up your naiveté around women once and for all. After you read this chapter, you'll see the problems coming and be able to get out of the way before they can overcome you.

GAUGING THE MAINTENANCE SPECTRUM

All relationships require some maintenance. Each person, man or woman, needs certain things to happen in order to feel as if someone cares about him or her, and to feel attracted. These needs in a woman are the maintenance you must do to keep her happy.

Women need varying degrees of maintenance. Some women's needs are fairly simple. If you are considerate, or don't treat them like dirt, they feel appreciated and attracted to you. Other women only feel attracted to you if you treat them poorly. Still others require constant compliments, gifts, and attention. Some even need to fight with you and have regular conflict in order to feel that the relationship is right for them.

You've probably heard men talk about women as "low maintenance" or "high maintenance." This is a very useful distinction to make. Here's how you tell the difference, early on, between low-maintenance women, medium-maintenance women and women who need too much to be worth it.

LOW-MAINTENANCE WOMEN

The low-maintenance woman is a gift to men. She doesn't require elaborate rituals to feel okay about you, and about dating you. Her needs will be simple and easy to figure out. She'll even help you, by telling you exactly what she needs, and meaning it.

Here's what you need to know about her:

- She takes very little in life personally. The low-maintenance woman won't jump on your every slip or boneheaded remark. When she is upset, she lets it go easily and is therefore easy to be with.

- She contains her feelings well. If she's upset, she doesn't show it, or doesn't take it out on you. She's responsible for her feelings.
- She is not unreasonable. She really tries to be reasonable at all times, thus making your life easier.
- She doesn't "flip out." If she feels anxious, upset, or stressed, she handles it responsibly, and often you never even know about it.
- She feels she has more to learn about everything, and doesn't jump to conclusions. She isn't overly attached to her own opinions.
- Her feelings in the moment are not too important to her. She listens to her feelings, but makes decisions in life from a rational and logical base.
- She consistently desires sex. She either wants it most of the time, or gives you sex because she wants to please you.
- She doesn't expect you to know what she needs; she is happy to tell you.
- She is emotionally consistent and doesn't have massive mood swings.
- She is not overly concerned about what other people think of her.
- She likes you and likes men.
- She is generative and creative and amuses herself well.
- She rarely complains.
- She does not feel she has the right to be difficult simply because she's upset. She works to stay reasonable at all times.

MEDIUM-MAINTENANCE WOMEN

You are more likely to encounter medium-maintenance women than low-maintenance. The medium-maintenance woman has more needs and takes more things you say and do personally than does the low-maintenance woman. At the same time, she isn't so wrapped up in her own feelings that she's impossible to deal with, like the high-maintenance woman. The medium-maintenance woman:

- Takes some things in life personally. There are some topics you'd better just avoid, like pornography, or other women's larger breasts. Fortunately, this isn't too difficult.
- Takes her feelings out on you occasionally. If she's in a bad mood she sometimes takes it out on you, and will be bitchy and start a fight.

She'll usually apologize for it afterward, though, and perhaps even apologize with sex.

- Is sometimes unreasonable.
- "Flips out," but feels bad about it later. When she has emotional scenes, she apologizes later.
- Can be emotional, but her moods are like the wind: They blow in, then blow out, and it's over like it never happened.
- Can be sensitive about her weight or looks.
- Is moderately creative, and moderately whiny.
- Likes sex, but sometimes says no and has some gripes about your performance.
- Has moods—one day she may be happy, the next sad, crying, or furious—but is mostly stable.
- Worries sometimes about how she looks to other people, and what other people think about *you*.
- Dates men, but sometimes likes them, sometimes doesn't.

TOO HOT TO HANDLE
(HIGH-MAINTENANCE WOMEN)

The high-maintenance woman is out of control. She exerts little control over her moods and behaviors and has constant problems with everything, most especially you.

The high-maintenance woman believes that she has the right to be as difficult as she likes. She is incredibly impulsive, and you have to deal with it. If she feels like yelling at a dangerous-looking stranger, she does it, and you have to handle the consequences. If she feels like screaming, or crying, or pouting, or generally acting like a baby, she would never dream of containing herself. She thinks nothing of yelling loudly at you and creating a scene during dinner at a nice restaurant. After all, she reasons, if she doesn't completely express her feelings at every moment, you are trying to repress her. The high-maintenance woman:

- Takes everything in life personally. If it rains out when she wants to go on a walk, she's angry at the weather.

- Takes her feelings out on you. If she's in a bad mood—and she is—she takes it out on you.
- Feels she has the right to be unreasonable. She never makes any attempt to be reasonable, and you have to just live with it.
- Feels she has the right to "flip out." If she feels anxious, upset, or stressed, she cries, or screams, or does whatever she feels like, wherever you might be, and you have to handle it.
- Feels she understands "God's opinion" about everything, and is happy to set you straight at all times about what you are doing wrong.
- Is insulted by everything you do.
- Believes that her feelings in the moment are the most important thing in the universe. She can never just "get off it" and get on with life. Has to process or fight about everything right now.
- Is impossible to give feedback to. If you tell her anything about her behavior, she flips out, screams, and cries, which she feels she has the right to do.
- Generates nothing, is not creative, complains constantly about being bored.
- Is incredibly sensitive. Will think you think she's fat, or not attractive, at the slightest provocation. You don't dare look at another woman while she's around.
- Is on or off sexually, and you never know which you are going to get. One night she'll be an incredibly hot vixen, the next she'll become furious at some little remark you make and kick you out of her house.
- Becomes furious if you don't instantly and automatically know what she needs at all times. Your inability to be psychic with her is proof, in her mind, of your insensitivity.
- Is incredibly inconsistent. One minute she may be happy, the next sad, crying, or yelling.
- Believes there's only one right way to do things, and you are doing it wrong.
- Worries continuously about how she looks to other people, and what other people think about *you*.
- Is very picky about your behavior.
- Dates men, but doesn't really like them. Sees men as a necessary evil.

Which type of woman do you tend to date? Is she the ultra-demanding high-maintenance type? Or is she the medium-maintenance, fairly demanding type? Understanding which degree of maintenance a potential date will pose is useful because it allows you to determine if it will be worth it to date her or not. Also, if you do date her, you can expect her to behave in the ways we've outlined. We are now going to cover how to handle many of the problems women will cause.

THE EIGHT SECRETS OF HANDLING
THE PROBLEMS WOMEN CAUSE

The biggest trap men fall into with women is that they handle the problems women cause incorrectly. Instead of diffusing the problem, they often make things worse. You've surely had this experience: You are with a woman, and she seems upset. You try to help, and end up fighting with her. She then complains that you are an insensitive bastard who's incapable of understanding her. This happened because you probably violated one or more of the following eight rules of handling the problems women cause. Follow these rules, and your fighting days are over:

1. Never solve a woman's problem,
or you will become her problem
Men who don't understand this get themselves into unending trouble with women. Solving a woman's problem is a big mistake, because if you do, she'll make *you* her problem. Here's how it works:

Women live with problems differently than men do. When men have problems, we want to solve them, pure and simple. And, by and large, we don't have a lot of tolerance for men who just want to complain about problems, but not try to solve them. If a man is designing a computer program, for instance, and can't get it to work, other men won't ask him, "Wow, how do you feel about that?" They won't spend time sharing how it felt when they had a similar problem with a program they were writing. They roll up their sleeves and get in there and try to fix it.

Similarly, men don't indulge each other complaining much about relationships. If two guys are at the gym, and one says, "I met this hot woman,

but she hasn't called me!" the other won't commiserate much about how bad that must feel. He'll more likely say, "What's the matter, forget how to use a phone? Call her up, you idiot!" Problem solved, and on to other topics of conversation.

Women, on the other hand, treat problems differently. Strange as it seems, women *like* problems more than men do. They use problems as opportunities to share their feelings with one another and to bond with one another. Women in the locker room will routinely complain about men they desire who don't call, and would never dream of solving one another's problems by saying, "Call him, you idiot!" *Simply having the problem, together,* is a way of bonding for women that men must learn to understand.

This difference between men and women is shown clearly in a *Cathy* comic strip. Cathy's car had broken down on a winter morning, and she couldn't leave the house to get to work. She called her boyfriend, Irving, and he said he'd come over to help her. As she waited for him, a fantasy formed in her mind. "He'll come over, and we'll be so happy to see each other. We'll drink coffee, and eat morning buns, and be brought together by this car problem. Everything else will disappear, and we'll be laughing and happy and in love on this cold winter morning."

At that moment, Irving entered. "I called a tow truck, it'll be here in ten minutes," he told her. "I also called a cab, so you'll be able to get to work. I must go, big meeting this morning." Whoosh, he was gone, and Cathy was left sulking in the final frame: "Men have no idea how to handle problems."

When a woman comes to you with a problem, you must not solve it. Let us repeat that, because it seems so strange: When a woman comes to you with a problem, you must not solve it. We feel odd even saying it. But it's true. If a woman presents you with a problem, and you try to solve it, she'll almost certainly be angry with you. She'll accuse you of not listening to her, or not being sensitive, and that's the thanks you'll get.

When a woman comes to you with a problem, be grateful. As long as she has that problem, she won't be making *you* her problem, and you are in the clear. Instead of fixing, we advise you to listen to her, be with her, and help her believe that you understand her feelings.

When Lenny first started dating Karen, everything seemed to be going

well. Then one day everything changed. He went to her house for a date and found her crying. "I didn't know what to say," he told us, "but I remembered not to solve her problem. Without saying a word, I just took her into my arms and allowed her to cry." This went on for five or ten minutes, and eventually she stopped. "Later she said to me, 'I can't believe how wonderful you were! You were just so perfect when I was so upset!' That blew me away, because I didn't actually do anything!" If he'd tried to "solve" her problem, she wouldn't have thought he was so wonderful, and perhaps would even have been angry.

You must try to be like Lenny and comfort a woman by just being with her, not fixing. If you must speak, here are some possible things to say:

- "Wow, tell me how that feels."
- "Sounds pretty intense. Tell me more, if you want to."
- "I just want to support you."
- "I really admire how you're handling this."
- "Is there anything I can say or do that would help?"

Don't worry if you find yourself repeating these phrases over and over. She simply wants to be heard. Your mind will be busy anyway, reminding yourself not to try to fix her problem. If you find yourself about to say any of the following things, stop yourself and say instead one of the platitudes listed above:

- "I think you should . . ."
- "Why don't you just . . ."
- "I don't see why it's such a big deal."
- "Have you tried . . ."

These statements will have you starting to fix her, and will get you into big trouble. Some men think that if they solve a woman's problems, she'll sleep with them. We discussed this thoroughly in Chapter 2, and will just remind you now that if you solve a woman's problem, she won't reward you with sex. All she'll do is think of the problem every time she sees you, and think of you as a friend.

2. Remember that fighting with a woman is like defusing a bomb

One of our students was a military demolitions expert. He told us about working with bombs. "Most of the time, you handle a bomb by sending in some sort of robot to just blow it up. No problem if you're not nearby. The real problem comes when you have to get in there and do it yourself. You really want to be patient, not jump to conclusions, and remember what you are up to when you are defusing a bomb."

It occurred to us that he was not only describing defusing a bomb—he was also describing fighting with a woman. If you can get someone else to take the blast, so much the better, but most of the time, you'll have to do it yourself.

Fighting with a woman is a delicate procedure. As in the bomb analogy, you can't let your mind wander from the most important thing. In dating, with a woman, the most important thing about a fight is to end it, quickly, and with the minimum stress. If you get caught up in some detail of the fight, or let your anger take over, you'll lose the fight, even if you "win" it technically. You might be able to badger her into admitting that you are right and she is wrong, but you will not have created harmony, and you won't be having sex later.

3. Keep asking yourself, "What's most important to me?"

It's easy to lose your head in a fight with a woman. She says things that hook you and make you want to defend yourself. This is almost as big a mistake as trying to solve a woman's problem. Consistently remember what your outcome is. If it is early on in your relationship and you haven't even had sex with her, we strongly urge you to avoid fighting with the woman altogether. If you must fight, remember what's most important to you: Is it more important to make her see that you are right, or is it more important that she desire you? Your answer to this question will guide your behavior in any fight you might encounter.

When Bob fights with a woman, he destroys any chance of being sexual with her. On his first date with Annette, he started telling her about his

favorite television program, *Lost*. "Geez," she responded. "My one wish in life is that people would stop telling me about *Lost*. I don't care about that science fiction stuff!" At this point, Bob needed to ask himself, "What's most important to me, sleeping with her, or arguing?" Had he done this, he might not have made the mistake of responding, "I don't know what you're so huffy about. It's only the best show ever made—everybody thinks so." Naturally, she took offense at this. "Oh, everybody does, do they? Well, *I* don't." They started having a little fight, which irritated Annette, and made her less attracted to Bob. "What am I doing with this jerk?" she asked herself. It was a good question.

It's important to realize that taking offense at what someone says is a choice. Have you ever been insulted by someone and simply let it roll off your back? Perhaps you thought to yourself, "It isn't worth it," and simply went on with your life. At that moment, your commitment to something else—having the life you want, perhaps—was more important than proving to someone that you wouldn't accept an insult.

If you haven't ever allowed yourself not to take offense at a potential insult, you had better learn to if you want romantic success with women. Women will give you plenty of opportunities to get angry. You must choose not to take the bait, and choose not to get offended by anything they say. If a six-year-old kid told you the same thing a woman did, it might seem obnoxious and annoying, but it wouldn't have the same impact as coming from a woman you are interested in dating. If you can "pretend" that she is that kid being silly, it will help you keep your mind on the seduction.

Our student Ivan made such a choice with Bonnie. He met Bonnie through a mutual friend, who was taking them both sailing on his boat. She was in her late twenties and looked good in her one-piece bathing suit. "She was cute enough," he told us, "and so I decided she'd be worth some effort." Their mutual friend mentioned that Ivan had self-published a book, and since he happened to have it with him, he showed it to her. "Women usually respond positively to it," he told us. "But Bonnie started finding all these errors in how it was typeset, and talking about how it wasn't put together properly. It really started pissing me off—after all, what had she ever done that she could talk about? But I kept asking myself, 'What's most important to me?' and I realized that I didn't care what she thought of the book. I just

wanted to get that suit off." He changed the subject, without fighting, and went on to other topics. He got her email address, seduced her first by email, then in person, and eventually had sex with her. "If I'd fought with her about the book, I would never have made it anywhere with her," he told us. "It really made a difference to ask myself what was most important."

4. Never reason with an upset woman

In the film *As Good As It Gets*, Jack Nicholson plays a writer who is asked, "How do you write female characters?" He answers, "I think of a man, and I remove the reason and the accountability." While this is by no means always true, you will be far more successful in fights with women if you act like it is.

If you are with a woman and she is upset, this is also the time she is likely to be unreasonable and difficult to be around. But this also holds true for everyone. When *you* are most upset, *you* are most likely to be unreasonable, too. Have you ever tried pointing out the lack of logic in an upset woman's thinking? How well has it worked for you? Our guess is not at all. Reason and logic will only make her more upset.

At a time like this, your job is *not* to influence her. Your job is to influence yourself. You must not get hooked, not try to fix it, and not try to make her see reason. Keep asking yourself what you are committed to, and go for that.

5. Don't take anything personally

Geena and Tony were on their seduction date. Their conversations were going fine until Geena said, "It must be hard not really being in the real world. I mean, since you only work at the university and are around eggheads all the time, it must make it hard to relate to real people." Not in the real world? Only work at the university? This might be an insult, or it might not be. Unfortunately, Tony decided to take it as one. "Well, what's that supposed to mean? I'm in the real world!" he said to her. He took something she said personally, and allowed a possible fight to begin.

Think back to a fight you've had with a woman. Most of the time, the conversation was going along fine. You two were talking and there was no problem. Suddenly, someone said something stupid that could be considered insulting. The other person took it personally, and a fight ensued. Sometimes the woman you are with will say boneheaded things that sound

like insults to you. Sometimes you will do the same thing to her. As the man and the seducer, it's your responsibility to make sure the date goes well. If you take something a woman says or does personally, you lose sight of your outcome, and the seduction will be ruined.

You must remember what your outcome is with a woman, especially in any stressful interaction. It's incredibly easy to take personally something she says or does, and to let yourself become insulted and start a fight. Here's a list of things women will do that you shouldn't take personally. As you date, you'll no doubt find other things to add to this list.

- Not calling you back
- Showing up late, or not showing up at all
- Canceling or changing dates at the last minute
- Not appreciating all the nice things you do for her
- Being cold, distant, insulted, or difficult to talk to
- Not responding to your seduction
- Ignoring you when you say hello

6. Handle female rudeness gracefully

So how should you handle these difficult behaviors if you can't take them personally? Little things, like not calling you back, you don't really have to deal with if you simply take it on that you will always do the calling. Ditto with a woman you've just met seeming cold or difficult to talk to. Handling that is your job as a man. But truly rude behavior, like missing several dates in a row, must be dealt with. If you let a woman seriously inconvenience you without responding, she will simply do it again, and worse.

The secret is to know how to handle female rudeness without getting into a fight, and the key to that is not taking what she did personally. Yes, you want to handle it, but just so she knows what's okay to do with you, and what isn't. You aren't mad, you aren't out of control; women won't respect men who act like this. It only scares them. But to set a boundary for a woman, you must be firm. If you don't take it personally, you'll be able to say what needs to be said, and to let it go. You'll be much more effective, and she'll respect you more for it.

Cindy missed two priming dates with Lyle. He didn't take it personally.

He reasoned that Cindy was pushing him, to see what she could get away with. Because he kept his mind clear, he was able to talk to her on the phone without starting a fight or making her feel bad. Instead, he said, "Listen, I like you and everything, but you've missed two dates. I have a rule you need to know about: If you miss another date, I can never talk to you again. So if you want to go out with me, you've gotta show up." His voice was firm but he was not yelling, and he was unapologetic. He set a boundary, and instead of whining about how rude she was, he gave her a simple choice: show up, or get lost. She showed up for their next priming date, which went directly into seduction, and then sex. "She was pushing to see how far she could go," he told us. "I wouldn't have talked to her again if she missed another date, but I'm glad she showed up." By not taking it personally, Lyle was able to handle the situation without getting caught up in his feelings.

7. Listen actively

Some guys think that listening is what you do when you are waiting for an opportunity to speak your piece. Other guys seem to think that listening is what happens in between her opening her mouth to talk and when you tell her how to fix her problem. If you are one of these men, have no fear. We're now going to show you exactly how to listen in the way that makes women feel the best.

Women we interviewed complained about not "feeling heard" by the men they talked with. You can overcome this if you follow the simple steps of active listening:

- *Look interested*. Remember when your teachers in school would ask, "Are you paying attention?" and you'd snap into focus? Think about what your body was doing before the teacher spoke to you. She thought you were bored because you looked bored. You were leaning back, slumped over, your eyes were unfocused, and you weren't looking at her. Now think about how you held your body when you wanted to look interested. You were leaning slightly forward, looking at the teacher; you were nodding, breathing deeply, and acting alert.

  Many men allow themselves to look bored when listening to

women they want to seduce. Even if you *are* listening, you won't look it if you are in a bored posture.

- *Repeat back what she said.* You don't want to be a parrot, like some annoying comedian who mimics everything everybody says. That would be bad. By repeating key parts back, however, you show her that what came out of her mouth actually went into your ears and is still in your brain. Believe us, she'll be impressed, and it will make anything she has to say to you easier and faster.

When Chuck's girlfriend Stacey was mad at him for flirting with other women, he used active listening very effectively. First he got himself into a posture that conveyed that he was interested in what Stacey was saying, even though the truth was that he'd rather have been just about anywhere than listening to her complain. "I don't like it when you flirt with other women at parties," she said. "It really makes me feel bad, like you don't love me." "Let me see if I'm getting what you're saying," he told her, "because it's important to me to really hear you. You don't like it when I flirt with other women at parties, and it makes you feel bad, like I don't love you. Is that right?" "Yeah," she responded, calming down. "I really want to feel like I'm there with you, as a couple." "Oh, I get it," he said back. "It's important to you that you feel like we're a couple when we are at parties. I didn't know you felt that way." By this time Stacey was calm enough to talk normally, and they were able to resolve the problem, all because Chuck was willing to employ active listening. You don't have to solve the problem, or even agree with her. A woman will calm down if she feels like you are listening, and an interested posture and repeating back are excellent ways to seem like you are.

8. Don't explain yourself

When you are in a conflict with a woman, you will be tempted to explain yourself, and to justify who you are and why you do things the way you do. Don't do it. A good rule of thumb is to only answer questions. If she asks you why you did something, tell her, but don't feel as though you owe her an explanation for every aspect of your behavior just because she is upset with you.

Remember, you are not out to get your validation in life from women.

You are getting that other places, remember? Women are an addition to your life that makes you feel good about yourself, not the central validating factor. If you violate this principle, you are more likely to be explaining yourself to women in conflicts. Simply remember what is most important to you, answer relevant questions, and get through the conflict.

THE THREE WAYS WOMEN FIGHT AND HOW TO HANDLE THEM

People fight in different ways, and each person tends to be consistent in his or her way of fighting. There are three basic modes that people default to. They either cry, yell, or manipulate. Let's discuss each one of these in detail, and show you how to handle women in each situation.

1. Crying

Some women love to cry. They default into crying at movies, weddings, even at long-distance phone service commercials. They get hurt easily, have tender feelings, and tend to cry right away when you have a conflict, rather than get angry or solve the problem.

How to Spot Her Early On. The crier gets moved easily. A wounded bird on the street causes her to rush out to save it. She seems to get upset at the slightest thing. If she is extremely emotional about anything, she is probably a crier. You can ask her how she feels about starvation, or the plight of Native Americans, and see how intense she gets about it. If she gets wide-eyed, and her voice gets urgent, she's probably a crier.

How to Fight With Her.

- *Don't get hooked.* The crier hooks you with her tears; she gets you upset and manipulates you. If you'll do anything she wants to stop her crying, you lose, while she wins. Ultimately, this can be a loss for her, too. Many of our students have made promises to a woman, which were so outrageous they couldn't be kept, only to stop her crying. When they broke their promises, even bigger fights happened.

Getting hooked by a woman's tears, and saying anything to get her to stop, just causes trouble down the road.

- *Don't be difficult by acting guilty.* Men who act guilty and ashamed when women cry often think they are being compassionate. Our interviews show the contrary. Women think men who act like this are the difficult ones. All of a sudden the women feel responsible for your being upset, too. It makes things worse for her and you. If a man acts guilty when a woman cries, he isn't paying attention to the woman. He's all wrapped up in himself, and seems selfish and self-absorbed. He needs the woman to tell him he's not guilty, and is generally very "me-centered." Women have told us time and again that they prefer men who aren't guilty. As one woman said, "If a guy's not going to do what it takes to make me happy, he might as well not feel guilty about it. That just makes him seem like an immature baby."

Understand this, because it is important: Your suffering and feeling guilty doesn't substitute for giving a woman what she wants from you. It only makes you harder to deal with. If you aren't going to give a woman what she wants, that's fine. But don't think that feeling guilty will make any positive difference in her experience.

What You Should Do.

- *Keep asking yourself "What's most important to me?"* There's not much more for us to say about this that hasn't already been said. Simply keep your outcome firmly in mind.
- *Don't try to fix the problem.* We don't need to go over this again in depth, but we do need to note that it is especially important with the crier. She doesn't so much need you to fix her problem, as she needs to think you are willing to hear about it. She wants you to be with her while she cries. This is not a time for solutions. Don't give them.
- *Say the right things.* It helps to know what to say to a crying woman. If you aren't going to suggest solutions, what can you say? Try these statements:
  - "I didn't know you felt that way."
  - "I can see why that would be rough for you."

- "I can see this is very upsetting for you."

You can repeat these as often as you need to. They help a crying woman feel understood, without getting in the way of her feelings.

- *Silence is golden!* The best thing you can say is nothing. If she's not upset about you, you can even hold her, silently, while she cries. It's amazing how often a man can be with a crying woman, saying nothing, but feeling like a world-class dork, only to have her say later, "You were so perfect when I was upset! How did you know not to say anything?" Silence is your best friend when you are with a crying woman.

If you don't allow yourself to be manipulated by them, the criers are the easiest to deal with. They eventually calm down and are clear about what they want and need. While they are crying, you must simply remember what's important to you, show her compassion for her suffering, and hold your position. Eventually she'll stop crying, and you can go on with your date.

2. Yelling

Women who default to yelling don't cry—they get *angry*. Subconsciously, they figure they can control you if they can scare you with their anger. If they can't, they will either respect you more, or get out of your life. Either way you win, so it's worth learning how to handle women who act this way.

How to Spot Her Early On. The yeller is a warrior by nature. She often likes to fight, looks tough, and is willing to take offense at the slightest thing you say. If you find that you have to tiptoe to keep her from getting angry, you are with a yeller. You can also spot one by her willingness to complain about service in restaurants, or by the stories she tells of conflicts she's been in.

How to Fight with Her. The yeller wants to scare you into submission. On some level she figures that if she is unreasonable enough, she can get her way. Besides, it's worked for her in the past. The solution is to avoid fighting and leave immediately. Later, after she has calmed down, you

can talk and resolve the conflict, if it seems worth it. But when she yells, or throws a fit, do not tolerate the abuse. Leave immediately.

3. Manipulating

You've probably heard the saying "Don't get mad, get even." The manipulator lives by this code, taking control of you indirectly and evening the score. Manipulators are the control freaks in life. They don't feel safe unless they are able to control everything around them. This tendency gets much worse when they are in conflict, because a conflict is a direct challenge to their control.

While the crier attempts to control you with tears, and the yeller tries to control you with anger, the manipulator tries to control you with mind games. She is especially preoccupied with being "right," and having "logical" arguments that prove her correctness. She will have justifications and arguments for why she is right, but will drive you crazy in a fight because her "logical" arguments won't be logical. She'll irrationally insist that they do make sense, all the while questioning your sanity as you get angrier and angrier about her inconsistency. She will portray herself as the soul of sanity, a civilized woman sadly drawn into having to defend herself from your unreasoning, brutish attack. This will make you even crazier, proving even more in her mind that you are unreasonable and therefore wrong. When she points out to you how crazy, and therefore wrong, you are acting, you're liable to lose your mind entirely. This is not a pretty sight.

How to Spot Her Early On. The woman who is a manipulator is often very intelligent, and may be in a field that requires a lot of "civilized" conflict, like law or administration. She may well be highly educated. These signs alone, however, are not enough; many women who aren't manipulators share these characteristics, and many woman who are manipulators don't.

When you are on a date with a manipulator, you'll find that she needs everything to be "just so." She is very particular about her needs and her comfort. It is often important for her to reject your idea, just so she is sure she has the power to do so. Her "reasons" strike you as incredibly lame. You may ask her out to a Chinese restaurant, for instance, only to have her

reject your choice by saying, "I had Chinese food last week." Last *week*? She's practicing her control. Watch out.

The manipulator is hard to please. There's always something just a little wrong with everything. Complaining, for her, is a way of establishing her control. She may send back her food at a restaurant, or want a drink with a particular brand of gin. If that brand is not available, she will, with a heavy sigh, have nothing at all. She may complain about details of the way you dress. You'll notice that you feel as if she is particularly controlling and persnickety. That's because she is.

How to Fight with Her.

- *Don't argue with her.* Watch out, this kind of woman can drive you crazy. The only way to keep from going insane with a manipulator is to not fall into the trap of arguing with her about the nonsense she is spewing forth. That will never work, and will only drive you insane. Your rebuttals will only perpetuate the fight. What the manipulator wants is control, not logic. She is afraid that if she loses control, something bad will happen to her. Pretending to care about logic and reason is her way of getting that control. She gets to drive you crazy, then demonize you as an illogical, wrong, out-of-control nutcase. If you argue with her about her logic, she has won immediately, and it's all over for you.

- *Tell her she's right.* Tell the manipulator that she is right as much as you can stomach doing it. If there is some small point that she is correct about, tell her, and emphasize that she is right about it. "You are right that this relationship is very important to us both," you might say. "That's very, very right." Try not to sound sarcastic. You are trying to give her as much control as you can, so she'll calm down, without letting her control *you*.

- *Apologize for not being logical.* It's also very powerful to tell the manipulator that you are sorry that your feelings aren't logical. She can insist that your feelings should be logical, but you can always come back with "I guess that's not the way I am." As long as you don't get drawn into an argument about whether or not you should be more

logical, you are safe. "It's just important to me to be able to go out with my ex-girlfriend as a friend," you might say. "I'm sorry it doesn't make any sense. I know how frustrating that must be. But it really is how I feel, and I don't think that's going to change."

- *Tell her how important she is to you.* Keep in mind, she's not a bad person, she's just scared of being out of control. It can help her calm down if she hears how important she is to you. If she's not important to you, you can find something about your relationship that is. You can almost always truthfully say that "I hope you know, it's important to me that you feel good and happy." Of course it's important—she's much easier to be with, and you get more of what you want, when she's happy. Just hearing that will often calm the manipulator down.
- *Change the scene.* You probably aren't going to get anywhere useful in argument with a manipulator, so you might as well get it over with as quickly as possible. See if you can leave, or get the two of you doing something else that doesn't allow you to argue, like seeing a movie or being with other people.

These are the three defaults of conflict for a woman. But don't think that only women fall into these categories. Men do, too, even *you*. Most men are yellers or manipulators; few are criers. You might want to look over this section again and see which kind of fighter you are, and see if that's really the way you want to be.

THE FOUR CLASSIC WOMEN TO AVOID

While all women cause problems, certain types cause more than they are worth, and you are better off avoiding them. For example, there are four classic psycho-types: the Flipped-Out Woman, the Paranoid Police-Caller, the Bitch Goddess, and the Street Fighter. You must know about them so you can spot them, and avoid having them mess up your life.

Craziness in women is on a continuum, and it's not always easy to tell when a woman is so crazy that you should avoid her. Here are the general warning signs that should alert you to the presence of a possible psycho woman:

- *She had an abusive childhood.* Psycho women were often abused, some-times more severely than you can imagine. Severe physical and sexual childhood abuse is tragically common, and psycho women are often the outcomes of such childhoods. If she tells you she was consistently beaten and raped as a child, she may very well be worth avoiding.
- *She tells you intimate details right away.* This often comes along with an abusive childhood. If a woman was abused, and she tells you about it the first time you meet her, that's an especially bad sign. It means she probably has very weak boundaries. The good side of this is that she might therefore be easy to get in bed. The bad side is that it won't be worth it when she flips out.
- *She's been in a lot of abusive relationships.* Same as above. Avoid her.
- *She seems like a hypochondriac.* If she seems to have a lot wrong with her physically, that can also be a sign of a mental problem, though this is by no means always true. It's our experience and that of our students that a woman with lots of allergies, for instance, or food sensitivities, can be trouble. A woman who needs to never be around perfume or in a room where someone once smoked a cigarette can be impossible and unstable in relationships. We don't know why, but it's true surprisingly often.
- *She is obsessive/compulsive.* Often such women will tell you right away. "I'm a really obsessive person," she might say, or "I've never let go of anything that didn't have claw marks from me holding on." It may seem strange that someone would show you such a disturbing part of her psyche right away, and it is. It's a warning sign to stay away, unless you want her to become obsessed with *you*.
- *A "red flag" goes up inside of you.* This is the most important guide-line of all. Men's good sense disappears when it looks like they might have an opportunity to have sex. They pursue sex even when it's with crazy women who they *know* will cause them unending problems. Don't be an idiot. If a "red flag" goes up inside of you, and you have a bad feeling about a woman, be a powerful, confident man and *stay away from her.* If you are smart enough to apply the techniques in this book consistently, you *will* be having sex. You don't need to hu-miliate yourself by making trouble with psychos. We say it again: If

you have a bad feeling about a woman, *stay away from her*. Listen to yourself, and trust your instincts.

The four types of women to avoid have these characteristics in abundance. Let's look at them more closely, one type at a time:

1. The Flipped-Out Woman

The Flipped-Out Woman is like the crier, only much more so. When she "flips out" and cries, it is often in the context of a sexual abuse flashback. She tends to hyperventilate as she cries, saying one word with each breath, so her speaking sounds like "I (gasp) am (gasp) feeling (gasp) very (gasp) scared (gasp) . . ." By hyperventilating, she unconsciously ensures that her brain chemistry will stay messed up, and that she will stay flipped out.

2. The Paranoid Police-Caller

This woman will tell you about men she's been stalked by, men she's called the police about, and men she has restraining orders against. It is critical for your future life out of jail that you stay away from this woman. She often has an abusive and crazy ex-husband or lover who she says still torments her. She changes her unlisted phone number every few months. This woman has been traumatized and learned that men are going to hurt her, and that the law is her only recourse. Eventually she will inevitably see you as a perpetrator, too. Stay away from her, no matter how hot her body is.

3. The Bitch Goddess

This woman is like the manipulator, only much more so. One such woman was Steve Martin's girlfriend in the film *L.A. Story*. At one point he says to her, "I don't think you understand how unattractive hate is." The Bitch goddess never does.

You are only likely to pursue such a critical, difficult woman because she's very physically attractive, and you think you can get her into bed. You ignore how negative and hate-filled she is, because you hope to have sex with her. Of all the types to avoid, this one is the most benign. If you can have sex with her a few times, then get rid of her, your suffering will be minimal. If you get into a relationship with her, however, you might as well castrate yourself now, because she's going to do it eventually.

It's good to start to notice such women and practice keeping away from them. By avoiding the most psycho of women, you will save yourself from much suffering.

4. The Street Fighter

The Street Fighter is the type who loves conflict. She can turn a wonderfully fun evening into an all-out crappy time. The fighter will constantly try to get you to argue with her, and the moment you fall for her ploys, you are in deep trouble. She tends to be mean-spirited, dramatic, and highly passionate.

Some signs of the Street Fighter are that she loves to criticize others and basks in being opinionated, asserting her opinion, and generally turning people off. She tends to be highly political, righteous, bitchy, and difficult to be around.

If you stay with a Fighter, you will get burned badly. She will eventually test your patience, and you will try to get out of the relationship. It will end in a huge blowout. The other threat is that this type will become violent with you and attack you. If a woman shows signs of being a conflict-lover early on, take it as a sign to get rid of her.

THE TWENTY-THREE PROBLEM WOMEN

All women are problems. (Don't get too smug about that, though. You are a problem, too, as we'll see later.) The faster you can recognize what kind of problem a woman is most likely to present, the faster you'll be able to deal with that problem, and the more likely the two of you will be to have a happy relationship. Here's a list of problem women. How many of them do you know?

- The rich bitch
- The alcoholic/druggie
- The therapist
- The princess
- The "I hate you for loving me"
- The bar-fighter/cat-fighter

- The depressed
- The angry feminist
- The arguer
- The complainer
- The religious moralist
- The drama queen
- The nag
- The wounded bird
- The stalker
- The anorexic
- The hypochondriac
- The enabler/rescuer
- The performance artist
- The control freak
- The know-it-all
- The look-gooder
- The earth mother

THE SIXTEEN PROBLEMS
CAUSED BY YOUR TENDENCIES

As we've mentioned, women are not the only source of problems in relationships. You cause problems, too. So it is just as wise to prepare for the problems you'll cause as it is to prepare for the ones she'll cause. Here's the list of problem men—which one are you?

The Sensitive New Age Guy

The Sensitive New Age Guy, or SNAG, tries to seduce women by being forever nice, helpful, artistic, and sensitive to women's issues. He wears crystals and lets his hair grow long. He may pretend to be a peaceful musician and play the drums, or may enjoy practicing guitar in the woods. The main problem is that he pretends, even to himself, that he's not a rutting sex-crazed beast, like other men. He's all full of light and goodness. When he does something mean to a woman—and he does—it is totally unconscious, and he's completely oblivious about it. Further, he never takes

responsibility for all the people he offends. He also has no vitality or masculine presence. If you are this guy, get more guy friends and start eating meat. Go see some strippers. Admit you have a dark side. Be more like other men, and you'll get more sex.

The Special Boy

Like the Sensitive New Age Guy, the Special Boy prides himself on not being like other men. He often has one or two "special" relationships, usually platonically, with women. He often dresses in an unusual way or wears very "special" items of clothing. Most women avoid him because he sends an immature message about himself. They say that there's something weird about him. Those women who don't avoid him like him, but only as a friend. If you are a Special Boy, you'll be happier and get more sex if you concentrate more on how you are like other men than on how you are different.

The Feminist Man

This well-meaning man has taken on women's feminist struggle as his own, but there's a subtext to his behavior that is disturbing to most women. He is able to talk easily about how men are the problem in the world, and how "all men" hurt women in various ways. It's as if he doesn't think of himself as a man. He may even say that he doesn't, preferring the term "person." The Feminist Man is deeply ashamed of his maleness, perhaps especially his sexual fantasies. On top of all this, he secretly thinks he can get sex by apologizing for being male.

If you are one of these men and you want to be successful with women, you have a problem. You must stop aligning yourself with a movement (feminism) whose leaders say, as Andrea Dworkin did, that "all men are rapists, and that's all they are." Practice saying, "I support equal rights and responsibilities for women, and I am not a feminist." You'll start to feel better about yourself immediately.

The Woman's Friend

As we've said before, you must limit your number of female friendships because they get you in the habit of not being women's lovers. If you must be friends with women, at least *try* to seduce them, even if only in a joking, flirty way. Never let it be forgotten that you are a man and that they are women.

The Woman's Friend thinks he can get sex from women by being friends with them. This ploy rarely works. If you use this method, and want sex, stop being their friends and get more friends who are men. It really is that simple.

The Beaten Down by Life/No Vitality Man

The fundamental message of this book can be boiled down to one statement: Be a generative, vital man, and women will want to give you more sex than you can handle. Everything else in this book is just telling you how to do that with women. The Beaten Down Man has given up on life. He has no energy, no vitality, and barely makes it through the day. He seems slumped, stressed, and depressed. Life is too hard for him. The Beaten Down Man is not attractive to women because he's not generative and vital. Who wants to be around someone who isn't fun, energetic, and who is overly serious?

If you are Beaten Down, you can overcome it. Taking on the practices in this book will increase your vitality and generativity. You may also need to look at your physical health, to change your diet, or exercise more regularly, or get a massage, or do *something* to bring more energy into your body. As you become more vital, women will desire you more.

The Beer-Drinking Jerk

The success of the drink-beer-be-jerk-get-girl strategy is almost directly related to age and physical attractiveness. If you are an attractive twenty-two-year-old weight lifter, being a drunken jerk in a bar can get you sex. If you are forty with a beer gut, however, this strategy is out-of-date. You not only have to study the techniques in this book, but also to unlearn your old ways of getting drunk, burping, and belching to get women. It won't work for you anymore.

The Know-It-All

This is the guy who has an answer for everything. Women hate it when men lecture them or talk down to them, all things the Know-It-All loves to do. He often works with computers, or in another technical field. He believes that the more knowledge he can share, the better person he is.

He thinks that the more technical language and examples he uses in conversation, the more people will like him. He often uses his knowledge as a way of one-upping himself over someone else. This helps him feel good about himself. When you show off your knowledge as a source of self-esteem, you are actually only showing off your level of insecurity. You are much better off developing your self-esteem from how you live your life, not from how much data you've absorbed.

If you think you might be a Know-It-All, practice saying "I don't know" at least once a day, even if you think you do know. Stick with your assertion that you don't know. If people around you seem more relaxed and friendly when you do this, you are probably a Know-It-All. Give it up.

The Control Freak

Did you think only women can be control freaks? Guess again: you, too, might also be one. The Control Freak has to control every little detail of everything. It's very hard for him to go with the flow, or follow someone else's leadership without criticizing. An insecure woman who has no self-esteem might be attracted to a man who provides so much structure, but eventually she'll rebel. If you notice that everybody always seems to end up doing what you say, you might be a Control Freak. Try doing what other people want occasionally. You'll be more attractive to women.

The Androgynous Boy

"Androgynous" means "appearing both male and female." Some men favor this feminized, non-masculine look. If this describes you, it will actually cause more problems with other men than it will with women. Some men are infuriated by men who seem "too feminine." One androgynous man we know is constantly hassled and harassed by men even though he is straight.

If the Androgynous Boy is cute in a boyish sort of way, some women will be attracted to him, while others will be repelled. Sadly, though, few will take him seriously as a fully mature, adult man. If he is not particularly attractive, however, it will be very hard for him to get sex. If you are androgynous and not attracting the women you desire, try wearing more masculine clothing and eating more meat.

The Comedian

The Comedian performs for women. He thinks that if he's funny enough, and entertaining enough, women will sleep with him. It is true that women tend to value a sense of humor in men they are attracted to, but alone it is not enough. Women will end up thinking of you as an entertainment machine, and expect you to perform, rather than as a man they could get romantic with.

Comedian men also show a certain level of insecurity through their constant need to make people laugh. It's as if they are always asking for some sort of validation from others that they should be getting from themselves. Women sense this, and relegate the comedian to the status of friend. If you find you are a comedian with women, joke less, have more opinions about things, and see what happens. They might find you more interesting.

The Geek Boy

It's more fashionable to be a geek now than it used to be, but it is still a bad seduction strategy. The Geek Boy's main problem is that he is more comfortable with machines than he is with people, especially women. He retreats into the world of computers or other machines, where he feels he understands what's going on.

This book is perfect for the Geek, because it presents a manual about seducing women. The Geek can become a good seducer because once he understands a system can be mastered, he masters it. Geeks do especially well with our system, and if you are a Geek, you are reading the right book. Read the damn manual, as technical support often says, and do what it says.

The Therapist

The Therapist breaks the cardinal habit of Highly Effective Seducers: Never be a prospect's therapist. The Therapist thinks that if he can only solve a woman's problems, she'll want to make love to him. As we said in Chapter 2, what happens in fact is that she wants to get away from him, and will then come to him about problems she's having with the jerk men she's having sex with. If you find yourself in this category, you have a choice to make. Do you want to be a woman's therapist, or do you want sex?

If you want sex, make the right choice today. If she brings up her problems, change the subject, and start seducing her.

The 12-Stepper

Twelve-step programs are important fellowships that has saved many lives, and we're not here to put them down. But it is worth mentioning that men deeply involved in a "program" create predictable problems when seducing women. If you are such a man, it's a good idea to know what to watch out for.

The 12-Stepper tends to take life a little too seriously. He screws up seduction by needing to talk too much about his emotional pain, and by his need to appear "vulnerable" by sharing his childhood traumas. He also turns women off with his need to think of everything in terms of addiction. If she wants a drink, he gets all concerned and asks if there is a history of alcoholism in her family; if she lights a cigarette, he lectures her on the perils of nicotine. Pleasure, it seems, is inherently suspect to him, and a woman notices this. Not wanting to hear him describe his sex addiction, she doesn't get sexual with him. Worrying about addiction and the free spirit of seduction don't necessarily go well together.

If you are in a 12-step program, more power to you. Stay with it; it can make a huge difference in your life. And when you try to seduce a woman, remember you are not at a 12-step meeting. She doesn't want to hear about your emotional pain, or about what an addict you are. Keep your outcome in mind, and focus on the seduction.

The Slave

The Slave thinks that any positive attention from a woman is a sign that he's on his way to having sex with her. To this end he does everything for a woman that she could possibly want. If she's hungry, he makes her dinner. If she needs his help moving furniture, he makes an elaborate show of canceling going to a party so he can be at her beck and call. He figures that her occasional compliments about how "sweet" he is, along with the obvious sacrifices he makes for her, will eventually and inevitably add up to sex for him. He keeps being her servant as he awaits that day.

The truth is that women hate Slave men, even as they use them merci-

lessly as handymen, cash machines, and secretaries. The day of sexual reward will always remain in the future, and the Slave will never get what he wants. It's like the *Dilbert* cartoon where he has a date with a woman to "grout the tile in her bathroom." That's not a date, it's being an idiot. If you find yourself being women's slave, you must stop right now, as you are destroying your chances with her sexually. Realize that every Slave action you take only builds her contempt for you, even as she praises you for your "sweetness." Take the actions we recommend in this book instead.

The Whiner

The Whiner is like the Beaten Down by Life guy, only louder. Rather than suffer in silence about what the world has done to him, the Whiner makes sure everybody knows about it. He sends a loud and clear message to women that says, "I am immature and you want to stay away from me." Women get the message and want nothing to do with him.

You may have every right to whine. You may have an especially rough life, and everybody may well be out to get you. We don't argue with that. Our point is that you'll get more women by dealing maturely with your problems than you will by whining about them. Like the Slave, the Whiner thinks that if he gets a positive, compassionate response from a woman, he *must* be on the road to sleeping with her. Like the Slave, he mistakes any positive reaction for arousal. The only difference is that, while the Slave seeks a "you're so sweet, you make me so happy" reaction, the Whiner seeks an "I feel so sorry for you" compassionate reaction. Neither approach works with women.

If you find yourself complaining to women about the difficulties of your life, stop it right now. They may appear compassionate about all you've suffered, but compassionate and aroused are completely different emotional states. Deal with your life, and seduce women. Don't complain to them.

The Desperate Man

We've talked a lot about the dangers of desperation to your seduction, so we'll only touch on it briefly here. The Desperate Man needs women to validate him; this results in a constant inability to relax around them. He is more like a puppy dog waiting for a treat. He seems heavy and awkward

to women because he is so afraid that he won't get the validation that he needs so desperately from them. If you are Desperate, you must learn to get your validation from your life, rather than from women. It is especially important that you pursue many, many women, so that any one woman's response to your seduction is not particularly meaningful. As you do this, your desperation will decrease, and you will have more success.

If there's one thing this section should show you, it's that women don't cause all the problems, after all. Too bad; it's much more satisfying to pin the blame on someone else, rather than on ourselves. A powerful man, however, is accountable for every area of his life and takes responsibility for how things turn out. As you figure out the kinds of problems you are likely to cause when seducing women, you can take responsibility for those problems, solve them, and be a much better seducer.

HOW TO HANDLE THE TOP PROBLEMS WOMEN CAUSE

You no longer have the excuses you once did for getting into out-of-control relationships with extremely difficult, demanding, unstable women. If you apply yourself to mastering the techniques in this book, you will be able to date as many women as you like. You'll be able to pick one that works best for you.

But trouble rears its ugly head even in the most "together" of women. To help you handle those inevitable breakdowns on the road to utter sexual fulfillment, we provide this emergency toolkit of ways to handle the common problems women cause.

Q: What should I do when she cries?

A: If a woman cries on a priming or seduction date, it's a very bad sign about her stability. There may be some extenuating circumstance—she just dropped an anvil on her foot, or her mother just died. But most of the time, she'll be crying because she's emotionally unstable and unable to contain her feelings. You may be able to have sex with her, but proceed with extreme caution. Keep an ear open for any indications that she's had to involve the police in any of her relationships. If she has, she might be unstable

enough to misinterpret something you do and call the police on *you*. If she has called the police, stay away from her. If you do decide to go ahead with her, be aware that you will probably want to have sex with her only a few times, because she's likely to be too unstable for anything long-term.

If she cries *after* you've been having sex with her for a while, it may simply be an isolated emotional episode, and you can follow the advice from earlier in this chapter and let it go. If a woman cries *while* you are having sex with her, you have to give up on the sex and deal with it. The bad news is, if she does this once, she's likely to do it again. If she hyperventilates while she cries, and gasps a lot and can't stop, she may be having a flashback and is reexperiencing some earlier sexual trauma. If this happens, you need to know that it probably is not going to stop happening anytime soon.

Q: What should I do when she's inconsistent?

A: Inconsistency and illogical behavior are commonalities shared by all humans, including you. She's probably marveling at how inconsistent *you* are. You've got to expect a woman to be inconsistent, and not worry about it. One minute she might like chocolate, the next hate it. Fine. One day she may think your new leather jacket looks great, the next bad. Okay. One date she may want to get away from you, the next have sex with you. Whatever. Don't take it personally.

Q: What should I do when she is moody?

A: Many women think that they have a perfect right to be moody, and a right to be as difficult as they want to be when they are in a mood. As one woman we interviewed told us, "I don't care if I am difficult to men!"

As usual, you must ask yourself what's most important to you, and not take her behavior personally. The most critical thing to know when dealing with a moody woman is how to not reward her for being in a bad mood. You may not think you reward women for being in bad moods, but you probably do. If you tiptoe around her, kowtow to her every demand, and are extra nice to her, all you are doing is training her that being in a bad mood is a great way to get you to treat her better. Guess what? She'll be faster to get back into a bad mood, and stay there longer, because of you.

The key for handling a woman's bad mood is to:

1. acknowledge it,
2. show some compassion for her problems,
3. stay upbeat and happy, and
4. get away from her as soon as you can. Let her work through her mood, and get together with you later when she's feeling better.

Here are some things you can say to take you through each of these steps:

1. *Acknowledge the mood.* "Had a bad day, eh?" "Not feeling so good today, eh?" "Having a rough time, eh?"
2. *Show a little compassion for her mood.* The key here is *never* to try to solve her problem. Just listen to her and show a little compassion. You might say: "Sounds rough. I know how bad a bad mood can be." "Wow, I'm sorry you are having a hard time."
3. *Stay upbeat.* This is critical. You must go on with your life, little affected by her bad mood. Otherwise, you are simply indulging her and rewarding her for being down. You shouldn't do this in a sarcastic or overly enthusiastic manner; just make it clear that her mood is not going to change yours.
4. *Get away from her as soon as you can.* If she's really down, she'll either want to sort it out with your help, sort it out alone, or take it out on you. If she wants your help, don't offer solutions: Just ask her clarifying questions so she can get clear on what she's upset about. Hopefully, it won't be *you.* If she wants to sort it out alone, or take it out on you, get away from her. You'll be happier later that you did.

Q: *What should I do when she has PMS?*

A: Premenstrual Syndrome is real, and has a profound effect on women's physiological and emotional states. If you don't believe such a thing is possible, remember back to a time when you felt so horny that you were about to lose your mind. Perhaps you hadn't had sex in a while, and felt particularly teased by all the lovely young women around you. Some men get so riled up that they start bar fights and get into trouble just to deal

with the hormonal mess that is going on in their bodies. PMS is equally real. The main difference is that a woman who behaves badly because of PMS has a medical excuse. When you behave badly because you are horny, you are still just a jerk. Oh well.

A woman who has constant problems with PMS may make a good short-term lover but, sadly, is very difficult to be in a long-term relationship with. If she gets angry or weird or difficult, then apologizes by explaining she has PMS, seriously consider dating someone else. This is not going to get better, only worse. If she is committed to handling it responsibly, and is treating it medically, she may be a good relationship partner. But if she handles it by taking it out on you, even once, consider looking elsewhere. If you are in a relationship with a woman who has PMS, stay away from her when she is at her worst.

Q: *What should I do when she has a flashback?*

A: A "flashback" occurs when a person, male or female, relives the emotions of a past trauma, as if it were happening right now. Flashbacks are part of a syndrome called post-traumatic stress disorder, and you are probably not qualified to handle it if the woman you are with has one. Flashbacks can involve hyperventilating, crying, touch-aversion, and even talking to people who aren't there. A woman in a flashback might scream, "He's coming to get me!" or "It's happening again!" If a woman was severely sexually abused, she may have a flashback while you are having sex. This is not fun for either of you, and a good reason to avoid having sex with any such person. Staying out of these situations is the best thing you can do.

While we are not putting ourselves in the position of giving you medical or therapeutic advice (which we are not qualified to do), we can tell you our anecdotal experience, which indicates that if you stay with her, the flashback will usually end in an hour or two. But sometimes it won't, and some people have to be hospitalized. If she starts to freak out in any way during sex, stop at once, and see if you can change her focus off the feelings in her body. Take her out for ice cream, or take her into a different room. Get her involved in a TV program. Ask her questions about her work. If you can get her mind involved in something else, she may not flash back. Then stop pursuing her romantically and find a more stable woman.

Q: *What should I do when she criticizes me?*

A: There are different levels of criticism. You have to balance the criticism against how attractive the woman is, and how fun you think she'll be in bed. If the criticism is small and her breasts are large, you may want to let it go. The best way to let it go is to not defend yourself. Simply say something like "Oh, that's interesting that you feel that way" or "I didn't know you felt that way." *Never* justify what she is criticizing, or explain yourself. That will get you into a conversation, or even an argument. Remember your outcome. You are there to seduce her, not prove how right you are and how much you are above her criticism. If you acknowledge it, and let it go, her criticism can go away as fast as it arrived.

It sometimes works best to nip criticism in the bud. She may not even know she is doing it and may need you to call her attention to it. You might calmly but firmly say, "Hey, you've never spoken to me like that before, and I didn't like it. Please don't talk to me like that again." If she is very critical, this will only start a fight, but you shouldn't be spending much time with very critical women anyway. As Madonna says, "Respect yourself." Have sex with her a few times, and when her critical nature gets unbearable, move on.

Q: *What should I do if she hits me?*

A: Leave instantly. Get your hat and coat and *go*. Say nothing. Ignore everything she says. Be out of her house or apartment within thirty seconds. We mean it. You want her to learn that striking you ends all interactions immediately. For a woman, that is a big punishment. You also want to leave her with the knowledge that she just hit you. When she thinks of you, you want her to remember that the last interaction the two of you had was her hitting you. That is more likely to change her future behavior than anything else.

It goes without saying that the stupidest thing you could possibly do is hit her back. You must *never* hit a woman, under any circumstances, do you understand? In the eyes of the law, when a woman hits you, even if she hits you first, it is almost always self-defense. If you hit her, no matter what she did to you, you are *always* domestically abusing her. Your pathetic whining that "she hit me first" will not keep you out of jail, especially if she denies it, which she will. Don't hit her back, and don't stay and argue. Leave at once. It's the best way.

Q: What should I do when she doesn't want sex?

A: Having an ample sex life means that you can pretty much have sex whenever you want it. There are plenty of women out there who love sex as much as you do, and who will almost never say no to you once you have become lovers. This is the kind of woman you are looking for.

If a woman doesn't want sex the first time you are in bed together, that may be a sign of a problem. If she simply wants to wait a date or two for the "big event," go ahead and wait. If she says that she simply doesn't feel like it, however, you may well be left wondering why she got into bed with you in the first place. She may have a very on-again, off-again relationship with her desire, one moment wanting sex, the next hating it. Such a woman will destroy your sense of sexual confidence, and you must get rid of her and sleep with somebody else.

If you are sleeping with a woman on a regular basis and she occasionally doesn't want sex, lighten up. It's not a big deal. If she consistently withholds sex, you aren't lovers anymore, and you should stop dating her.

Q: What should I do when she criticizes my sexual performance?

A: Not all people are sexually compatible. One of our students dated a woman who accused him of being sexually violent when he thought he was being gentle. One woman we interviewed told us that she was "riding" a lover, thinking she was displaying enthusiasm and passion, and he told her dryly that her movement up and down reminded him of a sewing machine. The point is, the message you think you are conveying sexually may not be what she is getting.

Some women simply can't be dealt with once they've started criticizing a lover. One man told us about a woman he dated who would cry during sex because "you are doing it all wrong." When he asked what she wanted different, she said, "You have to just know! Oh, someday I hope I have a lover who knows how to do it right!" He had a choice between this difficult woman and his sexual self-esteem. He broke up with her, and moved on.

Other times a woman's criticisms are worth listening to, and can improve her responsiveness. If she doesn't like her nipples pinched, and you pinch them, she'll be a happier and better lover if you listen when she tells

you to stop. The best way to avoid a woman's sexual criticism is to ask her questions about what she likes during the first time you have sex, and afterward. If you integrate these suggestions into your sexual play, she'll have less to criticize.

You can also find out a woman's lovemaking preferences before you first have sex with her by asking, "What do you think is important to women in a lover?" She'll then tell you what *she* likes, as if she was speaking about all women.

Q: What should I do when she hates my porn collection?

A: When you are seducing a woman for the first few times, she simply shouldn't be allowed to find out that you have pornography. The only exception is if she asks to see some while you are having sex, and this is rare. Put it away where she won't find it when she's looking for a shirt to wear while she makes coffee the next morning.

As you get to know her better, continue to keep your porn where she won't see it, until you can figure out how she feels about it. The main thing you need to know is that if she hates porn, you must never argue with her about it. Simply listen to what she has to say, then change the subject. Arguing about pornography will *never* change a woman's mind on the subject. Don't even try. And keep it away from her.

Q: What should I do when she doesn't like my friends?

A: When you are first seducing a woman, she shouldn't meet your friends. Your friends represent an unnecessary variable in the seduction equation. You don't know what kind of idiotic things they may say or do to screw up your seduction. They may even try to steal her from you! If you run into a friend when you are out with her, get rid of him as quickly as you can.

After you've been sleeping with a woman for a while, she may begin to get to know your friends. The thing to know is that you must never abandon a friend because a woman doesn't like him. Don't hang out with them at the same time, but don't write him off, either. Some men abandon their male friends when they get into a relationship with a woman, and they pay the price in loneliness later. Don't make this mistake.

Q: What should I do if she hates sports?

A: Ah, sports, the great divide between men and women! First and foremost, you don't indulge her desire to argue about sports. This is another instance where you can be as right as the day is long, and discussing it with a woman will still do nothing but cause trouble in your relationship. If you are in the process of seducing a woman, don't share the sports-loving part of yourself. No positive purpose is served by telling her that your idea of a great Sunday afternoon is to watch two football games and both the pregame and postgame shows. She'll find that out about you soon enough. If you are sleeping with her regularly, the rule is the same: Don't argue about it. If she wants to, acknowledge that she doesn't like it and change the subject.

Q: What should I do if I find unpleasant surprises under her clothes?

A: This can happen. Henry was a rock musician and, after a performance in a bar, picked up an extremely hot woman and took her home. "When I reached under her skirt, I discovered she was a 'he'!" Henry told us. "Needless to say, I told him to get the hell out of my apartment." This is an extreme example of the kinds of surprises you can get when you finally get a woman's clothes off.

One of our students took an attractive woman back to his apartment, only to discover that all of her body was covered by fine black hair. "It was an incredible turnoff," he told us. "I felt bad about it, but what could I do?" Another man told us about a date whose bustline turned out to be entirely padding. "I was so looking forward to getting my hands onto her breasts," he said. "I might as well have saved myself the time I spent seducing her and grabbed a box of tissues!" Another man told us of a woman who had a pungent, unpleasant smell once he got her in bed. It's tragic, but sometimes it happens that you want to get rid of a woman because you discover she just doesn't turn you on. What should you do?

Most of the time, it doesn't pay to tell her your specific gripe about her body. All you'll do is upset her about something she may have little or no control over. Why devastate her? Why be mean? Try saying something like "I know! Let's go get some ice cream!" Then jump up and start putting on your clothes. You can also say, "I really want to know you better before we

take this any further," to tactfully slow down unenjoyable sexual play. It's no fun to have to bail out on a sexual experience, but if you do, try to do it as gently as possible.

Q: What do I do if she wants to talk about marriage on the first date?

A: Sometimes relationship and marriage conversations can show up on the first date. Women who are over thirty years old often suddenly decide that it's time to get married. They will sometimes tell you this on the first date, or even before accepting your invitation to go out at all. "I have to tell you," she might say, "that in my twenties I was really into just dating around. Now I want a serious relationship. What do you think about that?" If you don't answer that you want a serious relationship, too, she probably won't go out with you.

The proper way to handle this is to be honest, but not to put her off. If you aren't really looking for a long-term relationship, remember that this doesn't mean you wouldn't get involved in one if you met the right woman. She might actually be that woman; you simply don't know. So you don't say, "I'm just looking to date around and have lots of unattached sex." She'll disappear instantly. Instead, try "I'm not really sure. I know that if I met the right woman, I'd be interested in the long term. I just don't know if I've met her yet." She'll stay interested, and you'll be able to go out.

You are now ready to handle the problems women cause. You can spot the women you should avoid, and understand the three modes of female fighting. Also, you've looked at the problems you cause in dating, and seen some steps you can take to stop creating the problems you have been having with women. You have a list of pro tips for handling specific problems. You are ready to roll.

More important, you now understand that no matter how skillful you are with women, problems are inevitable. You can let go of worrying that there is something wrong with you if the woman you are dating goes wacko on you. It's not personal, it's just part of dating.

12

Breaking Up Is Easy to Do

Bruce decided that after six dates and a few hot sex sessions with Belinda, he was ready to move on. Though they got along well, and he was attracted to her, he knew there was no way he was ready for a committed relationship. After deciding, Bruce waited a few days before calling her. During that time he went through the gamut of emotions: guilt, sadness, regret, everything.

Eventually, he decided to call her and break up. "Did I do something wrong?" she asked. "No, not at all," he said. "I really like you. Since the beginning, I told you that I wasn't looking for anything serious. If we keep going, I know it will probably develop into something I know I don't want. I thought it would be easier to break up now, and save us both the heartache later." Belinda began to cry.

Bruce tried to comfort her, and then began to feel guilty. He started to regret his decision and question his reasons. But then he remembered why it wouldn't work, and how if he continued to put off breaking up, it would end up being even more painful. "You have been a treasure to date, Belinda. I appreciate the time we've spent together. I've learned a lot from you and I think you are very special. I just can't keep going," Bruce said. They talked for a few more minutes, and finally Bruce ended the call. "I am sorry,

Belinda, but I must go. Is there someone else you can talk to about how upset you are?" Belinda decided to sleep at her sister's home, and they agreed to talk again soon.

Meanwhile, Bob had been dating Shirley for three months. They spent two or three nights per week together, and more time on weekends. He was never that interested in her, but continued dating her as something to do, in the hopes that a *better* woman came along. Bob figured it was better to spend time with *some* woman, rather than to be alone.

One night, after they got into a fight, Bob decided it was finally time to call it quits. The next night, while hanging out at her apartment, Bob told Shirley that the relationship was through. She was very upset. His announcement came out of the blue, and caught her off guard.

"What isn't working in our relationship?" she asked.

"The whole damn thing just sucks," Bob responded.

"Can't we work things out, Bob? I really like you, and want to keep building our relationship."

Bob responded, "We never *had* a relationship, Shirley. What we had were a few good times and some hot sex."

She began to cry. He did nothing to comfort her. "Quit crying, it isn't the end of the world. You are so damn emotional. Why do you always cry when it gets tough? That's part of why I want to break up," he told her.

"Maybe this is easy for you, Bob, but I am really hurt. I care very deeply for you. I thought we had something, something special. I counted on you. But now you are throwing that all away."

"Why are you arguing with me, Shirley? You are just too demanding. I need my space. We are through, and that's all there is to it." Bob got up, grabbed his coat, and left without saying another word.

One of the hardest parts of being a successful seducer is the breakup process. The more successful you get at seduction, the more frequently you'll be in the position of breaking it off. Cutting off a relationship is rarely easy, no matter how gently it's done. Unless you are a heartless jerk, both of you usually leave feeling upset. Breakups are a reminder that you are dealing with a living, breathing, feeling woman. It is important to learn how to end a relationship in the least painful manner, while still retaining a sense of integrity for yourself.

True to form, Bob makes mistakes in his split with Shirley. Primarily, he is unnecessarily cruel. Next, out of ignorance, he is unable to deal with her being upset by the split-up, and makes things worse by ignoring her cries for help. He also storms out of her apartment, leaving her in tears, and leaving their interaction incomplete. This will come back to haunt him. Last but not least, he fails to do the proper pre-work to make the breakup easier for her.

In a larger scope, Bob is oblivious to the fact that most women *will* take a relationship seriously and be hurt if a man suddenly, without mutual agreement, breaks up with them. In fact, dating for three months implies you are in a relationship, and requires more than simple conversation to break up.

Shirley has assumed that Bob spent so much time with her because he was interested in pursuing a relationship. She figured that he wanted to be her boyfriend and create a future together. In her mind, why else would a man spend so much time with a woman? In the end, she is left feeling heartbroken and confused.

Even though Belinda is upset when Bruce calls it quits, she isn't surprised. In fact, she knew it was coming a few weeks prior. Bruce had told her all along that he didn't want a girlfriend. He only wanted to casually date. When Bruce finally initiates breaking up, he makes sure to compliment her and show his appreciation for what they had. He reassures Belinda and makes sure she knows she did nothing wrong. At the same time, he doesn't argue with her, or feel intimidated when she begins to cry.

Bruce has thought out a strategy to break up in the least painful manner possible. Yet he doesn't fool himself into believing that it will be easy for her. He is willing to take any heat that may come his way and deal with the consequences of his actions. Though he has pangs of guilt, he stays true to his purpose and is able to ignore the disempowering thoughts about not breaking up and the regret inside his head.

While he talks to Belinda, he constantly asks himself what he could do to make the conversation and the breakup easier for her. By asking her if there is anyone else she could talk to, for example, Bruce makes sure she won't be alone while feeling so upset. He is, once again, taking care of her.

A few weeks after the breakup, Bruce still has his connection with Belinda. They agree not to date, or be sexual, but to be friends. Bruce figures that it is better to have another friend or acquaintance than it is to have an enemy. By allowing her the space to be upset, cry, and emote, Bruce makes sure that they will remain friends. In fact, because he is so skilled, Bruce rarely creates enemies when he breaks up with women.

Once you've moved through all the stages of dating—from meeting her and flirting to getting the date and seducing her—you will probably be left wondering if you should stick with the woman you've seduced or whether you should move on. This chapter will show you how to decide if the relationship you are developing works for you or not. From there, you can plan a breakup that is the most sensitive, yet easiest to accomplish.

TO COMMIT OR NOT TO COMMIT: THAT IS THE QUESTION

We have found that, eventually, most men want a long-term relationship. Contrary to popular belief, however, such a desire cannot be forced. It can only occur naturally and when the time is right. Wherever you are, wanting a relationship or a one-night stand, we support you, and are committed through the information in this book to giving you exactly what you want.

Bruce is clear that he is not ready to be in a relationship. He is content dating and flirting. He has moved from feeling intimidated by women, and afraid to flirt, to being on his way to mastery. Bruce has gone from being lonely on the weekends to having more dates than he can keep up with. He is living his dream life and only wants to bask in his success with women.

In the past, Daniel also was only looking for women to date. He wanted nothing to do with commitment. Since learning our material over the past two years, he has changed from being shy and sloppy to being a stud, always dating several women at once. Eventually, Daniel got tired of dating and decided to settle down with one woman. He credited his changes to first mastering short-term relationships. "It was only after I knew I could sleep with many women that a relationship seemed like a good idea. If I

hadn't waited, and had just committed to the first woman who seemed interesting, it just would have been another unsuccessful relationship. I would have been making decisions from a state of desperation rather than choice," he said.

Bruce and Daniel are each clear about what they specifically want from a woman. Bruce wants to continue dating. Daniel is happy being in a committed relationship. If you are in Daniel's position, ready and eager to commit for the long term, we think that's great and you should go for it. There are two bonus chapters at www.howtosucceedwithwomen.com/owners that will walk you through creating a committed relationship that will work for you.

SO YOU THINK YOU WANT TO BE A STUD . . .

No matter how many times we mention it, some men will remain unclear about what they want in a relationship. If you are one of the foggy ones, you are that way because you haven't yet chosen between dating and being in a committed relationship. Indecisiveness is debilitating. If you can't decide what you want, you will probably end up bouncing from woman to woman, unwilling to do the work of a seducer while simultaneously unwilling to do the work required for a committed relationship. Being unsure creates failure in either circumstance.

So we ask you again, what do you want? A committed, happy erotic relationship, or a harem of young nymphs?

Before giving your promise to a woman, we recommend that you first make sure that she has the qualities and characteristics you desire. We require all of our students to develop a list of their conditions for choosing a woman. Making this list is crucial for several reasons. For starters, if you don't know exactly what you are looking for, you will likely end up with someone who isn't right for you. Hence, the relationship will fail. Worse, you will likely end up with someone with whom you do not essentially connect. This will result in a constantly strained relationship.

Most men aren't clear about what they want and expect from a woman. They get into relationships, but act as if they didn't really choose to do so. You would think the relationship just mysteriously happened one day.

Contrast this to how these men behave when buying a car. Our bet is that most men bring a much higher degree of rigor to the process of selecting and purchasing a car than they do to finding the right woman to settle down with. In fact, most men know *exactly* what they want and expect from a car. Here are Simon's conditions:

1. It must cost no more than $30,000.
2. It must be at least a six-cylinder or a V-8.
3. It must be a stick shift.
4. It must have four-wheel drive.
5. It must have side-curtain airbags.
6. It must be black.
7. It must be domestically made.
8. It must have antilock brakes.

There are also a few conditions that he feels are not necessary, but would be great added extras:

1. It would be great if it had a sunroof.
2. It would be great if it had a DVD player.

If you are like most men, you have never sat down and given yourself the time to really think about what you want in a woman. Perhaps you have flirted with and dated women who caught your eye, or kept dating women because you felt too scared and guilty to break up with them. Making a list of conditions for choosing will greatly aid you in clarifying what you want. Note, however: It will likely be harder to decide, and figure out, conditions you require from a woman than it will be to decide what you require in a car. But it's worth the effort, and the difference it can make in your life is huge.

Follow these steps to make your list:

1. Set aside at least fifteen minutes.
2. Begin by listing qualities you require in a woman for a potential

committed relationship. Don't censor yourself. Start writing and let the ideas flow. If you get stuck, jot down the qualities you *don't* want in a woman. This will get you looking in the right direction.

Here is an example to help guide you:

Joe's List

- I must feel attracted to her.
- She must be shorter than me.
- She must enjoy science fiction movies.
- She must be punctual.
- She must want kids.
- She must have long blond hair.
- She must be a football fan.
- She must be emotionally stable.
- She must be willing to talk and resolve disagreements.
- She must have a sense of spirituality in her life.
- She must love me and act kindly.
- She must cook.
- She must have cool friends.
- She must be willing to have sex at least twice a week.
- She must love giving oral sex.
- She must not be offended when I burp.
- She must enjoy travel.
- She must have a stable job.
- She must enjoy hip-hop music.
- We must agree on political issues.
- She must be intelligent.
- She must love beer.

3. Now that you have the list, prioritize the requirements. Actually go through the list and mark which ones are flexible and which aren't. Remember, you are looking at qualities and conditions for a

long-term relationship. The emphasis is on *long-term*. When you take a long view of things, it usually decreases the significance of superficial qualities, like enjoying the same music or beer. As a rule of thumb, the shorter the duration of dating, the more significant the superficial things seem.

Here is Joe's revised list. He separated the qualities into three categories: things he was unwilling to be flexible about, qualities he was somewhat willing to be flexible about, and those that would be great if she had them, but are not necessary.

Unwilling to Be Flexible/Must Have

- I must be attracted to her.
- She must want children sometime.
- She must be fairly emotionally stable.
- She must be intelligent.
- She must be willing to have sex at least twice a week.
- She must be willing to talk and resolve disagreements.
- She must have a sense of spirituality in her life.
- She must love me and act kindly.

Somewhat Flexible/It Would Be Great If She Had These

- She must cook.
- She must have cool friends.
- We must agree on political issues.
- She must not be offended when I burp.
- She must enjoy travel.
- She must be shorter than me.
- She must be punctual.
- She must enjoy science fiction movies.
- She must have a stable job.
- She must enjoy giving oral sex.

Even Less Important/Won't Affect the Relationship Either Way

- She must enjoy hip-hop music.
- She must have long blond hair.
- She must be a football fan.
- She must love beer.

Now that Joe has a list, he can then choose a woman based on it. He can instantly measure if he and a potential mate are compatible based on his required qualities. If you are like Joe, you have a tendency to avoid commitment at any cost and actually make up, out of thin air, reasons *not* to commit. By clarifying what you want, it will be easier to overcome feelings of ambivalence. You will finally have something concrete to measure a woman against, rather than your moment-to-moment feelings, thoughts, and opinions.

WHY BREAK UP?

It is important to know when to keep a woman, when to break up, and when to do so. Cutting off relationships can be complicated. Even rock stars, actors, and mega-wealthy men know that relationships often don't work out.

Bad relationships are similar to broken-down cars. They get worse and worse, and constantly need more repair. At a certain point it makes more sense to junk the vehicle and get a new one. The other option is to maintain the car over the long haul, and never let it get junky in the first place. If you are willing to do the work necessary to keep the car running over time, and put in the necessary money and time, you can keep it going indefinitely.

Diagnosing where you in the commitment game

The longer you date a woman, the harder and more painful it will be to break up. The more extensively you get to know each other, the higher the investment and the greater the loss when it ends. We've developed a method to diagnose your level of existing commitment. This eight-type method shows the degree of commitment and the predicted level of difficulty in breaking up. Begin with where you are on the commitment scale.

THE EIGHT DEGREES OF COMMITMENT

1. One-night stand

One-night stands are eternally popular. Most women interested in only one night aren't looking for much else. There is no investment in a relationship on either side. The experience was probably purely sexual for both of you. A one-night stand requires no explanation. The best way to "end it" is to simply not call her again, or to call the next day to thank her and then not call her again. Most women expect you to call after you've had sex. If you don't, the possibility of any relationship will not just be cut; it will be annihilated. A one-night-stand woman probably likes you somewhat, but won't be crushed if she never sees you again.

2. An acquaintance

An acquaintance is a woman you just met, or have dated once or twice without being sexual. After dating once or twice, there is a minimal investment in a relationship between the two of you. Not enough time has elapsed for her to become crazy about you. We recommend using the same strategy as for a one-night stand. Simply not calling her back will end it without much upset on either side. If it doesn't, having a short conversation will be all that is necessary to cut things off. As with any breakup discussion, sensitivity and gentleness are required. Harshness will only hurt her, and actually prolong the situation.

3. Dated three or four times over the past few weeks

If you've been on three or four dates with a woman, she definitely likes you. Otherwise, why would she bother spending the time? After a few dates, your level of attraction is probably somewhere between finding each other sweet and interesting, and wanting to rip each other's clothes off and jump into bed.

Breaking up in person will be best. By this time, she has begun thinking of you as a potential boyfriend. If you've been having sex, it will be that much harder to cut off from her. Being honest about why you don't want to

be with her will be the easiest. At the same time, being diplomatic and not telling her details that will be interpreted as cruel is also suggested.

4. Slept with her a few times and realized it was going to become a problem

We discussed problem women in Chapter 11. These are the classic "psychos" who are potential stalkers, violent, cruel, hyperemotional, and all-around trouble. Maybe you didn't notice her psycho qualities at first, but they soon came up during conversation or during sex. Maybe you were so swept up with her beauty that you ignored our warnings. In any case, it is important to get away from such a woman quickly. The longer you are with a problem woman, the harder it is to break up, and the more trouble it will cause down the road.

Breaking up with a troubled woman will probably be difficult. She will most likely have a strong emotional reaction. It is important that you watch your safety; psychos can react violently. It is best to simply say that you are not ready to be in a relationship, or that you realize you can't give her what she wants from a man. You certainly can't tell her that she is psycho, or anything that will be construed as nasty. Be careful and try to be as gentle as possible.

5. She is an occasional sex partner

A woman who is having sex with you and not requiring a commitment is a wonderful find. First, examine why you are dismantling the relationship. If you are looking to date many women at once, this is the perfect one to keep. She is a perfect addition to your harem.

The likely reason to break up is that, after informal dating, she begins to want more. At first, being occasional sex partners worked, but now she has fallen for you and wants it to be serious. Meanwhile, you want it to remain informal. The other reason to call it quits is if you meet another woman and begin a committed relationship. In this case, the occasional sex partner will have to go. A simple phone call or in-person conversation will likely do. Just be honest, and the breakup will probably be easy. She'll likely understand, and may perhaps even congratulate you.

6. Dated for a month or less

A month is right around the time when things start to get serious. First, why do you want to break up? What in particular isn't working? Get clear about the specifics before you have a breakup conversation.

We recommend you use the breakup strategy employed in the third scenario, in which you have a face-to-face conversation and break up in the manner suggested. The best way to avoid this situation is to be clear from the start that you aren't looking for a girlfriend.

7. Dated for over a month

If you've been going out (and staying in!) for over a month, you are getting into the troubled waters of commitment. She obviously likes you; otherwise she wouldn't have dated you for so long. After being together this long, breaking up is best done over a few weeks. First, do the pre-work items, as suggested later in this chapter. Second, plan to discuss breaking up with her over several conversations, not simply during a one-shot thing. Be honest, tactful, and responsible for her reaction. You will likely have to have a few conversations with her for everything to be straightened out and the breakup to be done.

8. Dated for over three months

.   For all practical purposes, after three months you *are* in a relationship, and you *are* her boyfriend. Even if you don't think so, she most certainly does. A breakup at this stage must be well planned out. She will likely be hurt and angry.

PRE-WORK FOR THE BREAKUP

As with anything else in the dating game, there is always pre-work. Ceasing to date will be easier and less painful for both of you when it's planned out ahead of time. Creating a step-by-step plan will make everything go that much more smoothly. Find a way to be as compassionate as possible; being impulsive won't do.

Don't date a woman for more than a month

We know it sounds harsh, but after a month things will begin to get serious. If you want to make sure you don't hurt a woman by dragging things out, cease dating after a month. If you continue longer, she'll consider you her boyfriend. If, on the other hand, she is enjoying the informal nature of the relationship and doesn't appear to want more, initiate a "relationship discussion" after a month and tell her your future intentions. The clearer you are, the easier it will be. Remember that no matter what either of you says, you always run the risk after a month that she will become more and more attached to you.

Get all your things out of her home first

At least a week before the cutoff date, make sure to get all your stuff out of her home. This includes CDs, clothes, books—everything that you care about. Once you split up, your stuff is in jeopardy of being destroyed or thrown out. By taking your valuables out ahead of time, you have one less thing to worry about.

Make sure she doesn't view you as a long-term man

If you are not interested in having a serious relationship, don't lie and say that you are. Be honest with her from the start. If you string a woman along, telling her that you want a girlfriend when you don't, the breakup will be horrid, and she will likely end up hurt. If you lie, it is likely that you will feel guilty and worry if she'll find out the truth at a later time. Lying simply isn't worth it. If you are straight from the start, the woman won't be shocked when you stop dating. She will be aware ahead of time of the risks. It is cruel and unnecessary to put a woman through more crap in the dating arena than necessary.

Don't plan events with her far in advance

Naive men often make plans with women far into the future. The problem is that planning so far ahead deceives the woman into thinking a guy plans to be with her, and she begins to think of him as a longer-term mate. Given that most men have tunnel vision in relationships, and only focus

on the near future, if you start planning vacations six months later to France, or an end-of-the-year cruise, the woman will likely interpret this to mean that you plan to be with her for a long time. Hence, you are in a de facto committed relationship. The solution is simple: Only make plans for the near future, and make sure to avoid commenting on anything that could be interpreted to imply long-term plans.

Scott and Donna dated for a few months. From the start, he only wanted a sexual relationship. They both enjoyed international travel and frequently discussed exotic countries they both were interested in visiting sometime. In Donna's mind, he discussed these things because he wanted to visit those places with her. Scott even mentioned, informally, that they should visit Jakarta and New Zealand within the next fifteen months. She began telling her friends that Scott wanted to take her on a year-long world trip. When he initiated the breakup, Donna had a very hard time. All along, she'd assumed that they were planning a long trip together, and a relationship would bloom from there. If Scott had watched himself more carefully and avoided mentioning long-term plans, it would have been much easier.

Avoid talking about long-term plans to a short-term woman.

Don't be the perfect boyfriend

When we say, "Don't be the perfect boyfriend," we are *not* suggesting that you be mean, nasty, cruel, or hurtful. Instead, we are saying that if you act "perfect," for example, buying her flowers before every date, always being sweet, dressing well, calling her all the time, and generally taking care of her, you will come across as *the* perfect boyfriend, and she'll probably fall in love with you.

If you are not committed to being with her for the long term, you must realize that the more perfect you are, the more she will want a serious relationship. As a result, it will be harder to break up. We suggest that in this case you occasionally do things that are less than perfect, are obnoxious, or are annoying. If you want to break up, start increasing the frequency and number of behaviors and habits that she probably dislikes. If you act in ways she *doesn't* like, it will be easier for her to let you go. It may even prompt her to initiate the breakup and get rid of you.

You can start to get more into sports. This will likely put her off, without hurting her. A healthy love for cigars is also a turnoff. Dressing sloppy can help, as will a new love of avoiding deodorant and occasional swearing. Try making "That's what you said" a standard response to things that she says. More than anything, be aware that if you act perfectly, it will make breaking up harder. You can stop being the perfect boyfriend by reducing the number of awesome things you do, rather than by acting like a jerk.

THE THREE TYPES OF BREAKUPS

1. Mutual

A mutual breakup is the best kind. You both agree that things are not working, neither of you is getting what you need, and neither sees a future together. These types of breakups have the highest potential for your remaining friends.

After dating for a month, neither Andrew nor Pauline was satisfied. They had begun fighting, the spark was gone, sex turned boring, and they both only called out of obligation. During a walk, they both admitted that they weren't interested in dating anymore; it simply wasn't working. By mutually agreeing to break up, neither party felt responsible or guilty.

2. She breaks up with you

There are two forms of her breaking up with you. The obvious one is that you are interested in staying together and she isn't. She cuts you off. She finds something wrong with you, or the relationship, and she's done.

The second type is when you do things to get her to break up with you. For example, Heather told Robert that if he ever slept with another woman, she would break up with him. Several months later, Robert did just that and it prompted her to break up with him. There are many other examples of men crossing a line that leads to the woman officially doing the breaking up. When the breakup is examined, it becomes clear that the man was the one who caused it to occur.

3. You break up with her

Need we even explain this one? You decide that you don't want to go out with her, for whatever reason. You then do the pre-work necessary. Next, you break up, and deal with the fallout of your actions.

As mentioned earlier, some men break up out of fear. Deep down, they want to stay together, but they are scared of commitment. If you are going to break up out of fear, we recommend you rethink your decision and do what it takes to make it work.

If you are breaking up because it isn't working well, or is going in a direction you are not committed to, go ahead and do it. Use all the information in this chapter to help you.

THE EIGHT WARNING SIGNS
THAT IT'S TIME TO END IT

We all have blind spots—fears, motivations, or issues that we can't see. Before reading this book, Bob, for example, never realized that dressing sloppy would repel women. He simply had no idea that it made a difference, that he dressed in ways that kept women at bay. Men have many blind spots in relationships. They are issues they simply don't want to admit are problems, or potential problems. It is common for a man to ignore warning signs that a relationship is failing or that a woman he is involved with is dangerous and is psycho. Men don't register the warning signs as significant. They downplay the possibility of the dangers and hazards involved.

What follows are warning signs. If you are currently experiencing one or more of these signs, you should seriously consider ending the relationship. We have had too many students report horrible consequences of staying in dangerous and abusive situations. Get out quickly and avoid the inevitable headaches and heartaches.

1. You stop having the sex life with her that you want

A short-term relationship should be chock-full of sex. If it isn't, why are you in it? If the sex stops, the relationship is in a crisis. Women usually stop being interested in sex because of a problem in the relationship. Usu-

ally it is because the man stops doing the little things for her, all the maintenance items we've discussed throughout the book. If she has a problem with you, and you are unwilling to deal with it, the relationship will continue to decay until you either deal with it or get out. In a long-term relationship, you must deal with any problems that arise; that is part and parcel of the relationship.

2. You don't like yourself when you are with her

There are women in this world who bring out the worst in you. The worst temper, qualities, thoughts, feelings—everything. When you find yourself with such a woman, it's time to break up.

Jim, for instance, was dating a political activist named Hara. It always seemed to Jim as if he had to hold back his thoughts and opinions from her. He was always afraid they might get into an argument. Hara could share her opinions with him, however—and she did so all the time. Jim acted meek and timid around her, and hated himself for it. He felt as if he was groveling for sex and approval, and as if he was subservient to her whims and desires.

Finally Jim broke up with her, but he put up with too much suffering for too long before he did it. If Jim had paid attention to his fear and dislike of how he felt around her, and had remembered that there are plenty of other women to date, he would have saved himself a lot of hassle and would have broken up more quickly.

If you don't like how you act around a particular woman, either change your behavioral patterns or get out of the relationship. The cost is simply too high to stay in a messed up situation. Remember, if you feel bad around her, it is your responsibility to get out, not hers.

3. She doesn't like you

It may sound funny, but many men report dating (or even marrying) women who dislike them. Women have reported the same thing, being in relationships with men who seem to dislike them. In these situations, the couple stays together because there are qualities about the other that each likes and enjoys, but on the whole one party dislikes the other. The disdain comes across as constant criticizing, complaining, and general nastiness.

If the woman doesn't like you, get out.

4. She has constant emotional problems

Darlene was usually lovable. She was sweet, sincere, beautiful, and had a great job. At the same time, she was highly emotional and had constant emotional outbursts. It was nearly impossible to predict what would set her off. When she was angry, she would swear and throw things at anyone within range. When she was sad, she would hyperventilate and sob. Her full range of emotional outbursts scared David. He really liked her, but he felt that her emotional problems prevented him from getting to know her, and ever feeling comfortable.

Even though David liked Darlene, we still advised him to break up with her. She was simply too wild and too unpredictable. In a short-term relationship, someone like Darlene is unacceptable simply because she is too much work to date and maintain. While it may sound harsh, if you are dating an overly emotional woman, the best way to protect yourself is to break up. Be gentle in the process, and move on.

5. She is too demanding

Some women act as if you have no other purpose in life than to serve them. Perhaps they frequently call you at work and ask you to spend inordinate amounts of time talking when you should be doing something else. Maybe they stop by your home at all hours of the night, and bang on the door, wanting, wanting, wanting. Or they call and want you to pick up a huge grocery list of "female supplies" for them. Women who do these things all of the time can be too demanding.

The first solution is to start religiously using the magic word no in all your conversations with her. It may take a while to get your life back in order, but if you are strong-willed and can make friends with "no," it is imaginable that you could keep things going. If this doesn't work, or if she becomes even *more* demanding in the face of your refusals, then it's time to split up.

6. She tries to make you feel guilty about male things

Some of the ways men and women flirt are by teasing each other about "male" and "female" things. You tease her about how long it takes her to put on her makeup, and she teases you about loving sports. That is a fun-natured

banter. There are other women, however, who will try their hardest to hit you where it hurts. They will insult your masculinity and try to make you feel guilty about anything that can be construed to be manly. She might insult you for looking forward to your weekly ritual of watching Monday night football with your buddies. She might comment on how stupid the game is and how you are supporting a violent sport. She might also complain about your trips with the guys to auto shows, sporting events, action movies, or anything she thinks of as "male." Finally, she might constantly blame the problems of the country or the world on men and their "fragile male egos." She may claim that if the country was run only by women, everything would be fine. If you are with a woman who spouts off similar comments, welcome to a world of trouble. It is important for your self-esteem and sanity to cease being around a woman who dislikes you for being a man.

The fact that you have a penis is nothing to ever apologize for or feel ashamed of. If you respect her as a woman, you should expect the same in return. If not, go on to another woman.

7. You don't respect her

Why are you with a woman you don't respect? Is it that she is beautiful, rich, a stepping stone for your career, or what? If you don't respect someone you sleep with once, that is fine. After that, you are hurting both of you, and it will eventually weigh on you and chip away at your confidence. What does it say about you that you have to date women you don't respect?

8. She wants to come between you and your buddies

As we've said many times, close male friends are very important. The "lone rangers" in life, who only spend time alone or with their woman, will eventually bottom out. The nurturing, teasing, obnoxious, straight-with-one-another type of camaraderie and support men give each other is completely different from relationships between men and women. A good seducer has men he can talk to, support, and confide in.

When a woman tries to come between you and your buddies, she is trying to control your life. She is trying to cut off your contact with others; in essence, she is cutting off your mainline of masculine energy.

The bottom line is that no woman is worth cutting off your friends for. The women may come and go, but close male friendships will usually last forever.

THINGS TO WATCH OUT FOR
DURING THE BREAKUP CONVERSATION

She may try to entice you with sex

If a woman doesn't want to break up, she will often go to extreme measures to stop it. A woman will frequently offer sex as a way to get a man back. She thinks that if she offers him her body, he will remember how much he loves her and call off the breakup.

When Bob initiated the cutoff from Veronica, she began crying. Her next move was to unbutton her shirt and tell him that he would be missing out on a lot. "Don't you just want to make love one last time, for old times' sake?" she asked. Bob fell for it, and made love with her. The problem was, he didn't enjoy it. The whole time he felt guilty. "How can I make love with her and then just leave?" he thought to himself. After making love, Bob decided he should stay with her a few more weeks. Then he initiated the breakup again. She again tried to seduce him into staying; he fell for it again. After three cycles of breaking up and seduction, Bob finally learned not to have sex after breaking up or to let himself be seduced into staying.

While the possibility of sex is very tempting, it is rarely worth going for in a breakup situation. Stay strong and focused on the long-term happiness of both of you, rather than on the onetime sex experience, and it will be easier to break up.

She may argue with you

Most women will argue when you break up. It helps them understand and cope with the split. They want to know if there is anything they can do to avoid having you leave. The answer is to simply avoid long conversations or arguments with her. Our research shows that the more you argue, the harder it is to break up, and the more upset each of you becomes. Be kind, gentle, and honest; arguing won't work. If she won't stop arguing, leave the situation and talk to her later, if necessary.

Physical violence and threats

Rob had been dating Karen for a few months before he realized it wasn't working. She wanted to spend more and more time with him. When they were together, however, it constantly felt like work. Rob knew it was time to break up. He was scared, however, because during previous arguments, she had slammed doors, screamed, and cried. It turned out that Rob's fears were well justified. During their breakup talk, Karen screamed at him. She threatened to call his job and tell Rob's boss that he abused her. She grabbed a metal bowl and warned him that if he tried to leave, she would throw it at his head.

While it may sound unbelievable, these things do happen, and can be quite scary. If you are ever in a similar situation, we recommend that you leave immediately (and watch your head). You never want to endanger your own safety. Get out, and stay away from her forever. If you see the violent potential in a woman you are dating, avoid her and break up—in public, so there will be the calming influence of witnesses—as soon as you realize it.

She will promise to change

During the breakup process a woman may promise to change. She promises to eradicate any part of her personality you have ever complained about. She begs for one more chance. In response, you get drawn into all the drama and stop the breakup. Soon you will want to break up again and will, once again, be faced with her promises of changing. The problem, however, isn't whether or not the woman will change. She won't. (Neither will you.) All this only prolongs the inevitable breakup, and ultimately hurts her more. It is best to stay on course with why you are breaking up and never waver. Never be cruel, but don't fall into the trap of feeling guilty and let it back you down from the breakup. You are walking a thin line. Stay on course.

EXAMPLES OF CLEAN BREAKUPS

Craig thought he loved Bonnie. From the moment he laid eyes on her, she seemed perfect to him. They loved the same rock groups, the same food, and always had a great time when they partied. They saw each other all the time. After a few weeks, the "glow" wore off. They started fighting frequently. One night in a fit of rage Bonnie physically attacked him. She threw a plate at his head, and it nearly hit him. She then jumped on him and slapped and kicked him where no man wants to be kicked! Craig was in pain for a few days and vowed never to see her again. She apologized and begged him to come back. He couldn't help himself. Craig thought that he really did love her.

They got back together and things went smoothly for a few weeks. But then they fought again. This time she tried to shove him down a flight of stairs. Craig protected himself and avoided a potentially dangerous situation. At that point he knew they had to break up. He was scared, however, to initiate it. "What if she goes nuts again?" he asked himself. He spent the next few weeks gathering his things from her apartment while he planned the breakup. He decided to break up in public, where she would be less likely to kill him. He waited until they were sitting in a coffee shop to finally tell her that he didn't want to date anymore. She was upset, but accepted the breakup.

Ken met Mary Lou at a party. They drank, danced, and talked until 4:00 a.m., at which point he asked her to come home with him. She agreed. From the start, Ken had no desire for a girlfriend. Indeed, at the same time, he was dating three other women. Mary Lou went to his apartment, and they made love. In the morning, he took her out for breakfast. Over the meal, she confessed that she was looking for a boyfriend and thought that he might have potential. Ken told her that he would like to see her again, but she should know that he was dating others. She seemed mildly upset, but gave Ken her phone number and asked him to call for a date. They had a good time continuing the talking and flirting during the meal. After breakfast, he drove Mary Lou home.

After dropping her off, Ken threw her phone number out the window. While he enjoyed both sleeping with and talking to her, it seemed as

though her desire for a serious relationship would taint future interactions. Rather than having to tell her constantly that he didn't want a girlfriend, he decided to simply not call her again.

The sex was always intense, passionate, and wild between Kay and Alan. It was as if there were some magical chemistry between them. They saw each other three or four times per month, and sex was always a main part of the date. Both actively dated other people, and saw each other as only part-time lovers. After a few months, however, Kay wanted more. She was interested in being in a relationship with Alan.

One night, after sex, Kay confessed that she was falling in love with him. Rather than avoid discussing the topic, Alan said that he didn't feel the same way about her. He enjoyed the sex and closeness they shared, but didn't want to go further. She was upset. At the same time, she had known it was unlikely that he would feel the same way about her. They went their separate ways, and while Alan missed the sex, he knew that if he had continued, the breakup would have been much more difficult.

Bob and Diane had been dating for two months. They liked each other, but both were honest about the fact that they didn't see any long-term potential for them, and that they were dating other people. One evening, Bob noticed that Diane seemed more distant than normal, and he asked her if there was anything wrong. "Well," she told him, "I'm dating someone else, and it's starting to get serious. I really like you, but I have to stop seeing you, and just be with him."

"I understand," he told her. He was sad, but he also knew it was for the best. He let her go, and moved on to the next woman in his dating life.

In this chapter you've discovered how to break up with a woman when the time comes to do so. We began by asking you to decide what type of relationship you want to be in. We asked, do you want a long-term or a short-term erotic relationship? From there we discussed how many men avoid long-term relationships because of fear.

We then walked you through a step-by-step process to discover what you must have in a woman you commit to. We then showed you how to refine the process and come up with the qualities you require, the

qualities you desire, and the qualities that would be great but aren't necessary.

We talked about the eight stages of commitment, and basic strategies of breaking up in each stage. From there we discussed the pre-work we recommend you do before breaking up. This includes making sure all your things are out of her home, not being a perfect boyfriend to begin with, and making sure she doesn't view you as a long-term man.

Next we talked about the eight warning signs of trouble down the road. Some of the signs: a sudden reduction in how frequently you have sex; you don't like yourself when you are with her; she doesn't like you; she is too demanding; you don't respect her; she wants to come between you and your male friends; and she has constant emotional problems.

Then we warned you about the possible problems that may occur during the actual breakup discussion. Some things to watch out for: her enticing you with sex; her arguing with you, point for point, on why you are breaking up; her threatening you with physical violence and scaring you into not breaking up; and her promising to change and become your ideal girlfriend. All of these problems have a simple solution: Break up quickly and be done with the process.

No matter what your skill level, breakups are often full of pain. The master seducer deals with the pain and takes responsibility for himself, and for doing it as quickly and painlessly as possible. The more successful you are in seduction, the more often you will have to break up. If you are a man of integrity and sincerity, you will steer your way through possibly difficult situations with the least amount of difficulty.

CONCLUSION

It's now a year later and we see Bob walking down the sidewalk looking like a million bucks. At first glance it is hard to believe that this is the same guy who previously refused to wear nice clothes, had unkempt hair, had a bad attitude, and refused to alter his ways to impress a woman. Now he is looking sharp, his hair is stylishly done, and he looks and acts confident.

After decades of constant failure to meet and date women, Bob decided finally to take our advice and model himself after stylish men in the media. He focused on modeling their physiology, thoughts, clothing, attitude, and beliefs about dating. After some practice he was able to get himself psyched up and "in the zone," and since then success has become the norm.

A year ago, Bob wouldn't have been caught dead reading and studying men's fashion. Now he is always on the lookout for ways to improve his appearance. At first it felt funny, almost unnatural, to dress fashionably and concentrate on looking good, but after a while Bob noticed that women were treating him differently, and he felt differently about himself. Bob realized, as we hope you have, that the clothes a man wears, and the way he wears them, send a message to women. Before, he was unconsciously saying, "Stay away from me. I don't care what you think." His strategy was effective, and women kept away. Looking sloppy greatly contributed to his pattern of failure.

Bob also realized that the hot, young, and sexy twenty-one-year-olds he most wanted to date would never consider him a possibility if he dressed messy and didn't project confidence. Accepting this realization pushed

him to work out frequently, lose weight, and spend a few thousand dollars on clothing. "At first I thought the men's fashion stores were ripping me off, and I left feeling really pissed off. But then, after I thought about it for a while, I figured that it was an investment, like anything else, and it would lead to success down the road. With this attitude I took the advice of the salesclerks and bought outfits that looked good on me. Now I feel powerful when I walk down the street. Women check me out, and I actually feel like a movie star at times. It's fun."

When Bob began to change the way he dressed, he relied on the clothing and hygiene checklist from Chapter 3. This list includes things like making sure his glasses are both in good repair and fashionable, making sure his ear and nose hair are trimmed, making sure his lips are soft and kissable, shaving before every date, taking pens out of his shirt pockets before dates, wearing clean underwear, making sure socks match, and keeping all his clothing in good repair.

"There were many changes I had to make when I decided to seriously master seduction," Bob reports. "I completely altered my clothing and how I viewed things like exercise and diet. In the past I thought that being a stud was something you were either born with or you could never be. I've changed my tune."

Bob has gained the confidence with women, and in life, that he always wanted. He now knows that action is the key. Bob realized that having close guy friends was also essential for having the life he truly desired. "I always felt distant from other men," he reports. After being coached by us, he says, "I began talking to other men, getting to know them better. There are many topics I can talk about with guys that I can't with women. It has been a great help in seduction to have other men to bounce ideas off of, and egg each other on. I realized how fun it is to kick back, drink some beers, watch a game, and shoot the bull. It energizes me for the other areas of my life. Previously I used to think watching sports was for macho jerks. Now I know that I, too, am a 'jerk' like everyone else. There's nothing wrong with it—it's great fun!"

Another way Bob gained confidence with women was to admit that he was scared to date women. He was afraid of rejection, afraid that women wouldn't like him, afraid of not knowing how to talk to women, afraid of

people thinking he was macho and a womanizer. These fears kept him unsuccessful in his pursuit. It was only after he admitted his fears that he was able to move on and change them.

One solution was simply to flirt and talk to women all the time. Bob began doing so every day, and it quickly helped increase his confidence. At first, all he could do was say hi or ask what time it was, or directions to the nearest coffee shop. Slowly, he learned to use romantic questions, flirt, smile, memorize lines, and relax. Refusing to let rejections get him down, and having his new guy friends egg him on, helped him to keep going.

Looking over the year, Bob could see that he continued to make hundreds of mistakes, but he stayed on track. Most men would have given up, felt bad about themselves, and blamed everyone for their failures. Bob was persistent, and things slowly changed for him. He viewed learning seduction as an investment, something that took a lot of work on the front end to get results later.

On his first few seduction dates, Bob ignored our warnings that a man must have his car and home set up for romance. He continued to use his car as a roving garbage truck. He stored bottles and cans that would someday arrive at the recycling plant, hamburger wrappers from fast-food places, and a collection of tools, all within the confines of his old, loud, rusted, and dented compact car. Any woman who entered his car got out as quickly as she could. He later bought a decent, clean, used car, and this time modified it to be a certifiable sex mobile. He made sure to keep it clean, got a good stereo installed. And, of course, he hid a cache of condoms in the glove box.

Bob's home went through a similar transformation. He realized that a house full of garbage, dirty dishes, ragged furniture, and bad odors killed the romantic mood every time. Over a few months he replaced all the lamps in the living room and bedroom, making sure they each had a dimmer switch. Bob also purchased some new, soft, and comfortable furniture that invited romance and sensuality. He re-covered other pieces with matching material. His new bed was huge, inviting, and a joy to lie in. A collection of plants and framed pictures created a romantic mood in every room. Bob learned to clean his home before each date, and make sure that clean sheets and pillowcases were on his bed. He felt more comfortable in

his home, and several women commented that they felt truly comfortable in his space.

He greatly increased both his romance and flirting skills over the year as well. At first it seemed impossible to be effective at either romance or flirting, but after constant reading, practicing, and coaching from us, these skills became easy. In the past, Bob believed that flirting was simply talking without direction that would, hopefully, magically, lead to sex. He thought that since he had never had a one-night stand, and no single conversation had led to sex, he was a failure. Later, Bob realized that the essence of flirting is to play without an attachment to the outcome, and that a man rarely has sex with a woman after one flirting encounter.

As he learned to relax, he was able to flirt and interact with women with confidence. He learned to use flirting to prequalify women, to see if they were potentials for dating and for sex. He also learned to use flirting to anchor pleasurable feeling in the woman to seeing him. For instance, he began flirting and casually talking to the cashier at the convenience store near his job. Every few days, on his lunch break, he decided to go and talk to her about anything romantic. At first he was nervous, only saying a word or two; over time she grew to look forward to his visits.

Bob made many botched attempts at flirting before he learned the basics: not using crude humor, not joking as roughly as he would with guys, never joking about her appearance, never indulging in any disgusting behavior in front of her, and never making himself the butt of any joke. In the process of learning, he made all of these mistakes. But he soon learned to make jokes about things at hand, the importance of simply saying hi, focusing on eye contact, and describing romantic things during conversations.

Learning how to be romantic was equally difficult. In the beginning, he always forgot to make his romantic interest known right away. He often waited a few days before putting on the charm. The women usually felt put off by this behavior, however, having already decided he was a friend. Finally he realized that women usually decide within the first few minutes of meeting whether a man is a friend or a lover, and he changed his behavior to make it easier for women to think of him as having romantic potential rather than as "just a friend." Every week, he gave himself assignments to

understand and learn what women desired in a romantic situation. He decided that it was his job on dates to make the woman feel special and do the romantic things necessary to achieve that result.

One of the hardest things for Bob to learn was that women are generally concerned, at first, that a man is dangerous and will hurt them. This fear must be overcome before any further rapport can be built. He learned to overcome it and let go of his habitual anger with women. His new, lighter approach worked much better for him.

In the beginning of this book, Bob complained that there were no places to meet women. He was lonely, but nothing seemed to work for him. After taking our advice, Bob began experimenting with meeting women at alternative places. Some have paid off well, and led to dates, and others were not so productive. In any case, Bob has found that each and every place he goes is a possible place to meet women. He has learned to flirt and not take it personally if it doesn't lead to anything, or if he is rejected by the woman.

Bob started going to the same coffee shop every day. He became one of the regulars, and this made it easy to talk to women he saw routinely. They already had a connection—the coffee shop. He started eating at the same restaurants regularly and going to the gym to work out at a regular time. These, too, led to more opportunities to date and flirt. He talked with women at his favorite bookstore, and though it didn't lead to a date, he had some interesting discussions. Bob experimented with attending New Age events; he was even asked to leave one of them for teasing a psychic. He didn't get any sex that day, but he practiced his seduction skills and had fun being obnoxious, so in his mind it was a success.

He also attended ballroom dancing class a few times. He danced with some hot young women. He also met many women at dog training classes. He even signed up for a Japanese cooking class; he was the only man there. The other participants were mostly married, middle-aged women. But one of the students, Joyce, was younger and very friendly. They went out for drinks after one of the classes. Their drinking dates led to a short-term erotic relationship. Though they had little in common, the sex was good, and that was enough for them both.

Bob dated Joyce for a only a month. Though he wanted to date her

longer, he knew that if they continued, Joyce would likely want to be his girlfriend. Bob was able to cut off the potential relationship quickly, and Joyce was not surprised when he finally called it quits.

Bob made good use of the Internet for meeting women. He experimented with various online dating sites, creating several personas that he used to meet different kinds of women. He also set up accounts with several major social media sites, especially working his profile on Facebook .com—joining many groups, interacting with many women, and finding potential dates in surprisingly large numbers. He got good at moving women from first online contact to phone to dating to sex, and found that this was one of the best ways to meet women who fulfilled his desires.

Previously, one of Bob's biggest failures was to not notice all the women he came into contact with each day. He had acted as though there were no women to date. Now his days are much more like Bruce's in Chapter 4, flirting with and dating women all day and all night long.

One of his boldest moves was to attend a poetry reading and get up and read seductive poetry. He wrote several poems about sexuality and romance. He took our advice and created long poems out of romantic questions and by describing romantic states. "It shocked me to be up there. I never thought I would be so bold, but it was fun. After, I talked to six or more women. That was the best part. I got a few phone numbers. One woman, Rebecca, was a twenty-year-old tortured-artist type. She was all punky-looking, with tattoos and piercings on her face. She went home with me that night. I think that may have been the best I ever felt in my life."

Bob mastered the distinctions between priming and seduction dates. The goal of the first is to prime the woman and generate connection. He saw the importance of keeping that date short. If he went too long, he realized, it was easy to make mistakes, and not develop that connection.

Bob recently took Marsha, a woman he met at the gym, on a priming date at a coffee shop. They spent only forty-five minutes together, and it worked perfectly. Since she appeared to be having a great time, he decided to end the date even earlier than planned. Bob remembered that it wasn't a time to socialize. The work at hand was asking romantic questions and researching her requirements in a man and a mate. For example, he found

out what her first kiss was like, if she believed in love at first sight, what she valued in a relationship, and what she looked for in a boyfriend.

Bob, of course, brought his new book to read, in case Marsha failed to show up. He knew that many women wouldn't show up, and he was prepared, which made it easy for him to relax and be spontaneous. Because he had other women to date, he wasn't too concerned with Marsha's reactions to his questions or his behavior. He was able to take it all in stride.

One of Bob's biggest changes was becoming decisive. In the past he always relied on the woman to make the decisions, reasoning that it would make her feel comfortable. Now he knows that it is crucial that he make decisions during the date.

While the date with Marsha went well, he had been on dozens of failed priming dates throughout the year. He found a way to learn from each mistake he made and each thing he forgot to do. Before each date he went through the Before-the-Priming-Date Checklist from Chapter 7, and after each date, he went through his After-the-Date checklists to see what he could learn. He learned important priming date skills, like looking into the woman's eyes at least four times, asking romantic questions, touching her hand, making sure the date was no longer than seventy-five minutes, making decisions, making her smile and/or laugh at least once, being early, gathering information about her, complimenting her at least three times, and so on. Along with the After-the-Date checklists, he always examined how much he was willing to work to further the relationship. What would it take to move things to the next level? Bob created his own measurements to track the degree to which he was or wasn't interested in a woman.

Bob's next step was to study seduction dates. He wanted to master shifting the focus from building rapport to having sex. With Marsha, he knew she was ready to move things forward. She showed interest in him, flirted frequently, and responded well to his touch. On the seduction date he made sure to employ the key elements: making the date into a special event, picking a fun and romantic activity, making it memorable, paying for the date, being flexible with time, giving little gifts, making the woman feel special, planning for success, and making sure the date featured surprises.

Before the date, he made sure to look at the suggestions in Chapter 8 and to do all the pre-work. He assessed the attraction level between the

two of them, created sexual goals, made sure the date was at a convenient time, decided how much money to spend, had a backup plan, was prepared, and used the information from the priming date to guide his choices. During the date, Bob was punctual, polite, affectionate, complimentary, treated her like a woman, talked about upbeat topics, and was fun to be around. After the date he checked his after-the-priming-date checklists, seeing what he could learn in order to do better next time.

At first Bob failed to get a woman into bed, and when he did it ended up disastrously. Remember his situation with Barb we talked about in Chapter 10? Bob was in bed with her but didn't know how to touch her sensually. He was too rough and wanted to quickly move into intercourse. He refused to spend time on foreplay, kissing and petting, and the other necessary elements. With Marsha he did things differently. He kissed her during the seduction date, and they ended up in her bed. Because he had concentrated on learning about sensual touch and women's bodies, Bob touched Marsha just as she desired. He wasn't embarrassed by looking at her or asking questions. Bob kissed her and she moaned. He was full of confidence. His work on attitude in the bedroom paid great dividends.

Bob realizes that at this point in his life, his main goal is to be a true playboy. He sees himself in a long-term committed relationship within a few years, but for now he wants to continue dating and having many short-term erotic relationships. He knows what is needed to make a long-term relationship work when he is ready, but for now he wants to continue to play the field.

Another important skill Bob has learned that has come in handy on many dates is how to handle problem situations and problem women. Before, he would make mistakes regarding dating, including not dating more than one woman, not controlling all variables, confronting women when they didn't call him back or initiate things as much as he wanted them to. He would overwhelm a woman with sexual innuendoes, take the date too seriously, try to get validation and certainty from her, and check out other women when he was with her. He would not set limits and value his time, energy, and/or money. He tried to solve all women's problems, fought incessantly, and defaulted into yelling, screaming, and not managing his anger effectively.

Bob has dated a number of problem women during the year, and has learned to avoid them. He's dated women like the Flipped-Out Woman, the Paranoid Police-Caller, the Bitch Goddess, and the Street Fighter. He has learned to take his intuition seriously and avoid the women who could be dangerous. He has dated women who had constant emotional problems, who stopped being sexual, who interfered with his work, who degraded his self-respect, who tried to come between him and his buddies, who were overly critical, controlling, and violent. The moment any of these problems arose, he knew to promptly end the relationship.

Bob has also had to face many problems inside himself. The tendency to be a SNAG (Sensitive New Age Guy), for example, has pestered him for years. He was always trying to get women to have sex with him by being superficially nice, which never worked. He found out that women were looking for a confident man who was not so apologetic and who was not trying to impress them by being only nice. He also stopped being a control freak and a know-it-all on dates. He no longer lies to himself that he wants a relationship. Bob wants sex, and is not apologetic about it.

Bob credits his success to following our advice carefully, and never ceasing to work. He has faced more problems than most of our students, and he has come out successful with women. By taking the little steps along the way, you, too, will be like Bob and change the way you talk, act, and date women. This book is your bible for dating and sexual success. If you use our science and your own intuition, you are destined to succeed.

Remember, as an owner of this book you are entitled to two free bonus chapters, a mini-course on Making Women Pursue You, and a lot more at www.howtosucceedwithwomen.com/owners. Check it out now!

INDEX

Fight-or-flight syndrome, 104. *See also*
  Anxiety; Approaches; Fears; Rejection;
  Relaxation techniques
Fireplace, 303. *See also* Atmosphere
Flashbacks, 351
Flatulence, 77
Flexibility, 255–56, 364
Flirting, 4, 44, 117, 383–84. *See also*
  Approaches; Game; Playfulness
  with all women, 125, 127, 132–33, 386
  anchoring through, 157
  as "cold calling," 37
  elements of, 161–62
  with email, 186
  eye contact, 191, 229, 244
  fears and, 158–59
  as a game, 155–56
  generativity through, 161
  goal of, 156–57
  "good-bye" compliment, 191
  at grocery store, 34
  improving skills with, 189–90
  learning to stop, 190
  as outlet for self-expression, 122
  over a period of time, 184
  as qualifier, 158–59
  questions in, 191–92
  respect in, 172
  romance and, 160
  saying hi, 189–90
  on seduction date, 247
  smiling, 190
  text messaging, 186
  at volunteer event, 149
  waving, 190
  while shopping, 120
  winking, 190
"Flow," 255
Follow-up, 132
Football, 21
Foreplay, 305–6
Friends
  abandoning, 354
  dating set up by, 150
  encouragement from, with dating,
    131–32
  men, for support, 124, 131–32
  relationship with women vs. having,
    375–76
  when woman brings on priming date,
    236–37

Friendship, 50
  with men, 69, 96, 124, 131–32
  as ploy for sex, 51–52
  relationship and, 22
  romance vs., 6
  between shy guys and women, 102
  support and, 124, 131–32
  with women who don't want sex, 96
Frustration, 114. *See also* Anger; Resentment
Fun, 130, 234. *See also* Adventure; Game;
  Generativity; Playfulness

Game, 127, 130, 155–56. *See also* Numbers
  game
Gay men, 68
Geeks, 20
Generativity, 15–16, 161, 226–27, 253
Generosity, 206
Gifts, 194–96, 249–50, 263. *See also* Affection;
  Compliments; Romance
Giftwrapping, 249
Girlfriends, 114
Giving, 203, 325
Giving up, 292
Glasses, 74–75
Goals, 156–57, 258, 361
Goal-setting, 95
Goatees, 84–85
"Good-bye" compliment, 191
GQ (magazine), 68
Gratitude, 274
Grocery store, 34
Grooming, 107. *See also* Appearance; Body
  makeover; Clothing; Dress; Hygiene;
  Style
Groveling, 28–30
Guilt, 333
Guilt-tripping, 374–75
"Gurus," 2, 14

Habits
  being challenging, 55–59
  equanimity with "no," 31–36
  initiating, 42–44
  making it look easy, 54–55
  making life work for you, 46–50
  not groveling, 28–30
  numbers game, 36–40, 132
  outcomes in mind, 45–46
  prospecting, 44, 126
  of pursuit, 30–31, 40–42

Ron Louis and **David Copeland** have appeared as Dating Gurus on MTV, Fox News, CNN, UPN, *The Roseanne Show*, and *Good Day New York*. They have been featured in magazines including *Playboy, Maxim, Men's Fitness, Men's Health, GQ Active, Cosmopolitan, YM*, and others. They have been on thousands of radio shows including *The Dee Snider Show, The Man-cow Show, The Bill Handle Show*, and Playboy Radio. They have also been featured guests at Yale University's Sex Week. Visit their website at www .howtosucceedwithwomen.com.

For Lovers and Others...

• from •

Ron Louis and David Copeland

....

How to Succeed with Women

and

How to Succeed with Men

Both available from Prentice Hall Press

....

penguin.com